MAJOR PRINCIPLES
OF
MEDIA LAW

2003 EDITION

WAYNE OVERBECK

CALIFORNIA STATE UNIVERSITY, FULLERTON
MEMBER OF THE CALIFORNIA BAR

Australia • Canada • Mexico • Singapore • Spain • United Kingdom • United States

COPYRIGHT © 2003 Wadsworth, a division of Thomson Learning, Inc. Thomson Learning™ is a trademark used herein under license.

ALL RIGHTS RESERVED. No part of this work covered by the copyright hereon may be reproduced or used in any form or by any means—graphic, electronic, or mechanical, including but not limited to photocopying, recording, taping, Web distribution, information networks, or information storage and retrieval systems—without the written permission of the publisher.

Printed in Canada
1 2 3 4 5 6 7 05 04 03 02 01

Printer: Webcom, Ltd.

0-534-61911-8

For more information about our products,
contact us at:
Thomson Learning Academic Resource Center
1-800-423-0563

For permission to use material from this text,
contact us by:
Phone: 1-800-730-2214
Fax: 1-800-731-2215
Web: http://www.thomsonrights.com

Asia
Thomson Learning
5 Shenton Way #01-01
UIC Building
Singapore 068808

Australia
Nelson Thomson Learning
102 Dodds Street
South Street
South Melbourne, Victoria 3205
Australia

Canada
Nelson Thomson Learning
1120 Birchmount Road
Toronto, Ontario M1K 5G4
Canada

Europe/Middle East/South Africa
Thomson Learning
High Holborn House
50/51 Bedford Row
London WC1R 4LR
United Kingdom

Latin America
Thomson Learning
Seneca, 53
Colonia Polanco
11560 Mexico D.F.
Mexico

Spain
Paraninfo Thomson Learning
Calle/Magallanes, 25
28015 Madrid, Spain

TABLE OF CONTENTS

Preface   vii

Table of Cases   xiii

1) The American Legal System   1
  The Key Role of the Courts   2
  Structure of the Court System   3
  Types of Law   11
  Criminal and Civil Law   18
  Torts and Damages   18
  The Story of a Lawsuit   20
  How to Find the Law   27

2) The Legacy of Freedom   34
  Censorship in England   35
  Freedom in a New Nation   39
  The First Amendment   40
  First Amendment Scholars' Views   43
  Nineteenth-Century Press Freedom   45
  Sedition in the Twentieth Century   49
  The First Amendment and the States   52
  Postwar Sedition and Dissent   54
  Interpreting the Constitution   57
  The Future of Freedom in a Terrorist Era   60

3) Modern Prior Restraints   62
  Near v. Minnesota   63
  National Security and the "Pentagon Papers"   64
  Censoring "Hate Speech"   69
  Controls on Literature Distribution   75
  Prior Restraints and Abortion Protests   82
  Other Picketing and Related Issues   87
  Discriminatory Taxation as Censorship   94
  Other Prior Restraint Questions   97

4) Libel and Slander   111
  Libel Defined   113
  An Overview of Libel   114
  The Elements of Libel   118
  Libel Defenses   124

Libel and the First Amendment   136
Refining the Actual Malice Rule   145
Libel and Procedural Rights   150
Other Issues in Defamation Law   160
Ongoing Issues   169

5) The Right of Privacy   173
The History of Privacy Law   173
An Overview of Privacy Law   180
Intrusion   181
Disclosure of Private Facts   192
False Light and Fictionalization   200
Misappropriation   203
Privacy Defenses   213
Privacy Act of 1974   215
The Internet and Privacy   215
Ongoing Issues   218

6) Copyrights and Trademarks   222
An Overview of Copyright Law   224
The Fair Use Doctrine   237
Copyrights and Music Licensing   248
Cable Television Copyright Problems   251
Recording Technologies and Copyright Law   252
Computers, the Internet and Copyright Laws   255
International Copyrights   268
Unfair Competition   272
Trademarks   274
Ongoing Issues   283

7) Fair Trial-Free Press Conflicts   288
Prejudicial Publicity and Fair Trials   288
Closed Courtrooms   303
Cameras in Court   313
Ongoing Issues   319

8) Newsgatherer's Privilege   322
Contempt of Court   323
Reporter's Privilege   326
Statutory Shield Laws   338
Jailed Reporters: Three Notable Cases   344
Lawsuits by News Sources   348
Newsroom Searches   351
Ongoing Issues   352

9) Freedom of Information 355
  The Federal Freedom of Information Act   356
  Electronic Freedom of Information   367
  FoI Limitations   369
  Federal Open Meeting Legislation   378
  State Open Meeting and Record Laws   380
  Access to Other Places and Proceedings   383
  Practical Suggestions for Journalists   388
  Ongoing Issues   389

10) Obscenity and the Law 392
  Early Pornography Battles   394
  Changing Standards after 1900   395
  Setting a New Standard   401
  Other Forms of Censorship   408
  Municipal Pornography Regulation   416
  Ongoing Issues   421

11) Regulation of Electronic Media 424
  Broadcast Regulation: A Global View   426
  The Radio Spectrum   427
  The Birth of Broadcasting   431
  An Overview of the FCC   434
  Broadcast Licensing   436
  Broadcast Content Regulation   449
  Cable Television Regulation   476
  New Electronic Media Technologies   488
  Ongoing Issues   497

12) Media Ownership Issues 502
  An Overview of Antitrust Law   503
  The First Amendment and Antitrust Law   505
  Newspaper Antitrust Cases   507
  Joint Operating Agreements   510
  Broadcast Media Ownership Issues   515
  Broadcast Antitrust Cases   522
  Mass Media Buyouts and Antitrust Law   523
  Ongoing Issues   527

13) Advertising and the Law 530
  The First Amendment and Advertising   530
  Corporate Freedom of Speech   544
  Advertising and Media Access   546
  Federal Advertising Regulation   551
  State Advertising Regulation   566
  Self-Regulation   568

    Advertising on the Internet   570
    Ongoing Issues   571

14) Freedom of the Student Press   574
    The First Supreme Court Decision   575
    College Press Freedom Cases   577
    High School Cases before Hazelwood   583
    The Supreme Court Changes the Rules   587
    Freedom at Private Schools   594
    Practical Considerations   595
    Ongoing Issues   596

Index   599

PREFACE

This is the 14th edition of *Major Principles of Media Law* and the 12th published on an annual revision cycle. This edition covers new developments through the end of the Supreme Court's 2001-2002 term and will be in print in time for fall, 2002 classes.

Once again, the preface summarizes the year's new developments in communications law--and the changes have been numerous. The U.S. Supreme Court decided no fewer than 10 First Amendment and communications-related cases in 2001-2002, including seven cases on free expression issues and two interpreting the scope of the Buckley Amendment, a law that has hampered student journalists in their attempts to cover newsworthy issues on campus for years. Of the free expression cases, three involve attempts to define free speech rights in the areas of pornography, obscenity and Internet indecency. The court also handed down a decision that limits government power to regulate commercial speech and three others that address questions about free expression either in public forums or during judicial election campaigns.

Moving beyond the new Supreme Court decisions, nothing that happened during 2001 had more impact on mass media law than the events of Sept. 11. Although the full impact of those events on communications law may not be understood for years, the immediate effects are discussed in several chapters of this book. Among other things, a new policy statement on the Freedom of Information Act was sent to federal agencies a month after the attack, directing them to release less information and to favor secrecy over disclosure in borderline cases.

Several other issues in media law made headlines during 2001-2002. Among the more notable were freelance author Vanessa Leggett's jailing for 168 days for refusing to reveal confidential information, a series of court decisions forcing the Federal Communications Commission to reconsider many of its broadcast and cable ownership rules, the controversial new royalty rates for webcasting set by the Librarian of Congress, the ongoing battle over Internet copyrights and copy protection technologies and an *en banc* ruling of the ninth circuit U.S. Court of Appeals reinstating a jury verdict against "The Nuremburg Files," an anti-abortion website.

Here are some of the highlights of what has been added to the book since last year (in chapter order).

Chapter One (The Legal System) now includes:
* More coverage of online legal research methods; and
* Additional information about the federal appellate courts.

Chapter Two (The Legacy of Freedom) discusses:
* The impact of Sept. 11 on civil liberties in America.

Chapter Three (Prior Restraints) discusses:

* *Planned Parenthood v. American Coalition of Life Activists*, an *en banc* federal appellate court decision upholding much of a $107 million verdict against the creators of a controversial anti-abortion website after a three-judge panel of the same court had overturned the verdict on First Amendment grounds;
* *Watchtower Bible and Tract Society v. Village of Stratton*, a Supreme Court decision affirming the First Amendment right to do door-to-door soliciting for political, religious and other non-commercial causes without first obtaining a city permit;
* *Thomas v. Chicago Parks District*, a Supreme Court decision upholding a content-neutral permit system for large groups wishing to stage events in Chicago parks;
* New developments in the controversy over free expression rights on private property, including court decisions involving sidewalks on the Las Vegas Strip, a large gated apartment complex and retail centers; and
* A California Supreme Court decision overturning that state's "Son of Sam" law.

Chapter Four (Libel and Slander) discusses:
* *Suzuki Motor Corp. v. Consumers Union*, in which a federal appeals court declined to conduct an independent review of the evidence, overturned a summary judgment order and allowed a jury trial on Suzuki's evidence that CU's testing of the Suzuki Samarai was rigged;
* The trend for more states to enact anti-SLAPP laws and the effect of those laws on libel litigation; and
* A new $750,000 jury verdict for libel on the Internet.

Chapter Five (Privacy) discusses:
* New cases on the privacy of employer-owned computers and liability for flooding a company's e-mail system with hostile messages;
* New restrictions faced by journalists who monitor or tape telephone conversations or other confidential communications;
* New cases on the right of publicity, including one upholding a magazine's right to publish a digitally altered image of actor Dustin Hoffman as news and another denying a non-resident trust fund the right to sue the Franklin Mint for selling Princess Diana commemorative dolls; and
* The impact of the *Booth Rule* on recent right of publicity cases.

Chapter Six (Copyrights and Trademarks) discusses:
* Many Internet-related copyright issues, including the controversial (and, some say, prohibitive) royalty rates that webcasters must pay under a new decision by the Librarian of Congress, the Supreme Court's decision to hear a challenge to the length of copyright terms, a federal appellate court decision upholding censorship of information about DVD decryption techniques, new appellate court decisions on the use of deep linking and metatags, the ongoing debate about piracy and new developments in the battle over Internet file sharing as facilitated by Napster and its imitators;
* *Cavalier v. Random House*, an appellate court decision clarifying the extrinsic

and intrinsic tests for substantial similarity in copyright infringement cases.
* The settlement of the lawsuit over *The Wind Done Gone*, a parody of the novel, *Gone with the Wind*; and
* Continuing fallout from last year's *New York Times Co. v. Tasini* Supreme Court decision.

Chapter Seven (Fair Trial - Free Press) discusses:
* A decision by the South Dakota Supreme Court to admit cameras to many of its proceedings, which means that all 50 states allow cameras or video coverage of at least some proceedings in some courts; and
* *Republican Party of Minnesota v. White*, a Supreme Court decision certain to affect news coverage of judicial election campaigns by freeing candidates to announce their views on political and legal issues that they may have to rule on as judges.

Chapter Eight (Newsgatherer's Privilege) discusses:
* The story of Vanessa Leggett, the freelance book author who spent 168 days in a federal detention center, a modern record for jail time by a journalist protecting confidential information.

Chapter Nine (Freedom of Information) discusses:
* Attorney General John Ashcroft's memorandum directing federal agencies to be more cautious about releasing information under the Freedom of Information Act and to opt for secrecy in borderline cases;
* *Owasso Independent School District v. Falvo* and *Gonzaga University v. Doe*, two Supreme Court decisions on the scope of the Buckley Amendment; and
* *U.S. v. Miami University*, a federal appellate court decision reaffirming the secrecy of campus disciplinary records under the Buckley Amendment.

Chapter 10 (Obscenity and Pornography) discusses:
* *Ashcroft v. Free Speech Coalition*, a Supreme Court decision overturning the Child Pornography Prevention Act's ban on images that "appear to" depict minors in sexual activities;
* *Ashcroft v. Reno*, a Supreme Court ruling that community standards may be used to evaluate the content of the Internet, and ordering a lower court to reconsider First Amendment questions raised by the Child Online Protection Act;
* *City of Los Angeles v. Alameda Books*, a Supreme Court decision holding that it does not violate the First Amendment for a city ordinance to forbid adult bookstores to offer video viewing booths at the same location; and
* *American Library Association v. U.S.*, a three-judge federal court decision overturning the Children's Internet Protection Act's requirement that public libraries must install Internet filtering software to be eligible for federal funds.

Chapter 11 (Regulation of the Electronic Media) discusses:
* The Federal Communications Commission's third attempt to develop an

Equal Employment Opportunity Rule that will survive judicial review in the aftermath of the *MD/DC/DE Broadcasters Association v. FCC* ruling;
* The FCC's latest moves in its circuitous effort to enforce the Indecency Rule against broadcasters;
* The FCC's new bureau structure after the latest reorganization;
* The possible effect of the new campaign finance reform legislation on broadcast advertising of political issues;
* The dilemma posed by *National Public Radio v. FCC*, which barred the FCC from requiring non-commercial broadcast applicants to compete in auctions to win licenses; and
* The never-ending policy debates and uncertainties that threaten to delay the transition to digital television even further.

Chapter 12 (Ownership and Antitrust Issues) discusses:
* *Sinclair Broadcast Group v. FCC*, a federal appellate court decision rejecting the FCC's justification of the television duopoly rule and ordering the commission either to provide a better rationale or abolish the rule;
* *Fox Television Stations v. FCC*, a federal appellate court decision ordering the FCC either to eliminate or better justify its rule barring any company from owning television stations that reach more than 35 percent of TV households;
* Other pending changes in the FCC's ownership restrictions; and
* *National Cable & Telecommunications Association v. Gulf Power Co.*, the Supreme Court decision giving cable companies preferred rates for access to utility poles, even if the pole access is for Internet service as well as television.

Chapter 13 (Advertising Regulation) discusses:
* *Thompson v. Western States Medical Center*, the U.S. Supreme Court decision overturning Food and Drug Administration restrictions on advertising compounded drugs on First Amendment grounds;
* Recent developments in the war by many states against unsolicited e-mail advertising (spam), including a Washington Supreme Court decision upholding that state's anti-spam law; and
* Federal Trade Commission actions in response to Sept. 11, including a crackdown on Internet sites falsely advertising purported anthrax or smallpox remedies.

Chapter 14 (Student Press Law) discusses:
* A series of federal appellate court decisions clarifying First Amendment rights on college campuses in various contexts; and
* The problem of students being disciplined on campus for off-campus websites having content offensive to school officials.

* * *

All of this happened in the last year. As has been true ever since these annual revisions began, *Major Principles of Media Law* will be the first media law textbook in print with many of the year's new developments.

As this *Preface* has noted in previous years, having a textbook this current is possible only because of the emergence of desktop publishing technology--and because there are publishers willing to throw out the old production schedules for textbooks. A media law textbook produced on the traditional timetable is at least a year out of date when it arrives in college bookstores for the first time; it may be four or five years out of date before it is replaced by a new edition. That leaves those teaching a communications law class in the position of having to cover a lot of new developments in lecture or assign the students to read about them in a supplement--and then disregard the outdated parts of the textbook. After teaching the basic principles of communications law to more than 13,500 students on five campuses over the last 37 years, I'm convinced that having an up-to-date textbook makes teaching (and learning) this subject a lot easier.

Although much of the material is new, *Major Principles of Media Law* retains the primary goal it has had through 14 editions: to present a clear and concise summary of the law for mass communications students. If this book succeeds, much of the credit should go to the 35 reviewers who have offered so many helpful suggestions over the last 22 years. This year I particularly want to thank the new reviewers: Jens Koepke of California State University, Northridge, Gary Howard Mayer of Stephen F. Austin State University, Kathy Olson of Lehigh University and Mark Paxton of Southwest Missouri State University. They offered many valuable new insights.

Finally, I wish to thank Dean Rick Pullen of California State University, Fullerton, who wrote the original drafts of five chapters in 1980 and made many contributions as co-author of the first two editions of this book, as well as Janet and David Ewell, Lara Overbeck and Oli Rohrer, who proofread this year's manuscript as the deadline approached amidst late-breaking changes in communications law.

Wayne Overbeck, Ph.D., J.D.
July 1, 2002

Note: for information about major changes in communications law that occur during the 2002-2003 academic year, consult the author's website:

http://www.overbeck.com

TABLE OF CASES

44 Liquormart v. Rhode Island, 541
600 West 115th Street Corp. v. Von Gutfeld, 127

A&M Records et al. v. Napster, 262
Abrams v. U.S., 51
Action for Children's Television v. FCC, 465
Adarand Constructors Inc. v. Pena, 439
Adult Film Association v. Times Mirror, 570
Alabama Student Party v. Student Government Assn., 590
Alberts v. California, 396
Alden v. Maine, 13
Alderwood Associates v. Washington Environmental Council, 80
Alexander v. U.S., 417
Alpha Therapeutic Corp. v. Nippon Hoso Kyokai (NHK), 188
Alpo Pet Foods v. Ralston Purina, 566
Amalgamated Food Employees Local 590 v. Logan Valley Plaza, 79
American Library Association v. U.S., 414
American Life League v. Reno, 83
Ammerman v. Hubbard Broadcasting, 339, 340
Anderson v. Liberty Lobby, 156
Anheuser-Busch Inc. v. Schmoke, 542
Antonelli v. Hammond, 576
AP v. National Labor Relations Board, 506
ApolloMedia Corp. v. Reno, 413
Apple Computer Inc. v. Formula International, 257
Apple Computer Inc. v. Franklin Computer Corp., 256
Apple Computer Inc. v. Microsoft Corp., 257
Apprendi v. New Jersey, 72
Arkansas AFL-CIO v. FCC, 459
Arkansas Educational Television Commission v. Forbes, 455
Arkansas Writers' Project v. Ragland, 95
Armstrong v. H & C Communications, 199
Ashcraft v. Conoco Inc., 334
Ashcroft v. ACLU, 392, 415
Ashcroft v. Free Speech Coalition, 406
Ashton v. Kentucky, 169
Associated Press v. Walker, 138
Associated Press v. District Court, 311
Associated Press v. U.S., 506, 516
Associates & Aldrich v. Times Mirror, 547
Association of American Physicians and Surgeons v. Hillary Rodham Clinton, 376
Astaire v. Best Film and Video, 213
Astroline Communications v. Shurberg Broadcasting, 440
AT&T v. City of Portland, 525
Attorney General v. John Peter Zenger, 39

Austin v. Michigan State Chamber of Commerce, 546
Austin v. U.S., 417
Auvil v. CBS 60 Minutes, 162

Baez v. U.S. Justice Department, 366
Baker v. F & F Investment, 329
Baldwin v. New York, 324
Bally Total Fitness v. Faber, 283
Banzhaf v. FCC, 462
Barnes v. Glen Theatre, 418
Barron v. Baltimore, 52
Bartnicki v. Vopper, 182
Basic Books v. Kinko's Graphics Corp., 238
Batchelder v. Allied Stores Int'l, 80
Bates v. Arizona State Bar, 534
Batjac Productions v. GoodTimes Home Video Corp., 233
Bauer v. Kincaid, 374
Bauer v. Sampson, 583
Baughman v. Freienmuth, 585
Bay Guardian Co. v. Chronicle Publishing Co., 512
Bazaar v. Fortune, 577
Beahm v. Food and Drug Administration, 564
Beauharnais v. Illinois, 168
Bechtel v. FCC, 438
Becker v. FCC, 456
Behrendt v. Times Mirror Co., 122
Beilenson v. Superior Court, 158
Bell v. U.S., 361
Berger v. Hanlon, 185
Bernstein v. U.S. Department of Justice, 102
Bethel School District v. Fraser, 587
Bibles v. Oregon Natural Desert Assn., 363
Bigelow v. Virginia, 59, 532
Bilney v. Evening Star, 198
Bindrim v. Mitchell, 166
Black Citizens for a Fair Media v. FCC, 445
Bloom v. Illinois, 324
BMI v. Claire's Boutiques, 249
Board of Airport Commissioners v. Jews for Jesus, 88
Board of Regents v. Southworth, 581
Bock v. Westminster Mall Co., 80
Bolger v. Young Drug Products Corp., 408, 537
Boos v. Barry, 86
Booth v. Curtis Publishing, 208
Bose v. Consumers Union, 145
Bowers v. Hardwick, 177
Boy Scouts of America v. Dale, 91
Boyd v. U.S., 175
Bradbury v. Superior Court, 159
Braden v. Pittsburgh University, 594
Branch v. FCC, 456

Brandenburg v. Ohio, 56, 71
Brandywine-Main Line Radio v. FCC, 457
Branzburg v. Hayes, 327, 384
Braun v. Chronicle Publishing Co., 159
Braun v. Soldier of Fortune Magazine, 105
Bridges v. California, 324
Briggs v. Eden Council for Hope and Opportunity, 158
Bright v. Los Angeles Unified School District, 587
Briscoe v. Reader's Digest, 29, 192
Brookfield Communications v. West Coast Entertainment, 281
Brown and Williamson Tobacco Co. v. Jacobson, 112
Brown v. Board of Education, 14, 15
Brown v. Virginia, 336
Bruno & Stillman v. Globe Newspaper Co., 332
Bullfrog Films v. Wick, 99
Burch v. Barker, 593
Burnett v. National Enquirer, 153
Burstyn v. Wilson, 410
Butler v. Michigan, 396
Butterworth v. Smith, 107
Byers v. Edmonson, 105

Cain v. Hearst Corp., 200
Cairns v. Franklin Mint, 213
Calder v. Jones, 154
Caldero v. Tribune Publishing, 337
California First Amendment Coalition v. Calderon, 385
California v. American Stores, 504
Campbell v. Acuff-Rose Music Co., 246
Cantrell v. Forest City Publishing Co., 201
Capital Cities Cable Inc. v. Crisp, 480
Carey v. Population Services International, 533
Carson v. Here's Johnny, 204
Carter v. Helmsley-Spear Inc., 272
Cavalier v. Random House Inc., 229
CBS v. Democratic National Committee, 463
CBS v. FCC, 451
CBS v. Superior Court, 341
Central Florida Enterprises v. FCC, 445
Central Hudson Gas and Electric v. Public Service Commission of New York, 533
Chandler v. Florida, 315
Chaplinsky v. New Hampshire, 70
Cher v. Forum International, 207
Chesapeake & Potomac Telephone Co. v. U.S., 492
Chicago Joint Board - Amalgamated Clothing Workers of America v. Chicago Tribune, 547
Children of the Rosary v. City of Phoenix, 550
Chisholm v. FCC, 454
Christ's Bride Ministries v. Southeastern Pennsylvania Transportation Authority, 550
Church of Scientology v. Wollersheim, 159
CIA v. Sims, 363

Cincinnati v. Discovery Network, 93, 539
Cinevision Corp. v. City of Burbank, 101
Citizens Communications Center v. FCC, 444
Citizen Publishing Co. v. U.S., 510
Citizens Committee to Save WEFM v. FCC, 473
Citizens Committee to Preserve the Voice of the Arts in Atlanta v. FCC, 472
City of Corona v. Corona Daily Independent, 94
City of Erie v. Pap's A.M., 419
City of Ladue v. Gilleo, 82, 537
City of Lakewood v. Plain Dealer Publishing Co., 93
City of Los Angeles v. Alameda Books, 421
City of Los Angeles v. Preferred Communications, 486
City of New York v. FCC, 481
Clampitt v. Thurston County, 336
Clift v. Narragansett Television, 191
Coalition for a Healthy California v. FCC, 459
Cochran v. NYP Holdings, 134
Cohen v. California, 72
Cohen v. Cowles Media Co., 348
Cohen v. Illinois Institute of Technology, 595
Comedy III Productions v. Gary Saderup Inc., 211
Committee for an Independent P-I v. Hearst Corp., 513
Community Communications v. City of Boulder, 523
Community for Creative Non-Violence v. Reid, 235
Compco v. Day-Brite Lighting, 273
Conklin v. Sloss, 193
Consolidated Edison v. Public Service Commission of New York, 545
Corrigan v. Bobbs-Merrill, 166
Costco Companies v. Gallant, 81
Cox Broadcasting v. Cohn, 106, 193, 214
Cox v. Louisiana, 325
Craig v. Harney, 325
Curran v. Mt. Diablo Council of the Boy Scouts of America, 92
Curtis Publishing Co. v. Butts, 138

Debs v. U.S., 51
Delaney v. Superior Court, 342
Dennis v. U.S., 54
Denver Area Educational Telecommunications Consortium v. FCC, 487
Denver Publishing Co. v. Bueno, 200
Department of Defense v. Federal Labor Relations Authority, 35
Department of Revenue v. Magazine Publishers of America, 97
Department of the Air Force v. Rose, 362
Department of the Interior v. Klamath Water Users Protective Association, 365
Desilets v. Clearview Regional Board of Education, 592

Desnick v. American Broadcasting Company, 189
Deteresa v. ABC, 188
Diaz v. Oakland Tribune, 199
Dietemann v. Time Inc., 182
Dillon v. City and County of San Francisco, 333
DiSalle v. P.G. Publishing Co., 128
Dodds v. American Broadcasting Company, 134
Doe v. Methodist Hospital, 192
Dorsey v. National Enquirer, 129
Dr. Seuss Enterprises v. Penguin Books, 246
Dun & Bradstreet v. Greenmoss Builders, 146

East Canton Education Association v. McIntosh, 145
Eastwood v. National Enquirer, 209
Edison Brothers Stores v. BMI, 250
Edwards v. City of Santa Barbara, 86
Edwards v. National Audubon Society, 135
Eisner v. Stamford Board of Education, 584
El Vocero de Puerto Rico v. Puerto Rico, 310
Elyria Lorain Broadcasting v. Lorain Journal, 508
Engler v. Winfrey, 163
Equality Foundation of Greater Cincinnati v. City of Cincinnati, 92
Estate of Martin Luther King v. CBS, 241
Estes v. Texas, 314

Factors v. Pro Arts, 212
Farmers Educational and Cooperative Union v. WDAY, 130, 456
Farr v. Pitchess, 345
Farr v. Superior Court, 341, 344
FBI v. Abramson, 362
FCC v. ITT World Communications, 380
FCC v. League of Women Voters of California, 461
FCC v. Midwest Video, 479
FCC v. National Citizens Committee for Broadcasting, 519
FCC v. Pacifica Foundation, 465
FCC v. WNCN Listeners Guild, 473
FDA v. Brown & Williamson Tobacco, 542, 563
Federal Maritime Commission v. South Carolina State Ports Authority, 13
Federated Publications v. Swedberg, 303
Feist Publications v. Rural Telephone Service Co., 226
Fellows v. National Enquirer, 118
Feltner v. Columbia Pictures Television, 228
Ferguson v. Friendfinders, 570
Fiduccia v. Department of Justice, 358
First National Bank v. Bellotti, 544, 545
Fisher v. Dees, 245
Fiske v. Kansas, 54
Flanagan v. Flanagan, 189
Florida Bar v. Went for It Inc., 535, 536
Florida Publishing Co. v. Fletcher, 183
Florida Star v. B.J.F., 106, 194, 214

Florida v. Globe Communications Corp., 107, 194
Fogerty v. Fantasy, 228
Food Lion v. Capital Cities/ABC, 112
Forsham v. Harris, 362
Forsher v. Bugliosi, 193
Fortnightly v. United Artists, 251
Fox Television Stations v. FCC, 517
Frasca v. Andrews, 585
Freedman v. Maryland, 410
Friedman v. Rogers, 534
Friends of the Earth v. FCC, 463
Frisby v. Schultz, 82
Frohwerk v. U.S., 51
Fruit of the Loom v. Girouard, 277
FTC v. Colgate-Palmolive Co., 556
FTC v. R.F. Keppel & Brother, 551
FTC v. Raladam, 551
FTC v. Sperry Hutchinson Co., 559
FTC v. Standard Education Society, 551
FTC v. Winsted Hosiery Co., 551
Fujishima v. Board of Education, 584
Furumoto v. Lyman, 595
FW/PBS Inc. v. City of Dallas, 420

Galella v. Onassis, 183, 184
Galoob Toys v. Nintendo of America, 258
Gambino v. Fairfax County School Board, 585
Gannett v. DePasquale, 305, 384, 386
Garland v. Torre, 327
Garrison v. Louisiana, 169
General Media Communications v. Cohen, 409
Gentile v. State Bar of Nevada, 302
Georgia Television Company v. Television News Clips of Atlanta, 244
Gerawan Farming v. Lyons, 544
Gertz v. Welch, 119, 122, 141, 143, 147
Gill v. Curtis Publishing, 202
Gill v. Hearst Corporation, 202
Ginsberg v. New York, 400
Ginzburg v. U.S., 399
Gitlow v. New York, 52
Glickman v. Wileman Brothers & Elliot Inc, 544
Globe Newspaper Company v. Superior Court, 307
Golden Gateway Center v. Golden Gateway Tenants Association, 81
Goldstein v. California, 273
Gonzaga University v. Doe, 373
Gonzales v. NBC, 333
Greater Boston Television Corp. v. FCC, 444
Greater New Orleans Broadcasting Association v. U.S., 475, 540
Green Party of New Jersey v. Hartz Mountain Industries, 80
Green v. Alton Telegraph, 111
Greenbelt Publishing Assn. v. Bresler, 139
Griswold v. Connecticut, 176
Grosjean v. American Press, 94

Haelan Laboratories v. Topps Chewing Gum, 203
Halsey v. New York Society for the Suppression of Vice, 395
Hamling v. U.S., 403
Hanlon v. Berger, 186
Hannegan v. Esquire, 408
Harman v. City of New York, 69
Harper & Row Publishers v. The Nation Enterprises, 241
Harte-Hanks Communications v. Connaughton, 147
Hays County Guardian v. Supple, 579
Hazelwood School District v. Kuhlmeier, 574, 588
Healy v. James, 576
Heffron v. International Society for Krishna Consciousness, 87
Herbert v. Lando, 150
Hill v. Colorado, 86
Hoffman v. Capital Cities/ABC, 209
Holy Spirit Assn. v. Sequoia Elsevier, 132
Home Placement Service v. Providence Journal, 548
Hopewell v. Midcontinent Broadcasting Corp., 336
Houchins v. KQED, 383
Howard v. Des Moines Register, 197
Hudgens v. NLRB, 79
Hudnut v. American Booksellers, 417
Hurley v. Irish-American Gay Lesbian and Bisexual Group of Boston, 91
Hustler Magazine v. Falwell, 160
Hutchinson v. Proxmire, 128, 144

Ibanez v. Florida Department of Professional and Business Regulation, 535, 536
Immigration and Naturalization Service v. Chadha, 560
In re Aspen Institute and CBS, 454
In re Farber, 342
In re Farr, 345
In re Pappas, 328
In re Paulsen v. FCC, 455
In re R.M.J., 535
In re Taylor, 343
Intel Corp. v. Hamidi, 217
International News Service v. Associated Press, 273
International Shoe v. Washington, 154
Irvin v. Dowd, 293
Isaacs v. Temple University, 594

J.B. Williams Co. v. FTC, 554
Jacksonville Television Inc. v. Florida Dept. of Health and Rehabilitative Services, 301
Jacobellis v. Ohio, 398
Jacobs v. Indianapolis Board of School Commissioners, 585
Janklow v. Newsweek, 132
Jenkins v. Georgia, 403

John Doe Agency v. John Doe Corp., 364
Jones v. Opelika, 77
Journal-Gazette Co. v. Bandido's, 142
Joyner v. Whiting, 577
Junger v. Daley, 102

Kansas City Star v. U.S., 508
Kansas v. Alston, 301
Kansas v. Sandstrom, 336
Katz v. U.S., 176
Kay v. FCC, 452
Keenan v. Superior Court, 103
Keeton v. Hustler, 154, 155
Kelly v. Arriba Soft Corp., 283
Kennedy for President Committee v. FCC, 455
Khawar v. Globe Communications, 135
Kincaid v. Gibson, 591
Kissinger v. New York City Transit Authority, 549
Kissinger v. Reporters Committee for Freedom of the Press, 362
KOVR-TV v. Superior Court of Sacramento County, 199
KSDO v. Superior Court, 342
Kyllo v. United States, 176

Lake v. Wal-Mart Stores, 192
Lamothe v. Atlantic Recording Corp., 271
Lamprecht v. FCC, 441
Landmark Communications v. Virginia, 106, 194
Le Mistral Inc. v. CBS, 183
League of Women Voters v. FCC, 454
Leathers v. Medlock, 96
Lebron v. National Railroad Passenger Corp., 550
Lebron v. Washington Metropolitan Area Transit Authority, 550
Lee v. Board of Regents, 580
Lee v. International Society for Krishna Consciousness, 89
Leeb v. DeLong, 589
Lehman v. Shaker Heights, 549
Linmark Associates v. Willingboro, 532
Linnemeir v. Board of Trustees of Purdue University, 582
Lloyd Corp. v. Tanner, 79
Lloyd Corp. v. Whiffen, 80
Loeb v. New Times, 132
Long v. Internal Revenue Service, 358
Lorain Journal Company v. U.S., 507
Loretto v. Teleprompter Manhattan Cable Corp., 496
Lorillard Tobacco Co. v. Reilly, 542, 561
Los Angeles Free Press v. City of Los Angeles, 385
Los Angeles News Service v. KCAL-TV Channel 9, 245
Los Angeles News Service v. Reuters Television, 245
Los Angeles Police Department v. United

Reporting Publishing Co., 382
Lotus Development Corp. v. Borland International, 258
Lovell v. City of Griffin, 76
Lowe v. Securities and Exchange Commission, 97
Lugosi v. Universal Pictures, 212
Luke Records v. Navarro, 393, 405
Lutheran Church-Missouri Synod v. FCC, 441

M.G. v. Time Warner, 195
Madison v. Yunker, 153
Madsen v. Women's Health Center, 85
Mainstream Loudoun v. Board of Trustees, 414
Mangini v. R.J. Reynolds Tobacco Co., 562
Manual Enterprises v. Day, 397
Marbury v. Madison, 45
Maressa v. New Jersey Monthly, 342
Marsh v. Alabama, 78
Marshall v. U.S., 293
Masson v. New Yorker Magazine, 148, 149
Matthews v. Wozencraft, 210
McCulloch v. Maryland, 46
McIntyre v. Ohio Elections Commission, 90
MD/DC/DE Broadcasters Association v. FCC, 442
Meese v. Keene, 99
Melvin v. Reid, 192
Members of the Los Angeles City Council v. Taxpayers for Vincent, 536
Memoirs v. Massachusetts, 398
Memphis Development Foundation v. Factors, 212
Metro Broadcasting v. FCC, 439
Metromedia v. San Diego, 536
Miami Herald v. Department of Revenue, 97
Miami Herald v. Tornillo, 461, 547
Michigan Citizens for an Independent Press v. Thornburgh, 514
Midler v. Ford Motor Company, 205
Milkovich v. Lorain Journal Co., 131
Miller v. California, 401
Miller v. FCC, 453
Miller v. Superior Court, 342
Miller v. Transamerican Press, 332
Minneapolis Star and Tribune v. Minnesota Commissioner of Revenue, 95
Mississippi Gay Alliance v. Goudelock, 580
Mitchell v. Superior Court, 336
Moldea v. New York Times Co., 133
Monitor Patriot Co. v. Roy, 139
Montana v. Mercury News, 208
Morales v. TWA, 568
Motschenbacher v. R.J. Reynolds Tobacco, 204
Mutual Film Corp. v. Industrial Commission of Ohio, 409
Myers v. Boston Magazine, 132

National Cable & Telecommunications Association v. Gulf Power Co., 492, 525
National Endowment for the Arts v. Finley, 393
National Public Radio v. FCC, 438
NBA v. Motorola, 274
NBC Subsidiary v. Superior Court, 310
NBC v. U.S., 433, 516
Near v. Minnesota, 63, 64, 94
Nebraska Press Assn. v. Stuart, 299
New Era Publications v. Henry Holt & Co., 242
New Hampshire v. Siel, 336
New Jersey Coalition Against War in the Middle East v. J.M.B. Realty Corp., 80
New York Times Co. v. Superior Court, 342
New York Times Co. v. Tasini, 266
New York Times v. Sullivan, 20, 26, 28, 30, 121, 122, 123, 136, 139, 145, 146, 147, 165, 169, 181, 201
New York Times v. U.S., 64
New York v. Ferber, 405
Newcombe v. Adolf Coors, 208
Newton v. NBC, 146
Nitzberg v. Parks, 585

Ocala Star-Banner v. Damron, 139
Office of Communication of the United Church of Christ v. FCC, 443
Ohio ex rel. New World Communications v. Character, 301
Ohralik v. Ohio State Bar Association, 534
Oklahoma Publishing v. District Court, 106
Ollman v. Evans, 132
Olmstead v. U.S., 175
One Book Entitled 'Ulysses' v. U.S., 396
Organization for a Better Austin v. Keefe, 87
Orin v. Barclay, 582
Osborne v. Ohio, 405
Owasso Independent School District v. Falvo, 373

Pacific Gas & Electric Company v. Public Utilities Commission of California, 545
Pacific Telesis Group v. International Telesis Communications, 277
Panavision International v. Toeppen, 281
Papish v. University of Missouri Curators, 577
Pavesich v. New England Life Insurance Co., 174
Peavy v. WFAA-TV, 191
Peel v. Attorney Registration and Disciplinary Commission, 535, 536
Pell v. Procunier, 383
Penn Advertising v. Schmoke, 542
Pennekamp v. Florida, 325
People v. Croswell, 47
People v. Pawlaczyk, 343
Philadelphia Newspapers v. Hepps, 125, 131
Phoenix Newspapers v. U.S. District Court, 312
Pinkus v. U.S., 402
Pitt News v. Fisher, 580
Pittsburgh Press v. Pittsburgh Commission on Human Relations, 531
Pizza Hut Inc. v. Papa John's International Inc., 566

Planned Parenthood of Southeastern Pennsylvania v. Casey, 178
Planned Parenthood of the Columbia/Willamette v. American Coalition of Life Activists, 84
Planned Parenthood v. Clark County School District, 591
Playboy Enterprises v. Sanfilippo, 268
Playboy Enterprises v. Welles, 268, 281
Player's International v. U.S., 475
Plessy v. Ferguson, 14
Pope v. Illinois, 402
Posadas de Puerto Rico Associates v. Tourism Company of Puerto Rico, 537
Pottstown Daily News Publishing Company v. Pottstown Broadcasting, 273
Powell v. State of Georgia, 178
Press-Enterprise Co. v. Superior Court, 308
Press-Enterprise Co. v. Superior Court (P-E II), 309
Princeton University Press v. Michigan Document Services, 238, 239
Pring v. Penthouse, 112, 166, 167
Procter & Gamble Co. v. Banker's Trust Co., 108
Protect Our Mountain Environment v. District Court, 157
Pruneyard Shopping Center v. Robins, 79
Public Citizen v. Department of Justice, 375
Public Interest Research Group v. FCC, 463

Quad-City Community News Service v. Jebens, 385
Qualitex Co. v. Jacobson Products Inc., 277
Quality King Distributors v. L'Anza Research International, 260
Quarterman v. Byrd, 585

R.A.V. v. St. Paul, 70
Radio-Television News Director's Association v. FCC, 460
Randall v. Orange County Council of the Boy Scouts of America, 92
Recording Industry Association of America v. Diamond Multimedia Systems, 262
Red & Black Publishing Co. v. Board of Regents of the University of Georgia, 374
Red Lion Broadcasting v. FCC, 461
Redrup v. New York, 399
Regina v. Hicklin, 395
Reilly v. Hearst Corp., 515
Rendell-Baker v. Kohn, 595
Reno v. ACLU, 392, 412
Reno v. Condon, 378
Renton v. Playtime Theatres, 420
Renwick v. News and Observer, 200
Republican Party of Minnesota v. White, 302
Resorts International v. New Jersey Monthly, 342
Rex v. Tuchin, 38
Rice v. Paladin Enterprises, 104

Richmond Newspapers v. Virginia, 306, 384, 386
Richmond v. J.A. Croson Co., 439
Rideau v. Louisiana, 294
Riley v. Chester, 331
RKO v. FCC, 447
Roberson v. Rochester Folding Box Co., 174
Roe v. Wade, 7, 8, 176, 532
Romer v. Evans, 92, 178
Rosemont Enterprises v. Random House, 29, 239
Rosenberger v. Rector and Visitors of the University of Virginia, 581
Rosenblatt v. Baer, 138
Rosenbloom v. Metromedia, 140
Roth v. U.S., 396
Rowan v. Post Office, 408
Rubin v. Coors Brewing Co., 540
Rufo v. Simpson, 289
Rust v. Sullivan, 179
Ryan v. Hofstra, 595

S.O.C. v. The Mirage, 81
Sabelko v. City of Phoenix, 86
Sailor Music v. The Gap Stores, 249
Sanders v. ABC, 187
Saxbe v. Washington Post, 383
Saxe v. State College Area School District, 72
Schad v. Mt. Ephraim, 418
Schaffer v. Kissinger, 361
Schenck v. Pro-Choice Network, 85
Schenck v. U.S., 50, 64
Schiavone v. Fortune (AKA Time Inc.), 159
Schiff v. Williams, 578
Schneider v. State of New Jersey, 77
Scott v. The News-Herald, 145
Scoville v. Board of Education, 585
Sears Roebuck and Co. v. Stiffel, 273
Seattle Times v. Ishikawa, 303
Seattle Times v. Rhinehart, 107
SEC v. Wall Street Publishing Institute Inc., 98
Sega Enterprises v. Accolade Inc., 259
Senear v. Daily Journal-American, 336
Serafyn v. FCC, 463
Shanley v. Northeast Independent School District, 585
Shapero v. Kentucky Bar Association, 535
Sheldon v. MGM, 229
Shepherd v. Florida, 293
Sheppard v. Maxwell, 294, 325
Sherrill v. Knight, 385
Shoen v. Shoen, 334
Shuck v. Carroll Daily Herald, 547
Shulman v. Group W Productions, 186
Sidis v. F-R Publishing Co., 175
Sierra Life v. Magic Valley Newspapers, 1, 337
Silkwood v. Kerr-McGee, 332
Simon & Schuster v. New York State Crime Victims Board, 103
Sinatra v. Goodyear, 205
Sinclair Broadcast Group v. FCC, 517

Sipple v. Chronicle Publishing Co., 198
Smith v. Daily Mail, 106, 194
Snepp v. U.S., 67
Sony Computer Entertainment v. Bleem, 247
Sony Computer Entertainment v. Connectix Corp., 259
Sony Corp. of America v. Universal City Studios, 253
Southcenter Joint Venture v. National Democratic Policy Committee, 80
St. Amant v. Thompson, 139
Stanley v. Georgia, 400
Stanley v. Magrath, 578
Star v. Preller, 411
State of Minnesota v. Turner, 343
State of Washington v. Heckel, 570
State University of New York v. Fox, 538
Steaks Unlimited v. Deaner, 343
Stenberg v. Carhart, 179
Stewart v. Abend, 233
Stratton Oakmont Inc. v. Prodigy Services Co, 163
Stroble v. California, 293
Sussman v. ABC, 187
Suzuki Motor Corp. v. Consumers Union, 156
Syracuse Peace Council v. FCC, 459

TBG Insurance Services v. Superior Court, 217
Telecommunications Research Action Center v. FCC, 459
Teleprompter v. CBS, 251
Texas Monthly v. Bullock, 96
Texas v. Johnson, 73
The Gillette Co. v. Wilkinson Sword Inc., 566
The Miami Student v. Miami University, 374
Thomas v. Chicago Park District, 92
Thomas v. Granville, 585
Thompson v. Western States Medical Center, 564
Time Inc. v. Bernard Geis Associates, 240, 244
Time Inc. v. Firestone, 143
Time Inc. v. Hill, 200, 213
Time Inc. v. Pape, 139, 140
Time Warner Entertainment Co. v. FCC, 517
Time Warner Entertainment v. FCC, 485
Times Film Corp. v. Chicago, 410
Times Mirror Co. v. Superior Court of San Diego County, 196
Times Mirror v. U.S., 509
Times-Picayune v. U.S., 508
Tinker v. Community School District, 72
Tinker v. Des Moines Independent Community School District, 575
Toys R Us v. Akkaoui, 281
Trachtman v. Anker, 584
Trader Joe's Co. v. Progressive Campaigns Inc., 81
Triangle Publications v. Knight-Ridder Newspapers, 247
Trinity Broadcasting of Florida v. FCC, 449
Trujillo v. Love, 576
Turner Broadcasting System v. FCC, 484
Twentieth Century Music Corp. v. Aiken, 249
Two Pesos v. Taco Cabana, 278

U-Haul International v. Jartran, 566
U.S. Department of Justice v. Landano, 365
U.S. Department of Justice v. Reporters Committee for Freedom of the Press, 364
U.S. Department of State v. Washington Post, 362
U.S. ex rel. Milwaukee Social Democratic Publishing Co. v. Burleson, 52
U.S. v. Blucher, 404
U.S. v. C.I.O., 58
U.S. v. Cable News Network, 301
U.S. v. Cooper, 42
U.S. v. Criden, 331
U.S. v. Cuthbertson, 330
U.S. v. Edge Broadcasting, 474, 539
U.S. v. Eichman, 73
U.S. v. Hubbard, 333
U.S. v. Hudson and Goodwin, 46
U.S. v. Kaczynski, 313
U.S. v. Kokinda, 89
U.S. v. Marchetti, 67
U.S. v. Miami University, 375
U.S. v. Microsoft Corp., 504, 505
U.S. v. Midwest Video Corp., 479
U.S. v. Morison, 66
U.S. v. Morrison, 46
U.S. v. National Treasury Employees Union, 68
U.S. v. Nelson Brothers, 433
U.S. v. Nixon, 369
U.S. v. Playboy Entertainment Group, 488
U.S. v. Radio Corporation of America, 522
U.S. v. Reidel, 401
U.S. v. Southwestern Cable Co., 478
U.S. v. The Progressive, 66
U.S. v. Thirty-Seven Photographs, 401
U.S. v. Thomas, 404
U.S. v. Twelve 200-foot Reels of Super 8mm Film, 401
U.S. v. U.S. District Court, 406
U.S. v. United Foods Inc., 543
U.S. v. X-Citement Video Inc., 406
United Video v. FCC, 480
Universal City Studios v. Corley, 264

Vail v. Plain Dealer, 134
Valentine v. Chrestensen, 531
Valley Broadcasting Co. v. U.S. District Court, 312
Valley Broadcasting v. U.S., 475, 540
Vance v. Universal Amusement, 416
Varian Medical Systems v. Delfino, 164
Vaughn v. Rosen, 359
Venetian Casino Resort v. Local Joint Executive Board of Las Vegas, 81
Vermont v. St. Peter, 336
Virgil v. Time Inc., 196
Virginia State Board of Pharmacy v. Virginia

Citizens Consumer Council, 532

Waits v. Frito-Lay, 205
Wal-Mart Stores v. Samara Brothers, 278
Waller v. Georgia, 309
Ward v. Rock Against Racism, 100
Warner-Lambert Co. v. FTC, 555
Warren Publishing v. Microdos Data Corp., 226
Washington Post v. Kennedy, 121
Watchtower Bible and Tract Society v. Village of Stratton, 77, 90
WBAI-FM v. Proskin, 341
Webster v. Human Reproductive Services, 177
Weight Watchers International v. FTC, 558
Wendt v. Host International, 206
White v. Samsung, 206
Whitney v. California, 53, 57
Wilkinson v. Jones, 487
Williams and Wilkins v. U.S., 239
Williams v. Spencer, 586
Wilson v. A.H. Belo Corp., 453
Wilson v. Layne, 182
Winegard v. Oxberger, 335
Wirta v. Alameda-Contra Costa Transit District, 549
Wisconsin v. Mitchell, 71, 75
Wolston v. Reader's Digest Association, 144
Woodall v. Reno, 83
Worldwide Church of God v. Philadelphia Church of God, 243

Yates v. U.S., 56
Yeo v. Town of Lexington, 580, 591
Young v. American Mini-Theatres, 418

Zacchini v. Scripps-Howard Broadcasting, 210
Zauderer v. Office of Disciplinary Counsel, 535
Zelenka v. Wisconsin, 29, 336
Zeran v. America Online, 164
Zerilli v. Smith, 333
Zucker v. Panitz, 580
Zurcher v. Stanford Daily, 351

CHAPTER ONE

The American Legal System

America has become a nation of laws, lawyers and lawsuits. Both the number of lawsuits being filed and the number of people employed as lawyers have doubled since the 1970s. For good or ill, more and more people with grievances are suing somebody.

The mass media have not escaped this flood of litigation. The nation's broadcasters, cable and satellite television providers, newspapers, magazines, wire services, Internet providers and advertising agencies are constantly fighting legal battles. Just a few decades ago, media executives only rarely needed legal advice to perform their duties. But today, few major communications businesses operate without lawyers on their staffs, or at least on retainer.

Moreover, legal problems are not just headaches for top executives. Working journalists (and other mass communicators) run afoul of the law regularly: they are threatened with lawsuits and even jail sentences all too often. In fact, by now enough reporters have faced jail sentences for standing by their principles that the imprisonment of a journalist is no longer front-page news, except perhaps in the locality where it happens.

Million-dollar verdicts against the mass media are no longer unusual, and the big national media are by no means the only targets. For example, one medium-size newspaper in Idaho was ordered to pay $1.9 million in a libel case--not because the newspaper published some horribly libelous falsehood but merely because the paper refused to say who told a reporter where to find public records about wrongdoing by an insurance company. A higher court eventually set aside that ruling, but by then the paper had spent thousands of dollars on legal expenses to defend the case (*Sierra Life v. Magic Valley Newspapers*, 6 Med.L.Rptr. 1769). Likewise, those who do video production work, prepare advertising copy or even post messages on the Internet may risk lawsuits and threats of lawsuits for anything from libel to copyright infringement. More than ever before, a knowledge of media law is essential for a successful career in mass communications.

This textbook was written for communications students and media professionals, not for lawyers or law students. Perhaps we should begin by explaining how the American legal system works.

THE KEY ROLE OF THE COURTS

Mass media law is largely based on court decisions. Even though Congress and the 50 state legislatures have enacted many laws affecting the mass media, the courts play the decisive role in interpreting those laws. For that matter, the courts also have the final say in interpreting the meaning of our most important legal document, the U.S. Constitution. The courts have the power to modify or even overturn laws passed by state legislatures and Congress, particularly when a law conflicts with the Constitution. In so doing, the courts have the power to establish *legal precedent,* handing down rules that other courts must ordinarily follow in deciding similar cases.

However, not all court decisions establish legal precedents, and not all legal precedents are equally important as guidelines for later decisions. The United States Supreme Court is the highest court in the country; its rulings are binding on all lower courts. On matters of state law the highest court in each of the 50 states (usually called the state supreme court) has the final say--unless one of its rulings somehow violates the U.S. Constitution. On federal matters the U.S. Courts of Appeals rank just below the U.S. Supreme Court. All of these courts are *appellate* courts; cases are appealed to them from trial courts.

There is an important difference between trial and appellate courts. The major function of the appellate courts is to make precedent-setting decisions that interpret the meaning of law. The trial courts, on the other hand, are responsible for deciding factual issues (such as the guilt or innocence of a person accused of a crime). And this fact-finding process does not normally establish legal precedents. The way a judge or jury decides a given murder trial, for instance, sets no precedent at all for the next murder trial. The fact that one alleged murderer may be guilty doesn't prove the guilt of the next murder suspect.

In civil (i.e., noncriminal) lawsuits, this is also true. A trial court may have to decide whether a newspaper libeled the local mayor by falsely linking him to a scandal. Even if the paper did--and if the mayor wins his or her lawsuit against the paper--that doesn't prove the next newspaper story about a mayoral scandal is also libelous. Each mayor--or murder suspect--is entitled to his or her own day in court.

The trial courts usually have the final say about these questions of fact. An appellate court might rule that a trial court misapplied the law to a given factual situation, but the appellate court doesn't ordinarily reevaluate the facts on its own. Instead, it sends the case back to the trial court with instructions to reassess the facts under new legal rules written by the appellate court. For instance, an appellate court might decide that a certain piece of evidence was illegally obtained and cannot be used in a murder trial. It will order the trial court to reevaluate the factual issue of guilt or innocence, this time completely disregarding the illegally obtained evidence. Such a ruling may well affect the outcome of the case, but it is the job of the trial court to decide that question, just as it is the job of the appellate court to set down rules on such legal issues as the admissibility of evidence.

This is not to say trial courts never make legal (as opposed to fact-finding) decisions: they do so every time the law must be applied to a factual situation. But when a trial court issues an opinion on a legal issue, that opinion usually carries little weight as legal precedent.

Sometimes there is high drama in the trial courtroom, and that may result in extensive media coverage. According to the ratings, more Americans watched the announcement of the jury's verdict in the O.J. Simpson murder trial in October, 1995 than any other event in the history of television.

One trial verdict may even inspire (or discourage) more lawsuits of the same kind. Still, the outcome of a trial rarely has long-term legal significance. On the other hand, a little-noticed appellate court decision may fundamentally alter the way we live. That is why law textbooks such as this one concentrate on appellate court decisions, especially U.S. Supreme Court decisions.

STRUCTURE OF THE COURT SYSTEM

Because the courts play such an important role in shaping the law, the structure of the court system itself deserves some explanation. Fig. 1 shows how the state and federal courts are organized. In the federal system, there is a nationwide network of trial courts at the bottom of the structure. Next higher are 12 intermediate appellate courts serving various regions of the country, with the Supreme Court at the top of the system.

U.S. District Courts

In the federal system there is at least one trial court called the *U.S. District Court* in each of the 50 states and the District of Columbia. Some of the more populous states have more than one federal judicial district, and each district has its own trial court or courts.

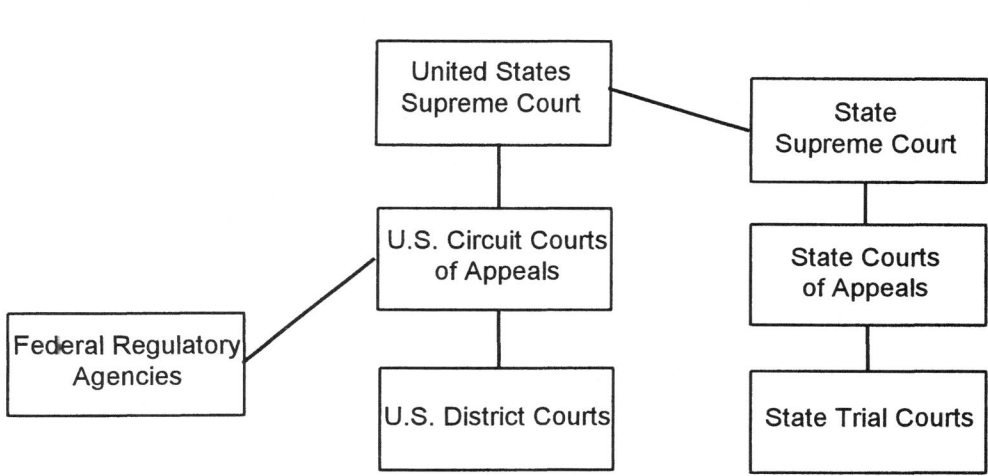

Fig. 1. Organization of the federal courts and a typical state court system.

4   The American Legal System

As trial courts, the U.S. District Courts have limited precedent-setting authority. Nevertheless, there are occasions when a U.S. District Court opinion is recognized as a precedent. The primary duty of these courts, however, is to serve as trial courts of *general jurisdiction* in the federal system; that is, they handle a variety of federal civil and criminal matters. Many times a trial in a U.S. District Court is newsworthy. These courts handle everything from civil disputes over copyrights to criminal trials of persons accused of acts of terrorism against the United States.

U.S. Courts of Appeals

The next level up in the federal court system is the U.S. Courts of Appeals, often called the *circuit courts* because the nation is divided into geographic *circuits* (see Fig. 2). That term, incidentally, originated in an era when all federal judges (including the justices of the Supreme Court) were required to be "circuit riders." That is, they spent much of their time traveling from town to town, holding court sessions wherever there were federal cases to be heard.

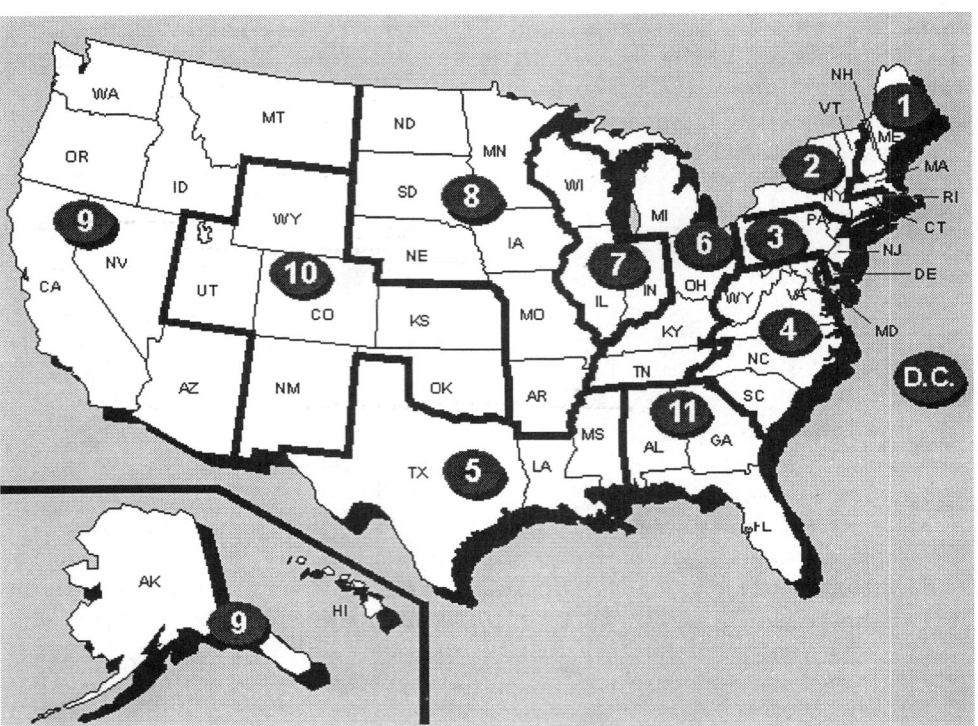

Fig. 2. Geographic "circuits" of the U.S. Courts of Appeals.

Each circuit court today serves a specific region of the country, and most of these courts still hear cases in various cities within their regions. There are 11 regional circuit courts. Fig. 2 shows how the United States is divided into judicial circuits. In addition, a separate circuit court (the U.S. Court of Appeals for the D.C. circuit) exists solely to serve Washington, D.C.; it often hears appeals of decisions by federal agencies, many of them involving high-profile issues. Many "D.C. circuit" judges are promoted to the Supreme Court. There is also a U.S. Court of Appeals for the Federal Circuit. Unlike the other circuit courts, this one serves no single geographic area. Instead, it has nationwide jurisdiction over certain special kinds of cases, including patent and customs appeals and some claims against the federal government. This court is the product of a merger of the old Court of Claims and the Court of Customs and Patent Appeals.

Some of the circuits have been divided over the years as the population grew. Until 1981, the fifth circuit included Alabama, Georgia and Florida, the states that now comprise the eleventh circuit. Lawyers and judges have discussed creating still another federal circuit court by dividing the far-flung ninth circuit, which serves Alaska, Hawaii and seven other western states. This idea is especially popular among lawyers in the Pacific Northwest, who say that the ninth circuit is too California-oriented because California's huge population has resulted in many of the ninth circuit's judges coming from that state. The ninth circuit has 28 active judges, by far the largest number of any circuit, and it rules on almost four times the number of cases that were handled by all of the circuit courts nationwide 50 years ago. The second largest circuit is the fifth, which has 17 active judges. Each court also has *senior judges* who are officially retired but still hear cases on a volunteer basis.

The losing party in most U.S. District Court trials may appeal the decision to the circuit court serving that region of the country. The decisions of the circuit courts produce many important legal precedents; on federal questions the rulings of these courts are second in importance only to U.S. Supreme Court decisions. Although each circuit court has a large number of judges, most cases are heard by panels of three judges. Two of the three constitute a majority and may issue the *majority opinion,* which sets forth the court's legal reasoning that led to the decision. Sometimes a case is considered so important that a larger panel of judges is assigned to decide the case. When that happens, it is called deciding a case *en banc.* Ordinarily, an *en banc* panel consists of all of the judges serving on a particular circuit court. As the circuit courts grew larger, Congress authorized smaller *en banc* panels in some instances. The ninth circuit U.S. Court of Appeals uses panels of 11 judges to hear cases *en banc*.

Since these appellate courts decide only matters of law, there are no juries in these courts. Juries only hear trial court cases, and even then their role is limited to deciding factual issues (such as the guilt or innocence of a criminal defendant) and not legal issues. Appellate cases are always decided by judges alone, unassisted by a jury--both in the federal and state court systems.

One point should be explained about the significance of the legal precedents established by the federal circuit courts. As long as the decision does not conflict with any U.S. Supreme Court ruling, each circuit court is free to arrive at its own conclusions on issues of law, which are then binding on lower courts in that circuit. A circuit court is not required to follow precedents established by other circuit courts around the country, although precedents from other circuits usually carry considerable weight and are often followed.

There are occasions when two different circuit courts will rule differently on the same legal issue. When that happens, the trial courts in each region have no choice but to follow the local circuit court's ruling. Trial courts located in other circuits may choose to follow either of the two conflicting precedents, or they may follow neither. Since this kind of uncertainty about the law is obviously bad for everyone, the U.S. Supreme Court often intervenes, establishing a uniform rule of law all over the country.

Circuit courts of appeals have jurisdiction to hear cases from a variety of sources. As already indicated, appeals from the federal trial courts go to the circuit courts. But in addition, appeals of the decisions of many special-purpose courts and federal administrative agencies are routed to the circuit courts. For instance, decisions of both the Federal Trade Commission and the Federal Communications Commission may be appealed to these courts. Such cases are often heard by the U.S. Court of Appeals for the D.C. circuit.

The U.S. Supreme Court

The U.S. Supreme Court is, of course, the highest court in the country. Its nine justices are the highest-ranking judges in the nation, and its decisions represent the most influential legal precedents, binding on all lower courts.

Because of this court's vast authority, it is common for people involved in a lawsuit to threaten to "fight this all the way to the Supreme Court." However, very few cases have any real chance to make it that far up through the system. The U.S. Supreme Court is, after all, only one court, and it can only decide a limited number of cases each year. The Supreme Court accepts only a few hundred cases annually for review--out of at least 5,000 petitions for a hearing. In the end, the court issues formal signed opinions in no more than about 100 cases each year. In recent years the court has produced even fewer: an average of 80 or 90 per term. Obviously, some screening is required to determine which cases will get that far.

In doing the screening, the Supreme Court tries to hear those cases that raise the most significant legal issues, those where the lower courts have flagrantly erred, and those where conflicting lower court decisions must be reconciled. However, the fact that the Supreme Court declines to hear a given case does not mean the high court necessarily agrees with the decision of a lower court. To the contrary, the Supreme Court may disagree with it, but it may choose to leave the decision undisturbed because it has a heavy caseload of more important matters.

The fact that the Supreme Court declines to review a lower court decision establishes no precedent: for the Supreme Court to refuse to hear a case is not the same as the Supreme Court taking up the case and then affirming the lower court's ruling. When the Supreme Court declines to take a case, the lower court ruling on that case remains in force--but it is still just the decision of a lower court. There are occasions, however, when the Supreme Court accepts a case and then merely affirms the opinion of a lower court instead of issuing its own opinion, thereby giving the lower court's opinion the legal weight of a Supreme Court decision.

The nine justices vote to decide which cases they will hear of the many appealed to them. Under the Supreme Court's rules of procedure, it takes four votes to get a case on the high court's calendar.

Cases reach the U.S. Supreme Court by several routes. For one, the Constitution gives the Supreme Court *original jurisdiction* over a few types of cases (that is, it may be the first court to hear those cases). Disputes between two states and cases involving ambassadors of foreign countries are examples of cases in which the Supreme Court has original jurisdiction. Even these cases may sometimes be heard in lower courts instead--with the blessing of the Supreme Court's nine overworked justices.

Then there are a few cases in which the losing party in the lower courts has an automatic right to appeal to the Supreme Court. For example, when a lower federal court or the highest court in a state rules an Act of Congress unconstitutional, the U.S. Supreme Court must hear an appeal if asked to do so by the government. The Supreme Court is required to accept these cases for review.

Finally and most important, there are a vast number of cases that the Supreme Court may or may not choose to review; it is not required to hear these cases. In these cases the losing party in a lower court asks the Supreme Court to issue a *writ of certiorari*. Technically, a writ of certiorari is an order from the Supreme Court to a lower court to send up the records of the case. *Certiorari granted* means the Supreme Court has agreed to hear an appeal, while *certiorari denied* means the Supreme Court has decided not to hear the case.

This certiorari procedure is by far the most common way cases reach the Supreme Court, although many more petitions for certiorari are denied than granted. Cases may reach the Supreme Court in such appeals from both lower federal courts and from state courts. The U.S. Supreme Court often hears cases that originated in a state court, but only when an important federal question, such as the First Amendment's guarantee of freedom of the press, is involved. Most of the Supreme Court decisions on libel and invasion of privacy that will be discussed later reached the high court in this way.

The U.S. Supreme Court will consider an appeal of a state case only when the case has gone as far as possible in the state court system. That normally means the state's highest court must have either ruled on the case or refused to hear it.

It would be difficult to overstate the importance of the nine justices of the U.S. Supreme Court in shaping American law. That is why bitter battles are so often fought in the U.S. Senate over the confirmation of those nominated to be Supreme Court justices. The makeup of the court can determine the scope of First Amendment freedoms, what due process rights are afforded to those accused of crimes, whether abortions remain legal and a thousand other major issues. As Chapter Five explains, in 1992 the Supreme Court upheld the basic principle of *Roe v. Wade*, the landmark abortion decision, by a 5-4 vote. Three justices appointed by presidents who opposed abortions (Anthony Kennedy and Sandra Day O'Connor, appointed by Ronald Reagan, and David Souter, appointed by George Bush) formed the nucleus of the majority that upheld *Roe v. Wade*. Had any of them voted as the president who nominated them probably expected, *Roe v. Wade* would have been overturned. But no one can predict how a jurist will vote once on the high court. Souter, considered a conservative when he replaced the liberal William Brennan, has written some surprisingly liberal opinions, including a stirring defense of the free press (see Chapter Eight). In contrast, Clarence Thomas, who replaced Thurgood Marshall (the first African-American ever to serve on the Supreme Court and an avowed liberal), has taken a decidedly more conservative course as a jurist than his predecessor.

With the retirement of Justice Byron White in 1993, a Democratic president had the opportunity to appoint a Supreme Court justice for the first time since the 1960s, and President Clinton nominated longtime federal appellate judge Ruth Bader Ginsburg to replace White. A year later, Justice Harry A. Blackmun, who was perhaps best known for writing the court's main opinion in *Roe v. Wade*, also retired. Clinton then made Stephen G. Breyer, another federal appellate judge, his second nominee for the Supreme Court. Both Ginsburg and Breyer were viewed as moderates. Ironically, they replaced a conservative justice appointed by a liberal president (White, appointed by John F. Kennedy) and a moderately liberal justice appointed by a conservative president (Blackmun, appointed by Richard Nixon).

The Supreme Court is sometimes closely identified with its chief justice, who may set the tone for the entire court. For example, the "Warren Court," named for Earl Warren, who served as chief justice from 1953 to 1969, had an enormous influence on the modern interpretation of the First Amendment. Later in this chapter and in Chapter Four there are references to the Warren Court's major role in reshaping American libel law. But the Warren Court did far more than that: it also rewrote American obscenity law and greatly expanded the rights of those who are accused of crimes, to cite just two examples. In the decades since the era of the liberal Warren Court ended, more conservative justices have dominated the Supreme Court. Under the current chief justice, the conservative William Rehnquist, the court has begun to overturn precedents established by the Warren Court, particularly in such fields as criminal law. And yet, many of the Warren Court's landmark decisions still stand, a tribute to the influence wielded by Warren and his judicial colleagues. An interesting footnote: although the term, the "Warren Court," is synonymous with judicial *liberalism*, Warren was a longtime Republican, appointed to the Supreme Court by Dwight D. Eisenhower, a Republican president.

The State Courts

Each of the 50 states has its own court system, as already indicated. Larger states such as California, New York, Ohio, Pennsylvania, Texas, Illinois and Michigan have two levels of state appellate courts plus various trial courts, duplicating the federal structure.

In these states, the intermediate appellate courts (usually called simply "courts of appeal") handle a variety of cases that the state supreme court has no time to consider. The state supreme court then reviews only the most important cases. Worth special note is the New York system, which is structurally similar to the systems in other populous states, but with opposite nomenclature. In New York, the "supreme court" is a trial court that also has intermediate appellate jurisdiction; there are many such courts in the state. New York's highest court is called the Court of Appeals. Maryland also calls its highest court the Court of Appeals.

In smaller states, the trial courts send cases directly to the state supreme court, which may have from three to nine or more justices to hear all appeals in the state. As both the population and the volume of lawsuits increase, more and more states are adding intermediate appellate courts.

The states tend to have a much greater variety of trial courts than does the federal government, since the state courts must handle many minor legal matters that are of no concern to the federal courts. A typical state court system includes some kind of local court that handles minor traffic and civil matters and perhaps minor crimes. Such courts are often called municipal courts, county or city courts, justice courts, or the like.

In some states the highest trial courts not only hear the most important trials but also perform some appellate functions, reviewing the verdicts of the lower trial courts.

State and Federal Jurisdiction

It may seem inefficient to have two complete judicial systems operating side by side. Wouldn't it be simpler and less expensive to consolidate the state and federal courts that operate in each state? Perhaps it would, but one of our strongest traditions is power sharing between the federal government and the states. We'll have separate state and federal laws--and separate court systems to interpret them--throughout the foreseeable future.

How then is authority divided between the federal and state courts? State jurisdiction and federal jurisdiction sometimes overlap, but basically the state courts are courts of *residual jurisdiction*; that is, they have authority over all legal matters that are not specifically placed under federal control. Anything that isn't a *federal question* automatically falls within the jurisdiction of the state courts. In addition, the state courts may also rule on certain issues that are federal questions (for instance, First Amendment rights).

What makes an issue a federal question? The Constitution declares that certain areas of law are inherently federal questions. For instance, the Constitution specifically authorized Congress to make copyright law a federal question. And Congress, acting under the authority of the Constitution, has declared copyrights and many other matters to be federal questions. Congress has used its constitutional power to regulate interstate commerce as a basis for federal regulation of broadcasting, for instance. Thus, certain legal disputes are inherently federal questions because of their subject matter.

In addition, federal courts may intervene in state cases if a state court ruling conflicts with the U.S. Constitution. Much of mass communications law is based on cases of this type. In almost every area of state law discussed in this textbook, the U.S. Supreme Court has intervened at one time or another, interposing federal constitutional requirements on the states. Most often, of course, the constitutional issue is freedom of expression as protected by the First Amendment; the Supreme Court has often overruled state laws and court decisions that violated the First Amendment.

In addition to these federal questions, there is another reason the federal courts will sometimes agree to hear a case: *diversity of citizenship*. This principle applies only when a citizen of one state sues a citizen of another state. For example, if a New Yorker and a Pennsylvanian are involved in a serious auto accident, each may be able to avoid a lawsuit in the other's state courts under the diversity principle. If there is a lawsuit, it may well be removed to a federal court instead of being heard in a state court.

The framers of the Constitution felt it would be unfair to force anyone to fight a lawsuit on someone else's "home turf," so they ordered the federal courts to provide a neutral forum to hear these disputes involving citizens of two different states. The theory is that a state court might be biased in favor of its own citizens and against outsiders. When a federal court hears a case that would be a state matter if it involved two citizens of the same state, it is said to be a federal case because of *diversity jurisdiction* rather than *federal question jurisdiction*. In diversity lawsuits, the trial may still occur in the home state of one of the litigants, but in a federal rather than a state court.

 There are limits on diversity jurisdiction. If there were not, the federal courts might be overwhelmed by minor cases. To avoid that problem, federal courts accept diversity-of-citizenship cases only when the dispute involves more than $75,000. This jurisdictional threshold has been increased repeatedly over the years. Until it was raised from $10,000 to $50,000 in 1988, the federal courts had to handle many relatively minor civil lawsuits--cases that federal judges felt should rightfully be left to the state courts.

 Another limitation on diversity jurisdiction is the requirement of *complete diversity*. That is, all of the parties on one side of a lawsuit must come from a different state than anyone on the other side. That means, for instance, that a lawsuit by a New Yorker against both an individual from Pennsylvania and an insurance company in New York would not usually qualify as a diversity case.

Sometimes there is considerable legal maneuvering when a case does qualify for federal jurisdiction, either because a federal question is involved or because there is diversity of citizenship. One side may want the case kept in state court, while the other prefers a federal court. Such a case may be filed in a state court, removed to federal court, and eventually sent back to a state court.

One more point about federal-state relationships bears explaining. As we have already said, certain legal matters are exclusively federal concerns, either under the Constitution or an act of Congress. In those areas, the federal government is said to have *preempted the field*. That is, no state law in this area is valid; the federal government has exclusive jurisdiction. Copyright law is one such area.

In certain other areas of law, Congress has enacted some federal laws without preempting the field. The states may also enact laws in these areas, providing that the state laws do not conflict with any federal laws. These are called areas of *concurrent jurisdiction*. Examples of this in media law include the regulation of advertising, antitrust law and trademark regulation. A typical dividing line in such an area of law is the one that exists in trademark regulation, where the federal Lanham Act protects trademarks of businesses engaged in interstate commerce, while many states have laws to protect the trademarks of local businesses.

In addition to the areas of law preempted by the federal government and areas of concurrent jurisdiction, of course, a large number of legal matters are left to the states--unless a state should violate some federal principle in the exercise of that authority. Libel and invasion of privacy are two areas of media law that are essentially state matters. Recently the U.S. Supreme Court has been refining the concept of federalism by limiting the power of Congress to curtail the traditional authority of the states, a trend that is discussed later.

TYPES OF LAW

Although the courts play a major role in shaping the law, the other branches of government also have the power to make laws in various ways. In fact, the term *law* refers to several different types of rules and regulations, ranging from the bureaucratic edicts of administrative agencies to the unwritten legal principles we call the *common law*. This section explains how the courts interact with other agencies of government in shaping the various kinds of law that exist side by side in America.

The Constitution

The most important foundation of modern American law is the U.S. Constitution. No law that conflicts with the Constitution is valid. The U.S. Constitution is the basis for our legal system: it sets up the structure of the federal government and defines federal-state relationships. It divides authority among the three branches of the federal government and limits their powers, reserving a great many powers for the states and their subdivisions (such as cities and counties).

The First Amendment to the Constitution is vital to the mass media. In just 45 words, it sets forth the principles of freedom of the press, freedom of speech and freedom of religion in America. The First Amendment says:

> Congress shall make no law respecting an establishment of religion, or prohibiting the free exercise thereof; or abridging the freedom of speech, or of the press; or the right of the people peaceably to assemble, and to petition the government for a redress of grievances.

What do those words mean? The job of interpreting what they mean has fallen to the appellate courts, which have written millions of words in attempting to explain those 45 words. For instance, the First Amendment sounds absolute when it says "Congress shall make no law...." However, the courts have repeatedly ruled that those words are not absolute, and that freedom of expression must be balanced against other rights. In practice, the First Amendment should really be read more like this: "Congress shall make *almost* no laws..." or "Congress shall make *as few laws as possible*...abridging freedom of speech, or of the press....." The chapters to follow will discuss the many other rights that the courts have had to balance against the First Amendment.

Another point about the First Amendment is that it originally applied only to Congress and to no one else. It was written that way because its authors did not think it was their place to tell the state governments not to deny basic civil liberties; their purpose was to reassure those citizens who feared that the new federal government might deny basic liberties. They felt that many basic liberties were so firmly rooted in the *common law* that no written declaration was needed to assure that the states would safeguard these liberties. However, it became clear over the years that state and local governments, like the federal government, may violate the rights of their citizens from time to time. Hence, the Supreme Court eventually ruled that the First Amendment's safeguards should apply to state and local governments as well.

Chapter Two describes the evolution of freedom of expression in America. It is sufficient here to remember that the U.S. Constitution plays the central role in American law. No law may be enacted or enforced if it violates the Constitution. The courts--particularly the U.S. Supreme Court--play the central role in interpreting what the Constitution means, often in practical situations that the founding fathers never dreamed of when they wrote the document more than 200 years ago.

Perhaps the Constitution has survived for more than 200 years because the courts do adapt it to meet changing needs, and because it can be amended when there is strong support for this step. The Sixteenth Amendment, for example, was approved in 1913, authorizing the federal income tax at a time when the federal government needed to find a way to bring in more revenue. And the Twenty-first Amendment, approved in 1933, abolished prohibition (thus ending an era that began when the Eighteenth Amendment was enacted to ban alcoholic beverages). The normal procedure for amending the Constitution is for each house of Congress to approve a proposed amendment by a two-thirds vote, after which it must be ratified by three fourths of the states.

In addition to the federal Constitution, each state has its own constitution, and that document is the basic legal charter for the state. No state law may conflict with either the state's own constitution or the federal Constitution. Each state's courts must interpret the state constitution, overturning laws that conflict with it.

Likewise, many cities and counties have *home rule* charters that establish the fundamental structure and powers of local government. Like the state and federal constitutions (which local governments must also obey), local charters are basic sources of legal authority. On the other hand, many local governments operate under the general laws enacted by state legislatures instead of having their own local charters.

In all of these circumstances, the courts must decide when a government action--be it an act of Congress or the behavior of the local police department--violates one of these basic government documents. When that happens, it is the job of the courts to halt the violation.

The Common Law

The common law, which began to develop out of English court decisions hundreds of years ago, is our oldest form of law. It is an amorphous collection of legal principles based on thousands of court decisions that have been handed down over hundreds of years. It is *unwritten* law in the sense that you cannot sit down and read it all in one place as you can with the statutory laws enacted by Congress. Starting nearly 1,000 years ago, English judges began to follow *legal precedents* from previous cases. Each new decision added a little bit to this accumulated body of law. As it grew, the common law came to include rules concerning everything from crimes such as murder and robbery to non-criminal matters such as breach of contract.

When the American government took its present form with the ratification of the Constitution in 1789, the entire English common law as it then existed became the basis for the American common law. Since then, thousands of additional decisions of American courts have expanded and modified the common law in each state.

It should be emphasized that the common law is mainly state law and not federal law; an important U.S. Supreme Court decision so ruled years ago. Each state's courts have developed their own judicial traditions, and those traditions form the basis for that state's common law, which may vary from the common law of other states.

Several controversial U.S. Supreme Court decisions in recent years underscored the continuing power of the common law as a force that even Congress cannot ignore. In *Alden v. Maine* (527 U.S. 706, 1999) and several other cases, the high court looked back to the status of the common law before the Constitution was ratified in 1789 and concluded that a concept called *sovereign immunity* was firmly entrenched in the law then--and was not abrogated by the Constitution. Sovereign immunity exempts the "sovereign" from being sued in the courts. In eighteenth century England, the sovereign was the king or queen. In the pre-constitutional United States, the individual states had sovereign immunity.

How does sovereign immunity affect modern America? In these recent decisions, a 5-4 majority of the Supreme Court said the states still enjoy sovereign immunity, and Congress does not have the right to authorize lawsuits against the states either in federal courts or in state courts. The result: the court held that the states are largely exempt from various federal laws that purport to allow private parties (such as individuals and corporations) to sue a state. The court said the states (but not private parties) are exempt from many patent (and copyright) infringement lawsuits, for example. In 2002, the Supreme Court held that the states are immune not only to many lawsuits but also to some actions brought by federal regulatory agencies (*Federal Maritime Commission v. South Carolina State Ports Authority*, 122 S.Ct. 1864).

These decisions were widely criticized in the media. They are based on an expansive view of common law concepts that are routinely taught in law school and that still apply today--in the opinion of the Supreme Court majority. Of course, the states have all *voluntarily* agreed to set limits on their own sovereign immunity over the years by enacting laws to allow lawsuits against themselves under various circumstances.

Like federal constitutional law, the common law can grow and change without any formal act of a legislative body precisely because it is based on court decisions. When a new situation arises, the appellate courts may establish new legal rights, acting on their own authority. A good example of the way the common law develops a little at a time through court decisions is the emergence of the right of privacy. As Chapter Five explains, there was no legal right of privacy until the twentieth century. But as governments and the mass media both became more powerful and pervasive, the need for such a right became apparent. The courts in a number of states responded by allowing those whose privacy had been invaded to sue the invader, establishing precedents for other courts to follow.

In addition to privacy law, several other major areas of mass media law had their beginnings in the common law tradition, among them libel, slander and the earliest forms of copyright protection.

If this all happens through judicial precedent, with the courts expected to follow the example set by earlier decisions, how can the common law correct earlier errors?

The common law system has survived for nearly a thousand years precisely because there are mechanisms to allow the law to change as the times change. Courts don't always follow legal precedent; they have other options.

When a court does adhere to a previous decision, it is said to be observing the rule of *stare decisis*. That Latin term, roughly translated, means "Let the precedent stand." However, courts need not always adhere to the rule of stare decisis. Instead, a court faced with a new factual situation may decide that an old rule of the common law should not apply to the new facts. The new case may be sufficiently different from previous ones to justify a different result. When a court declines to follow a precedent on the ground that the new case is a little different, that is called *distinguishing* the previous case. When an appellate court does that, the common law grows and keeps up with changing times.

Another option, of course, is for a court to decline to follow precedent altogether, even though the factual circumstances and issues of law may be virtually identical. That is called *reversing* or *overruling* a precedent; it is considered appropriate when changing times or changing conditions have made it clear that the precedent is unfair or unworkable.

A good example of the way this process works is provided by the 1954 ruling of the U.S. Supreme Court in the famous school desegregation case, *Brown v. Board of Education* (347 U.S. 483). Although this case is based on an interpretation of the Constitution and is therefore an example of the development of constitutional law rather than the common law, it provides a good illustration of just how the law develops over the years. When the high court took up the *Brown* case, there was a judicial precedent, an 1896 Supreme Court decision called *Plessy v. Ferguson* (163 U.S. 537). In that earlier case, racial segregation had been ruled constitutionally permissible as long as the facilities provided for different races were "separate but equal." But in 1954 the Supreme Court pointed out that more than half a century's experience under the *Plessy v. Ferguson* rule proved that the "separate but equal" approach didn't work. The Supreme Court noted that segregated facilities were almost always unequal--and ruled that the public schools of America had to be desegregated. As a result of that new decision, the precedent from the 1896 case was no longer binding and a new precedent replaced it. In the end, *Brown v. Board of Education* became one of the most important court decisions of the twentieth century.

Statutory Law

The third major type of law in America is the one most people think of when they hear the word *law*. It is statutory law, a sweeping term that encompasses acts of Congress, laws enacted by state legislatures and even ordinances adopted by city and county governments.

If constitutional and common law are largely unwritten (or at least uncodified) forms of law because they are the result of accumulated court decisions, statutory law is just the opposite. It is law that is written down in a systematic way. Statutory laws are often organized into *codes*. A *code* is a collection of laws on similar subjects, indexed and arranged by subject matter. Much federal law is found in the *United States Code*. Each *title* of the U.S. Code deals with a particular subject or group of related subjects. Title 17, for example, deals with copyright law, discussed in Chapter Six. On the state level, much statutory law is similarly organized, although not all states refer to their compilations of statutory laws as codes.

Although statutory law is created by legislative bodies, the courts have an important place in statutory lawmaking just as they do in other areas of law. That is true because the courts have the power to interpret the meaning of statutory laws and apply them to practical situations. For this reason, law books containing statutory laws are often *annotated*. This means each section of the statutory law is followed by brief summaries of the appellate court decisions interpreting it. Thus, one can quickly learn whether a given statutory law has been upheld or if it has been partially or totally invalidated by the courts. Annotated codes also contain cross-references to other relevant analyses of the statutory law, such as attorney general's opinions or articles in law reviews.

Why would a court invalidate a statutory law? It can happen for several reasons. First, of course, if the statute conflicts with any provision of the appropriate state or federal constitution, it is invalid. In addition, there are sometimes conflicts between two statutory laws enacted by the same state legislature or by Congress. When that happens, the differences must be reconciled, and that may mean reinterpreting or even invalidating one of the laws. In addition, courts may void laws that conflict with well-established (but unwritten) common law principles. For instance, Chapter Eight explains that a number of state legislatures have enacted *shield laws* to protect journalists' news sources. But several courts have overruled these shield laws on the ground that they infringe on judicial prerogatives guaranteed by constitutional or common law principles.

There is considerable interplay between the courts and legislative bodies in the development of statutory law. As already indicated, often a new legal concept is recognized first by the courts, whose decisions will make it a part of the common law. At some point, a legislature may take note of what the courts have been doing and formally codify the law by enacting a statute covering that subject. The courts may then reinterpret the statute, but the legislature may respond by passing yet another statute intended to override the court decision.

We will see precisely this sort of interplay between a legislative body and the courts in several areas of mass media law, particularly in such areas as copyright, shield laws and broadcasting. For example, the Supreme Court once ruled that most private, at-home videotaping of television shows is legal under the U.S. Copyright Act, for reasons explained in Chapter Six. Congress then considered legislation that would have revised the Copyright Act to overturn that court decision and outlaw home videotaping. That legislation was rejected because most members of Congress believed public opinion supported the court's interpretation of the law. On the other hand, if the Supreme Court had said a constitutional principle (such as the First Amendment) protected the right to make home videotapes of TV shows for personal use, the only way to reverse that ruling would have been by amending the Constitution--or waiting for the court to reverse its own earlier decision. Congress cannot pass a statutory law to overrule a Supreme Court decision *interpreting the meaning of the Constitution*. Congress can, of course, propose a constitutional amendment and submit it to the states for ratification. Short of that, the most Congress can do when a statutory law is ruled unconstitutional is to revise it to bring it into compliance with the Constitution.

Administrative Law

Another important kind of law in America is administrative law. Within the vast bureaucracies operated by the federal government and by the states, there are numerous agencies with the power to adopt and enforce administrative regulations, and these regulations have the force of law. The term *administrative law* may seem contradictory, but these agencies do have law-making powers.

In fact, such agencies often have so much authority that it would seem to violate the traditional concept of separation of powers. They may write the rules, enforce them and try alleged violators, handing out de facto criminal penalties to those convicted. For example, the Federal Communications Commission is a regulatory body with that kind of authority over the electronic media. The Federal Trade Commission exercises similar authority over the advertising industry.

While these agencies have considerable power, there are important checks and balances that limit their authority. For example, their decisions may be appealed to the courts, and that gives the appellate courts a veto power over the rules adopted by these agencies.

In addition, many of these agencies were created by legislation, and in recent years Congress and the various state legislatures have proven that they can take back some of the authority they handed out, either directly by rewriting the enabling legislation or indirectly by making budget cuts. A notable example of this is the limitations imposed on the Federal Trade Commission by Congress in 1980 (see Chapter 13). Also, while the policy-making boards and commissions of these agencies are rarely elected, the commissioners are usually appointed by the president or the governor of a state, who is elected. Also, their appointments must usually be confirmed by a legislative body.

Among the thousands of government agencies with administrative rule-making powers, some of the most important (in addition to the FCC and FTC) are the Interstate Commerce Commission, the Federal Aviation Administration and the Nuclear Regulatory Commission on the federal level, and the state-level regulatory bodies that determine the rates charged by public utilities.

Actions in Equity

One final kind of "law" that should be mentioned here is not really a form of law at all but an alternative to the law: a remedy for legal wrongs called *equity*.

Hundreds of years ago in England, it became obvious that courts sometimes caused injustices while acting in the name of justice. There are some circumstances in which faithfully applying the law simply does not result in a fair decision. For example, the common law has always held that *damages* (money) would right a wrong, and that the courts should not act until an injury actually occurred--and even then they could do nothing except to order a payment of money to compensate the injured party. Obviously there are times when letting a court sit back and wait for an injury to occur just isn't satisfactory. The harm that could result might be so severe that no amount of money would make matters right. In those situations, courts have the power to act in *equity*: they can issue an *injunction* to prevent a wrong from occurring. A good example of an occasion when an action in equity would be appropriate is when highway builders are about to excavate and thus destroy an important archeological site. Those seeking to preserve the site cannot wait until after an injury occurs and sue for damages. The artifacts that would be destroyed might be priceless.

The concept of equity is an old one: it developed in medieval times. Early in the development of the English common law, people facing irreparable injuries began to appeal to the king, since he was above the law and could mete out justice when the courts could not--or would not. As the volume of requests for this sort of special consideration increased, kings began to appoint special officers to hear appeals from those who could not get justice in the courts of law. Such officers came to be known as *chancellors* and their court became known as the *court of the chancery*. As time went on, this brand of justice based on the dictates of someone's conscience came to be known simply as equity.

The concept of equity works in much the same way today, but in America the same courts that apply the law usually entertain actions in equity, too.

Unlike the law, which has elaborate and detailed rules, equity is still a system that seeks to offer fairness based on the dictates of the judge's conscience. Equity is only available in situations where there is no adequate remedy under the law, and only then if the person seeking *equitable relief* is being fair to the other parties in a dispute.

There are certain kinds of legal actions that are based on equity rather than law. Probably the most important for our purposes are injunctions, which are court orders requiring people to do something they are supposed to do (or to refrain from doing something that would cause irreparable harm). Chapter Three discusses several attempts by the federal government to prevent the publication of information that government officials felt would cause irreparable harm to national security. When a court orders an editor not to publish something, that is ordinarily an example of an action in equity.

CRIMINAL LAW AND CIVIL LAW

Another major distinction in the law is the distinction between criminal and civil law. Although criminal and civil law are not categories comparable to statutory law, the common law or administrative law, there are important differences between civil and criminal cases.

In a criminal case, someone is accused of committing an act that is considered to be an offense against society as a whole--a crime such as murder, rape or robbery. Therefore, society as a whole ("the people," if you will) brings charges against this individual, with the taxpayers paying the bill for the people's lawyer, often called the district attorney (or U.S. attorney in federal cases). If the person accused of the crime (*the defendant*) is impoverished, the taxpayers will also pay for his or her defense by providing a lawyer from the local (or federal) public defender's office. Defendants who are more financially secure will hire their own defense lawyers, but the basic point to remember is that the legal dispute is between the defendant and "the people"--society as a whole. Moreover, because the defendant's life or liberty may be at stake, the prosecution must prove guilt *beyond a reasonable doubt*. That is a difficult standard of proof.

In a civil case, it is a different matter. Here, one party claims another party injured him or her individually, without necessarily doing something so bad it is considered a crime against society as a whole. It's just a dispute between two individuals (or two corporations, or two government agencies, etc.). The courts simply provide a neutral forum to hear a private dispute. The burden of proof is correspondingly lower in civil cases: to win, a litigant must usually prove his or her case by *the preponderance of the evidence*, but not necessarily *beyond a reasonable doubt*, as in criminal cases.

Don't assume that all legal matters are either criminal or civil matters--some are both. The same series of events may lead to both civil and criminal litigation. For instance, someone who has an auto accident while intoxicated may face criminal prosecution for drunk driving as well as civil lawsuits by the victims for personal injuries and property damage, among other things.

TORTS AND DAMAGES

Two other legal concepts that should be explained here are the concepts of *torts* and *damages*.

Most civil lawsuits not based on a breach of contract are tort actions. A tort is any civil wrong that creates a right for the victim to sue the perpetrator. Almost any time one party injures another, the resulting lawsuit is a tort action.

For example, if you are walking across the street and you're struck by a car driven by a careless driver, you have a right to sue for your personal injuries in a tort action for *negligence*. Suppose you need surgery as a result of the accident. If the doctor at the hospital should forget to remove a sponge from your body after the emergency surgery, you could sue for the tort of *medical malpractice*.

On the other hand, if you could prove that the car struck you not because the driver was careless but because a manufacturing defect caused the steering to fail, you could sue the manufacturer for the tort of *products liability*.

Finally, you could sue for *libel* if the local newspaper falsely reported that you had just committed a crime and were fleeing from the crime scene when you were hit by the car.

All of these legal actions and dozens of others fall into the broad category called torts. The person who commits the wrong is called the *tortfeasor*; he or she becomes the *defendant* in the lawsuit while the victim is the *plaintiff*.

Several of the important legal actions affecting the mass media are tort actions. Examples include libel and slander, invasion of privacy and unfair competition.

To win a tort lawsuit the plaintiff generally has to show that there was some sort of wrongful act on the part of the tortfeasor, often either negligence or a malicious intent. The plaintiff also has to show that he suffered some kind of *damages*, although courts are sometimes permitted to presume damages when certain kinds of wrongful acts have occurred.

This brings us to the definition of damages, which is a central point in this introduction to mass media law. In many states, there are three basic kinds of damages: general damages, special damages and punitive damages.

General damages are a form of monetary compensation for losses incurred under circumstances in which the injured party cannot place a specific dollar amount on the loss. In an auto accident where you suffer personal injuries, for instance, you may win general damages to compensate you for your pain and suffering, which is obviously an intangible. In a libel suit, the plaintiff seeks general damages to compensate for embarrassment and loss of prestige in the community--another intangible.

Special damages are a little different. Here, the plaintiff must prove out-of-pocket monetary losses to win compensation. In the auto accident we've been using as an example, perhaps you can show that your doctor and hospital bills came to a certain amount of money. Maybe you can also show that you were unable to work for several months or years, or maybe you needed in-home nursing care or rehabilitation. These are all things for which courts can establish specific dollar values. Special damages are intended to compensate for these kinds of provable losses.

On the other hand, *punitive damages* are not based on any tangible or intangible loss. Instead, they are intended as a punishment for the person who commits a maliciously wrongful act. For the victim, they constitute a windfall profit--and the Internal Revenue Service taxes them as such. For the wrongdoer, they're a form of noncriminal punishment, imposed by the court to deter such wrongful actions. Punitive damages are only awarded in those tort actions where the victim can prove there was malice on the part of the tortfeasor. As we'll see in Chapter Four, the term *malice* has more than one meaning in law. For the purpose of winning punitive damages in most tort actions, it means ill will or evil intentions toward the victim. In libel cases, it has a different meaning, but either way, it is difficult to show malice--unless the tortfeasor actually set out to injure someone deliberately.

As we'll see later, keeping track of these three kinds of damages is important in several areas of mass media law. Sometimes one type of damages is available but not another. It is not unusual for a plaintiff in a libel suit, for example, to be denied a right to sue for anything but special damages because a newspaper has printed a retraction.

Sometimes other terms are used to describe the various types of damages. *Actual damages* or *compensatory damages* means provable losses, including out-of-pocket losses (special damages) and, in some instances, some intangible but nonetheless real losses (i.e., general damages). *Presumed damages* are damages that a court assumes occurred without any proof. For many years, libel plaintiffs were awarded presumed damages without having to prove the defamation actually caused any injury. In some kinds of lawsuits such as copyright infringement cases, *statutory damages* may be awarded by a court without proof of a tangible or intangible loss. Instead, the damage award is based on legal rules set forth in a statutory law such as the Copyright Act. In some areas of law, *treble damages* (three times the actual damages) are awarded as a means of discouraging improper behavior. For example, federal antitrust and advertising fraud laws allow treble damages.

THE STORY OF A LAWSUIT

Perhaps the best way to illustrate how the legal system works is to follow a lawsuit through the courts, step by step. We'll trace a civil case called *New York Times v. Sullivan* (376 U.S. 254), a libel suit that is usually remembered for the very important legal precedent it established. Its effect on libel law is discussed in Chapter Four. However, *New York Times v. Sullivan* is also an excellent case to illustrate court procedures, since the case was carried through almost every step that occurs in civil lawsuits.

Anyone who thinks a newspaper story has injured his or her reputation has a right to sue the newspaper for monetary damages to compensate for his/her losses. This case involved such a lawsuit between an individual named L. B. Sullivan and the company that publishes the *New York Times*.

The case began after the *New York Times* published an advertisement from a group of African-American civil rights leaders that described instances of alleged police brutality in the South. Some of the incidents occurred in Montgomery, Alabama. The ad was essentially accurate for the most part, but it did contain several errors of fact.

The ad did not name any individual as responsible for the alleged police misconduct. Nevertheless, Sullivan, who was one of three elected commissioners in Montgomery and the man in charge of police and fire services there, contended that his reputation had been damaged by the ad, so he hired a lawyer and sued the

New York Times for libel. He contended that to criticize the police was to criticize the city commissioner who oversees the police department. The result was a lawsuit that went all the way to the U.S. Supreme Court after a variety of intermediate steps.

Initiating the Lawsuit

When Sullivan's lawyer filed the papers required to initiate the lawsuit (a document called the *complaint*), the clerk of the trial court assigned the case a number for record-keeping purposes, and the case became known as *Sullivan v. New York Times*. In our legal system, court cases are identified by the names of the parties to the dispute, with a little "v." (for versus) between the two names. When there are multiple parties on either side, the case is popularly identified by the name of the first person listed on each side. The name of the party bringing the lawsuit (the plaintiff) appears first, followed by the name of the party defending (the defendant). When the defendant loses the case in the trial court and then appeals, the two names are sometimes reversed. Hence, this case later became known as *New York Times v. Sullivan*.

As the plaintiff, Sullivan was seeking an award of monetary damages. The *New York Times*, of course, wanted to convince the court it had done nothing to injure Sullivan and that damages should therefore not be awarded.

Sullivan could have chosen to sue the *New York Times* in the New York state courts or even in the federal courts (based on diversity of citizenship). However, at that point in history many southerners bitterly resented northern efforts to promote the civil rights of African-Americans in the South. To many in Alabama, the *New York Times* symbolized all that they disliked. Thus, Sullivan's lawyer knew his client would have a much more sympathetic jury in Alabama than in New York. Besides, it would certainly be more convenient for them (but not for the *Times*) to try the case there.

Having filed the complaint in the proper Alabama trial court, the next step was to serve the *New York Times*. That is, a *process server* had to deliver a copy of the papers announcing the lawsuit to an appropriate representative of the newspaper. Some states permit the plaintiff to simply mail a copy to the defendant, depending on the nature of the case.

Serving the *New York Times* was a bit of a problem for Sullivan, since the paper didn't have any offices or regular employees in Alabama. Shortly after Sullivan initiated his law suit, a *Times* reporter visited the state to cover a civil rights demonstration, but *Times* lawyers in New York advised the reporter to leave the state before Sullivan's process servers could catch up with him, and he did so.

Sullivan ultimately served the papers on an Alabama resident who was a "stringer" (a part-time correspondent) for the *New York Times*. The *Times* immediately filed a motion in the Alabama courts to *quash* (invalidate) the service of process. Anxious to gain jurisdiction over the *Times*, the Alabama court denied the motion--and then found a technicality in the *Times*' legal petition that enabled the Alabama courts to hear the case.

Given the sentiments of many Alabama residents toward the *New York Times*, this would seem to have been an ideal case to be tried in federal court on a diversity of citizenship basis. However, the Alabama courts ruled that the *Times* had voluntarily consented to Alabama jurisdiction by the manner in which the motion to quash the process service was worded.

Although it had a daily circulation of only 390 in the entire state and about 35 in the Montgomery area, the *New York Times* was forced to submit to the jurisdiction of the Alabama state courts due to a legal technicality.

Once the Alabama court established jurisdiction, the paper was obliged to respond to the lawsuit. The newspaper filed a reply (called the *answer*), denying Sullivan's claims. If no answer had been filed, the *New York Times* would have *defaulted*. That means the court would have been free to award Sullivan whatever he asked for, without the paper having any say in the matter. But the *Times* did file an answer, denying any *liability* (responsibility for the alleged wrong).

Pretrial Motions

The *Times* also initiated a series of legal motions designed to get the case thrown out of court before trial by saying, in effect, "Look, this is nothing but a harassment lawsuit, and we shouldn't be put to the expense of a full trial."

Two kinds of pretrial motions can lead to a dismissal of the case before trial. One is called a *demurrer* (or simply a *motion to dismiss*) and it contends that there is no *legal basis* for a lawsuit, even if every fact the plaintiff alleges is true. The other kind is a motion for *summary judgment*, and it is often based on the defendant's contention that there is no *factual basis* for the lawsuit to proceed further even if all the facts that the plaintiff alleges are completely true. A summary judgment motion may also be made when either side contends that there is no real disagreement between the parties about the facts, and that the judge should simply decide the case without further proceedings.

The *Times* filed a series of demurrers to argue that, among other things, the ad in no way referred to Sullivan and thus there was no legal basis for Sullivan to sue. (Someone must be identified and libeled before he/she can sue for libel, as Chapter Four explains.)

Demurrers and motions for summary judgment are particularly important for the mass media, because the media are often sued by people who may be embittered over unfriendly news coverage but who have no valid basis for a lawsuit. In such cases, the media may be entitled to a dismissal without the expense of a full trial. However, pretrial dismissals deny plaintiffs their day in court. Thus, a court reviewing such a request must give the plaintiff the benefit of every doubt. A pretrial dismissal is improper if there is any reasonable possibility the plaintiff could win at a trial.

This point is important because a number of the Supreme Court decisions affecting the media have come on appeals of motions to dismiss a case before trial. When a newspaper or television station, for instance, is denied a pretrial dismissal and the U.S. Supreme Court affirms the denial, that does not mean the Supreme Court thinks the plaintiff will eventually win the lawsuit. Rather, it merely says that the plaintiff might have some slight chance to win and, in our system of justice, has a right to try. If you keep that point about court procedures in mind, some of the seemingly anti-media decisions we discuss later may not appear quite so harsh.

Returning to the Sullivan case, the Alabama court denied all of the *Times'* motions to dismiss the case before trial, and a trial was eventually scheduled.

Discovery

After the legal maneuvering over motions for summary judgment and demurrers, there is another very important pretrial procedure: the process of *discovery*. It is a process that allows each side to find out a great deal about the strengths and weaknesses of the other side's case. Each *litigant* (party to the lawsuit) is permitted to ask the opposition a variety of oral questions (at *depositions*) and written questions (*interrogatories*). During *depositions*, each side is permitted to meet and question hostile witnesses who are under oath (i.e., the witness has taken an oath promising to tell the truth).

As a result of the discovery process, a defendant might find out how substantial the plaintiff's losses really were, for instance. A plaintiff who says the wrong thing during a deposition can devastate his or her own case. And each litigant can size up the other's witnesses to see whether they will be credible in court. Much important information is revealed during discovery.

Why do courts allow discovery? Experience has shown that allowing discovery encourages many out-of-court settlements of lawsuits that would otherwise clog up the courts. If you find out that your opponent really does have a good case against you, you'll be much more likely to make a generous settlement offer. Actually taking a case to trial costs time and money, so it is in everybody's interest to see cases settled out of court whenever possible. The more each side knows about the other's case, the more likely they are to reach an agreement on their own.

However, in this case Sullivan and the *New York Times* were hopelessly far apart; no settlement was possible. Sullivan was suing for half a million dollars, and the *Times* was contending that this was ridiculous. With a circulation of only 35 in Sullivan's county, and with him never mentioned either by name or title, the *Times* felt there was simply no way the ad could have done $500,000 worth of damage to the man's reputation.

The Trial

Sullivan and the *New York Times* squared off in a courtroom for trial. The first step in the trial was the selection of a jury, a process that raises another interesting point about civil cases.

Jury rights in civil cases differ somewhat from those in criminal cases. A defendant's right to a trial by a jury is one of the cornerstones of our criminal justice system, but no such stringent constitutional safeguards are involved in civil cases. There is a growing trend toward reducing the size of civil juries from the traditional panel of 12 to as few as six persons, and to allow verdicts to be rendered by nonunanimous civil juries. Only a few states allow nonunanimous juries or juries of fewer than 12 persons to decide major criminal cases.

In fact, many civil cases are tried without any jury because the losing side could be stuck with a bill for the jury, a risk neither side wishes to take. (By contrast, the defendant never has to pay for asserting his constitutional right to a jury trial in a criminal case.) Moreover, as a matter of strategy some civil litigants avoid jury trials because they feel they will fare better if a judge decides the facts as well as the law. But on the other hand, there are instances where a civil plaintiff may insist on a jury trial in the hope that the jurors will become emotional and award a big judgment. That happened in the Sullivan case.

Sullivan's lawyers were not unaware of the hostility many white southerners felt toward both the civil rights movement and the *New York Times* in the early 1960s when this case was tried. Blacks were still rare on Alabama juries at that point. The lawyers felt--correctly--that their client would do well before a jury.

Thus, the trial began. Sullivan, as the plaintiff, presented his evidence first, and then the *New York Times* responded. The plaintiff always goes first, the defendant last. A variety of witnesses testified for each side, with Sullivan's witnesses saying that they indeed associated him with the actions of the Montgomery police, and that they would think less of him if they believed the charges in the *New York Times* advertisement. Other witnesses testified about what they claimed were inaccuracies in the ad.

In its response, the *Times* contended that publishing the ad was protected by the First Amendment and that the ad in no way referred to Sullivan. The significance of these arguments will become more clear in Chapter Four, which discusses what one must prove to win a libel suit and what a newspaper must prove to defend itself in such a suit.

After all of the evidence was in, the judge instructed the jury on the law. He told the jurors the material was libelous as a matter of law. Thus, their job was to decide only whether the *Times* was responsible for the publication and whether, in fact, the ad referred to Sullivan. The judge ruled that Sullivan did not need to prove any actual monetary losses because of the ad, since damages could be presumed from any libelous statement under Alabama law.

Eventually the jurors adjourned to a private room and arrived at a verdict: a judgment of half a million dollars (the full amount requested) for Sullivan. They would see to it the *Times* would pay for its decision to publish an ad alleging police brutality in Montgomery, Alabama.

After that verdict was rendered, the *New York Times* took two important procedural steps. The first was to file a motion for a new trial, citing what it claimed were errors and irregularities in the original trial. That motion was promptly denied in this case, but that doesn't always happen.

If a trial court judge feels the jury improperly weighed the evidence or was not impartial, or if improper evidence was presented at the trial, or if various other procedural errors occurred during the trial, the losing side may be entitled to a new trial. In this case, the motion for a new trial was denied. Then the *Times* exercised its other option, appealing the verdict to the Alabama Supreme Court.

The Appeal

When a case is appealed, the nomenclature changes a little. The party that appeals the case becomes the *appellant,* while the other party becomes the *respondent.* When the losing side at the trial level appeals, the names may be reversed, as we already suggested would happen in this case. Hence, the *New York Times* became the appellant and Sullivan the respondent: the case became known as *New York Times v. Sullivan.*

The Alabama Supreme Court agreed to hear the *New York Times v. Sullivan* case. When an appellate court grants an appeal such as this one, several things occur. First, each side submits a *brief* which is an elaborate argument of the legal issues involved in the case: a *brief* is not always brief. The appellant's brief must argue that the trial court erred in applying the law to the facts at hand, while the respondent must defend the trial court's decision.

After the briefs are filed and read by the appellate justices, oral arguments are usually scheduled. At oral arguments the lawyers for each side are given a short period of time to highlight their main points. The justices may ask them questions, sometimes on obscure points, perhaps forcing the lawyers to use up their time allotment without ever getting to their most important arguments. Sometimes the lawyers (and knowledgeable spectators such as journalists who regularly cover the court) can guess which side will win from the kind of questions the justices are asking. Appellate court justices sometimes reveal their own sympathies by the nature of their questions.

After the oral arguments, the justices informally vote on the case to see how they will rule. Once the positions of the various justices are clear, one justice will be assigned to write the *majority opinion*--the opinion that will prevail and become a legal precedent. If other justices disagree with this opinion, they may write *dissenting opinions* in which they argue that the majority is in error. Or a justice may agree with the result reached by the majority but disagree with some of the reasoning. When that happens, the result is a *concurring opinion.* A justice may also concur with another's concurring or dissenting opinion.

Dissenting and concurring opinions are important, because as times change it is not unusual for a new majority to coalesce around what was once a minority viewpoint. A dissenting opinion may become the foundation for a later majority opinion. Chapter Two cites an example of that happening in cases involving fundamental First Amendment rights.

When the appellate opinion is then published--that is, printed in a law book that provides a verbatim record of all published decisions of the particular court--that decision officially becomes a legal precedent, adding a little more to the ever-growing body of law.

Not all appellate opinions are published: many courts publish only their most important opinions. The unpublished ones have little weight as legal precedents because they are not readily available to judges or to lawyers arguing later cases. In many federal and state appellate courts, only a small percentage of all appellate court rulings are published, and the unpublished ones are not considered to be legal precedents at all. The California Supreme Court sometimes eliminates lower appellate court rulings that it dislikes by simply ordering them *decertified for publication*. A decertified lower court decision may still appear in law books, but officially it no longer exists as a legal precedent.

There are other occasions when an appellate court decision will lose its significance as a legal precedent. For instance, this also occurs when a higher court decides to review the decision and issue its own ruling on the issue.

In the *New York Times v. Sullivan* case, the Alabama Supreme Court affirmed the judgment of the trial court in full, upholding the half-million-dollar libel award to Sullivan. In an elaborate legal opinion, the Alabama Supreme Court defended the trial court's finding that it had jurisdiction over the *New York Times*. Then the court upheld the trial judge's controversial jury instructions, in which he told the jurors Sullivan didn't need to prove any actual losses to win his case. Finally, the state supreme court affirmed all other aspects of the decision, including the large award of damages.

After this setback, the *New York Times* had one hope left: the chance that the U.S. Supreme Court might agree to hear the case in spite of the fact that civil libel had traditionally been purely a matter of state law. The *Times* petitioned for a *writ of certiorari*, contending that this kind of a libel judgment violated the First Amendment because it would inhibit public discussion of controversial issues such as civil rights.

To the amazement of some legal experts, the U.S. Supreme Court agreed to hear the case.

The U.S. Supreme Court Ruling

When the *New York Times v. Sullivan* case reached the U.S. Supreme Court, all of the steps just described happened again. Elaborate briefs were filed by both sides, and oral arguments were heard by the nine Supreme Court justices. Then the justices conferred privately and Justice William J. Brennan was selected to write a majority opinion in what was destined to become the most famous court decision of all time on libel law.

Chapter Four describes the legal reasoning of the Supreme Court in this landmark decision. At this point, we'll simply say the *New York Times* won. The decisions of the Alabama courts were *reversed and remanded*. That means the Supreme Court invalidated the lower court decisions and ordered the Alabama trial court to reconsider the facts of the case under new legal rules set down by the Supreme Court.

As a practical matter, sometimes a decision like this one terminates the case, because the plaintiff knows he cannot hope to win a trial conducted under the new legal ground rules. When the U.S. Supreme Court *reversed and remanded* the Alabama court's decision, this case was terminated--in fact if not in legal theory.

Other Options

In addition to reversing and/or remanding a lower court ruling, there are several other options open to an appellate court. The decision can be upheld (*affirmed*) or it can be affirmed in part and reversed in part. Then a new trial may be scheduled later. But whatever the ultimate outcome of the case at trial, often the most important aspect is the precedent-setting ruling of an appellate court. In the study of mass media law, you will encounter cases where the discussion centers on a major legal issue--and the final disposition of the lawsuit isn't discussed at all. After a landmark appellate ruling, it may take many more years to complete all of the various legal maneuvers at the trial court level and conclude a lawsuit--or the matter may be terminated as soon as a high appellate court rules.

Certainly a valid criticism of the American legal system is the length of time it takes to get a case to trial, up through the appellate courts and then back to trial again if necessary. If "justice delayed is justice denied," as critics of the system have suggested, the route through the American court system often includes enough detours to deny justice to many.

Another ethical issue raised by all of this, of course, is the prohibitive cost of justice. By the time a case reaches the U.S. Supreme Court, each side will typically have spent several hundred thousand dollars in legal fees, court costs and even printing bills.

HOW TO FIND THE LAW

Once you understand the various kinds of law and how the American legal system fits together, it isn't difficult to learn the law on any given subject. Legal research (i.e., the process of finding out what the law is on a subject), involves nothing more than knowing how to use some basic online reference tools or books that every well-stocked law library keeps on its shelves. Most larger county courthouses either have a law library or are located near one since judges who must make legal decisions every day need ready access to the laws on which to base their decisions. Also, every accredited law school has an extensive law library. Most of these law libraries are open to the public. You can go in and look up the law for yourself.

More than ever before, it is also possible to use the Internet, or a computer data base such as Lexis-Nexis or Westlaw, to do legal research. These computer data bases, once so costly that only the best-heeled law firms could afford them, are now accessible online via many university libraries, although the collegiate version of Lexis-Nexis lacks some features used in legal research.

In the absence of a specialized legal data base, the Internet itself has become a powerful legal research tool, as a growing number of state and federal courts, as well as many other government agencies, have begun posting the full text of their decisions, regulations and other documents on their web sites. For example, there is a wealth of regulatory information about advertising on the Federal Trade Commission's web site (**www.ftc.gov**) and about the electronic media on the Federal Communications Commission's web site (**www.fcc.gov**). Among more general online legal resources, some of the most popular include Thomas (**thomas.loc.gov**), the Library of Congress legislative information website, FindLaw (**www.findlaw.com**), a comprehensive privately maintained website, the Cornell

Legal Information Institute site (**www.law.cornell.edu**), widely regarded as one of the best law sites, and Oyez (**oyez.nwu.edu**), Northwestern University's multimedia U.S. Supreme Court site that has audio of oral arguments before the court, among other things. The official website of the federal court system (**www.uscourts.gov**) also has the full text of most recent federal court decisions, including those of the Supreme Court and the U.S. Courts of Appeals.

The amount of legal information available on the Internet is enormous and growing daily--a trend that is revolutionizing legal research.

This chapter explains some basic principles of legal research, principles that are applicable whether you are consulting books in a law library or accessing the same legal information via a computer.

Court Decisions

Precedent-setting appellate court decisions are not difficult to look up, because there's a *citation* system that will tell you where to find each case. Throughout each chapter in this book you'll find citations to important court decisions in that area of media law. After the names of the two parties in the case, you'll see the case citation (a series of numbers and letters). We've already discussed the landmark libel decision, *New York Times v. Sullivan*. When you look up that case in this or any other law-oriented book, you'll see this legal citation after the name of the case: 376 U.S. 254. The letters and numbers tell you exactly where to find the full text of the Supreme Court's ruling in a law book.

The "U.S." in the middle tells you which court ruled on the case because it stands for *United States Reports,* a series of books carrying the official text of Supreme Court decisions. Thus, to find the decision in print, you'd ask the law librarian where the "U.S. Supreme Court Reports" are kept. When you find this large collection of identical-looking volumes, the rest is simple. The first number in the citation (376) refers to the volume number of the law book in which the *New York Times v. Sullivan* case appears. You would look down the row, find the volume labeled "376" on the binding and pull it out.

Now you're there. The number after the "U.S." is the page number where the text of the case begins. Turn to page 254 in volume 376 of the United States Reports, and there's *New York Times v. Sullivan*. Before the actual text, there are introductory notes explaining the decision, designed to facilitate a quick review of the highlights of the case. Some citations conclude with the year of the decision. For example, *New York Times v. Sullivan* is cited as 376 U.S. 254, 1964.

When doing online research, it's possible to search by the case name, the citation, or both--or to search for key words in the text of the case. To find *New York Times v. Sullivan* using Lexis-Nexis Academic Universe, for example, first select "legal research," then select "federal case law." At that point, there are several options. Probably the easiest is to select "guided search" instead of "basic search" and then choose "all available dates" under the date option. Next choose to search for the "citation" (not "full text") and enter "376 U.S. 254". That will bring up the link to *New York Times v. Sullivan*. One more click will put the full text of the decision on your screen. There are other ways to get to that point, but entering the citation under the "guided search" option gets you to the case you want without a lot of other "hits" (other cases that have cited *New York Times v. Sullivan,* of which there are many).

You can also look up any other published appellate court decision in exactly the same way. Chapter Six mentions a well-known copyright decision, *Rosemont Enterprises v. Random House,* and its legal citation is "366 F.2d 303." That case was decided by a federal circuit court of appeals, not the U.S. Supreme Court, and the letters in the middle tell you that. "F.2d" means *Federal Reporter, second series,* which is a set of law books containing decisions of the various U.S. Courts of Appeals. Why *second series*? The publisher of these books began producing them many years ago, and after a time the original editorial treatment and even the style of the binding seemed old-fashioned. Thus, the publisher modernized the book and started a second series, beginning again with volume number one in the new series. In 1993, the publisher launched a *third series,* once again starting with volume number one. If you see a citation to "F.3d," the case is a 1993 or later decision of a U.S. Court of Appeals.

How would you find the *Rosemont* case, for example? You would first locate the Federal Reporter, second series, in the law library. Then you'd select volume 366 and turn to page 303. To find a case with a "F.2d" or "F.3d" citation on Lexis-Nexis, follow all of the steps described above except one: at the opening page of the "guided search" under "federal case law," select "Court of Appeals," not "Supreme Court."

In this textbook you will see a variety of other legal citations to court decisions, and in each instance the letters in the middle tell you which court decided the case. Those decisions of the federal district courts that are published as legal precedents (many are not) appear in the *Federal Supplement* (abbreviated "F.Supp." in citations).

The citation system works much the same way in the state courts. In Chapter Five there's a reference to a privacy case called *Briscoe v. Reader's Digest,* 4 C.3d 529. That is a decision of the California Supreme Court, and the case appears in the *California Supreme Court Reports, third series.* To find the case, you would find volume 4 of that series and turn to page 529. Chapter Eight cites a case on reporter's privilege named *Zelenka v. Wisconsin,* 266 N.W.2d 279. It's a decision of the Wisconsin Supreme Court, but the citation refers to the *Northwestern Reporter, second series.* That series carries important court decisions from a number of midwestern states. It is a part of the *National Reporter System,* one publishing house's collection of regional reports that taken together cover all 50 states.

By the way, don't assume that your local law library only has reports of your own state's precedent-setting court decisions. Any large law library will have the National Reporter system and perhaps other sets of volumes reporting the major cases of the state appellate courts around the country. Whether you're in New York, Florida or Alaska, you'll probably find the text of state supreme court decisions in the other states.

In many instances, you will discover that your law library has more than one set of law books reporting the most important court decisions. This is true in part because there are competing legal publishing houses, each seeking to offer a full set of reports of the major appellate cases. To illustrate by returning once again to *New York Times v. Sullivan*, here is a more complete set of citations to that case: 376 U.S. 254, 84 S.Ct. 710, 11 L.Ed.2d 686 (1964). Don't be intimidated by all those numbers: let's take it a step at a time. You already know what "376 U.S. 254" means, and that's all you need to know to find the case in volume 376 of the official United States Reports. But suppose that volume is unavailable when you visit the law library. No problem. Just go to the next citation. "S.Ct." means *Supreme Court Reporter,* and if you pull down volume 84 and look on page 710, there's your case. Or you could go to "L.Ed.2d", which means *Lawyer's Edition, U.S. Supreme Court Reports, second series,* and pull down volume 11 and look on page 686. In each of these law books, the text of the Supreme Court decisions is exactly the same, but the introductory matter and editorial treatment may vary somewhat. Many law libraries keep all three of these sets of Supreme Court rulings in their collections, at least partly because the privately published versions are usually in print long before the official U.S. Reports become available.

Occasionally a blank citation may appear in this book (for example, 122 S.Ct. ____). That means the case was decided so recently that the full citation was not available when the book went to press. Some recent cases are shown with citations to a computer data base such as Lexis-Nexis. In fact, the growing use of computer data bases may soon lead to wholesale changes in the legal citation system described here. The page numbering system used in traditional citations has been based on *book pages*, of course. However, the pagination of a case is quite different on a computer screen, which typically consists of about 24 lines per "page." Colorado, Louisiana and Wisconsin have adopted new citation systems more compatible with computerized research methods. Several other states and the federal government are considering similar changes in legal citations.

In the mass communications field, another convenient way to look up court decisions is to check the *Media Law Reporter.* One volume is published each year, and it carries the full text of most precedent-setting court decisions on media law, including Supreme Court decisions, lower federal court rulings and state cases. In this book there are several citations to the Media Law Reporter (abbreviated in citations as Med.L.Rptr.).

When doing legal research online, you can not only look up a case such as *New York Times v. Sullivan* by searching for the name or the citation--you can also search for key words in the opinion itself (words such as *actual malice* in this instance, to note just one of many examples). In addition, you can quickly find later cases in which a particular case is mentioned. The ability to do these key word searches makes electronic legal research much faster than traditional paper-bound methods.

Legal Encyclopedias

We have just described the method of looking up the text of any major appellate court decision, but what happens if you don't know the names of any court decisions and you want to learn something about the law on a particular topic?

In that case, one place you might look is a legal encyclopedia. Legal encyclopedias are just like the regular encyclopedias you've used for years--except that they discuss only legal subjects. There are two leading legal encyclopedias in America, produced by different publishing houses: *American Jurisprudence,* or "AmJur" for short, and *Corpus Juris Secundum,* or "CJS." The publisher of the "CJS" (Latin for "body of the law, second edition") is now publishing a set called *Corpus Juris Tertium,* or "body of the law, third edition."

Despite their intimidating names, these sets of legal encyclopedias are not difficult to use. The many legal topics they treat are listed in alphabetical order with brief summaries of the major legal principles in each area. The only trick is knowing where to look for a particular subject, and for that there's a comprehensive index at the end of each set. If you want to know more about libel law, for instance, you would look up the word "libel," and you would be told where to go for more information. It's not always that straightforward, because the name you have in mind may not be the key word under which that subject is indexed; you may have to think of some synonyms. Once you find the right word in the index, it will lead you directly to a summary of the law you want, whether it's bankruptcy or crimes, unfair competition or medical malpractice.

As well as these national legal encyclopedias--which try to summarize the general rules of law around the country--there are legal encyclopedias that specifically summarize the laws of one state. Most of the populous states have such encyclopedias, bearing names such as *Florida Jurisprudence, California Jurisprudence, Texas Jurisprudence* or *New York Jurisprudence.*

One thing you need to be aware of when you consult a legal encyclopedia is the existence of *pocket parts*. The law changes every year, often drastically. What a legal encyclopedia says in its main text is supplemented by annual updates that are tucked into a pocket at the back of each volume. Make it a habit to check the pocket part first, lest you waste time learning something that is no longer valid law.

Because there have been thousands of important court decisions, and because many of them have reached seemingly inconsistent conclusions, the American Law Institute has commissioned groups of legal scholars to write summaries of the law as it has developed over the years through court decisions. These are called *Restatements* of the law, and the courts give them considerable weight. The *Restatement (Second) of Torts* summarizes libel, privacy and other areas of tort law, and is an important reference work in these fields. The Restatements carry far more legal weight than any legal encyclopedia, although they might seem less user-friendly to newcomers doing their first legal research.

Annotated Codes

Once you have read a survey of your subject in a legal encyclopedia, you might want to learn more about the subject by actually reading some of the court decisions and statutory laws summarized in the encyclopedia. We've already described the method of finding court decisions by working from the case citations found in any law book. Looking up the text of a statutory law is often even easier.

Many of the important state and federal laws are organized by subject matter. To look up a statutory law, you locate the appropriate book of state or federal statutes: a legal encyclopedia will refer you to statutory laws as well as court decisions that pertain to your subject. If you wanted to read the federal Copyright Act, for instance, you would use its legal citation, which is "17 U.S.C.A. 100 et seq." That means Title 17 of the United States Code, section 100 and following sections. To find the text of the Copyright Act, you would ask the law librarian where the U.S. Code volumes are kept, and then look up section 100 in Title 17. The number before the name of a state or federal code is always the title, book, or volume number, and the number after the name will lead you to the correct chapter and section. The nomenclature varies somewhat from state to state, but the principles are the same.

There are two things to remember in looking up statutory laws in this fashion. One is that the most complete sets are annotated. That is, they contain brief summaries of court decisions interpreting the statutory laws as well as the text of the laws themselves. It's important to look through these annotations to make sure the law you're learning has not been overruled by a court decision.

Another thing you must do to make sure your law is still in effect is to once again check the pocket part. Almost any code book that isn't completely revised every year (or more frequently) will contain a pocket part, just as a legal encyclopedia does. That pocket part will tell you of amendments to the law, if any, and of any new court decisions interpreting it.

Like encyclopedias, the annotated collections of statutory laws are extensively indexed. If you want to learn what the law of libel is in West Virginia, for instance, you can simply look up libel in the index to the *West Virginia Code* and then turn to the appropriate sections to find both statutes and summaries of cases mentioned in the annotations. In some chapters of this book, there are suggestions for simple legal research you can do to learn exactly what the laws are on the particular topic in your state. No comprehensive national survey textbook can hope to summarize the law in each state in great detail, but you can fill in those details for your own state in this fashion.

If you are doing legal research online, many web sites and data bases offer statutory laws as well as court decisions and regulatory information.

Administrative Regulations

Administrative law is such a vast and amorphous thing that we will not devote much space to the problems of researching it here. However, students with a special interest in broadcasting, for instance, should be aware that the regulations of the Federal Communications Commission are organized to facilitate research.

Title 47 of a legal work called *The Code of Federal Regulations,* or "CFR" for short, contains the FCC's rules and regulations. Working from the table of contents, you can quickly look up the FCC's rules on a particular point of broadcast regulation in CFR. CFR is updated frequently, since the administrative agencies whose regulations appear in it are constantly changing their rules.

There are also privately published summaries of the actions taken by major administrative agencies. In the case of the FCC, a set of legal reports known as "Pike and Fisher" provides information about the agency's actions. Many major law libraries keep complete sets of specialized legal reference materials such as Pike and Fisher. And, of course, many regulatory agencies now have their own Internet web sites that include compilations of their regulations, summaries, news releases and reports.

Further Information

In summarizing the methods of legal research, we have attempted to do in a few pages what an entire course does in law school. This section doesn't cover all of the details. But on the other hand, you probably won't be preparing a legal brief to be filed at the U.S. Supreme Court right away. All you need now is a general overview of the subject.

However, there are some additional things to remember if you undertake a serious legal research project. One is that the courts are constantly interpreting and reinterpreting previous decisions. Before you cite any court decision, you need to make sure it has not been reversed by a higher court or a later decision. A good way to do that is to consult a cross-reference index called *Shepard's Citator*. If you're involved in serious legal research that involves cases, ask someone at the law library to explain how to use "Shepard's" so you won't make the mistake of writing 10 pages about a court decision that has been reversed.

Finally, you should feel free to ask questions when you visit a law library or go online using a computer data base. The people at the help desk are paid to help you, and they often encounter visitors who know far less about the law than you do if you've read this far. Don't refrain from asking a question out of fear you'll sound ignorant. If you don't know where something is--or don't quite know what you're looking for--ASK.

CHAPTER TWO

The Legacy of Freedom

Americans are sometimes accused of taking freedom for granted. It is easy to talk about the First Amendment almost as if it were a universal law of nature, a principle that always existed and always will.

That, of course, is not the case. The kind of freedom of expression that is permitted today in the United States and a few dozen other democracies is unique in world history. Our freedoms were won through centuries of bitter struggle, and they could easily be lost. Even today, fewer than half of the world's people live in countries that fully recognize such basic freedoms as freedom of speech, freedom of the press and freedom of religion. Government leaders in many countries consider "national security" (or their own personal security in office) more important than their peoples' freedoms. Many leaders see the mass media only as tools of propaganda or national development--weapons to be used against their rivals, both foreign and domestic. Even in America, the threat of terrorism has prompted some new restrictions on civil liberties in the aftermath of the events of Sept. 11, 2001. For example, the USA Patriot Act, passed shortly after the Sept. 11 attacks, broadened the federal government's power to monitor telephone and Internet communications, among other things.

In much of the world it is still commonplace for governments to censor the mass media directly. And even in some countries where the media are nominally free of censorship, journalists and others who advocate democratic reforms are sometimes arrested, tortured and murdered. Journalists "disappear" so often in some countries that the outside world hardly notices. Short of that, government officials may control the media in more subtle ways, such as by offering lucrative government "advertising" that looks and sounds just like bona fide news when it is published or broadcast. Without that government subsidy, many news media would quickly go broke--a fact that makes it very difficult for them to maintain any semblance of editorial independence.

Most Americans and Western Europeans were delighted in 1989 and the early 1990s when communist governments all across Eastern Europe were replaced by non-communist governments that implemented democratic reforms, including freedom of the press. Even the former Soviet Union, long the prime symbol of totalitarianism to many westerners, entered an era of *glasnost* and *perestroika*--a time of openness and restructuring that led to free elections and new freedom for the mass media, and ultimately to the breakup of the Soviet Union itself.

However, 1989 was also the year when thousands of Chinese students and intellectuals who demonstrated for democracy in Beijing were slaughtered en masse by the Chinese army, which was apparently acting on orders of the government. Unfortunately, what happened in China was not unique. While the transition from one-party rule to democracy was remarkably non-violent in many countries, hundreds or perhaps thousands of people who dared to demonstrate for freedom were also massacred in Romania before that country's hard-line communist government fell. And it was not long ago that those who advocated basic civil liberties were brutalized in many other countries that now permit free expression and free elections. The story of how earlier generations won the freedoms we enjoy today is an important part of this summary of mass communications law.

CENSORSHIP IN ENGLAND

This summary of the evolution of freedom of expression could begin in the ancient world, were this a survey of the philosophical underpinnings of modern civilization. Powerful arguments for freedom of expression were made thousands of years ago in ancient Greece and several other places around the globe. But our tradition of freedom of expression traces its roots most directly to England about 400 years ago.

In the 1600s, England was caught up in a battle that mixed politics and religion. The monarchy and the government-sponsored Church of England were determined to silence dissenters, many of them Puritans. Moreover, the religious and political struggle was closely linked with an economic battle between the aristocracy and the rising middle class.

Leaders on both sides of this ideological battle understood the importance of the printing press and sometimes resorted to heavy-handed efforts to censor ideas they considered dangerous. In those days more than one Englishman was jailed, tortured and eventually executed for expressing ideas unacceptable to those in power. Brutality that would be shocking to Americans--or Britons--today was fairly commonplace in England in that period.

Official censorship was enforced through a licensing system for printers that had been introduced as early as 1530. The licensing denied access to printing presses to people with unacceptable ideas, but it also enabled government representatives to preview and pre-censor materials before publication. Moreover, by making the possession of a license to print a coveted privilege, the government was often able to control underground printing. The licensed printers themselves helped to ferret out bootleg presses to protect their own self-interests.

Milton and the Puritans

By the early 1600s censorship was being used to suppress all sorts of ideas that threatened the established order. This inspired some of the leading political philosophers of the day to write eloquent appeals for freedom of expression as a vital adjunct to the broader freedom from religious and political oppression they sought. An early apostle of freedom of expression was John Milton, who in 1644 wrote his famous argument against government censorship, *Areopagitica*. Milton's appeal to the Long Parliament for freedom contained this statement:

> Though all the winds of doctrine were let loose to play upon the earth, so Truth be in the field, we do injuriously by licensing and prohibiting to misdoubt her strength. Let her and Falsehood grapple; who ever knew Truth put to the worse in a free and open encounter?

Out of this passage several modern ideas emerged, including the concept that a *self-righting process* would occur through open debate of controversial issues. In effect, Milton said censorship was unnecessary because true ideas would prevail over false ones anyway. Milton advocated something of a *marketplace of ideas.* That was a revolutionary idea: almost no one in Milton's time believed that freedom of expression should be universal. But even to Milton, this freedom had its limits. Although he favored far more freedom than most of his contemporaries, Milton did not think free expression rights should be extended to persons who advocated ideas that he considered dangerously false or subversive. His appeal for freedom specifically excluded "popery (support for the Roman Catholic Church) and open superstition" and ideas that were "impious or evil."

In fact, after the Puritan movement led by Oliver Cromwell gained control of England and executed King Charles I in 1649, Milton accepted a government appointment that required him to act as something of a government censor. One of his duties was to license and oversee the content of an official newssheet, *Mercurius Politicus*. By 1651--only seven years after he appealed to the government to allow true and false ideas to struggle for popular acceptance--Milton was engaged in the prior censorship of ideas. And he was serving in a government that imposed strict Puritan beliefs on England and showed little tolerance for the beliefs of other religious groups.

Was Milton's later employment inconsistent with the spirit of *Areopagitica*? Perhaps it was, but even today scholars disagree about the role Milton actually played in Cromwell's government. Some doubt that Milton really did much censoring. Whatever Milton later did--or did not do--to earn a living, his *Areopagitica* was an eloquent appeal for freedom of expression and an important influence on later English political thought.

In fairness to Cromwell's followers, we should also point out that there were some who went further than Milton did in advocating freedom of expression. For instance Roger Williams, a onetime Puritan minister in the Massachusetts Bay colony who was exiled to Rhode Island for his controversial religious ideas, later returned to England and wrote *Bloudy Tenent of Persecution for Cause of Conscience* in the same year as Milton's *Areopagitica*. Williams urged freedom of expression even for Catholics, Jews and Moslems--people Milton would not have included in his marketplace of ideas.

Perhaps even more emphatic in their arguments for freedom from censorship in the 1640s were the Levellers, a radical Puritan group. Their tracts consistently contained passages condemning censorship and the licensing system. In their view, free expression was essential to the religious freedom and limited government authority they so fervently sought.

In a 1648 petition to the Parliament, the Levellers appealed for a free press. When "truth was suppressed" and the people kept ignorant, this ignorance "fitted only to serve the unjust ends of tyrants and oppressors." For a government to be just "in its constitution" and "equal in its distributions," it must "hear all voices and judgments, which they can never do, but by giving freedom to the press."

Despite the rhetoric of the Puritans, England restored the monarchy in 1660 and the licensing of printers continued (although Parliament by then had a much larger say in the process). Although the post-1660 Restoration period was marked by unprecedented freedom--and even bawdiness--in English literature, it was also a time of religious repression. A 1662 act of Parliament, for instance, limited the number of printing presses and prohibited the printing of books contrary to the Christian faith as well as seditious or anti-government works.

John Locke and Natural Rights

As the struggle between the monarchy and Parliament became more intense in the late 1600s, new philosophers of free expression emerged. Perhaps chief among them was John Locke. His ideas were not necessarily original, but he presented them so eloquently that he is remembered as one of the most important political theorists of his time. Locke's famous *social contract* theory said that governments were the servants of the people, not the other way around. Locke believed men were endowed with certain natural rights, among them the right to life, liberty and property ownership. In effect, Locke said the people make a deal with a government, giving it the authority to govern in return for the government's promise to safeguard these natural rights.

Central to these natural rights, Locke felt, was freedom of expression. Thus, when the English licensing system came up for review in 1694, Locke listed 18 reasons why the act should be terminated. The act was allowed to expire, primarily because of "the practical reason arising from the difficulties of administration and the restraints on trade." For a fuller description of the struggle for freedom of expression in England, see Fred Siebert's classic work, *Freedom of the Press in England, 1476-1776* (Urbana: University of Illinois Press, 1952).

Other forces in English society were also providing impetus for freedom of expression. For one, Parliament gained a major victory over the monarchy in the Glorious Revolution of 1688. James II, an avowedly Catholic king so offensive that several warring factions united against him, fled the country that year. Then in 1689 Parliament enacted a Bill of Rights and invited William of Orange and his consort Mary, James' Protestant daughter, to assume the throne with strictly limited powers. In the Declaration of Rights, William and Mary accepted these conditions, ending England's century-long struggle between Parliament and the monarchy.

In addition, a two-party system was emerging in England; the times were ready for open, robust political debate. The two parties, the Whigs and Tories, both relied extensively on the printing press in taking their views to the people.

Seditious Libel as a Crime

If official censorship by licensing the press was a thing of the past as England moved into the 1700s, the crime of seditious libel (i.e., the crime of criticizing the government or government officials) remained a viable deterrent to those who might publish defamatory tracts.

A good illustration of this problem was the 1704 case of John Tuchin, who was tried for "writing, composing and publishing a certain false, malicious, seditious and scandalous libel, entitled, *The Observator*" (see *Rex v. Tuchin*, 14 Howell's State Trials 1095).

Tuchin was convicted of the crime, and in the process the presiding judge defined the common law on seditious libel:

> To say that corrupt officers are appointed to administer affairs, is certainly a reflection on the government. If people would not be called to account for possessing the people with an ill opinion of the government, no government can subsist. For it is very necessary for all governments that the people should have a good opinion of it. And nothing can be worse to any government, than to endeavor to procure animosities, as to the management of it; this has been always looked upon as a crime, and no government can be safe without it be punished.

This common law rule did not go unchallenged for long. Free press advocates, perhaps strengthened by their success in abolishing licensing, opened the eighteenth century with a flurry of articles and tracts advocating greater freedom. Nevertheless, criticism of the government remained a crime throughout the century, with the truthfulness of the criticism not a defense against the charge. The prevailing legal maxim was, "the greater the truth, the greater the libel."

How could this be? The assumption underlying this philosophy was reminiscent of Milton: if a printer publishes a false attack on the government, it will be disregarded by the people; if, on the other hand, a truthful attack is published, the people are likely to lend it credence and perhaps revolt, causing disorder and anarchy.

Parliament itself recognized the abuses possible under the common law of seditious libel, and in 1792 the Fox Libel Act was passed. That act permitted juries, rather than judges, to decide whether a statement was libelous. Prior to that time, the law allowed the jury to determine only whether the defendant was guilty of printing the libelous publication. The judge ruled on the legal question of whether the material was actually libelous.

This legal reform did not eliminate seditious libel prosecutions, but it did make it more difficult for a government to punish its critics because a jury, whose members might well sympathize with the defendant's allegedly libelous statements, could decide if the statements were libelous.

An additional reform came in 1843, further strengthening the rights of those who would criticize the government in England. In that year, Parliament passed Lord Campbell's Act, establishing truth as a defense in all seditious libel cases.

Thus, the old maxim, "the greater the truth, the greater the libel," was at last abolished.

While the struggle for freedom of expression was being fought in England, a parallel battle was under way in the American colonies.

FREEDOM IN A NEW NATION

Although many of the early colonists in North America left England or the European continent to escape religious or political oppression, they found (or created) an atmosphere of less than total freedom in some of the colonies here. As the Puritans gained control in New England, they established close church-state ties, and persons with unpopular religious or political ideas were hardly more welcome here than they had been in England.

In fact, the first laws that restricted freedom of the press in North America preceded the first newspaper here by some 30 years. Even without any specific authority, colonial rulers often simply assumed they had the right to censor dissenting publications because the authorities had that right in England. Even after licensing was abolished in England, colonial leaders continued to act as if they had licensing powers, and several colonial newspapers carried the phrase "published by authority" in their mastheads years after the right to publish without government permission was won in England.

Moreover, in North America as in England, seditious libel prosecutions were used as a means of controlling the press, as were laws that placed special tax burdens on newspapers. The Stamp Act of 1765, for instance, taxed newspapers by forcing publishers to purchase revenue stamps and attach one to every copy. The result was such blatant defiance of British authority by colonial publishers that it helped inspire the eventual revolution against the mother country.

The Zenger Libel Trial

Early in the colonial publishing experience there was a seditious libel case that became a cause celebre on both sides of the Atlantic: the trial of John Peter Zenger in 1735 (*Attorney General v. John Peter Zenger*, 17 Howell's State Trials 675).

Zenger, a German immigrant, was the publisher and printer of the *New York Weekly Journal*. His paper became a leading voice for the opposition to a particularly unpopular royal governor, William Cosby. After some legal maneuvering, the governor was able to have Zenger jailed and charged with "printing and publishing a false, scandalous and seditious libel, in which ...the governor ...is greatly and unjustly scandalized, as a person that has no regard to law nor justice."

Zenger was fortunate enough to have Andrew Hamilton of Philadelphia, one of the most respected lawyers in the colonies, make the trip to New York for his defense. And Hamilton, ignoring the orders of Cosby's hand-picked judge, appealed directly to the jury. He urged the jurors to ignore the maxim of "the greater the truth, the greater the libel" and to decide for themselves whether the statements in question were actually true, finding them libelous only if they were false.

"Nature and the laws of our country have given us a right--and the liberty--both of exposing and opposing arbitrary power ...by speaking and writing truth," Hamilton said.

In urging the jurors to ignore the judge's instructions and acquit Zenger if they decided the statements were true, Hamilton was clearly overstepping the bounds of the law. A less prestigious lawyer might have been punished for an action so clearly in contempt of the court's authority. However, Hamilton was not cited, and his eloquent appeal to the jury worked: the jury returned a not-guilty verdict even though there was little question that Zenger was the publisher of the challenged statements.

It would be difficult to overstate the importance of the Zenger trial in terms of its psychological impact on royal governors in America. Still, its direct effect on the common law was minimal in America and England itself. Even in those days, a criminal trial verdict established no binding legal precedent. English courts continued to punish truthful publications that were critical of government authority. For instance, the trial of John Wilkes for publishing a "wicked and seditious libel," a 1763 English case, made it clear that the common law had not been changed by the Zenger trial.

Nevertheless, the argument was made again and again that mere words critical of the government--and especially truthful words--should not be a crime. In 1773 the Rev. Philip Furneaux wrote that only overt acts against a government should be punished:

> The tendency of principles, tho' it be unfavourable, is not prejudicial to society, till it issues in some overt acts against the public peace and order; and when it does, then the magistrate's authority to punish commences; that is, he may punish the overt acts, but not the tendency which is not actually harmful; and therefore his penal laws should be directed against overt acts only.

THE FIRST AMENDMENT

When a series of incidents strained relations between England and the colonies past the breaking point, the colonists declared their independence in 1776. Yet even in breaking with England, the Americans borrowed heavily from the mother country. Thomas Jefferson's ideas and even some of his language in the Declaration of Independence were borrowed from English political philosophers, notably John Locke. Locke's natural rights and social contract ideas appear repeatedly in the declaration.

After independence was won on the battlefield, the new nation briefly experimented with a weak central government under the Articles of Confederation and then became a unified nation under the Constitution, which was ratified by the states in 1788. Despite its ratification, many Americans feared the new federal government, particularly because the Constitution had no guarantees that basic civil liberties would be respected. Although the defenders of the Constitution argued that these civil liberties were firmly entrenched in the common law we had inherited from England, many were wary. Some states ratified the Constitution only after they received assurances that it would be amended quickly to add a Bill of Rights.

That promise was kept. In the first session of Congress, the Bill of Rights was drawn up and submitted to the states to ratify. It was declared in force late in 1791. Of paramount concern to the mass media, of course, is the First Amendment, which reads:

> Congress shall make no law respecting an establishment of religion, or prohibiting the free exercise thereof; or abridging the freedom of speech, or of the press; or the right of the people peaceably to assemble, and to petition the Government for a redress of grievances.

Taken literally, the First Amendment is almost everything that a free press advocate might hope for, but those words have not often been taken literally. In fact, the exact meaning of the First Amendment has been vigorously debated for more than 200 years now.

Early First Amendment Questions

The record of the Congressional discussions when the Bill of Rights was drafted is sketchy: it is impossible to be certain what Congress had in mind. Constitutional scholars have advanced various theories, but most doubt that the majority of the framers of the Constitution intended the First Amendment to be an absolute prohibition on all government actions that might in any way curtail freedom of the press.

The crucial question, then, and the one that is the focus of the rest of this chapter, is this: which restrictions on freedom are constitutionally permissible and which ones are not? Many scholarly works have been published attempting to answer this question; several historians have dedicated much of their lives to examining records, debates and documents of the period in an attempt to find the answers. Some of their conclusions will be presented shortly.

Whatever the first Congress intended in drafting those words, it was only a few years later that Congress passed laws that seemed to be a flagrant violation of the First Amendment. In 1798 Congress hurriedly approved the Alien and Sedition Acts, a group of laws designed to silence political dissent in preparation for a war with France, a war that was never declared. The Sedition Act made it a federal crime to speak or publish seditious ideas. The law had one important safeguard: truth was recognized as a defense. Nevertheless, a fine of up to $2,000 or two years' imprisonment was prescribed for any person who dared to:

> ...(W)rite, print, utter or publish, or ...knowingly and willingly assist or aid in writing, printing, uttering or publishing any false, scandalous and malicious writing or writings against the government of the United States, or either house of the Congress of the United States, or the President of the

United States, with intent to defame the said government, or either house of said Congress, or the said President, or to bring them, or either of them, into contempt or disrepute; or to excite against them, or either or any of them, the hatred of the good people of the United States, or to stir up sedition within the United States.

There were about 25 arrests and 15 indictments under the act. All were aimed at opponents of President John Adams and the Federalist Party, which then controlled Congress and had enacted the law over the opposition of Jefferson and his followers. Even though the Federalist press was often guilty of vicious attacks on Thomas Jefferson and other non-Federalist government officials, no Federalist was ever prosecuted under the Sedition Act. A two-party system was emerging, and the Jeffersonian, or anti-Federalist, opposition party was the real target of the Sedition Act.

One historic trial resulting from the Sedition Act was that of Dr. Thomas Cooper, who was charged with publishing a list of mistakes he thought Adams had made as president (*U.S. v. Cooper*, 25 F. 631, 1800).

Cooper, who later became president of what is now Columbia University, made statements at his trial that were widely circulated, condemning the restrictions placed on the press by the Sedition Act. Cooper pointed out that "in the present state of affairs, the press is open to those who will praise, while the threats of the law hang over those who blame the conduct of the men in power."

Furthermore, he said that if freedom of discussion is stifled, then the avenues of information are closed. The electorate cannot wisely select political leaders then, since those in power have thrown "a veil over the grossest misconduct of our periodical rulers," Cooper said.

In reply, Samuel Chase, the Federalist judge who presided over Cooper's trial at a federal court in Pennsylvania, told the jury:

> All governments which I have ever read or heard of punish libels against themselves. If a man attempts to destroy the confidence of the people in their officers, their supreme magistrate, and their legislature, he effectually saps the foundation of the government.

The jury convicted Dr. Cooper. Elsewhere in the United States, about seven others were similarly convicted, and several of them became folk heroes among a populace that was increasingly dissatisfied with the Federalist leadership.

The emerging opposition political party of Thomas Jefferson capitalized on this unrest and gained a wide base of popular support in part because of the heavy-handedness of the Federalists.

Jefferson, by then the vice president, strenuously opposed the Alien and Sedition Acts. The Kentucky and Virginia legislatures passed resolutions, backed by Jefferson, that purported to "nullify" these laws, thus raising questions about states' rights that would not be resolved until the Civil War.

James Madison, later to be Jefferson's secretary of state and then the nation's fourth president, made it clear in drafting the Virginia Resolution that he felt the

Sedition Act was a violation of the First Amendment. Madison believed the First Amendment was supposed to be an absolute prohibition on all actions of the federal government that restricted freedom of the press.

Jefferson probably agreed. In one letter to a friend, he wrote: "I am ...for freedom of the press and against all violations of the Constitution to silence by force and not by reason the complaints or criticisms, just or unjust, of our citizens against the conduct of their agents."

When Jefferson ran for president in 1800, he made the Alien and Sedition Acts a major issue; public discontent over these laws was certainly an important factor in his victory. Immediately after his inauguration, Jefferson ordered the pardon of those who had been convicted under the Sedition Act.

However, Jefferson's record as a champion of a free press was not entirely unblemished. During his presidency he was subjected to harsh personal attacks by some opposition newspapers. Although he usually defended the right of his foes to express their views, he eventually became so annoyed that he encouraged his backers to prosecute some of his critics in state courts.

FIRST AMENDMENT SCHOLARS' VIEWS

The Sedition Act expired in 1801, and it was more than 100 years before Congress again attempted to make criticism of the government a federal crime.

However, this does not prove the First Amendment was intended to eliminate seditious libel as a crime, and the debate over that issue continued well into the twentieth century. Historian Leonard Levy, a leading constitutional scholar, once wrote:

> What is clear is that there exists no evidence to suggest an understanding that a constitutional guarantee of free speech or press meant the impossibility of future prosecutions of seditious utterances.... The security of the state against libelous advocacy or attack was always regarded as outweighing any social interest in open expression, at least through the period of the adoption of the First Amendment.

Levy argued that most likely the framers of the First Amendment weren't certain what its full implications were, but that most of the framers believed future prosecutions for seditious utterances were possible.

However, later in his life Levy rethought that conclusion based on extensive additional research into the content of early American newspapers. He ultimately decided that the framers must have intended for the First Amendment to provide "a right to engage in rasping, corrosive, and offensive discussions on all topics of public interest." His earlier, more narrow view of the First Amendment was presented in a 1960 book, *Legacy of Suppression: Freedom of Speech and Press in Early American History*. In 1985, he published a revised and enlarged edition of the book that he retitled, *Emergence of a Free Press*. For those with an interest in such matters, Levy's dramatic reversal of his position--described in his 1985 edition--makes fascinating reading. In the preface to his new edition, Levy wrote:

> I was wrong in asserting that the American experience with freedom of political expression was as slight as the conceptual and legal understanding was narrow.... Press criticism of government policies and politicians, on both state and national levels, during the war (for independence) and in the peaceful years of the 1780s and 1790s, raged as contemptuously and scorchingly as it had against Great Britain in the period between the Stamp Act and the battle of Lexington. Some states gave written constitutional protection to freedom of the press after Independence; others did not. Whether they did or not, their presses operated as if the law of seditious libel did not exist.

In revising his views, Levy came much closer to agreeing with several other noted legal historians. For example, Harvard Professor Zechariah Chafee wrote that the First Amendment was indeed intended to eliminate the common law crime of seditious libel "and make further prosecutions for criticism of the government, without any incitement to law-breaking, forever impossible in the United States."

Chafee, in his 1941 work, argued that freedom of expression is essential to the emergence of truth and advancement of knowledge. The quest for truth "is possible only through absolutely unlimited discussion," Chafee said. Yet, he noted that there are other purposes of government, such as order, the training of the young, and protection against external aggression. Those purposes, he said, must be protected too, but when open discussion interferes with those purposes, there must be a balancing against freedom of speech, "but freedom of speech ought to weigh heavily on that scale."

Chafee argued against prior restraint of expression unless it was very clear that such expression imperiled the nation. He wrote:

> The true boundary line of the First Amendment can be fixed only when Congress and the courts realize that the principle on which speech is classified as lawful or unlawful involves the balancing against each other of two very important social interests, in public safety and in the search for truth. Every reasonable attempt should be made to maintain both interests unimpaired, and the great interest in free speech should be sacrificed only when the interest in public safety is really imperiled, and not, as most men believe, when it is barely conceivable that it may be slightly affected. In war time, therefore, speech should be unrestricted by the censorship or by punishment, unless it is clearly liable to cause direct and dangerous interference with the conduct of war.

Chafee's boundary line, then, is that point where words will incite unlawful acts. As we'll see later, that is precisely the point at which the Supreme Court has drawn the line in recent decisions on the meaning of the First Amendment.

A third noted constitutional scholar, Alexander Meiklejohn, agreed for the most part with Chafee's interpretation of the First Amendment. He said that only expression that incites unlawful acts should be punishable. Further, he said, incitement does not occur unless an illegal act is actually performed and the prior words can be directly connected to the act. Then, and only then, can words be punished in spite of the First Amendment.

Meiklejohn said that the First Amendment was written during a time when large sections of the population were hostile to the form of government then being adopted. Thus, the framers knew full well that a program of political freedom was a dangerous thing. Yet, Meiklejohn said, the framers chose to write the First Amendment as it is and not the way the courts have rewritten it during the twentieth century. He said that if the framers had wanted the federal government to control expression, the First Amendment could have read:

> Only when, in the judgment of the legislature, the interests of order and security render such action advisable shall Congress abridge the freedom of speech.

Both Chafee and Meiklejohn felt that the voters must be well informed to make wise decisions. Both endorsed Milton's "marketplace of ideas" concept, and Meiklejohn supported Milton's view that truth will prevail in this clash of ideas:

> No one can deny that the winning of the truth is important for the purposes of self-government. But that is not our deepest need. Far more essential, if men are to be their own rulers, is the demand that whatever truth may become available shall be placed at the disposal of all the citizens of the community. The First Amendment ...is a device for the sharing of whatever truth has been won.

Much of what we have just discussed is quite theoretical, but the views of scholars such as Chafee, Meiklejohn and Levy have often influenced the U.S. Supreme Court when it was forced to make difficult decisions about the scope and meaning of the First Amendment in the real world.

NINETEENTH-CENTURY PRESS FREEDOM

Whatever the framers of the Constitution and Bill of Rights intended, the question received little attention in the 1800s. The nineteenth century was a time when Americans were preoccupied with such overriding issues as national expansion and slavery. There was surprisingly little attention given to the meaning of the First Amendment, during most of that century. Instead, the country and the courts were looking at other issues for the most part.

The Supreme Court and Judicial Review

In 1803, the Supreme Court gained the power to declare acts of Congress unconstitutional and thereby invalidate them. In the landmark case of *Marbury v.*

Madison (1 Cranch 137), what the court really did was simply to *declare* that it had the power to overturn acts of Congress. Perhaps the court got away with it mainly because President Jefferson and his followers were happy with the outcome of the case.

Just before his term expired, John Adams, the lame-duck Federalist president, had appointed a number of federal judges. Because of their belated appointments, they came to be called "midnight judges." The new judges were Federalists, and the Jeffersonians were anxious to keep them from taking office. James Madison, Jefferson's secretary of state, refused to give William Marbury, one of the would-be judges, his signed commission (the document appointing him to office). Marbury sued to get the commission. The Jeffersonians were not displeased when the high court, under its famous chief justice, John Marshall, dismissed Marbury's claim by overturning the Judicial Act of 1789, on which the would-be judge had based his lawsuit. In the convoluted politics of the day, Marshall--a Federalist--had sided with the Jeffersonians on a small matter (Marbury's commission), but in so doing Marshall had prevailed on the larger issue: the right of the court to review actions of other branches of government for compliance with the Constitution.

Ironically, Chief Justice Marshall had himself been appointed by John Adams during the final year of his presidency. Although the Federalist Party faded away, never winning another national election, Marshall served as chief justice for 34 years, allowing the Federalist philosophy to have an ongoing impact on American law long after the Federalist Party disappeared from the scene.

Marshall's Supreme Court asserted its authority in many other areas, attempting to define the scope and limits of federal power. In 1812, the Supreme Court ruled that the federal courts had no authority to entertain actions involving common law crimes such as criminal libel. In *U.S. v. Hudson and Goodwin* (7 Cranch 32), the high court said this area of law fell within the exclusive domain of the states, a philosophy that has remained largely unchanged ever since. On the other hand, in *McCulloch v. Maryland* (4 Wheat. 316), an 1819 decision that is among Marshall's most famous, the court upheld the right of Congress to create a national bank and regulate the economy even though a narrow, literal reading of the Constitution might not permit it. Having so ruled, Marshall then declared once and for all that the states may not tax agencies of the federal government.

When the Bill of Rights was added to the U.S. Constitution, its authors wanted to be certain that the federal government's powers would be strictly limited so as to avoid usurping the powers of the states. The Tenth Amendment reads, "The powers not delegated to the United States by the Constitution, nor prohibited by it to the states, are reserved to the states respectively, or to the people."

To the amazement of many Americans, the Supreme Court reasserted the principle of a strictly limited federal government in a series of decisions 200 years later. For example, in 2000, the Supreme Court overturned the Violence against Women Act of 1994, holding that Congress had invaded an area of law reserved for the states (i.e., the prosecution of crimes such as rape) by passing this law (*U.S. v. Morrison*, 529 U.S. 598).

While the federal government stayed out of mass communications law during much of the nineteenth century, the states filled that void. Throughout the century, the states were expanding the common law and adopting statutory laws in such areas as libel and slander.

One of the best known state cases was the 1804 libel trial of Harry Croswell in New York (*People v. Croswell*, 3 Johnson's Cases 336). Croswell attacked President Jefferson in print and was prosecuted for criminal libel. He was convicted, but he appealed to a higher state court. His defense attorney, Federalist leader Alexander Hamilton, argued that truth plus "good motives for justifiable ends" should be a defense in such cases.

Although Croswell lost when the appellate panel of four judges deadlocked 2-2, the concept that truth should be a libel defense was sometimes called the *Hamilton Doctrine* and was adopted in a number of states during that era. For instance, the New York legislature recognized the truth defense by statute in 1805--and added a provision empowering the jury to determine whether the statement in question was actually libelous. Some states had recognized truth as a libel defense even before that time and, of course, the 1798 Sedition Act had recognized it on the federal level. Nevertheless, what Andrew Hamilton, the distinguished Philadelphia lawyer, had argued for in the Zenger trial 70 years earlier gained general acceptance in American law only after another distinguished lawyer named Hamilton made it his cause as well.

Alexander Hamilton, of course, didn't live long enough to enjoy whatever recognition the *Hamilton Doctrine* might have brought him: a newspaper account of something he purportedly said during the Croswell trial led to the infamous duel in which he was killed by Aaron Burr, then the vice president of the United States.

Slavery and Free Expression

Aside from the gradual evolution of libel law, probably the most significant conflict over American freedom of the expression in the 1800s resulted from the struggle over slavery and the War Between the States.

As the national debate over slavery intensified in the early 1800s, a number of southern states enacted "gag laws" that prohibited the circulation of newspapers and other materials advocating the abolition of slavery. Although these laws were clearly acts of prior censorship and violated the spirit of the First Amendment, the First Amendment had not yet been made applicable to the states, and these laws were never tested for their constitutionality.

Some northern states also attempted to curb abolitionist literature through various laws; these laws too escaped constitutional scrutiny because the Bill of Rights did not yet apply to the states.

Even Congress adopted rules to suppress debate about slavery that violated the spirit and probably the letter of the First Amendment. When anti-slavery groups began submitting petitions to Congress asking that the slave trade in Washington, D.C. be abolished, the House of Representatives adopted internal "gag rules" to prevent these petitions from being introduced and considered. These rules not only censored anti-slavery members of Congress but also took direct aim at the First Amendment's provision guaranteeing the right to petition the government. Rep. John Quincy Adams of Massachusetts, who returned to Congress after serving as the nation's sixth president, led the fight against these gag rules. At one point he arrived in Washington with anti-slavery petitions signed by more than 50,000 persons. When he was barred from presenting them formally, he left the petitions stacked high on his desk in the House of Representatives as a silent protest against the gag rules. In 1844, Adams--by then 77 years old--finally garnered enough support to have the Congressional gag rules eliminated.

During the Civil War itself, a vigorous antiwar movement emerged in the North, and antiwar editors came to be known as Copperheads. Some of them tested freedom of the press in wartime to the limit, openly advocating a southern victory.

The Copperheads' rhetoric often hindered recruiting for the Union Army. On several occasions, military commanders in the North acted against Copperheads, creating a difficult dilemma for President Lincoln, who was deeply committed to the First Amendment but also wanted to end the war quickly. He is generally credited with exercising great restraint in the face of vicious criticism from the Copperhead editors. On one occasion he actually countermanded a general's decision to occupy the offices of the *Chicago Times* to halt that paper's attacks on the war effort.

However, in 1864 Lincoln reached his breaking point when two New York newspapers published a false story claiming there was to be a massive new draft call--an announcement sure to stir violent antidraft riots. The president allowed the editors to be arrested and their papers occupied by the military until it was learned the newspapers got the story from a forged Associated Press dispatch that they had every reason to believe was authentic. As it turned out, the story was fabricated by an unscrupulous journalist who hoped to make a stock market killing in the panic he expected the story to produce.

After the end of the Civil War, the Fourteenth Amendment was approved, requiring the states to safeguard the basic civil liberties of all of their residents. The relevant part of the Fourteenth Amendment reads as follows:

> No state shall make or enforce any law which shall abridge the privileges or immunities of citizens of the United States; nor shall any State deprive any person of life, liberty or property, without due process of law; nor deny to any person within its jurisdiction the equal protection of the laws.

Like the First Amendment, this amendment had far-reaching consequences that were not fully understood when it was adopted. Its immediate impetus came from the desire to protect the former slaves from oppressive legislation in southern states. But during the twentieth century the "liberty" clause of the Fourteenth Amendment was relied upon repeatedly to make the various federal rights guaranteed in the Bill of Rights--including the First Amendment--applicable to the states. Under a modern understanding of constitutional law, no state could enact and enforce a gag law of the sort adopted by many states before the Civil War.

John Stuart Mill's Philosophy

While the United States was preoccupied with the struggle over slavery, John Stuart Mill, an English political philosopher, was refining the theoretical concept of freedom of expression.

Mill's *On Liberty,* first published in 1859, defined the limits of freedom and authority in the modern state. He said that by the mid-1800s the important role of the press as one of "the securities against corrupt or tyrannical government" was well recognized--at least in such countries as England and the United States. He stressed that any attempt to silence expression, even that of a one-person minority, deprives the people of something important. He said that "if the opinion is right, they (the people) are deprived of the opportunity of exchanging error for truth; if wrong, they lose what is almost as great a benefit, the clearer perception and livelier impression of truth, produced by its collision with error."

Mill presented four basic propositions in defense of freedom of expression. First, he said an opinion may contain truth, and if one silences the opinion, the truth may be lost. Second, there may be a particle of truth within a wrong opinion; if the wrong opinion is suppressed, that particle of truth may be lost. Third, even if an accepted opinion is the truth, the public tends to hold it not on rational grounds but as a prejudice unless forced to defend it. And fourth, a commonly held opinion loses its vitality and its effect on conduct and character if it is not contested from time to time.

In these terms, Mill expanded upon Milton's "marketplace of ideas" concept. The impact of these ideas on the evolution of freedom of expression became evident in the twentieth century.

SEDITION IN THE TWENTIETH CENTURY

Wars and the threat of wars tend to make lawmakers worry more about national security and less about such ideals as freedom of speech. The Alien and Sedition Acts of 1798 were passed at a time when war with France seemed imminent, and the Civil War created pressures for censorship of those who opposed that war effort.

Early in the twentieth century, this nation became involved in what many Americans thought would be the war to end all wars: World War I. In preparing the country for this all-out war, Congress again decided that domestic freedom would have to be curtailed. The result was the Espionage Act in 1917, which was expanded by the Sedition Act in 1918.

In passing these laws, Congress was not merely expressing its own collective desire to suppress unpopular views. In fact, there was a growing worldwide movement for fundamental social change, a movement many Americans found threatening. Already, Marxist revolutionaries were on the move in Russia, and socialists, anarchists and Marxists were also highly visible in this country. Moreover, we were about to undertake a war against Germany, and yet there were millions of persons of German descent living in America. In addition, labor unions such as the International Workers of the World (the "Wobblies") were gaining wide support and calling for basic changes in the capitalist system.

The Espionage Act was passed shortly after the United States entered World War I. It prohibited seditious expression that might hurt the war effort. This federal law was particularly aimed at those who might hamper armed forces recruiting, and it was written so broadly that it was once used to prosecute a grandmother who wrote a letter urging her grandson not to join the army.

Unlike the 1798 Sedition Act, which resulted in only a handful of prosecutions, the 1918 Sedition Act was vigorously enforced. About 2,000 persons were arrested for violating the Espionage and Sedition acts and nearly 1,000 were convicted. Several of the convictions were appealed to the U.S. Supreme Court, which upheld every conviction it reviewed.

Early Free Expression Decisions

The first Espionage Act or Sedition Act case to reach the Supreme Court was *Schenck v. U.S.* (249 U.S. 47) in 1919. Charles T. Schenck, general secretary of the Socialist Party, and another socialist were convicted under the Espionage Act and state anarchy and sedition laws for circulating about 15,000 leaflets to military recruits and draftees. The tracts denounced the draft as an unconstitutional form of involuntary servitude, banned by the Thirteenth Amendment. They urged the draftees not to serve and called the war a cold-blooded venture for the profit of big business.

When their conviction was reviewed by the Supreme Court, the socialists argued that their speech and leaflets were protected by the First Amendment. The court was thus compelled to rule on the scope and meaning of the First Amendment. In a famous opinion written by Justice Oliver Wendell Holmes Jr., the court rejected the socialists' argument:

> We admit that in many places and in ordinary times the defendants in saying all that was said in the circular would have been within their constitutional rights. But the character of every act depends upon the circumstances in which it is done. The question in every case is whether the words used are used in such circumstances and are of such a nature *as to create a clear and present danger* that they will bring about the substantive evils that Congress has a right to prevent. (emphasis added)

In short, the Supreme Court said the First Amendment is not absolute. Congress may abridge freedom of speech whenever that speech presents a "clear and present danger" to some other national interest that is more important than freedom of speech at the moment.

In reaching this conclusion, Holmes made his famous analogy: "free speech would not protect a man in falsely shouting fire in a theatre and causing a panic." Thus, he wrote, free speech can never be considered absolute. Instead, each abridgment of freedom must be weighed against its purpose to decide if it is an appropriate or inappropriate one.

Although the *clear and present danger* test has proved to be vague and difficult to administer, it replaced a common law test for allegedly dangerous speech that was even more difficult to administer without unduly inhibiting freedom. The old common law test, known as the *reasonable tendency* or *bad tendency* test, was established in England in the 1700s and adopted as American common law along with the rest of the English common law. This test could be used to forbid any speech that might tend to create a low opinion of public officials, institutions or laws. It gave prosecutors wide latitude to prosecute anyone charged with the crime of seditious libel.

Whatever its limitations, the clear and present danger test was more precise and offered more protection for unpopular speech than the old reasonable tendency test.

Following the *Schenck* decision, the Supreme Court quickly upheld the convictions of two other persons charged with violating the Espionage Act: Jacob Frohwerk, a German language newspaper editor, and Eugene V. Debs, the famous leader of the American Socialist Party who later received nearly a million votes for president of the United States while in jail.

Eight months after the *Schenck*, *Frohwerk v. U.S.* (249 U.S. 204) and *Debs v. U.S.* (249 U.S. 211) decisions, the Supreme Court ruled on another Espionage Act case, *Abrams v. U.S.* (250 U.S. 616). The convictions of Jacob Abrams and four others who had published antiwar leaflets were upheld, but this time the court had a new dissenter: Justice Holmes had rethought his position and wrote an eloquent defense of freedom of expression that was joined by Justice Louis Brandeis.

In the majority opinion that affirmed the convictions, Justice John Clarke said:

The plain purpose of their propaganda was to excite, at the supreme crisis of the war, disaffection, sedition, riots, and, as they hoped revolution, in this country for the purpose of embarrassing and if possible defeating the military plans of the Government in Europe.

The primary goal of Abrams and his co-defendants, Clarke said, was to aid the enemy. That constituted a clear and present danger to national interests. But on the other hand, Holmes and Brandeis replied:

It is only the present danger of immediate evil or an intent to bring it about that warrants Congress in setting a limit to the expression of opinion where private rights are not concerned. Congress certainly cannot forbid all effort to change the mind of the country. Now nobody can suppose that the surreptitious publishing of a silly leaflet by an unknown man, without more, would present any immediate danger that its opinions would hinder the success of the government aims or have any appreciable tendency to do so.

Elsewhere in the dissenting opinion, Justice Holmes echoed the views of John Milton and John Stuart Mill in writing this appeal for a free exchange of ideas:

...When men have realized that time has upset many fighting faiths, they may come to believe even more than they believe the very foundations of their own conduct that the ultimate good desired is better reached by free trade in ideas--that the best test of truth is the power of the thought to get itself accepted in the competition of the market, and that truth is the only ground upon which their wishes safely can be carried out.

This opinion was very influential in later years, but at the time it was a minority view. Neither the country nor the Supreme Court was in a mood to be tolerant toward political radicals.

In the last Espionage Act case it reviewed, the Supreme Court affirmed a lower court ruling that denied second-class mailing privileges to the *Milwaukee Leader,* the best known Socialist paper in the country. The high court found that articles in the *Leader* "sought to convince readers... that soldiers could not be legally sent outside the country," and thus the sanctions were appropriate (*U.S. ex rel. Milwaukee Social Democratic Publishing Co. v. Burleson*, 255 U.S. 407, 1921).

By today's standards, these Supreme Court decisions seem repressive. The expression of views that would have been considered well within the protection of the First Amendment in more recent times led to criminal prosecutions during World War I. Obviously, First Amendment law was in its infancy at that point. The courts felt little obligation to observe the niceties of constitutional law at a time when leftists seemed threatening to many Americans.

THE FIRST AMENDMENT AND THE STATES

During the first part of the twentieth century, at least 20 states enacted their own laws against various kinds of political radicalism. The common element in these laws was a fear of groups that sought to change the American political and social system and advocated force as a means of accomplishing their goals. The constitutionality of these laws was soon challenged by those convicted under them, and it wasn't long before some of these cases reached the U.S. Supreme Court.

Probably the most important of these state sedition cases was *Gitlow v. New York* (268 U.S. 652), which reached the Supreme Court in 1925. Benjamin Gitlow, a New York socialist, and three others were convicted of violating a state criminal anarchy law by writing a document called the "Left Wing Manifesto." They were also convicted of distributing a paper called *The Revolutionary Age*.

Gitlow argued that the New York law violated his freedom of expression, as guaranteed under the First Amendment. In so doing, he was asking the high court to reverse an 1833 decision that said the Bill of Rights only applied to the federal government (*Barron v. Baltimore*, 7 Peters 243). Gitlow contended that the Fourteenth Amendment's requirement that the states safeguard the "liberty" of their residents meant the civil liberties guaranteed in the Bill of Rights could no longer be violated by the states.

Enacted after the Civil War and intended to safeguard the civil rights of the former slaves, the Fourteenth Amendment applies specifically to the states.

Among other things, it has a provision known as the *due process clause*, which says, "...nor shall any state deprive any person of life, liberty or property, without due process of law...." Gitlow argued that "liberty," as the term is used in the Fourteenth Amendment, includes all of the freedoms guaranteed in the First Amendment.

By making this argument, Gitlow won a tremendous long-term victory for freedom of expression, but he lost his own appeal. In an amazingly brief passage, the Supreme Court completely rewrote the rules on constitutional law, acknowledging that the Fourteenth Amendment had indeed made the First Amendment applicable to the states. But then the court said the First Amendment did not protect Gitlow's activities, thus upholding the New York conviction.

The court said, "a state in the exercise of its police power may punish those who abuse this freedom by utterances inimical to the public welfare, tending to corrupt public morals, incite to crime, or disturb the public peace."

Although Gitlow's conviction was affirmed, the Supreme Court had almost offhandedly rewritten the basic rules governing free expression rights at the state and local level. By requiring the states (and their political subdivisions such as city and county governments) to respect freedom of speech, press and religion, the Supreme Court had vastly expanded the rights of Americans.

Two years after the *Gitlow* decision, the Supreme Court affirmed another state conviction in a case that produced a famous opinion defending freedom of expression. In that case (*Whitney v. California*, 274 U.S. 357), Charlotte Anita Whitney was prosecuted for violating a California criminal syndicalism law, a law that made it a felony to belong to a group that advocated forcible change. Whitney was a member of the Communist Labor Party, but she had argued against its militant policies at a meeting just before her prosecution.

Despite these mitigating circumstances, the Supreme Court affirmed her conviction. For technical reasons, Justice Brandeis concurred in the court's decision rather than dissenting, but his concurring opinion (which Justice Holmes joined) was a powerful appeal for freedom:

> Those who won our independence by revolution were not cowards. They did not fear political change. They did not exalt order at the cost of liberty. To courageous self-reliant men, with confidence in the power of free and fearless reasoning applied through the processes of popular government, no danger flowing from speech can be deemed clear and present, unless the incidence of the evil apprehended is so imminent that it may befall before there is opportunity for full discussion. If there be time to expose through discussion the falsehood and fallacies, to avert the evil by the processes of education, the remedy to be applied is more speech, not enforced silence.

Brandeis said he believed that free speech should be suppressed only in times of emergency and that it was always "open to Americans to challenge a law abridging free speech and assembly by showing that there was no emergency justifying it."

The Supreme Court finally reversed a conviction for expressing radical ideas for the first time in another 1927 case, *Fiske v. Kansas* (274 U.S. 380). In that case, a defendant was prosecuted merely for belonging to the International Workers of the World, and the primary evidence against him was the preamble to the "Wobblies'" constitution. There was no evidence that he had advocated or engaged in any violent or otherwise unlawful acts. The court said the preamble simply didn't present sufficient evidence of unlawful goals to justify the conviction.

POSTWAR SEDITION AND DISSENT

The 1918 Sedition Act, like its 1798 predecessor, was only in force a short time: most of its provisions were repealed in 1921. Major portions of the 1917 Espionage Act were not repealed, but that law was specifically written so that it only applied in wartime. Thus, for nearly two decades after 1921, there was no federal law prohibiting seditious speech. But as World War II approached, those who felt the need to curtail freedom in the interest of national security again gained support in Congress. Finally, a sedition law was attached to the Alien Registration Act of 1940, popularly known as the Smith Act because one of its sponsors was Congressman Howard Smith of Virginia.

Not only were the new sedition provisions attached to an essentially unrelated bill, but the whole thing happened so quietly that many free speech advocates didn't realize what had happened until months later.

Among other things, the new sedition law made it a crime to advocate the violent overthrow of the government or even to belong to a group that advocated overthrowing the government by force. In addition, there were provisions making it a crime to proselytize for groups having such goals. The law did not require proof that the group might actually carry out any of those goals before its members could be prosecuted; mere advocacy was sufficient. Nor did this law apply only during wartime.

The 1940 law was rarely used at first. In fact, compared to other wars, World War II elicited little domestic opposition, perhaps because of the manner in which the United States became involved in that war as well as the widely publicized atrocities of the Nazis. However, during the tense "cold war" era that followed World War II, the Smith Act was used to prosecute numerous members of the American Communist Party.

The Smith Act's constitutionality was first tested before the U.S. Supreme Court in a 1951 case involving 12 alleged Communists, *Dennis v. U.S.* (341 U.S. 494). Eugene Dennis and the others were tried on charges of willfully and knowingly conspiring to overthrow the U.S. government by force. After a controversial nine-month trial, they were convicted and the Supreme Court eventually upheld the convictions.

Chief Justice Fred Vinson's opinion, in which three other justices joined, didn't specifically apply the clear and present danger test to the activities of the defendants. Instead, the court adopted a test that had been formulated by Learned Hand, a famous appellate court justice who heard the case before it reached the Supreme Court. Justice Hand's test is this:

> In each case (courts) must ask whether the gravity of the "evil," discounted by its improbability, justifies such invasion of free speech as is necessary to avoid the danger.

By using Justice Hand's modified version of the *clear and present danger* test, it was possible for the Supreme Court to sustain the convictions without any evidence that there was a real danger that the Communists could achieve their stated goals. Justice Vinson ruled that the American Communist movement, tiny though it was, constituted a sufficient "evil" to justify the limitations on freedom of speech inherent in the Smith Act. For the moment, it would be unlawful even to belong to an organization that advocated the violent overthrow of the government. Chief Justice Vinson wrote:

> Certainly an attempt to overthrow the Government by force, even though doomed from the outset because of inadequate numbers or power of the revolutionists, is sufficient evil for Congress to prevent.

Justice Vinson continued:

> Overthrow of the Government by force and violence is certainly a substantial enough interest for the Government to limit speech. Indeed, this is the ultimate value of any society....

After winning the *Dennis* case, the U.S. Justice Department began a new series of prosecutions under the Smith Act. During the early 1950s at least 121 persons were prosecuted under the act's conspiracy provisions, and many others were prosecuted under the provisions outlawing mere membership in organizations advocating the violent overthrow of the government.

This may seem to be an alarming violation of the American tradition of free speech, but it was in keeping with the mood of the times. The early 1950s were the heyday of McCarthyism, a time when prominent Americans were accused of pro-Communist sympathies, often with little or no proof. For example, a number of well-known writers and motion picture celebrities were blacklisted in the entertainment industry after undocumented charges were made against them. In Congress, the House Committee on Un-American Activities conducted investigations that its critics felt were little more than witch-hunts designed to harass those with unpopular ideas.

However, the times were changing, and so was the makeup of the U.S. Supreme Court. Senator Joseph McCarthy of Wisconsin, the man whose name is synonymous with the red scare, was censured by his Congressional colleagues, and public disapproval of his tactics increased notably by the time of his death in 1957. Meanwhile, the Supreme Court had gained several new members, most notably Chief Justice Earl Warren, who led the court into an unprecedented period of judicial liberalism. Warren was appointed in 1953 after the death of Chief Justice Vinson.

In 1957 the Supreme Court responded to these changes by modifying the

Dennis rule in another case involving the prosecution of alleged Communists under the Smith Act, *Yates v. U.S.* (354 U.S. 298). In this case, the Supreme Court reversed convictions or ordered new trials for a total of 14 persons charged with Communist activities. In so ruling, the high court focused on the distinction between teaching the desirability of violently overthrowing the government as an abstract theory and actually advocating violent action. The court said the convictions had to be invalidated because the jury instructions did not require a finding that there was any tendency of the advocacy to produce forcible action.

The court said the Smith Act could only be used against "the advocacy and teaching of concrete action for the forcible overthrow of the Government, and not of principles divorced from action." The Supreme Court did not return to the clear and present danger test as such, and the court insisted it was not abandoning the *Dennis* rule. But the new requirement of proof that the defendant was calling for action rather than teaching an abstract doctrine made it very difficult to convict anyone under the Smith Act. As a result, this controversial law was almost never used against political dissidents after that time.

Changing Times: the 1960s

Perhaps it was fortuitous timing that the Smith Act was rarely used against radicals after 1957, because in the 1960s there was a period of political dissent unprecedented in twentieth-century America. Thousands--and eventually millions--of Americans came to disagree with their government's handling of the Vietnam War, and countless numbers of them vociferously demanded changes in the political system that led to this unpopular war. Had that happened at a time when the government was prepared to vigorously enforce the Smith Act (and when the courts were willing to brush aside the First Amendment and let it happen) far more people than were jailed under the World War I Sedition Act might have been imprisoned for opposing the government during the Vietnam War.

The First Amendment protection for those accused of seditious speech was again expanded in a controversial 1969 Supreme Court decision involving a Ku Klux Klansman. In that case, *Brandenburg v. Ohio* (395 U.S. 444), a man convicted of violating an Ohio criminal syndicalism law contended that his conduct was protected under the First Amendment. Brandenburg spoke at a Klan rally that was filmed. Part of the film was later televised nationally. Much of what was said was incomprehensible, but the meaning of other remarks was quite clear. Brandenburg urged sending "niggers" back to Africa and Jews to Israel, and also talked of the need for "revengeance."

Was this a call for action that could be prosecuted under the *Yates* rule, or was it merely the teaching of abstract doctrine? In resolving that question, the Supreme Court went beyond the constitutional protection it had afforded speech in the *Yates* decision. In *Brandenburg*, the court said the First Amendment even protects speech that is a call for action, as long as the speech is not likely to produce *imminent* lawless action. Thus, the point at which the First Amendment ceases to protect seditious speech is not when there is a call for action, but when that call for action is persuasive and effective enough that it is likely to produce imminent results. The court said:

> ...(T)he constitutional guarantees of free speech do not permit (state regulation) ...except where the speech is directed to inciting or producing imminent lawless action, and is likely to incite or produce such action.

Brandenburg's criminal conviction was reversed, and the Supreme Court invalidated the Ohio criminal syndicalism law itself. In so doing, the Supreme Court reversed the 1927 *Whitney v. California* decision, in which a state law virtually identical to Ohio's had been upheld. This provides an interesting illustration of the way a dissenting or concurring opinion of one generation can inspire a majority opinion in another. Justice Brandeis' concurring opinion in *Whitney* argued for an imminent danger requirement: Brandeis said the First Amendment should not permit sanctions for political speech unless it threatens to provoke imminent lawless action. More than 40 years later, the Supreme Court adopted that view in the *Brandenburg* decision, repudiating the majority opinion in *Whitney*.

Even now--many years after the *Brandenburg* decision--millions of Americans feel passionately that the Supreme Court was wrong: the Ku Klux Klan and other racist organizations do not deserve First Amendment protection, they believe. During the 1980s and 1990s, there was a major national controversy about "hate speech." Many states passed laws forbidding that kind of speech, and the Supreme Court ultimately stepped into the debate by ruling on the issue twice, in 1992 and 1993. Those cases are in Chapter Three, which deals with today's First Amendment questions.

INTERPRETING THE CONSTITUTION

In tracing the development of First Amendment freedoms, we have noted several philosophies and "tests" that have been proposed to aid in interpreting what the First Amendment means. Because interpreting the First Amendment (and the rest of the Constitution) is so central to the study of mass media law, we will summarize some basic principles of constitutional interpretation at this point.

Almost every dispute about constitutional rights involves some kind of a *balancing test*. The courts must weigh conflicting rights and decide which is the most important. That means sometimes one constitutional principle must give way to another: there are few absolutes in constitutional law.

That fact, of course, is unfortunate for the mass media. Were the First Amendment an absolute, many of the legal problems the media face would not exist. Given an absolute First Amendment, there would be no such thing as sedition or prior restraint, and it is doubtful the media could even be held accountable for libel and slander, invasions of privacy, or copyright infringements. Certainly there would be no obscenity law and no limits on media coverage of the criminal justice system. But if that were the case, many of society's other interests would be forced to yield to freedom of speech and freedom of the press.

Fortunately or unfortunately, depending on your point of view, the *absolutist theory* of the First Amendment has never been the majority view on the U.S. Supreme Court. Some of the founding fathers, such as James Madison, may have considered the First Amendment something of an absolute safeguard for free speech, and two well-known Supreme Court justices who served during the 1950s and 1960s (Hugo Black and William O. Douglas) took an absolutist position. However, the majority view has always been that the First Amendment must be weighed in the balances against other rights and social needs. Thus, the task for the courts over the years has been to develop appropriate guidelines to assist in this balancing process.

One of the best-known of these guidelines for balancing the First Amendment against other interests has been the clear and present danger test. As already noted, it was first cited by Justice Oliver Wendell Holmes in the 1919 *Schenck* decision. In the years since, it has sometimes been applied to political speech cases, although in recent years the Supreme Court has not mentioned it in the leading decisions on free speech. As Chapter Eight explains, the Supreme Court has also applied the clear and present danger test in resolving conflicts between the media and the courts. In many of those cases, the Supreme Court has been forced to weigh the First Amendment guarantee of a free press against judges' rights to exercise their contempt of court powers; the concept of clear and present danger has been used in this balancing process.

Some constitutional scholars argue for a *preferred position* test as an alternative to balancing the First Amendment against other rights and social interests. In their view, the First Amendment should occupy a preeminent place in constitutional law and should rarely give way to other interests. Some believe that during the era when Earl Warren was chief justice, the Supreme Court leaned toward that view of the First Amendment. Indeed, many of the decisions most favorable to the media were handed down by the "Warren Court," as it came to be known.

In a more general way, the Supreme Court always uses a kind of preferred position test in weighing constitutionally protected interests against other values. In *U.S. v. C.I.O.* (335 U.S. 106), a 1948 case, Justice Wiley Rutledge articulated this view. He noted that the normal rule of judicial interpretation requires the courts to adopt a presumption in favor of the validity of legislative acts. However, he said, when a legislative act restricts First Amendment rights, the presumption must be reversed so that there is a presumption against the validity of the law rather than in favor of its validity. Thus, he advocated a "reverse presumption of constitutionality" when a statutory law is challenged on constitutional grounds.

The concept that the rights protected by the Bill of Rights occupy a preferred position compared to other interests has been mentioned in a number of other Supreme Court decisions. However, on a practical level that bias in favor of constitutional rights does not necessarily translate into tangible results. What the court still does is balance the competing interests--albeit with the scales tipped slightly toward constitutional rights.

The Supreme Court has also developed a series of more specific guidelines to use in evaluating claims that a given statutory law or government action violates a constitutional right.

When a statute (or a state's application of the common law) is challenged, the court normally looks for nothing more than a *rational relationship* between the law and a legitimate government goal. When a state law is challenged, for instance, the state may attempt to defend it by showing that the law bears a rational relationship to its police power or its duty to promote the health and welfare of its citizens.

However, when the claim is that the statute violates a fundamental right protected by the Constitution, the state must show a *compelling state interest* to justify the statute. The state must, in effect, convince the court that its objective in enacting this statute is of such overriding importance that a fundamental right (such as freedom of expression) must give way. A good example of this is described in Chapter 13, where the Supreme Court's landmark decisions on the First Amendment and commercial speech are discussed. In some of those cases, the high court has forced the states to show a compelling state interest to justify restrictions on the right to advertise (see, for instance, *Bigelow v. Virginia*, 421 U.S. 809, 1975).

Another way the courts, and particularly the U.S. Supreme Court, evaluate challenged state and federal statutes is to decide whether they are *vague* or *overly broad*. If a law that limits constitutionally protected rights is so broad that it inhibits freedom more than is necessary to achieve a legitimate government purpose, or if it is so vague that it is difficult to know exactly what speech or conduct is prohibited, it may be invalidated for overbreadth or vagueness.

If a court is going to invalidate a statutory law, it has two options: (1) to find that the law is unconstitutional and thus void under all circumstances; or (2) to find that it is unconstitutional only as it has been applied to the person challenging the law. Moreover, given an ambiguous law, the courts have an obligation to resolve the ambiguity in such a way as to avoid a constitutional conflict if possible. The U.S. Supreme Court has the final say in construing the language in federal statutes, but the state courts have the final say in interpreting state laws. The U.S. Supreme Court can only decide whether a state law is unconstitutional as interpreted by the state courts; it cannot reinterpret a state statute.

This means the U.S. Supreme Court sometimes has to send a case back to a state court to find out what a state law means. Once the state court spells out the meaning, the nation's highest court can then decide whether the law--as interpreted by the state court--actually violates the U.S. Constitution. If it does, it is invalid, of course. But if the state court can interpret the law in such a way as to avoid a conflict with the U.S. Constitution, the law is valid.

Obviously, determining whether a given statute or government action violates the Constitution is a difficult and subjective job. The Supreme Court has a variety of guidelines that it may choose to follow (or choose to ignore) in any given situation. Critics of the process suspect that whatever test is or isn't applied in a particular case, the ultimate outcome of the case depends more on the values and priorities of the nine justices than on how the facts measure up against one or another set of guidelines. In short, whatever other test may be applied, cases are decided on the basis of a rather subjective balancing process in which various competing values, interests and social objectives are weighed.

In his autobiography, former Justice William O. Douglas described a very revealing conversation he had with then-Chief Justice Charles Evans Hughes soon after being appointed to the Supreme Court:

Hughes made a statement to me which at the time was shattering but which over the years turned out to be true: "Justice Douglas, you must remember one thing. At the Constitutional level where we work, 90 percent of any decision is emotional. The rational part of us supplies the reasons for supporting our predilections."

In the end, most Supreme Court-watchers would probably agree. Bruce Sanford, longtime First Amendment lawyer for the Society of Professional Journalists, most likely would. After seeing the Supreme Court staunchly uphold *unpopular* First Amendment principles in three different 1989 decisions--and then limit First Amendment freedoms in two other cases where most of the public probably didn't care either way, Sanford said the First Amendment remains "the most unpredictable area of Supreme Court jurisprudence." He also said, "There is no clear consensus on First Amendment theory and the manner in which it is applied to cases."

So much for theories that purport to rationalize and reconcile the court's seemingly inconsistent rulings on the meaning of the First Amendment...

THE FUTURE OF FREEDOM IN A TERRORIST ERA

In this chapter, we have traced nearly 400 years of struggles for freedom of expression. Of the total history of humanity, that is but a tiny portion. Where, then, is freedom going in the next 400 years? Perhaps more to the point, what will be the future of freedom in the near future--an era that may be dominated by the threat of terrorism in many parts of the world?

Obviously, no one can answer these questions. The status of freedom in America will depend on who runs the country--and the world. It also depends on who is appointed to the U.S. Supreme Court, the federal appellate courts and the appellate courts of the 50 states. And it depends on who is elected to national, state and local offices. It is those people who will shape the law.

In a larger sense, the future of freedom is always decided by the changing mood of the times. As several later chapters explain, there is a growing sentiment in America today in favor of more restrictions on free expression. Polls often show that large numbers of people think the First Amendment should not protect the work of artists, musicians and others whose choice of language or subject matter may be offensive. Another growing controversy concerns the extent to which the Internet should be a free marketplace of ideas--as opposed to a government-controlled forum. And the contemporary pressure to be politically correct has surely reduced the freedom to express offensive words and unpopular ideas, particularly on college campuses and in the mass media.

However, the overriding factor in determining the status of freedom in the United States in the near future is likely to be the progress of the war against terrorism. Already, legal controversies are raging over issues such as the propriety of trying some of those accused of terrorist acts in military as opposed to civilian courts, as President George W. Bush has decreed by executive order. Military courts lack some of the safeguards guaranteed by the U.S. Constitution in civilian courts.

Whenever a society feels threatened by subversive forces within or powerful enemies abroad, freedom suffers. Over the past 200 years, First Amendment freedoms have been curtailed repeatedly when war seemed imminent. Chief Justice William Rehnquist wrote a book in 1998, several years before the Sept. 11 events, tracing some of this history. In *All the Laws but One: Civil Liberties in Wartime*, the chief justice focused on crucial Supreme Court decisions concerning the constitutionality of military trials for those accused of subversive activities.

In a 2002 speech to a judicial conference in Williamsburg, Va., Rehnquist summarized a few highlights of his book and said, "These cases (Supreme Court decisions on the use of military courts) suggest that, while the laws are surely not silent in time of war, courts may interpret them differently then than in time of peace." But Rehnquist's book also concluded that with each war, Americans have become more protective of civil liberties and less willing to abandon constitutional rights even during what seems to be a national emergency.

Will that still prove to be true in a era of terrorism? The events of Sept. 11 prompted several government actions in addition to the decision to try some alleged terrorists in military courts. As noted early in this chapter, Congress passed the USA Patriot Act, expanding government surveillance powers, soon after Sept. 11. While the curtailment of First Amendment freedoms since Sept. 11 has been minimal compared to the restrictions imposed during World War I, for example, recent events once again underscored the difficulty of preserving civil liberties while safeguarding national security during an international crisis.

Looking beyond the effect of terrorist threats on civil liberties, there are other issues that should not be ignored. The behavior of the mass media themselves may help determine how much freedom we have. Journalistic sensationalism, inaccuracy and arrogance--as well as monopolistic media business practices--invite punitive responses by governments. If the media are to preserve their freedom, they must stand firm against abuses by governments at all levels, but they must also be responsible in exercising their freedom.

CHAPTER THREE
Modern Prior Restraints

Censorship. That word has a lot of emotional impact today, just as it has ever since colonial times. But its meaning has shifted over the years. Today, censorship in a legal sense usually means *prior restraint* of communications by an agency of government, not *subsequent punishment* for disseminating an unlawful form of communication. As Chapter Two explains, the First Amendment is not absolute: the courts have allowed a variety of limitations to be placed on freedom of expression. But most of those limitations would be classified as subsequent punishments, not prior restraints. For example, lawsuits that charge someone with libel or invasion of privacy involve the threat of subsequent punishments, not prior restraints. The media are free to disseminate defamatory communications or communications that invade someone's privacy, but they must be prepared to face the legal consequences--afterward.

However, there are some occasions when prior restraints are permitted--times when an agency of government actually engages in some form of prior censorship. And prior restraints are usually considered a far greater threat to freedom than subsequent punishments. If the media are free to publish controversial or unpopular facts and opinions without government interference beyond the threat of punishment afterward, at least a few courageous publishers or broadcasters will take the risk and make the questionable material public. If the material turns out to be of social importance, the publisher may still be punished, but at least the people will have the information and a public dialogue can begin. However, if government authorities can prevent the publication from ever occurring, the public may never know about important facts or ideas, and the democratic process may be thwarted. A democratic society cannot long survive if prior censorship by government is commonplace.

Only a few forms of prior restraint are permitted in America today; many communications that are highly offensive to someone (or perhaps to almost everyone!) are protected by the First Amendment and may not be censored. Nevertheless, there are times when prior censorship does occur, or is attempted, at least. The result may be a major controversy--and perhaps a landmark court decision. For example, sometimes government officials attempt to censor the news media to prevent the dissemination of information that they see as a threat to national security. And sometimes unpopular groups are denied the right to demonstrate or distribute literature in public places such as city sidewalks or parks. Another form of prior restraint involves laws that have been enacted to forbid "hate speech" that expresses hostility on the basis of ethnicity, religion, gender or sexual orientation. Also, discriminatory taxation of the mass media can be a form of government censorship. And there are other examples of prior restraints: government censorship of controversial films, bureaucratic attempts to regulate stock market newsletters, and rules that forbid the media to publish confidential information such as the names of juvenile offenders or rape victims. In all of these diverse situations, there is one common element: a government agency or official is attempting to censor some kind of communication that is considered unacceptable--and that action raises First Amendment questions. In this chapter, we look at these and a few other forms of prior restraint.

NEAR V. MINNESOTA

A good place to begin any discussion of prior restraints is a landmark Supreme Court decision about 70 years ago--a case that resolved some of the most basic issues in this field of law. In the 1931 case of *Near v. Minnesota ex rel. Olson* (283 U.S. 697), the U.S. Supreme Court made it clear that prior restraints are generally improper in America. The case resulted from a Minnesota state law that allowed government officials to treat a "malicious, scandalous and defamatory newspaper" as a public nuisance and forbid its publication. Under this law, a county attorney brought suit to shut down *The Saturday Press,* a small weekly newspaper produced by Howard Guilford and J. M. Near.

Guilford and Near had published several articles critical of certain public officials over a period of two months. In their attacks, they charged that a gangster controlled gambling, bootlegging and racketeering in Minneapolis. They claimed law enforcement agencies did little to stop this corruption. In particular, they accused the police chief of gross neglect of duty, illicit relations with gangsters and participating in corruption.

A trial court ruled the paper a public nuisance under the Minnesota law and banned its further publication. The Minnesota Supreme Court affirmed the ruling, and Near appealed to the U.S. Supreme Court, contending that his First and Fourteenth Amendment rights had been violated.

In a decision that made constitutional history, the Supreme Court overturned the lower courts and allowed Near to continue publishing. In a narrow 5-4 decision, the high court traced the history of prior restraints and concluded that a newspaper may not be censored before publication except under very exceptional circumstances. Chief Justice Charles Evans Hughes wrote:

> The fact that for approximately one hundred and fifty years there has been almost an entire absence of attempts to impose previous restraints upon publications relating to the malfeasance of public officers is significant of the deep-seated conviction that such restraints would violate constitutional rights. The general principle that the constitutional guaranty of the liberty of the press gives immunity from previous restraints has been approved in many decisions under the provisions of state constitutions.

In reaching this conclusion, the court cited James Madison's interpretation of the First Amendment as well as the views of William Blackstone, a highly respected British jurist of the eighteenth century. Blackstone argued against prior restraints but in favor of punishments afterward for those whose publications turn out to be unlawful.

The Supreme Court also pointed to the *Schenck v. U.S.* case (discussed in Chapter Two) as an example of an exceptional circumstance in which prior restraint might be proper. Chief Justice Hughes said that, in addition to prior censorship in the interest of national security, prior restraints might be proper to control obscenity and incitements to acts of violence. The court said, "the constitutional guaranty of free speech does not protect a man from an injunction against uttering words that may have all the effect of force."

In the decades since the landmark *Near v. Minnesota* decision, the closeness of the Supreme Court's vote against prior restraints has often been overlooked. The dissenters in *Near*, who needed just one more Supreme Court justice on their side to prevail, would have allowed prior restraints under many more circumstances. In fact, their reading of history led them to believe that the only form of prior restraint the First Amendment was actually intended to prohibit was licensing of the press by the executive branch of government.

Despite the closeness of the decision, the *Near v. Minnesota* case established a pattern that the Supreme Court has followed ever since. The court has often invalidated prior restraints on the media, declaring that prior censorship would be possible under the right conditions but usually failing to find those conditions.

NATIONAL SECURITY AND THE "PENTAGON PAPERS"

One of the most controversial forms of prior restraint has involved government efforts to censor the news media to prevent potential breaches of national security. In 1971 the Supreme Court decided a very significant case involving censorship in the name of national security, a case that pitted then-President Richard Nixon against two of the nation's leading newspapers, the *New York Times* and the *Washington Post*. The case came to be known as the "Pentagon Papers" case, although its official name is *New York Times v. U.S.* (403 U.S. 713). For the first time in American history, the federal government was seeking to censor major newspapers to prevent them from publishing secret documents that would allegedly endanger national security.

A secret Defense Department study of American policy during the war in Vietnam was surreptitiously photocopied and portions of it were given to several newspapers. It revealed questionable decisions by four presidents (Truman, Eisenhower, Kennedy and Johnson) that led the country into the Vietnam War. Although the Pentagon Papers only covered the period through 1968, and thus did not cover Nixon's presidency (Nixon took office in 1969), the *Times*' and *Post*'s editors knew Nixon would be outraged if these secret documents were published. Nonetheless, after consulting with several First Amendment lawyers, the *Times* and *Post* went ahead.

When the first installment of a planned series based on the Pentagon Papers appeared in each newspaper, the Nixon administration demanded that the *Times* and *Post* halt all further stories on the subject. When they refused, the Justice Department secured a temporary order from a federal district judge forbidding the *Times* to publish any more articles on the "Pentagon Papers." The judge then changed his mind and vacated the order, but a federal appellate court reinstated it. The case was immediately appealed to the U.S. Supreme Court. Meanwhile, another federal appellate court refused to stop the *Post* from publishing more stories about the "Pentagon Papers."

In view of the flagrant prior censorship inherent in the order against the *Times*, the U.S. Supreme Court justices decided the case only two weeks after the controversy arose, working during what might otherwise have been their summer recess. The Nixon administration argued that publication of the "Pentagon Papers" would endanger national security and damage U.S. foreign relations.

The newspapers replied that this was a clear-cut First Amendment issue involving information of great importance to the American people. Further, the newspapers contended that the entire classification system under which these documents were declared secret should be revised. The system existed only by presidential order; it was not established by an act of Congress. And at least one Pentagon official had conceded in Congressional testimony that only a few of the millions of classified documents actually dealt with bona fide military secrets or other material affecting national security.

The Supreme Court voted 6-3 to set aside the prior restraint and allow the publication of articles based on the "Pentagon Papers." Journalists proclaimed the victory as if it were the outcome of the Super Bowl. *Newsweek*, for instance, put "Victory for the Press" in bold yellow type on its cover. Inside, the magazine said this: "Few clearer gauges of the sanctity of the First Amendment freedoms, few plainer demonstrations of the openness of American society, could be imagined than the High Court's ruling in favor of the press."

Unfortunately, it wasn't that clear cut.

In a brief opinion, the court had simply said the government had failed to prove that the articles would endanger national security sufficiently to justify prior restraint of the nation's press. In the majority were Justices Black, Brennan, Douglas, Marshall, Stewart and White. The minority consisted of Justices Harlan and Blackmun and Chief Justice Burger.

In addition to the brief opinion by the court, the nine justices wrote their own separate opinions explaining their views. When legal scholars began analyzing those opinions, they realized the decision was no decisive victory for the press.

Only two of the justices (Black and Douglas) took the absolutist position that prior restraints such as the government sought would never be constitutionally permissible. Justice Marshall said the courts should not do by injunction what Congress had refused to do by statutory law (i.e., authorize prior censorship). Justice Brennan said the government simply hadn't satisfied the very heavy burden of proof necessary to justify prior censorship in this particular case.

However, the other five made it clear they either favored censorship in this case or would at least condone criminal sanctions against the nation's leading newspapers after publication of the documents. At least two justices (Harlan and Blackmun) favored prior restraint in this case, while Chief Justice Burger voted to forbid publication at least until the lower courts had more time to consider the matter, although he didn't really address the substantive issue of prior restraint. Justice White, in an opinion joined by Justice Stewart, said the government had not justified prior censorship but also suggested (as did Burger) that the editors could face criminal prosecution after publication for revealing the secret documents.

Thus, the "Pentagon Papers" case was not a clear-cut victory for freedom of expression, but at least the nation's press was allowed to publish stories based on the documents. No journalist was ever prosecuted in connection with the "Pentagon Papers," although the government unsuccessfully prosecuted Dr. Daniel Ellsberg, the social scientist who copied the documents in the first place.

The United States government has also criminally prosecuted those who revealed classified information on other occasions. For instance, in *U.S. v. Morison* (844 F.2d 1057), a widely noted 1988 decision, the U.S. Court of Appeals upheld Stanley Morison's conviction for giving secret information about U.S. military hardware to *Jane's Defence Weekly*, a respected British publication that reports on military technology worldwide. The court rejected Morison's argument that he should have a First Amendment right to give military information to a recognized publisher of such information.

The question of prior restraint in the interest of national security also arose in a controversial 1979 case, *U.S. v. The Progressive* (467 F. Supp. 990). Unfortunately, this case was never given full consideration even by a court of appeals, let alone by the Supreme Court, so it has limited value as a legal precedent. Nevertheless, it did dramatize the conflict between freedom of the press and the need for national security.

The Progressive, a liberal magazine, was planning to publish an article entitled, "The H-bomb Secret: How We Got It, Why We're Telling It." The author, Howard Morland, had assembled an apparently accurate description of a hydrogen bomb through library research. The magazine sent the article to the federal government prior to publication with a letter requesting that its technical accuracy be verified. The U.S. Department of Energy responded by declaring that publication of the article would violate the secrecy provisions of the 1954 Atomic Energy Act. The U.S. Justice Department sought a court order prohibiting publication.

Federal Judge Robert Warren issued an order forbidding the magazine to publish the article. He said the article could "accelerate the membership of a candidate nation in the thermonuclear club." He distinguished this case from the "Pentagon Papers" case in that he said the H-bomb article posed a current threat to national security. Also, he ruled, a specific statute prohibited publication of this article, whereas there was no statutory authorization to censor the "Pentagon Papers." Ultimately, though, he offered a pragmatic rationale for censorship:

> Faced with a stark choice between upholding the right to continued life and the right to freedom of the press, most jurists would have no difficulty in opting for the chance to continue to breathe and function as they work to achieve perfect freedom of expression.

Doubting that the issue was quite that black and white, *The Progressive* appealed Warren's ruling. However, before a federal appellate court could decide the case, articles describing an H-bomb in similar detail appeared in other publications, rendering the case moot. Once the information was published elsewhere, the government dropped its attempt to censor the magazine article.

Therefore, the *Progressive* case left many important issues unresolved. One of the most troubling is that the information for the article was gleaned from non-classified sources, yet when it was put into an article questioning the classification system, the U.S. government tried to censor it. Also, Judge Warren's abandonment of the First Amendment invited appellate review. In reviewing Warren's order, a higher court might have clarified the extent to which the national security classification system overrides the First Amendment.

Censoring Present and Former Government Employees

Should government employees have the same First Amendment rights as other citizens? What about employees of agencies such as the Central Intelligence Agency (CIA), who have access to government secrets and are required to sign an agreement that they will not disclose these secrets? What about other government employees--people who have no particular access to government secrets?

A major challenge to the national security classification system came from two former employees of the Central Intelligence Agency, both of whom published books on their CIA experiences. In both instances, the agency attempted to censor the ex-employees' writings under a provision of their employment contracts that prohibited them from publishing information they gained as CIA agents without the agency's prior approval. Both employees contended these contract provisions violated their First Amendment rights.

The first case, *U.S. v. Marchetti* (466 F.2d 1309, 1972) arose after Victor L. Marchetti left the CIA and published both a book and a magazine article critical of CIA activities. When the agency learned he was about to publish still another book, it got a court order temporarily halting the project. After a secret trial (much of the testimony was classified), the court ordered Marchetti to submit everything he might write about the CIA to the agency for approval. Marchetti appealed that decision, but it was largely affirmed by the U.S. Court of Appeals.

However, the appellate court said the CIA could only censor classified information, and after further legal maneuvering a district court allowed the agency to censor only 27 of 166 passages in the new book that the agency wanted to suppress.

Although the U.S. Supreme Court refused to review the *Marchetti* case, in 1980 the court did rule on a similar case, *Snepp v. U.S.*, (444 U.S. 507). Former CIA agent Frank Snepp resigned in 1976 and wrote a book alleging CIA ineptness in Vietnam. He did not submit it for prior CIA approval, as required by his employment contract. After its publication, the U.S. government filed a breach of contract suit against Snepp. Snepp contended the contract violated his First and Fifth Amendment rights.

A trial court ordered Snepp to turn over all his profits from the book to the government and submit any future manuscripts about the CIA to the agency for prior approval. An appellate court reversed that ruling in part, prompting the Supreme Court to hear the case.

The Supreme Court reinstated the trial court's order against Snepp without even hearing full arguments from both sides: the court never let Snepp present his case. But the high court upheld the validity of the contract, ignoring the prior censorship implications of such contracts. The court said: "He (Snepp) deliberately and surreptitiously violated his obligation to submit all material for prepublication review. Thus, he exposed the classified information with which he had been entrusted to the risk of disclosure."

The *Snepp* case, then, was decided as it was because of the provisions of Snepp's CIA employment contract and would not be applicable to persons who had not signed such contracts. However, thousands of present and former CIA employees are subject to such contracts--and the CIA has now reviewed and censored many other manuscripts written by former employees. Moreover, many journalists began to wonder what would happen if the government decided to impose similar restrictions on the free expression rights of other government employees. They didn't have to wonder for long.

In 1983, President Ronald Reagan issued a presidential directive requiring more than 100,000 government employees to sign agreements consenting to "prepublication review" of their writings by government censors--for the rest of their lives. The order applied to high-level employees of the Defense, State and Justice Departments, among others. The directive produced immediate protests from civil libertarians, the mass media and members of Congress. Congress eventually passed legislation to delay implementation of the plan, and Reagan later dropped the proposal.

Another controversy over restrictions on the free speech rights of government employees arose in 1989 when Congress amended the Ethics in Government Act to bar not only members of Congress but virtually all federal workers from receiving "honoraria"--payments for writing articles or giving speeches--even if the subject has little to do with their official duties.

Few would question the wisdom of telling federal officials they cannot be paid for giving talks about job-related subjects to special interest groups that they regulate. But the federal regulations written to implement the law did not stop there. One Internal Revenue Service worker pointed out that she had been supplementing her $22,000 annual salary by earning about $3,000 a year as a free-lance writer. Her articles were about camping and the outdoors, a subject that had nothing to do with her job, but the new rules prohibited her from being paid for her writing. Other workers who wrote or gave talks about subjects such as African-American history, the Quaker religion and dance performances also objected to the rules. Several lawsuits were filed by government workers who had been paid for writing or speaking about subjects unrelated to their work, contending that they should have the same right as other citizens to be paid for writing and speaking.

In 1995, the Supreme Court ruled on this question in *U.S. v. National Treasury Employees Union* (513 U.S. 454). The court said the ban on federal employees receiving pay for writing articles or giving speeches was excessively broad and a violation of the First Amendment. The court's 6-3 majority held that Congress had gone too far by banning payments for speeches and articles not only by senior government officials but also by rank and file employees of the executive branch. The court ruled that lower level employees (those below federal grade GS-16) could not be barred from accepting payments for speeches and articles. Writing for the majority, Justice John Paul Stevens agreed that there is a legitimate basis for the ban on senior government officials being paid for speaking and writing about policy issues that relate to their official duties, but he said lower level government employees should have the same First Amendment rights as other citizens, including the right to be paid for their articles and speeches. The high court overturned the ban entirely as it applied to lower level government employees, although Justice Stevens said Congress might be able to rewrite the ban so that it would be valid if it applied only to speeches and articles directly relating to an employee's official duties.

Meanwhile, in 1993 Congress expanded the free expression rights of federal workers in another way by amending the Hatch Act, which had prohibited most partisan political activities by federal employees for more than 50 years. Under the 1993 amendments, most federal workers may now work in political campaigns, do political fund-raising and hold positions in political parties--as long as they do it on their own time. Federal workers are still barred from holding partisan elective offices, however. About 85,000 workers in sensitive federal jobs, such as many law enforcement and national security-related positions, are not covered by the 1993 Hatch Act amendments. They are still barred from partisan political activities, even on their own time.

A related question that often arises among journalists and public relations practitioners is whether government employees can be forbidden to talk to a reporter without first seeking approval of a public affairs officer or other government officials. The second circuit U.S. Court of Appeals held that such a requirement violates the First Amendment in *Harman v. City of New York* (140 F.3d 111), a 1998 decision.

In this case, a radio station interviewed a child-welfare worker about the death of a young child. When the interview was aired, the employee was suspended for speaking to the media without first getting approval from New York's Media Relations Office as required by city policy. The worker then sued, and the appellate court held that the city could not justify such censorship of government workers. Even though the city contended that the policy did not really prevent city employees from speaking to the media, the court rejected the policy because it allowed city officials to delay an employee until his/her comments were no longer newsworthy. Also, the policy was overly broad, the court held.

CENSORING "HATE SPEECH"

One of the most troubling First Amendment questions being debated in America today concerns what is called "hate speech." During the late 1980s and 1990s, several hundred colleges adopted rules forbidding hostile remarks aimed at persons of any racial or ethnic group, gender or sexual orientation. These rules are intended to foster a campus environment that is not perceived as hostile by members of any group. But because many of these rules were written so broadly that they could be used to prohibit the expression of unfashionable viewpoints on social issues, critics of these rules charged that they really enforced "politically correct" speech. Meanwhile, more than 40 states adopted laws criminalizing "hate speech" in various forms. Like many of the campus speech rules, some of these laws forbid the expression of ideas, as opposed to forbidding violent acts.

Because these rules and laws are intended to punish those who express bigoted ideas, they have staunch defenders, including many civil libertarians. But do they really square with the First Amendment? Their defenders say that they do, and they cite the *Fighting Words Doctrine* expounded by the U.S. Supreme Court in a famous case more than 50 years ago: *Chaplinsky v. New Hampshire* (315 U.S. 568, 1942). In that case, the high court upheld the criminal conviction of a man who used words likely to produce an immediate violent response--a breach of the peace. Thus, speech likely to cause a fight, such as calling someone a "damned fascist" during the heyday of Hitlerism (as happened in *Chaplinsky*), may be prohibited, the court ruled. Like calling someone a fascist then, "hate speech" can be banned today under the fighting words rationale, the defenders of these laws and rules say.

However, in 1992 the Supreme Court revisited this controversial issue--and ruled that "hate speech" cannot be banned on the basis of its content--although violent action can, of course, be prohibited. Ruling in the case of *R.A.V. v. St. Paul* (505 U.S. 377), the high court overturned a St. Paul, Minn. ordinance intended to punish those who burn crosses, display swastikas or express racial or religious hatred in other ways. The case involved a Caucasian youth who burned a homemade cross in the front yard of an African-American family's home. He could have been prosecuted for a variety of other offenses, including arson and trespassing, but city officials chose to prosecute him under the "hate speech" law. Because he was a juvenile, "R.A.V." was originally identified only by his initials. Later he was indentified in the media as Robert A. Viktora.

In ruling against the St. Paul law, Justice Antonin Scalia said:

Let there be no mistake about our belief that burning a cross in someone's yard is reprehensible. But St. Paul has sufficient means at its disposal to prevent such behavior without adding the First Amendment to the fire.

In an opinion that was a wide-ranging defense of the First Amendment right to express unpopular and offensive ideas, Scalia said that governments may not punish those who "communicate messages of racial, gender or religious intolerance" merely because those ideas are offensive and emotionally painful to those in the targeted group.

The Supreme Court was unanimous in overturning the St. Paul "hate speech" ordinance, but they disagreed about the legal rationale for doing so. Four justices (Byron White, Harry Blackmun, Sandra Day O'Connor and John Paul Stevens) argued that the ordinance was unconstitutional only because it was overly broad--not limited to expressions that could lead to violence under the Fighting Words Doctrine.

The other five joined in a majority opinion taking a much broader view of the First Amendment rights of those who engage in "hate speech." They said that any law is unconstitutional if it singles out expressions of "bias-motivated hatred" for special punishment. While the majority did not specifically overturn *Chaplinsky v. New Hampshire*, they made it clear that the Fighting Words Doctrine cannot ordinarily be used to suppress the expression of racial, religious or gender-based hostilities. That kind of viewpoint discrimination violates the First Amendment, they said.

The *R.A.V. v. St. Paul* decision stirred a new national controversy about the meaning of the First Amendment--and it created deep rifts among traditional allies. The St. Paul youth was represented by the American Civil Liberties Union, which strongly argued that St. Paul's "hate speech" law violates the First Amendment. But other traditionally liberal, pro-civil-liberties groups such as People for the American Way criticized the Supreme Court ruling.

The *St. Paul* ruling raised serious doubts about the constitutionality of many other "hate speech" laws, as well as many of the campus speech codes adopted in recent years. However, this was by no means the first time the courts had held that "hate speech" is protected by the First Amendment. Several universities' speech codes had been overturned by lower courts prior to the Supreme Court's ruling in the *St. Paul* case.

The Supreme Court's 1992 decision on "hate speech" was reminiscent of *Brandenburg v. Ohio* (395 U.S. 444), the court's 1969 decision upholding the First Amendment rights of a Ku Klux Klan member. As Chapter Two explains, that case represented an expansion of the scope of the First Amendment in that the court upheld the Klansman's right to make an offensive (and bigoted) speech at a Klan rally, as long as the speech did not create an imminent danger of violent action.

On the other hand, when an act of violence is motivated by hatred based on race, religion, national origin, gender or sexual orientation, the First Amendment does *not* protect the violent act. Indeed, a state may impose harsher penalties for violent acts motivated by hatred than it would otherwise for the same violent acts. The Supreme Court so held in a unanimous 1993 decision, *Wisconsin v. Mitchell*, (508 U.S. 476). The case arose when several African-American youths watched the movie, "Mississippi Burning," and then attacked a white youth. After seeing the movie, Todd Mitchell, then 19, asked his friends, "Do you feel all hyped up to move on some white people?" Then Mitchell saw a 14-year-old youth across the street and said, "There goes a white boy. Go get him." The victim spent several days in a coma, but survived. Mitchell was convicted of aggravated battery, and his sentence was increased under a state hate-crime law.

Writing for a unanimous court, Chief Justice William Rehnquist said, "A physical assault is not by any stretch of the imagination expressive conduct protected by the First Amendment."

In so ruling, the court upheld the law in Wisconsin--and similar laws in many other states--that treat hate crimes as more serious offenses than crimes in which hate cannot be proven to be the motivation. In 2000, the Supreme Court added a proviso to this: if there is a *sentence enhancement* for a hate crime (i.e., a crime is punished more severely if motivated by hate), that extra sentence must be imposed by the jury--not added later by the judge (*Apprendi v. New Jersey*, 530 U.S. 466).

Some years earlier the Supreme Court ruled that still another form of inflammatory and offensive speech is protected by the First Amendment in *Cohen v. California* (403 U.S. 15, 1971). In that case, Paul R. Cohen was criminally prosecuted for appearing in a Los Angeles courthouse wearing a leather jacket emblazoned with the motto, "Fuck the Draft." At the time, several people who had demonstrated against the Vietnam-era military draft were standing trial. The Supreme Court ultimately held that this was a constitutionally protected expression of opinion, despite the offensiveness of the word. Writing for the court, Justice John Marshall Harlan said:

> While the particular four-letter word being litigated here is perhaps more distasteful than most others of its genre, it is nevertheless often true that one man's vulgarity is another's lyric. Indeed, we think it is largely because governmental officials cannot make principled distinctions in this area that the Constitution leaves matters of taste and style so largely to the individual.

Perhaps the main point of all of these cases is that the First Amendment protects the expression of opinions in many forms, however unenlightened or vulgar the speaker's ideas (or choice of words or symbols) may seem to be. However, the First Amendment does not protect unlawful conduct such as acts of violence, arson or trespass.

By the early 2000s, the controversy over hate speech and campus speech codes appeared to be subsiding a little. A number of colleges eliminated or revised their speech codes after several courts overturned such codes on First Amendment grounds. In one case that attracted national attention, Stanford University, a private institution, did not appeal a trial judge's ruling against its speech code. The judge held that the code violated a California state law under which the free speech guarantees of the First Amendment were extended even to private colleges.

In 2001, the third circuit U.S. Court of Appeals issued a sweeping ruling against a school district's anti-harassment policy, which prohibited many kinds of "verbal, written or physical conduct" that might create an "intimidating, hostile or offensive environment" based on anyone's race, religion, gender, sexual orientation or disability, among other things. Two Christian students and their guardian challenged the policy, arguing that it prevented them from expressing their religious belief that homosexuality is a sin. In *Saxe v. State College Area School District* (240 F.3d 200), the court said the policy violated the free-speech rights of students. The court said the school district had failed to explain how the banned expression would "disrupt school operations or interfere with the rights of others," the showing required to justify a denial of students' rights under the landmark student First Amendment case, *Tinker v. Community School District* (393 U.S. 503), which is discussed in Chapter 14.

Flag Burning and the First Amendment

While the constitutional ramifications of laws forbidding "hate speech" are being debated at colleges, in the media and in the nation's courtrooms, there has also been much debate concerning a related free-expression issue: flag desecration. Americans have been bitterly divided over two Supreme Court decisions holding that flag-burning is a protected form of expression. Like cross-burning, the act of burning the American flag stirs strong feelings in many people--and they find it hard to see the value of permitting this kind of symbolic "speech."

When this issue gained national attention, it became clear that millions of Americans believed the American flag was a national symbol that deserved special protection. A political protester should never be allowed to desecrate the flag as a form of symbolic free speech, many felt. But like Ku Klux Klan members, those who desecrate the flag were given First Amendment protection by the Supreme Court. The court, like most civil libertarians, concluded that there is a higher principle involved in these cases, and that a truly democratic society must extend free expression rights even to those whose ideas or political activities are reprehensible to most people.

In 1989 and 1990, the Supreme Court handed down two separate decisions on flag-burning as a form of symbolic speech protected by the First Amendment. In the 1989 case, *Texas v. Johnson* (491 U.S. 397), the court declared that a man named Gregory Johnson could not be punished for burning an American flag during the 1984 Republican National Convention to protest then-President Reagan's policies. In a decision that produced strong dissenting opinions by four justices, the majority ruled that flag desecration is a protected form of symbolic speech, particularly when it occurs in a clearly political context (as it did in this case).

Like the Ku Klux Klan decision of 1969 and the "hate speech" decision in 1992, the flag desecration ruling brought vehement objections from many people. President George Bush, for example, called for a constitutional amendment to overturn the *Johnson* ruling and restore flag desecration as a crime.

On the other hand, many civil libertarians feared that such a constitutional amendment would end up including restrictions on other First Amendment freedoms such as the right to express controversial views on racial issues and the right of consenting adults to possess erotic but non-obscene literature.

After a major public debate over this question, Congress enacted the Flag Protection Act of 1989, a federal law that carried penalties of up to a year in jail and a $1,000 fine for flag desecration. President Bush allowed this act to go into effect without his signature, declaring that he still favored a constitutional amendment instead of a statutory law that could be overturned by the courts.

Predictably, the new law was challenged in court as soon as it went into effect. Recognizing the importance of this question, the Supreme Court agreed to hear this new case on an expedited schedule. In 1990--just a year after its first decision on this issue--the court declared the new flag protection law to be unconstitutional.

Ruling in the case of *U.S. v. Eichman* (496 U.S. 310), the same 5-4 majority reaffirmed its earlier holding that flag desecration is a form of symbolic political speech protected by the First Amendment. Justice William Brennan, who authored the majority opinion, said, "(T)he bedrock principle underlying the First Amendment... is that the government may not prohibit the expression of an idea simply because society finds the idea itself offensive or disagreeable."

During oral arguments on the *Eichman* case, Justice Anthony Kennedy (a conservative jurist who joined the majority in voting to extend First Amendment protection to flag-burners) pointed out that flag desecration has become an internationally recognized form of political protest. He observed that the national flag was desecrated by protesters in almost every Eastern European country during the 1989 upheavals that led to the collapse of communist governments throughout that region.

While the four dissenting justices again advanced legal arguments to explain why they felt that the First Amendment should *not* protect those who desecrate the flag--as they did a year earlier--in the 1990 decision they also took the unusual step of criticizing public officials who exploited the popular emotions on this issue for their own partisan gain. Writing for the four dissenters, Justice John Paul Stevens said the integrity of the flag is tarnished "by those leaders who seem to advocate compulsory worship of the flag even by individuals it offends, or who seem to manipulate the symbol of national purpose into a pretext for partisan disputes about meaner ends."

Nevertheless, the *Eichman* decision immediately triggered a new campaign for a constitutional amendment that would modify the First Amendment to exclude flag desecration from its scope. Congress quickly took up the issue again in 1990. But this time, much of the debate centered on the question of whether it was wise to amend the First Amendment for the first time in American history. In June of 1990, only days after the *Eichman* ruling, the proposed anti-flag-burning amendment was killed when the House of Representatives failed to give it the two-thirds majority required for constitutional amendments. As the debate reached its conclusion, many members of Congress argued that the flag is a symbol of American freedom--including even the freedom to burn the flag itself as a political protest.

For several years after the 1990 vote in Congress, public concern--and Congressional concern--about flag desecration seemed to be subsiding. However, during more recent years new proposals for a constitutional amendment were introduced several more times--but never cleared both houses of Congress.

In 1995 a flag protection amendment was quickly approved by the required two-thirds majority in the House. However, in 1996 that measure fell three votes short of a two-thirds majority in the Senate. In the next Congress, yet another constitutional amendment to protect the flag was introduced, and it was approved in the House of Representatives by a 310-114 vote in 1997. However, the measure was never brought to a vote in the Senate before that term of Congress ended in 1998. The proposal was introduced again in 1999, and it once again gained the necessary two-thirds approval in the House but fell short of a two-thirds majority in the Senate. The flag protection amendment was introduced once again in 2001, and this time it cleared the House with the required two-thirds majority, but it still faced an uncertain future in the Senate as of mid-2002.

Because the legislatures of 49 states have already endorsed such a constitutional amendment, it could well be ratified by the necessary three-fourths of the states if it clears both houses of Congress.

The most recent version of the proposed constitutional amendment says only this: *The Congress shall have the power to prevent the physical desecration of the flag of the United States.*

Perhaps voicing a widely held sentiment in Congress in the late 1990s, House Judiciary Committee Chairman Henry Hyde, R-Ill., said a flag protection constitutional amendment should be seen in the larger sense as "an effort by mainstream Americans to reassert community standards. It is a popular protest against the vulgarization of our society."

A flag protection amendment is indeed popular: according to a 1998 poll reported by The Freedom Forum, about 75 percent of Americans support such an amendment.

Does the *St. Paul* decision--upholding the First Amendment rights of people who may be racial or religious bigots--and the *Johnson* and *Eichman* rulings--which upheld the First Amendment rights of flag-burners--mean that the First Amendment never allows speech or symbolic speech to be made a crime unless there is a call for action that may actually lead to unlawful acts? Generally, the answer has been yes--even if the speech is highly offensive. But if unlawful acts of violence do occur, the violent acts are not protected by the First Amendment, as the Supreme Court pointed out in *Wisconsin v. Mitchell*.

In addition, the Supreme Court has also ruled that in some circumstances speech itself may be censored. For example, the high court has often ruled that the First Amendment does not protect speech or writings that are legally obscene. The problem in that area, of course, is deciding whether a particular work is obscene or merely pornographic but not legally obscene. That task has fallen to the Supreme Court, which has sometimes had to decide on a case-by-case basis whether specific films, books and photographs are obscene. Chapter 10 discusses the problems of obscenity, pornography and the First Amendment. Another category of speech that has not always been given full First Amendment protection is *commercial speech* (including commercial advertising), although that appears to be changing now (see Chapter 13). In addition, broadcasting does not enjoy the same First Amendment protection as other mass media. The courts have sometimes upheld government controls on broadcast content when similar controls would be unconstitutional if applied to other media (see Chapter 11).

CONTROLS ON LITERATURE DISTRIBUTION

If the First Amendment does not permit the direct censorship of such offensive forms of expression as "hate speech" or flag burning, are there other ways governments can control those who want to engage in these forms of expression? Could a local government simply refuse to let a group like the Ku Klux Klan or the American Nazi Party hold rallies or distribute literature on public property? What about other groups whose views are controversial, such as Operation Rescue, an anti-abortion group known for large and sometimes confrontational demonstrations?

Over the years, there have been hundreds of court decisions about questions such as these. The basic answer is that federal, state and local governments may adopt *content-neutral* time, place and manner restrictions on First Amendment activities--but groups wishing to express controversial views cannot be censored through the use of laws governing public assemblies or literature distribution. For example, a government agency may require that all groups obtain a permit before holding a parade on the public streets or a large rally in a public park. And the permit could impose reasonable time limits or noise limits for such events. Similarly, a government agency may set reasonable limits on the places where groups hand out their literature or collect signatures on petitions. However, no government may issue permits for rallies, parades and literature distribution to groups with which it agrees, while denying permits to groups with which it disagrees unless there is a *compelling state interest* that justifies such a content-based restriction on First Amendment activities. The Supreme Court has repeatedly ruled on cases involving these issues, holding that governments may not arbitrarily deny controversial or unpopular groups the right to distribute literature or hold rallies or demonstrations in a *public forum*--a public place where First Amendment activities are regularly permitted.

Jehovah's Witness Cases

The constitutionality of restrictions on literature distribution was first tested in connection with the proselytizing activities of the Jehovah's Witness movement. Since this religious group engages in door-to-door and street-corner soliciting for a cause unpopular with many Americans, its efforts led to restrictive ordinances in a number of cities by the late 1930s. The Witnesses challenged these limits on their First Amendment rights in a series of lawsuits, several of which reached the U.S. Supreme Court by the early 1940s, establishing new free-expression safeguards that benefitted not only Jehovah's Witnesses but also the advocates of many other religious and political causes. In 2002, the Supreme Court revisited these issues again in still another Jehavah's Witness case, illustrating the timelessness of these issues.

The first of these Jehovah's Witness cases was *Lovell v. City of Griffin* (303 U.S. 444), decided in 1938. Alma Lovell, a Witness, circulated pamphlets in Griffin, Ga., without the city manager's permission, something a local law required. She was fined $50, but she took her case all the way to the Supreme Court and won.

The Supreme Court found the ordinance invalid, saying it "strikes at the very foundation of the freedom of the press by subjecting it to license and censorship." The city claimed the First Amendment applied only to newspapers and magazines and not to Lovell's pamphlets. The Supreme Court disagreed: "the liberty of the press is not confined to newspapers and periodicals. It necessarily embraces pamphlets and leaflets. These indeed have been historic weapons in the defense of liberty."

Moreover, the court emphasized that the First Amendment protects the right to distribute literature as well as the right to publish it.

Elsewhere, a number of communities attempted to curb Jehovah's Witnesses by using anti-littering ordinances against them. Several of these laws were considered by the Supreme Court in a 1939 case, *Schneider v. State of New Jersey* (308 U.S. 147).

The court said a city indeed has the right to prevent littering, but it must do so by punishing the person who actually does the littering, not by punishing someone who hands literature to willing recipients. The person handing out a pamphlet cannot be punished even if the recipient later throws it away, the high court said.

In *Schneider*, the Supreme Court also invalidated a city ordinance that required anyone seeking to distribute literature door to door to get police permission first.

The court said giving the police discretion to decide which ideas may and may not be advanced by neighborhood canvassing is a violation of the First Amendment. The court said a city may limit the hours of door-to-door soliciting, but requiring a permit in advance is unconstitutional when the permit system gives the police discretion to approve permits for causes they like and deny permits to unpopular causes.

In 1942, the Supreme Court first approved and then invalidated another city ordinance that had been used against a Jehovah's Witness, this one simply requiring a $10 "book agent" license for all solicitors. In this case (*Jones v. Opelika*, 316 U.S. 584), the high court initially upheld the license requirement. But some 11 months later, the court vacated its decision and adopted what had been a dissenting opinion as the majority view. The court's final decision was based on the fact that the ordinance gave city officials discretion to grant or revoke these licenses without explaining why the action was taken.

To the amazement of many, 60 years later the same kind of questions were addressed again in still another Jehovah's Witness Supreme Court decision, *Watchtower Bible and Tract Society v. Village of Stratton* (2002 U.S. Lexis 4422). Stratton, a small town in Ohio, adopted an ordinance that made it a misdemeanor for door-to-door "canvassers" to promote "any cause" without first obtaining a permit from the mayor's office. The ordinance also made it a misdeamor for anyone to go to a private home where a "no solicitors" sign was posted--a provision the Jehovah's Witnesses did not challenge.

After lower courts largely upheld the Stratton ordinance, the Supreme Court overturned its permit requirement on an 8-1 vote. Writing for the court, Justice John Paul Stevens said extending such a permit requirement to religious and political advocates and other non-commercial canvassers violates the First Amendment. The court did not rule out permit systems that apply only to commercial solicitors.

Stevens said the Stratton ordinance is overbroad and "offensive--not only to the values protected by the First Amendment, but to the very notion of a free society." He condemned laws that require citizens, "in the context of everyday public discourse," to first inform the government of their desire to speak "and then obtain a permit to do so."

Stevens emphasized the right, first recognized by the Supreme Court long after the earlier Jehovah's Witness cases, of religious and political advocates to engage in anonymous speech. Any permit system for these canvassers necessarily violates that constitutional right and also precludes spontaneous acts such as going across the street to talk to a neighbor about a cause. Stevens said some citizens might "prefer silence to speech licensed by a petty official."

Responding to the town's argument that the ordinance was needed to preserve residents' privacy and protect them from crime, Stevens noted that criminals would not be likely to obtain permits before going to someone's door and said that a "no soliciting" sign is a suitable protection for those who do not want to be disturbed.

Only Chief Justice William H. Rehnquist dissented in the *Stratton* case. He said "(the majority) renders local governments largely impotent to address the very real threat that canvassers pose." And he predicted that the decision might actually lead to less door-to-door communication by forcing more residents to put up "no soliciting" signs.

As a result of these and other Jehovah's Witness cases, it is now a settled principle of constitutional law that government authorities may not arbitrarily grant solicitation permits to those advocating popular ideas while denying permits to advocates of unpopular ideas. Even a *content-neutral* permit system that merely controls the time, place and manner of free expression raises constitutional questions because it precludes anonymous religious or political speech and forces those who want to engage in this kind of activity to ask a government for prior permission.

However, these cases all involved the acts of government agencies that attempted to control the dissemination of ideas in public forums or by door-to-door canvassing. Is the rule different if the activity is to occur in a company-owned town or a private shopping center?

Private Property and Literature Distribution

The Supreme Court first addressed the question of literature distribution on private property in a 1946 case, *Marsh v. Alabama* (326 U.S. 501). The case arose in Chickasaw, Alabama, a company town owned by Gulf Shipbuilding. The distribution of literature without permission of the town's authorities was forbidden.

The case arose when a Jehovah's Witness tried to pass out tracts there. She was told that permission was required before solicitation was allowed, and that she would not be given permission. She was ordered to leave, and when she refused she was prosecuted for trespassing.

Even though the entire town was privately owned, the high court stood by its earlier decisions in the *Marsh* case. Noting that for all practical purposes this company town was a city, the court applied the same rules to it as had been applied to other cities. The court pointed out that the town was in fact open to the public and was immediately adjacent to a four-lane public highway. Even though the streets were privately owned, the public used them as if they were public streets. The court said:

> Ownership does not always mean absolute dominion. The more an owner, for his advantage, opens up his property for use by the public in general, the more do his rights become circumscribed by the statutory and constitutional rights of those who use it.

More than 20 years later, the Supreme Court applied the same kind of logic to a private shopping center in *Amalgamated Food Employees Local 590 v. Logan Valley Plaza* (391 U.S. 308, 1968). This case involved union picketing, which had been forbidden on shopping center premises. The union challenged this rule and won.

The Supreme Court compared the private shopping center to the private town in *Marsh,* and said the same right to distribute literature existed here. However, the court said a factor in its decision was that the case involved a labor dispute to which a merchant in the shopping center was a party. The court did not say whether the First Amendment would have applied if there had not been a close relationship between the picketing and a merchant in the shopping center.

However, in 1972 the Supreme Court decided *Lloyd Corp. v. Tanner* (407 U.S. 551), a case involving a shopping center where there was no relationship between the material being distributed and the business of the shopping center. This decision allowed a very large shopping center in Portland, Oregon, to ban anti-Vietnam War protesters who wanted to pass out literature.

In the years between the *Logan Valley* decision and this one, four Nixon appointees had replaced key members of the liberal Warren court, and these four justices helped create a new majority that backed away from the court's previous rulings about literature distribution on private property. The court said there was no constitutional right to distribute literature in this case, particularly because there was no relationship between the literature and the business being conducted at the shopping center. However, the majority opinion did not specifically say it was overruling the *Logan Valley* decision.

In 1976 the Supreme Court came full circle, specifically stating it had reversed the *Logan Valley* decision as it decided another shopping center case, *Hudgens v. NLRB* (424 U.S. 507). This case involved warehouse employees of the Butler Shoe Company who were on strike. When they picketed a Butler store in an Atlanta shopping center, the center's management ordered them out of the mall. The National Labor Relations Board held this to be an unfair labor practice, and the shopping center owner appealed.

The *Hudgens* majority made it clear that there is no longer any constitutional right to distribute literature at a private shopping center, even if the literature specifically involves a labor dispute with a merchant doing business there. The court said that, if First and Fourteenth Amendment rights are involved, the content of the material should be irrelevant; it shouldn't matter whether the literature has anything to do with the business being conducted at the shopping center or not. Whatever the subject matter of the literature, there is no constitutional right to distribute it at a private shopping center, the *Hudgens* majority ruled. However, this would not prevent the NLRB from ordering an employer to allow picketing on another legal basis; the court merely ruled out any such right under the federal Constitution. For example, the NLRB could rule that to deny picketing rights was an unfair labor practice, in violation of federal labor laws.

There were those who thought *Hudgens* settled the matter of literature distribution at private shopping centers, but they were wrong. In 1980, the Supreme Court made another sharp turn in its circuitous route through this area of law in the case of *Pruneyard Shopping Center v. Robins* (447 U.S. 74).

80 Modern Prior Restraints

This case presented the conservative majority on the Supreme Court with a classic confrontation between private property rights and states' rights, two causes that have sometimes been rallying cries of conservatives. At a shopping center near San Jose, California, a group of high school students tried to distribute literature opposing a United Nations resolution against "Zionism." They were refused permission, and they sued in California's state courts. The state Supreme Court said that the California Constitution provides a broader guarantee of free expression than the federal Constitution. The California court said there is a right to distribute literature in private shopping centers in California, even if no such right is guaranteed by the federal Constitution.

The center's owners appealed to the U.S. Supreme Court, contending that this California Supreme Court ruling denied them their property rights and due process rights under the federal Constitution. The respondents replied, of course, in states' rights terms, asserting the right of a state to afford its citizens more free speech rights than the federal Constitution mandates.

In a 7-1 opinion, Justice William Rehnquist chose states' rights over property rights, ruling that the California Supreme Court decision violated no federal right of the shopping center owners that was as important as a state's right to define freedom for its citizens. Rehnquist said the U.S. Supreme Court's earlier rulings on access to shopping centers were not intended to "limit the authority of the state to exercise its police power or its sovereign right to adopt in its own Constitution individual liberties more expansive than those conferred by the Federal Constitution."

In short, the Supreme Court affirmed California's right to create broader rights than the federal Constitution requires. The effect of the *Pruneyard* decision is to leave it up to other state legislatures and courts to decide whether to grant literature distribution rights in private places similar to those recognized in California.

In the years since the *Pruneyard* decision, the highest courts in several other states have recognized at least a limited right to engage in various forms of free expression at private shopping malls. These decisions have been based on several different legal grounds, including general free expression provisions in state constitutions and the right to circulate petitions for ballot measures, also recognized in some state constitutions.

The states that have recognized free expression rights at large malls include Massachusetts (*Batchelder v. Allied Stores Int'l*, 445 N.E.2d 590), Oregon (*Lloyd Corp. v. Whiffen*, 849 P.2d 446), Colorado (*Bock v. Westminster Mall Co.*, 819 P.2d 55), Washington (*Alderwood Associates v. Washington Environmental Council*, 635 P.2d 108, but also note *Southcenter Joint Venture v. National Democratic Policy Committee*, 780 P.2d 1282, which curbed free expression other than petition-circulating at malls in Washington) and most recently New Jersey (*New Jersey Coalition Against War in the Middle East v. J.M.B. Realty Corp.*, 650 A.2d 757, and *Green Party of New Jersey v. Hartz Mountain Industries*, 752 A.2d 315).

In New Jersey, for example, the state Supreme Court ruled in the *Coalition Against War* case that the owners of large regional shopping malls must permit leafletting and similar political speech, subject to reasonable time, place and manner restrictions. In the *Green Party* case, decided in 2000, the New Jersey

Supreme Court ruled that a mall could not require those who want to do leafletting to obtain a $1 million liability insurance policy. Such insurance is prohibitively expensive if it can be obtained at all, the court noted. Nor can mall managers limit groups that want to do leafletting to just one day a year. Those restrictions are not reasonable, the New Jersey Supreme Court ruled. However, the court also emphasized that it was authorizing only literature distribution, not bullhorns, megaphones, placards, picket signs, parades or similarly intrusive actions. And the court emphasized that it was authorizing free-expression activities only at large regional malls, not at smaller shopping centers, football stadiums, theaters or other private places that may attract crowds.

The New Jersey cases closely parallel post-*Pruneyard* decisions of the California courts in allowing leafletting only at large shopping malls. In 1999, for example, a California appellate court held that there is no right to circulate petitions outside a stand-alone store--as opposed to a mall with many stores (*Trader Joe's Co. v. Progressive Campaigns Inc.* (73 C.A.4th 425). In 2000, 2001 and 2002 several other California courts ruled similarly, upholding bans on free expression on private property surrounding stand-alone stores, even large ones (see, for instance, *Costco Companies v. Gallant*, 96 C.A.4th 740).

In 2001, the California Supreme Court went a step further, rejecting any right to circulate literature inside a large, gated apartment complex (*Golden Gateway Center v. Golden Gateway Tenants Association*, 26 C.4th 1013). In this case, the court ruled 4-3 that the California Constitution does not protect free speech on private property unless it is "freely and openly accessible to the public," carving out an exception to the *Pruneyard* rule for places that are not the functional equivalent of downtown sidewalks--places where there is no state action, the court said. However, Justice Janice Rogers Brown, writing for the majority, said the decision "does not give apartment owners carte blanche to stifle tenant speech." She said tenants may communicate with one another in many ways without leaving unsolicited newsletters at doorways, which is what the tenants association wanted to do.

In Nevada, a similar legal controversy has involved literature distribution on the heavily-used sidewalks along the Las Vegas Strip. When the street was widened in the early 1990s, local authorities allowed several large hotels to retain ownership of the new sidewalks as their private property.

Hotel owners then banned leafletting on the new sidewalks for "erotic" entertainment, arguing that as private property, the sidewalks are not a public forum. The county also restricted commercial leafletting along the Strip in general. In 2001, a divided Nevada Supreme Court upheld the right of the casinos to ban leafletting for outcall services and similar businesses. Three justices joined in an opinion saying the sidewalks are not a public forum. Two others said that even if the sidewalks are a public forum, the leafletting in question is not protected by the First Amendment because it represents a commercial message for an apparently illegal activity (*S.O.C. v. The Mirage*, 23 P.3d 243, 2001).

However, the hotel owners quickly learned that it wouldn't be that easy to control the privatized sidewalks. Two months later the ninth circuit U.S. Court of Appeals held that the sidewalks along the Strip are in fact a public forum to which the First Amendment applies (*Venetian Casino Resort v. Local Joint Executive

Board of Las Vegas, 257 F.3d 937). In a case involving picketing by a labor union, the federal court rejected The Venetian's attempt to render the sidewalks off limits to free expression. The U.S. Supreme Court declined to hear the hotel's appeal in 2002, leaving the ninth circuit decision as a binding precedent and protecting the right to engage in traditional First Amendment activities such as union picketing along the Strip. Whether the hotels and local authorities can sustain the ban on commercial leafletting against new legal challenges remains to be seen.

Still another aspect of the problem of First Amendment rights on private property led to an important Supreme Court decision in 1994: the question of local ordinances that forbid property owners to place signs containing political messages on their own property. In *City of Ladue v. Gilleo* (512 U.S. 43), the Supreme Court overturned an ordinance in Ladue, Mo. (an upscale suburb of St. Louis) that barred almost all signs in the front yards of private homes.

The case arose when a Ladue woman, Margaret Gilleo, put up a sign in her yard protesting the Persian Gulf War in 1990. It was stolen, so she put up another sign. Someone knocked that sign down, and she reported this vandalism to police. She was then told her signs were illegal and she sued, alleging that the city was violating her First Amendment rights. After a lower court ordered the city not to enforce its sign ordinance, Gilleo placed a sheet of paper in a window that read, "For Peace in the Gulf." That, too, was probably a violation of Ladue's rules, but it didn't matter: the Supreme Court ruled that the town's strict sign ordinance was unconstitutional. The court said this ban on almost all yard signs precluded an entire category of speech, thereby violating the First Amendment. The court conceded that Ladue could ban most commercial signs in front yards (but not "for sale" signs: see Chapter 13 for a discussion of that issue). However, this ordinance went too far by censoring all political and religious messages that might be conveyed in yard signs.

PRIOR RESTRAINTS AND ABORTION PROTESTS

During the 1980s and 1990s, the growing controversy over abortion led to other conflicts concerning the scope and meaning of the First Amendment. Congress, the courts and state and local governments have all become involved in the emotion-charged debate not only about abortion itself but also about the methods used by demonstrators who oppose abortions. There are several related questions involved. Under what circumstances may demonstrations near medical clinics be restricted? When may demonstrations that target the homes of doctors and other clinic workers be restricted? And when does the First Amendment protect the fiery rhetoric of abortion foes?

The Supreme Court first addressed the question of whether a town may ban demonstrations near the homes of doctors and other abortion clinic workers in a 1988 case, *Frisby v. Schultz* (487 U.S. 474). In this case the town of Brookfield, Wisconsin, a small suburb of Milwaukee, banned demonstrations near private homes after anti-abortion protesters picketed several times in front of a doctor's home. Sandra Schultz and other anti-abortion demonstrators sued Russell Frisby and other town officials, charging that the ordinance violated their First Amendment rights.

The court affirmed Brookfield's right to ban targeted picketing at a specific private home. In essence, the majority held that while residential streets in general are a public forum, the space in front of a specific home is not. That means a city must allow protesters to walk down residential streets carrying signs, but if they stop and linger too long near one particular residence, that conduct is not protected by the First Amendment. If a local government wishes to do so, then, it may forbid targeted picketing at someone's home.

The court based its decision largely on the idea that a person is entitled to a certain amount of privacy and freedom from harassment in his or her own home. Writing for the court, Justice Sandra Day O'Connor said:

> The First Amendment permits the government to prohibit offensive speech as intrusive when the 'captive' audience cannot avoid the objectionable speech.... The target of the focused picketing banned by the Brookfield audience is just such a 'captive.' The resident is figuratively, and perhaps literally, trapped within the home, and because of the unique and subtle impact of such picketing is left with no ready means of avoiding the unwanted speech.

In the years since the *Frisby v. Schultz* case was decided by the Supreme Court, the controversy over abortion demonstrations has become even more heated. Some anti-abortion groups have launched major campaigns targeting the homes of doctors and others who work at clinics that perform abortions. By 2000, many cities had adopted restrictions on picketing individual homes patterned after the Brookfield ordinance and the Supreme Court had ruled on anti-abortion protests in two more cases.

During the 1990s many cities and states--and eventually Congress--passed laws to curtail demonstrations not only near clinic workers' homes but also near clinics where abortions are performed. In 1994, Congress enacted the Freedom of Access to Clinic Entrances (FACE) Act, which prohibits protesters from blocking access to abortion clinics or intimidating patients and employees. First offenses carry fines of up to six months in prison and $10,000 fines. Those convicted of repeated violations of the law could face life imprisonment and fines of up to $250,000.

Almost as soon as the new federal law went into effect, anti-abortion demonstrators challenged it in court. Among other things, they contended that it unduly restricts their First Amendment freedoms and violates the ban on cruel and unusual punishments in the Eighth Amendment by imposing such severe sentences on persons who are doing nothing more than civil rights and antiwar demonstrators did in the 1960s: engaging in civil disobedience as an act of conscience. In 1995, all of those arguments were rejected in two federal appellate court decisions, *Woodall v. Reno* (47 F.3d 656) and *American Life League v. Reno* (47 F.3d 642). Deciding the two cases simultaneously, the fourth circuit U.S. Court of Appeals ruled that the FACE Act did not violate the First Amendment because it targets only unprotected acts such as obstructing doorways, not activities protected by the First

Amendment such as peaceful picketing.

Censoring "The Nuremburg Files"

The FACE Act was also the basis for a controversial appellate court decision in 2002 that upheld part of a large monetary judgment against anti-abortion activists and also affirmed a judge's order censoring a website that allegedly advocated violence against abortion clinic workers.

Ruling in *Planned Parenthood of the Columbia/Willamette v. American Coalition of Life Activists* (2002 U.S. App. Lexis 9314), the ninth circuit U.S. Court of Appeals ruled on a 6-5 vote that the judgment did not violate the First Amendment rights of anti-abortion activists. The case involved a website named "The Nuremburg Files" that called abortion doctors "baby butchers" and included names, home addresses and license plate numbers as well as names of spouses and children of some doctors who performed abortions. If such a doctor was killed, as three who were depicted in "wanted" posters on the website had been, the site showed a line drawn through the doctor's name.

When a group of abortion providers sued under the FACE Act, a federal jury awarded $107 million in actual and punitive damages. Over the objections of five dissenters, the six-judge majority on the U.S. Court of Appeals upheld the actual damages but ordered the trial court to reconsider the amount of the punitive damages. The majority also upheld an injunction by the trial judge ordering some of the "wanted" posters taken down, an order that was undisputedly a prior restraint of communications on a controversial public issue.

Eleven judges participated in the decision instead of the usual panel of three because the court was reconsidering the case *en banc*. Earlier, a three-judge panel of the ninth circuit had upheld the website and posters as protected speech in a ruling that was set aside by the en banc decision.

The majority ruled that the language of the website constituted "true threats" to health care workers even though there were no explicit threats on the site. Writing for the majority, Judge Pamela Rymer said a true threat is one "where a reasonable person would foresee that the listener will believe he will be subjected to physical violence upon his person, (and) is unprotected by the First Amendment."

"It is not necessary that the defendant intend to, or be able to carry out his threat; the only intent requirement for a true threat is that the defendant intentionally or knowingly communicate the threat," Rymer wrote.

In three separate opinions, the five dissenters said the majority was weakening the First Amendment by its dismissal of the free expression rights of abortion foes. Judge Alex Kozinski, joined by four judges, wrote: "While today it is abortion protesters who are singled out for punitive treatment, the precedent set by this court... will haunt dissidents of all political stripes for many years to come."

In another disenting opinion, Judge Marsha Berzon said the abortion foes who faced this large monetary penalty "have not murdered anyone." She added, "neither their advocacy of doing so nor the posters and website they published crossed the line into unprotected speech... If we are not willing to provide stringent First Amendment protection and a fair trial to those with whom we as a society disagree as well as those with whom we agree...the First Amendment would become a dead letter."

Some of the defendants said they would ask the Supreme Court to hear an appeal of the ninth circuit's decision.

Supreme Court Rulings on Abortion Protests

Prior to the "Nuremburg Files" decision, the activities of abortion protesters near clinics led to three U.S. Supreme Court decisions, all of which required the court to balance the rights of protesters against those of clinic patrons and staff.

In a 1994 case, the Supreme Court upheld a Florida court's injunction ordering demonstrators to stay 36 feet away from the entrances to an abortion clinic (*Madsen v. Women's Health Center*, 512 U.S. 753). In that case, the Supreme Court's 6-3 majority, in an opinion by Chief Justice William Rehnquist, said the 36-foot buffer zone was not an undue restriction on demonstrators' First Amendment rights.

However, in *Madsen* the Supreme Court overturned several other parts of the Florida court order, including a provision that barred demonstrators from approaching patients anywhere within 300 feet of the clinic. The court also overturned a portion of the Florida order that banned demonstrations within 300 feet of the residences of clinic workers. Rehnquist said that was too broad a restriction on the First Amendment rights of anti-abortion demonstrators, although a smaller buffer zone around workers' homes, coupled with limits on the time and duration of residential demonstrations, might be acceptable. In so ruling, Rehnquist adhered to the holding in *Frisby v. Shultz*, discussed earlier in this section. In the *Madsen* case, the Supreme Court also overturned a portion of the Florida court order that prohibited demonstrators from displaying "images observable" by patients in the clinic. Rehnquist said the complete ban on signs was overly broad, although a ban on signs carrying threats might be acceptable. On the other hand, Rehnquist's opinion upheld a part of the Florida order that banned excessive noise during abortion protests.

In 1997, the Supreme Court went further to protect the First Amendment rights of anti-abortion demonstrators, overturning a New York judge's order that required them to stay 15 feet away from clinic patrons and workers. Ruling in *Schenck v. Pro-Choice Network* (519 U.S. 357), an 8-1 majority of the court held that demonstrators have a right to approach patrons on public sidewalks. The court overruled the judge's order establishing a 15-foot "floating bubble" around patrons that abortion foes could not enter. But the court upheld another part of the judge's order that created a 15-foot no-demonstration zone around clinic entrances.

Again writing for the court, Chief Justice Rehnquist emphasized that picketing, leafletting and even loud protesting are "classic forms of speech that lie at the heart of the First Amendment." Rehnquist noted that sidewalk protesters have no right to grab, push or stand in the way of persons going to abortion clinics, but he also said the New York judge's ban on approaching patrons or workers was overly broad.

"We strike down the floating buffer zones around people entering and leaving clinics because they burden more speech than is necessary" to protect the free flow of traffic and public safety, the chief justice explained.

In ruling on all of these specific restrictions on demonstrations, the Supreme Court held that they were *content-neutral* (that is, they would apply to everyone, regardless of the issue addressed by demonstrators). Therefore, the restrictions were valid unless they imposed a greater burden on First Amendment freedoms than was necessary to serve a *significant government interest*. The court's majority concluded that there was a significant government interest in protecting the safety of clinic workers and patients, and in assuring that they could enter and leave the clinic freely. The court held that small buffer zones around clinic entrances are sufficient to accomplish those goals, and that larger buffer zones or floating buffer zones around clinic patrons or workers create an undue burden on free expression.

Lower federal courts applied these principles similarly in several cases decided after *Schenck v. Pro-Choice Network*. For example, in 1997 a federal appellate court overturned several provisions of a Phoenix, Ariz. city ordinance in *Sabelko v. City of Phoenix* (120 F.3d 161), including a requirement that protesters step back eight feet from clinic patients and workers even when they were much farther than 15 feet from a clinic entrance. The same court ruled similarly in overturning a Santa Barbara, Calif. ordinance that established an eight-foot floating buffer zone around clinic workers and patients (*Edwards v. City of Santa Barbara*, 150 F.3d 1213, cert. den. 526 U.S. 1004, 1999).

In 2000, however, the Supreme Court *upheld* a Colorado state law that included an eight-foot floating buffer zone. Ruling in *Hill v. Colorado* (530 U.S. 703), the court's 6-3 majority said the Colorado law was narrowly tailored enough to pass constitutional muster. The law established a 100-foot zone around every health care facility's entrance. Inside that perimeter, no one could distribute leaflets, display signs or engage in sidewalk counseling within eight feet of another person unless that person consented to being approached. Displaying signs within the perimeter, but not within eight feet of any person, was legal.

After first ruling that the Colorado law is content neutral, the court held that it is a valid time, place and manner regulation of speech. The court noted that protest signs can be read, and normal conversations can occur, at a distance of eight feet. The court called that distance a "normal conversational distance." The court said the ban on approaching people does not prevent leafletting because a protester can stand in one place and hand out leaflets as people approach the person doing the leafletting.

"This statute simply empowers private citizens entering a health care facility with the ability to prevent a speaker, who is within eight feet and advancing, from communicating a message they do not wish to hear," Justice John Paul Stevens wrote for the court.

In short, the majority in *Hill* said this floating buffer zone is sufficiently different from the one overturned in *Schenck* to be constitutional.

Several years earlier, the Supreme Court ruled on another right-to-demonstrate question: the right to picket near a foreign government's embassy in Washington, D.C. In *Boos v. Barry* (485 U.S. 312, 1988), the court overturned some of the provisions of a Washington, D.C. local ordinance aimed at preventing embarrassing demonstrations outside foreign embassies.

The court held that Congress, in passing local ordinances to govern Washington, could not forbid picket signs that might say embarrassing things. Writing for the majority, Justice Sandra Day O'Connor said, "The display clause of (the ordinance) is unconstitutional on its face. It is a content-based restriction on political speech in a political forum, and it is not narrowly tailored to serve a compelling state interest."

However, the high court affirmed another part of the ordinance: a provision requiring protesters to stay 500 feet away from the embassy that is the target of the picketing if police believe the protesters pose a threat to the security of the embassy.

OTHER PICKETING AND RELATED ISSUES

If picketing in front of a private home can be banned to avoid disrupting the lives of the occupants, is it possible to ban other First Amendment activities that might be disruptive, inconvenient or embarrassing to an unwilling audience? The U.S. Supreme Court has addressed that kind of question several times.

In 1971 the Supreme Court was confronted with such a prior restraint issue in the case of *Organization for a Better Austin v. Keefe* (402 U.S. 415). Jerome Keefe was a real estate broker who allegedly engaged in "blockbusting" tactics in the community of Austin, near Chicago, Ill. That is, he was accused of attempting to panic white residents into selling at low prices to escape an influx of blacks that he claimed were moving into their neighborhoods. The Organization for a Better Austin (OBA), trying to halt this white flight, began circulating fliers attacking Keefe for his "panic peddling" tactics. Keefe got a court order that prohibited the OBA from distributing its fliers or picketing. The order was affirmed by an Illinois appellate court, and OBA appealed to the U.S. Supreme Court.

The Supreme Court invalidated the injunction, noting that peaceful pamphleteering is protected by the First Amendment, and its prohibition is a prior restraint. The court said:

> Any prior restraint on expression comes to this court with a 'heavy presumption' against its constitutional validity. Respondent thus carries a heavy burden of showing justification for the imposition of such a restraint. He has not met that burden.

The Supreme Court has dealt with somewhat more difficult First Amendment problems in a series of cases involving the Hare Krishna movement, cases reminiscent of the early Jehovah's Witness cases.

In a 1981 case, *Heffron v. International Society for Krishna Consciousness* (452 U.S. 640), the court had to decide how much access to a state fair Hare Krishna believers should have.

Like members of the Jehovah's Witness movement, Hare Krishna adherents believe their faith requires them to distribute literature and solicit donations from the public. Krishna members have attempted to promote their faith and solicit funds in many public places where people gather, often citing the earlier Jehovah's Witness cases to support their right to do so. The *Heffron* case arose when Krishna members were refused permission to distribute literature and solicit funds freely at the Minnesota State Fair. They were told they could only do so at a single booth. Under the fair's rules, booths were available to all groups on a non-discriminatory first-come, first-served basis.

The Krishna movement challenged the rules as a violation of the First Amendment, and the case eventually reached the U.S. Supreme Court. Krishna followers argued that distributing literature and soliciting funds are actually part of the movement's religious ritual, required of all members. To limit these activities is a violation of the First Amendment as interpreted in the *Schneider* and *Lovell* cases (discussed earlier), they contended. Minnesota fair officials conceded that Krishna followers, like Jehovah's Witnesses or anyone else, have a constitutional right to propagate their views at the state fair. However, they said it was necessary to restrict all such groups to booths to keep the fair orderly.

The Supreme Court majority agreed. The court said it is not a violation of the First Amendment to require Krishna followers to practice their religion at a booth rather than at large throughout the state fair. The majority opinion pointed out that Krishna members remained free to mingle with the crowd and orally present their views, but it upheld the rule limiting solicitations and literature distribution to individual booths at the fair. The court explained that if the Krishnas were allowed to proselytize throughout the fairgrounds, all other groups would have to be given the same privilege.

Access to Public Airports

If religious pamphleteering can be curtailed at government-sponsored events such as a state fair, can it also be restricted at other government-owned facilities where it might be disruptive, such as major airports?

The Supreme Court has addressed that issue in two cases inspired by the activities of Hare Krishna believers. In a 1987 case, *Board of Airport Commissioners v. Jews for Jesus* (482 U.S. 569), the court overturned a rule adopted by the government agency in charge of Los Angeles International Airport that flatly prohibited all First Amendment activities at this government-owned facility.

After lower courts overruled several earlier attempts by the airport commissioners to ban literature distribution by Hare Krishna believers, the board adopted a complete ban on all First Amendment activities at the airport. Under this rule a clergyman associated with Jews for Jesus, an evangelical Christian organization, was barred from distributing leaflets there. The Jews for Jesus organization decided to challenge the validity of the ban on First Amendment grounds.

The high court unanimously held that the regulation was so sweeping as to be unconstitutional on its face. Writing for the court, Justice Sandra Day O'Connor said almost any traveler might violate such an all-encompassing ban on First Amendment activities--by doing something as commonplace as talking to a friend or reading a newspaper, for instance. However, the court did not rule out the possibility that more narrowly drawn regulations limiting the time, place and manner of literature distribution might pass constitutional muster. Nonetheless, by 2002--15 years after the Supreme Court ruling--Los Angeles airport authorities still had not managed to draft a soliciting ordinance that would withstand judicial scrutiny. Federal judges repeatedly rejected various ordinances intended to regulate soliciting at Los Angeles International Airport.

In 1992 the Supreme Court ruled on another case resulting from Hare Krishna members' First Amendment activities at airports. This time the court ruled that soliciting donations can be banned, although handing out literature must be permitted at appropriate places in public airports. Ruling in *Lee v. International Society for Krishna Consciousness* (505 U.S. 830), a 6-3 majority of the court held that Hare Krishna members could be barred from fund-raising at New York's three public airports. Five of the justices also agreed that unlike city streets and parks, airports are not traditional public forums for First Amendment activities. However, in a separate opinion the court ruled by a 5-4 vote that airports must still be open for First Amendment activities that are less intrusive than soliciting money (for example, handing out free literature).

By holding that distributing literature but not soliciting money at airports is protected by the First Amendment, the court was following the pattern set two years earlier in a case involving U.S. Post Offices: *U.S. v. Kokinda* (497 U.S. 720, 1990). In that case, the court upheld regulations of the Postal Service that prohibit all soliciting at post offices. The case began when several representatives of the National Democratic Policy Committee were criminally prosecuted for setting up a table to distribute literature and solicit contributions at the Bowie, Md., post office. They argued that their activities should be protected by the First Amendment.

In a 5-4 decision that produced a strongly worded dissent by Justices Brennan, Marshall, Blackmun and Stevens, the court upheld regulations that banned soliciting (but not all First Amendment activities) at post offices. Writing for the court, Justice O'Connor said Postal Service regulations forbidding soliciting were justified because soliciting at post offices had often caused disruptions that interfered with the mail service. Post offices had never been First Amendment forums, she concluded, adding: "Whether or not the Service permits other forms of speech, it is not unreasonable for it to prohibit solicitation on the ground that it inherently disrupts business by impeding the normal flow of traffic."

Justice Anthony Kennedy concurred in the outcome of the case, but on a different rationale. He said post offices may well be public forums, but he also said the ban on soliciting was a reasonable time, place and manner restriction on free expression--and therefore valid. The four dissenting justices said they thought post offices were public forums and that in their view the ban on soliciting was *not* a reasonable time, place and manner restriction.

As a result of these cases, fund-raising can be prohibited not just at airports and post offices but also at many other government-owned facilities that are open to the public but are not traditional public forums. However, governments must allow other First Amendment activities such as literature distribution at many of these same places. And there is still a First Amendment right to solicit donations at places that *are* traditional public forums--subject only to the authorities' right to impose reasonable restrictions on the time, place, and manner of free expression activities.

On the other hand, purely private facilities such as shopping centers are not ordinarily First Amendment forums. First Amendment activities may usually be banned in such places whenever the owners choose to do so. Of course, if the owners wish to allow free expression activities--or if a state chooses to require the owners to allow such activities--they can occur on private property even though the United States Constitution does not guarantee any literature distribution rights on private property.

The Supreme Court has ruled on one other aspect of literature distribution rights that should be noted here: the right to distribute *unsigned* political literature. In an important 1995 case, *McIntyre v. Ohio Elections Commission* (514 U.S. 334), the high court overturned laws in almost every state that banned the distribution of anonymous political handbills. Based on the idea that anonymous political "hit pieces" are unfair, inaccurate and often libelous, most states have had laws requiring that political literature carry the originator's name and address. But in the 1995 decision, the court held that the concern about possible fraud and libel in unsigned political literature did not justify such a sweeping restriction on First Amendment rights. Ohio's ban on unsigned leaflets applied even to those that were completely truthful, the court noted. Under the *McIntyre* decision, there is now a constitutional right to distribute unsigned political literature. In 2002, the high court concluded that this right also undergirds the right to do door-to-door non-commercial soliciting without first obtaining a city permit. Any permit requirement compels canvassers to give up their constitutionally protected anonymity, as the court noted in *Watchtower Bible and Tract Society v. Village of Stratton*, discussed earlier.

Access to Parades, Parks and Organizations

Another issue that has stirred much controversy in recent years has been the question of whether privately sponsored parades and fairs that are held on public property are First Amendment forums open to all viewpoints, or whether the sponsors have a First Amendment right to decide who will participate. A focal point of this debate has been the efforts of homosexual groups to participate in St. Patrick's Day parades. In New York, the Ancient Order of Hibernians, a Roman Catholic fraternal organization, sponsors the nation's oldest formal St. Patrick's Day parade: it was first held in 1762. Based on their religious beliefs, the Hibernians have refused to allow gay and lesbian groups to join the parade, which annually attracts as many as 150,000 participants and two million spectators. In 1993, a federal judge ruled that the Hibernians have a First Amendment right to exclude groups with which they disagree.

On the other hand, the largest St. Patrick's Day parade in Boston has been sponsored by veterans' groups rather than a religious group, and in 1994 the veterans were ordered by a Massachusetts court to include a gay and lesbian group in the parade under a state law guaranteeing homosexuals equal access to public facilities. The veterans groups decided to cancel the parade instead. In 1995, they replaced the St. Patrick's Day Parade, in which marchers traditionally have carried green banners, with a protest march in which the marchers carried black flags to protest the court order. Meanwhile, the veterans also appealed to higher courts. The Massachusetts Supreme Court upheld the lower court's order, but in 1995 the U.S. Supreme Court disagreed and ruled in favor of the veterans.

In *Hurley v. Irish-American Gay, Lesbian and Bisexual Group of Boston* (515 U.S. 557), the Supreme Court ruled unanimously that the veterans groups have a First Amendment right to choose which other groups they will include in their parade. Writing for the court, Justice David Souter said the state could not use its public accommodations law to force a private group to admit anyone with whom it disagreed to a parade.

Souter said that a parade by its nature is an expressive activity, and that its sponsors have the right to decide what their message is to be. Souter noted, "One important manifestation of the principle of free speech is that one who chooses to speak may also decide what not to say."

Souter noted the "enlightened purpose" of the public accommodations law (to prevent discrimination against homosexuals), but said the state cannot force a private organization to alter its own message. Souter also noted that individual gays and lesbians are entitled to march in the parade as members of any group that is admitted to the parade, and that the gays and lesbians are certainly free to conduct their own parade on city streets (and presumably, to exclude veterans' groups if they wish).

A related issue has arisen concerning groups such as the Boy Scouts of America, an organization that has traditionally barred homosexuals from being scoutmasters. Do state laws guaranteeing equal access to public facilities or forbidding discrimination against homosexuals by business enterprises apply to private organizations? How can those laws be reconciled with a private organization's First Amendment freedom of association rights? Also, do these laws require the Boy Scouts' to admit members who are unwilling to take the Scouts' oath affirming a belief in God?

The U.S. Supreme Court ruled on this issue in a widely anticipated 2000 decision, *Boy Scouts of America v. Dale* (530 U.S. 640). The court's 5-4 majority ruled that the Boy Scouts may exclude gays as troop leaders, declaring that a private organization has the right to set its own moral code and espouse a viewpoint.

In so ruling, the high court overturned a New Jersey Supreme Court decision that said the Boy Scouts had to allow gay scoutmasters under that state's law banning discrimination in public accommodations.

Writing for the court, Chief Justice William Rehnquist said the Boy Scouts have a First Amendment right to freedom of association, including the right to include or exclude persons based on their beliefs or their sexual orientation. Thus, the Scouts could exclude James Dale, a one-time Eagle Scout and assistant scoutmaster who was dismissed after Scout leaders learned he was gay.

"It appears that homosexuality has gained greater societal acceptance. But this is scarcely an argument for denying First Amendment protection to those who refuse to accept those views," Rehnquist wrote.

"Dale's presence in the Boy Scouts would, at the very least, force the organization to send a message, both to the youth members and the world, that the Boy Scouts accepts homosexual conduct as a legitimate form of behavior," the chief justice also wrote.

The U.S. Supreme Court's *Dale* decision is consistent with two 1998 California Supreme Court rulings on the same question. The court held in *Curran v. Mt. Diablo Council of the Boy Scouts of America* (17 C.4th 670) that the Scouts have the right to exclude gays as scoutmasters. In *Randall v. Orange County Council of the Boy Scouts of America* (17 C.4th 736), the same court upheld the right of the Boy Scouts to exclude those who are unwilling to profess a belief in God.

In 1996, the U.S. Supreme Court addressed another issue that touched upon the constitutional rights of homosexuals and their critics. Although it is not a First Amendment case as such, it should be noted here. In *Romer v. Evans*, 517 U.S. 620), the high court overturned a Colorado ballot initiative banning state and local laws giving legal protection to the rights of homosexuals. The initiative was approved by a majority of Colorado voters in 1992. In a 6-3 ruling, the court said a state cannot single out a group for "disfavored treatment" based on "animosity." Writing for the majority, Justice Anthony Kennedy said "...Amendment 2 (the ballot initiative) classifies homosexuals not to further a proper legislative end but to make them unequal to everyone else. This Colorado cannot do." This decision does not necessarily guarantee homosexuals equal rights in all areas of the law. However, it does mark the first time the Supreme Court has overturned a law intended to legalize discrimination against them.

On the other hand, in 1998 the Supreme Court declined to review a decision of the sixth circuit U.S. Court of Appeals *upholding* a Cincinnati, Ohio, city charter provision that eliminated special protections for gays and lesbians. The Cincinnati charter provision ruled out "any claim of minority or protected status, quota preference or other preferential treatment" for gays and lesbians (*Equality Foundation of Greater Cincinnati v. City of Cincinnati*, 128 F.3d 289, cert. den. 525 U.S. 943).

The Supreme Court has also addressed the question of when government regulations concerning the use of a public place such as a park become a form of censorship. In *Thomas v. Chicago Park District* (534 U.S. 316), the high court in 2002 upheld the reasonableness of Chicago's rules for deciding whether to grant permits to demonstrators seeking to stage an event in a public park.

The court ruled unanimously that the city's 13-point guidelines, which require groups of more than 50 people to prove they have insurance, among other requirements, does not violate the First Amendment because it applies equally to all groups regardless of their viewpoint. Chicago officials defended the policy as necessary to assure fair access to local parks by individuals as well as large groups.

Writing for the court, Justice Antonin Scalia said, "the licensing scheme at issue here is not subject-matter censorship but content-neutral time, place and manner regulation of the use of a public forum." He added, "the picknicker and soccer player, no less than the political activist or parade marshal, must apply for a permit if the 50-person limit is to be exceeded."

The case was initiated by advocates of legalizing marijuana who frequently applied for permits to demonstrate in Chicago parks, sometimes gaining permission but sometimes being denied a permit.

Newsrack Ordinances

Another difficult First Amendment issue concerns newsracks on public property. Many states and cities have adopted laws regulating the size and placement of newsstands on sidewalks, for instance. Some have banned newsracks altogether. This has produced a variety of conflicting court rulings. In 1988, the Supreme Court squarely addressed this issue for the first time, and in so doing handed the news media a significant victory.

In *City of Lakewood v. Plain Dealer Publishing Co.* (486 U.S. 750), the court voted 4-3 to overturn a Lakewood, Ohio, ordinance that gave the town's mayor broad discretion to grant or deny publishers' requests to place newsstands on public sidewalks. The court ruled that newsracks are a legitimate form of expression in a public forum protected by the First Amendment. As a result, the court ruled that a city may not base decisions to grant or deny newsrack space on the content of the publication.

The case began when the mayor of Lakewood, a suburb of Cleveland, rejected the *Cleveland Plain Dealer*'s request to place newsracks at 18 locations in the town. The newspaper argued that the decision was arbitrary and violated the First Amendment.

Writing for the majority, Justice William Brennan said, "The Constitution requires that the city establish neutral criteria to insure that the licensing decision (i.e., to allow newsracks) is not based on the content or viewpoint of the speech being considered."

Brennan acknowledged that a city could flatly prohibit all newsracks, but he said a city may not ban some while permitting others based on arbitrary decisions about their content. The Supreme Court sent the case back to a lower court to determine if the Lakewood ordinance would be valid if the provisions allowing discrimination based on content are deleted.

Justice Byron White and two others joined in a vigorous dissenting opinion that compared newsracks to soft-drink vending machines and questioned their right to enjoy First Amendment protection. White said the majority's reasoning would, in effect, force many cities to allow private companies to do business on the public sidewalks. Chief Justice William Rehnquist and Justice Anthony Kennedy did not participate in the court's decision.

In 1993, the Supreme Court went even further in upholding the right to distribute literature in newsracks on public property. In *Cincinnati v. Discovery Network* (507 U.S. 410), the court said the city of Cincinnati could not flatly ban newsracks for commercial literature while allowing newspaper vending machines. City officials ordered Discovery (the publisher of a free magazine describing adult educational and recreational courses) and the publishers of a free real estate magazine to remove 62 newsracks from city property. Meanwhile, the city allowed more than 2,000 newspaper vending machines to remain on public property.

Voting 6-3, the court rejected the city's contention that the free flyers could be banned because they were merely commercial speech. The court ruled that commercial speech enjoys considerable First Amendment protection, and cannot be banned by a government agency unless the agency has a reasonable basis for doing so. The court rejected Cincinnati's argument that banning the 62 commercial newsracks would enhance the appearance of the city at a time when the city was not acting to remove newspaper racks. This commercial speech aspects of this case are discussed in Chapter 13.

DISCRIMINATORY TAXATION AS CENSORSHIP

One of the oldest forms of government control over the mass media is discriminatory taxation. Authorities in seventeenth- and eighteenth-century England used taxes as a means of controlling the press. One of the major grievances of the colonists before the revolutionary war was the Stamp Act, which singled out newspapers and legal documents for heavy taxation. Taxes may be burdensome for everyone, but if governments can levy high taxes on the news media and exempt other kinds of businesses, governments can force crusading news organizations into bankruptcy--or force them to become docile to avoid punitive taxation.

For many years after independence, attempts to single out newspapers for special taxes were rare in America, but a classic example of such a tax cropped up in the 1930s. And during the 1980s and 1990s, there were repeated lawsuits charging that various tax schemes singled out the media for unfair treatment in violation of the First Amendment.

In 1936, just five years after its landmark *Near v. Minnesota* decision, the Supreme Court decided *Grosjean v. American Press* (297 U.S. 233). This case arose because the state of Louisiana, dominated by Governor Huey "Kingfish" Long's political machine, had imposed a special tax on the gross receipts of the 13 largest papers in the state, 12 of which opposed Long. The tax applied to total advertising receipts of all papers and magazines with a circulation over 20,000 copies per week.

The newspapers challenged the tax in court and a federal district court issued an order barring the tax as a violation of the First Amendment. The Supreme Court heard the case on appeal and unanimously affirmed the lower court.

In an opinion by Justice George Sutherland, the court traced the history of taxes on knowledge in England and America. Sutherland said the First Amendment was intended to prevent prior restraints in the form of discriminatory taxes. He noted that the license tax acted as a prior restraint in two ways. First, it would curtail advertising revenue, and second, it was designed to restrict circulation. The Louisiana tax, Sutherland said, was "not an ordinary form of tax, but one single in kind, with a long history of hostile misuse against the freedom of the press."

This Supreme Court decision, however, did not free the media from their normal tax obligations as businesses. That principle was illustrated in a 1953 California case, *City of Corona v. Corona Daily Independent* (115 C.A.2d 382). The *Daily Independent* refused to pay a $32 city business license fee, claiming the fee was a violation of the First Amendment. The appellate court ruled:

> There is ample authority to the effect that newspapers and the business of newspaper publication are not made exempt from the ordinary forms of

taxes for the support of local government by the provisions of the First and Fourteenth Amendments.

The U.S. Supreme Court refused to review that decision. Taxation as a means of controlling or punishing the media is clearly prohibited by the First Amendment; routine taxation of all businesses (including media businesses) is not.

More recently, the Supreme Court has overturned three other state tax systems that improperly singled out the media for unconstitutional taxation. In 1983, the Supreme Court overturned a Minnesota plan that taxed some--but not all--newspapers.

Minnesota created a "use" tax on the ink and newsprint used by newspapers in 1971. But after some of the smaller papers complained of the economic hardship the tax caused, the legislature rewrote the law to exempt the first $100,000 in newsprint and ink each newspaper purchased annually. Thus, the law in effect exempted small newspapers or, to put it another way, singled out the large newspapers for a special tax. By 1974, one newspaper company--the *Minneapolis Star and Tribune*--was paying about two-thirds of the total amount the state collected from all Minnesota newspapers through this tax. Citing the *Grosjean* precedent, the *Star and Tribune* company challenged the constitutionality of the tax.

In *Minneapolis Star and Tribune v. Minnesota Commissioner of Revenue* (460 U.S. 575, 1983), the Supreme Court voted 8-1 to overturn Minnesota's tax on ink and newsprint. Justice Sandra Day O'Connor, writing for the court, warned that because such a tax "targets a small group of newspapers," it "presents such a potential for abuse that no interest suggested by Minnesota can justify the scheme." Justice William Rehnquist dissented, arguing that the use tax in question was less of a burden than the normal sales tax paid by other businesses. (Minnesota had exempted newspapers from the state sales tax, a practice that was common in other states as well.) Rehnquist said the state was actually conferring a benefit on the press, something the states may do without violating the First Amendment.

However, the majority's view was that the Minnesota tax *was* a problem precisely because it singled out certain newspapers for a tax not paid by others. Had Minnesota merely imposed a uniform sales or use tax on all businesses (including newspaper publishers), there would have been no First Amendment issue.

Also, Justice O'Connor emphasized that this case was not comparable to *Grosjean* in that there was no evidence that Minnesota's discriminatory tax was established to punish large newspapers for their editorial views. But the potential for such abuses was enough to render the tax unconstitutional, O'Connor said.

In 1987 the Supreme Court overturned another state taxation scheme that singled out some media for taxes not paid by others. This case involved an Arkansas sales tax that applied to general interest magazines but not to newspapers or to specialized magazines (e.g., religious, professional, trade and sports publications). In *Arkansas Writers' Project v. Ragland* (481 U.S. 221), the Supreme Court ruled the tax unconstitutional, relying on much the same rationale as in the *Minneapolis Star and Tribune* case.

In fact, the court said the Arkansas tax was even more flagrantly unconstitutional than the one in Minnesota because it required government officials to base a tax break on the *content* of the media. "...(O)fficial scrutiny of the content of publications as the basis for imposing a tax is entirely incompatible with the First Amendment's guarantee of freedom of the press," Justice Thurgood Marshall wrote for the majority.

Marshall was saying, in effect, that any tax giving some media favorable treatment while not extending the benefit across the board is unconstitutional. However, the court did not specifically rule out the possibility that a state could impose a tax on *entire categories* of media, taxing all newspapers while exempting all magazines, for instance.

The ruling produced a strong dissent from Justices Antonin Scalia and William Rehnquist (who was by then the Chief Justice). Writing the dissenting opinion, Scalia said that instead of promoting press freedom, the ruling would actually undermine other government tax breaks based on content, such as subsidies of public broadcasting, educational publications and the arts in general.

In 1989, the Supreme Court continued in this pattern by overturning a Texas tax system that granted sales tax exemptions to religious books, magazines and newspapers but not to secular publications. In *Texas Monthly v. Bullock* (489 U.S. 1), the majority ruled that the Texas tax scheme was unconstitutional because it violated the First Amendment's requirement of separation of church and state. In effect, the tax break was an unconstitutional state action to subsidize religion, they ruled. In a separate opinion, Justice Byron White said the tax scheme was invalid because it violated the First Amendment's free-press guarantees. Either way, the Texas plan was held to be just as unconstitutional as other methods of taxing some media while exempting others based on their content or size.

On the other hand, in 1991 the Supreme Court again made it clear that the media are subject to the same taxes as other businesses--as long as the tax does not improperly single out the media. Ruling in *Leathers v. Medlock* (499 U.S. 439), the court voted 7-2 to uphold an Arkansas sales tax that applied to cable and satellite television services--as well as to utilities, hotels and a variety of other businesses. Writing for the court, Justice Sandra Day O'Connor said this tax was not like the taxes on the media that the high court had previously overturned. Justice O'Connor wrote:

> The (Arkansas) tax does not single out the press and does not therefore threaten to hinder the press as a watchdog of government activity....There is no indication in this case that Arkansas has targeted cable television in a purposeful attempt to interfere with its First Amendment activities.

Justices Thurgood Marshall and Harry Blackmun dissented, arguing that this kind of sales tax could be used to inhibit freedom of expression. They were especially troubled by the fact that the Arkansas tax applied to pay-TV services but not to newspaper and magazine subscriptions. Nonetheless, the court upheld the tax.

The Supreme Court did, however, send the case back to the Arkansas state courts to determine whether cable companies should get a tax refund for a two-year period when the tax applied to cable systems but not to other pay-TV services. (When the tax was first imposed on cable TV, it did not apply to satellite TV, but the Arkansas Legislature changed that to avoid the legal problems inherent in singling out one type of pay-TV service for a tax that did not apply to other pay-TV services).

A week after it upheld the Arkansas cable television tax, the Supreme Court disposed of three other cases involving taxes on the media. The court declined to review state court decisions on media taxes in Tennessee and Iowa. But in the third case, *Miami Herald v. Department of Revenue* (499 U.S. 972), the high court issued an order directing the Florida Supreme Court to reconsider the validity of a sales tax that applied to magazines but not newspapers. The state court complied with the U.S. Supreme Court's order--and again ruled that the state cannot tax just magazines. Such a tax is improper because it is based on the content, the court ruled in 1992 (*Department of Revenue v. Magazine Publishers of America*, 604 So.2d 459).

To summarize, these Supreme Court decisions on media taxation basically say that the media may not be taxed in a discriminatory fashion. If some media must pay a tax that does not apply to others based on their content or their size, the tax is unconstitutional. But if the tax applies across the board to similar media--and especially if it applies to other businesses as well--it is valid.

OTHER PRIOR RESTRAINT QUESTIONS

The twentieth century was a time of government regulation, an era when many forms of activity were brought under government supervision for the first time. When the targeted activity involved the communication of ideas or information, however, the regulation has often been challenged as a violation of the First Amendment. This has forced the nation's courts--and ultimately the Supreme Court--to look at the propriety of government control of expressive activities of many kinds. This section summarizes some of the most important of these questions.

Censorship of Financial Newsletters

Does the federal government have the right to prohibit the publication of newsletters offering advice to stock market investors by people with questionable backgrounds? Is this kind of prior restraint acceptable despite the First Amendment? Or does the First Amendment protect the right to publish such newsletters, regardless of the publisher's past misdeeds?

That question was raised in a 1985 Supreme Court decision, *Lowe v. Securities and Exchange Commission* (472 U.S. 181). Under the federal Investment Advisers Act, the SEC is empowered to regulate the dissemination of investment advice, even when the advice is in the form of a publication that would seem to be protected by the First Amendment. The act exempts "bona fide" newspapers and magazines.

Christopher Lowe was convicted of mishandling a client's funds, and the SEC canceled his registration as an investment adviser. However, he continued to publish a financial newsletter. When the SEC tried to stop him from publishing his newsletter, he argued that he had a First Amendment right to publish it.

The Supreme Court ruled that Lowe's newsletter was in fact a "bona fide" publication and therefore exempt from regulation by the SEC. The high court did not rule on the larger issue of whether the SEC's registration process violates the First Amendment when it is used to prevent a person from communicating investment advice. But the court did affirm Lowe's right to publish his newsletter.

Writing for the majority, Justice John Paul Stevens noted that Lowe's newsletter contained disinterested investment advice intended for numerous readers, not personalized advice for specific individual clients. The court said the SEC could regulate those who give individualized advice, as opposed to publishers who offer their analyses of various investments to a general audience. Lowe's newsletter was published regularly, and it did not promote any stocks in which Lowe had a financial interest, the court pointed out. Thus, Lowe qualified as a "bona fide" publisher, not as an investment adviser.

In short, the court liberally interpreted the Investment Advisers Act's exemption for "bona fide" publications, and thereby avoided the First Amendment implications of the act's restrictions on giving investment advice. The court did not resolve the question of when the right to communicate opinions about the stock market is protected by the First Amendment.

However, a year after it lost the *Lowe* case at the Supreme Court, the SEC abandoned many of its efforts to regulate publications and broadcasts that give investment advice or discuss economic issues. Nevertheless, the SEC continued to act against financial publications that allegedly published misleading information that might affect the stock market. In 1988, the SEC lost such a case in the U.S. Court of Appeals, *SEC v. Wall Street Publishing Institute Inc.* (851 F.2d 365). That firm, the publisher of *Stock Market Magazine*, was accused of publishing articles that were little more than corporate "flackery" (as a federal judge put it)--articles that were written by the companies or their public relations agencies and that were uniformly flattering.

The SEC wanted a court order requiring *Stock Market Magazine* to disclose the origin of these articles. The appellate court ruled that neither the SEC nor the courts can delve into the sources or origins of magazine articles without violating the First Amendment. However, the appellate court did send the case back to a trial judge to determine whether some of the articles might have been paid advertising disguised as news. The court said that if the magazine was accepting payment for publishing the articles, the SEC might have the authority to force the magazine to disclose that fact. Accepting payment to publish an article would make the article a form of advertising; it should be identified as such.

"Political Propaganda" and Foreign Films

Is it a form of censorship for the federal government to force motion picture theaters to label foreign films that the government dislikes as "political propaganda?" How would you feel if you went to see such a film, and there was a large warning notice at the beginning, written by the United States attorney general, calling the film "political propaganda?" Would that affect your attitude toward the film? Would it affect the First Amendment rights of the film's producers if you told your friends not to see the film because of the warning label? Would you think less of the movie exhibitor for showing a film that was "political propaganda?" Is there a stigma attached to those words that might affect the exhibitor's First Amendment rights?

Those were some of the questions the Supreme Court faced in a 1987 case, *Meese v. Keene* (481 U.S. 465). Under an obscure provision of the Foreign Agents Registration Act of 1938, the Justice Department has the right to require that foreign films be so labeled if the attorney general considers them to be political propaganda.

Attorney General Edwin Meese ordered that the "political propaganda" label be placed on three Canadian films, including an Academy-Award-winning short film entitled, "If You Love This Planet." All three films advocated greater efforts to protect the environment. Two of the films addressed the problem of acid rain--in which pollution from U.S. power plants causes environmental damage in Canada (as well as the United States).

The case began when Barry Keene, the California State Senate majority leader and a Democrat, arranged to show the films and objected to being stigmatized as an exhibitor of foreign "political propaganda." Keene won an order from a lower court removing the warning label.

The Supreme Court, in a 5-3 ruling, overturned the lower court and said the "political propaganda" label does not violate the First Amendment but instead gives the public additional information about the film. Writing for the court, Justice John Paul Stevens said the label "has no pejorative connotation" and is not tantamount to censorship. In effect, Stevens was saying this: when Congress has given the attorney general the authority to label foreign films that the government dislikes as "political propaganda," the labeling is not a form of censorship.

Dissenting, Justice Harry Blackmun, joined by two others, replied that "...it simply strains credulity for the court to assert that propaganda is a neutral classification." They said the term still has negative connotations, just as it did long ago when it was widely associated with the government information practices of Nazi Germany. For the government to be able to so stigmatize films that it dislikes clearly has a chilling effect on First Amendment freedoms, they argued.

Censoring American Films Overseas

There have also been legal battles concerning an issue that is the reverse of the one just discussed. While the U.S. government labels foreign films with which it disagrees as "propaganda," the government has also taken steps to prevent American filmmakers from exporting films with which it disagrees. That practice led to a court decision in 1988, and this time the government's film policies were held to violate the First Amendment.

In *Bullfrog Films v. Wick* (847 F.2d 502), the U.S. Court of Appeals ruled that the U.S. Information Agency may not grant or deny a certification that a film is "educational" based on whether the USIA agrees with the film's content. Under a

1949 international treaty called the Beirut Agreement, "educational, scientific and cultural films" (i.e., documentaries) are exempt from the very high import tariffs levied on foreign commercial movies by many countries. (Entertainment-oriented movies often draw large audiences and generate enough revenue to pay the import tariffs; documentaries usually do not. As a result, it is often economically unfeasible to export a documentary that is not classified as "educational, scientific or cultural" by its country of origin.)

Bullfrog Films produced a series of award-winning documentaries that dealt with such subjects as nuclear war, the Sandinista government of Nicaragua and the use of Agent Orange in Vietnam. The USIA denied them the educational classification, thus effectively making it impossible to distribute them overseas. Bullfrog argued that the regulations under which its films were denied the educational classification gave the USIA a free hand to approve films with which it agreed while rejecting films critical of U.S. policy.

The Court of Appeals agreed and ordered the USIA to draft content-neutral regulations to be used in determining which U.S.-made films will be given the overseas tax benefits inherent in being labeled as educational, scientific or cultural.

The *Bullfrog Films* case was not the end of the matter, however. In 1988, the USIA adopted new rules that still consider the content of the film in deciding whether it will be certified for tax-free export. USIA Director Charles Z. Wick announced that if the new rules should be declared unconstitutional by the courts, the USIA would simply withdraw from the Beirut Agreement and not certify any U.S. films as educational, scientific or cultural. That would make it very difficult for American documentary filmmakers to export their works and would create a new prior restraint question.

Rock Concerts and the First Amendment

If motion pictures are generally protected from government censorship by the First Amendment, what about rock concerts? May a city restrict the sound levels at rock concerts in a city park without violating the First Amendment?

In 1989, the Supreme Court ruled on this question in *Ward v. Rock Against Racism* (491 U.S. 781). For a number of years a group called Rock Against Racism sponsored annual concerts at a bandshell in New York City's Central Park. The group provided its own sound equipment and technicians--and drew repeated complaints from other park-goers and nearby residents about the sound level at RAR concerts.

Eventually the city set limits on the sound level and placed monitors beyond the seating area to measure the sound. When the prescribed volume was repeatedly exceeded during a concert sponsored by RAR, city officials ordered the sound turned down. The concert promoters refused to lower the volume and were cited for excessive noise several times as the concert continued. The city finally cut off electric power to the bandshell to halt the concert--and refused to allow RAR to hold future concerts in Central Park. The city also decided to use its own equipment and sound technician so the volume could be controlled at other rock concerts.

RAR eventually sued the city, contending that the restrictions on the sound level at rock concerts violated the First Amendment. RAR especially objected to the city's decision to use its own sound technician, arguing that this gave government officials excessive control over the content of protected expression.

When the case reached the Supreme Court, the court acknowledged that rock music is a form of expression protected by the First Amendment. However, the court also ruled that the city's limits on sound level were a reasonable time, place and manner restriction, not an abridgement of the First Amendment. The court majority said the city's policy has "no material impact on any performer's ability to exercise complete artistic control over sound quality." The court conceded that the city's use of its own technician to control sound levels was not the least intrusive means of achieving the city's goal (i.e., keeping the volume down). The city could have continued to monitor sound levels, issue citations, and halt concerts if the sound level remained too high. In earlier cases, governments had been required to use the least intrusive means of regulating the time, place and manner of First Amendment activities. However, the court dropped that requirement and said that it is no longer necessary that time, place and manner restrictions on First Amendment freedoms be as non-intrusive as possible.

Dissenting, Justices Marshall, Brennan and Stevens objected to the broad sweep of the court's decision:

> No one can doubt that government has a substantial interest in regulating the barrage of excessive sound that can plague urban life. Unfortunately, the majority plays to our shared impatience with loud noise to obscure the damage that it does to our First Amendment rights. Until today, a key safeguard of free speech has been government's obligation to adopt the least intrusive restriction necessary to achieve its goals. By abandoning the requirement that time, place and manner regulations must be narrowly tailored, the majority replaces constitutional scrutiny with mandatory deference (to local officials' decisions).

Justice Marshall protested that giving the city a free hand to set volume limits before a concert was an improper prior restraint. Nevertheless, the court's decision settled the question of government regulation of sound levels at rock concerts: the sound level may be limited--and government employees may be placed in charge of the equipment to make sure the limits are observed--without that violating the First Amendment. However, that does not mean government officials are free to control other aspects of performances at government-owned amphitheaters and arenas. For example, when officials in Burbank, California, banned all rock concerts while allowing other kinds of performances at a city-owned amphitheater, the U.S. Court of Appeals overturned that action as a First Amendment violation (*Cinevision Corp. v. City of Burbank*, 745 F.2d 560, 1984).

Censoring Computer Encryption Software

Another prior restraint controversy that arose recently involved government restrictions on the distribution and especially the export of computer encryption software--software that allows computer messages to be encoded so unauthorized persons cannot read them. The federal government imposed these restrictions out of fear that terrorists or others who might threaten national security could use the encryption technology to engage in secret communications that could not be intercepted and monitored by law enforcement authorities.

Eventually these export restrictions were undermined by two federal appellate court decisions--and dropped by the federal government itself--in a series of legal actions that extended First Amendment protection to computer *source code* (i.e., the basic computer instructions built into software).

First, the ninth circuit U.S. Court of Appeals overturned the restrictions in *Bernstein v. U.S. Department of Justice* (176 F.3d 1132, 1999). The court rejected the government's concerns that the unregulated spread of encoded messages would aid criminals and terrorists, ruling 2-1 that the restrictions constituted an impermissible prior restraint. The court said the regulations gave virtual veto power to federal bureaucrats to prevent the free distribution of computer source code needed by cryptography academicians and scientists to exchange ideas about encryption.

Judge Betty Fletcher wrote that the regulations "strike at the heartland of the First Amendment" because this prior restraint applies "directly to scientific expression, vests boundless discretion in government officials, and lacks adequate procedural safeguards."

Shortly after the original *Bernstein* decision, the ninth circuit Court of Appeals voted to withdraw the ruling and reconsider the case *en banc*--with 11 judges on the ninth circuit considering the case instead of the usual panel of three judges. But then the federal government itself liberalized the rules concerning the overseas distribution of encryption software. Under the new rules, most limitations on the export of encryption software were dropped altogether, leaving Americans free to export even the most powerful data-scrambling software without an export license. That also left Americans free to post encryption software on the Internet--something else the federal government had opposed on the ground that it would make encryption software accessible overseas. After the rules were changed, the ninth circuit sent the *Bernstein* case back to a trial court to determine if the new regulations still constitute an unconstitutional prior restraint.

Meanwhile, in 2000 another federal appellate court ruled decisively that computer source code, including the code used for encryption, is fully protected by the First Amendment. In *Junger v. Daley* (209 F.3d 481), the sixth circuit U.S. Court of Appeals upheld law professor Peter Junger's right to place encryption software on his website, even though that would make it readily accessible to Internet users overseas. Ironically, the federal government had allowed Junger to export his computer law textbook, which contained the same encryption software. But the government refused to authorize him to put the software on his website.

After affirming that computer code is protected by the First Amendment, the sixth circuit ordered a lower court to decide if Junger had a basis for challenging the newly liberalized federal rules governing the export of encryption software. But whatever the outcome of this convoluted series of lawsuits, one thing appears to be settled: computer software, including encryption software, is protected by the First Amendment.

Seizing Criminals' Royalties

Is it an unlawful form of censorship for a state to seize profits or royalties a criminal receives for telling or writing about his/her crimes? Many states and the federal government have laws allowing the authorities to take criminals' publishing profits and give them to the victims of their crimes. These laws are often called "Son of Sam" laws because New York's pioneering law of this type was enacted after serial killer David Berkowitz, who called himself by that name, received lucrative offers to tell his story.

The Supreme Court addressed this issue in 1991. The court held that New York's "Son of Sam" law was unconstitutional because it imposed a special financial burden on communications--based on the content of the message. In *Simon & Schuster v. New York State Crime Victims Board* (502 U.S. 105), the court said New York would have to show a compelling state interest to justify a law that burdened First Amendment activities in this way--and that the state had failed to do so.

Writing for the court, Justice Sandra Day O'Connor said the law was "overinclusive" and therefore unconstitutional because it would apply to many legitimate literary works. Had it been in effect in an earlier era, the law would have allowed the state to seize the profits from works such as Henry David Thoreau's *Civil Disobedience*, O'Connor wrote. She added that some other laws of this type might be sufficiently different from New York's law to be valid.

Under the New York law, criminals were required to give up the royalties and profits from books, movies and other communications that in any way concerned their crimes. The money was then placed in a fund to compensate crime victims.

The law was challenged by the publishing house of Simon & Schuster, which paid Henry Hill, a former mafia figure, nearly $100,000 for his story about his life as a mobster who became a government informant. The resulting book, *Wiseguy*, became a best seller and was made into a widely acclaimed movie, "Goodfellas." Simon & Schuster was holding another $27,000 that it owed to him when the Crime Victims Board demanded the money. Instead of complying, the publisher challenged the Son of Sam law--and prevailed when the Supreme Court declared the law to be unconstitutional.

In the years since the *Simon and Schuster* Supreme Court decision, several states have enacted narrower laws to give crime victims any money earned by convicted felons for telling the stories of their crimes. These laws generally apply only to persons actually convicted of a crime and are limited to money earned for a specific, detailed account of the crime.

While some of these laws have survived legal challenges, in 2002 the California Supreme Court overturned such a law in the case of *Keenan v. Superior Court* (27 C. 4th 413). Barry Keenan, who kidnapped Frank Sinatra, Jr., son of the famous vocalist, in 1963, earned a reported $1 million for the movie rights to his story three decades later. The court rejected Sinatra's attempt to seize Keenan's earnings under the California "Son of Sam" law, holding that the law was so broad that it could be used to interfere with the right of authors to profit from works that happen to discuss a crime in detail.

The California legislature responded to the *Keenan* decision by considering a replacement law that would allow victims of major crimes to sue the perpetrators under a greatly extended statute of limitations: it would allow lawsuits until 10 years after the offender's release from prison. This proposal makes no distinction between book or movie income and wealth the ex-convict might acquire in some other way--seemingly avoiding a First Amendment problem.

Liability for Inspiring Crimes

Another troubling First Amendment question involves holding the communications media accountable for crimes committed by readers or viewers who were allegedly inspired by a movie, website, television show, book, news story, magazine article or an advertisement. A number of such cases have arisen recently. Although they may involve subsequent punishments rather than prior restraints, the First Amendment issues they raise should be discussed here.

In 1998, the Supreme Court refused to intervene in a case where a book allegedly facilitated a crime: *Rice v. Paladin Enterprises*, (128 F.3d 233, 1997). In this case, the publisher of a book called *Hit Man: A Technical Manual for Independent Contractors* was sued by the families of three people who were killed by a man who followed the detailed instructions in *Hit Man*. The publisher sought to have the lawsuit dismissed on First Amendment grounds, but a federal appellate court held that this book, with its "extraordinary comprehensiveness, detail and clarity" in describing how to commit murder, is not exempted from civil lawsuits by the First Amendment. The court held that a publisher can be sued by those who are injured (or the families of those who are killed) in this type of situation.

The appellate court called the 130-page book a "step-by-step murder manual, a training book for assassins." Because it was intended to train potential murderers and not merely to entertain, it falls outside the scope of the First Amendment, the appellate court ruled.

When the Supreme Court refused to intervene, the families were free to take their case against the publisher to trial. This case caused alarm among media organizations. Publishers, broadcasters and filmmakers, among others, urged the Supreme Court to hear the case, arguing that the same rationale could be used in lawsuits alleging that a variety of books, magazines, scientific and military manuals, movies and other media might have inspired or assisted someone who committed a crime.

Similar issues were also raised in several other widely publicized recent cases, including one in which an Oakland, Mich. jury ordered the producers of the *Jenny Jones* television talk show to pay $25 million in damages to the family of a man who was killed by another man who appeared with him on the show. The victim said (on camera) that he had a homosexual interest in the man who later shot and killed him. This verdict was being appealed at this writing.

In 1999, the U.S. Supreme Court declined to intervene in a similar case where a Louisiana appellate court held that the family of a shooting victim could sue the producers of the movie, *Natural Born Killers*, if they could prove that the producers *intended to* inspire others to commit violent acts. In *Byers v. Edmonson* (712 So.2d 681, cert. den. 526 U.S. 1005), the Supreme Court refused to hear an appeal of the Louisiana court's ruling, which cleared the way for a lawsuit by the family of Patsy Byers, a convenience store clerk who was seriously wounded by a couple who had repeatedly watched *Natural Born Killers* and then went on a crime spree.

The Byers family never proved that filmmaker Oliver Stone and others involved in producing this movie actually *intended to* inspire violent acts by viewers, and a Louisiana judge eventually dismissed the case, ruling that Stone and the movie's distributor were protected by the First Amendment. However, this legal victory, coming only after lengthy (and costly) litigation, does little to protect the media from other lawsuits by crime victims or their families when a crime is committed by someone who watched a movie or television program--or read a book, a news story or a magazine article--about a similar crime.

Although lawsuits alleging that the media inspired a crime are becoming more commonplace, this is not a new phenomenon. Nearly a decade before these cases arose, a family sued *Soldier of Fortune Magazine* and won a large damage award because the magazine published an advertisement that led to a murder for hire. A federal appellate court eventually upheld the award and dismissed the magazine's First Amendment arguments (*Braun v. Soldier of Fortune Magazine*, 968 F.2d 1110, 1992).

In 1985, the magazine carried an ad from an unemployed Vietnam veteran who described himself as a "37-year-old professional mercenary (who) is discrete (sic) and very private. Body guard, courier and other special skills. All jobs considered." He accepted an assignment to kill a man in Atlanta and was later caught and convicted of the crime. The family sued the magazine for wrongful death; a jury awarded the family the $4.3 million.

A number of publishers and industry groups joined in a petition to the Supreme Court to review this decision, arguing that it could have a serious chilling effect on First Amendment freedoms. However, the high court declined to hear the case, leaving the judgment undisturbed.

Censoring Confidential Information

Another form of prior restraint results from laws and court orders forbidding the media to publish confidential information, often concerning crimes and court proceedings. This creates legal problems that fall into several areas, including fair trial-free press (discussed in Chapter Seven) and the privacy rights of crime victims (discussed in Chapter Five). This chapter discusses a series of Supreme Court decisions concerning the censorship questions inherent in these laws.

One of the most difficult problems in this area involves laws forbidding the media to reveal the names of crime victims, particularly sex crime victims. Although a good case can be made for protecting the privacy of crime victims, the

Supreme Court has held that the media have a First Amendment right to publish their identities if the information was lawfully obtained from public records. The court so ruled in 1975, overturning a Georgia privacy judgment against a broadcaster who published a rape victim's name. In that case (*Cox Broadcasting v. Cohn*, 420 U.S. 469), a television reporter had obtained the victim's name from a court record, and the station later faced a civil invasion of privacy suit for broadcasting it. (No criminal charges were filed against the station, although publishing the name was illegal.) The U.S. Supreme Court said the First and Fourteenth Amendments do not permit either criminal sanctions or civil invasion of privacy lawsuits for the publication of truthful information lawfully obtained from *official court records*. However, the states can keep victims' names secret if they wish.

Two years later the U.S. Supreme Court overturned an Oklahoma court order that banned publication of the name of an 11-year-old boy allegedly involved in a fatal shooting, in *Oklahoma Publishing v. District Court* (430 U.S. 377, 1977).

Reporters attended the boy's initial detention hearing and learned his name there. Local newspapers and broadcasters carried the name, but a judge ordered them not to publish the boy's name or picture again, and the Oklahoma Publishing Company appealed the order to the state Supreme Court, which upheld it. The U.S. Supreme Court reversed, ruling that the order amounted to prior censorship in violation of the First and Fourteenth Amendments. The high court relied on *Cox Broadcasting* as a precedent and said there was no evidence that the press acquired the information unlawfully or even without the state's permission.

In 1979, the Supreme Court overturned a West Virginia law that imposed criminal sanctions on newspapers for publishing the names of juvenile offenders. In this case (*Smith v. Daily Mail*, 443 U.S. 97), a newspaper published the name of a youth who killed another student at a junior high school. Reporters learned his name by monitoring police radio broadcasts and talking to eyewitnesses.

The Supreme Court again ruled that the media cannot be punished for publishing truthful information that was lawfully obtained. One aspect of the law that particularly amazed Justice William Rehnquist, who wrote a concurring opinion, was that it prohibited newspaper publication of juvenile names while not outlawing a broadcast of the same information.

The publication of another kind of confidential information produced a 1978 U.S. Supreme Court decision, *Landmark Communications v. Virginia* (435 U.S. 829). The case involved the *Virginian Pilot*'s coverage of the proceedings of a state commission reviewing a judge's performance in office. The paper published the name of the judge, among other information. Virginia had a law making these proceedings confidential. The paper was criminally prosecuted and fined for publishing this information and the state Supreme Court affirmed the judgment.

The U.S. Supreme Court ruled that the Virginia law violated the First Amendment. The high court said judges have no greater immunity from criticism than other persons or institutions. When a newspaper lawfully obtains information about a proceeding such as the one in question, the paper may not be criminally punished for publishing what it learns.

In 1989, the Supreme Court again addressed this kind of issue in *Florida Star v. B.J.F.* (491 U.S. 524). Under Florida law in effect then the media were forbidden to publish the names of sex crime victims. However, a reporter for the weekly *Florida Star* copied the name of a rape victim from a police report that was posted on the Jacksonville Sheriff's pressroom wall. The name was published, and the crime victim sued. She won a $97,000 judgment from the newspaper, but the Supreme Court overturned the verdict, ruling that the newspaper could not be penalized for publishing the name when it was lawfully obtained from a police record--even though the police may have violated the Florida law by making the information available to a reporter. However, the court's 6-3 majority declined to rule that the media are *always* exempt from liability for publishing information that they lawfully obtain. The court said that *Cox Broadcasting* and the other earlier cases had actually stopped short of ruling out all liability for the truthful publication of lawfully obtained information. But when judicial records are involved, the court seemed to be saying that the media are free to publish whatever information they can lawfully obtain.

An interesting footnote to the *Florida Star* case is that the state law forbidding the mass media to publish the names of sex crime victims was eventually ruled unconstitutional by the Florida Supreme Court. In *Florida v. Globe Communications Corp.* (648 So.2d 110, 1994), the state court ruled that the Florida law was too broad because it banned the publication of victims' names without any consideration of the circumstances--and also too narrow because it applied only to the mass media. This case arose when the Globe, a tabloid newspaper, published the name of the woman who accused William Kennedy Smith, a nephew of former President John F. Kennedy and Sen. Edward Kennedy, of rape. As was true in the *Florida Star* case, the Globe lawfully obtained the alleged victim's name, and the woman eventually agreed to the release of her name--even appearing on national television after Smith was acquitted of the charge. When the Globe was criminally prosecuted for publishing the name, a trial court, a state appellate court and eventually the Florida Supreme Court all agreed that the state law was unconstitutional.

Less than a year after the *Florida Star* decision, the Supreme Court ruled on another Florida case involving the right to publish information that was lawfully obtained. In *Butterworth v. Smith* (494 U.S. 624, 1990), a reporter who had testified before a grand jury wanted to write about the things he told the grand jury--including alleged wrongdoing by a local public official. But under Florida law, it was illegal for a grand jury witness to disclose his/her testimony *ever*.

In overturning the Florida law, the Supreme Court ruled that it is an unconstitutional prior restraint to prohibit a witness from publicly disclosing his own testimony even after the grand jury investigation ends. Writing for the court, Chief Justice William Rehnquist pointed out that this case did not involve the reporter disclosing anything he *learned from a secret grand jury investigation*. Instead, it was merely a case of a journalist being forbidden to publish information that was already in his possession before he testified. And that violates the First Amendment, the court held.

One noteworthy limitation on the media's right to publish lawfully obtained information involves the pretrial discovery process when a news organization is involved in a lawsuit. The Supreme Court has held that a judge can forbid a newspaper to publish information it obtains during discovery. In *Seattle Times v.*

Rhinehart (467 U.S. 20, 1984), the high court said the *Seattle Times* and another paper could be forbidden to publish information they learned while defending a libel suit against a religious group. During discovery, the plaintiff (a minister) was ordered to provide his organization's membership lists, tax returns and other financial information. The Supreme Court upheld the trial judge's order forbidding the newspapers to publish this material. The court said they would be free to publish the same information if they learned of it independently, but when a plaintiff is compelled to hand it over in a libel case, the judge is entitled to require that it remain confidential. Such a court order may be a prior restraint, but the Supreme Court held that it was a legitimate one, despite the First Amendment.

In 1990, a somewhat similar prior restraint situation arose in connection with the drug trafficking trial of former Panamanian dictator Manuel Noriega. Cable News Network obtained tape recordings of some of Noriega's telephone conversations with his lawyers. After CNN broadcast a portion of the tapes, a federal judge ordered CNN not to air any more of them. The Supreme Court rejected an emergency appeal by CNN, leaving the order in effect. The judge eventually set aside the order, ruling that the tapes would not threaten Noriega's right to a fair trial. However, in 1994, the U.S. Attorney's office in Miami filed criminal contempt of court charges against CNN for airing excerpts from the tapes while the order was in effect. As Chapter Seven explains, CNN was convicted of contempt and fined.

The question of judicial censorship arose again in 1995 in a widely noted case involving Business Week magazine. Business Week obtained 300 pages of documents that Procter & Gamble Co. had filed in a complex lawsuit against Banker's Trust Co. In the lawsuit, P&G alleged that it suffered large losses on its investments because of the misdeeds of Banker's Trust. The documents, like many others filed with the court during the pretrial discovery process, were sealed--not open for public inspection. Business Week obtained them from one of the lawyers involved in the case, but a federal judge ordered Business Week not to publish information from the documents. After a series of legal maneuvers, the magazine was eventually permitted to publish information from the documents. Later, the sixth circuit U.S. Court of Appeals ruled that it was improper for the judge to censor the magazine in the first place. In *Procter & Gamble Co. v. Banker's Trust Co.* (78 F.3d 219), a 2-1 majority ruled that the judge did not have the very compelling legal reasons needed to justify an act of prior restraint of the press. The majority noted that the documents were nothing more than routine filings in a lawsuit; their publication would not endanger any fundamental government interest. While the appellate court ruling was a victory for freedom of the press, the case also raised new questions about the routine practice of sealing documents filed during lawsuits so they are off limits to the press and public.

Why was this case decided differently than the *Seattle Times* case, where the Supreme Court upheld a judge's right to order a newspaper not to publish court documents? The Seattle Times was a party to a lawsuit, and the opposing side was compelled by a court order to hand over confidential information. Here Business Week was not a party to the underlying lawsuit and obtained the court documents independently and lawfully. Under those circumstances, there was a far less compelling justification for a judge to impose a prior restraint on the media. The *Seattle Times* case is a rare exception to the rule that the media may not be forbidden to publish court documents that they lawfully obtain.

A SUMMARY OF PRIOR RESTRAINTS

What Is a Prior Restraint?

A prior restraint is an act of government censorship to prevent facts or ideas that the government considers unacceptable from ever being published or broadcast. It is a far greater abridgment of freedom of expression than a subsequent punishment system, which allows publication but punishes the publisher afterward for any harm that may result.

Are Prior Restraints Permitted in America?

Under the First Amendment, prior restraints are permitted only under extremely compelling circumstances, with the government agency that seeks to impose such censorship required to carry a very heavy burden of proof to justify it.

When Would a Direct Prior Restraint Be Constitutional?

In the "Pentagon Papers" case, the Supreme Court ruled that prior censorship of the news media would be permissible if the government could prove that irreparable harm to national security would otherwise occur. However, the government was unable to prove national security was sufficiently endangered to justify prior restraint in that case.

Are There Other Rules Concerning Prior Restraints Today?

Governments may lawfully regulate the *time, place and manner* in which First Amendment activities occur, provided the rules are *content neutral*. Laws or government actions that unduly restrict literature distribution or other free expression activities on public property may constitute prior restraints; they have often been invalidated by the courts. Private property owners, on the other hand, may usually prohibit First Amendment activities on their property, although some states recognize limited free expression rights at quasi-public places such as large shopping malls. Discriminatory taxes that single out some media for special treatment have also been declared unconstitutional as prior restraints. Government actions that limit the freedom to export motion pictures or that unduly restrict rock music performances at publicly owned concert facilities have also been overruled as improper prior restraints. Laws forbidding racial and religious "hate speech" also have been overturned on First Amendment grounds.

May the Media Be Forbidden to Identify Crime Victims?

Laws or court orders forbidding the media to publish information they lawfully obtain are usually unconstitutional, even if the information is legally confidential (e.g., some crime victims' names). While the media may not have a right of access to this kind of news, governments cannot ordinarily prevent its publication once the media have it--particularly if it was obtained from a public record.

CHAPTER FOUR
Libel and Slander

Ever since American journalists won their basic First Amendment freedoms, their most serious ongoing legal problem has been the danger of being sued for *defamation*--libel or slander. Other threats to journalistic freedom arise from time to time, but over the past two centuries libel has been a continuing legal problem, with thousands of lawsuits resolved by the courts--and thousands more settled out of court. Even the fear of libel suits often leads journalists to suppress newsworthy stories they would otherwise publish, thus engaging in a form of self-censorship that may not be in the public interest.

A libel is a *written defamatory statement*; a slander is a *spoken* one. Libel and slander laws exist to protect people whose reputations have been wrongfully damaged. Clearly, there is a need for that kind of protection. However, many libel suits are filed by persons who were not actually libeled, but who are angry about unfavorable but true (and thus non-libelous) publicity. And hostile juries sometimes hand out enormous punitive damage awards against the mass media without worrying much about the validity of the libel claim itself.

A single libel suit can be financially devastating even to a powerful media corporation. The Libel Defense Resource Center, a New York-based organization that monitors libel cases nationally, reported that there were six libel judgments against the mass media exceeding $10 million each during 1990 and 1991 alone. In 1996, the LDRC reported that the *average* judgment in libel and related cases lost by the mass media was $2.8 million.

Although most of the large libel judgments are eventually overturned by appellate courts, the cost of defending such a lawsuit often runs into millions of dollars. For a small-market broadcaster or newspaper publisher, the cost of one libel suit--even one that is eventually won in court--can put the company on the brink of bankruptcy. For example, the *Alton Telegraph*, a small Illinois newspaper, filed for bankruptcy court protection after losing a $9.2 million libel judgment in the 1980s. The plaintiffs in the case eventually agreed to accept a $1.4 million settlement, and the paper managed to borrow enough money to stay in business--but just barely (see *Green v. Alton Telegraph*, 438 N.E.2d 203, 1982).

If small local newspapers are targets in libel suits, well-known national media are even bigger targets for angry jurors. A jury once awarded a former "Miss Wyoming" beauty contest winner $26.5 million for a *Penthouse* magazine article about a fictitious "Miss Wyoming" who resembled her. An appellate court eventually set aside the verdict and dismissed the case, but by then *Penthouse* had spent more than a million dollars on legal fees (*Pring v. Penthouse*, 695 F.2d 438, 1983). And $26.5 million is not the all-time record for a libel judgment: there have been several larger verdicts.

In 1990, a jury awarded Philadelphia lawyer Richard A. Sprague $34 million in a libel case against *The Philadelphia Inquirer*; that award was reduced to $24 million by an appellate court in 1994. The paper charged that as a prosecutor Sprague had once dropped a murder investigation as a favor to a police official whose son was present when the murder occurred. Less than a year after Sprague won his record jury verdict, that record was shattered when a jury in Waco, Texas, awarded $58 million to a former district attorney who was accused by Dallas television station WFAA of accepting payoffs to drop drunk driving cases. Both of these verdicts were appealed and then settled for undisclosed (but surely large) sums of money. The Sprague case was especially noteworthy because the alleged libel occurred in 1973; the case was settled in 1996, 23 years later.

All of these judgments seem small compared to a 1997 verdict in which a Houston jury ordered the *Wall Street Journal* to pay $222.7 million (including $200 million in punitive damages) to an investment brokerage that went out of business shortly after the *Journal* reported on the firm's alleged difficulties. However, the judge later threw out the $200 million punitive damage award, and he eventually set aside the remainder of the judgment as well, ruling that the brokerage withheld crucial evidence that would have corroborated the *Journal* story. But by then the *Journal* had spent several years and thousands of dollars defending itself in court.

One of the most controversial judgments against a news organization in many years was $5.5 million in punitive damages that a jury awarded to the Food Lion grocery chain in 1997 because ABC's PrimeTime Live had two of its staff members obtain jobs at Food Lion under false pretenses. The ABC staffers used hidden cameras to document the mishandling of foods. Although Food Lion did not even allege that ABC's report was libelous, the jury found ABC guilty of trespass, fraud and other wrongs in connection with its undercover newsgathering. The trial judge later reduced the punitive damage award to $315,000. In 1999, the fourth circuit U.S. Court of Appeals overturned that award, upholding only $2 (yes, two dollars) in damages against ABC for trespass and a breach of the duty of loyalty to an employer by the two ABC staffers who took jobs at Food Lion only to get the story (see *Food Lion v. Capital Cities/ABC*, 194 F.3d 505).

From the outset, ABC's defenders saw Food Lion's lawsuit as an end run around the libel laws by a company that could not prove the ABC report was false but wanted to sue anyway. The appellate court verdict largely vindicated ABC, but only after years of litigation and enormous legal bills for the network.

Although appellate courts often overturn or reduce these multimillion-dollar judgments against the media, that does not always happen. In 1987 the U.S. Court of Appeals in Chicago affirmed a $3.05 million libel judgment against CBS and a television journalist in a case called *Brown and Williamson Tobacco Co. v. Jacobson* (827 F.2d 1119). The Supreme Court refused to hear a further appeal in 1988, rendering the U.S. Court of Appeals decision final. The case resulted from broadcasts by Chicago news anchor Walter Jacobson accusing tobacco companies of targeting young people in their advertising. He cited as an example an advertisement that was never actually used.

While these are extreme examples, libel and slander lawsuits are a daily concern of the mass media. And the fear of lawsuits can have a serious chilling effect on First Amendment freedoms: it causes some news organizations to avoid controversial stories to minimize the risk of being sued for libel or slander.

This point has never been better illustrated than by the continuing campaign of the tobacco industry against media reporting of the alleged misdeeds of tobacco companies. It turned out that Brown and Williamson's libel victory in 1987 was only the beginning. More recently B & W and other large tobacco companies have continued to sue or threaten to sue the major media in an apparent bid to discourage hard-hitting reporting about the risks of tobacco and the practices of the tobacco industry.

In 1994, ABC reported on its Day One program that tobacco companies were regulating the amount of nicotine in their products, in effect spiking cigarettes to keep smokers hooked. Philip Morris filed a $10 *billion* libel suit, and in 1995 ABC paid Philip Morris $15 million to drop the case. ABC also apologized twice in prime time--even though the journalists who produced the award-winning program insisted that they could document their charges. Day One producer Walt Bogdanich, a Pulitzer-Prize-winning broadcast journalist, refused to sign the apology--and then announced that he was moving to CBS to join 60 Minutes.

Did this huge settlement and apology have a chilling effect on reporting of the tobacco controversy by other networks? Bogdanich later said in *Broadcasting & Cable* magazine that it would. "I fear that we're going to start picking on the small fry," while ignoring the misdeeds of huge corporations, he said.

Ironically, a few months before Bogdanich made that statement, CBS chose not to air a planned interview with a former B & W scientist on 60 Minutes, citing fears of another lawsuit by B & W. Mike Wallace, reporter/co-editor of 60 Minutes, was widely quoted as criticizing this decision, even though the interview was aired several months after the initial decision to pull it off the program. "We continue to go after the big ones because it's the big ones that count," Wallace told a conference of investigative journalists in 1996.

Maybe so, but how does all of this affect smaller media organizations--the ones that couldn't begin to write a $15 million check to get out of a lawsuit?

LIBEL DEFINED

Just what are libel and slander?

They are legal actions to compensate the victims of defamatory communications--communications that tend to injure someone's reputation. As noted earlier, libel is a lawsuit based on a *written* defamatory statement; slander is similar but based on a *spoken* defamation. The differences between the two are less important today than they once were, as a result of recent Supreme Court decisions and the growing influence of the electronic media. Because libel is a far more common lawsuit than slander, we will often say *libel* when referring to both kinds of defamation.

Libel and slander suits are almost as old as the English common law from which they emerged. Even before this country was colonized, libel and slander were recognized legal actions. In fact, the concept that a person's good name is something of value, and that anyone who damages it has committed a wrong, can be traced back at least to the time of the ancient Romans.

Most libel cases today are handled as civil tort actions, private disputes between two parties in which the courts merely provide a neutral forum. In earlier times, libel was often treated as a criminal matter: the prevailing view was that defamatory words might lead to a breach of the peace, and should be regarded as a crime. This was especially true in the case of seditious libel (the crime of criticizing the government), for reasons explained in Chapter Two. While many states still have criminal libel laws on their books, these laws are rarely enforced today. Some have been ruled unconstitutional. Thus, the bulk of this chapter will be devoted to civil rather than criminal libel.

Libel suits are ordinarily state cases, not federal ones. The U.S. Supreme Court has intervened in some state libel cases in recent years, reminding the states that their libel laws can have a chilling effect on freedom of the press. But aside from the Supreme Court's role in setting constitutional limits for libel suits, this remains a field of law reserved for the states.

However, that does not mean that libel suits are never tried in federal courts. State libel cases are sometimes heard in federal courts when the two parties live in different states, but even then, the federal courts apply state law rather than federal law.

Although libel is a matter of state law, its basic principles are much the same all over the United States, as is true of many kinds of law that grew out of the English common law. Moreover, the Supreme Court's rulings have tended to make libel law more uniform in the various states. Nevertheless, there are still important state-to-state variations; you may wish to supplement this national overview by learning your own state's libel laws.

AN OVERVIEW OF LIBEL

In studying a complex legal subject such as libel, it is easy to get lost in the details, overlooking some of the major principles. This section summarizes the basics of libel law.

A libel occurs whenever the *elements* of libel are present. As you look at the list of these elements, you will realize that many libelous statements are published and broadcast every day. But that doesn't mean numerous libel suits are filed against the mass media every day. Instead, most libelous publications and broadcasts are unlikely to produce lawsuits because they are covered by one or more of the legal *defenses* that apply in libel law. Thus, to decide whether a given item is likely to produce a libel suit, you have to determine not only whether the elements of libel are present but also whether there is a viable defense.

For a libel to occur, at least four elements must be present--with a fifth one required in many cases. The elements are these:

1. The statement must actually be *defamatory*--it must tend to hurt someone's reputation.
2. The statement must *identify* its intended victim, either by name or by some other designation that is understood by persons other than the victim.
3. The statement must actually be *communicated*: it must be published or broadcast in such a fashion that at least one person other than the victim and the perpetrator hears or sees it.
4. In most instances, there must also be an element of *fault* (the U.S. Supreme Court has ruled that in libel cases involving issues of public concern there must be proof that a falsehood was disseminated, and that the publisher was guilty of actual malice or at least negligence in publishing it).
5. In cases where the victim cannot prove the publication resulted from actual malice, there must be proof of damages (i.e., losses that may be compensated in money). Until the Supreme Court added this requirement, state courts sometimes held the media strictly accountable for libelous statements and *presumed* that damages existed without proof of any actual injury.

Once these elements are present, a libel has occurred. It doesn't matter whether the defamatory statement is in a direct quote, a letter to the editor, an advertisement, a broadcast interview, or whatever. With few exceptions, anyone who contributes to the libel's dissemination may be sued for it, even if the libel was originated by someone else. That means the reporter who writes a story, the editor who reviews it, and everyone else in the production process may be named as a defendant in a libel suit. Of course, the normal legal strategy is to go after the "deep pocket"--the person with enough money to make it worthwhile. Therefore, the prime defendant is usually the owner or publisher, not the hired hands who actually processed the libelous material. If you were defamed in a letter to the editor, you might want to sue the letter writer and the editor who chose to print it, but your prime defendant would probably be the owner. In this era of corporate and chain ownership of the mass media, this is more true than ever before.

After you determine whether the elements of libel are present in a given situation, the next crucial question is whether any of the defenses apply. What are the defenses? Three major ones developed under the common law and have been recognized for many years. In addition, a few defenses of lesser importance are also recognized at least in some states, and these will be noted later. The major defenses are these:

1. *Truth*: any statement that is substantially truthful is protected. Truth is the oldest common law defense in libel cases, but recent Supreme Court decisions have made it even stronger. Those who sue the media usually must bear the *burden of proving falsity*: they must prove not only that the defamatory statement is false but also that it resulted from either negligence or actual malice;

2. *Privilege*: fair and accurate accounts of what occurs during many proceedings of legislative bodies, the courts and the executive branch of government--and also accurate reports of many types of government documents--are privileged, which means they are protected even if libelous;

3. *Fair comment*: a statement of *opinion* about the performance of a person who places himself in the limelight (e.g., a politician, actor, sports celebrity, etc.) is protected under the common law fair comment defense. (In addition, expressions of opinion are sometimes protected by the First Amendment under recent Supreme Court decisions.)

If one or more of these defenses is present, the mass media may publish libelous material without fear of losing a libel suit. However, many lawsuits are filed by people who know they have little chance of ultimately winning. The mere opportunity to force a newspaper or broadcaster into court may seem inviting to someone who feels he or she has been subjected to unfair publicity. Thus, the cost of defending a libel suit is in itself a deterrent to publishing some stories that may be controversial, no matter how strong the defenses are.

In addition to the classic defenses of truth, privilege and fair comment, the Supreme Court's new requirement that libel plaintiffs prove negligence or actual malice has sometimes been referred to as the "constitutional privilege" or "First Amendment" defense. This concept would more correctly be viewed as an element of the plaintiff's case instead of a libel defense, but it is occasionally called a defense and is mentioned here in the interest of completeness.

In short, to be libelous a statement must be defamatory, it must identify a victim in some understandable way, it must be disseminated, usually there must be some fault on the part of the media, and the libel victim must suffer some provable injury. But even if all of these *elements of libel* are present, the statement may or may not lead to a successful libel suit, depending on whether any of the recognized *libel defenses* applies. In addition, there are certain other factors to consider in deciding if any particular defamatory statement could lead to a successful lawsuit.

Who May Sue for Libel

The first step in analyzing any potentially libelous item is to determine whether there is a *plaintiff*--a party who may sue for libel. Generally, the rule is that any living person or other private legal entity (such as a corporation or an unincorporated business) may sue for libel. The right to sue for libel is what is called a *personal* right, not a *property* right. This means that the right dies with the individual: most states follow the common law rule that the heirs cannot sue on behalf of a deceased person unless they were also personally libeled. New Jersey and Pennsylvania do allow a libel victim's heirs to sue under certain circumstances, but that is the exception. However, a number of states allow the heirs to *continue an existing lawsuit* if a libel victim dies before the case is resolved.

On the other hand, corporations are not limited by the life span or tenure in office of any individual. They may pursue a lawsuit for decades, regardless of the departure of individual officers. But for a corporation to sue for libel, the organization itself must have been defamed, not just an individual officer.

It may seem surprising that a big company can sue for libel. Nevertheless, the courts have often ruled that a corporation has the same right as an individual to sue for libel when its reputation is besmirched by a false and defamatory statement. However, special rules sometimes apply when the defamation is directed at a product rather than the company itself. Many states allow a special legal action called *product disparagement* or *trade libel*. In a trade libel suit, the suing company usually has to prove that the libelous statement actually damaged its business, something that is sometimes difficult to prove.

Product disparagement laws were rarely used for many years, but they enjoyed a new surge in popularity during the 1990s, when at least 13 states passed new laws intended to protect perishable food products from negative media publicity. These so-called "veggie libel" laws are discussed later in this chapter.

If companies can sue for libel, what about nonprofit associations and other unincorporated organizations? They, too, may sue for libel in some states, but the rule on this point varies somewhat around the country.

And what about government agencies? On this question, the law does not vary: governments may not sue for libel anywhere. However, government officials may sue *as individuals* if their personal reputations are damaged by a libel.

Group Libel

What about a libel of a group of people? May the individuals sue? A long-recognized rule of law is that individuals may sue for libel when a group to which they belong has been defamed, but only if one of two conditions is met: (1) the group must be small enough that the libel affects the reputations of the individual members; or (2) the libelous statement must refer particularly to the individual who is suing.

A libel of a five-member city council could very well hurt the reputations of all the individual members. But what about a libel directed against a big organization, such as the United States Army? Would it be legally safe to say, "all soldiers are stupid"?

The courts settled that sort of group libel question long ago. No individual may sue for libel when the libelous statement is directed toward such a large group. The cutoff seems to be somewhere between five and 100 people, depending on which court you listen to. A court once allowed individual football players to sue when the University of Oklahoma football team was libeled. But other courts have refused to allow individuals to sue when groups considerably smaller than a college football team were libeled. In general, the bigger the group is, the less the chance an individual may be able to sue for libel.

To summarize: any living individual may sue if he or she is libeled, as may a corporation. Unincorporated organizations may sue in some states but not in others. Government agencies may not sue for libel, although government officials may sue if they are personally libeled. Individuals may sue for libel if they belong to a sufficiently small group that has been libeled.

In analyzing an item for possible libel, the next step after you decide there is a potential plaintiff is to check off the elements of libel and see if all are present. If so, then you should check off the defenses and see if any will protect you. That kind of analysis requires a more detailed summary of the elements of libel and the defenses.

THE ELEMENTS OF LIBEL

Defamation

Of the various elements of a libel case, the one that is sometimes the hardest to remember is the most obvious: the requirement that a statement actually be libelous (i.e., defamatory). Without defamation there is no libel, so the first step in analyzing a statement for potential libel is to decide whether there really is a defamation.

Over the years the courts have recognized a wide variety of statements as defamatory, dividing them into two categories: libel *per se* and libel *per quod*. Libel per se is the classic kind of defamation where the words themselves will hurt a person's reputation. Words such as "murderer," "rapist," "racist" and "extortionist" are obvious examples, but there are thousands of others. Any word or phrase is likely to be libelous if it falsely accuses a person of a heinous crime, public or private immorality, insanity or infection by some loathsome disease (e.g., AIDS), or professional incompetence. Even words that don't fall into any of these categories may be ruled libelous if they cause other people to shun and avoid the person.

When the words themselves communicate the defamation with no additional explanation necessary (as the words would in the examples just cited), you have libel per se. But when, on the other hand, it is not immediately apparent that the words are libelous, or when one must know additional facts to understand that there is a defamation, it is called libel per quod.

A classic example of libel per quod arose in a case called *Fellows v. National Enquirer* (42 C.3d 234, 1986). The *Enquirer* reported that television director Arthur Fellows was "steady dating" a famous actress. That statement would not ordinarily be libelous--except for the fact that he had been married to someone else for many years. The paper didn't mention that he was married, and very few readers knew this additional fact that made the statement libelous per quod. If the *Enquirer* had said he was committing adultery, that would probably qualify as libel per se. But merely to say he was dating an actress without mentioning his marriage would only be libel per quod (unless the fact that he was married was widely known).

When Fellows sued, he presented evidence that he was not dating the famous actress or anyone else besides his wife, but he lost because he could not prove *special damages* (any provable monetary loss). Many states require a showing of special damages in libel per quod cases, whereas only general damages (pain and suffering or merely embarrassment due to the loss of reputation) are typically required in cases of libel per se. Fellows may have been embarrassed by the article in the *Enquirer*, but he didn't suffer any significant financial losses (if anything, the libelous story might have helped his career).

Nevertheless, the distinction between libel per se and libel per quod is becoming less important today. For many years, the courts generally ruled that libel per se was automatically actionable; that is, the plaintiff didn't even have to prove general damages. Instead, the courts would *presume* damages merely because a libelous statement had been published. But on the other hand, if it was only a matter of libel per quod, the plaintiff had to prove special damages.

However, the *Gertz v. Welch* (418 U.S. 323) Supreme Court decision, a landmark 1974 decision that we will return to later, prohibited presumed damages in many libel suits against the media. The plaintiff today must be prepared to prove that he or she suffered at least general damages whether the defamatory statement was libel per se or libel per quod. The only time damages may be presumed in cases involving the media is when the plaintiff proves actual malice (i.e., that a falsehood was published knowingly or with reckless disregard for the truth). Some states have even eliminated presumed damages in non-media cases.

As a result, there is not usually much difference between libel per se and libel per quod today when the mass media are involved. If a statement is libelous (either on its face or only because of unique circumstances in the context of the statement) the media may have to defend a libel suit, provided the victim of the libel can prove the rest of the elements of libel.

Several types of subject matter result in disproportionate numbers of libel suits. For instance, the reporting of crime news has probably produced more libel suits than any other kind of journalism. In the American system of justice, a person is presumed innocent until proven guilty: stories that label people as "rapists" or "murderers" before they are convicted by a court are particularly dangerous. The best way to avoid lawsuits is to be as accurate and specific as possible in reporting the news. If someone has been detained for questioning in connection with a certain crime, say that much and nothing more. If the person has been formally charged, report that but don't go beyond what the facts will support. If the person has been arraigned, indicted, bound over for trial, released on bail, or whatever, be careful to report only what has actually happened and no more. If the police are seeking someone for questioning, be wary of a story that identifies him as a suspect prematurely.

Several other areas of journalism also produce more than their share of libel suits. In recent years a number of libel suits have resulted from stories accusing someone of having "Mafia" or organized crime connections. Another dangerous area--because of the ease with which special damages can be proven--is any statement that reflects upon a professional person's competence. Professionals such as physicians, psychologists and attorneys rely on public confidence for their continued livelihood to a greater extent than most other persons. Should the local paper publish a story questioning a doctor's or lawyer's integrity or competence and his/her business thereafter declines, special damages can often be proven. A false or misleading statement (or even an innuendo) about a professional person invites a libel suit.

Those seeking public office are another group of people who generate a lot of libel suits. Although the media now have strong constitutional safeguards when sued by a public official or public figure, public officials are frequently inclined to file libel suits as a means of saving face if nothing else. Even if there is little chance that the politician will ultimately win in court, the cost of defending a libel suit may force some publishers and broadcasters to think twice about carrying a story that reflects upon the character or competence of a politician.

Another problem area is gossip about the private lives of the famous. Some publications that deal in this sort of "news" as their basic commodity expect (and are prepared for) frequent libel suits as a result. Of course, many celebrities would prefer to let the matter drop and thus avoid the cost and additional publicity a libel suit would bring, rather than sue a supermarket scandal sheet. But those who do sue may have a good chance of success: tales about the private lives of celebrities that a publisher knew or should have known to be false are beyond the First Amendment's protection.

These, then, are some of the areas where defamatory statements are a special risk; of course there are others.

The Dissemination Element

Once there is a defamatory statement, the next element required for a libel suit is that it be published or broadcast. The rules in this area are quite liberal: any time someone besides the party making the defamatory statement and the victim sees or hears it, there has been a publication. Actually, the plaintiff in a lawsuit may have a tough time proving he or she suffered any damages if only a few people saw or heard the defamatory statement. Nevertheless, there have been cases where communicating a libel to only a handful of people resulted in a lawsuit for the perpetrator of the libel.

In most instances, of course, libel suits against the mass media result from statements that were actually published or broadcast; proving the dissemination element is not difficult in those cases.

It should be reiterated that everyone who furthers the dissemination of a libel can be sued. Even though the defamation first appeared in a letter to the editor, in a public speech, or even in a wire service dispatch, with few exceptions every publisher or broadcaster who further disseminates it can be sued (as can the originator of the libel or slander). Unless one of the defenses is available, the media can be sued for accurately reporting what someone else said. The speaker may be sued--but in many instances so may everyone who further disseminates the libelous statement. You need not be the originator of a libel to be sued for it.

The Identification Element

The third element the plaintiff must prove in a libel suit is identification: at least some of the readers or listeners must understand to whom the defamatory statement refers.

Where a person's name is used, there is usually little difficulty in proving identification. However, there are a great many ways a person may be identified other than by name. Any reference--no matter how oblique--is sufficient if the plaintiff can produce witnesses who testify convincingly that they understand the libelous statement to refer to him or her.

Perhaps the classic example of an oblique reference producing a libel suit is the situation that led to the famous *New York Times v. Sullivan* (376 U.S. 254) decision of the Supreme Court. As Chapter One indicated, the plaintiff in that case was a city commissioner in Montgomery, Alabama. What prompted the lawsuit was a *New York Times* ad that alleged police misconduct in the South (including Montgomery) but never mentioned Sullivan either by name or as a city commissioner. He was able to convince a jury that the criticism of the conduct of the local police injured his reputation because many people knew that one of his responsibilities as a city commissioner was to oversee the police. In reversing the judgment years later, the U.S. Supreme Court expressed doubt that the ad really referred to Sullivan. But in the meantime, the case had gone all the way up through the American legal system at a cost of thousands of dollars.

In short, don't expect to escape a libel suit by using a vague identification. If even a few of your readers understand whom you are talking about, the identification requirement for a libel suit has been met.

Another problem that leads to many libel suits is an identification so vague that it can refer to more than one person. A famous libel case more than half a century ago proved this point. Two lawyers in the Washington, D.C., area were named Harry Kennedy. One used his middle initials; the other did not. The one who normally used his middle initials was arrested for a serious crime. The *Washington Post* reported the fact, but omitted the middle initials. The other Harry Kennedy sued for libel, claiming that his reputation had been damaged, and he won (*Washington Post v. Kennedy*, 3 F.2d 207, 1924).

The moral of this story is an obvious one: when you publish or broadcast a defamatory but true statement, be sure to identify the person or persons involved as completely as possible, lest you inadvertently also identify an innocent party. This is one of the reasons it is good journalistic practice to identify people by full name, address and occupation whenever the story involves potential libel.

Some publishers go so far as to make a special note of who is *not* involved in a libelous story. When news broke of the 1978 Jonestown massacre, in which several hundred followers of the Rev. Jim Jones were murdered or committed suicide in a South American jungle, one of the persons implicated was a young man named Larry Layton. Thousands of miles away in Los Angeles another man named Larry Layton was a prominent lawyer. One Los Angeles newspaper published a separate news story to tell its readers that the Larry Layton involved in Jonestown was not the same person as the prominent local attorney--even though none of the news stories about Jonestown had in any way suggested otherwise.

Beyond the dangers inherent in publishing a story with libelous content when more than one person has the same name, there are pitfalls to avoid when two people have similar names, given that journalists do make errors. A notable example is the case of Ralph A. Behrend and R. Allen Behrendt, two medical doctors who had worked at the same hospital in Banning, Calif. The *Los Angeles Times* reported that Dr. Behrendt had been arrested for theft and using narcotics. Sure enough, it was really Dr. Behrend who was arrested--and Dr. Behrendt had a great libel suit against the *Times* as a result of this copy desk error (*Behrendt v. Times Mirror Co.*, 30 C.A.2d 77, 1939).

If newspapers of the stature of the *Los Angeles Times* and the *Washington Post* have identification problems and face libel suits as a result, you can see why this sort of thing is a serious problem.

The Element of Fault

Until 1964, our summary of the things a plaintiff must prove to win a libel suit would have been basically complete at this point. However, in that year the U.S. Supreme Court handed down its landmark *New York Times v. Sullivan* decision. A decade later, the Supreme Court announced another very important libel decision, *Gertz v. Welch*. Both cases are discussed in depth in the section on Libel and the Constitution, but in the interest of offering a logical presentation of the elements of libel, their basic provisions are summarized here.

In *New York Times v. Sullivan*, the Supreme Court ruled that public officials who sue for libel or slander must prove *actual malice*, which the court defined as publishing a falsehood with knowledge of its falsity, or with *reckless disregard for the truth*. In the *Gertz* case, the Supreme Court extended this principle by ruling that in all libel cases involving matters of public concern, the plaintiff must prove some degree of *fault*. No longer would the media face libel suits under a legal doctrine called *strict liability*, a doctrine assuming that whenever a wrong occurs its perpetrator will be held strictly responsible (no matter whose fault it was). Without this protection, the Supreme Court ruled, the fear of libel suits would unduly inhibit the media in covering controversial stories that should be reported in a free society. Therefore, these safeguards were required to protect First Amendment freedoms.

In essence, the Supreme Court in the *Gertz* case set up two levels of fault for the media: *negligence* and *actual malice*. The court said the states could not allow libel suits by public figures and public officials unless they could prove actual malice, something the court had already said in *New York Times v. Sullivan* and several other cases before *Gertz*. But the court also said (for the first time) that private citizens as well as public figures had to prove some fault on the part of the media to win libel cases. The court ruled that the states could allow private citizens to sue by showing a lower level of fault than actual malice, perhaps just negligence. Alternately, any state that wished to do so could also impose the tough actual malice requirement on private citizens as well as public figures who sue the media for libel. The *Gertz* case raised two legal problems:

1. What is negligence, and how does it differ from actual malice?
2. Who is a public figure, and who is a private person?

Negligence is a term that has a long legal history in other kinds of tort actions, but it had not previously been used in libel cases. It refers to a party's failure to do something that he has a duty to do, and that a reasonable person would do. In libel cases, it has come to mean failing to adhere to the standards of good journalism by doing such things as checking the facts. Courts in several states have ruled that private persons must prove something more than negligence--but less then actual malice--in most libel cases against the media.

Malice is another old legal term, but the Supreme Court gave it a special meaning in connection with libel suits in *New York Times v. Sullivan* by saying that it meant publishing a falsehood knowingly or with reckless disregard for the truth. "Reckless disregard" generally means publishing a false story when you strongly suspect it to be false--or should entertain such suspicions. That is very hard to prove in a libel case.

Since it is harder to prove actual malice than it is to prove negligence, the *Gertz* decision made it important to determine who is a private person (and therefore required to prove only negligence in most states) and who is a public figure (and required to prove actual malice).

Why should it be harder for public figures to win libel cases? The court's rationale for this approach was twofold. First, public officials and public figures have much greater access to the media to reply to libelous charges than do private persons. Second, those who place themselves in the limelight have to expect some adverse publicity, while private persons should not be unduly subjected to publicity they do not seek.

Because winning a libel suit is usually much easier for a private person than a public figure, almost everyone who files a libel suit wants to be classified as a private person. The media, of course, want most plaintiffs classified as public figures. Several Supreme Court decisions since *Gertz* have helped to clarify who is and is not a public figure for libel purposes.

Proving Damages

Another way in which the Supreme Court's *Gertz* decision changed libel law was that, as mentioned earlier, it abolished what were called "presumed" damages except in those cases where the plaintiff was able to prove actual malice.

Under the old presumed damage rules, many states allowed plaintiffs in libel suits to simply skip the difficult matter of proving that they were really injured by the libelous publication or broadcast. If there was a libel, the courts would simply presume there were damages, without any proof.

The Supreme Court's *Gertz* decision changed all that. Now all plaintiffs who cannot prove the media guilty of actual malice--even private persons--must prove damages to win their cases. Plaintiffs can win special damages by proving their out-of-pocket losses, of course. But in addition, the Supreme Court ruled that plaintiffs may also collect general damages for such intangibles as embarrassment and loss of reputation. Obviously, no dollar amount can be placed on such losses, but if the plaintiff can prove he or she was injured, the court (i.e., the judge or a jury) may then decide how many dollars the plaintiff should be given as compensation.

How is this different from presumed damages? It's subtle, but the difference is this: under the old presumed damages doctrine, plaintiffs didn't even have to offer any proof of their loss of reputation in the community. The court would just assume the bad publicity must have had a bad effect. Now plaintiffs must prove their reputations were damaged. How can this be done? For example, a plaintiff may bring in witnesses to testify about the effect the defamatory statement had on his or her reputation. Often plaintiffs themselves testify that their former friends shunned them after a libel occurred.

In the *Gertz* decision, the Supreme Court went a step further in placing limits on damages in libel suits: it also held that punitive damages should not be awarded--even to private persons--without proof of actual malice (i.e., knowing or reckless publication of a falsehood) by the media. Previously, the courts in some states allowed punitive damage awards (which can involve huge amounts of money) on proof of a different sort of malice. That kind of malice involved showing that the publisher or broadcaster harbored ill will or evil intentions toward the plaintiff. Under that rule, a publisher could face a massive punitive damage award without being guilty of actual malice as the Supreme Court had defined the term for libel cases.

As indicated earlier, punitive damage awards by no means disappeared in libel cases since the *Gertz* decision, but at least all plaintiffs now must prove actual malice under the new definition to win punitive damages.

LIBEL DEFENSES

In analyzing a given news item (or advertisement, press release or whatever) for libel, the next step after determining if the elements are present is to decide whether any of the recognized libel defenses apply. At this point, however, the analysis must be approached a little differently. In order to win a libel case, the plaintiff must convince the court that the elements of libel are present; that is not the defendant's task. The plaintiff bears the *burden of proof* in that part of the case. But when it comes to building an affirmative defense against a libel suit, it's often the other way around: the defense bears the burden of proof. Thus, in many cases it isn't enough for publishers or broadcasters to believe they have a libel defense: they may have to prove it under a court's rules of evidence.

That can be a problem. The rules of evidence make it difficult to prove many things that are discovered through investigative journalism. A reporter may be absolutely convinced of the correctness of a story: the sources may be completely reliable and the reporter may have extensively double-checked the facts. But that doesn't mean the facts can be proven in court. For example, under a court's rules of evidence, hearsay (statements made by one person to another, with the second person testifying about what he was told) is often inadmissible. A good deal of the information a reporter gathers would be considered hearsay.

Another problem arises when journalists promise to keep the identities of sources confidential. Many important stories could not be developed without the use of such sources, but in a libel suit a journalist may have to choose between revealing his sources and losing the case. A judge won't take his word that the source exists; the source may have to be identified during the discovery process, or may even have to testify. If the source cannot be produced without compromising journalistic ethics, the case may be forfeited.

With these problems in mind, you should check off the defenses that might apply to a potentially libelous item. Only if there is a defense--and it could be proved in court--should the item be considered safe. There may be times when it is necessary to take a chance and publish an important story without the certainty that it could be defended in court, but the decision to gamble in that way should only be made intelligently, after calculating the risks.

Truth

The oldest of all libel defenses--and certainly the most obvious--is truth (sometimes called *justification*). Since the early days of American independence, courts have been allowing publishers to prove the truth of what they printed as a means of defending against civil libel suits.

For many years, there was a catch: in some states the proof of truth had to be accompanied by proof that the publisher's motives were not improper. For instance, a publisher sometimes could be sued for engaging in character assassination of an enemy (often a rival publisher), even if all of the charges were true.

And, of course, there was the additional catch that only those truthful facts that could be proved under a court's rules of evidence would be considered true in deciding the case. As just suggested, that has been a serious problem for journalists.

However, the U.S. Supreme Court has lately revised the rules on truth as a libel defense, particularly by shifting the burden of proof from the media to the plaintiff. As indicated earlier, in its *Gertz* decision the Supreme Court said it was not constitutionally permissible to allow a libel judgment against the mass media unless the plaintiff could prove fault, with fault meaning the publication of a false statement of fact due to negligence or malice.

The Supreme Court reinforced this in a 1986 decision, *Philadelphia Newspapers v. Hepps* (475 U.S. 767). In that case, the *Philadelphia Inquirer* had published several articles linking beverage distributor Maurice Hepps to organized crime. When he sued for libel, he was unable to prove the charges false, but neither could the reporters fully document the charges in order to prove them true.

Pointing out that conclusively proving that type of charge can be very difficult, the Supreme Court said that to prevent self-censorship of important stories by journalists, those who sue for libel must now bear the burden of proving the story false, at least when issues of public concern are involved. In such cases, no state may require the media to prove that a statement is true; the person suing must prove that it is false.

Explaining the new ruling, Justice Sandra Day O'Connor wrote for the majority:

> To ensure that true speech on matters of public concern is not deterred, we hold that the common-law presumption that defamatory speech is false cannot stand when a plaintiff seeks damages against a media defendant for speech of public concern.... There will always be instances when the fact-finding process will be unable to resolve conclusively whether the speech is true or false. It is in those instances that the burden of proof is dispositive.

Thus, the rule today is that to win a libel case resulting from the media's coverage of any issue of public concern, the plaintiff always bears the burden of proving that the libelous statement is false. But what about libel cases not involving issues of public concern? The Supreme Court left that up to the states: the states are constitutionally required to place the burden of proof on plaintiffs only in cases involving public issues. However, some states have completely abandoned the common law rule that presumed all libelous statements to be false and now require all plaintiffs to prove the falsity of every allegedly libelous statement. Also, in most cases the old requirement of truth plus good intentions is no longer valid. As a general rule, there can be no successful libel suit against the media unless the material is proven false--period. If it cannot be proven false, the publisher's motives no longer matter in most libel suits.

If the publisher's motives are now irrelevant when a publication is truthful, they are very relevant if a publication turns out to be false. In that circumstance, the key issue may be whether the publisher or broadcaster knew or should have known that the libelous statement was false. If so, a court may find that there was actual malice, which means that even a public official or public figure may win a libel case against the media. And in cases involving private persons rather than public figures, publishing a false statement negligently but unknowingly--because of sloppy fact-checking--may be enough to lose a libel suit.

Also, in flatly stating that the First Amendment does not permit libel judgments against the media for truthful publications about public issues, we should emphasize that libel is not the only potential legal problem for the mass media. For example, a publisher or broadcaster may also be sued for invasion of privacy. As Chapter Five explains, truth is not always a defense in a privacy suit. The fact that a statement is truthful may preclude a successful libel suit, but not necessarily an invasion of privacy lawsuit.

Privilege

The legal concept of *privilege* is an old one, and it creates a strong libel defense for the media.

A privilege is an immunity from legal liability, and the term is used in a variety of legal contexts. Chapter Eight discusses *reporter's privilege,* the concept that a journalist should be exempt from being forced to testify about his sources of information and unpublished notes. Other privileges excuse lawyers and doctors from testifying about much of what their clients and patients tell them in confidence.

As the term is used in libel and slander law, privilege means an immunity from a lawsuit. The concept was recognized in Article I, Section 6 of the U.S. Constitution, which created an absolute privilege for members of Congress engaged in debates on the floor of Congress. They may never be sued for anything they say there; they have absolute freedom of speech during Congressional debates.

Over the years, this concept of absolute privilege has been broadened to encompass many other government officials, government proceedings and government documents. Today, there is a broad privilege for local, state and national legislative bodies, and it extends to major officials in the executive branch of government and to court proceedings. When performing their official duties, many government officials now have an absolute privilege; they cannot be sued for libel or slander as a result of what they do while conducting their official duties.

As this privilege for government officials was developing, the courts also recognized that in a democracy the news media need to be free to report to the public on what their elected leaders are doing and saying. This led to the concept of *qualified privilege*, sometimes called *conditional privilege*, or the *fair reports privilege*.

Qualified privilege is a libel defense that allows the media to report on government proceedings and records without fear of a libel suit, provided they give a fair and accurate account. A biased account or one that pulls a libelous quote out of context may not be protected by the qualified privilege defense. However, this defense is broad enough to allow the media to publish many stories based on government documents or statements by government officials--without worrying about whether the statements themselves are true. If a charge of wrongdoing is contained in a government document such as a court record, for example, the media may publish it even if it later turns out to be false. Nevertheless, this defense raises at least two major legal questions:

1. What officials and records are within its scope?
2. Under what circumstances does it apply--when are officials conducting official business, and when are they doing something else?

It would take a detailed state-by-state summary to describe which officials and what records are covered by the qualified privilege defense, but some general rules have developed over the years. First of all, this defense clearly applies to official legislative proceedings from the local level to Congress, but not necessarily to informal and unofficial functions. What a local government official says during a meeting of a city council or commission is privileged, but what the same official says at a service club meeting or a campaign appearance (or writes in a press release, as will be explained shortly) may sometimes be a different matter.

In the executive branch of government, most states apply the privilege to the official conduct of senior elected officials, but not necessarily to lesser officials or appointees. The state attorney general's remarks on an official occasion may be privileged, for example, but not necessarily the statements of his deputies. In general, the less official the occasion and the lower the status of the person making the statement, the less likely it is to be privileged. However, many courts recognize the privilege defense even in situations involving unofficial public events where matters of public concern are discussed. On the other hand, in some states the courts are moving in the opposite direction, declining to extend the privilege defense beyond government officials. In New York, for instance, the Court of Appeals has held that an allegedly libelous statement by a private citizen at a New York City Community Board meeting is *not* privileged (*600 West 115th Street Corp. v. Von Gutfeld*, 80 N.Y.2d 130, 1992).

In the judiciary, the privilege applies to public court proceedings and official records. It may not apply to proceedings and records that are not open to the

128 Libel and Slander

public, however. If a particular type of proceeding is routinely closed to the public (as divorce and juvenile proceedings are in some states), the reporter who surreptitiously covers such a proceeding or publishes information taken from the secret records of the proceeding may not be protected by the privilege defense. Also particularly dangerous are false charges appearing in non-public documents that are "leaked" to the press.

Even if a document is obtained from court files that are open to the public, there are pitfalls for journalists. The *Pittsburgh Post-Gazette* had to pay nearly $3 million in damages and interest for publishing information that was obtained from a deposition in an old lawsuit in the case of *DiSalle v. P.G. Publishing Co.* (544 A.2d 1345, 1988). The *Post-Gazette* published a story saying an attorney who later became a judge had helped prepare a false will as a favor to a woman with whom he was having an affair. The accusation was made--or at least implied--in a deposition (a sworn pretrial statement) by the woman's brother, who was then challenging the validity of the will. The story was published *after* a court had ruled that the will was *not* fraudulent. The U.S. Supreme Court declined to hear the newspaper's appeal, thus leaving intact a Pennsylvania court's ruling that the newspaper acted with actual malice in publishing the story.

Another problem in reporting court news involves documents that have been filed but have not yet received any review by a judge. A number of states recognize a rule that court documents are not privileged (even though they may be available to the public) until they are in some way acted upon by a judge.

One of the most serious privilege problems involves reporting the police beat. Law enforcement officials sometimes let journalists see police files that are not public records. A story based on such reports may not be protected by the qualified privilege defense: if the police privately suspect someone of a crime and they're wrong (i.e., guilt isn't proven in court), there is a danger of libel. Beware of undocumented charges leveled against a potential suspect, charges that may never be substantiated or placed in a public record. Stories about a person's arrest and booking are almost always privileged; stories quoting police hunches usually are not.

This is not to suggest that journalists should never report the progress of a law enforcement investigation aimed at someone suspected of a serious crime until charges are formally filed or an arrest is made. There are occasions when such a story is important news. At times, it may be necessary to report information that will not be protected by the qualified privilege defense. But when that step is taken, it should be done with a full awareness of the potential for libel that may exist. At that point, the precise wording of the story may be crucial. To qualify a story by saying someone is only an "alleged" murderer probably will not help if he has not been charged with the crime, but to say he was "detained for questioning in connection with" a crime may--if that is really what has happened.

Equally troubling is the problem of government officials who engage in activities beyond the scope of their official duties. A 1979 U.S. Supreme Court decision provided a classic example of a United States senator engaged in a thoroughly newsworthy activity in which he was not--the court ruled--protected by privilege. The case, *Hutchinson v. Proxmire* (443 U.S. 11), involved the "Golden Fleece of the

Month Awards," presented to various individuals and organizations by Sen. William Proxmire (D-Wis) because he felt they were wasting the taxpayers' money in a conspicuous way.

One of the winners of this tongue-in-cheek award was Dr. Ronald Hutchinson, a mental health researcher who had received nearly a half million dollars in government grants to study such things as the teeth-clenching habits of monkeys under stress. Dr. Hutchinson sued, claiming this satirical award damaged his professional reputation. Inasmuch as Senator Proxmire regularly issued press releases publicizing his selections for the "Golden Fleece" award, Hutchinson was able to show the elements of libel, including a publication beyond the limits of Proxmire's absolute privilege as a senator. The Supreme Court said this privilege covered the senator's remarks in the *Congressional Record* but didn't cover the press release even though it was almost a verbatim copy of those remarks.

This Supreme Court decision is mainly remembered for its ruling that Hutchinson was not a public figure, and thus did not need to prove actual malice. That aspect of the decision will be discussed later. But the Supreme Court also ruled that the privilege defense did not protect Proxmire. The senator had gone beyond his official capacity in issuing a press release, even if it said the same thing he had said on the floor of Congress.

If a U.S. senator who pokes fun at what he considers wasteful government spending is not protected by the privilege defense, it should be apparent that this libel defense has its limitations. However, it should be noted that the libel suit was against the senator, and not against the media that reported the award. Probably no state would entertain (nor would the First Amendment allow) a libel suit against a news medium that accurately reported the contents of the Congressional speech in which Proxmire announced the award. The senator's mistake was republishing his own remarks off the floor of Congress.

The *Proxmire* decision troubled many journalists, because the "golden fleece" awards were not only newsworthy but also dealt with a matter of great public concern (wasteful government spending). For better or worse, the Supreme Court chose to restrict the scope of the constitutional absolute privilege of members of Congress. But that had little effect on the qualified privilege of the media to report on issues of public concern; that privilege has been expanding in recent years. Nor did it affect the right of other public officials to issue press releases: at least two other court decisions have extended public officials' common law privilege to their press releases. All *Proxmire* really did was to limit the constitutional privilege of those who serve in Congress.

As a means of protecting the media when they fairly and accurately report public records and public proceedings, qualified privilege represents an important safeguard. When a public official engages in slander during a government proceeding, or when an official public document carries a libelous charge, the privilege defense enables the media to report this newsworthy item to the public.

The breadth of the privilege defense was illustrated by a 1991 federal appeals court decision upholding the *National Enquirer*'s right to reveal that entertainer Engelbert Humperdinck had been accused of having the AIDS virus--even though the newspaper staff was told the charge was false. In *Dorsey v. National Enquirer*

(952 F.2d 250), the court reaffirmed that the privilege defense covered a court document filed by a woman who had a daughter by Arnold Dorsey (Humperdinck's real name), and who was seeking additional support payments on the ground that Dorsey was HIV positive. The *Enquirer* said in a page-one headline, "Mother of His Child Claims in Court... Engelbert has AIDS virus." A photo caption contained Humperdinck's denial that he was HIV positive.

Reporting false charges that may appear in a public record does, of course, raise very serious ethical questions. However, from a legal standpoint it is usually permissible--as long as the report is a fair and accurate account of the record. That kind of reporting may invite a lawsuit, but as the *Dorsey* case illustrates, the privilege defense generally applies.

In addition to the qualified privilege defense, there is one circumstance under which the mass media are afforded an absolute privilege defense. Under Section 315 of the Communications Act, broadcasters are required to provide equal opportunities for air time to all candidates for a given public office. And the act denies the broadcaster any control over the content of a candidate's remarks made on the air under this provision. Thus, the broadcaster has no way to prevent a politician from defaming someone during such a broadcast. In fact, the rhetoric of a political campaign invites defamation.

In a 1959 decision (*Farmers Educational and Cooperative Union v. WDAY*, 360 U.S. 525), the U.S. Supreme Court afforded broadcasters an absolute immunity from libel and slander suits under these circumstances. Since they are forbidden to censor or otherwise control the content of political speeches required under Section 315, broadcasters are powerless to prevent a defamation and should not be held accountable if one occurs, the court ruled.

Some states carry this logic a step further: they exempt broadcasters from liability for defamatory statements made as a part of network programming they are not allowed to edit locally (although the network remains liable).

Fair Comment and Criticism

Another of the classic common law libel defenses is called *fair comment*. Although it has been partially superseded by the constitutional protection for the media created by the Supreme Court in recent years, it remains important in many states and should be described here.

The fair comment defense protects expressions of *opinion* about the public performances of persons such as entertainers and politicians who voluntarily place themselves before the public. The courts recognized long ago that reviewing public figures' performances is a legitimate function of the press and should be protected, even if it sometimes means excusing defamation.

As this defense was expanded by the courts, it came to protect even hostile expressions of opinion as long as two qualifications were met: the expression had to be based on facts that were correct and accurate, and it had to be a critique of the person's public performance rather than his or her private life.

In recent years, many states have eliminated these requirements, extending libel protection to all expressions of opinion that are clearly labeled as such, while allowing libel suits only for items that could be taken to be false statements of fact. This trend was greatly encouraged by the majority opinion in the Supreme Court's *Gertz* decision, which said:

> Under the First Amendment there is no such thing as a false idea. However pernicious an opinion may seem, we depend for its correction not on the conscience of judges and juries but on the competition of other ideas.

That language seemed to rule out libel suits for expressions of opinion. However, in 1990 the Supreme Court added an important qualification to this in the case of *Milkovich v. Lorain Journal Co.* (497 U.S. 1). In *Milkovich*, the court allowed a high school wrestling coach to sue a sports columnist who accused him of lying under oath during an investigation of a melee that broke out at a campus wrestling match. A lower court ruled that the entire sports column was an expression of opinion and therefore not libelous.

The Supreme Court held that expressions of opinion enjoy no *separate* Constitutional protection in libel suits. However, the court reaffirmed its holding in *Philadelphia Newspapers v. Hepps* (475 U.S. 767, 1975), a case that is discussed more fully later. The *Hepps* case held that libel plaintiffs must prove the falsity of any allegedly libelous statement, at least in cases involving matters of public concern. And because opinions by their nature cannot be proven true or false, expressions of opinion cannot be the basis for a successful libel suit. However, in *Milkovich* there was more than an expression of opinion: there were potentially false factual allegations. For example, to accuse a coach of lying under oath is to accuse him of a crime. This was a column of opinion--but it also contained factual allegations that might be proven false. The Supreme Court ruled that the states may allow libel suits in such situations. Chief Justice William Rehnquist, writing for the court, used an example to explain the difference between fact and opinion:

> (U)nlike the statement, 'In my opinion Mayor Jones is a liar,' the statement, 'in my opinion Mayor Jones shows his abysmal ignorance by accepting the teaching of Marx and Lenin,' would not be actionable.

While a pure expression of opinion cannot be the basis for a libel suit, an opinion that carries a false factual implication (like the charge that "Mayor Jones is a liar") is not constitutionally protected. If the writer or speaker cannot prove that Mayor Jones actually told a lie on at least one specific occasion, the statement may be an actionable libel, not a protected expression of opinion. To say that someone told a lie is a factual allegation that may be proved or disproved; to say a person is "abysmally ignorant" is just someone's opinion.

The distinction between a fact and an opinion is often a very subtle one. As a result, it may be necessary to have a full libel trial in which a jury determines whether a given statement is a protected expression of opinion or a false and libelous factual allegation.

Nevertheless, the fair comment defense offers excellent protection for those who disseminate pure opinions. Fair comment often protects the media from liability even for vitriolic political rhetoric, social commentary and criticism of the arts. This defense allows the media to use intemperate language and get away with it, as long as a statement is clearly an expression of opinion. It has been said that the fair comment defense protects *rhetorical hyperbole*. For instance, during a single year various courts allowed the media to: accuse a church of "Nazi-style anti-Semitism," call someone the "worst" sports announcer in town, and refer to a newspaper publisher as a "near-Neanderthal" whose paper is published "by paranoids for paranoids." (See *Holy Spirit Assn. v. Sequoia Elsevier*, 426 N.Y.S.2d 759, 1980; *Myers v. Boston Magazine*, 403 N.E.2d 376, 1980; and *Loeb v. New Times*, 497 F.Supp. 85, 1980.)

Two federal court decisions may help to explain the difference between a statement of fact (which could lead to a successful libel suit if false) and an expression of opinion (which could not). In a 1985 case, *Ollman v. Evans* (750 F.2d 970), and a 1986 case, *Janklow v. Newsweek* (788 F.2d 1300), two different federal circuit courts faced the problem of separating fact from opinion.

The first case arose when syndicated columnists Rowland Evans and Robert Novak accused Bertell Ollman, a political science professor at New York University, of not only being an avowed Marxist but also of wanting to use his teaching position as a platform for political indoctrination. He sued the columnists for libel.

In the second case, William Janklow, the governor of South Dakota, was described in a *Newsweek* magazine article as having had a long-running feud with Native American activist Dennis Banks. *Newsweek* implied that as South Dakota's attorney general, Janklow had prosecuted Banks to get revenge after Banks falsely accused him of raping an Indian girl. Janklow sued *Newsweek* for libel.

In both cases, the federal courts had to distinguish facts from opinion. In both, the courts found the statements to be opinions and thus not the proper basis for a libel suit. Both decisions are especially significant because they are *en banc* decisions--rulings by all judges of the particular circuit court instead of the usual panel of three judges.

Adapting and slightly modifying the guidelines developed in the *Ollman* case, the *Janklow* decision listed the following four criteria to be used in determining whether a statement is a potentially libelous fact or a protected expression of opinion:

1. The precision and specificity of the disputed statement. Calling someone a "fascist" is indefinite and therefore an opinion; charging someone with a specific wrongful act would be a statement of fact.
2. The verifiability of the statement. "If a statement cannot plausibly be verified, it cannot be seen as 'fact,'" the court said.
3. The literary context in which the statement is made. A court may look at the type of publication, its style of writing and intended audience to determine whether a statement is fact or opinion.
4. The "public context" of the statement. A statement made in "a public, political arena" or which "implicates core values of the First Amendment" is much more likely to be an expression of opinion than a statement of

fact.

Concluding its analysis of the context of the *Newsweek* article, the *Janklow* ruling says:

> Here we have criticism of the conduct of a state attorney general who now serves as governor, as well as questions about the actions of three other governors of two other states, all involving an issue of national importance, the treatment of Indian people. Few other discussions of public concern could make a greater claim for First Amendment protection.

While this four-part test may not be accepted by all courts dealing with fact-or-opinion questions, it has now been adopted by several federal circuit courts. It will probably be used elsewhere.

In 1994, a prominent federal court caused near panic among book reviewers and others who write critical reviews by holding that a book reviewer could be sued for expressing the opinion that a book contains "too much sloppy journalism." However, the court changed its mind and reversed itself a few months later, causing widespread relief among reviewers. In *Moldea v. New York Times Co.* (15 F.3d 1137, and 22 F.3d 310, 1994), the U.S. Court of Appeals in Washington, D.C. issued this surprising pair of opinions.

The case began when *New York Times* sports writer Gerald Eskenazi did a review of *Interference: How Organized Crime Influences Professional Football*, a book by Dan E. Moldea. The review, published in the New York Times Book Review, offered a number of examples from Moldea's book to back up the charge that it contained "sloppy journalism."

Moldea sued for libel, charging that the *New York Times* book review destroyed his career as an author. A trial court dismissed the lawsuit almost immediately and Moldea appealed. At first, the appellate court reinstated the lawsuit, but then the three-judge panel that ruled on the case took the unusual step of reversing itself. In the second ruling, the court held that to escape libel, a book reviewer's criticism must be "rationally supportable by reference to the actual text he or she is evaluating." In short, what a book review says about a book need not be more than a *supportable interpretation* of the book.

Had the earlier decision stood, it could have severely curtailed the freedom of book reviewers and other critical journalists to express negative views about the books or performances they review. But in its second ruling, the appellate court made it clear that in the context of a book review, a charge such as "sloppy journalism" is not libelous as long as it is backed up with valid examples from the book.

To summarize the fact-versus-opinion distinction, a false charge that someone committed a crime is likely to be ruled a libelous statement of fact, even if it appears on an "opinion" page of a newspaper, in a direct quote or in a letter to the editor or an advertisement. (However, if the charge is made by a public official or during a government proceeding, the *privilege* defense may apply even though the charge is a false statement of fact and not a protected expression of opinion).

On the other hand, a clearly labeled column or editorial accusing a public figure of incompetence is likely to be ruled an opinion, protected by the fair comment defense. But between the extremes of falsely calling someone a murderer (almost certainly a statement of fact) and accusing a celebrity of lacking talent or accusing a politician of incompetence (which would usually qualify as an expression of opinion), there is a large gray area. In this ill-defined middle ground between fact and opinion, the courts must often decide on a case-by-case basis whether a statement is fact or opinion. If anything, the gray area is a little bigger as a result of the Supreme Court's 1990 decision in the *Milkovich* case.

However, one thing has become clear about the *Milkovich* decision: most states are continuing to dismiss libel cases based on statements that are clearly expressions of opinion as opposed to verifiably true or false statements of fact. When the *Milkovich* case was decided, many journalists feared an avalanche of lawsuits by persons criticized in columns, reviews, editorials and op-ed pieces. Except where an opinion piece also contains an allegedly false factual statement, that has simply not happened. Even in Ohio, where the *Milkovich* case began, the state Supreme Court has extended broad protection to expressions of opinion under the state constitution (see *Vail v. Plain Dealer*, 649 N.E.2d 182, 1995).

In the years since the *Milkovich* decision, most courts have continued to interpret the fair comment defense liberally, extending broad protection to expressions of opinion. Perhaps a 1998 decision of the ninth circuit U.S. Court of Appeals illustrates the degree to which the courts are refusing to allow libel suits based on expressions of opinion. In *Dodds v. American Broadcasting Company* (145 F.3d 1053), the court dismissed a lawsuit filed by a judge after ABC's PrimeTime Live depicted him as incompetent. Writing for the court, Judge Stephen Reinhardt said, "part of our American heritage is the right of all citizens to express their views about politicians, officeholders and umpires, frequently in highly unfavorable terms."

"Indeed, were we to conclude otherwise, millions of citizens and hundreds of political pundits would currently be committing libelous and slanderous acts on a daily basis," Reinhardt wrote, adding that the First Amendment protects "statements of opinion concerning whether a person who holds high public office is fit for that office or is competent to serve... whether or not those statements are supportable, verifiable or based on facts or premises that are disclosed." In 1999, the U.S. Supreme Court declined to hear an appeal of this ruling.

These principles apply not only to "politicians, officeholders and umpires" but also to many other people who may be newsworthy, allowing the media to criticize them as well. For example, after the O.J. Simpson murder trial, *New York Post* columnist Andrea Peyser wrote that Johnnie Cochran, Simpson's lead attorney, "will say or do just about anything to win, typically at the expense of the truth."

Peyser also said Cochran was part of a team of "legal scoundrels" who "dazzled a Los Angeles jury into buying his fantasy tale of a citywide police conspiracy in order to set free a celebrity who slaughtered his ex-wife."

In 2000, a federal appellate court upheld a trial judge's decision to dismiss Cochran's libel suit. The court said Peyser was merely exercising her constitutionally protected right to criticize Cochran's defense strategy, not accusing him of unethical conduct, lying or anything else that would be actionable as a libel (*Cochran v. NYP Holdings, 210 F.3d 1036).

Minor Defenses

In addition to the generally recognized libel defenses, there are other defenses that have been recognized by some courts. Also, two purely technical defenses should be noted here.

Perhaps the most interesting of the less-recognized defenses is one called *neutral reportage*. It got its main impetus from a 1977 federal appellate court decision in the case of *Edwards v. National Audubon Society* (556 F.2d 113, 2d.cir. 1977). That case involved a *New York Times* story reporting a heated dispute between the National Audubon Society and a group of scientists the society had accused of being "paid to lie" by pesticide companies. The paper attempted to cover both sides on this controversy and was sued by some of the scientists for reporting the charge against them, even though the reporter attempted to present their side of the story too. The appellate court recognized a special libel defense for this situation, pointing out that the paper was attempting to be neutral in reporting both sides of a controversial issue.

Although the idea of a neutral reportage defense is highly appealing to those who believe the mass media should be able to cover all sides of a controversy without risking a libel suit, the concept has not been universally accepted by other courts. For instance, shortly after the *Edwards* decision another federal appellate court declined to follow the precedent and refused to recognize the defense in a seemingly similar situation. Some state courts (in Florida, for instance) have recognized neutral reportage, while others (in New York and Michigan, for example) have not. In Illinois, one appellate court recognized neutral reportage but another appellate court rejected the concept.

In 1998, the California Supreme Court rejected neutral reportage in a widely noted case where a tabloid, *The Globe*, republished charges made in an obscure book that a farmer who had once been a photojournalist was the real assassin of Sen. Robert F. Kennedy. The former photojournalist was covering the election-night celebration where Kennedy was killed, but none of the investigations of the assassination ever linked him to the crime. In rejecting neutral reportage as a libel defense in cases involving private persons such as this farmer, the California court held that it could be used by the media to escape liability for republishing known falsehoods about private persons who have little access to the media and therefore little opportunity to reply to the charges against them (*Khawar v. Globe Communications*, 19 C.4th 254). The U.S. Supreme Court later declined to hear an appeal of this decision.

In short, while neutral reportage has been accepted as a new libel defense in some jurisdictions, it has not yet gained the broad acceptance that many journalists hoped it would.

Another occasionally recognized defense is called *right of reply*. It should not be confused with the broader concept of a right of reply to mass media attacks, discussed in Chapter 13. In libel cases, it involves a situation in which two parties--often two publishers--have been exchanging libelous charges. Finally one sues the other, and the defendant responds by pointing out that he was merely replying in kind to a previous attack the plaintiff had directed against him. It has sometimes been accepted as a valid libel defense by state courts, but it is not generally recognized today.

Among the technical (as opposed to substantive) libel defenses, two should be mentioned here: consent and the statute of limitations. Where it can be proved that a plaintiff gave an actual consent to a libelous publication, he or she cannot thereafter sue for libel. If the consent was voluntarily and intelligently given, it precludes a libel suit. Likewise, where the statute of limitations (the time limit during which a law suit must be filed) has run, the defendant is entitled to an easy dismissal without the trouble and expense of a trial.

LIBEL AND THE FIRST AMENDMENT

The extent to which the U.S. Supreme Court has reshaped American libel law in recent years is probably best shown by the number of times we have already mentioned the Supreme Court in this chapter.

Until 1964 we could have concluded our discussion of libel law with almost no mention of the Supreme Court. For nearly 200 years of American jurisprudence, the nation's highest court took the position that civil libel suits were purely a state matter and none of its business. But in 1964 the historic *New York Times v. Sullivan* decision was handed down, establishing once and for all that there are constitutional limits to what the states may do in awarding libel judgments.

What prompted this landmark Supreme Court decision was a half-million-dollar libel judgment against the *New York Times*. In making this award, an Alabama jury was allowed to presume that a massive injury had occurred simply because it found the wording of an advertisement libelous to L. B. Sullivan, a Montgomery city commissioner. The ad never mentioned Sullivan, and in fact only a few copies of that issue of the *Times* were ever distributed in Sullivan's community.

What did the advertisement say to produce such a large libel judgment? It said, among other things, that the Montgomery police had taken certain actions against civil rights demonstrators that they in fact had not. We could devote several pages of this chapter to the charges contained in the ad and the means by which Sullivan's lawyers convinced a jury that the ad defamed him even though he wasn't mentioned. However, Chapter One discussed this case to illustrate court procedures, so we'll not repeat the details here. But Sullivan won at the trial level, and the Alabama Supreme Court affirmed the judgment in its full amount.

Meanwhile, other Montgomery public officials filed additional libel suits against the *New York Times*, seeking total damages of $3 million. The *Times* was going to pay dearly for publishing a pro-civil rights advertisement that contained some factual errors and then distributing a few dozen copies of the paper in Montgomery, Ala.

Had the U.S. Supreme Court not chosen to review the case--instead maintaining its long tradition of leaving civil libel law completely up to the states--the threat of censorship via libel suits would have been a serious one. The Supreme Court broke with tradition and agreed to hear the case precisely because lawsuits such as this one were a serious threat to First Amendment freedoms.

Writing for a unanimous court, Justice William Brennan ruled that the huge libel judgment against the *Times* could not stand--for three reasons. He said to allow such a judgment would in effect sanction a new form of government censorship of the press via civil libel suits. To avoid lawsuits by local officials in various communities to which the nation's major newspapers are mailed, the major papers would have to steer clear of controversial subjects. Moreover, Brennan wrote, the mass media need some "breathing space" in their handling of controversial issues--including some protection when errors inevitably occur during the "robust" debate of these issues.

Finally, Brennan pointed out that public officials voluntarily move into the public arena when they seek office, subjecting themselves to much more scrutiny than private citizens should have to face. Criticism is something they must expect. In return, public officials gain more access to the media to present their side of the story than a private citizen enjoys. Thus, public officials need less libel protection than other citizens.

Under this rationale, the Supreme Court ruled that public officials could no longer win libel judgments against the mass media unless they could prove *actual malice*:

> The constitutional guarantees require, we think, a federal rule that prohibits a public official from recovering damages for a defamatory falsehood relating to his official conduct unless he proves that a statement was made with 'actual malice'--that is, with knowledge that it was false or with reckless disregard of whether it was false or not.

This language is among the most important ever written on mass media law in America. If you remember any single concept from this discussion, you should remember that public officials must prove actual malice to win libel suits, and you should remember how actual malice is defined. First, actual malice means *publishing a falsehood*. Second, it means publishing that falsehood either with *knowledge* that it was false, or with *reckless disregard* for whether it was false or not.

Malice is a legal term that has other meanings in other contexts, often referring to bad intentions. But in libel law it was given a special meaning in the *New York Times v. Sullivan* decision.

When a landmark Supreme Court decision is handed down, there are often unanswered questions--issues that must be clarified by additional Supreme Court rulings. The *New York Times* case had exactly that result. First of all, what public officials are included in its coverage? Does it apply only to elected officials or does it also apply to public figures who hold no office? And does it apply to all public servants or just to certain prominent ones? And equally important, exactly what does "reckless disregard for the truth" mean?

Post-Sullivan Rulings

In the years that followed the *New York Times* decision, the Supreme Court attempted to resolve these ongoing questions by handing down a series of additional libel rulings. First, in a 1966 case (*Rosenblatt v. Baer*, 383 U.S. 75) the court said the actual malice requirement would apply to minor public officials. A. D. Rosenblatt, a New Hampshire newspaper columnist, had accused the former supervisor of a county skiing and recreation area of mishandling public funds. The Supreme Court said even a public employee of that rank would henceforth have to prove actual malice to win a libel suit. The "public official" designation would apply to all who have "substantial responsibility for... the conduct of governmental affairs," the court ruled. More recent rulings have cast doubts on the applicability of the actual malice requirement to minor public employees, but for the moment the rule was that almost anybody who was on the public payroll and made policy decisions would have to prove actual malice.

Then in 1967 the high court applied the actual malice rule to public figures who held no office and also offered guidance on the meaning of the "reckless disregard" concept in two cases it decided together, *Curtis Publishing Co. v. Butts* and *Associated Press v. Walker* (388 U.S. 130).

The *Curtis* case arose when the *Saturday Evening Post,* published by Curtis, carried an article entitled, "The Story of a College Football Fix." The article claimed that Wally Butts, athletic director at the University of Georgia, had given Alabama coach Paul "Bear" Bryant information in advance about Georgia's game plans for an upcoming football game between the two schools. The story was based on information provided by an insurance agent in Atlanta who said he had overheard a telephone conversation between Butts and Bryant through an electronic error.

Although there was no deadline pressure and the article was published some time after the game, the *Post* did not double-check the story with anyone knowledgeable about football to see whether the information the insurance man claimed he overheard would in fact have helped Alabama or hurt Georgia.

The *Walker* case differed in several respects. It resulted from an AP dispatch detailing the activities of former U.S. Army General Edwin Walker, who resigned his command and engaged in conservative political activities, often speaking out against school desegregation. Walker was present at the University of Mississippi during the initial desegregation of the campus. A group of whites attacked the federal marshals who were protecting the first black student enrolled at the university. Walker had addressed the crowd of whites. The AP dispatch, moved over the wires within minutes after the fast-breaking events occurred, said ex-General Walker led the charge of the whites.

Walker admitted being present and addressing the gathering of whites, but he claimed he had called for a peaceful protest and counseled against violence. He denied leading the charge.

Butts and Walker each won a libel judgment of about half a million dollars; both Curtis Publishing and the Associated Press appealed to the U.S. Supreme Court. The Supreme Court voted 5-4 to affirm Butts' libel judgment against the

Saturday Evening Post, but unanimously overruled Walker's judgment against the AP. The court took the occasion to compare the two situations as a way of illustrating what reckless disregard for the truth means.

But first, a majority of the Supreme Court justices agreed that both men were public figures and should be subject to the *New York Times v. Sullivan* rule, although neither was a public official at the time of the respective libel suits. Walker was no longer an officer in the U.S. Army, and Butts received his salary from the Georgia Athletic Association, a private corporation, not from the state.

However, both men were involved in issues "in which the public has a justified and important interest." Although the court was not unanimous in deciding that the *New York Times* rule as such should apply to public figures as well as public officials, the precedent has held up in the years since and is now settled law. Thus, both men had to show reckless disregard for the truth to win their libel suits.

Why, then, did Butts win while Walker lost? The Supreme Court pointed out that there was a big difference between the kind of reporting that went into the two stories. The AP was under intense deadline pressure and had no time to double-check its information; the *Post* was not. The AP had a reporter with a good reputation for accuracy on the scene; the *Post* relied on the uncorroborated statements of a non-journalist, a man who was in fact an ex-convict, and the magazine's staff never checked the story with anyone who had special expertise in football. Further, the conduct AP's reporter attributed to Walker was consistent with Walker's previous statements on the issue of school desegregation.

In short, because the Supreme Court found a substantial difference between the *Saturday Evening Post*'s reporting practices and AP's, the libel judgment against the *Post* was affirmed while the one against AP was reversed.

After the 1967 *Curtis* and *AP* rulings, the Supreme Court handed down several libel decisions that continued the trend toward protecting the media, almost to the point of abolishing libel as a legal hazard for journalists. Some of these decisions are considered to be relatively unimportant today, including *St. Amant v. Thompson* (390 U.S. 727), decided in 1968, and *Greenbelt Publishing Assn. v. Bresler* (398 U.S. 6), a 1970 case. *St. Amant* overruled a libel judgment where a series of false charges had not been fully investigated; the case is remembered mainly because the court said reckless disregard means something more than merely failing to investigate: it means there must be evidence the publisher "in fact entertained serious doubts as to the truth of his publication." *Greenbelt* disallowed a libel judgment where the word "blackmail"--traditionally a word that constitutes libel per se--had been used during spirited public debates before a city council. The court felt the word was not used in a sense that connoted actual malice: it was political rhetoric, not a statement of fact.

The Supreme Court continued its trend of reversing libel judgments against the media with three cases it handed down on the same day in early 1971, *Monitor Patriot Co. v. Roy* (401 U.S. 265), *Ocala Star-Banner v. Damron* (401 U.S. 295) and *Time Inc. v. Pape* (401 U.S. 279). The *Monitor-Patriot* case stemmed from a syndicated column that branded a candidate for the U.S. Senate as a "small time bootlegger" because of a conviction in the 1920s. The plaintiff contended the publisher was vulnerable to a libel judgment because the conviction involved his private life long ago and had nothing to do with his public performance. The Supreme Court ruled the actual malice requirement had not been met, and the libel case could not be sustained, to no one's surprise. After all, the accusation was basically true.

In *Ocala*, the Supreme Court overruled a libel judgment where a newspaper had confused two brothers, identifying a candidate for office as having been convicted of perjury when in fact it was his brother who had been convicted. The Supreme Court said there was no reckless disregard for the truth in this copy desk error. At the time, this seemed to free the media from liability when a public official or public figure is the victim of an accidental misidentification problem such as those discussed earlier in this chapter.

The *Time Inc. v. Pape* case involved a libel contained in a U.S. Commission on Civil Rights report, disseminated in a *Time* magazine article. *Time* had changed the reported information somewhat, but the Supreme Court found no reckless disregard for the truth in *Time*'s reporting of a statement charging a Chicago police officer with brutality--even though the story did not make it clear these were mere allegations. *Time*'s imprecise reporting was forgiven in large part because the report itself was ambiguous and subject to more than one interpretation.

The theme in all three of these 1971 cases seemed clear: the traditional rules of libel must give way when a public official is the plaintiff, lest the threat of libel suits unduly inhibit the reporting of public affairs.

Almost Abolishing Libel: The Rosenbloom Case

Moreover, later in 1971 the Supreme Court handed down a decision that was heralded by some as the ultimate victory for the mass media over the threat of libel: *Rosenbloom v. Metromedia* (403 U.S. 29). Although there was no majority opinion, the three-justice plurality opinion seemed to foreclose libel judgments against the media whenever the plaintiff was involved in an issue of public interest, no matter how private a citizen he or she might be.

George Rosenbloom, a Philadelphia magazine dealer, was arrested during a police campaign against obscenity, and he was called a "smut distributor" and a "girlie-book peddler" on radio station WIP, owned by Metromedia. He was never convicted, and a court granted an injunction ordering the police to leave him alone, since the books were not legally obscene. Rosenbloom sued the station and won a $275,000 libel judgment. An appellate court reversed the judgment, although Rosenbloom contended that he was a private citizen rather than a public figure and should not be required to prove actual malice to win a libel suit.

The U.S. Supreme Court agreed on a 5-3 vote that he should not win a libel judgment, but only three justices (Brennan, Burger and Blackmun) joined in the plurality opinion. Justices Black and White concurred in the result, but on a different rationale. What made *Rosenbloom* memorable was the sweep of the language in that plurality opinion. Justice Brennan, writing for the court, said the distinction between public officials and public figures on the one hand and private citizens on the other "makes no sense." He said that in the future the criterion for applying the actual malice requirement should be whether the plaintiff was involved in a matter of "public or general interest." Thus, the court seemed to be saying the media could bootstrap themselves out of libel suits by publicizing a private person's activities so as to generate public interest and then avoid a lawsuit because of that public interest.

After *Rosenbloom,* it seemed that virtually everyone whose name appeared in a newspaper or in a radio or television newscast was going to have to prove actual malice. And because proving actual malice turned out to be so difficult, it appeared for a time in the early 1970s that the media were at last virtually free from their most troubling legal problem, the libel suit.

Malice, Negligence and Gertz

However, three years later the hope that libel was being abolished vanished when the Supreme Court handed down its famous *Gertz v. Welch* decision in 1974. Much has already been said of this decision, which profoundly changed the law of libel in all 50 states--and thus laid the foundation for modern libel law when private persons are involved.

Elmer Gertz, a Chicago lawyer, represented the family of a young black man who had been killed by a Chicago police officer (the officer was later prosecuted for the act). With Gertz's help, the family was seeking civil damages in a lawsuit for *wrongful death* in the late 1960s.

An article appeared in *American Opinion,* the magazine of the ultraconservative John Birch Society, claiming that Gertz was part of a communist conspiracy to discredit law enforcement. Gertz was called a "communist-fronter" and a "Leninist." The article also falsely accused Gertz of various subversive activities.

Gertz sued Robert Welch Inc., publisher of *American Opinion,* and initially won a $50,000 jury verdict against Welch. However, the trial judge set aside the verdict and ruled that Gertz was a public figure who could not win a libel judgment without proving actual malice, something he had not proved during the original trial. Then the Supreme Court's *Rosenbloom* decision was announced, and an appellate court upheld the trial judge's decision that Gertz would have to prove actual malice to win a libel judgment against Welch. Gertz asked the Supreme Court to review the determination that he was a public figure.

In a narrow 5-4 decision that Justice Blackmun said he joined only because the country needed a clear-cut majority opinion on an issue as important as libel law, the Supreme Court backed away from the *Rosenbloom* decision and reinstated the distinction between private persons and public figures. The court said that Gertz, although he was a prominent Chicago lawyer, had done nothing to seek public figure status in this context. Thus, he should not be constitutionally required to prove actual malice to win a libel suit.

The court said the states should feel free to allow private persons such as Elmer Gertz to win libel suits against the media by proving a level of fault short of actual malice. However, in no case could the media be held on the "strict liability" (or "liability without fault") basis that had been the prevailing rule of law for at least 200 years. The court said the media had to be guilty of something beyond merely publishing a falsehood--there had to be some level of fault. Still, the Supreme Court didn't say every state had to allow private persons to prove mere negligence.

The court just said the states could allow this lesser standard of proof for private plaintiffs if they wished. But the court also said any state that wished to could still require private persons to prove actual malice.

As a result, in all 50 states public figures still have to prove actual malice. But in most states that is not required of private persons. Most states have accepted the Supreme Court's invitation and adopted rules under which private persons must prove only some level of negligence to win a libel case against the mass media. However, some state courts have chosen to require all libel plaintiffs--private persons as well as public figures--to prove actual malice in any libel case involving an *issue of public or general concern* (see, for instance, a 1999 Indiana Supreme Court decision that so held: *Journal-Gazette Co. v. Bandido's*, 712 N.E.2d 446).

Now both of these terms--actual malice and negligence--have special meanings in law. There is no way we can define them in a way that would be applicable in all states. We already indicated that negligence is a less serious breach of the standards of good journalism than reckless disregard for the truth. Negligence may well mean nothing more than publishing a falsehood as a result of sloppy reporting, or perhaps even because an innocent error slipped past the copy desk. Some states say it means failing to do the kind of checking a "reasonable man" would do under the circumstances.

In addition to its ruling that private persons could be allowed to sue for libel without proving actual malice, the *Gertz* case had an important effect on the award of damages in libel suits, as already mentioned. In the interest of continuity and completeness, that aspect of *Gertz* will be reiterated here.

The *Gertz* ruling required most private libel plaintiffs to prove at least general damages (sometimes called actual damages). The court said that in the absence of a showing of actual malice, there could be no punitive or presumed damages. Instead, plaintiffs who could only prove negligence and not actual malice could win only such damages as they could prove, although those damages would not be limited to just out-of-pocket losses (special damages).

As a result of these sweeping changes in American libel law, a new period of reassessment occurred, as the courts and legislatures tried to adapt their rules to the new constitutional boundaries. It quickly became apparent that the crucial issue in future libel suits would often be whether the plaintiff was a public figure or a private person. To assist in resolving this question, the *Gertz* ruling offered this observation about public figures and private persons:

> For the most part those who attain this status (public figure) have assumed roles of especial prominence in the affairs of society. Some occupy positions of such persuasive power and influence that they are deemed public figures for all purposes. More commonly, those classed as public figures have thrust themselves to the forefront of particular public controversies in order to influence the resolution of the issues involved. In either event, they invite attention and comment.

Thus, the Supreme Court was saying that many public figures are so classified only because they have thrust themselves into the *vortex* of a particular controversy.

These people might be called *vortex public figures,* and the courts were to look mainly to a libel plaintiff's own conduct in deciding whether the definition applied.

Despite this guidance, in the five years following the *Gertz* decision, the U.S. Supreme Court found it necessary to render three more rulings to clarify the issue of who is a public figure and who is not.

There is one ironic footnote to the *Gertz* case: after the landmark Supreme Court decision, Elmer Gertz patiently waited as his case meandered through pretrial procedures and finally went to trial again. Although the Supreme Court decision emphasized that non-public figures such as Gertz didn't necessarily have to prove actual malice, during the second trial a jury agreed that he *did* prove actual malice and awarded him $400,000 in damages (including $300,000 in punitive damages). The new judgment was affirmed by a federal appellate court in 1982--eight years after the Supreme Court decision and 14 years after the police shooting that led to the original libel (*Gertz v. Welch,* 680 F.2d 527).

Private Persons and Public Figures

In the aftermath of the *Gertz* decision, the Supreme Court repeatedly had to decide whether libel plaintiffs were public figures (who had to prove actual malice to win their lawsuits) or private persons (who could win by proving just negligence). The first of these cases, *Time Inc. v. Firestone* (424 U.S. 448, 1976), involved a divorce in a wealthy and socially prominent Florida family. Russell Firestone, an heir to the tire company fortune, sued his wife Mary Alice for divorce on the grounds of extreme cruelty and adultery, and the case received extensive publicity. When the divorce was granted after a trial in which there was considerable evidence of marital infidelity on both sides (enough evidence "to make Dr. Freud's hair curl," the judge said), *Time* magazine reported that one of the grounds for the divorce was adultery.

However, the judge was vague about the legal grounds for the divorce, and in fact an obscure provision of Florida law would have prohibited the award of alimony if adultery had been a ground for a divorce. Since Firestone had been granted alimony, her alleged adultery couldn't have been one of the legal grounds on which the divorce was granted. This rather obscure point of Florida law escaped the *Time* correspondent--but that could hardly be called publishing a falsehood with reckless disregard for the truth. (Was it even negligent reporting?)

Obviously, if Firestone were ruled a public figure she would have less chance to win a libel judgment. There was some evidence that she was indeed a public figure and even sought publicity: she held two press conferences to discuss the divorce with the media and subscribed to a press clipping service. The story was covered in no fewer than 45 articles in one local newspaper.

However, the Supreme Court ruled that she was *not* a public figure. She had not voluntarily thrust herself into any public controversy. The court said: "Dissolution of marriage through judicial proceedings is not the sort of 'public controversy' referred to in *Gertz,* even though the marital difficulties of extremely wealthy individuals may be of interest to some portion of the reading public." The court said Firestone had really done nothing more than she was required to do--avail herself of the courts to terminate a marriage.

The Supreme Court seemed to be saying this: while some celebrities and politicians are so pervasively famous that they are all-purpose public figures, most people do not become public figures unless they voluntarily inject themselves into a public debate on a controversial issue. As a result, some relatively well known persons may not be considered public figures should they sue for libel based on a reference to their personal lives. And when it comes to persons involved in a crime, the Supreme Court's *Firestone* ruling made it clear they will not ordinarily be classified as public figures:

> While participants in some litigation may be legitimate "public figures," either generally or for the limited purpose of that litigation, the majority will more likely resemble respondent (Firestone), drawn into a public forum largely against their will in order to attempt to obtain the only redress available to them or to defend themselves against actions brought by the state or by others. There appears little reason why these individuals should substantially forfeit that degree of protection which the law of defamation would otherwise afford them simply by virtue of their being drawn into a courtroom.

After the Supreme Court ruled that Firestone was not a public figure, she chose not to pursue her lawsuit further, and the case was eventually dismissed.

It would be difficult to overemphasize the extent to which the thinking in the *Firestone* case is a retrenchment from the libel protection the media enjoyed in the late 1960s and early 1970s. However, the Supreme Court continued the same trend away from classifying newsworthy persons as public figures in a pair of 1979 decisions, *Hutchinson v. Proxmire* (443 U.S. 111) and *Wolston v. Reader's Digest Association* (443 U.S. 157).

The *Hutchinson* case (involving Senator Proxmire's Golden Fleece Award) was discussed earlier in connection with its adverse effect on the privilege defense. At this point, we will simply add that it offered the media little comfort on the issue of who is a public figure, either. The court said that Dr. Hutchinson was not a public figure, despite the fact that he was the research director of a major state-controlled mental health facility--and had won large grants from tax monies.

The *Wolston* case followed the same policy of narrowing the definition of a public figure, thus freeing more individuals to sue for libel without proving actual malice. Ilya Wolston had an aunt and uncle who had pleaded guilty to charges of spying for the former Soviet Union, and he had been cited for contempt himself when he failed to comply with a Congressional subpoena. Other than that contempt citation, he was never convicted of any offense. Many years later, a *Reader's Digest* publication included his name in a list of "Soviet agents" in the United States. He sued for libel and a lower court dismissed his case, ruling that he was a public figure who could not prove actual malice. The Supreme Court reversed, finding that he had done nothing to inject himself into a public controversy.

Once again, a libel plaintiff was ruled to be a private person who did not need to prove actual malice to win his case, thereby reducing the media's First Amendment protection and making it much easier for the plaintiff to win.

The definition of a public figure or public official was clearly changing. If some of the Supreme Court's early libel rulings were decided under the new standards, would Athletic Director Butts be a public figure--or a public official? What about Baer, the ski resort manager? Or Pape, the Chicago policeman?

In the decades since the *Firestone*, *Hutchinson* and *Wolston* decisions, the public figure-private person question has been addressed in literally thousands of lower court cases. If there is a general rule today, it is that many people whose names are in the news are *not* public figures--unless they inject themselves into a public controversy or take other actions that would be likely to place them in the limelight. Even people who hold newsworthy but non-elective government positions may not necessarily be classified as either public figures or public officials. For example, in a surprising 1999 decision, the Ohio Supreme Court held that a public high school *principal* was neither a public official nor a public figure for libel purposes and therefore do not have to prove actual malice (*East Canton Education Association v. McIntosh*, 709 N.E.2d 468, cert. den. 528 U.S. 1061). In contrast, the Ohio Supreme Court had previously ruled that a public school superintendent *was* a public official (*Scott v. The News-Herald*, 496 N.E.2d 699, 1986), while courts in some other states have found *principals* to be public officials. So who is a public figure or public official today? The answer depends on which court decides the question.

REFINING THE ACTUAL MALICE RULE

Once someone is ruled to be a public official or public figure, he/she faces the difficult challenge of proving actual malice--as defined by the Supreme Court--to win a libel case. During the 1980s and 1990s, the high court clarified the scope of the actual malice rule, applying it in several difficult fact situations.

One of the most important of these cases to the media was *Bose v. Consumers Union* (466 U.S. 485). This 1984 case was a strong reaffirmation of the constitutional safeguards journalists enjoy under *New York Times v. Sullivan*, a decision handed down almost exactly 20 years before the *Bose* ruling. The case began when the Bose Corporation, a manufacturer of high-fidelity speakers, sued *Consumer Reports* magazine for a product review that commented negatively and hyperbolically about the performance of Bose speakers. In a 1970 article, the magazine said that with these speakers music "tended to wander about the room." A Consumers Union engineer had written a report that said the speakers made violins seem "about 10 feet wide."

The manufacturer sued for product disparagement and won a six-figure damage award. During the trial, the judge concluded that the engineer should have said Bose speakers made music sound as if it wandered "along the wall," not "about the room." This, he said, was evidence of actual malice. On appeal, the first circuit U.S. Court of Appeals reversed that judgment, ruling that the magazine was not guilty of actual malice in its product review even if some of the engineer's words and conclusions were debatable.

Normally, appellate courts are not supposed to second-guess a trial court's assessment of the evidence in deciding factual issues (such as whether there was actual malice in this *Consumer Reports* article), but that is exactly what the Court of Appeals did in this case. The Supreme Court upheld that decision, ruling that the media need the additional protection of being able to appeal a trial court's determination of actual malice. To rule otherwise, the court said, would unduly erode First Amendment freedoms by denying the media the right to challenge some libel judgments that are improperly awarded by trial judges or juries.

In concluding that there was no actual malice in this case, Supreme Court Justice John Paul Stevens, writing for the majority, said, "...we agree with the Court of Appeals that the difference between hearing violin sounds move around the room and hearing them wander back and forth fits easily within the breathing space that gives life to the First Amendment."

Thus, the *Bose* case represents a significant expansion of the protection the mass media enjoy under the *New York Times v. Sullivan* rule. When a judge or a jury finds actual malice in a publication or broadcast where there was little or no evidence of "reckless disregard for the truth," the media now have a second shot at that verdict.

Having the appellate courts empowered to re-evaluate the evidence in libel cases can be vital to the news media, as a 1990 decision involving entertainer Wayne Newton illustrated. Newton sued NBC after the network alleged that he had engaged in questionable business dealings and was in contact with persons involved in organized crime, among other things. A federal jury in Las Vegas--where Newton was a very popular celebrity--ruled that he was libeled and awarded him $5.3 million in damages. But the ninth circuit U.S. Court of Appeals overturned the verdict and ordered the case dismissed, ruling that Newton did not prove actual malice and that NBC's statements were basically correct (*Newton v. NBC*, 930 F.2d 662).

Narrowing Gertz

In 1985, the Supreme Court took a major step to narrow the scope of the *Gertz* case: it ruled that *Gertz* applies only to issues of public concern, not to libel cases arising from discussions of purely private matters. That happened in the case of *Dun & Bradstreet v. Greenmoss Builders* (472 U.S. 749).

This case began after Dun & Bradstreet, a credit reporting agency, falsely informed several of its clients that Greenmoss, a Vermont construction company, had filed for bankruptcy. The false credit report resulted from a young worker's negligent (but nonmalicious) error in record-checking. Although Greenmoss could not prove actual malice, it won a $350,000 libel judgment against Dun & Bradstreet. The award included punitive damages, despite the *Gertz* case's holding that even non-public figures must prove actual malice to win punitive damages. The judgment was eventually upheld by the Supreme Court.

Affirming the libel verdict, a three-justice plurality ruled that credit rating reports are not a matter of public concern and therefore should not be subject to the actual malice requirement as set forth in *New York Times v. Sullivan* and expanded in *Gertz v. Welch*. This represented a new distinction in libel law: the plurality said the actual malice rule from *Gertz* should continue to apply to libel cases involving issues of public concern, but not to cases involving purely private matters.

While the three justices in the plurality (Lewis Powell, William Rehnquist and Sandra Day O'Connor) voted to create this new exception to the *Gertz* principle, two others (Chief Justice Warren Burger and Justice Byron White) filed concurring opinions in which they agreed that *Gertz* was inapplicable to this situation. But both also said they would overturn *Gertz* itself if given the opportunity. They were dissenters when the *Gertz* decision was handed down in 1974.

The remaining four justices dissented in the *Greenmoss* decision, arguing that the *Gertz* principle should apply to this case. Justice William Brennan, who authored the majority opinion in *New York Times v. Sullivan* in 1964, joined Thurgood Marshall, Harry Blackmun and John Paul Stevens to argue that credit reporting is a legitimate matter of public concern and therefore should be subject to the actual malice requirements of *Gertz*.

Nevertheless, the plurality of three justices who carved out this exception to *Gertz*--together with the two justices who would overturn *Gertz* altogether--constituted a majority of the Supreme Court, a majority that said *Gertz* simply does not apply to libel cases involving non-public issues. In such cases, the states are free to allow libel plaintiffs to win without proving either actual malice or negligence. (However, some states have chosen to continue requiring proof of actual malice or negligence in all libel cases, despite this Supreme Court ruling. The five justices were merely saying that the states are not *constitutionally required* to make plaintiffs prove actual malice or negligence in libel cases involving purely private matters.)

Affirming an Actual Malice Ruling

Proving actual malice is so difficult that few libel cases are won by public officials or public figures, the people who must prove actual malice to win any libel case that involves an issue of public concern. It is perhaps ironic that in 1989--almost exactly 25 years after the actual malice rule was created by the *New York Times v. Sullivan* decision--the Supreme Court upheld a libel decision involving actual malice for the first time since the 1960s.

Ruling in *Harte-Hanks Communications v. Connaughton* (491 U.S. 657), the Supreme Court unanimously affirmed a lower court's finding that the *Hamilton (Ohio) Journal-Beacon* was guilty of actual malice. The newspaper falsely reported that Daniel Connaughton, who was running for a judgeship in an election, wrongfully tried to discredit an opponent.

The Supreme Court reaffirmed the guidelines it had set down in the *1984 Bose* case (discussed earlier), requiring appellate courts to independently review the evidence in libel cases involving alleged actual malice. But the court then affirmed the appellate court's conclusion that actual malice was present in this case. Writing for the court, Justice John Paul Stevens noted the newspaper's failure to check its own news sources--and the fact that an editor declined an opportunity to listen to tape recorded interviews that could have cast doubts on the accuracy of the story.

Those newsroom practices constitute more than just a departure from normal professional standards of journalism; they create evidence of actual malice, the court concluded.

A jury had awarded Connaughton $5,000 in compensatory damages and $195,000 in punitive damages. The Supreme Court affirmed that verdict.

Actual Malice and Direct Quotations

Is it possible to libel people by misquoting them? When a book, newspaper or magazine uses quotation marks, do readers assume the words inside the quotes are the speaker's exact words? Suppose a reporter knows that a quotation is not precisely what the speaker said. Does that mean the reporter has published a knowing or reckless falsehood--and is therefore guilty of actual malice if a libel suit results from the quotation?

In 1991, the Supreme Court ruled on a libel case that raised those questions, *Masson v. New Yorker Magazine* (501 U.S. 496). The court said a serious misquotation that hurts a person's reputation may be libelous. But at the same time, the court upheld the right of journalists to rephrase what a person says without risking a libel judgment, unless the rephrasing results in a "material change in the meaning."

The case began when Jeffrey Masson, a psychoanalyst who once was the archivist for Sigmund Freud's papers, sued free-lance writer Janet Malcolm and *New Yorker* magazine, among others, for publishing a lengthy article about him containing at least six quoted statements that he denied making. Malcolm conducted 40 hours of tape-recorded interviews with Masson. She also claimed there were additional non-recorded interviews during which she took detailed notes; Masson disputed that claim. He said she took no notes during most of the non-recorded interviews, and Malcolm could not find her notes at the time.

Among other things, Malcolm quoted Masson as calling himself an "intellectual gigolo" and "the greatest analyst who ever lived." Those phrases were not in the taped interviews, but Malcolm claimed Masson did say those things during the non-recorded interviews. Masson flatly denied making those statements, charging that he was seriously misquoted--and that the resulting misrepresentation of his views injured his reputation.

Lower federal courts dismissed Masson's libel suit before trial, ruling that the quoted statements were "rational interpretations" of things Masson did say on the tape and therefore not actionable. But the Supreme Court reinstated the case and remanded it to a federal appellate court to determine if the case should go to trial or be dismissed.

Writing for the Supreme Court, Justice Anthony M. Kennedy Jr. said that journalists could not be expected to be absolutely precise in every direct quote. However, he said that the quoted statements in the article differed significantly enough from the taped statements that Masson was entitled to a jury trial (at which he will still have to prove that Malcolm did misquote him, did so knowingly or recklessly, and thereby damaged his reputation). Justice Kennedy said:

We reject the idea that any alteration beyond correction of grammar or syntax by itself proves falsity in the sense relevant to determining actual malice under the First Amendment.... In some sense, any alteration of a verbatim quotation is false, but writers and reporters by necessity alter what people say, at the very least to eliminate grammatical and syntactical infelicities. If every alteration constituted the falsity required to prove actual malice, the practice of journalism, which the First Amendment standard is designed to protect, would require a radical change, one inconsistent with our precedents and First Amendment principles.

Thus, journalists who make minor changes in quoted statements by public figures are protected by the actual malice rule. But if the meaning is knowingly or recklessly changed in a "material" way, and the change hurts the person's reputation, then the person may have a case. (Private persons would only need to prove that they were libeled by a *negligent* misquote rather than by a knowing or reckless one under the libel law of most states). In short, the *Masson v. New Yorker Magazine* Supreme Court decision gives journalists some leeway in handling direct quotes, while holding them accountable for changing the meaning of a quote in a way that harms the quoted person's reputation.

When he wrote the court's opinion in *Masson*, Justice Kennedy also offered a suggestion concerning the actual malice rule itself--one that might have been drawn from his experience as a law professor before he joined the Supreme Court. He said the term "actual malice" is confusing and should not be used in jury instructions. Instead, he said judges should merely tell jurors to decide if a falsehood was published knowingly or with reckless disregard for the truth. The problem, of course, is that many people who have never read a media law textbook assume (with the encouragement of most dictionaries) that "actual malice" means ill will or evil intentions. In libel cases involving public figures or public officials, it doesn't mean that at all.

Armed with the Supreme Court's holding that he could win if he could prove he was misquoted in a way that materially changed the meaning and thereby defamed him, Masson got a federal appellate court to refer the matter back to a federal trial court. In a 1993 trial, the jury agreed that he was libeled but deadlocked on the amount of damages to award (if any), and a mistrial was declared. In a second jury trial a year later, the jury ruled against Masson, concluding that he failed to prove his case. Masson then appealed once more, and in 1996 a federal appellate court upheld the jury's verdict. This could mark the end of a complex and costly 12-year legal battle (*Masson v. New Yorker Magazine*, 85 F.3d 1394).

By 1996, Malcolm's legal expenses exceeded $2.5 million. Ironically, in 1995 Malcolm said she finally found her long-lost notes from the non-recorded interviews, and they included several key statements that Masson denied making, including the "intellectual gigolo" quote. She said her two-year-old granddaughter pulled a stack of old books and papers off a shelf, including a red notebook containing the missing notes from the Masson interviews. If she could have produced those notes in 1984, the case might have been disposed of much earlier, saving her and her publishers a fortune in legal expenses during a protracted lawsuit!

LIBEL AND PROCEDURAL RIGHTS

The details of courtroom procedure often seem to be arcane and irrelevant technicalities--certainly not issues that should concern journalists. However, on three occasions in recent years the Supreme Court has ruled against the mass media on procedural issues that can be vitally important in libel cases. On the other hand, the Supreme Court has ruled in favor of the media in several other libel cases that were decided on legal technicalities.

In the first of these rulings, the Supreme Court held in 1979 that libel plaintiffs have the right to inquire into journalists' thought processes at the time when an allegedly libelous story was being prepared.

Ruling in the case of *Herbert v. Lando* (441 U.S. 153), the Supreme Court said that since libel plaintiffs often have to prove actual malice or at least negligence on the part of journalists, they are entitled to use the pretrial *discovery* process (explained in Chapter One) to check on journalists' attitudes and thought processes.

The *Herbert* case caused considerable alarm among journalists when the Supreme Court ruled that the First Amendment does not excuse journalists from providing state-of-mind evidence to libel plaintiffs who are looking for proof of actual malice. Actually, though, the decision did little more than to uphold a long-recognized principle of discovery: each party is permitted to use discovery to gather information about the other side's case. Where the plaintiff must prove actual malice to win his case, the rules have allowed plaintiffs to seek evidence of malice.

The *Herbert* case arose when a military officer sued the producers of the CBS television program, 60 Minutes, for libel and then sought state-of-mind evidence during the discovery process. The show's producers refused to cooperate, citing the First Amendment, but the high court ruled that the First Amendment provides journalists with no special immunity from the normal rules of discovery.

Where does the *Herbert* case leave the mass media? Technically, it leaves the media in the same position they were in before this Supreme Court decision: required to cooperate in the discovery process even if it means responding to questions designed to determine whether there really was actual malice present when an allegedly libelous story was prepared.

However, the *Herbert* decision appears to have had an important psychological impact on libel cases. The Supreme Court has in effect endorsed and encouraged the aggressive use of discovery procedures by libel plaintiffs as a means of ferreting out evidence of actual malice or negligence. In the years since *Herbert*, discovery has been an increasing burden for the media in libel cases. Ironically, Herbert eventually lost his libel suit when a federal appellate court dismissed the bulk of his case against CBS in 1986--12 years after the lawsuit began.

Discovery and News Sources

The discovery process has produced a new dilemma for the media in more and more libel suits. If a plaintiff must prove fault on the part of the media, that means he or she must inquire into a journalist's reporting methods to see if there was negligence or actual malice.

As a result, more and more libel plaintiffs are demanding to know where a reporter got the information that appeared in an allegedly libelous story. That means the plaintiff wants to identify the reporter's news sources so they can be interviewed and possibly called as witnesses in a libel trial. However, one of the strongest ethical standards of journalism is the principle of keeping confidential sources confidential (see Chapter Eight for further discussion of this point). In recent years a number of journalists facing libel suits have refused to reveal their sources during the discovery process.

This has sometimes caused problems for the media. Under the normal rules of discovery, if one party to a lawsuit refuses to cooperate in turning over requested evidence to the other side, that evidence may be presumed not to exist. Some judges have responded to a reporter's refusal to reveal his sources in a libel case by simply ruling that there were no sources. Consequently, the court may conclude that story was published with reckless disregard for the truth--no matter how reliable the sources actually were. The result is almost certain defeat in a libel suit.

Many states have shield laws that exempt reporters from having to reveal their sources. However, these laws often protect the reporter only from a contempt of court citation; such laws may not override the rules of discovery in civil litigation. In some instances, there is simply no way a publisher or broadcaster can defend a libel suit without revealing confidential sources, so he or she must choose between violating a promise to a news source and losing a big libel suit.

A good illustration of this problem was the $60 million libel suit that former Iranian hostage Jerry Plotkin filed against the Los Angeles *Daily News*. Shortly after the hostages were released, the paper reported that Plotkin--the only American captured in the U.S. embassy takeover who was not there on government business--was in Iran to conduct large-scale drug purchases.

The two reporters who wrote the story relied on secret sources. During pretrial discovery, Plotkin demanded to know the identity of the sources, but the paper at first refused to name them. The trial judge ordered a default, clearing the way for Plotkin to win a big libel judgment without proving the story was libelous or false.

At that point, the newspaper replaced original lawyers and adopted a new legal strategy: the paper ordered the reporters to reveal their sources and asked the judge to set aside the default against the publishing company, in effect leaving the reporters on their own.

The judge eventually reinstated the case--but ruled that "as a matter of law" no sources existed for the story other than those who were named. The reporters eventually identified their sources: an FBI agent and an official of the Drug Enforcement Agency. Thus, the reporters themselves escaped a certain defeat in a libel case--but only after they were able to persuade their sources to go public. In the end, the *Daily News* settled the lawsuit out of court for an undisclosed sum of money.

While the *Plotkin* case set no legal precedent, that case and several similar cases that have arisen elsewhere illustrate the serious problem facing journalists who use confidential sources for investigative stories.

This problem is so severe that some libel insurance policies are invalid unless the publisher or broadcaster agrees to reveal confidential news sources if a libel suit is filed. It may cost a publisher thousands (or possibly millions) of dollars to maintain source confidentiality; the result could even be bankruptcy. This can create a serious ethical dilemma for journalists and their employers.

The Role of Retractions

In at least 33 states, publishing (or in some instances broadcasting) a retraction or correction of a libelous item reduces the likelihood of a successful lawsuit against the mass media or at least reduces the risk of a news organization facing a large damage award. One of the aspects of libel law that a communications professional needs to understand is his or her own state's rule on retractions.

In most states that have retraction laws, publishing a timely retraction of a libel (and placing the retraction in as prominent a place as the original libel) limits the damages that may be won. In many states, a retraction restricts the plaintiff to special damages (provable out-of-pocket monetary losses, which are often difficult to show). Therefore, publishing a retraction may effectively preclude a lawsuit in many instances.

The provisions of the retraction laws vary widely from state to state. Some of the strongest ones are found in midwestern and western states, such as Arizona, California, Idaho, Nebraska and Nevada. These states all have laws that require a potential plaintiff to demand a retraction within a fixed period of time (often 20 days after learning of the libel). After that, the media usually have another 21 days to publish or broadcast the retraction.

Under these retraction statutes, if the plaintiff fails to demand a retraction or if a suitable retraction is published or broadcast, the plaintiff is limited to special damages (provable out-of-pocket monetary losses). In these states a plaintiff may win other damages only if: (1) a retraction was demanded in a timely fashion; *and* (2) a legally adequate retraction was not published or broadcast in a timely fashion. To be legally adequate, a retraction usually must retract all of the libelous charges without further libeling the potential plaintiff. Also, the retraction must be as prominent as the original libel.

On the other hand, some states have retraction laws that simply say a libel defendant can show that a retraction was published as a way to "mitigate" damages, or perhaps to defend against charges of malice.

Not all retraction laws are equally comprehensive in their protection of the mass media, however. About half of the states that have retraction laws specifically include broadcasters within their coverage. Several other states have laws that cover "all libel suits" or "all media." But several states have retraction laws that apply only to the print media or, more specifically, only to newspapers. California's retraction law is unusual in that respect: it protects newspapers and radio and television stations but not magazines. That was a crucial factor in actress Carol Burnett's libel suit against the *National Enquirer* (mentioned earlier in this chapter): the trial court ruled the *National Enquirer* a magazine and not a newspaper, thus denying it the protection of the retraction statute. An appellate court affirmed that ruling (*Burnett v. National Enquirer*, 144 C.A.3d 991, 1983).

Montana's retraction law, on the other hand, was once so comprehensive that it was ruled unconstitutional. The Montana Supreme Court ruled that the law violated the state constitution because it in effect denied libel plaintiffs any reasonable remedy for the wrongs they might have suffered (see *Madison v. Yunker*, 589 P.2d 126, 1978).

The Montana legislature responded to that decision by rewriting the state retraction law in 1979. As rewritten, Montana's retraction law was weaker than those found in many neighboring states: it required a demand for a retraction prior to a libel suit only if the plaintiff was going to seek punitive damages. And publishing a retraction prevented only punitive damages. With or without a retraction, the media might still have to pay general as well as special damages.

Retraction statutes are obviously useful in situations where the media have made an honest error, but they do little good in many of the circumstances that produce lawsuits--situations in which the publisher does not feel he or she made an error and is in no mood to back down. Moreover, there is a natural human tendency to believe the original charge--not anyone's later denial. To accuse someone of a crime in print and then retract, saying it was all a mistake, is certain to leave some readers with a strong suspicion that it really wasn't a mistake. For this reason, some people question whether retraction statutes are really fair to libel victims.

Nevertheless, many states have such laws, and they have an important impact on libel litigation in those states.

Because retraction laws vary so much from state to state, there has been a movement in recent years to standardize and strengthen these laws. In 1994, the American Bar Association approved a model retraction law called the *Uniform Correction or Clarification of Defamation Act*. While ABA approval does not necessarily lead to a model law being adopted in any particular state, it does increase the likelihood that various state legislatures will consider it. The model law, written by the National Conference of Commissioners on Uniform State Laws, gives libel victims 90 days after a defamatory statement is published to request a correction or clarification. Then the publisher has 45 days to publish a correction or clarification. The model law provides that no libel plaintiff may sue for damages without first seeking a correction or clarification, and limits plaintiffs to special damages (for provable monetary losses) if a suitable correction or clarification is published.

The uniform law's drafters said it was designed to give a libel victim a "quick and complete vindication of his or her reputation" while giving publishers a "quick and cost-effective means of correcting or clarifying alleged mistakes and avoiding costly litigation." Whether it will be widely adopted remains to be seen.

Long-Arm Jurisdiction

Another growing burden for the media--albeit once again not really a new burden--is the cost of defending libel suits in courts thousands of miles from home.

For many years the law has said persons and companies that engage in interstate commerce may be sued in any state where they have *minimum contacts.* The Supreme Court so ruled in 1945, in a case called *International Shoe v. Washington* (326 U.S. 310).

However, some journalists have argued that they should not be forced to defend a libel suit in a faraway state merely because copies of their newspaper or magazine are distributed there or their material is broadcast there. That argument has gotten nowhere with the Supreme Court, which has ruled twice that the First Amendment should not be considered in such cases. Instead, the court said, lawsuits against journalists should have to meet only the same test of fairness as would a lawsuit against another kind of business. In short, if it would be fair for a company that makes cars or lawnmowers to be hauled into court in a distant state where its products are sold, it is also fair for the mass media to be sued in that state if their "product" is sold there.

In two cases decided on the same day in 1984--*Calder v. Jones* (465 U.S. 783) and *Keeton v. Hustler* (465 U.S. 770)--the high court unanimously rejected the argument that forcing journalists to defend themselves in faraway courts would have any chilling effect on freedom of the press.

That means the national media and their employees may be sued in any state--and a libel plaintiff is entitled to engage in *forum shopping.* A plaintiff can select the state with the most favorable laws and file a libel suit there, regardless of where any of the prospective defendants live or maintain offices.

The *Calder v. Jones* case arose when the *National Enquirer* published a story claiming that producer Marty Ingels had driven his wife, actress Shirley Jones, to drink. "...(B)y 3 o'clock in the afternoon she's a crying drunk," the *Enquirer* said. Jones and Ingels both sued the sensational tabloid in California, where they live. Although headquartered in Florida, the *Enquirer* itself did not challenge the California court's jurisdiction. However, John South, the writer of the story, and Iain Calder, editor of the *National Enquirer*, both argued that they should not have to defend themselves in a courtroom nearly 3,000 miles from home.

The Supreme Court unanimously ruled that the writer and editor were subject to California jurisdiction even though neither one went to California to research or write the story. Justice William Rehnquist, who wrote the court's opinion, pointed out that the *Enquirer* was selling about 600,000 copies of each issue in California--twice as many as in any other state. "An individual injured in California need not go to Florida to seek redress from persons who, though remaining in Florida, knowingly cause the injury in California," Rehnquist wrote.

Shortly after the Supreme Court's *Calder v. Jones* decision, Jones and Ingels reached a settlement with the *National Enquirer* to terminate the case. The paper agreed to print a retraction and an apology, and to pay a large cash settlement. Neither side would reveal the amount of the settlement, but Ingels released a statement that said the amount took into account the fact that he and his wife had spent $300,000 in attorney's fees by then.

Although the Supreme Court's decision in the *Jones* case was troubling to some journalists, the *Keeton v. Hustler* case seemed far more so. At least Jones and Ingels had filed suit in the state where they lived and worked; they could hardly be accused of "forum shopping." But in *Keeton*, neither the plaintiff nor the defendant seemed to have any particularly good reason for suing in New Hampshire, the state where the suit was filed. Rather, the choice of New Hampshire was clearly a matter of forum shopping: it was apparently the only state whose statute of limitations (i.e., the deadline) for filing libel suits was not past when the suit was filed.

Kathy Keeton, an executive at *Penthouse* magazine, sued for libel after *Hustler* ran a cartoon suggesting that she had contracted a venereal disease from *Penthouse* Publisher Robert Guccione. She initially sued in Ohio (where *Hustler* was then headquartered), but her case was dismissed because she missed the Ohio filing deadline. By then, it was apparently too late to sue for libel anywhere but New Hampshire, which permitted libel suits as long as six years after publication (that deadline has since been shortened to three years).

When this case was filed, *Hustler* was selling about 10,000 copies of each issue in New Hampshire, but it had no other ties to the state. And Keeton had no ties to the state at all: she lived and worked in New York. Both the federal district court in New Hampshire and the first circuit U.S. Court of Appeals ruled that the jurisdictional requirements were not satisfied. The appellate court suggested that libel cases should be subject to tougher jurisdictional standards than other kinds of lawsuits in order to protect First Amendment freedoms.

The Supreme Court overturned that ruling and reinstated Keeton's lawsuit. "...(T)here is no unfairness in calling (*Hustler*) to answer for the contents of that publication wherever a substantial number of copies are regularly sold and distributed," Justice Rehnquist wrote for the court.

Libel and Summary Judgment

Like several earlier Supreme Court decisions on libel, the *Calder* and *Keeton* cases involved attempts by the media to terminate libel suits before trial by means of a motion for summary judgment or a motion to dismiss on other procedural grounds. As explained in Chapter One, a summary judgment is a ruling in which the court decides the case without trial, saving the expense and trouble of a prolonged lawsuit.

However, because a pretrial dismissal denies the plaintiff his or her day in court, it is only supposed to be granted when it is absolutely certain the plaintiff could not win.

In recent years, some courts have recognized that many libel suits against the media are filed not in the hope of winning but as a means of harassment. Thus, libel suits have sometimes been thrown out of court under summary judgment proceedings. This procedure has been particularly applicable in situations where a public official or public figure is suing but is clearly unable to prove actual malice.

In 1986 the Supreme Court addressed this problem--and endorsed the idea that many of these questionable libel suits should be dismissed on summary judgment. Deciding the case of *Anderson v. Liberty Lobby* (477 U.S. 242), the court said that public figures must provide "clear and convincing" evidence that a jury could find actual malice on the part of the media--or have their lawsuits dismissed on motions for summary judgment.

The *Anderson* case involved three magazine articles written by syndicated columnist Jack Anderson concerning Willis Carto, founder of the Liberty Lobby (an ultraconservative political organization). Anderson called Carto a "neo-Nazi," a "racist" and "anti-Semitic," among other things.

Carto sued but a trial judge dismissed the case, ruling that Carto was a public figure who could not prove that the statements in question were made with actual malice. The judge noted that there had been extensive research to document Anderson's articles, a fact that would have made it extremely difficult to prove Anderson guilty of "reckless disregard for the truth." Carto appealed the dismissal; his case eventually reached the Supreme Court.

The high court ruled by a 6-3 majority that if a libel plaintiff such as Carto cannot show by "clear and convincing" proof that he could win the case if it went to a full trial, the case should be dismissed without subjecting the media to the expense of a trial.

Both media lawyers and lawyers for libel plaintiffs agreed that this decision would have an enormous dollars-and-cents effect on libel law. Both sides agreed that it represented a clear invitation to trial judges to dismiss libel suits on summary judgment instead of letting them go to trial. Media attorneys generally predicted that the *Anderson* case would reduce the high cost of defending libel cases for the news media.

In the years since the *Anderson* decision, these predictions have generally come true. At least four different federal appeals courts have held that *Anderson* requires them to conduct an independent review of the record when they decide whether to allow summary judgment in a libel case, and to dismiss the case if the plaintiff is someone who must prove actual malice--but cannot do so by clear and convincing evidence.

However, in 2002 the ninth circuit U.S. Court of Appeals disagreed in a case involving alleged fabrication of product testing results by *Consumer Reports* magazine. In *Suzuki Motor Corp. v. Consumers Union* (2002 U.S. App. Lexis 12405), the court declined to uphold a trial judge's grant of summary judgment. The appeals court said it would not conduct an independent review of the record and grant summary judgment but would instead allow a jury trial on the merits of the case.

Suzuki submitted evidence that the Suzuki Samarai, which *Consumer Reports* said rolls over too easily, in fact never tipped during 37 tests on the magazine's test course in 1988 and was rated highest of the SUVs tested, until a senior editor demanded changes to increase the likelihood of a roll. The National Highway Traffic Safety Administration later criticized Consumers Union's testing as unscientific.

Suzuki pointed out that the magazine repeatedly cited its testing of the Samarai in publications and promotions during the decade following the original tests. The magazine rated the car's performance not acceptable because it is "likely to roll over during a maneuver that could be demanded of any car at any time."

Suzuki also alleged that Consumers Union was doing fund-raising at the time of the tests and needed a "blockbuster" story to bring it national attention. The appellate court held that the claim of financial motivation combined with evidence of rigged testing could allow a jury to find actual malice, something Suzuki would have to prove to win this case.

"We conclude that the evidence of motive and test-rigging, in combination, is sufficient to preclude summary judgment and therefore requires reversal (of a trial judge's grant of summary judgment)," Judge Wallace Tashima wrote for the 2-1 majority. In dissent, Judge Warren Ferguson said the majority "failed to apply the full procedural protections afforded by the First Amendment," thereby curtailing free expression on two important topics, consumer protection and public safety.

Several media attorneys said the *Suzuki* decision would make editors more reluctant to do hard-hitting stories that might lead to a costly and protracted lawsuit.

Getting "SLAPP" Lawsuits Dismissed

A lawsuit can be an intimidating form of harassment, as journalists have sometimes discovered. The whole point of the *Anderson* case was to allow journalists to get harassment libel suits dismissed quickly on summary judgment. In recent years, it has also become commonplace for citizen activists to be sued for libel or slander by wealthy corporations when they speak against a corporate project at public hearings or circulate petitions to oppose a project. These lawsuits are often nothing more than a form of intimidation--an attempt to silence a corporation's critics. A new acronym to describe these lawsuits has gained wide acceptance lately: SLAPP (*strategic lawsuits against public participation*).

Because it is so costly to defend a lawsuit, citizens who oppose corporate activities in the public arena may have no choice but to back down in the face of a threatened lawsuit. Typically, leaders of a citizens' group that opposes a project such as a large real estate development receive letters from the developer's lawyers telling them they will be sued for libel or slander if they don't stop criticizing the project. Such lawsuits have been given the SLAPP acronym because they take aim at the very foundation of democracy: the right of citizens to speak out on local issues at public hearings where the whole point is to solicit comments from citizens.

The SLAPP acronym was first used by Penelope Canan and George W. Pring, two Denver University professors who advocated legislation to curb these lawsuits in an article published by the California Western University Law Review in 1990.

By 2002, anti-SLAPP laws had been enacted in various forms in at least the following states: California, Delaware, Florida, Georgia, Indiana, Maine, Massachusetts, Minnesota, Nebraska, Nevada, New York, New Mexico, Oklahoma, Oregon, Pennsylvania, Rhode Island, Tennessee, Utah and Washington.

In Colorado, the state Supreme Court recognized a right of citizen activists to get harassment lawsuits dismissed quickly under the common law even without an anti-SLAPP law (see *Protect Our Mountain Environment v. District Court*, 677 P.2d 136, 1984).

California is widely regarded has having the most sweeping anti-SLAPP law in the country. This law requires anyone who sues someone else because of his/her exercise of free speech in the public arena to show at the outset that there is a "probability" the lawsuit has a valid basis and is not merely a form of harassment. If a court determines that there is not a "probability" that the plaintiff has a valid case, the lawsuit is to be dismissed quickly, sparing the defendant the expense of fighting a prolonged legal battle that could have a chilling effect on free speech.

Plaintiffs who file these harassment lawsuits must pay defendants' legal expenses if such a lawsuit is dismissed before trial. On the other hand, under California's anti-SLAPP law defendants must pay the plaintiff's legal expenses incurred in opposing the motion for dismissal if a court rules that the lawsuit is valid enough that it should not be dismissed before trial.

Perhaps what is most notable--and controversial--about California's anti-SLAPP law is that it allows even a large corporation that is being sued by an individual to dispose of a questionable lawsuit quickly and then collect attorney's fees *from the individual*. This could make a private citizen who believes he or she has been libeled think twice about suing a large media corporation, restricting citizens' access to the courts.

In a notable 1999 case, the California Supreme Court held that the anti-SLAPP law should be interpreted very broadly to protect a wide variety of people and entities who are sued for speaking out in a government proceeding or investigation. In *Briggs v. Eden Council for Hope and Opportunity* (19 C.4th 1106), the state high court said the anti-SLAPP law prevents an apartment owner from suing a housing advocacy council that accused him of being a racist and "redneck" in a complaint to federal housing investigators. The apartment owner was eventually cleared of all charges of wrongdoing by federal officials, and he sued the council. His case was ordered dismissed as a SLAPP case by the California Supreme Court, which held that the anti-SLAPP law applies to *any* discussion in a public proceeding.

Most other state anti-SLAPP laws are generally similar to California's but more narrowly drawn. Some do not include the provision requiring plaintiffs to pay a defendant's legal expenses in all cases. The New York law specifically applies only to those who speak out concerning land-use issues being considered by government bodies such as zoning boards.

By 2002, thousands of lawsuits had been dismissed under the various state anti-SLAPP laws. In California alone, there had been no fewer than 50 reported appellate court decisions interpreting the scope of the anti-SLAPP law, including 17 in 2001 (four of which the state Supreme Court was reviewing in 2002).

Perhaps typical of many of the SLAPP cases is one that arose in Minnesota. In this case, a retired wildlife biologist was sued shortly before his 80th birthday for speaking out against a developer's plans to build townhouses across Lake Amelia from his home of 40 years. The biologist contended that the townhouses would disrupt the breeding places of threatened species of birds near the lake. After running up more than $20,000 in legal expenses, he settled the lawsuit--under terms he was forbidden to discuss. Minnesota adopted its anti-SLAPP law amidst the public outcry about this case.

In other notable cases, courts have held that a *politician* may use an anti-SLAPP law to dispose of a meritless lawsuit based on *campaign literature* (*Beilenson v. Superior Court*, 44 C.A.4th 944, 1996), a former church member can use the law to halt harassment lawsuits by the church (*Church of Scientology v. Wollersheim*, 42 C.A.4th 628, 1996) and government officials may use the anti-SLAPP law to halt lawsuits resulting from their statements about matters in the public record (*Bradbury v. Superior Court*, 49 C.A.4th 1108, 1996).

In another major victory for the news media, in 1997 a California appellate court handed down a sweeping affirmation of the *San Francisco Chronicle's* right to cover a controversial state investigation of alleged wrongdoing at a university medical center that led to the firing of the center's director--without fear of a harassment lawsuit (*Braun v. Chronicle Publishing Co.*, 52 C.A.4th 1036). In this case, the court tossed out the former director's libel suit against the *San Francisco Chronicle* and one of its reporters.

Taken together, these cases illustrate how valuable an anti-SLAPP law can be in protecting the news media as well as individuals from frivolous (yet costly) lawsuits when they cover newsworthy public issues. However, these laws remain controversial because they require even individual plaintiffs to make their case at the very outset--or risk not only having the case dismissed but also being hit with a bill for the defendant's legal fees.

"Magic Words" in Libel Lawsuits

Although the technicalities of the law sometimes work to the detriment of journalists in libel cases, at other times just the opposite is true. Time Inc. once escaped liability in a major lawsuit because the plaintiff failed to properly identify this large media conglomerate in legal papers.

In *Schiavone v. Fortune (AKA Time Inc.)* (477 U.S. 21), a 1986 case, the Supreme Court let Time Inc. off on a very arcane technicality.

Fortune, a business magazine owned by Time Inc., published an article in 1982 that linked several New Jersey men to organized crime and to alleged wrongdoing by Raymond Donovan, then the Secretary of Labor in the Reagan Administration. Ronald Schiavone and two others attempted to sue *Fortune* for libel--but they never got a chance to make their case because of a series of procedural foul-ups by their lawyer.

Under the laws of many states (including New Jersey, where this case began), libel lawsuits have a one-year statute of limitations. If the lawsuit is not filed within the year, it may not be filed at all. Just before the year expired, Schiavone's lawyer filed a libel suit against "Fortune," without naming the magazine as a subsidiary of Time Inc.

Realizing the mistake, Schiavone's lawyer then amended the legal papers, revising the name of the defendant to "Fortune, also known as Time Inc." However, by then the one-year statute of limitations had run: the would-be libel plaintiffs had missed their deadline.

Lawyers for Time Inc. noticed that the original papers had an incomplete name and moved to have the case dismissed because Schiavone had missed the deadline. They contended that the name "Fortune" is merely a trademark owned by Time Inc. and not a separate entity that could be sued. Since the original lawsuit didn't name the parent company, the entire lawsuit was null and void, they contended. A trial judge agreed and dismissed the case.

Schiavone appealed, and the Supreme Court eventually affirmed the dismissal of the lawsuit by a 6-3 vote. That prompted a stinging dissent from Justice John Paul Stevens. The majority said that the rules governing this sort of thing are clear--and Schiavone's lawyer did not comply with those rules. To that, Justice Stevens responded by accusing the majority of following a "sporting theory of justice" by allowing the entire lawsuit to be thrown out just because the original complaint failed to include "the magic words ...'also known as Time Inc.'" Stevens said that the point of these rules is to make sure the party being sued has actual notice of the lawsuit. There was no disputing the fact that Time's lawyers received the notice of the lawsuit on time and understood that it was aimed at one of their publications, *Fortune* magazine. They simply found a way to avoid having to defend the lawsuit because of a legal technicality.

Despite Stevens' strongly worded dissent, the Supreme Court's decision stands. Libel plaintiffs' lawyers have been given fair warning that they had better use the full and correct legal name of the prospective defendant or else get ready to be defendants themselves--in legal malpractice lawsuits filed by their own disgruntled clients.

OTHER ISSUES IN DEFAMATION LAW

A number of other questions and problem areas in defamation law have arisen in recent years. This section discusses some of these issues.

Libel and Emotional Distress

Libel is only one of many legal theories on which a lawsuit may be based. When someone sues for libel, he or she may also sue on some other legal theory such as invasion of privacy. It is entirely possible to lose a libel case but win on a different legal basis--because the elements and defenses may be different under the two legal theories. A plaintiff may have a weak libel case (because of the truth defense, for example) but a strong invasion of privacy case (truth is not always a defense on those cases). In recent years it has become common for those who sue the media for libel to add other charges, often invasion of privacy or even *the intentional infliction of emotional distress*, a trend that is discussed in Chapter Five.

That trend led to a 1988 Supreme Court decision that presented about as clear a contrast between plaintiff and defendant as any lawsuit discussed in this book: *Hustler Magazine v. Falwell* (485 U.S. 46). Although widely reported as a libel case, it was primarily an *emotional distress* case. But in the end, the high court disposed of it by applying the classic *New York Times v. Sullivan* doctrine as if it had been a libel case.

The case began when *Hustler* magazine published a satirical purported advertisement suggesting that the Rev. Jerry Falwell, founder of the Moral Majority and arch-enemy of *Hustler* publisher Larry Flynt, had his first sexual experience in an outhouse with his mother. The Falwell pseudo-ad was a take-off on an advertising campaign for Campari liquor that used "the first time" as its theme. Falwell, whose Moral Majority movement vigorously opposed pornography, frequently attacked Flynt, whose magazine is widely regarded as one of the more explicit erotic publications. The purported ad was Flynt's satirical reply. It was clearly labeled as fiction, not to be taken seriously.

Nevertheless, Falwell sued *Hustler* on two legal grounds: libel and the intentional infliction of emotional distress. A jury awarded Falwell $200,000 on the emotional distress rationale, while ruling against him in the libel case. Because Falwell was clearly a public figure, he would have had to prove actual malice to win his libel case. And the ad was obviously satirical; it could not be understood as presenting facts that the reader was supposed to take literally. Thus, Falwell could not prove actual malice. However, in affirming the jury verdict, a lower federal court had said Falwell did not need to prove actual malice to win an emotional distress case.

That verdict alarmed many journalists because it suggested that numerous other public figures who could not win libel cases could get around the protection provided by the actual malice rule by suing for intentional infliction of emotional distress instead of libel.

However, the Supreme Court voted unanimously to overturn the verdict for Falwell. Writing for the court, Chief Justice William Rehnquist said that public figures must henceforth prove actual malice to win damages for emotional distress, just as they must in libel cases. To rule otherwise would force political cartoonists, among others, to heavily censor their work. Rehnquist wrote:

> The appeal of the political cartoon or caricature is often based on exploration of unfortunate physical traits or embarrassing events--an exploration often calculated to injure the feelings of the subject. Lincoln's tall, gangling posture, Teddy Roosevelt's glasses and teeth and Franklin D. Roosevelt's jutting jaw and cigarette holder have been memorialized by political cartoons ...and our political discourse would have been poorer without them.
>
> There is no doubt that the caricature of (Falwell) published in Hustler is at best a distant cousin of the political cartoons described above and a rather poor relation at that.... But we doubt that there is any standard (which would allow a court to distinguish political cartooning from the allegedly 'outrageous' Hustler ad). 'Outrageousness' in the area of political and social discourse has an inherent subjectiveness about it which would allow a jury to impose liability on the basis of the jurors' tastes or views, or perhaps on the basis of their dislike of a particular expression.

What encouraged many journalists the most about the *Falwell* decision was that it was not only a strongly worded defense of freedom of the press, but that it was authored by Rehnquist, who had rarely taken a broad view of the First Amendment in his earlier Supreme Court decisions. Rehnquist had often dissented when the court expanded First Amendment rights. For instance, he objected when the court said libel cases could be based only on statements of fact, not on expressions of opinion. But in this 1988 case, he endorsed the court's earlier holding that expressions of opinion cannot be libelous, however offensive an opinion may be to some readers or viewers. (In the 1990 *Milkovich* case, mentioned earlier, Rehnquist went into some detail in explaining his view on the distinction between constitutionally protected expressions of opinion and statements that sound like opinion but have a false factual component).

The media still face many emotional distress lawsuits. In fact, media lawyers sometimes call emotional distress a "tag-along tort" because plaintiffs' lawyers so often toss in this claim when they sue for libel. But in the years since the *Falwell* case, it has become clear that a plaintiff must prove that the media engaged in clearly *outrageous* conduct that was either *deliberate* or *reckless*, and caused *severe* emotional distress to win this kind of lawsuit. That is not often easy to do. And, of course, public-figure plaintiffs now have to prove actual malice as well if the lawsuit is based on the *content* of something that appeared in the media. (As Chapter Five explains, the media are often sued for *newsgathering torts* based on the *behavior* of media representatives instead of the content of what was published or broadcast.)

Product Disparagement and "Veggie Libel"

During the 1990s, an old legal action that is a close relative of libel--product disparagement--became a newsworthy topic after many years of obscurity. Farmers and ranchers in some areas became alarmed about what they considered to be overly sensational media accounts of alleged health hazards associated with food products. They cited examples in which food producers suffered large losses when public demand for a perishable product suddenly dwindled after the media reported claims that the product might be unsafe. Food producers lobbied for state laws allowing them to sue in response to such media publicity; these laws came to be known as "veggie libel" laws.

This trend began with a case in which Washington state apple growers sued CBS for a 60 Minutes segment that said a chemical used by some growers to enhance the growth and appearance of apples could cause cancer. There was a large decline in apple consumption, and growers claimed the CBS report was false or at least exaggerated--and cost them $130 million. Their lawsuit was eventually dismissed; a federal appellate court ruled that the growers could not prove the CBS report was false--as they would have to in order to win a product disparagement lawsuit (*Auvil v. CBS 60 Minutes*, 67 F.3d 816, 1995).

In response to the CBS story linking apples to cancer-causing chemicals, a number of states passed new laws that were much tougher than traditional product disparagement laws, authorizing growers to sue whenever false information is published claiming that a perishable food product is unsafe. By 2002, such laws had been passed in at least 13 states: Alabama, Arizona, Colorado, Florida, Georgia, Idaho, Louisiana, Mississippi, North Dakota, Ohio, Oklahoma, South Dakota and Texas. Most of these laws define false information as information not based on "reliable scientific data." Allowing growers to sue under these circumstances raises First Amendment questions because growers, journalists and consumer groups are not likely to agree about what is "reliable" scientific data.

Such laws made national headlines in 1997 and 1998 when a group of Texas cattlemen sued talk show host Oprah Winfrey after a guest on her show discussed mad cow disease, an illness that had caused the death of at least 20 persons in Britain, and raised questions about whether this illness could spread to the United States. Cattle prices dropped sharply, and growers sued Winfrey under Texas' "veggie libel" law.

Amidst what many called a media circus, the case went to trial in Amarillo, Texas. Winfrey moved production of her television show there for the duration of the trial. But the case went badly for the cattlemen almost from the beginning. With little explanation and no written opinion, the trial judge dismissed the part of the lawsuit that was based on the "veggie libel" law, allowing the cattlemen to continue the case only under a general business defamation law. In the end, the growers were unable to persuade the jury that Winfrey or her guest intended to harm the Texas cattle industry by making knowingly false statements about the cattle industry, as required by the business defamation law. The jury quickly ruled against the cattlemen--in a case that was far more newsworthy than it was legally significant. In 2000, a federal appellate court upheld this verdict (*Engler v. Winfrey*, 201 F.3d 680).

Nonetheless, many media attorneys expressed fears that future "veggie libel" lawsuits could seriously chill the First Amendment right of the media to report legitimate health questions about food products.

Libel and the Internet

Traditionally, most libel and slander lawsuits have resulted from newspaper and magazine articles and radio or television broadcasts. However, recently a whole new source of potential libel suits appeared: cyberspace. (As the term is used in this book, "cyberspace" refers to all forms of computer communications, including the Internet, bulletin board systems, commercial online services and data bases such as Lexis-Nexis, among other things).

Online communication has grown explosively: today there are millions of websites with even more millions of users who post literally billions of words of new material on the Internet and commercial online services every week. Inevitably, some of that material is libelous.

When a libelous message is posted at a website, a bulletin board, a "chat room" or a newsgroup, it is obviously disseminated: many persons are likely to see it. But is anyone other than the originator of the message legally responsible?

In 1995, a New York trial judge ruled that Prodigy, a commercial provider of computer communications, could be sued for libel because a subscriber posted a message accusing an investment firm of criminal conduct (*Stratton Oakmont Inc. v. Prodigy Services Co*, No. 11063/94). The judge ruled that Prodigy assumed *editorial control* and thus became the legal equivalent of a publisher by *attempting to monitor the content of incoming messages* with text scanning software (i.e., software that checks for offensive words or phrases). Therefore, the online service could be sued for libel, the judge said. Although the ruling caused concern among online service providers, Prodigy eventually settled the case by doing nothing more than issuing an apology.

A provision of Title V of the Telecommunications Act of 1996 overruled the basic thrust of the *Prodigy* decision by declaring that Internet service providers are not to be treated as publishers and held liable for the content of the messages they carry, regardless of whether they employ a content filtering system to screen out objectionable material or merely deliver all messages without any review. Internet service providers are now free to screen out material they consider obscene or otherwise inappropriate without assuming liability for everything they *do not* screen out. Even if an Internet service provider is notified of an allegedly libelous posting and does not then delete it, the provider is exempt under this law, according to a 1997 decision of the fourth circuit U.S. Court of Appeals (*Zeran v. America Online*, 129 F.3d 327). In sweeping terms, the appellate court held that online services are exempt from liability under state libel laws for any message posted by a third party. In 1998, the U.S. Supreme Court declined to review this decision, leaving it intact.

If the Internet service provider is exempt from liability, those who create a libelous website are not. Many individuals have faced lawsuits based on the content of their sites or even e-mail messages that were widely disseminated. In 2002, for example, a jury in California's Silicon Valley ordered two research scientists to pay $775,000 in punitive and compensatory damages to a high-tech company and two of its managers for posting thousands of defamatory messages on Internet message boards (*Varian Medical Systems v. Delfino*, #780187). The trial judge also issued an injunction barring the two from posting any more defamatory messages--an order that raised First Amendment questions. Moreover, the order was impossible to enforce. Soon after it was announced, many anonymous messages were posted on Internet message boards protesting the injunction and criticizing the company. Some included links to the two scientists' websites and several discussed topics the judge had banned. The scientists said they would appeal the verdict.

Libel Insurance Policies

Because a single libel suit can be disastrous, many publishers and broadcasters carry libel insurance, just as they carry insurance to protect them from other business calamities. However, private libel insurance is difficult to secure in some states. Moreover, few insurance carriers are willing to underwrite certain high-risk media.

To solve these problems, several major communications industry trade associations have arranged libel insurance protection for their members through private carriers.

The National Association of Broadcasters, for instance, arranged for two levels of insurance coverage: a policy covering libel and invasion of privacy suits and another that also covers other First Amendment problems for a 50 percent additional fee. Significantly, this did not require the broadcaster to agree to reveal confidential sources as a condition of insurance coverage. But the plan did include surcharges in certain high-risk states. The policy would pay judgments as high as $2 million and cover lawyer's fees as well as the judgment.

How much does libel insurance cost? The NAB's plan required radio stations to pay an annual premium of 10 times their highest rate for a one-minute spot advertisement. Television stations were assessed the rate they received for carrying one hour's prime time network programming. The one-hour rate ranges from a few hundred dollars for stations in small markets up to sums in excess of $5,000 for stations in cities such as New York, Los Angeles and Chicago.

When this package was introduced, the NAB estimated that nearly half of all commercial broadcasters lacked libel insurance.

Libel insurance can be costly, but at least it helps protect publishers and broadcasters from catastrophic libel judgments. However, libel insurance often does not cover punitive damages, and large punitive damage awards are becoming increasingly commonplace, as noted earlier. In fact, some states have laws forbidding insurance companies to cover punitive damages: the idea is that punitive damages are a punishment and they should *hurt*.

Another serious shortcoming of some libel insurance policies is that they cover only libel *judgments* and not the prohibitive cost of defending a libel suit. The major cost of libel litigation is not paying off the few judgments that are ultimately upheld by appellate courts, but rather the very high cost of fighting a long legal battle. In addition, libel insurance sometimes does not protect a media organization if a reporter refuses to identify the news sources used to prepare an allegedly libelous story.

Nevertheless, insurance plays an important role in protecting the media from libel judgments--for those media that can afford it. Ironically, the small-market publishers and broadcasters who can least afford to defend a libel suit on their own are also the least likely to be able to afford to carry libel insurance.

Libel and Fiction

The fundamental question in many libel cases is truth or falsity: only if a statement is false can it be the basis for a successful libel case. But what about libelous innuendoes in a work of fiction--which by its very nature is *intended* to be false? Most publishers and broadcasters didn't worry about this problem until the 1980s, because courts rarely allowed libel suits based on works of fiction. A more serious legal problem had been the threat of lawsuits for invasion of privacy by those who recognized themselves--or thought they did--in fictitious works.

However, in the late 1970s and early 1980s that began to change. Courts started finding sufficient identification in works of fiction to support libel judgments. The result for the media has become a vicious circle: to avoid identifying any real person, those who write novels, short stories and scripts must carefully fictionalize their characters. However, if a real person nevertheless can convince a court he has been identified in the fictitious work, every respect in which the fictional character differs from the real person is a "falsehood" and thus exacerbates the libel. The *New York Times v. Sullivan* rule sometimes has been applied--some say misapplied--in these situations with disastrous results for the media. In a work of fiction, the characters necessarily differ from real people, but some courts have ruled that fictionalization equals knowing or reckless falsehood, thus proving actual malice and opening the door to punitive damages.

The case that initiated this trend toward libel judgments for fictionalization was *Bindrim v. Mitchell* (92 C.A.3d 61, 1979; cert. den. 444 U.S. 984), a California appellate court ruling. As a decision of an intermediate appeals court in a single state, it carries little weight as a precedent, but it encouraged other fiction-based libel cases, including the Wyoming judgment against *Penthouse* cited in the introduction to this chapter (*Pring v. Penthouse*, 695 F.2d 438, 1983).

In *Bindrim*, novelist Gwen Davis Mitchell described a fictitious "nude encounter marathon" similar to therapy sessions conducted by Dr. Paul Bindrim, a psychologist. In fact, Mitchell had attended one of Bindrim's sessions and signed an agreement not to write about it. But in Mitchell's book, entitled *Touching*, the psychologist who conducted the sessions had a different name and did not physically resemble Bindrim. The main thing the real man and the fictional character had in common was that they both conducted nude encounters on the theory that nudity made the therapy sessions more effective.

Nevertheless, a jury found that Bindrim was identified and libeled by the fictional account in the novel, and awarded Bindrim $75,000 in total damages against Mitchell and her publisher, Doubleday and Company. The award was later reduced to $50,000.

Both the California and U.S. Supreme Courts refused to review the lower appellate decision, which affirmed the judge's determination that Bindrim was sufficiently identified for a libel suit. "The test is whether a reasonable person, reading the book, would understand that the fictional character was, in actual fact, the plaintiff," the appellate majority wrote.

The *Bindrim* ruling was widely criticized by writers and publishers, and the Writers Guild of America filed a brief urging the U.S. Supreme Court to review the case. The guild reminded the justices that many previous literary works have been based on fictionalizations of real people. The guild cited the classic movie, *Citizen Kane*, as a work that could not be produced under the *Bindrim* precedent. In that movie, the fictional Charles Foster Kane was far more similar to William Randolph Hearst, the newspaper publisher, than the character in *Touching* was to Bindrim. If a movie like *Citizen Kane* were done about a person living today, it would invite a *Bindrim*-type libel suit. To allow libel judgments for works of fiction will severely inhibit literary freedom, the guild warned.

Those arguments notwithstanding, no higher court was willing to review the *Bindrim* decision. This was by no means the first time a libel judgment had ever been based on a work of fiction: as early as 1920 the New York Court of Appeals had ruled similarly (see *Corrigan v. Bobbs-Merrill*, 228 N.Y. 58). Several other courts reached similar conclusions later, but none with quite the impact of *Bindrim*, which caused widespread alarm among writers and publishers.

However, fiction writers could take some comfort in the ultimate decision in the "Miss Wyoming" libel suit against *Penthouse*. The 10th circuit U.S. Court of Appeals reversed the multimillion-dollar jury verdict, and the Supreme Court declined to hear a further appeal.

The case stemmed from a *Penthouse* article describing a fictitious "Miss Wyoming" who competed in the Miss America Pageant, a champion baton twirler who had an even more interesting talent: oral sex. The story said she performed an act of oral sex at the pageant before a national television audience, and the recipient of her favors was levitated--he rose up in the air in defiance of the laws of gravity. Kim Pring, a champion baton twirler who once represented Wyoming in the Miss America Pageant, claimed the story was about her and damaged her reputation, so she sued. A Wyoming jury agreed and awarded $26.5 million in damages ($25 million of it in punitive damages).

The appellate court overturned the jury verdict because it found the story to be "physically impossible in an impossible setting," and therefore not something the reader could reasonably understand as describing actual events involving Pring.

The court called the *Penthouse* story "gross, unpleasant, crude," but said the First Amendment "is not limited to ideas, statements or positions... which are decent and popular...." The court also offered some guidance on the murky issue of libel and fiction:

> The test is not whether the story is or is not characterized as 'fiction,' 'humor,' or anything else in the publication, but whether the charged portions in context could be reasonably understood as describing actual facts about the plaintiff or actual events in which she participated. If it could not be so understood, the charged portions could not be taken literally.

Thus, the court said the *Penthouse* story was too incredible and obviously false to be libelous to Kim Pring or anyone else. However, this decision offers little comfort for serious fiction writers. If a story is an accurate portrayal of life, it may be a more powerful (and artistically sound) literary work--but it is also more likely to be the basis for a libel suit. In effect, the *Pring v. Penthouse* decision says fairy tales are immune to libel judgments, but realistic literature is not.

Libel and Broadcasting

So far this summary of the principles of libel law has made almost no distinction between the print and electronic media. That was done in the interest of clarity and simplicity--and because it is generally justified. There are, however, some special libel problems when the broadcast media are involved.

Not the least of these problems is the question of whether a broadcast defamation is really a libel at all or is in fact a slander. Before broadcasting came along, slander (a spoken defamation) was a limited legal action for the obvious reason that an oral statement was a fleeting thing, while a printed one might be read by thousands of people over many years. In view of slander's limited nature, the courts generally ruled that one could only win a slander suit by proving special damages unless the slander fell into one of several particularly offensive categories that were sometimes called *slander per se*. Because of these restrictions, successful slander suits were relatively rare.

But when broadcasting developed, the potential for harm in a spoken defamation became at least as great as in a written one. Recognizing the pervasiveness of

168   Libel and Slander

a broadcast defamation, some states simply declared that broadcast defamation would be regarded as libel, not slander. Other states such as California classified broadcast defamation as slander but liberalized the requirements for a successful slander suit so there was little difference between libel and slander. Some states even adopted the rule that a defamation contained in a script would be treated as a libel (since it was written down, after all), while an ad-libbed one would be treated as slander. Only a few states still adhere to that rule today.

These variations in broadcast defamation law may seem quaint--and perhaps they are today. Whatever its name, broadcast defamation is a viable legal action in all states. As noted earlier, some states exempt local broadcasters from liability for defamation occurring during network programs they have no power to edit, but even then the network remains liable. And, as already noted, the Supreme Court has exempted broadcasters from liability for defamation occurring during political advertising that broadcasters are forbidden to censor under Section 315 of the Communications Act.

Aside from these exceptions, a defamation that is broadcast is just as actionable as a printed one, and perhaps more so because of the massive audiences the electronic media attract. In evaluating a defamation that was broadcast rather than published, the same rules normally apply.

However, there are other practical problems in broadcasting. If broadcasters are going to be held accountable for slanders by all the various people whose voices are broadcast, how can broadcasters hope to protect themselves? Various solutions have been developed in the industry, among them the practice of putting as much programming as possible on tape or film to expedite pre-broadcast review. Talk shows have produced problems for broadcasters in this respect; those who call in can hardly be expected to obey (or even know about) the rules of libel. One common solution is the use of a short time delay to allow the broadcaster to bleep out potentially offensive remarks. That means, of course, that the talk show host or producer must be able to recognize defamation--and delete it--quickly.

Criminal Libel

At the beginning of this chapter we said many states still have criminal libel laws on their books, but that these laws are rarely used. For that reason, the entire discussion so far has been devoted to civil libel.

The reason we can touch criminal libel so lightly in a text such as this is that it has become an obsolete legal action because of both common law traditions and a pair of U.S. Supreme Court decisions in the 1960s.

Criminal libel laws generally cover situations in which civil libel law is inapplicable. For instance, some states still make it a crime to libel a dead person--a form of libel that is rarely actionable in civil suits. In addition, some state laws still forbid distributing literature so defamatory that it might cause a breach of the peace.

The Supreme Court once upheld an Illinois criminal libel law that was used to prosecute a man who distributed racist literature. In a 1952 ruling (*Beauharnais v. Illinois*, 343 U.S. 250), the court said the First Amendment does not protect the kind of racist literature involved in that case. Few legal scholars believe this case would be decided the same way now, given the court's more expansive interpretation of the First Amendment since then.

Shortly after handing down its landmark *New York Times v. Sullivan* civil libel ruling in 1964, the Supreme Court rendered another important criminal libel decision: *Garrison v. Louisiana* (379 U.S. 64). That case arose when New Orleans prosecutor Jim Garrison severely criticized a group of judges, calling them sympathetic with "racketeer influences" and "vacation-minded." Prosecutor Garrison was himself prosecuted under a Louisiana law that made it a crime to defame public officials.

The Supreme Court said Garrison's prosecution was not permitted by the First Amendment unless it could be proved that he made false statements either knowingly or with reckless disregard for the truth. In short, the court said the same tough standards that apply in civil libel suits by public officials also apply in criminal prosecutions for defamation of public officials: actual malice must be shown.

That decision was perhaps the final blow for seditious libel laws in this country. Some states still have such laws, but they are almost never used. Such laws are likely to be overruled on constitutional grounds by the state courts when they are used.

The U.S. Supreme Court dealt another blow to criminal libel in the 1966 case of *Ashton v. Kentucky* (384 U.S. 195), a decision stemming from circulation of a pamphlet that attacked various local officials. The circulator was prosecuted for criminal libel because the pamphlet allegedly threatened to cause a breach of the peace. The Supreme Court unanimously reversed the conviction, ruling the law overbroad and in violation of the First Amendment.

As a result of these Supreme Court decisions and parallel rulings by a number of state courts, criminal libel prosecutions are rare in modern America. Those criminal statutes that remain in force constitute a minimal legal threat to the mass media today. If the remaining criminal libel laws were vigorously enforced, few of them could withstand a constitutional challenge at this point in our history.

ONGOING ISSUES

Although libel and slander are very old concepts, there are several new problems in this field, problems that will not be easy to resolve.

Through most of American history, the threat of being sued for libel has been the most serious continuing legal hazard for the mass media, and today that threat may be more serious than ever. For a time, it appeared that the libel problem was subsiding. After *New York Times v. Sullivan*, the Supreme Court handed down a series of decisions in the 1960s and early 1970s that made it more and more difficult for plaintiffs to win libel suits. By the time of *Rosenbloom v. Metromedia* in 1971, even private persons involved in public issues were being required to prove actual malice (that a falsehood had been published with knowledge or with reckless disregard for the truth).

However, the 1974 *Gertz v. Welch* decision reversed that trend. While *Gertz* rewrote the common law of libel in all 50 states by forcing even private plaintiffs to prove at least negligence in most cases (something that was not usually required before), it also reclassified many people as private persons when they were previously considered public figures. As a result, many persons who would previously have been required to prove actual malice can now win libel cases by proving nothing more than negligence.

But to talk of negligence, actual malice, private persons and public figures is to dwell on legal theory. The real problem today is that juries in libel cases tend to ignore the law: they often hand out monstrous damage awards without worrying about whether the material in question is really libelous. By now there have been at least 100 verdicts in excess of $1 million in libel cases. Granted, most big libel judgments are eventually overturned by appellate courts, but by then the bill for legal expenses may be bigger than the judgment was.

Moreover, the high cost of defending a libel suit will surely go even higher in the aftermath of the Supreme Court's *Keeton v. Hustler* and *Calder v. Jones* decisions, which permit *forum shopping* in libel cases. Few people would question the fairness of requiring a major corporation to defend a lawsuit in any state where it injures someone while doing business there. Years ago the Supreme Court authorized the states to exercise what is called *long-arm jurisdiction* over companies having *minimum contacts* with a particular state. But the Supreme Court now says that selling a few thousand copies of a magazine constitutes minimum contacts.

Many journalists and lawyers disagree with that conclusion, but what is even more troubling about *Keeton* and *Calder* is that they allow individual writers and editors to be sued in courts thousands of miles from where they live and work. Where, one might ask, are the minimum contacts to justify a distant state taking jurisdiction over these individuals? It is one thing to force a major corporation to defend itself in the courts of all 50 states; it is quite another to place that burden on individual journalists whose employers may or may not pay their legal expenses.

In addition, the Supreme Court's *Milkovich v. Lorain Journal* decision in 1990 might have sent a message to the states to give expressions of opinion less protection in libel cases. While statements of pure opinion are still exempt from libel suits, that is not necessarily true of mixed statements that include false factual allegations within an expression of opinion. Editorials, letters to the editor, columns, reviews and "op-ed" pieces often combine factual assertions with expressions of opinion; they now enjoy less protection from libel suits. Fortunately for the media, most states continue to afford strong protection to statements that are clearly opinion and not false factual allegations.

On the other hand, the Supreme Court has given the news media some good news in the libel field too. The *Hepps v. Philadelphia Inquirer* decision declared that the burden of proof in virtually all libel cases involving the mass media falls to the plaintiff. The media need not prove the truth of an allegedly defamatory statement; the plaintiff must prove it is false. And the *Bose v. Consumers Union* decision told the appellate courts to review the evidence in libel cases to be certain that actual malice has really been shown when it is required to be.

These court decisions have resolved some of the major problems in libel law, while perhaps creating new ones. Nevertheless, the biggest problem is still the cost and complexity of libel lawsuits. Many people in and out of the communications industries question whether the legal system offers the ideal solution to the libel problem. There will inevitably be persons who believe they have been wronged by the mass media--with varying degrees of justification. However, these people rarely have anywhere to go with their complaints except to a lawyer's office and then to court.

Because of these problems, there have been many proposals for reform of the libel and slander laws. For example, the Annenberg Washington Program sponsored a Libel Reform Project and brought together a group of experts to study this problem. They proposed sweeping changes in libel laws, among them a system to determine the truth or falsity of an allegedly libelous statement without all of the legal formalities that are now required. Although their plan would rule out money damages, the loser would pay the winner's attorney's fees. However, the Annenberg proposal has not been implemented anywhere, even on a trial basis. Nor has any other major reform of the way libel cases are handled in the American legal system.

Perhaps the nearest thing to a libel "reform" that has occurred recently has been the adoption of anti-SLAPP laws in numerous states to curb *strategic lawsuits against public participation*. Although these laws are intended primarily to protect citizen activists who speak out on controversial issues, in some states they also protect the media from harassment lawsuits. Even in states lacking an anti-SLAPP law, of course, media defendants can always seek to have nuisance libel suits dismissed before trial by seeking summary judgment, a tactic encouraged by the Supreme Court's *Anderson v. Liberty Lobby* decision. Unfortunately, a summary judgment motion cannot be made until later in a lawsuit than a dismissal motion under most anti-SLAPP laws, running up the legal expenses for both sides.

Ultimately, our discussion of libel must end where it began: with the observation that the system is very, very costly and cumbersome--and that libel is now and will likely remain a serious legal problem for the mass media.

A SUMMARY OF LIBEL AND SLANDER

What Are Libel and Slander?
Libel and slander are legal actions to compensate someone whose reputation has been wrongfully damaged. Traditionally, a written defamation was called libel and a spoken defamation was called slander, but the distinction between the two became blurred as the influence of the broadcast media expanded. In many states the two are virtually identical today.

Who May Sue or Be Sued for Libel?
Individuals and corporations--but not government agencies--may sue. Unincorporated associations may sue in some states but not in others. An individual may sue for *group libel* if the group is very small and the libel refers particularly to that individual. Usually anyone who contributes to the publication--or republication--of a libelous statement may be sued, even if the libel appears in a direct quote, a live interview, an advertisement or a letter to the editor.

To Win a Libel Suit, What Must a Plaintiff Prove?
To win, the plaintiff (the person who initiates the lawsuit) must prove all of the elements of libel, which are: (1) *defamation*; (2) *identification*; (3) *publication*; (4) in cases involving issues of public concern, *fault* on the part of the publisher or broadcaster (i.e., dissemination of a falsehood due to either negligence or actual malice); (5) in many instances, *actual damages*.

What Defenses Are There?
Even though all of the elements of libel may be present, the plaintiff will not prevail if the defendant can prove that any of the recognized defenses apply. The major ones are: (1) *truth*; (2) *fair comment and criticism*; (3) *privilege*. The Supreme Court has ruled that the plaintiff usually *bears the burden of proof*; he/she must prove the falsity of a libelous statement--the defendant does not have the burden of proving truth.

Are There Different Rules for Public Figures and Private Persons?
The Supreme Court has ruled that public officials and public figures must prove actual malice, meaning the publication of a falsehood with knowledge of its falsity or with reckless disregard for the truth. With the Supreme Court's blessing, most states now permit private persons to win libel cases by proving merely negligence on the part of the media, not actual malice. In cases involving purely private matters rather than issues of public concern, the high court has held that the states may allow private persons to win libel cases without proving any fault at all.

What Does Publishing a Retraction Accomplish?
In many states publishing a timely retraction--as prominently as the original libel--limits the plaintiff to special damages (i.e., provable monetary losses).

CHAPTER FIVE
The Right of Privacy

The legal concept called *the right of privacy* has much in common with libel and slander. Like libel, invasion of privacy is usually a tort action--a civil lawsuit in which an injured party sues for monetary compensation. Moreover, privacy, like libel, is basically a state legal matter, although the U.S. Supreme Court has sometimes stepped in to place constitutional limits on state actions in this area just as it has in libel law. In fact, some of the major Supreme Court decisions on libel are cited in privacy lawsuits--and Supreme Court decisions on invasion of privacy are sometimes cited in libel cases.

Invasion of privacy and libel are so similar that persons offended or embarrassed by media publicity often sue for both--hoping to win on at least one of the two legal theories. Libel and invasion of privacy overlap enough to invite this sort of double-lawsuit strategy, particularly because the two actions have slightly different defenses. It is entirely possible to have an excellent libel defense in a given situation--but a weak defense against an invasion of privacy suit.

However, there are important differences between libel and invasion of privacy, including their histories. Libel was incorporated into the English common law hundreds of years ago, but invasion of privacy is a relatively new legal action. It was not widely recognized by the courts or legislatures until the twentieth century.

Although privacy law developed only recently, it grew to become one of the most important and controversial aspects of communications law in the late 1990s. Even before the tragic death of Princess Diana--in a 1997 auto accident reportedly caused by her driver's recklessness while attempting to elude paparazzi photographers--there was an upsurge of lawsuits resulting from aggressive and allegedly intrusive newsgathering activities.

THE HISTORY OF PRIVACY LAW

The legal concept of a "right of privacy" developed only after the mass media, corporations and government agencies became powerful enough--and technically sophisticated enough--to threaten individual privacy. That happened early in the twentieth century.

By 1900, the biggest newspapers had achieved circulations of nearly a million copies a day--and they did it with a heavy emphasis on stories about crime and scandal, stories that were not always truthful and tasteful. It became obvious that the media could destroy someone's reputation, sometimes in a way that did not make a libel suit a good remedy. Suppose, for instance, that a sensational newspaper revealed intimate (but truthful) details of a person's private life. The truth defense would preclude a successful libel suit, but shouldn't there be some way for the injured party to win justice in court?

In one of the most widely quoted law review articles of all time, Samuel D. Warren and Louis D. Brandeis addressed this issue in 1890. (Brandeis later served on the U.S. Supreme Court and wrote several well-known opinions on freedom of expression in America.) Their essay in the *Harvard Law Review* contended that there should be a right of privacy either under the common law or state statutory law. Such a right, they felt, should protect prominent persons from gossipy reporting of their private affairs. The article was prompted at least in part by the experiences of Warren's family, which had occasionally found its name mentioned in unflattering ways in the Boston press.

"The press is overstepping in every direction the obvious bounds of propriety and of decency," they wrote. "Gossip is no longer the resource of the idle and of the vicious, but has become a trade, which is pursued with industry as well as effrontery."

Influential as that law review article became later, it did not create an overnight legal revolution. In fact, it was a dozen years later when a case based on the Warren-Brandeis theory finally reached a New York appellate court--and the court didn't buy the idea. The case (*Roberson v. Rochester Folding Box Co.*, 64 N.E. 442, 1902), was brought by Abigail Roberson, whose picture was used without her permission in a flour advertisement. She sued, but the court ruled that "the so-called 'right of privacy' has not yet found an abiding place in our jurisprudence...."

However, Roberson's defeat in court quickly was turned into a victory in the New York legislature, which responded to a public outcry over the court decision by passing the nation's first statutory law on privacy. Acting in 1903, the legislature enacted what are now Sections 50 and 51 of the New York Civil Rights Law, which read in part:

> ...(T)he name, portrait or picture of any living person cannot be used for advertising purposes or for purposes of trade, without first obtaining that person's written consent.

Obviously, this was not a sweeping law: it failed to address the sort of invasion of privacy Warren and Brandeis had in mind. All it did was outlaw commercial exploitation of a person's name or likeness without consent--a separate legal wrong that we call invasion of the *right of publicity* today. It said nothing about situations in which the media reveal intimate details about a person's private life in a news story or engage in intrusive newsgathering activities.

Two years after the New York privacy law was enacted, a state supreme court judicially recognized a right of privacy in connection with the media for the first time. In that 1905 case (*Pavesich v. New England Life Insurance Co.*, 50 S.E. 68), the Georgia Supreme Court upheld the right of an artist named Paolo Pavesich to sue New England Life for using his likeness in an advertisement without permission. The ad included a photo of Pavesich and a testimonial implying that he endorsed the company's insurance.

Another famous early privacy case raised a different question, one that has plagued the courts (and journalists) ever since: can a public figure return to a private life and then sue for invasion of privacy if the press does a "where-is-he-now" story years later? In *Sidis v. F-R Publishing Co.* (113 F.2d 806, 1940), William J. Sidis sued the publisher of the *New Yorker* magazine for doing an article about him. He was a one-time mathematical genius who graduated from Harvard University at age 16. The article, published some 20 years later, revealed that he was living in a shabby rooming house and working as a low-salaried clerk. It ridiculed him and even included a cartoon with a caption calling him an "April fool."

Should someone like William Sidis be able to sue the *New Yorker* for invading his privacy? A federal appellate court ruled that the case should be dismissed, pointing to the newsworthiness of the story. The court said that someone who becomes a celebrity even involuntarily (as Sidis had) cannot completely avoid publicity later in life.

The *Sidis* case did not settle this issue, of course. Old-but-true-facts cases continue to arise--and the media try to justify their coverage of such stories by citing the continued public interest in the subject. Publicity-shy plaintiffs, of course, argue that they should not be forced to have their past deeds revealed to people who have forgotten (or never knew) about them.

However, two legal concepts were emerging from these early privacy cases. First, there is the idea that the news media do not need anyone's consent to do stories about *newsworthy* subjects. But on the other hand, when a person's name or likeness is used for commercial purposes (as in advertising), it must be with the person's permission. Most states have now recognized at least these aspects of the right of privacy, either by statute or court decision.

Meanwhile, the U.S. Supreme Court began to recognize that there is also a limited constitutional right of privacy, although none of the early Supreme Court decisions actually involved the mass media. Rather, the early cases all involved the right of individuals to be free of excessive *government* intrusions into their private lives. The high court acknowledged the right of privacy in a law enforcement context as long ago as 1886, in *Boyd v. U.S.* (116 U.S. 616). In that case, the court said the Fourth and Fifth Amendments provide protection against governmental invasions of the "sanctity of a man's home and the privacies of life."

Then in 1928, Louis Brandeis--by then a Supreme Court justice--wrote a famous dissenting opinion in which he urged recognition of the right of privacy in *Olmstead v. U.S.* (277 U.S. 438). That case involved government eavesdropping to gain evidence against suspected bootleggers in the prohibition era, and the majority opinion held that there was no violation of any right of privacy unless the federal agents committed a physical trespass in order to listen in. But in his dissent, Brandeis called for a "right to be let alone." He said the framers of the Constitution intended "to protect Americans in their beliefs, their thoughts, their emotions and their sensations.... They conferred, as against government, the right to be let alone--the most comprehensive of rights and the right most valued by civilized man."

Since then, the Supreme Court has specifically recognized the right of privacy, both in media cases and in other areas. For instance, the *Olmstead* majority opinion--which allowed government eavesdropping as long as there was no physical trespass--was reversed some 40 years later in *Katz v. U.S.* (389 U.S. 347). In that 1967 case, federal agents had used monitoring devices atop a public telephone booth to gather evidence against alleged bookmakers (i.e., persons taking illegal bets on horse races). The Supreme Court said a person's right to privacy extends to all areas where there is a justifiable expectation of privacy. Unauthorized law enforcement surveillance activities need not involve a physical trespass to constitute a violation of the Fourth Amendment, the court ruled.

In the decades since *Katz*, the Supreme Court has repeatedly ruled on the privacy issues raised by the use of other technologies by law enforcement investigators to conduct searches without a search warrant. In 2001, the court ruled against federal agents who used heat-sensing equipment to detect an indoor marijuana farm. In *Kyllo v. United States* (533 U.S. 27), a 5-4 majority of the court declared that the use of thermal imaging equipment violated the right of privacy guaranteed by the Fourth Amendment even though there was no physical intrusion into the home. This was true even though the imaging equipment merely detected heat radiating out from the home, and did not involve looking into the house, the court said.

Writing for the court, Justice Antonin Scalia made a distinction between using a technology that is in widespread public use (such as binoculars, which the court had previously allowed police to use in surveillance of private homes), and an exotic technology such as this one--which detected heat coming out of rooms where the resident was using heat-generating lights to grow about 100 marijuana plants. Scalia said there *is* an expectation in privacy in this instance.

The Supreme Court also relied largely on a privacy rationale in reaching its famous and controversial decisions on birth control and abortion. In the 1965 ruling that overturned state laws against contraceptive devices (*Griswold v. Connecticut*, 381 U.S. 479), Justice William O. Douglas said the various rights listed in the Bill of Rights, taken together, add up to a right of privacy that bars the state from involving itself in individuals' sexual relations in marriage. Although some of the other justices based their decision on a different rationale, Douglas' view was widely quoted later in support of a limited constitutional right of privacy. A couple's decision to use contraceptives was a private matter and none of the state's business, Douglas was saying. Thus, the Connecticut law banning the use of contraceptives (even by married couples) was ruled unconstitutional.

In the landmark 1973 Supreme Court decision that overturned state laws against abortions (*Roe v. Wade*, 410 U.S. 113), the court focused on concepts related to personal privacy in reaching the decision that abortions were a private matter between a woman and her physician, at least during the early months of pregnancy.

In the years since 1973, *Roe* has become the most controversial Supreme Court decision of the twentieth century. Millions of Americans vehemently disagree with the ruling that a state cannot prohibit abortions during the first six months of pregnancy when the fetus is not viable outside the womb. Millions of others strongly support the court's holding that there is a right of privacy in this area.

In 1989, a deeply divided court had stopped just short of overturning *Roe v. Wade* in a case called *Webster v. Human Reproductive Services* (492 U.S. 490). In that case, the court did uphold some restrictions on abortions that had been adopted in Missouri. The court affirmed Missouri's ban on abortions in public hospitals and abortion counseling by public employees as well as a law requiring doctors to test the fetus for viability before performing an abortion if the fetus appeared to be at least 20 weeks old.

Even before the *Webster* ruling, the Supreme Court had begun to limit the constitutional right of privacy--or at least to avoid expanding it further. In 1986 the Supreme Court declined to recognize constitutional privacy rights for homosexuals in *Bowers v. Hardwick* (478 U.S. 186). In *Bowers*, the court upheld a Georgia law forbidding sex acts such as sodomy even between consenting adults in private. The Georgia law, which was similar to laws then in effect in more than 20 other states, made sodomy a crime for everyone including heterosexual married couples, although it was primarily enforced against homosexuals. Georgia officials said there had been few prosecutions in modern times.

The case began when police entered the home of Michael Hardwick because he had not paid a traffic ticket. An officer found Hardwick in his bedroom sodomizing another man (police were allowed to enter the house by a third occupant who had been asleep and was apparently unaware Hardwick was at home). Hardwick was arrested, but local authorities decided not to prosecute him. Nonetheless, Hardwick sued Georgia Attorney General Michael J. Bowers, contending that the anti-sodomy law violated his constitutional right of privacy. The Supreme Court ruled that it did not.

In refusing to overturn the sodomy law, the court said that the authors of the Constitution were surely not trying to protect the rights of homosexuals when they wrote the Bill of Rights. Although the court earlier had held that the Constitution includes a right of privacy in connection with contraception and abortion, a five-justice majority ruled that the same privacy rights do not exist when the private sex lives of homosexuals are concerned. Writing for the court, Justice Byron R. White said:

> We think it is evident that none of the rights announced in those cases (the cases involving contraception, abortion, and similar questions) bears any resemblance to the claimed constitutional rights of homosexuals to engage in acts of sodomy.

The *Bowers v. Hardwick* decision was--and still is--controversial, particularly because Justice Lewis Powell, who said at the time that he had joined the five-member majority only reluctantly, later said he had changed his mind. Speaking to New York University law students in 1990 (after his retirement from the court), Powell said of his vote in the *Bowers* case, "I think I probably made a mistake." With Powell's vote on the other side, of course, the 5-4 decision would have gone the other way, and the court would have recognized a constitutional right of privacy for homosexuals, just as it had earlier in the areas of contraception and abortion. Nevertheless, *Bowers v. Hardwick* stands as a legal precedent, denying homosexuals any privacy rights under the *federal* Constitution.

Since the *Bowers* decision a number of states have recognized a right of privacy for homosexuals under their own *state* constitutions, ruling that these state constitutions provide a broader right of privacy than the U.S. Constitution does. One of these states is Georgia. In a widely noted 1998 decision, the Georgia Supreme Court held that the sodomy law under which Michael Hardwick was charged violates the privacy guarantees of the Georgia Constitution (*Powell v. State of Georgia*, 510 S.E.2d 18). And in 1996, the U.S. Supreme Court ruled that the voters of Colorado could not legalize discrimination against homosexuals by passing a ballot initiative to invalidate existing state and local laws protecting homosexuals' rights. That decision, *Romer v. Evans*, is discussed in Chapter Three.

In view of the *Bowers v. Hardwick* ruling and several later decisions that took a narrow view of the right of privacy in personal matters--and in view of the replacement of the last two liberal justices (William Brennan and Thurgood Marshall) with conservatives (David Souter and Clarence Thomas), almost everyone on both sides of the abortion controversy expected the Supreme Court to overturn *Roe v. Wade* in 1992. But to almost everyone's astonishment, a new coalition of moderate conservatives led the court in a 5-4 vote to reaffirm the basic holding of *Roe v. Wade* in the closely watched case of *Planned Parenthood of Southeastern Pennsylvania v. Casey* (505 U.S. 833). In that case, Justice Sandra Day O'Connor formed a coalition with Justices Anthony Kennedy and David Souter to rule that the states may not place an *undue burden* on a woman's right to choose an abortion during the early months of pregnancy. When the decision was announced, O'Connor said she was personally very opposed to abortions, but she added, "Our obligation is to define the liberty of all, not to mandate our own moral code...."

The court upheld Pennsylvania laws establishing a 24-hour waiting period for adult women who want an abortion and requiring teen-agers to get a parent's or a judge's permission for an abortion. Those were *not* undue burdens, the court held. But the court overturned Pennsylvania's requirement that married women had to notify their husbands of their plans. That, they said, *was* an undue burden.

Justice Harry Blackmun, who wrote the court's opinion in *Roe v. Wade* 19 years earlier, concurred in the 1992 decision to reaffirm it, as did Justice John Paul Stevens. Chief Justice William Rehnquist and three other conservatives dissented, indicating that they would overturn *Roe v. Wade*. Blackmun, who had been widely quoted as predicting that the court would overturn *Roe*, was at least as surprised as anyone else. In what may be among his most memorable words as a Supreme Court justice, Blackmun wrote:

> ...(N)ow, just when so many expected the darkness to fall, the flame has grown bright.... Make no mistake, the joint opinion of Justices O'Connor, Kennedy and Souter is an act of personal courage and constitutional principle.

But Blackmun also included this surprisingly candid and personal statement in his concurring opinion:

> I am 83 years old. I cannot remain on this court forever, and when I do step down, the confirmation process for my successor may well focus on the issue before us today. That, I regret, may be exactly where the choice between the two worlds will be made.

Of course, the confirmation battles involving Justices Kennedy, Souter and Thomas had all focused on this issue. All three were appointed by Republican presidents staunchly opposed to abortions, but two of them voted to uphold the basic tenets of *Roe v. Wade*. Ironically, when Blackmun did leave the court two years after the *Planned Parenthood* decision, the debate over the confirmation of his successor (Stephen G. Breyer) focused mainly on other issues. Nevertheless, no one--including the presidents who appoint Supreme Court justices--can predict which way the next Supreme Court decision on a volatile issue such as abortions will go.

In 2000, the Supreme Court decided its first abortion case since *Planned Parenthood*. The court ruled that a Nebraska law forbidding "partial birth abortions" placed an undue burden on a woman's constitutional right to terminate a pregnancy and is therefore unconstitutional (*Stenberg v. Carhart*, 530 U.S. 914). The Nebraska law defined partial birth abortion as a procedure in which a person "...intentionally delivers into the vagina a living unborn child, or a substantial portion thereof, for the purpose of performing a procedure" that the person knows "will kill the unborn child."

In essence, the court said this law (and similar laws banning partial-birth abortions in about 30 other states) is too broad, precluding abortion methods that are safer for the mother than some alternative methods used in late-term abortions. Chief Justice William Rehnquist and Justices Antonin Scalia, Anthony Kennedy and Clarence Thomas dissented, writing four separate opinions. In essence, they argued that a state should be free to ban partial birth abortions for various reasons. Scalia said, "The method of killing a human child... proscribed by this statute is so horrible that the most clinical description of it evokes a shudder of revulsion."

A year before the *Planned Parenthood* decision, the Supreme Court was called on to decide whether the federal government could tell health care providers who receive federal funds not to mention abortions to their patients. In *Rust v. Sullivan* (500 U.S. 173), the Supreme Court upheld such federal regulations. In so ruling, the court's 5-4 majority ruled that doctors do *not* have a First Amendment right to inform their patients about abortions. (However, the federal rules were later rewritten to eliminate this ban on federally-supported doctors mentioning abortions to their patients). Dissenting in the *Rust* case, Justice Harry Blackmun called the case a major retreat from previous decisions protecting First Amendment rights as well as the right of privacy. Blackmun wrote:

> One must wonder what force the First Amendment retains if it is read to countenance the deliberate manipulation by the government of the dialogue between a woman and her physician.

Thus, Blackmun was clearly surprised a year later when a 5-4 majority of the

Supreme Court declined to overturn *Roe v. Wade* itself. But while the Supreme Court's decisions about privacy rights in these controversial areas have made more headlines, the court has also recognized a right of privacy in several areas that directly affect the mass media. The rest of this chapter concerns the purely media-related aspects of privacy law.

AN OVERVIEW OF PRIVACY LAW

In 1960 William L. Prosser, one of the greatest legal scholars of his era, published an analysis of privacy law in which he said the concept of invasion of privacy really breaks down into four different legal rights. His classification has been widely accepted and provided the basis for many of the court decisions in this field that have followed. Prosser wrote:

> The law of privacy comprises four distinct kinds of invasion of four different interests of the plaintiff, which are tied together by a common name, but otherwise have almost nothing in common except that each represents an interference with the right of the plaintiff, in the phrase coined by Judge Cooley, 'to be let alone.' Without any attempt to (write an) exact definition, these four torts may be described as follows:
>
> 1. Intrusion upon the plaintiff's seclusion or solitude, or into his private affairs;
> 2. Public disclosure of embarrassing private facts about the plaintiff;
> 3. Publicity which places the plaintiff in a false light in the public eye;
> 4. Appropriation, for the defendant's advantage, of the plaintiff's name or likeness. (48 Calif. Law Review 383, 1960)

Courts in a number of states had recognized these four kinds of invasion of privacy before Prosser wrote his classic analysis; many others have done so in the years since. Even today, though, not all states recognize all four kinds of invasion of privacy as a legal wrong that may be remedied in a civil lawsuit. For example, at least 10 states have declined to recognize Prosser's third kind of invasion of privacy, that of holding someone up before the public in a false light. The false light concept closely parallels libel, and some states have chosen not to recognize it as a separate legal action apart from libel. But for the most part, Prosser's four-category breakdown of privacy law remains valid, and this chapter is organized around the four concepts.

The *intrusion* concept is based on a journalist's conduct as a newsgatherer. Reporters--and especially photographers or video crews--who pursue someone too aggressively may face this kind of lawsuit. The late 1990s saw an explosion in litigation of this kind.

Private facts cases usually result from the dissemination of intimate or embarrassing information about a person's private life or past--information that may be factually correct, thus precluding a successful libel suit.

Lawsuits based on holding a person before the public in a *false light* resemble libel suits because there must be an element of falsity in the communication. The basic difference between libel and false light privacy is that the latter does not necessarily require proof that the false statement is defamatory.

The fourth kind of invasion of privacy occurs most often in advertising and entertainment-related communications. Alternately called *misappropriation* or an invasion of the *right of publicity*, it prohibits the unauthorized use of a person's name, likeness, voice or some other element of his/her public persona for someone else's commercial gain.

As in libel law, there are defenses that the media may assert to escape liability in lawsuits for invasion of privacy. The two most widely recognized ones are *newsworthiness* (or *public interest*) and *consent*. If the media show that the subject matter of a news story or news broadcast is newsworthy, the plaintiff in a private facts lawsuit will normally lose in court. However, the newsworthiness defense is of little help when the alleged invasion of privacy involves an intrusion or holding a person before the public in a false light. Even celebrities have some right to be free of harassment by journalists, although that right is limited. And no amount of newsworthiness will excuse a story that holds someone up before the public in a false light. Nor is newsworthiness a helpful defense when the issue is an unauthorized commercial use of a person's name or likeness (in an advertisement, motion picture or poster, for instance). In fact, the more newsworthy a person is, the greater the potential injury is likely to be if his or her name or likeness is used commercially without consent.

The consent defense is most applicable in misappropriation cases: celebrities regularly give their consent to commercial uses of their names and likenesses, but for a fee. The consent defense could also be useful in other kinds of privacy lawsuits, provided it could be shown that the person suing actually gave consent.

In addition to these two common law defenses, the U.S. Supreme Court has created constitutional defenses in privacy cases, just as it has in libel cases. In fact, the *New York Times v. Sullivan* principle has been transplanted from libel to privacy law and applies in certain kinds of privacy cases. In addition, the Supreme Court has also recognized a constitutional right of the media to publish the contents of some public records that are lawfully obtained, notwithstanding anyone's claim that publishing the information is an invasion of privacy.

Although these defenses often enable the mass media to defeat invasion of privacy claims in court, the fact remains that serious legal hazards exist in this area. For that reason, the four major categories of invasion of privacy warrant a more detailed summary here.

INTRUSION

The concept of *intrusion* is based more on the conduct of a reporter, photographer or video crew than on the content of the mass media. It is a legal action to compensate a person when a journalist unduly intrudes into his or her *physical solitude or seclusion* or *private affairs*. It often involves snooping, eavesdropping, using a hidden camera or simply being in the way when someone has a reasonable right to expect a little peace and quiet.

In general, journalists have a right to ask questions or take pictures in public places without risking a lawsuit for this kind of invasion of privacy. In fact, in this era of miniaturized electronic listening devices and long telephoto lenses, technology has created a variety of new newsgathering opportunities (or threats to personal privacy, depending on your point of view). While the law affords journalists a good deal of latitude in gathering the news, there are limits to this right: journalists are sometimes sued for stepping over the bounds of propriety in their pursuit of a story or visual image. The growing popularity of "tabloid television" shows led to a number of new controversies and lawsuits in this area, as video crews aggressively pursued their subjects--often into their own private homes during "ride-alongs" with law enforcement officers. This has led to a series of new court decisions holding that the media may sometimes be sued for intrusive newsgathering, including two notable U.S. Supreme Court decisions in a two-year period.

Media ride-alongs were severely curtailed by a 1999 U.S. Supreme Court decision. In *Wilson v. Layne* (526 U.S. 603), the high court ruled that it violates the Fourth Amendment for law enforcement officers to allow the media to accompany them into private homes when they enter with search warrants or arrest warrants.

While *Wilson v. Layne* was a serious defeat for some newsgatherers, the second Supreme Court decision was a significant victory. In *Bartnicki v. Vopper* (532 U.S. 514), the high court held in 2001 that the media have a First Amendment right to broadcast a private cellphone conversation recorded by an unknown third party if it concerns a newsworthy subject. Both of these cases are discussed later.

Early Intrusion Cases

Long before cellphone eavesdropping and media ride-alongs with law enforcement officers became national issues and led to Supreme Court decisions, a number of individuals charged that intrusive newsgathering invaded their privacy. These early cases played a major role in shaping the modern concept of intrusion.

The pioneering case of *Dietemann v. Time Inc.* (449 F.2d 245, 9th cir., 1971) is a good example of an intrusion by journalists that violated someone's privacy. Two reporters for *Life* magazine investigated a man suspected of practicing medicine without a license by posing as a patient and her husband. They visited the man at his home--where he practiced his craft--and surreptitiously took photographs. They also carried a hidden transmitter so law enforcement personnel nearby could monitor and record the conversation. The result was a criminal prosecution and an article in *Life* called "Crackdown on Quackery."

The man accused of medical quackery sued for invasion of privacy and ultimately won $1,000 in general damages, but only after several years of litigation and an appeal to the U.S. Court of Appeals. In a 1971 decision the appellate court agreed that the pictures and story were newsworthy but said the reporters had intruded upon Dietemann's privacy in gathering the information. The magazine had a right to publish the story but it did not have the right to use hidden electronic devices in the man's home to get the information.

If the news media may not surreptitiously enter a private home to get a story, may journalists go into a private home that is the scene of a fire and take pictures at the invitation of a public official? The Florida Supreme Court addressed that question in a 1976 case, *Florida Publishing Co. v. Fletcher* (340 So.2d 914). A photographer took a picture of a silhouette left on the floor by a girl's body after a fire, and the girl's mother sued, claiming a trespass and an invasion of privacy, among other things.

The Florida Supreme Court found no actionable trespass or invasion of privacy in the photographer's actions. In fact, a fire marshal had asked the photographer to take the picture when the marshal's own camera ran out of film. The court said, "The fire was a disaster of great public interest and it is clear that the photographer and other members of the news media entered the burned home at the invitation of the investigating officers." The court noted that it was customary for journalists to accompany public officials to the scene of such disasters. In 1977 the U.S. Supreme Court refused to review this case. However, as noted earlier, in 1999 the high court ruled that when *law enforcement* officials enter private property with a search warrant and allow the media to go along, in many instances they are violating the Fourth Amendment and inviting a lawsuit.

Long before this, there were circumstances in which journalists who went onto private property without permission of the owner or tenant could be sued successfully. In one early case of this type, *Le Mistral Inc. v. CBS* (402 N.Y.S.2d 815, 1978), a New York court partially affirmed a trespass judgment against WCBS-TV. The case arose because a news camera crew photographed the interior of a swanky French restaurant over management objections in covering a story on health code violations.

The *Fletcher* and *Le Mistral* cases raise questions about the rights of photographers under privacy law. It is difficult to generalize on this subject because the rules vary somewhat from state to state, but in most states photographers who trespass to get a picture may face both civil and criminal sanctions unless they have consent to be there from someone authorized to give it. On the other hand, photographers in public places may generally shoot any subject within view for news purposes--but not for commercial or advertising purposes, for reasons that will be explained later in this chapter. There are occasional exceptions, but the general rule is that anything within camera range of a public place may be photographed for journalistic purposes. If the picture has even a little newsworthiness, and if no false impression is created with a misleading caption, it is usually safe.

Nevertheless, even in public places a photographer may not lawfully be so offensive in taking pictures that he seriously interferes with his subject's right to be left alone. The classic example of harassment by a photographer is the case of *Galella v. Onassis* (487 F.2d 986, 2d cir., 1973). Ron Galella, a free-lance photographer who made something of a career of photographing the late Jacqueline Kennedy Onassis and her children in the late 1960s and early 1970s, was ordered by a federal appellate court to stay 25 feet away from Onassis and even farther from her children. This was by no means a typical case: Galella's conduct prior to the court order had been outrageous. He had engaged in a variety of offensive activities, some of which actually endangered the safety of Onassis and her children. He followed her and her children, bumped into other people while taking pictures, spooked a horse her son was riding, and was generally underfoot at all hours.

In fact, a decade after the original lawsuit Onassis again hauled Galella into court for invading her privacy. She contended that he had repeatedly violated the original court order by failing to stay far enough away, among other things. The court agreed and found Galella in contempt (*Galella v. Onassis*, 533 F.Supp. 1076, 1982). The court emphasized--again--that Galella had a right to photograph Onassis (or any other celebrity) in public places, or to write articles about her if he wished. But Galella's conduct was so outrageous as to justify some restrictions on his activities, the court said. This was, in short, a rather unusual situation.

In more typical circumstances, there is little that celebrities can do about those who photograph them in public places, except perhaps to surround themselves with bodyguards whose job is to make it impossible for anyone to get an unobstructed shot. Occasionally, in fact, those who try to photograph the famous actually encounter violence from bodyguards. In those cases, photographers may well have grounds for their own lawsuits--against the celebrity's protectors. But that does nothing to salvage the pictures that the guards may either destroy or prevent the photographer from taking.

In recent years, however, the ability of journalists using powerful microphones and telephoto lenses to see and hear the activities of people in their own homes and other private places without trespassing has led many to rethink whether journalists should be free to report everything they can see or hear from a public place.

The Hazards of Intrusion: Ride-Alongs

By 2002, many lawsuits had been filed in state and federal courts charging journalists--particularly photographers, television crews and reporters with hidden cameras--with various wrongful acts. Many of these lawsuits alleged not only an invasion of privacy (intrusive newsgathering) but also an intentional infliction of emotional distress (see Chapter Four). By now many of these lawsuits have reached the appellate courts. The resulting court decisions have raised questions about the proper line between the First Amendment freedoms of journalists and the privacy rights of celebrities and others who are involved in newsworthy situations such as accidents.

In fact, this area of law has acquired a new name: *newsgathering torts*, a term that encompasses a variety of different legal theories being advanced by those who want to sue because of journalists' *newsgathering behavior*--as opposed to suing because of the *content* of what appears in the media. Those who are angry about journalists' newsgathering activities may sue for intrusion, of course, and for the infliction of emotional distress. In addition, the media are being sued for trespass, fraud and "outrage," which some states recognize as a tort.

The U.S. Supreme Court's *Wilson v. Layne* decision in 1999 made it clear that the media--and law enforcement officers--risk liability for media ride-alongs that allow journalists to enter a private home, even if the officers have a search warrant. The court held that while a search warrant gives officers the right to enter a private home, it is nevertheless a violation of the Fourth Amendment's ban on illegal searches and seizures for journalists to go into a home without the consent of residents.

The court reached this conclusion in considering appeals by several different persons whose homes (or in one case, a large ranch) were invaded by the news media during ride-alongs with officers. The *Wilson* case itself began when law enforcement officers, armed with an arrest warrant, entered the home of Charles and Geraldine Wilson at 6:45 a.m. to arrest their son, who turned out not to be living there. A *Washington Post* reporter and photographer entered the home with the officers and observed a scuffle between officers and Charles Wilson, who came out of his bedroom wearing only briefs to ask the officers why they were in his home. No photographs of the incident were ever published, but the Wilsons sued the officers for allowing journalists to enter their home.

The Supreme Court ruled that law enforcement officials are violating the Fourth Amendment in most instances when they allow the media to accompany them onto private property to conduct a search or make an arrest. Writing for the court, Chief Justice William Rehnquist said that the Fourth Amendment's protection against unreasonable searches and seizures "embodies centuries-old principles of respect for the privacy of the home.... It does not necessarily follow from the fact that the officers were entitled to enter (a suspect's) home that they (were) entitled to bring a reporter and a photographer with them."

The court stopped short of ruling that the officers could be sued in the *Wilson v. Layne* case--as opposed to future cases. Rehnquist noted that the law on ride-alongs may not have been clear before this definitive Supreme Court ruling. But in the future, there can be no doubt that officers who allow the media to accompany them onto private property to conduct searches or make arrests are inviting lawsuits for violating the Fourth Amendment.

Another case that troubled many journalists (and contributed to the Supreme Court's decision to hear *Wilson v. Layne*) was *Berger v. Hanlon* (129 F.3d 505), a 1997 decision of the ninth circuit U.S. Court of Appeals.

In the *Berger* case, Cable News Network arranged to send a television crew with federal wildlife agents on a raid of a 75,000-acre ranch in Montana. The federal agents suspected that Paul Berger, the elderly owner of the ranch, had killed American bald eagles in violation of the Endangered Species Act. An agent wearing a hidden microphone searched the ranch and questioned Berger and his wife inside their home.

The court said that by agreeing to cooperate with CNN, the federal agents had "transformed the execution of a search warrant into television entertainment." Judge Mary Schroeder held that the federal agents and CNN could both be sued for an allegedly unlawful intrusion, adding, "Law enforcement authority was used to assist commercial television, not to assist law enforcement objectives."

Berger was later acquitted of charges of killing protected species and convicted only of a misdemeanor pesticide charge that carried a $1,000 fine. In turn, the Bergers sued the federal agents--and CNN--for $10 million for the alleged invasion of privacy.

Responding to the appellate court ruling in the Bergers' favor, their attorney told the media, "Twenty armed agents carrying weapons in 10 trucks rolled onto my clients' property looking for something that didn't exist. What they were doing was performing for the cameras."

The *Berger* case was appealed to the U.S. Supreme Court. The high court considered it along with *Wilson v. Layne* and then sent the *Berger* case back to the U.S. Court of Appeals to reconsider the issue of law enforcement liability based on *Wilson v. Layne*. The high court said that the federal officers should be given *qualified immunity* for allowing the *Berger* ride-along because the law was not clear when the ride-along occurred. The appellate court then followed that reasoning, granting legal protection to the officers who authorized the ride-along, while holding that CNN itself was not entitled to qualified immunity, thereby leaving the network in a difficult legal position (see *Hanlon v. Berger*, 526 U.S. 808).

Even before *Wilson v. Layne*, media attorneys were warning of the legal hazards of intrusive journalism based on earlier adverse court decisions. In 1998, the California Supreme Court alarmed many media lawyers by ruling that a television producer may be sued when a crew shoots video of an accident victim being freed from a car and receiving emergency medical care in a rescue helicopter. In *Shulman v. Group W Productions* (18 C.4th 200), the court ruled that Ruth Shulman, the accident victim, had a right to go to trial with her claim that the video crew's coverage of her auto accident was unduly intrusive. Although the state Supreme Court was deeply divided in its reasoning, five of the seven justices agreed that the media can be sued for intruding on an accident victim's privacy, even if the accident itself is newsworthy. On the other hand, the justices agreed that the media could *not* be sued for the revelation of private facts in a situation as newsworthy as an accident scene near a major highway.

Writing the court's lead opinion, Justice Kathryn Mickle Werdegar said, "...the state may not intrude into the proper sphere of the news media to dictate what they should publish and broadcast, but neither may the media play tyrant to the people by unlawfully spying on them in the name of newsgathering.... A jury could reasonably believe that fundamental respect for human dignity requires the patient's anxious journey be taken only with those whose care is solely for them and out of sight of the prying eyes of others (via cameras)."

What appeared to trouble the justices most about the *Shulman* case was that the video crew secretly recorded Shulman's post-accident conversations with emergency workers at the scene and in the helicopter by using microphones hidden on paramedics.

The use of hidden cameras or microphones has been central to several other cases in which the courts have ruled that journalists could be sued for intrusive newsgathering. In the aftermath of these cases, most media attorneys are cautioning their clients that it is legally hazardous *ever* to do photographic or video coverage during a law enforcement ride-along in which journalists accompany officers onto private property, even if the photos are never published and the video is never aired. And now very few officers are willing to risk being sued by allowing ride-alongs that enter private property (unless someone with authority to do so gives consent for the media's presence).

The Hazards of Intrusion: Hidden Cameras and Secret Taping

The courts are also showing a growing impatience with the use of hidden cameras in private or semi-private places. In a widely noted 1999 decision, the California Supreme Court ruled that ABC could be sued for having reporter Stacy Lescht pose as a psychic and use a hidden camera to videotape the conversations of workers who were paid to give psychic advice via telephone. Ruling in *Sanders v. ABC* (20 C.4th 907), the high court ordered a lower court to consider reinstating $1.2 million in damages and attorney's fees that had been won by two employees of the telepsychic operation who were shown on ABC's PrimeTime Live.

Writing for a unanimous court, Justice Kathryn Mickle Werdegar said that even workers who talk openly to co-workers can have "a limited, but legitimate, expectation that their conversations and other interactions will not be secretly videotaped by undercover television reporters." However, she also said that the *Sanders* decision does not preclude all use of hidden cameras by journalists in the state. She said a violation of privacy only occurs if the intrusion is "highly offensive to a reasonable person," and that the determination of reasonableness should include consideration of the motives of newsgatherers. The media can still argue that the use of hidden cameras is justified in a specific situation by a legitimate need to gather news that could not be obtained in any other way.

In the *Sanders* case, the telepsychics worked in cubicles in a large room that was off limits to nonemployees. Lescht, the ABC reporter, sometimes stood on her chair and looked around the room. Unbeknownst to other employees, she had a camera hidden in a flower on her hat and a microphone attached to her brassiere. That, the court concluded, was unduly intrusive even though the resulting story revealed the newsworthy fact that the telepsychics did not always take the advice they were giving to 900-line callers very seriously.

The same ABC undercover investigation also led to a ninth circuit U.S. Court of Appeals decision in 1999. In this federal case, the court ruled that the subjects of hidden-camera exposes' cannot sue for federal wiretap violations unless they can show that a news organization *intended* to commit a crime or a civil wrong. This ruling came in *Sussman v. ABC* (186 F.3d 1200, cert. den. 528 U.S. 1131),

In *Sussman*, 12 employees of the telepsychic operation claimed that by surreptitiously recording their conversations and then airing them on PrimeTime Live, ABC had violated the federal anti-wiretapping statute. By adopting this legal strategy, their attorneys hoped to establish a precedent that would permit lawsuits against the media even in states that do not follow the *Sanders* precedent. But it didn't work. Writing for a unanimous federal appellate panel, Judge Alex Kozinski seemed to be saying that *Sanders* defines the outer limit of media liability for a hidden-camera expose'. He wrote: "Although the ABC taping may well have been a tortious invasion of privacy under state law, plaintiffs have provided no probative evidence that ABC had an illegal or tortious purpose when it made the tape."

The *Sanders* and *Sussman* cases are reminiscent of another case in which ABC was slapped with a $5.5 million jury verdict for having two PrimeTime Live staffers take jobs at the Food Lion grocery store chain in North and South Carolina--and use hidden cameras to record alleged health hazards in food processing. As noted in Chapter Four, that verdict was reduced to $315,000 by the trial judge and later reduced to a token amount ($2) by a federal appellate court. But ABC spent at least a million dollars by most estimates for its legal defense.

On the other hand, some recent court decisions have upheld the right of journalists to use hidden cameras and microphones. A notable example is *Deteresa v. ABC* (121 F.3d 460), a 1997 decision in which the ninth circuit U.S. Court of Appeals interpreted California privacy law to allow a television network to secretly tape a conversation between a producer and a reluctant news source on her front porch and then use a small portion on the air. The court dismissed a lawsuit against ABC by Beverly Deteresa, a flight attendant who worked the flight that carried O.J. Simpson to Chicago the night of the murders of Nicole Brown Simpson and Ron Goldman.

A week after the murders, an ABC producer went to Deteresa's condominium to ask her to appear on an ABC program and discuss the flight. She declined, but she also volunteered that she was "frustrated" to hear news reports about the flight that she knew were false. Among other things, she challenged news accounts that Simpson kept his hand in a bag of ice during the flight. After further conversation, she said she would "think about" appearing on ABC.

The producer called Deteresa the next day and again asked her to appear. When she declined, the producer told her he had recorded their conversation the previous day on her porch, and that an ABC cameraperson had videotaped them talking from a public street nearby. She hung up on the producer; later her husband called the producer and demanded that the tape not be aired.

ABC did air a five-second clip on Day One, along with a summary of her recollections of Simpson's behavior during the flight.

The appellate court held that Deteresa had no reasonable expectation of privacy when she talked to a TV producer on her front porch, in plain view of a nearby street. The court said ABC did not violate California's wiretap law, which forbids surreptitious taping of any "confidential communication" because that law applies only when someone reasonably expects *the content* of a conversation to be confidential. Deteresa knew she was talking to a media representative and that others could see and hear the conversation, the court pointed out. And she continued to talk to him about what she saw on the flight. Based on these facts, there was no violation of the wiretap law. Nor was there an actionable invasion of privacy by intrusion, the federal appellate court concluded. The U.S. Supreme Court later declined to hear an appeal of the *Deteresa* case.

Illustrating the complexity of the rapidly evolving law of hidden-camera journalism, the same court that upheld ABC's right to air secretly-taped video of Beverly Deteresa on her doorstep later ruled against another news organization that did something similar.

In 1999, the ninth circuit U.S. Court of Appeals ruled in *Alpha Therapeutic Corp. v. Nippon Hoso Kyokai (NHK)* (199 F.3d 1078) that it may be an invasion of privacy for a broadcaster to secretly tape an interview on someone's doorstep and then air the tape without consent. This time the court said a medical director and his company could sue because NHK, Japan's government-backed television network, did about the same thing that ABC did--but aired much more of the tape.

An NHK reporter went to the home of Alpha Therapeutic Medical Director Clyde McAuley and interviewed him at his door while wearing a hidden microphone. The conversation was secretly videotaped in a van parked on the street, as in the *Deteresa* case. However, NHK aired the audio tape of the interview. NHK used much of the actual interview in an hour-long program aired only in Japan. The program concerned charges that Alpha had shipped AIDS-tainted blood products to Japan. However, a shorter segment of the interview was also aired in the United States. The appellate court held that NHK was partially exempt from liability as an agency of a foreign government. But the court also ruled that the broadcast and newsgathering in the U.S. were actionable. The case was remanded to a lower court for a later trial.

In the *Alpha Therapeutic* case, the appellate court said a jury could conclude that the surreptitious taping was an invasion of privacy because McAuley knew only that he was talking to a reporter--he did not know the conversation was being taped. The court said "a person may reasonably expect privacy against the electronic recording of a communication, even though he or she had no reasonable expectation as to confidentiality of the communication's contents." The court held that a jury could find the taping to have been conducted in a private place, and to be "highly offensive" to a reasonable person--the two elements required for an actionable intrusion under California law. (Like *Deteresa*, this was a federal case based on diversity of citizenship, which requires the federal court to apply state law.) This court also cited California's wiretap law, which permits civil lawsuits by victims of surreptitious taping of any "confidential communication."

Unlike some state laws and the federal wiretap law, the California wiretap law requires all parties to a "confidential communication" to give consent for the conversation to be taped or monitored by others.

The California Supreme Court in 2002 adopted a very broad definition of the term, "confidential communication," increasing the number of conversations that would be considered confidential and therefore off-limits for secret taping or monitoring. The court disavowed the more narrow definition of "confidential communication" used by the federal court in the *Deteresa* case, underscoring the pitfalls for journalists who tape a conversation without the knowledge of all parties. In *Flanagan v. Flanagan* (27 C.4th 766, 2002), the court said a communication is confidential, and therefore cannot be secretly taped, whenever any party believes it is not being taped or monitored by anyone else. Under this definition, even a party who knows the *content* of a conversation is not confidential may have a reasonable expectation of privacy that precludes secret taping.

Again illustrating the complexity and contradictions on this area of law, another federal appellate court *upheld* the right of ABC to use hidden cameras for newsgathering in another part of the country in a 1995 decision, *Desnick v. American Broadcasting Company* (44 F.3d 1345). In this case, ABC's PrimeTime Live equipped seven persons with hidden cameras and had them pose as patients at clinics that did cataract procedures. The resulting story suggested that the Desnick Eye Centers, a chain of 25 eye clinics in Illinois, Indiana and Wisconsin, did unnecessary cataract surgeries for Medicare patients. The seventh circuit U.S. Court of Appeals held that Desnick did not have a right to sue for intrusion even though

ABC had people posing as patients enter the clinics with hidden cameras. The *Desnick* decision was particularly notable because the court's opinion was written by Richard A. Posner, one of America's best-known appellate judges and a widely quoted expert on privacy law.

The Hazards of Intrusion: A Supreme Court Ruling

The question of surreptitious monitoring and recording of telephone conversations--and then broadcasting them--resulted in a U.S. Supreme Court decision in 2001.

As noted earlier, that happened in the case of *Bartnicki v. Vopper*. In that case, the high court ruled that a broadcaster had a First Amendment right to air a newsworthy but pirated tape recording of a private cellphone call. By a 6-3 vote, the court rejected the argument that airing such a tape is a violation of the federal wiretap law.

In this case, a Pennsylvania broadcaster, Frederick Vopper, was given a tape of a conversation between two teacher's union officials. Whoever made the tape gave it anonymously to a local anti-tax crusader amidst a controversy over teachers' salaries. The anti-tax crusader then passed it on to Vopper, who broadcast it on his talk show several times. The tape included some fiery rhetoric aimed at local school leaders. At one point, one union official said to the other, "we're going to have to go to their homes...to blow off their front porches" if school board members resisted the union's demands for a pay raise. Gloria Bartnicki and another union leader sued Vopper for airing the tape of their conversation.

No one disputed the point that whoever monitored the phone call and made the tape violated the law. But the court ruled that when such a tape *concerns an issue of public concern and the media lawfully obtain it from a third party without participating in or encouraging the illegal taping*, the media have a First Amendment right to air the tape.

In reaching this conclusion, Justice John Paul Stevens relied heavily on the "Pentagon Papers" case (*New York Times v. U.S.*, discussed in Chapter Three), in which the court allowed the *Times* to publish excerpts from the so-called Pentagon Papers even though they had been illegally copied and then given to the *Times*.

"A stranger's illegal conduct does not suffice to remove the First Amendment shield about a matter of public concern," Stevens said.

However, two justices, Stephen G. Breyer and Sandra Day O'Connor, wrote a separate concurring opinion in which they took a narrower view than Stevens did of the media's rights in such cases. They said the media would not have the right to air a tape that reveals gossip about someone's private life, as opposed to a discussion of a major local issue such as teachers' salaries. And there were three dissenters, Chief Justice William Rehnquist and Justices Antonin Scalia and Clarence Thomas. They said the media should *not* be free of liability for airing a bootlegged tape of a private phone conversation even if it addresses an issue of public concern.

Thus, the result was a victory for the media, but a narrow one. The right to air a pirated tape extends only to a tape of a conversation about an issue of public concern--usually a political or social issue. Also, new telephone technologies have made the interception of private phone calls much more difficult in recent years. Media lawyers were widely quoted as hailing the *Bartnicki* decision as a good one--while emphasizing that it may have little real impact on personal privacy because of improvements in telephone privacy protection in the digital age.

Significantly, shortly after deciding *Bartnicki* the Supreme Court refused to intervene in another case where a television station played a more active role in illegal taping: *Peavy v. WFAA-TV* (221 F.3d 158, 2000). In this case, the fifth circuit U.S. Court of Appeals said the station could be held liable because a reporter cooperated with a family that illegally monitored and taped a neighbor's cordless telephone conversations. The neighbor, Carver Dan Peavy, was an elected Dallas, Texas school trustee. The taped conversations led the TV reporter to believe that Peavy had taken kickbacks on school insurance purchases. The tapes were *not* aired, but they were used by WFAA-TV in preparing several stories about alleged wrongdoing by Peavy. Peavy sued, but a trial court dismissed the case on First Amendment grounds. The appellate court reinstated the case.

The Hazards of Intrusion: Other Problems

With only a few exceptions, the clear trend today is for the courts to take a narrow view of aggressive newsgathering methods that allegedly intrude upon someone's physical solitude. And in the aftermath of Princess Diana's death, journalists are beginning to encounter statutory restrictions on their right to pursue newsworthy persons or use high-tech hardware to observe people in private places. In 1998 Congress considered legislation intended to curb paparazzi photographers and others who engage in aggressive newsgathering. A federal Personal Privacy Protection Act was drafted but not adopted.

A state anti-paparazzi law *was* enacted in 1998 in California. Under this law, it is a *constructive invasion of privacy* for journalists even to *attempt to* capture images or sounds of "personal or familial activities" on private property where there is a reasonable expectation of privacy if "enhancing devices" such as a boom microphone or telephoto lens are used to capture images or sounds that could not be obtained without these devices. And if journalists trespass to obtain such images or sounds, that is also an invasion of privacy--regardless of whether they use enhancing devices. In either case, victims may sue for *treble damages* (three times the actual damages).

Even in states without this kind of law, aggressive journalists may risk not only civil lawsuits but also criminal sanctions. At various times journalists have been charged with trespassing, assault and reckless driving, among other things.

Of the many tabloid television cases that have been litigated, few are as notable--and troubling--as *Clift v. Narragansett Television* (688 A.2d 805), in which a news person spoke by phone with a man who was barracaded in his home, threatening to commit suicide. The man apparently watched the television news, which included a taped excerpt from the phone call, at 6:04 p.m. and then killed himself at 6:07--with his television set still on and tuned to the station that aired the newscast. His widow sued the station on various legal grounds, and in late 1996 the Rhode Island Supreme Court denied the station's motion to have the case dismissed.

DISCLOSURE OF PRIVATE FACTS

The second widely recognized kind of invasion of privacy is the *public disclosure of private facts*. In many states, to win a private facts case, a plaintiff has to prove that there was a public disclosure of a private fact that is not newsworthy and in a manner that is offensive or objectionable to a reasonable person. A few states including Oregon allow private facts lawsuits only if the revelation is truly outrageous (*outrage* as a legal concept is discussed later in this chapter). And several states, including New York and North Carolina, do not recognize this form of invasion of privacy. In 1997, a plurality of the Indiana Supreme Court rejected private facts as a legal action in that state (*Doe v. Methodist Hospital*, 690 N.E.2d 681). On the other hand, in 1998 the Minnesota Supreme Court broke new legal ground by recognizing not only the private facts concept but also intrusion and misappropriation as actionable forms of invasion of privacy in that state (*Lake v. Wal-Mart Stores*, 582 N.W.2d 231).

A legal action for the revelation of private facts provides a remedy for a person who has been embarrassed by a publication but may have little chance to win a libel suit because the facts revealed are accurate. In many states this type of invasion of privacy causes problems for journalists, often because it is hard to anticipate which stories may lead to lawsuits. What may seem clearly newsworthy to journalists may seem to be a flagrant instance of revealing private facts to someone else. Perhaps a summary of some of the situations that have led to lawsuits will help illustrate the problem.

In some states, publishing or broadcasting information about a person's shady past may lead to litigation, especially if the person has changed his way of life. Over the years California courts have led the nation in this area, entertaining lawsuits in several instances where details of a person's embarrassing past were revealed. The earliest--and perhaps still the best known--of these old-but-true-facts cases is a 1931 California Appellate Court ruling, *Melvin v. Reid* (112 C.A. 285). The case resulted from a motion picture that revealed the past activities of a former prostitute who had been charged with murder and acquitted. Her maiden name was used in the movie advertising. However, after the murder trial the woman had moved to another town, married and adopted a new lifestyle. She said her new friends were unaware of her past. The court ruled that she was entitled to sue for invasion of privacy. In so doing, the court created a *social utility* test to determine whether the newsworthiness defense should apply. In *Melvin* and some later California cases, courts held that if a communication had little social utility or social value, the newsworthiness defense might not apply.

Actually, the movie producer in the *Melvin* case was guilty of two different kinds of invasion of privacy: revealing private facts and commercially exploiting the woman's name without permission. The latter type of invasion of privacy is discussed later.

In several rulings since the *Melvin* case, California courts have reiterated their position that a person's privacy may sometimes be invaded by the republication of old news if the republication has little social utility. In the 1971 case of *Briscoe v. Reader's Digest* (4 C.3d 529), the California Supreme Court allowed a lawsuit to proceed where the *Reader's Digest* had published the name of a man convicted of truck hijacking 11 years earlier. The man had been rehabilitated and started a family in another place. His new family and friends first learned of his past from the magazine article. Although the man ultimately lost his case, the state Supreme Court said there was a legal basis for a lawsuit under such circumstances.

In 1978, a California appellate court handed down a similar ruling in a case called *Conklin v. Sloss* (86 C.A.3d 241). That one involved a small newspaper's "Twenty Years Ago..." column. The paper republished the story of a local man's murder conviction, and the man sued, contending that he had paid his debt to society and acquired new friends unaware of his past. The appellate court said he, too, had a right to pursue his contention that his privacy had been invaded. Like Briscoe, he lost at the trial court level, but the precedent from both cases--that a person in this situation has a right to sue--may still be valid, at least in California. Even in California, though, this principle doesn't necessarily apply to anyone except rehabilitated criminals, according to a 1980 state Supreme Court ruling (*Forsher v. Bugliosi*, 26 C.3d 792).

Moreover, these decisions have been followed in few other states. Most state courts have not been willing to entertain invasion of privacy lawsuits based on factually accurate revelations of a person's past misdeeds. In fact, in *Cox Broadcasting v. Cohn* (420 U.S. 469, 1975) and several later cases the U.S. Supreme Court ruled that it is unconstitutional for the media to be held accountable under privacy law for an accurate publication of information they lawfully obtain from court records and perhaps other public documents.

The *Cox* Supreme Court decision resulted from a news broadcast that identified a rape victim in Georgia. A Georgia law prohibited publishing or broadcasting the identity of rape victims, but a reporter was given a copy of the court records during criminal proceedings against several young men accused of the rape. The victim, Cynthia Cohn, was identified in these public records, and Cox Broadcasting used the name in its coverage of the trial. The victim's father, Martin Cohn, sued Cox Broadcasting, contending that the broadcasts identifying his daughter invaded his privacy.

The Georgia Supreme Court upheld the law against publishing rape victims' names and also ruled that the father could sue under common law invasion of privacy principles. However, in 1975 the U.S. Supreme Court reversed that decision. Writing for an 8-1 majority, Justice Byron White ruled that a state may not impose sanctions against the media for accurately reporting the contents of open court records such as those involved in this case. Quoting an earlier opinion by Justice William O. Douglas, Justice White said: "A trial is a public event. What transpires in the courtroom is public property."

At the time, this decision was widely viewed as a victory for the mass media. As noted in Chapter Three, the Supreme Court has also applied this principle in some other circumstances. A later Supreme Court decision suggested that the *Cox* rule was not limited to court records:

> Our holding there (in *Cox*) was that a civil action against a television station for breach of privacy could not be maintained consistently with the

First Amendment when the station had broadcast only information which was already in the public domain. (*Landmark Communications v. Virginia*, 435 U.S. at 840, 1978)

A widely respected summary of tort law, the *Restatement (Second) of Torts*, takes the same position on this point, declaring, "The case (*Cox*) ...holds that under the First Amendment there can be no recovery for disclosure of and publicity to facts that are a matter of public record."

However, in a 1989 decision, *Florida Star v. B.J.F.* (491 U.S. 524), the Supreme Court avoided broadly interpreting the *Cox* rule, as Chapter Three explains. While the 1989 case also overturned an invasion of privacy judgment against a news organization for publishing a rape victim's name, the 1989 decision is more limited in scope. In fact, this time the court said that the media are not necessarily exempt from all lawsuits even when they accurately report information that they lawfully obtain. If the information is obtained lawfully from court records, it is safe to publish. But the Supreme Court stopped short of saying that the same thing is always true when the information is obtained elsewhere. On the other hand, state laws banning the publication or broadcast of sex crime victims' names have also faced constitutional challenges in state courts. As noted in Chapter Three, the Florida Supreme Court overturned such a law in 1994 in *Florida v. Globe Communications Corp.* (648 So.2d 110).

If *Cox v. Cohn* and the newer *Florida Star* case give the media the right to publish information they lawfully obtain from court records, does that mean state laws against publishing the names of juvenile offenders are invalid? The U.S. Supreme Court has also addressed that issue.

Naming Juveniles and other Ethical Issues

Obviously, there are ethical as well as legal issues involved in publishing the names of sex crime victims and juvenile offenders. But in both areas, many of the legal issues have now been resolved in favor of the media. The Supreme Court in 1979 ruled that no state may impose *criminal sanctions* where the media have disseminated the names of juvenile offenders, even if that information was secured from sources other than public records. The high court didn't rule out *civil* invasion of privacy lawsuits where such information is secured from unofficial sources, but at least criminal prosecution of journalists was forbidden.

The 1979 case (*Smith v. Daily Mail*, 443 U.S. 97) was a test of a West Virginia law making it a crime for a newspaper to publish the name of any young person involved in juvenile court proceedings. The case arose when two newspapers were indicted after they identified a 14-year-old boy charged with fatally shooting a schoolmate. The shooting occurred at a junior high school, and journalists learned the name from eyewitnesses. They also heard the name by monitoring a police band radio.

After the indictments, the West Virginia Supreme Court overturned both the indictments and the state law, and the U.S. Supreme Court agreed. Chief Justice Warren Burger wrote:

At issue is simply the power of a state to punish the truthful publication of an alleged juvenile delinquent's name lawfully obtained by a newspaper.

In voiding this West Virginia law, the court said that the magnitude of the state's interest in protecting the anonymity of juvenile crime suspects is not sufficient to justify imposition of criminal penalties on the newspapers.

However, Burger warned that the court might uphold a similar law if there were an issue of "unlawful press access to a confidential judicial proceeding" or an issue of "privacy or prejudicial pretrial publicity," or if the publication were false.

Still, this represented another instance when the Supreme Court felt it necessary to intervene to protect the right of the media to disseminate lawfully obtained information. The *Smith v. Daily Mail* case did not create a new privacy defense, but it did make it clear that criminal prosecution of the media is not an appropriate way to prevent the dissemination of juvenile names (and presumably other kinds of information that could be embarrassing).

Another important point to remember about *Smith v. Daily Mail* is that it did not prohibit invasion of privacy lawsuits for publication of personal information that is not part of a public record; the Supreme Court only banned criminal sanctions. Moreover, the Supreme Court has not created any special right of access to the names of rape victims and juvenile offenders. It is still constitutionally permissible for a state to keep that kind of information secret--and many states do so. But if the media do obtain the information lawfully, it may be published without fear of criminal prosecution. And, as just explained, the *Cox* case and several later Supreme Court decisions generally protect the media from civil suits for invasion of privacy when they lawfully obtain the names of sex crime victims from public records. But there are several unresolved problems in this area--particularly where the media obtain the information from confidential sources instead of public records.

The ethical problems in this area were underscored by the nationally televised 1991 rape trial of William Kennedy Smith, a nephew of Sen. Edward Kennedy, D-Mass. While most of the media honored the Florida law that barred publishing alleged rape victims' names (a law that was later ruled unconstitutional, as noted previously), the *New York Times* and several other leading news media published the woman's name. (After the name appeared in *The Times*, many *Times* staffers held a rally to protest that editorial decision.) After Smith's acquittal by a jury, the woman agreed to be interviewed on camera by ABC-TV. At that point, most news media began using her name.

Still another case that raised powerful ethical questions as well as legal ones is *M.G. v. Time Warner* (107 Cal. Rptr.2d 504), in which a California appellate court allowed Little League parents to sue because *Sports Illustrated* published a photo of their children alongside their coach, who turned out to be a child molester. Although none of the children was named, they were identifiable in the photo. The appellate court refused to dismiss the lawsuit, ruling that the photo was not necessarily newsworthy and that publishing it could be an "intrusion" that "outweighs the values of journalistic impact and credibility." Time Warner attorneys assailed the decision, which cleared the way for a trial, as legally wrong, allowing a lawsuit for publication of "truthful, nonprivate information on a subject of legitimate importance."

Another unresolved question is whether it is still constitutionally proper for a state to allow lawsuits for the publication of information taken from *old* public records. As noted earlier, California, for instance, has continued to allow such lawsuits despite the *Cox* decision. If the Supreme Court has said state courts may not impose liability for any publication of information obtained from court records, shouldn't that apply to old as well as new public records? Taken together, the *Cox* and *B.J.F.* cases seem to say that the media may report the contents of any judicial record they lawfully obtain--including old records.

Moreover, California and several other states have been reluctant to apply the *Cox* rule across the board--especially in difficult situations. For example, there was a troubling 1988 case about the naming of a woman who could identify a murderer: *Times Mirror Co. v. Superior Court of San Diego County* (198 C.A.3d 1420). In this case, a woman returned home just after her roommate had been raped and murdered. As she arrived, she saw the murderer leaving. The *Los Angeles Times* published her name and said she had discovered the body, but did not identify her as the person who also saw the fleeing suspect. Nonetheless, she sued, contending that publishing her name while the suspect was at large endangered her safety.

The *Times* argued that the use of the name was absolutely privileged because the name was in the official coroner's report, a public record. However, a California appellate court declined to order the case dismissed on a 2-1 vote. Although the dissenting judge said the ruling could have a chilling effect on First Amendment freedoms, the other two judges who heard the appeal concluded that the First Amendment does *not* necessarily apply here. They were clearly troubled by the facts of this case: a major newspaper publishing the name of someone who could identify a suspected murderer who was not in custody.

When no higher court was willing to hear the *Times*' appeal, the newspaper settled the case by paying an undisclosed sum of money to the woman.

For the moment, at least, it appears that some courts will continue to allow invasion of privacy lawsuits under a few circumstances when information from a public record is revealed, despite the *Cox Broadcasting* and *B.J.F.* Supreme Court decisions.

Private Facts: Other Contexts

In addition to the kinds of cases discussed so far, there are other situations that produce private facts lawsuits. Often the facts are contemporaneous and correct but simply embarrassing for some reason. In these cases, the crucial issue is usually whether the facts fall within the newsworthiness defense.

There have been many such cases litigated over the years, and most of them were ultimately won by the mass media. However, the litigation is often protracted and costly, and the threat of such a lawsuit is often a deterrent to publishing stories containing embarrassing personal information. A good example of such a lawsuit is *Virgil v. Time Inc.* (527 F.2d 1122, 9th cir., 1975). This case involved Mike Virgil, a surfing enthusiast who was profiled in an article in *Sports Illustrated*. The writer of the article had interviewed Virgil at great length and had also received Virgil's permission to photograph him. Before the article was published, Virgil revoked all consent for publication of the article and photographs because he feared the article would focus on bizarre incidents in his life that were not directly related to surfing.

The fact that Virgil revoked his consent for the publication did not mean the article could not be published. The news media routinely publish and broadcast stories about people who don't want publicity. When an item is published or broadcast without the subject's consent, it merely means the publisher or broadcaster must be certain it is newsworthy enough to preclude a successful lawsuit for invasion of privacy.

The article about Mike Virgil was published over his objections, and it contained this quotation:

> Every summer I'd work construction and dive off billboards to hurt myself or drop loads of lumber on myself to collect unemployment compensation so I could surf at The Wedge.

The article also said he had extinguished a cigarette in his mouth and had eaten spiders and insects.

Virgil sued for invasion of his privacy, and his lawsuit reached the ninth circuit Court of Appeals on a motion to dismiss the case before trial. The appellate court said that unless a subject is newsworthy, the publicizing of private facts is not protected by the First Amendment. The court said:

> In determining what is a matter of legitimate public interest, account must be taken of the customs and conventions of the community, and what is proper becomes a matter of the community mores.

The U.S. Supreme Court refused to review the circuit court's ruling that Virgil had a right to take his case to trial. The case went back to a federal district court, which ruled that *Sports Illustrated* published a "newsworthy" article that in fact generally portrayed Virgil in a positive way in the context of prevailing social mores (424 F.Supp. 1286, 1976).

Thus, the magazine eventually won the *Virgil* case, but only after a protracted and expensive legal battle. Moreover, the appellate court's ruling left much room for uncertainty about which stories are protected by the newsworthy defense and which ones are not. Newsworthiness is a broad but vague privacy defense.

The newsworthiness defense also was used successfully by the *Des Moines Register* in a 1979 case of an entirely different sort, *Howard v. Des Moines Register* (283 N.W.2d 289). This case was filed by Robin Howard after a news story disclosed that she had been involuntarily sterilized while a resident in a county facility. Howard said that the newspaper had invaded her privacy by giving unreasonable publicity to her private life. She said that friends and acquaintances were not aware of her surgery and that such publicity humiliated her, causing mental pain and anguish.

The trial court granted summary judgment in the case on the grounds that the information in its context was newsworthy. The article focused on the facility's alleged poor care and lax administration. The Iowa Supreme Court affirmed the trial court and ruled that "the disclosure of plaintiff's involuntary sterilization was closely related to the subject matter of the news story." The court went on to say: "...they had a right to treat the identity of victims of involuntary sterilizations as matters of legitimate public concern. The subject is one of grave public interest." The court also said:

> The article is an example of investigative journalism. Its obvious purpose was to bring the problems of the Jasper County Home to public attention. In chronicling alleged abuses in the home, defendants portrayed a pattern of incidents which cumulatively established more reason for public concern about management of the home than would any one incident viewed in isolation. This journalistic technique is basic and legitimate.

Another private facts case where the newsworthiness or public interest defense prevailed for the media involved stories in both the University of Maryland *Diamondback* and the *Washington Star* reporting that six University of Maryland basketball players were in academic trouble. The university newspaper even published the players' grade point averages.

The six players sued the newspapers, seeking $72 million in damages for an invasion of privacy and mental duress. Both a lower court and the Maryland Court of Special Appeals agreed that the players had sought the "limelight" by joining the team. Therefore, they "will not be heard to complain when the light focuses on their potentially imminent withdrawal from the team." The court, in putting the facts in perspective, said basketball in Maryland was a big-time sport and information about team members was a matter of legitimate public interest (*Bilney v. Evening Star*, 406 A.2d 652, 1979).

But what about the people who aren't basketball players, champion surfers, or patients in a public custodial institution? Suppose an ordinary citizen happens to be in the right place at the right time to do something heroic, and as a result the whole world learns intimate details of his or her life. Has that person's privacy been invaded?

A very good example of this problem is the case of Oliver Sipple, who may have saved former President Gerald Ford's life during an assassination attempt in 1975. When Sara Jane Moore, the would-be assassin, took aim at the president, Sipple struck her arm and caused her shot to miss. He was hailed as a hero, but soon the media also revealed the fact that he was a homosexual, an active member of the San Francisco gay community. He sued for invasion of privacy, but the California Court of Appeal ruled that the stories about his sexual preferences were newsworthy, given all of the circumstances (*Sipple v. Chronicle Publishing Co.*, 10 Med.L.Rptr. 1690, 1984).

However, the court ordered that its decision in the *Sipple* case not be published in the official reports of California appellate court decisions. Under California law, unpublished decisions may not be cited as legal precedents. This is, nonetheless, an interesting case that raises difficult ethical and legal issues.

Another case that raises troubling ethical as well as legal issues is *Diaz v. Oakland Tribune* (139 C.A.3d 118, 1983). Toni Ann Diaz was originally a male, but she underwent surgery to change her sex. Then she enrolled at a community college and was eventually elected student body president. Apparently no one on campus was aware of the sex change operation until it was revealed in a column in the *Oakland Tribune*. She sued for invasion of privacy and won a jury verdict of $775,000. But an appellate court overturned the verdict and ordered a new trial, ruling that the trial judge erred in requiring the newspaper to prove the story newsworthy. Instead, the burden should have been on Diaz to prove that the story was *not* newsworthy, the appellate court held. As student body president, Diaz had often been in the news; she dropped the case rather than go through a second trial at which she would have to prove that the story was not newsworthy. Nonetheless, the newspaper's decision to reveal the interesting but perhaps irrelevant fact of Diaz' sex change raises ethical questions.

Perhaps even more troubling--and a good illustration of the legal hazards of journalistic sensationalism--is an Orlando, Florida case in which a television station showed a video of a police officer holding the skull of a six-year-old girl who was kidnapped and murdered. The girl's family--and thousands of other viewers--were shocked by the video, shown on the evening news without any warning, even to the family. In *Armstrong v. H & C Communications* (575 So. 2d 280), a Florida appellate court ruled that showing the skull was not an actionable invasion of privacy because of the public interest in the girl's abduction and the discovery of her remains. On the other hand, the court ruled that the family could sue the station on the legal theory that showing the video was an outrageous act.

Like a number of other states, Florida recognizes *outrage* as a separate basis for a lawsuit--a legal wrong somewhat akin to the *intentional infliction of emotional distress* (see Chapter Four). In states that recognize outrage as a legal wrong, a person may be sued for engaging in a course of conduct that would make a reasonable person angry enough to say, "that is outrageous," even though the wrongful act may not fit into any other category that is recognized as a basis for a lawsuit. In the *Armstrong* case, there was evidence not only that the video angered many viewers but also that it was shown over the objections of some members of the station's staff, and that the station later expressed regrets when it became clear that many viewers were offended. Those facts could form the basis for a lawsuit against the station, the Florida court held. A California appellate court reached a similar conclusion in a case where a television reporter confronted several children and told them two neighborhood children were killed by their mother, who then killed herself. The reporter asked the children for their reaction to this news. The court said the reporter and the television station could be sued for the intentional infliction of emotional distress under these circumstances (*KOVR-TV v. Superior Court of Sacramento County*, 31 C.A.4th 1023, 1995).

These cases involving outrage or emotional distress are often reminiscent of the situations that may lead to lawsuits for the *intrusion* form of invasion of privacy. There is clearly an overlap among the various areas of privacy law and some of the similar legal actions that have evolved in recent years.

To summarize, the private facts area of privacy law is by no means clearly defined. Usually the media win private facts lawsuits by asserting the newsworthiness defense, but even then, a court may allow the lawsuit to go to trial on some other legal basis. Also, no one--not the courts, not legal scholars, and indeed not even journalists--can precisely define newsworthiness. Another unresolved issue is when the media may be sued for revealing allegedly private facts contained in public records, given the *Cox* case's strong affirmation of the constitutional protection for news reports of information lawfully obtained from public records.

The conflict between the individual's right to keep private facts private and the media's right to report the news raises a number of other ethical questions, too. For instance, should the media be able to make a person a celebrity by intensive coverage and then defend against a privacy lawsuit by citing that celebrity status? Does mere publicity make a person newsworthy, or must one already be newsworthy before publicity is permitted? Moreover, when the media make the judgment that someone is newsworthy and publicize his or her activities, should the First Amendment permit the courts to second-guess that judgment?

FALSE LIGHT AND FICTIONALIZATION

The third area of privacy law that has produced litigation for the media is sometimes referred to as *false light* invasion of privacy. It involves publicity that places the plaintiff in a false light before the public. This kind of privacy case might be described as a libel case but without the defamation.

As noted earlier, false light is recognized in most states, but it has been rejected as a valid basis for a lawsuit in at least 10 states. For example, in 1984 the North Carolina Supreme Court rejected the false light concept in that state (*Renwick v. News and Observer*, 312 S.E.2d 405). A decade later, the Texas Supreme Court ruled similarly, rejecting the false light concept in Texas (*Cain v. Hearst Corp.*, 878 S.W.2d 577). The Texas Supreme Court said it was rejecting the false light concept because it "substantially duplicates the tort of defamation (i.e., libel and slander) while lacking many of its procedural limitations." By 2000, appellate courts in Massachusetts, Minnesota, Mississippi, Missouri, Ohio, Virginia, Washington and Wisconsin had joined the Texas and North Carolina courts in refusing to recognize false light invasion of privacy. In 2001, the Colorado Supreme Court agreed to decide whether false light should be recognized as a basis for a lawsuit in that state (*Denver Publishing Co. v. Bueno*, 2001 Colo. Lexis 813).

Where it is recognized, a person may sue when portrayed falsely in a manner that would be highly offensive to a reasonable person.

Photographers (or more correctly, those who write captions for photographs) have been especially vulnerable to this kind of lawsuit, but other journalists should also be aware of the pitfalls in this area. In fact, two different false light privacy cases stemming from inaccurate reporting have reached the U.S. Supreme Court.

The first of these false light Supreme Court decisions came in 1967. The case, *Time Inc. v. Hill* (385 U.S. 374), involved the James J. Hill family, which gained notoriety when it was taken hostage in its own home by three escaped convicts in 1952. The incident was clearly newsworthy, especially because two of the three convicts were eventually killed in a shoot-out with police.

One year after the event, novelist Joseph Hayes published *The Desperate Hours*, a story about a family taken hostage by escaped convicts. Later the novel was made into a play and a motion picture. The story line differed in significant ways from the Hill family's experiences, although there were similarities. For example, the escaped convicts were not brutal to the Hill family during the real hostage situation, but in the book the escapees did commit acts of violence toward the fictional hostage family.

An invasion of privacy suit was filed by the Hill family in 1955 after an article was published in *Life* magazine reviewing the play based on Hayes' book. *Life* directly stated that the play was based on the Hill family incident. The Hills sought damages on grounds that the magazine article "was intended to, and did, give the impression that the play mirrored the Hill family's experience, which, to the knowledge of defendant ...was false and untrue."

The Hill family won a $30,000 judgment in the New York state courts, but Time Inc., appealed the case to the U.S. Supreme Court, which in 1967 reversed the New York judgment.

Justice William Brennan, writing for a divided court, applied the *New York Times v. Sullivan* libel rule to this kind of privacy lawsuit. Brennan said persons involved in a matter of public interest could not win a false light privacy suit unless they could show that the falsehood was published either knowingly or with reckless disregard for the truth. Although some have suggested that the Hills could have proven reckless disregard for the truth if they had opted to pursue the case through a second trial, they dropped the case instead.

In transplanting the *New York Times v. Sullivan* rule into privacy law, Justice Brennan emphasized that it was to be applied only in the "discrete context of the facts of the Hill case." Nevertheless, Brennan's opinion has often been applied by state courts and was cited in a later U.S. Supreme Court ruling on false light invasion of privacy.

That later ruling, *Cantrell v. Forest City Publishing Co.* (419 U.S. 245, 1974), presented the U.S. Supreme Court with the chance to abandon the *Time Inc. v. Hill* requirement in privacy cases the same year the court limited application of the *New York Times* rule to public figures in libel cases, but the court didn't address that issue. Instead the court upheld an invasion of privacy judgment against a newspaper by saying the paper was guilty of "calculated falsehoods" and "reckless untruth." The court did not say what the outcome of the case would have been if the newspaper had been guilty of nothing more than negligence.

The *Cantrell* case resulted from newspaper coverage of the consequences of the collapse of a bridge across the Ohio River. A man named Melvin Cantrell was among 44 victims, and Joseph Eszterhas, a *Cleveland Plain Dealer* reporter, followed up the tragedy with a feature story about how the man's death affected his widow and children. Several months after the accident, Eszterhas and photographer Richard Conway visited the Cantrell residence to gather information for the follow-up story. Margaret Cantrell, the widow, was not home, so Eszterhas talked to the children and Conway took many pictures. The resulting feature appeared as the lead story in the *Plain Dealer*'s Sunday magazine. It stressed the family's abject poverty and contained a number of inaccuracies including a description of Margaret Cantrell's mood and attitude, with statements clearly implying that Eszterhas had talked to her.

Mrs. Cantrell brought an action for invasion of privacy against the publisher of the newspaper. When the U.S. Supreme Court reviewed the case in 1974, it upheld a $60,000 judgment in her favor. The Supreme Court said the evidence showed that the newspaper "had published knowing or reckless falsehoods about the Cantrells." The court also said much of what was published consisted of "calculated falsehoods and the jury was plainly justified in finding that ...the Cantrells were placed in a false light through knowing or reckless untruth."

Interestingly enough, the Supreme Court ruled that the photographer who took the pictures should not be held liable since there was no misrepresentation inherent in his pictures. In comparison, there was an obvious misrepresentation in the feature story itself.

The *Hill* and *Cantrell* cases are notable because they reached the U.S. Supreme Court--but they are not necessarily representative of all false light privacy lawsuits. As indicated earlier, another common source of false light privacy lawsuits is misleading photo captions. Two California Supreme Court decisions in the 1950s nicely illustrate the problem in this area.

Both lawsuits were initiated by John and Sheila Gill, a couple who operated a candy and ice cream store at Farmer's Market, a tourist attraction in Los Angeles. Noted photographer Henri Cartier-Bresson caught the couple sitting side by side at the counter in their shop. John had his arm around Sheila, and they were leaning forward with their cheeks touching. The photo, taken without permission on private property that was open to the public, was published in both *Harper's Bazaar*, a Hearst publication, and *Ladies Home Journal*, a Curtis publication.

The Hearst publication used the photo to illustrate an article entitled, "And So the World Goes Round." The couple was described as "immortalized in a moment of tenderness." However, the Curtis publication used the photo in a different context. There, it illustrated an article on the dangers of "love at first sight," with statements such as this one: "Publicized as glamorous, love at first sight is a bad risk." Further, the article went on to condemn this sort of thing as love based on "instantaneous powerful sex attraction--the wrong kind of love."

The Gills sued both publishers, but the two lawsuits produced opposite results. In *Gill v. Hearst Corporation* (40 C.2d 224, 1953), the couple lost. The California Supreme Court found no misrepresentation of their status, and thus no basis for an invasion of privacy lawsuit. But in *Gill v. Curtis Publishing* (38 C.2d 273, 1952), the couple won: the court found that the Gills had been held up before the public in a false light, since there was no basis for saying their relationship was "love at first sight" or based merely on "instantaneous ...sex attraction."

The two *Gill* cases are typical of many others that have been filed since. If there is a general rule in these situations, it is that a photograph is reasonably safe if the caption is not misleading, provided it was taken in a public place and is used in a manner that falls within the newsworthiness defense. However, if the caption creates a false impression about the people in the picture, or if it is used for a commercial purpose such as advertising (as opposed to a journalistic purpose), the risk of a lawsuit for invasion of privacy is often much greater.

MISAPPROPRIATION

The fourth type of invasion of privacy protects people from the unauthorized commercial use of their names, photographs and other aspects of their "public personas." This concept has been given several names, including *misappropriation* or *commercial appropriation*. Today it is often referred to as a violation of the *right of publicity*. Perhaps it has more than one name because it is a very broad legal concept; no one term really describes all of the kinds of legal issues involved in this field. Whatever its name, this concept is quite different from the other three kinds of privacy law: it usually involves the economic rights of people whose names are well known, not the personal rights of private individuals who just want to be left alone.

Although right of publicity lawsuits are occasionally filed by private persons whose names or photographs were used for someone else's commercial gain, more often the plaintiffs in these lawsuits are celebrities, people whose names have great commercial value. Usually the problem isn't that the celebrity objects to publicity; what he or she objects to is not being adequately *paid*. An endorsement or an appearance by a celebrity may be worth thousands (or even millions) of dollars, and the celebrity's lawyers want to make sure their client collects. There are times, of course, when a celebrity doesn't want to endorse a particular product at all, regardless of what fee may be offered. And some celebrities simply refuse to do *any* endorsements.

The media have the right to do *news stories* and publish newsworthy photographs of celebrities as often as they wish--with or without permission. No celebrity has the right to keep his or her name or picture out of the news media. What the right of publicity prevents is the unauthorized *commercial exploitation* of the celebrity's name or likeness (in advertising or product endorsements, for example).

The right of publicity is the oldest privacy right to be recognized by the law. The 1902 *Roberson* case, discussed in the section on the history of privacy, would be called a right of publicity case if it were decided today. The New York statutory privacy law that was enacted in response to the *Roberson* decision is fundamentally a right of publicity law--it protects a person's name and likeness from unauthorized commercial exploitation.

In the years since that pioneering New York case, most states have recognized the right of publicity in some form, either by statute or court decision. The concept was given its contemporary name in a 1953 U.S. Court of Appeals decision, *Haelan Laboratories v. Topps Chewing Gum* (202 F.2d 866, 2d cir., 1953). The case involved the right of baseball players to control the commercial use of their names and photos on baseball trading cards, and the court said this:

> We think that in addition to an independent right of privacy ...a man has a right in the publicity value of his photograph, i.e., the right to grant the exclusive privilege of publishing his picture.... This right might be called a

"right of publicity."

A variety of state laws and court decisions have reiterated the point made in the *Haelan* case: no one may commercially exploit a person's name, public persona, or likeness without consent. Various courts have said the right protects sports figures, entertainment celebrities, and even people who would be classified as public figures only because of their involvement in controversial public issues.

Nor does the right of publicity just protect a person's name and likeness. A number of courts have ruled that the right extends to the commercial exploitation of other aspects of a celebrity's public persona. A memorable illustration of this point is the 1983 federal appellate court decision in a case called *Carson v. Here's Johnny* (698 F.2d 831).

The case arose after Here's Johnny Portable Toilets Inc. began marketing its products in 1976. Entertainer Johnny Carson, longtime host of NBC's "Tonight Show," was introduced to viewers with the phrase "Here's Johnny" from the time he became the host in 1962 until he retired 30 years later. Carson was obviously not amused when the toilet company not only called its product "Here's Johnny" but also added the phrase, "the world's foremost commodian." Carson sued, alleging a violation of his right of publicity, among other things.

Overruling a trial judge who had dismissed Carson's lawsuit, the appellate court held that the use of "Here's Johnny" as a brand name did violate Carson's right of publicity. The court emphasized that a person's full name need not be used for his right of publicity to be violated, especially in a case involving a celebrity as well known as Johnny Carson. Clearly, the phrase "here's Johnny" is associated with Carson in the minds of millions of television viewers. In fact, at one point in the case the company had conceded that it was trying to capitalize on Carson's reputation.

In deciding the *Here's Johnny* case in this way, the appellate court cited another case it had ruled on about 10 years earlier: *Motschenbacher v. R. J. Reynolds Tobacco* (498 F.2d 821). In that case, the court held that a race car driver's right of publicity was violated by an advertisement in which R. J. Reynolds used a photo of his car, even though the driver's face was not visible. The car's markings were so distinctive that the car fell within the driver's public persona, the court ruled.

Thus, the right of publicity protects celebrities and others from the commercial use of far more than just their names and likenesses. Catch phrases and even tangible objects that are closely associated with a celebrity in the public mind may be off limits to advertisers (unless permission is negotiated and paid for).

However, there are limits to this rule. Another federal appellate court decision permitted a tire company ad to use actresses dressed in miniskirts and boots, a style that singer Nancy Sinatra had popularized, even though the advertisements also featured a revised version of "These Boots are Made for Walkin'," one of her popular songs. In *Sinatra v. Goodyear* (435 F.2d 711), the court said it was clear that Nancy Sinatra was neither singing the song nor appearing on camera in the ad, which promoted Goodyear's "Wide Boots" tires. The court said Sinatra's right of publicity had therefore not been violated. (Note that the use of the song itself was not an issue. The advertiser had made arrangements with the copyright owner for use of the song.)

A similar question arose in a 1988 right of publicity case much like the *Sinatra v. Goodyear* case--but with a different result. In *Midler v. Ford Motor Company* (849 F.2d 460), singer-actress Bette Midler sued Ford and Young & Rubicam, Ford's ad agency, for using a Midler sound-alike vocalist in advertising for the Mercury Sable. The ad agency asked Ula Hedwig, who was Midler's backup singer for a decade, to sing a Midler hit song, "Do You Wanna Dance," and to "Sound as much as possible like the Bette Midler record." Before employing Hedwig to do the singing, the ad agency had asked Midler's agent to have Midler sing in the commercial--and was turned down.

Although the ad agency had obtained permission to use the copyrighted song, Midler contended that the recording sounded so much like her performance that many listeners would believe it was her. Citing the *Motschenbacher* case as a precedent, a federal appellate court said there were adequate grounds for Midler to pursue her lawsuit. Like the cigarette ad showing the race car driver's auto, this ad campaign might lead many people to conclude that Midler was endorsing the product, the court said. The case was sent back to a trial court to assess damages; in 1989, a jury awarded Midler $400,000. In 1992, the U.S. Supreme Court declined to review that decision.

Why was this case decided differently than the *Nancy Sinatra* case? Perhaps the most significant reason was that there was more likelihood of the public being deceived into believing there was an endorsement by Midler. In reality, the Midler decision was based on the idea that the impersonation itself was wrong; there was no actual misappropriation of Midler's name, likeness or voice. On the other hand, there was no impersonation in the *Sinatra* case: it was obvious in the Goodyear ad that Nancy Sinatra was neither on camera nor doing the singing--although the Goodyear ad used a song closely identified with Sinatra, just as the Ford ad did with Midler.

The *Sinatra v. Goodyear* and *Midler v. Ford* cases raise the question of how far an advertiser can go in using celebrity impersonations. Traditionally, the rule has been that celebrity imitations do not violate a celebrity's right of publicity as long as the public is not deceived into thinking the celebrity is actually appearing in the ad or endorsing the product.

Advertisers have often relied on the phrase, "celebrity voice impersonated," for protection when they did sound-alike ads. However, the *Midler* decision led many advertising agency lawyers to believe that a disclaimer may not be enough. They are becoming especially wary of celebrity impersonations--with or without a disclaimer--in the aftermath of an even bigger damage award to a celebrity in an impersonation case: more than $2 million! In *Waits v. Frito-Lay* (978 F.2d 1093, 1992), the ninth circuit U.S. Court of Appeals upheld almost all of a $2.5 million jury verdict against the manufacturer of Doritos brand corn chips for doing commercials featuring a song made popular by singer Tom Waits, using a close imitation of his vocal style. The Supreme Court declined to review that decision.

At about the same time as the *Waits* case, the same appellate court also ruled that game show hostess Vanna White had the right to sue Samsung Electronics and its advertising agency, David Deutsch, for ads featuring a blond robot wearing a gown and jewelry reminiscent of White's on-air style, and standing in front of a large game board. Although Judge Arthur Alarcon dissented, arguing that there was little likelihood of the public mistaking a mechanical robot for Vanna White, the 2-1 majority ruled that this could be a wrongful commercial exploitation of White's public persona--and allowed her to take her case to trial (*White v. Samsung*, 971 F.2d 1395, 1992).

Samsung then asked the Court of Appeals to rehear the case *en banc*. That request was denied, but it gave one of the nation's most quotable appellate judges, Alex Kozinski, a chance to issue a colorful opinion objecting to the court's decision not to rehear the case. Kozinski blasted the court for its expansion of the right of publicity. Among other things, he said:

> Something very dangerous is going on here....The panel's opinion is a classic case of overprotection. Concerned about what it sees as a wrong done to Vanna White, the panel majority erects a property right of remarkable and dangerous breadth: Under the majority's opinion, it's now a tort for advertisers to *remind* the public of a celebrity. Not to use a celebrity's name, voice, signature or likeness; not to imply the celebrity endorses a product; but simply to evoke the celebrity's image in the public's mind. This Orwellian notion withdraws far more from the public domain than prudence and common sense allow. It conflicts with the Copyright Act and the Copyright Clause. It raises serious First Amendment problems. It's bad law, and it deserves a long, hard second look.

Perhaps encouraged by Kozinski's passionate arguments, Samsung then appealed to the Supreme Court, but as in the *Midler* and *Waits* cases, the court refused to hear an appeal of this case. White then took her case to trial, and in 1994 a jury awarded her $403,000 in damages, which Samsung and its ad agency agreed to pay instead of appealing the case again. In return, White agreed not to appeal for a chance to seek an even larger judgment.

Still another similar dispute led to the case of *Wendt v. Host International* (125 F.3d 806, 1997). George Wendt and John Ratzenberger, the actors who played Norm and Cliff in the "Cheers" television series, sued Host for placing animatronic robotic figures resembling them in airport bars modeled after the set of "Cheers." They contended that the robots resembled them sufficiently to be a possible misappropriation, and a federal appellate court agreed, ruling that they had a right to take their case to trial. In a series of subsequent rulings in this case, various courts held again and again that Host could be sued for invading the two actors' right of publicity even though Host had purchased the right to depict the "Cheers" bar scene from Paramount Studios, the copyright owner. Eventually the U.S. Supreme Court refused to review this case, clearing the way for a trial. In 2001, Paramount and the two actors settled the lawsuit under undisclosed terms.

In essence, the courts were saying in *Wendt* that a copyright and the right of publicity are separate legal rights: a copyright clearance does not give someone the right to depict the actors who appeared in the copyrighted show. To depict actual people without consent and for commercial gain is a violation of the right of publicity.

Although the *Midler*, *Waits*, *Wendt* and *White* cases were all federal cases, they were based primarily on California state law--either the statutory right of publicity in the California Civil Code or state common law principles.

However, the recent trend toward courts refusing to allow celebrity impersonations in advertising began in New York. In 1984 a New York judge ruled that the use of a celebrity look-alike in an ad violated Jackie Onassis' right of publicity, and he ordered an ad agency to stop using an Onassis look-alike to promote Christian Dior clothes. The judge issued this order without finding that anyone was actually deceived into thinking Onassis was appearing in the ad or endorsing the product.

These cases were all based on state law because the right of publicity is an area of state law, not federal law. There have been proposals for a federal right of publicity law, including one from the American Bar Association, but Congress has not acted on any of these proposals.

Misappropriation and the News

If celebrities have a right to prevent the unauthorized commercial use of their names and likenesses--and sometimes even the right to prevent advertisers from *reminding* the public of them (as Judge Kozinski put it)--where does that leave a journalist who wants to write news stories about the famous?

That is an important issue, and the answer is relatively clear: the right of publicity does not apply to news situations, even though the media are commercial enterprises. The print and broadcast media are free to use a person's name and likeness whenever the situation creates newsworthiness--and the courts have tended to be very liberal in defining newsworthiness for these purposes. Even if a news medium engages in advertising to promote itself and reproduces a photograph of someone famous that appeared in print or on the air, that advertisement does not usually fall within the right of publicity.

However, if a newspaper, magazine, or radio or TV station uses the name or photograph of a celebrity in a way that implies an *endorsement*, it is a different matter. Cher, the singer and actress, was involved in a case that illustrated this point in 1982.

In *Cher v. Forum International* (692 F.2d 634), Cher had granted an interview to a free-lance writer who hoped to write an article for *Us* magazine. The article was rejected by *Us*, and the writer then sold it to the publishers of two other magazines, *Star* and *Forum*. Both published it. *Star* carried the article with a headline that offended Cher. The headline read, "Exclusive Series ...Cher: My life, my husbands, and my many, many men."

Cher disliked the idea that the interview ended up being published in *Star* instead of *Us*, and she disliked the headline even more. But what apparently offended Cher the most was that *Forum* not only ran the article but also used her name and likeness in advertising that implied she endorsed and read the magazine. One ad in the *New York Daily News* included Cher's photograph and the words, "There are certain things that Cher won't tell *People* and would never tell *Us*. She tells *Forum*.... So join Cher and *Forum*'s hundreds of thousands of other adventurous readers today."

In deciding the legal issues raised by this series of events, the **ninth circuit U.S. Court of Appeals** overturned a trial verdict against the free-lance writer and the publisher of *Star*. They did not violate Cher's right of publicity by writing and publishing a newsworthy article, the court decided. The writer, for instance, had never promised Cher any control over where the article would be published. If the writer had made such promises and then published the article elsewhere, Cher could have sued him for breach of contract. But in the absence of any contractual commitment, the writer had the same right to freely publish his article as would any other journalist.

In contrast, what *Forum* did was another matter: that magazine promoted the article in a way that clearly implied an endorsement by Cher. Although *Forum*'s publication of the article itself did not violate Cher's right of publicity, the advertising for it did, the court ruled.

This case, then, illustrates the principle that the media may freely publish stories about newsworthy people--but not advertisements that imply an endorsement--without violating their right of publicity. On the other hand, if the ad had simply promoted the story by saying something like "Read an interesting article about Cher in *Forum*," it would probably have been safe.

Former football star Joe Montana discovered a similar legal principle when he tried to prevent a newspaper from publishing promotional posters and a souvenir edition based on earlier news coverage of his football heroics. In *Montana v. Mercury News* (34 C.A. 4th 790, 1995), a California appellate court upheld the right of the *San Jose Mercury News* to publish materials celebrating the San Francisco 49ers four Super Bowl victories during the 1980s. Even though individual pages of the souvenir edition were sold--and the cover included an artist's drawing of Montana--the court held that the paper had the right to publish these items about newsworthy events such as Montana's triumphs in the Super Bowl.

The *Montana* and *Cher v. Forum* decisions were both based in part on the **Booth Rule**, an old principle of privacy law that says the media may use previously published newsworthy materials in later advertising of the publication itself as long as no endorsement is implied. This concept originated with *Booth v. Curtis Publishing* (182 N.E.2d 812), a 1962 New York Court of Appeals decision that allowed *Holiday* magazine to use a previously published photo of actress Shirley Booth in later advertising for the magazine.

On the other hand, a different legal issue was raised when the Coors brewery did advertising that included a drawing based on a news photograph of baseball star Don Newcombe pitching for the Brooklyn Dodgers in the 1949 World Series. A federal appellate court said Newcombe had the right to sue Coors and its ad agency for misappropriation (*Newcombe v. Adolf Coors*, 157 F.3d 686, 1998). A newspaper that published the photo in 1949 could republish it to advertise itself later, but others cannot. Newcombe particularly objected to the use of his image in beer advertising because of his own acknowledged problems with alcoholism.

May a magazine digitally alter a photo? Actor Dustin Hoffman won a $3 million jury verdict against *Los Angeles Magazine* in 1999 after the magazine used a digitally altered photo of Hoffman's head superimposed on a model in a designer dress. The jury concluded that the magazine's use of Hoffman's image was commercial misappropriation, not news coverage, even though it was one of a series of digitally altered photos depicting celebrities in modern, fashionable attire. In 2001 the ninth circuit U.S. Court of Appeals reversed the jury verdict, holding that the magazine had a First Amendment right to publish the altered photograph of Hoffman as news, particularly because he made *Tootsie*, a movie in which his character cross-dresses (*Hoffman v. Capital Cities/ABC*, 255 F.3d 1180).

Although this is unusual, a celebrity won a lawsuit stemming from news coverage in a 1997 case, *Eastwood v. National Enquirer* (123 F.3d 1249). In this case, the ninth circuit U.S. Court of Appeals *upheld* a large damage award won by actor Clint Eastwood against the *National Enquirer* for merely publishing an article about him when he had not submitted to an interview with that publication. On its face, this seemed very similar to the case Cher lost against the *Star*. The *National Enquirer* billed the story as "exclusive" when in fact it had appeared earlier in a British tabloid, but the *Enquirer* pointed out that it had purchased exclusive U.S. rights to the story from the British author. Eastwood objected to the implication that he would grant an exclusive interview to the *Enquirer* (just as Cher did when she sued the *Star*), but Eastwood won $150,000 in damages, plus at least $650,000 in attorney's fees. Eastwood claimed that the purported interview never occurred at all, and that his quotes were fabricated by a British journalist (and then reprinted in the *Enquirer*). Eastwood apparently prevailed because the court thought calling the story "exclusive" was a misappropriation of his name (an argument that the court did not accept in Cher's case). The only real difference between the Cher and Eastwood cases may be the fact that Cher admitted being interviewed by the writer of the article, while Eastwood denied even sitting for an interview. But both publications claimed they had an "exclusive" story when the celebrity never agreed to be interviewed by that publication.

Perhaps the best conclusion here is that anyone can write and publish an article about Cher or Clint Eastwood (or reprint someone else's article with permission of the copyright owner), but saying it's "exclusive" is dangerous--sometimes. And don't even consider using the celebrity's name in an advertisement that implies an endorsement of the publication--that goes beyond what the Booth Rule allows. Virtually every other form of commercial advertising (as opposed to news coverage) falls within the restrictions of the right of publicity. In most advertising, you cannot include photographs of recognizable people, be they famous or unknown, unless you get their consent. This rule applies equally to advertising in the print and electronic media: you can be sued if you use a street scene in a television ad without getting the consent of everyone recognizable on the street.

The right of publicity also applies to the entertainment media. When someone produces a motion picture, all of the people appearing on the screen who are recognizable must give their consent--which is why producers commonly use "extras" who are on the payroll instead of just photographing anyone who happens to be walking past for use in scenes showing public places. These rules do not apply, of course, to most news and public affairs productions. Nor do they ordinarily prevent accurate portrayals of newsworthy persons in docudramas based on news events. But in movies produced for entertainment purposes, the unauthorized use of a person's likeness invites a lawsuit.

Nonetheless, the major television networks routinely broadcast docudramas without obtaining the consent of every single person depicted. Where the story is based on facts that have already been reported by the news media, there is little risk of a successful right of publicity lawsuit by anyone who was involved in the story. This is especially true where the facts are in the public record (in court documents, for example).

A noteworthy 1994 federal court decision reaffirmed the right of authors and motion picture producers to tell a person's life story without violating that person's right of publicity. In *Matthews v. Wozencraft* (15 F.3d 432), the fifth circuit U.S. Court of Appeals upheld the right of author Kim Wozencraft to use a character based on her ex-husband and fellow police officer Creig Matthews in her book, *Rush*. Their story received extensive media publicity: they served as undercover narcotics officers in Texas, became romantically involved, used marijuana and cocaine themselves (but later denied it under oath), and falsified evidence to win a drug conviction. They eventually served time in federal prison and were divorced. Wozencraft later earned a master's degree at Columbia University and published *Rush*, which was based on their life stories. She eventually sold the movie rights to the book for $1 million and Matthews sued, alleging that she violated his right of publicity by using his life story without permission. The court held that a person's life story does not fall within Texas' right of publicity and affirmed a lower court decision to dismiss Matthews' lawsuit. In so ruling, the court noted that their story had already received extensive news coverage. The court also held that Wozencraft had a First Amendment right to publish a book about these events without Matthews' consent.

On the other hand, even a news presentation may lead to a lawsuit for invasion of the right of publicity under some circumstances. An excellent example is a case that produced a U.S. Supreme Court decision--the only one to date dealing with the right of publicity.

The case was *Zacchini v. Scripps-Howard Broadcasting* (433 U.S. 562, 1977), and it involved Hugo Zacchini, who called himself "the human cannonball" and had an "act" in which he was shot from a cannon into a net at fairs and other exhibitions. His entire "act" was filmed and broadcast as news by Scripps-Howard Broadcasting despite his objections to the filming. He sued for invasion of his right of publicity under Ohio law, but the state Supreme Court said the First Amendment precluded any recovery by Zacchini because the newscast covered a matter of "legitimate public interest."

However, in 1977 the U.S. Supreme Court modified the Ohio ruling by declaring that the First Amendment did not protect a broadcaster who took a performer's entire act and showed it without consent as news. The Supreme Court didn't rule that Zacchini's rights had necessarily been invaded: that was a matter for the Ohio state courts to decide. But the high court did say that Scripps-Howard was not constitutionally exempt from being sued if the state courts cared to entertain such a suit.

The case was returned to the Ohio courts, and Zacchini won his lawsuit. To deny him a right to sue when his entire act was broadcast without his consent would deny him the economic value of his performance, the state court said.

The *Zacchini* decision is troubling to many journalists, particularly because it seems to suggest that other people whose ability to earn money is somehow damaged by a news story could also sue. Also, the court didn't really consider whether Scripps-Howard actually profited from the telecast at Zacchini's expense.

There is obviously a fine line between news coverage of a celebrity's activities and the commercial exploitation of the person's name and likeness. Normally the courts give the news media considerable leeway in this area, but the rule is different in a situation such as the *Zacchini* case where all or most of a performer's act is broadcast without consent.

The test of what is improper commercial exploitation and what is legitimate news coverage would seem to be somewhat like the test used to determine what is a fair use under copyright law (discussed in Chapter Six). Thus, a purported news story or news broadcast that seriously impairs a celebrity's ability to make a profit by exercising his or her right of publicity is less likely to be considered proper than one using only a small portion of a performance and having little effect on the celebrity's profit opportunities.

Even news coverage of people who aren't celebrities sometimes produces right of publicity lawsuits. A number of people whose photographs have been used in newspapers and news programs without their consent have sued for an alleged invasion of their right of publicity, but they have almost always lost in court if the photograph was taken in a public place and the use was even minimally newsworthy. The news media clearly have the right to use people's names and show their likenesses in covering the news--without violating anyone's right of publicity. Of course, there is still the danger that the combination of a photograph and text matter may place someone in a false light. If that happens, a false light invasion of privacy lawsuit may result, even though there may be no basis for a right of publicity lawsuit.

One more question that often arises is whether an artist may sell products featuring a rendering of a celebrity--on T-shirts, for example. In 2001 the California Supreme Court ruled against an artist who sold thousands of T-shirts bearing his sketch of the Three Stooges. The court unanimously ruled that the sketches were far more "imitative" than "creative," and therefore a violation of the comedy trio's heirs' rights. Artist Gary Saderup's "undeniable skill is manifestly subordinated to the overall goal of creating literal, conventional depictions of The Three Stooges so as to exploit their fame," Justice Stanley Mosk wrote for the court, rejecting the artist's claim of a First Amendment right to draw (and sell) sketches of celebrities (*Comedy III Productions v. Gary Saderup Inc.*, 25 C.4th 387).

A Personal or Property Right?

One unsettled point about the right of publicity is whether it is a *personal right* or an inheritable *property right*. Courts in various regions of the United States have taken conflicting positions on this question.

In a widely noted case involving Bela Lugosi, the star of the original *Dracula* film, the California Supreme Court ruled that the right is a personal right and dies with the person. The case, *Lugosi v. Universal Pictures* (25 C.3d 813), was decided in 1979.

The California court had to mediate a long-standing dispute between Universal and the widow and son of the late actor. The Lugosis contended that Universal was violating their inherited publicity rights by marketing tee shirts and other "Dracula" souvenirs using the actor's likeness after his death. The state Supreme Court said they had no right to sue, because the right of publicity could not be inherited. Even if a person builds a business marketing his name or likeness during his lifetime, the court said the most his heirs could inherit would be monies from the use of his name or likeness during his lifetime--not the right to control the commercial exploitation of his right of publicity after his death.

The California state legislature eventually passed the Celebrity Rights Act, a new law giving the heirs of deceased celebrities the right to profit from the commercial use of their names and likenesses for 50 years (later extended to 70 years) after their deaths. This law effectively overturned the *Lugosi* decision and made the right of publicity a fully inheritable property right in California.

The death of an even more famous deceased celebrity, rock and roll musician Elvis Presley, produced conflicting federal appellate court decisions on this question. Almost as soon as Presley died, unauthorized commercial exploitation of his name and likeness began. In a 1978 decision (*Factors v. Pro Arts*, 579 F.2d 215), the second circuit U.S. Court of Appeals ruled that Presley's right of publicity was a property right and survived his death. Moreover, the court said that the right could be transferred to a business, which could maintain its exclusive right to exploit Presley's name after his death.

However, two years later another federal circuit court ruled in just the opposite way regarding Elvis Presley. The sixth circuit ruled, in *Memphis Development Foundation v. Factors* (616 F.2d 956, 1980), that Presley's right of publicity did not survive his death. Thus, the court said Factors did not have an exclusive right to exploit the rock and roll star's name and likeness. At issue was the foundation's right to sell $25 pewter replicas of a statue of Presley it planned to erect in Memphis. The court said, "after death, the opportunity for gain shifts to the public domain, where it is equally open to all."

Further confusing matters, after the *Memphis Development Foundation* decision was published, the court that decided *Factors* (the second circuit U.S. Court of Appeals) reversed itself. In a 1981 ruling (*Factors v. Pro Arts*, 652 F.2d 278), the court followed the sixth circuit's lead, concluding that Presley's right of publicity did *not* survive his death. The second circuit made this abrupt switch because it felt obligated to follow the law of Tennessee, Presley's home state, as it had been interpreted by a court in that region (the sixth circuit U.S. Court of Appeals).

The *Factors* decision did not settle the matter: Tennessee and several other states joined California in enacting statutory laws forbidding the unauthorized commercial exploitation of a deceased celebrity's name or likeness for 50 years or longer (the Tennessee law has no cutoff date, giving the owners of Presley's right of publicity the exclusive right to exploit his name and likeness in perpetuity.) New York, on the other hand, refused to recognize that the right of publicity extends beyond a celebrity's lifetime.

Also, the court decisions on the inheritability of the right of publicity do not affect the *copyright* on a celebrity's recordings or motion pictures. As the next chapter explains, copyrights are always property rights rather than personal rights, and they do NOT terminate at the artist's death. Only the inheritability of the right of publicity, not the inheritability of copyrights, is unclear in some states. However, once a copyright expires, the work falls into the public domain and is available for all to use.

The boundary line between copyrights and the right of publicity was illustrated in a 1998 court decision resulting from the efforts of Robyn Astaire, the widow of Fred Astaire, to control and often to prevent the commercial exploitation of the celebrated actor's public persona. A federal appellate court held that she could not prevent a company from using stock public domain footage of Astaire in instructional videos, as opposed to commercial endorsements (*Astaire v. Best Film and Video*, 136 F.3d 1208).

Another difference between copyrights and the right of publicity is that the latter does not extend to non-residents, at least under the California law. That became clear when a charity trust fund established to control uses of the late Princess Diana's public persona tried to stop the Franklin Mint from selling a Princess Di commemorative doll. The ninth circuit U.S. Court of Appeals held that the trust fund could not prevent the sale of the dolls, in part because the trust fund is based in Great Britain (*Cairns v. Franklin Mint*, 2002 U.S. App. Lexis 12032).

PRIVACY DEFENSES

Throughout this chapter we have repeatedly talked about the legal defenses available to the mass media in various kinds of privacy cases, but in the interest of completeness we should separately reiterate them here.

In most cases where the mass media are defendants, the best defense is *newsworthiness*, often called public interest. If it is possible to convince a court that a given story, broadcast, or photograph is newsworthy, the plaintiff will not win a private facts lawsuit. The trend just about everywhere is for the courts to define newsworthiness liberally, recognizing that even sensational reporting is permissible as long as it is not inaccurate. Therefore, the media do not often lose private facts cases, although the cost of defending a lawsuit alone may deter coverage of some kinds of stories.

However, if there are inaccuracies, it is a different matter. False light privacy cases against the media are more often successful, with the constitutional standards first established in libel cases sometimes used to evaluate the media's conduct. The Supreme Court created a limited First Amendment defense for false light privacy cases in its *Time Inc. v. Hill* decision. That defense protects the media from false light privacy suits for non-malicious but erroneous publications involving matters of public interest. If a journalist has not been guilty of actual malice, a person involved in a newsworthy event has little chance of winning a false light privacy suit. If, on the other hand, there has been wrongful conduct by the media, plaintiffs fare about as well in false light privacy cases as in libel cases.

Much the same is true in intrusion cases. The inquiry focuses on the conduct of the media when a court tries to decide if someone's right of privacy has been invaded. The newsworthiness of a story is not a defense for unscrupulous reporting methods. A journalist who resorts to unlawful acts in getting a story (or otherwise intrudes upon someone's right to be let alone) may face a privacy lawsuit.

In areas other than news-editorial journalism, the best (and often the only) privacy defense is *consent*. Persons who consent to a use of their names or likenesses have no recourse when the use to which they consented occurs. But even then, journalists must remember a few legal technicalities about consent.

First, the consent must be in a form that is legally enforceable, and that means there must be a contract that complies with the formalities of contract law. The person who enters the contract must be of age, and the contract must be supported by some form of consideration. Consideration is often thought of as another way of saying money, but it can be other things, even intangibles. Any time the person who is giving the right to use his or her likeness commercially gets something of value in return, that is consideration enough. For instance, photo release forms are one of the most common kinds of contracts granting consent, and they sometimes simply say that the person posing gives his or her consent for publication of a picture in return for the free publicity that may result. Publicity is a valid form of consideration.

To be valid, the consent must be voluntarily entered into. And it must be given in a manner that lends itself to proof in court, if necessary. For that reason, a written consent is much better than an oral one, and infinitely better than the implied consent a photographer tries to establish when he says, "...but he posed willingly."

Another caution is that the consent must be all-encompassing enough to apply to all situations in which a person's name or likeness is likely to be used. A consent for one commercial use may not imply any consent for subsequent uses of the same photograph, for example. And a consent to use a picture at one time may not be a consent to use it later. All of these kinds of problems are contract law problems, and the solution lies in writing a contract that leaves no loopholes.

In addition to the newsworthiness and consent defenses, the Supreme Court has, in effect, created another separate constitutional defense for publication of information lawfully obtained from court records. The *Cox Broadcasting v. Cohn* and *Florida Star v. B.J.F.* decisions included language assuring the media's right to report information lawfully obtained from court records and possibly other public records. That right may not include a right to report on rehabilitated criminals' past activities--additional decisions will be needed to clarify that issue--but in other respects the right to report the contents of lawfully obtained court records appears to be firmly entrenched.

These, then, are the defenses in privacy law. Because they differ from the defenses in libel cases, it is possible to publish something that is safe from a libel standpoint but risky under privacy law (or vice versa). In evaluating stories that may defame or embarrass someone, you should keep that point in mind. Once you have analyzed any sort of material that you plan to publish or broadcast for potential libel and concluded it is safe, you must also run through the possible invasion of privacy problems. At a time when many lawyers routinely add allegations that there was an invasion of privacy to almost any libel suit they file, mass communicators must also think in terms of both of these legal actions.

PRIVACY ACT OF 1974

After years of debate, a comprehensive federal privacy law was passed by Congress in 1974. That law recognized the individual's "right to be left alone." The act gives all citizens the right to inspect most of the government files maintained on them, to prevent improper distribution of those records, and to challenge errors. The act flatly prohibits indiscriminate government snooping and prying. Federal agencies are under orders to streamline their files and to stop accumulating information that has no relevance to the job they were set up to do.

Meanwhile, many states have enacted similar laws forbidding activities by state and local government agencies that improperly impinge upon individual privacy.

These laws have sometimes interfered with the work of journalists seeking to gather news because they place many records containing personal information off limits. The conflict between the journalist's struggle for access to information and the growing body of statutory privacy law is one of the major challenges for journalists. By 2002, the explosive growth of the Internet had given this problem a whole new dimension, with records that have been public for years--but were not easily accessible to the uninitiated--turning up online where millions of net surfers can access them quickly and easily from their homes. This has led to new demands for government secrecy to protect individual privacy, and in many instances resulted in the loss of public access to public records. These problems are discussed further in Chapter Nine, which includes a longer summary of the Privacy Act.

THE INTERNET AND PRIVACY

Perhaps no technical advance of the twentieth century created greater concern about personal privacy than the explosive growth of personal computer technology--and especially the Internet--during the 1990s. By the end of the decade, Internet privacy had become a major national issue. This led to legislation and calls for legislation in many places. Certain aspects of this question involve the privacy issues of the sort addressed in this chapter, including legislation to protect the public from unscrupulous data-gatherers and the legal questions surrounding the use of people's names and images on the Internet without consent.

Internet Privacy: Protecting Children--and Adults

Responding to concerns expressed by many parents and community groups, Congress passed the 1998 Children's Online Privacy Protection Act to limit the collection of information from children under age 13 without parental consent. This law should not be confused with the Child Online Protection Act, a different

1998 law intended to curtail access to adult materials by minors. That law is discussed in Chapter 10.

The Children's Online Privacy Protection Act limits the ability of children under 13 to have e-mail accounts without parental consent, and it requires those who gather data to deal with parents before dealing with their children. A website cannot simply have children fill in personal information on an electronic form and then click "send" when they're finished. It is a partial response to a proposal of the Federal Trade Commission that had similar provisions. The act includes federal preemption: the states may not enact conflicting laws governing the collection of information from children. The law also includes provisions for self-regulation by industry groups that develop their own programs to protect the privacy of children. The FTC is charged with supervising and approving these self-regulation programs. In 1999, the FTC adopted regulations to implement this law.

In 2000, the FTC issued a report asking Congress to pass a law restricting the collection of personal information about *adults* on the Internet. The FTC proposed a four-point program to protect consumer privacy built around the ideas of "notice, choice, access and security." Anyone who gathers personal information would have to give notice, allow each person to opt in or opt out and allow people to see their own computer data file to correct errors. Finally, the legislation proposed by the FTC would regulate how personal information that is gathered online is used to prevent abuses. However, Congress did not act on this proposal during 2000, and by 2002 the issue appeared to be less of a priority for Congressional leaders.

Although the United States has not enacted a comprehensive Internet privacy law, the European Union has done so--and placed U.S. corporations in the position of having to comply with European standards if they wish to do business in Europe. The EU law requires member countries to implement data-protection standards to prevent the inappropriate use of personal information obtained over the Internet. The rules also forbid companies doing business in Europe to transfer data to any country that does not have suitable data privacy standards (e.g., the United States). In 2000, the U.S. Department of Commerce, working with EU authorities, announced a set of data privacy *safe harbor* rules that were acceptable to the EU so U.S. companies could continue doing business and exchanging data with European countries.

Under the safe harbor rules, companies that need to meet European standards must: 1) give individuals *notice* of the purpose for collecting personal data and how it will be used; 2) give users a *choice* to refuse to disclose personal information to any third party for purposes other than those originally disclosed at the time of collection; 3) give users *access* to their own personal information for verification purposes; 4) provide *security* to prevent interception or misuse of personal data; 5) take steps to ensure *data integrity* (i.e., accuracy and completeness); and 6) provide an *enforcement mechanism* to protect individual privacy rights. Websites that certify to the Department of Commerce that they meet these standards are then eligible to transfer data to and from EU countries.

By mid-2002, relatively few companies had agreed to comply with the safe harbor rules--a development that concerned Department of Commerce officials. It appeared that some large corporations were simply ignoring the safe harbor and the EU rules--and getting away with it for the time being. However, other companies were *not* getting away with it. In late 2001 data-protection authorities in Spain imposed a penalty of about $60,000 on Microsoft Corporation for improperly transferring personal data to the United States in violation of the EU rules.

Internet Privacy: Intercepting E-mail

Another controversial aspect of Internet privacy concerns the interception of e-mail and surreptitious monitoring of closed discussion groups, often by an employer.

In general, employers have succeeded in defeating legal challenges to the common practice of monitoring employees' e-mail that passes through a corporate server. Both government and private employers often monitor e-mail, and there is little that employees can do about it, aside from using an outside e-mail server to avoid having their messages read by supervisors. Several courts have upheld the right of employers to monitor employees' e-mail, and even to prevent a disgruntled former employee from flooding the e-mail system with messages (*Intel Corp. v. Hamidi*, 94 C.A.4th 325, 2001). Even if an employer provides a computer to an employee for *home* use, but with the provision that it is to be used for company business only, the employee has no reasonable expectation of privacy that would prevent the employer from getting a court order to examine files on that computer (*TBG Insurance Services v. Superior Court*, 96 C.A.4th 443, 2002).

Misappropriation and the Internet

As the Internet has become a pervasive medium of communication, many questions have arisen concerning the unauthorized use of the names and images of celebrities and sometimes others. This question has led to many lawsuits but few precedent-setting appellate court decisions.

In one of the first cases to be resolved, television actress Alyssa Milano won a $238,000 default judgment against a Minnesota man and got several other website operators to pay undisclosed settlements for posting nude photographs of her. In a series of lawsuits, she accused website operators of violating her right of publicity. She contended that these website operators were making thousands of dollars a month in access fees paid by users to view their websites.

Many other celebrities have considered filing similar lawsuits, given the rampant unauthorized use of their images--with or without clothing--on various websites.

As explained earlier, the news media have a First Amendment right to use the name and image of anyone, including private persons as well as celebrities. This is true regardless of whether the news medium is delivered to the public at no charge, as is broadcast television, or sold, as are newspapers and magazines. The mere fact that a fee is charged for a newspaper or magazine (or access to a website) does not automatically make its use of someone's name or image a commercial misappropriation. But there have been many lawsuits that questioned where the boundary should be drawn between coverage of the news and commercial misappropriation.

At this point, the few courts that have addressed the unauthorized use of someone's name or likeness on the Internet have generally found the uses to be misappropriations, not journalistic uses. However, it remains clear that news coverage is not a form of misappropriation. Where a website is clearly engaged in covering the news, it can use celebrities' (and other people's) names and images without permission. If a website is not covering the news, its owner can be sued for the unauthorized use of peoples' names or images.

There is another issue inherent in this: the potential for lawsuits in faraway courts. Because of the worldwide reach of the Internet, a website operator could be sued in many different places. A celebrity could shop around for the state whose laws are most favorable for his or her case and sue there if the website operator has sufficient contacts for the courts to assume jurisdiction. (As Chapter Four explains, the Supreme Court has held that selling magazines or newspapers in a place satisfies this requirement, although other courts have held that it takes more than a website being accessible in a state to give that state jurisdiction over the website.)

Still another factor that must be considered when images are posted on a website without consent is *copyright ownership*, which is discussed in the next chapter. It may not be a misappropriation to publish someone's picture on the Internet in a journalistic context. But whoever owns the copyright to the picture may sue for copyright infringement even if the person in the picture has no recourse under privacy law.

ONGOING ISSUES

Privacy law is still a growing field with many unresolved questions. Some of the most heated public debates of our time concern the conflict between individual privacy rights and the right of governments to regulate individual moral choices. The Supreme Court will continue to face intense pressure from those who firmly believe that abortion or homosexuality is wrong--and from those who believe just as strongly that the government has no business regulating such private matters.

While few of the privacy issues directly involving the mass media generate that level of emotion, they are nonetheless important--and difficult to resolve. In *Cox Broadcasting v. Cohn* and several similar cases, the Supreme Court has ruled that journalists may truthfully report the contents of court records and often other public records without civil liability. However, the court has refused to extend that principle across the board to all other types of information that the media may lawfully obtain. And what about reporting the name of an eyewitness to a crime? If the person's name is in a court record, the media would have a legal right to publish it. But when the suspect is still at large, at least one appellate court has simply refused to follow the *Cox Broadcasting* rule. Is that right? Should the media voluntarily refrain from publishing the names of rape victims, eyewitnesses to crime, and others with similar concerns about their privacy and safety?

The trend toward "tabloid television" has produced new ethical and legal dilemmas in the privacy area. When (if ever) is it acceptable for journalists to go under cover or use hidden cameras to get a story? Does it matter if the story is truthfully reported, if the newsgathering is too intrusive?

What about law enforcement ride-alongs? The Supreme Court has now ruled that it violates the Fourth Amendment for officers to take journalists with them when they enter private property with a search warrant or arrest warrant. Was this decision right? Which should take priority--the right of privacy inside one's own home or the news value of showing people who are suspected of serious crimes at the moment of their arrest?

And what about paparazzi photographers? They do what they do because there are media willing to buy their pictures. And there are media willing to buy these pictures because a large segment of the public wants to see candid pictures of celebrities--and is willing to pay for the privilege. But what about the right of celebrities to enjoy some semblance of personal solitude? Do celebrities abandon all of their privacy rights when they become famous? How can a balance be struck between First Amendment freedoms and the right of celebrities to be left alone, if they have any such right? Is California's pioneering anti-paparazzi law a needed protection for those who are targets of paparazzi journalism or a violation of the First Amendment right to gather the news?

There are also other contexts in which the rules on privacy remain unclear or controversial. When, for example, may a journalist report embarrassing but truthful private facts? It will take more court decisions to fully outline the scope of the newsworthiness defense. Are there *any* private facts when public figures are involved? Should there be?

Also unsettled is the extent to which the *New York Times v. Sullivan* doctrine applies in false light privacy cases. Must all public figures prove actual malice to win such privacy lawsuits? Are there some matters of public interest that should not fall under the actual malice rule, despite the *Time Inc. v. Hill* decision? How should the rules in false light privacy cases differ from those in libel cases? Ultimately, the courts must strike a balance between the public's right to know and the right of individuals to be left alone. Do the media have too much freedom in this area, at the expense of individual privacy? Or do they have too little?

One more unsettled question in privacy law surrounds the scope of the right of publicity. Does that right survive a person's death, making it unlawful to commercially exploit a deceased celebrity's name and likeness? Should it? When the press and public bestow celebrity status on someone, with all of the accompanying rewards and burdens, should that person have the same right to control the use or his/her name or likeness as a private citizen does? Where do the Bette Midler, Tom Waits and Vanna White cases leave advertisers? Is federal appellate Judge Alex Kozinski correct in saying that it is now illegal for advertisers to create an image or sound that merely *reminds* the public of a celebrity? If so, is that an unreasonable restriction on advertising? Perhaps someday the Supreme Court will hear a case on these issues. So far, the high court has consistently avoided getting involved.

Finally, what about Internet privacy? The European Union has adopted strict privacy standards to govern the collection of personal data on the Internet, something the United States has not done so far. But in order to do business in Europe, many U.S. companies have had to observe the EU standards, or at least follow the U.S. Department of Commerce's *safe harbor* rules. Is this right? Should the EU be able to dictate U.S. privacy rules in this back-door fashion? Has Congress been remiss in failing to adopt stricter U.S. privacy standards?

Chapter Five 221

A SUMMARY OF THE RIGHT OF PRIVACY

What Is Invasion of Privacy?
Invasion of privacy is a legal action to compensate persons whose right of privacy has been interfered with. There are four generally recognized types of invasion of privacy: (1) *intrusion upon a person's physical solitude*; (2) *publication of private facts, causing embarrassment*; (3) *placing a person before the public in a false light*; (4) *unauthorized commercial exploitation of a person's name or likeness*. (commercial use)

Are These Rights Universally Recognized?
No. Some states have recognized all four kinds of invasion of privacy, while others allow lawsuits for only some of them. However, statutory laws or court decisions in virtually all states recognize that a person's name or likeness may not be exploited in commercial advertising without permission.

What Is the Right of Publicity?
Misappropriation and violation of the *right of publicity* are terms for the fourth type of invasion of privacy listed above (the commercial exploitation of a person's name or likeness). The right of publicity is fundamentally different from the other types of privacy in that it involves a *property right* that is inheritable in many states rather than a *personal right* that is extinguished when the victim of an invasion of privacy dies. Those who use a person's name, voice, photograph or any other element of his/her *public persona* for a commercial purpose must have consent.

What Defenses Are There?
The courts have recognized several defenses as applicable to one or more of the four kinds of invasion of privacy. The primary ones are: (1) *newsworthiness* or *public interest* (which applies mainly in private facts cases); (2) *consent*; and 3) a constitutional *public record* defense (which also applies mainly in private facts cases).

Is Invasion of Privacy a Serious Legal Problem for the Media?
Compared to libel, invasion of privacy was traditionally a less serious legal problem for the news media. While the media lose privacy lawsuits on occasion, the courts have broadly interpreted the newsworthiness defense to protect the media from many types of privacy lawsuits. However, right of publicity lawsuits are an increasingly serious problem for advertisers, the entertainment industry and others who exploit celebrities' public personas for commercial gain. And "tabloid television" has created new controversies and lawsuits that raise difficult questions about hidden cameras and intrusive or undercover newsgathering.

CHAPTER SIX
Copyrights and Trademarks

How can anyone *own* words, images, sounds or ideas?

Shouldn't the arts, information and ideas belong to everyone in a free society? Why should copyright owners--who are rarely the actual creators of artistic, musical or literary works--be able to lock up someone else's creative endeavors and treat them as private property, denying their use to others? Specifically, why should record companies, publishing houses and Hollywood producers be able to buy other people's creative works and then profit from them, depriving even the creators of any say about the future use of their works? Should a television distribution company be able to purchase the rights to classic movies and then change them despite the strenuous objections of the people who made those movies into classics in the first place?

The growth of the Internet has created enormous new problems for copyright owners. It has become easy for millions of Internet users around the world to share copyrighted materials. Even worse, in the view of some copyright owners, the Internet also makes it easy to share software that defeats the copy-protection schemes built into some digital audio and video products.

In recent years many other copyright questions have arisen. Motion picture writers, actors and directors objected bitterly to the "colorization" of classic black and white movies by the distribution companies that now own the copyrights. Authors chronically complain about the things publishers do to their manuscripts, including publishing them electronically after contracting only to publish in traditional printed formats. And those who write and perform music sometimes watch helplessly as others take control of their music--and profit from it. Much has been written about singer Michael Jackson's purchase of the copyrights to many of the Beatles' songs--and about Courtney Love's lawsuit against her record label in which she contends that the long-term contracts recording artists are forced to sign are so unfair as to be invalid as a matter of law.

For years singer-composer John Fogerty refused to perform his biggest hits from his days with the Credence Clearwater Revival group to avoid encouraging his fans to buy those now-classic recordings. Why didn't he want people to buy his early recordings? Because his former manager and music publisher received some of the profits from those recordings--and Fogerty was locked in a bitter fight with the former manager. The ex-manager sued Fogerty for copyright infringement because Fogerty wrote new songs that allegedly sounded too much like his own older recordings. (A federal jury ruled in Fogerty's favor in that case.)

Copyright law creates a maze of problems for the entire creative community. To make a video and distribute it legally, one must obtain copyright clearances from many sources, including the owner of the underlying story, the author of the script, music composers and publishers, recording artists and record companies, among others.

Clearly, there are difficult philosophical questions in all of this; there are no satisfactory answers to some of them. But the fact remains that creative works, like inventions and trademarks, are often treated as private property--property that can be bought and sold or even rented out, if you will.

Collectively, the law governing this kind of property is called *intellectual property law*. It includes copyrights, trademarks, unfair competition and patent law. Mass communicators are primarily concerned with copyrights (which protect creative works such as books, periodicals, manuscripts, music, film and video productions, computer software and works of art) and trademarks (which protect words, phrases and symbols identifying products and services). Unfair competition, a legal concept that sometimes protects works not covered by copyright or trademark law, is also important to some communicators. Patents, on the other hand, typically protect inventions and scientific processes. They are usually more important to scientists and engineers than to mass communicators.

Intellectual property law exists to encourage creativity by protecting the creator's right to make a profit from the dissemination of his or her works. The basic rationale for it is that creative people are just as entitled to profit from their labors as are the people who make consumer goods. However, in practice the creators of copyrighted works frequently find it necessary to sell their works to others--often at low prices--just to make a living. As a result, by the time a creative work becomes highly profitable, someone other than the creator is often entitled to the bulk of the profits.

The fact that someone other than the creator often profits from copyrights is troubling to some people. Another troubling aspect of intellectual property law is that it creates monopolistic controls on knowledge. For that reason educators, librarians, scientific researchers and even newsgatherers sometimes find copyrights and patents to be a major annoyance.

Even antitrust lawyers for the U.S. government have been known to oppose copyright laws because of their monopolistic tendencies. For instance, during the Congressional debate over a comprehensive revision of the U.S. Copyright Act in the mid-1970s, the Justice Department lobbied to weaken the proposed amendments to minimize the restraints on competition inherent in copyright protection.

Though intellectual property law may be monopolistic and an abridgment of free expression, it has a long history in the United States. It is unlikely this form of monopoly will soon disappear, the First Amendment notwithstanding.

Intellectual property law originally evolved within the English common law, but the framers of the U.S. Constitution considered it so important that they specifically recognized it, making both copyrights and patents federal matters right from the time the Constitution was ratified.

Article I, Section 8 of the Constitution includes this language:

The Congress shall have the power to promote the progress of science and the useful arts, by securing for limited times to authors and inventors the exclusive right to their respective writings and discoveries.

Shortly after the Constitution was ratified, Congress accepted that invitation and enacted the first federal copyright law, the Copyright Act of 1790. That law has been revised several times since, as technology created new problems that could not have been anticipated by the framers of the Constitution. The 1976 Copyright Act--the most recent comprehensive revision of the law--attempted (not always successfully) to deal with such troublesome new problem areas as photocopying, audio and video recording, satellite communications and cable television.

Critics of modern copyright law like to point out that the Constitution says copyrights and patents are supposed to be *for limited times*. The 1790 Copyright Act decreed that copyrights would last for 14 years, renewable for another 14--far less than today's 95-year term for corporate copyrights. Because copyright owners have done a better job of lobbying than consumers, librarians, educators, journalists and others who would often benefit from shorter copyright terms, Congress has repeatedly extended the duration of copyrights.

Whatever the unresolved problems in copyright law, the history of Congressional involvement makes copyright law fundamentally different from some of the other areas of mass media law: it is an area of federal statutory law, not primarily a form of state statutory or common law. If the problems of copyright law are to be solved at all, they must be resolved mainly by Congress, with help from the federal courts.

There is another way in which copyrights and other kinds of intellectual property law differ from such areas of law as libel and invasion of privacy. As Chapters Four and Five point out, the right to sue for libel, slander or most kinds of invasion of privacy is a purely personal right; it dies with the aggrieved party. That person's heirs usually have no basis for a lawsuit unless they were also personally injured. Copyrights and trademarks are entirely different in this respect. They create property rights rather than personal rights, rights that may be passed on to one's heirs. In fact, copyright law is specifically written to provide legal rights many years after the death of a work's creator.

AN OVERVIEW OF COPYRIGHT LAW

To summarize very briefly, the owner of a copyright has the *exclusive right* to reproduce the copyrighted work, to create *derivative works* based on it, and to distribute copies, perform the work or display it to the public. Anyone else who does these things without the copyright owner's permission is guilty of *copyright infringement* unless what that person does qualifies as a *fair use*. To prove an infringement, the copyright owner must show *substantial similarity* between the original work and the allegedly infringing work. The owner must also show that his/her copyright is *valid* and the infringer had *access* to the original work and violated one of the exclusive rights just listed. When the copyright eventually expires, the work then falls into the *public domain*; at that point, the once-exclusive rights belong to everyone.

If the basics of copyright law can be summarized in a paragraph, it takes far longer to fill in enough details to provide useful information for those who may need to protect their own works and use the copyrighted works of others.

What Copyright Law Covers

The Copyright Act of 1976 continued a tradition begun in earlier U.S. copyright laws, setting up a system under which people may protect their creative works from unauthorized copying. The 1976 law was a major rewrite of the 1909 Copyright Act, and the 1976 law has been amended a number of times since then.

What sorts of things may and may not be copyrighted under this law?

Generally, all kinds of creative endeavors may be copyrighted. That includes literary works (fiction and non-fiction, prose and poetry), musical works (and any accompanying words), dramatic works (including music), choreographic works and pantomimes, pictorial, graphic and sculptural works (including both photographs and paintings), computer software, maps, architectural designs, recordings, motion pictures and radio or television productions (whether dramatic or news/documentary in nature). Just about everything that is printed or broadcast may be copyrighted.

However, there are some very important exceptions to that rule. Probably the most important one for the mass media is that the news itself cannot be copyrighted, although a *description* of a news event can be. The first reporter to reach the scene of a plane crash, for instance, cannot prevent others from reporting the fact that the plane crashed or the details of how it happened. The most that this reporter can deny to others is his or her account of the event. Others may tell the story in their own words.

Thus, it is commonplace for journalists to rewrite each other's stories. Whenever one reporter scores an important "scoop," others quickly pick up the story, carefully putting it in their own words and perhaps giving credit to the original source. Even though this is permissible under copyright law, it should be emphasized that one news medium cannot systematically purloin all of its news from a competitor to avoid having to employ its own news staff. To do that is called *unfair competition,* and on several occasions courts have awarded damages for that kind of wrongdoing even though it may not be a copyright infringement. Systematic "news piracy," as it has been called, is not permissible. More will be said of unfair competition later.

There are several other important categories of material that cannot be copyrighted. Like news, other forms of factual information cannot be copyrighted. Historical or scientific information, for instance, is available to everyone. (However, remember that a particular description of the facts can be copyrighted, and that a scientific process may be patented.) And ideas, processes and inventions may not be copyrighted; usually they may be protected only by patent law. Copyright law protects the style of presentation, not the underlying factual information.

In an important 1991 case, the U.S. Supreme Court emphasized the point that only an *original* arrangement of facts can be copyrighted, not the facts themselves. The court held that the information in a telephone directory lacks the requisite originality and creativity to be copyrightable (*Feist Publications v. Rural Telephone Service Co.*, 499 U.S. 340). However, in recent years data base compilers have lobbied Congress to amend the Copyright Act to override the *Feist* ruling. They contend that compilations of factual information should have copyright protection even if the facts were originally obtained from public records that are available to all. Congress has not complied, and in 1997 another widely noted court decision went against the compilers of data bases: the 11th circuit U.S. Court of Appeals denied copyright protection to *The Television & Cable Factbook*, a large compilation of factual information. The Supreme Court declined to review that case (*Warren Publishing v. Microdos Data Corp.*, 115 F.3d 1509).

Another thing that cannot be copyrighted is a word or short phrase, including the words that constitute *trademarks* and *service marks*. As will be explained later, they may be protected under state and federal trademark registration laws, but they cannot be copyrighted. You cannot be sued for copyright infringement for mentioning someone's trademark in a book or news story, for example. However, you may face a trademark infringement lawsuit if you wrongfully exploit a protected trademark as if it were your own. Within the limits of libel law, you can write anything you like about a product with a registered trademark such as Coca-Cola, but you cannot make soft drinks and call them Coca-Cola.

Securing a Copyright

Once you have a creative work that is eligible for copyright, obtaining copyright protection is easy. Basically, copyright protection is automatic: you don't have to do anything to copyright a work once it is *fixed in a tangible medium of expression*. You can *register* the copyright, and you should put a *copyright notice* in the work. However, the failure to do those things does not cause you to forfeit your copyright.

Although it is no longer mandatory, you normally announce to the world that your work is copyrighted by inserting a notice in a prominent place that says the work is copyrighted. The notice says something like this: "Copyright (C) 2002 by J.J. Author." The "C" is supposed to have a circle around it; that is a standard symbol to indicate that a work is copyrighted.

The 1976 Copyright Act was amended in 1988 to make it far more flexible regarding the insertion of this copyright notice. Under the 1909 version of the Copyright Act, the failure to include the notice--or even putting it in the wrong place--generally meant forfeiture of copyright protection. Under the 1988 amendments to the 1976 Act, there was a complete liberalization of the rules on inserting copyright notices. Now even if you should fail to insert the notice, your copyright is valid, although innocent infringers (those who do not know the work is copyrighted) have some legal protection until they are notified of the copyright.

For full copyright protection, it is also desirable to register the copyright. You are still required to register the copyright before filing any lawsuit against an infringer, and if you register within 90 days of publishing the work--or at least *before* an infringement occurs--you have better legal protection than you would otherwise.

What happens to a work if you do not insert the copyright notice or register the copyright? You still have a valid copyright, but you must notify any infringer that the work is copyrighted. Of course, if you choose not to claim copyright protection, the work falls into the *public domain.* That means the work belongs to everyone, and anyone who wishes may reproduce or perform it as if he or she owned the copyright.

How do you register a copyright? First, you secure the proper forms from the U.S. Copyright Office, Library of Congress, Washington, DC 20559 (or on the Copyright Office's website, www.lcweb.loc.gov/copyright/). For most works that are primarily text, you will need Form TX. For serial publications (newspapers, magazines, etc.), use Form SE. For sound recordings, Form SR is required. For films, broadcast works and the like, request Form PA. For visual arts works, Form VA is required. The Copyright Office also has a free package of copyright information that will be sent on request or can be downloaded.

To complete registration, you fill out the forms, pay the prescribed fee and send in one or in some cases two copies of the work to be deposited in the Library of Congress. There are some exceptions to this deposit requirement for bulky works such as motion pictures and certain works of art. The basic fee to register a copyright is still $30. It was not raised when many of the U.S. Copyright Office's other fees (for services such as registering multiple issues of a serial publication) were increased on July 1, 2002.

You have to complete these steps for each edition you want to register. Some critics of the system have argued that the deposit requirement allows the Library of Congress to acquire most of the major works published in America--for free. Some have even challenged the validity of the deposit system in court, but to no avail.

By dropping the mandatory registration requirement, the new Copyright Act legalized a practice that had become commonplace: merely inserting the copyright notice without doing anything further unless an infringement occurs. The new law legitimized this practice by eliminating copyright registration as a precondition to the validity of a copyright. However, registering either within 90 days of publication or before an infringement occurs still gives you more legal remedies than you would have if you do not register until later, and you still must register before suing an infringer. However, Congress has considered legislation that would make copyright registration *completely voluntary*: a copyright owner would not even have to register the work before filing a lawsuit for infringement. This change, if enacted, would bring U.S. copyright law into line with the provisions of international copyright law, which is discussed later.

Remedies for Infringements

Copyright protection would mean little if the law had no enforcement provisions. Thus, the Copyright Act provides a variety of legal remedies for copyright owners to use against infringers. When a copyright *is* registered, the remedies available include the right to seek an injunction (a court order to stop the infringement), a court order to impound all pirated copies, court-ordered payment of the copyright owner's attorney's fees by the infringer, and either actual or statutory damages. Owners of unregistered copyrights retain some (but not all) of these rights, as will be explained shortly.

In 1994, the U.S. Supreme Court ruled that the provision for attorney's fees cuts both ways: both plaintiffs (those who sue, claiming that someone infringed their copyright) and defendants (those who are sued for copyright infringement) can ask the court to order the other side to pay their attorney's fees if they win. That ruling came in *Fogerty v. Fantasy*, (510 U.S. 517), the case in which singer John Fogerty was sued by his former manager and music publisher, who claimed that Fogerty's new songs were so similar to his older songs that they infringed the copyrights on the older songs (which were owned by the publisher). Fogerty won the case, and the Supreme Court said the trial court could order the publisher to pay Fogerty's attorney's fees. A trial court later awarded Fogerty over $1.3 million in attorney's fees, and that ruling was upheld by an appellate court in 1996 (*Fogerty v. Fantasy*, 94 F.3d 553).

Statutory damages are an arbitrary sum of money a court may award when actual damages (i.e., the infringer's net profits) are either hard to prove or very nominal (perhaps because the infringer made little or no profit). Congress increased the amount of statutory damages by 50 percent in 1999. Now the damages for each infringement may range from $750 to $30,000 at the judge's discretion, although awards as low as $300 are authorized for innocent infringements, with amounts as high as $150,000 permitted in the case of a flagrantly intentional infringement.

In an important interpretation of the Copyright Act in 1998, the U.S. Supreme Court ruled that the defendant has a constitutional right to a jury trial in copyright infringement lawsuits seeking statutory as well as actual damages (*Feltner v. Columbia Pictures Television*, 523 U.S. 340). Previously, statutory damage cases were decided by judges without a jury.

Of course, if the infringer made a great deal of money, the copyright owner would seek actual damages rather than statutory damages.

When a copyright is unregistered at the time of an infringement, the copyright owner may still seek several remedies. First, however, he or she must register the copyright, following the procedures described earlier. Only then may a lawsuit for copyright infringement be initiated. After registering the copyright, the owner may sue the infringer for actual damages--but not statutory damages. He or she may also seek an injunction or court-ordered impoundment of the pirated copies, but not attorney's fees.

Thus, if your copyright is unregistered when an infringement occurs, you lose the right to sue for your attorney's fees and statutory damages. This means owners of unregistered copyrights are protected from large-scale infringements in which there may be substantial damages. But small-scale infringements--those where actual damages are minimal and the lawyer's fees would be disproportionately high--are more likely to go unchallenged if a copyright is unregistered.

Nevertheless, the viability of an unregistered copyright should not be overlooked. Actual damages alone can be a substantial deterrent because of the manner in which they are calculated. To collect actual damages, the copyright owner sues for both his losses and the infringer's gross profits. The infringer then must prove all of his or her expenses in order to get them deducted from that gross profit figure. Thus, actual damages are supposed to take away all of the net profit from an infringement.

However, this provision can be so harsh to an infringer that courts have been known to refuse to enforce it fully. For instance, there was a famous 1940 U.S. Supreme Court decision involving a pirated script that was made into a major-studio motion picture, complete with high-priced promotion and big-name stars.

After deducting all costs, the profits for the movie (*Letty Lynton*, starring Joan Crawford and Nils Asther) came to nearly $600,000--a very large sum for the time. A trial court complied with the Copyright Act and awarded that full amount to the author of the pirated script. However, the Supreme Court set aside the provisions of the Copyright Act and apportioned the profits, awarding the author only about $120,000. Much of the profit was attributable to factors other than the script, the high court held (*Sheldon v. MGM*, 309 U.S. 390).

Despite the *Sheldon* decision, large actual damage awards do occur. Moreover, the infringer could face criminal sanctions. The law was designed to make copyright infringements painful and expensive, whether the copyrighted work is registered or not.

Proving an Infringement

Suppose someone publishes a work that you feel was pirated from a similar work that you created. What can you do about it?

As already pointed out, there are many remedies available if you sue the infringer and win your lawsuit. But to win a copyright infringement lawsuit, there are several things you have to prove. One is that the alleged infringer had some access to your work. Another is that there is substantial similarity between the two works. And, of course, you have to prove that your copyright is valid in that it covers a legitimate, original work.

In the case of a verbatim copy of a copyrighted work, proving these things is usually not difficult, but what happens if the infringer was skillful enough to modify the original work? At that point, you must prove there is substantial similarity between your work and the allegedly infringing work--and that is not always easy. Where literary works are involved, authorities on literature are sometimes brought in as expert witnesses to testify about the subtle similarities of plot, character development and theme. For the substantial similarity test to be met, there must be similarity in the specific expressive elements of the two works (including plot, themes, dialogue, mood, setting, characters and sequence of events). This is called the *extrinsic test* for similarity, an objective test. In addition, the works must be substantially similar under the more subjective *intrinsic test*, which considers whether an ordinary, reasonable audience would find the works substantially similar in total concept and feel. (For an explanation of the two tests as they have evolved, see *Cavalier v. Random House Inc.*, 2002 U.S. App. Lexis 9554).

To show substantial similarity between two works, there must be proof of similarity of the *protectible elements*, not just the underlying historical facts--which cannot be copyrighted. For example, if someone were to make a new movie about the 1912 sinking of the ocean liner Titanic, it could include the same historical characters and events depicted in the James Cameron movie, *Titanic*. It could not use characters and plot lines substantially similar to the fictitious aspects of the movie, such as the story of the aristocratic Rose DeWitt Bukater falling in love with the free-spirited artist Jack Dawson and fleeing her arrogant, wealthy fiance, Cal Hockley.

After all of this legal analysis of what constitutes substantial similarity is completed, the original copyright owner ultimately has to convince a judge or jury that the average person (not just an expert) would see the new work as similar enough to have been pirated from the original.

Not only is substantial similarity sometimes difficult to prove when a pirated work is not an exact copy of the original, but there can be problems in proving access to the original work. If someone who has never seen nor heard of your copyrighted work creates a similar work, that is not a copyright infringement. If you cannot prove the alleged infringer had some opportunity to learn of your work, you can't prove he or she copied it. If the second work is truly an independent creation by someone who had no access to your original work, he or she can copyright it and go into business reproducing and selling it, as far as copyright law is concerned. (However, he or she may have other legal problems in the unfair competition and trademark areas, to be discussed shortly).

Given the pervasiveness of the mass media today, though, it is rare for creative persons to be able to prove that they had no access to any earlier published work that is substantially similar to theirs. For example, musician George Harrison spent several years in court trying to prove that his 1971 hit song, "My Sweet Lord," was not copied from "He's So Fine," a 1963 song that a group called the Chiffons made into a big hit on the charts. The two songs have virtually the same melody, but Harrison vehemently argued that he was not familiar with the earlier song and had no intention whatever to plagiarize it. In the end, a court ruled that he could not have avoided hearing the earlier song at some time or other, and that he must have been inspired by its catchy tune, *at least at the subconscious level*. (Ironically, during a contract dispute with Harrison, his former managers purchased the rights to "He's So Fine." Because of his managers' resulting conflict of interest, a court later required Harrison to pay only a small penalty and then awarded him the ownership rights to both "My Sweet Lord" and "He's So Fine" in several countries!)

How do you prove that your work is independently created and original when you plan to submit it to someone else for possible publication? How do you prevent an editor, for instance, from taking the work and using it without payment? There are various ways to amass evidence that could be used in court to prove your original authorship, should a lawsuit be necessary. The classic advice was to mail a copy to yourself before submitting the work to anyone else, retaining the copy in the sealed (and postmarked) envelope. However, the 1976 Copyright Act provided a much more dependable approach: you may now copyright the unpublished work under federal law and register it with the U.S. Copyright Office. Then your copyright is protected, prior to the work's submission to anyone who might be tempted to claim it as his or her own. It is far better to register the copyright than to merely mail yourself a copy and keep it in a sealed envelope.

The Duration of Copyrights

The duration of copyright protection has been extended repeatedly. As noted at the outset, U.S. copyrights were originally valid for 14 years and could be renewed for another 14. In 1831, Congress extended the term to 28 years, renewable for 14 more. Under the 1909 Copyright Act, copyrights were valid for 28 years and could be renewed for another 28 years. The 1976 Copyright Act extended the basic term of a copyright to the author's life plus 50 years. For works created anonymously or for hire, the term was extended to 75 years from the date of publication. For unpublished "works made for hire" and for unpublished anonymous or pseudonymous works, the term was set at 100 years from the year of creation by the 1976 act.

In 1998, Congress added 20 more years to all of these copyright terms in the Sonny Bono Copyright Term Extension Act. Therefore, the basic term now is the author's life plus 70 years, or 95 years for works created anonymously or for hire, which means most corporate copyrights are valid for 95 years. Unpublished works made for hire or created anonymously are now protected for 120 years from the year of creation. The 20-year extension applies retroactively to all works created after Jan. 1, 1978 as well as to new works. Copyrights now expire on December 31 of the expiration year.

How do these extensions of copyright periods affect works copyrighted earlier? For pre-1978 works that still held a valid copyright when the 1998 law went into effect, the term was extended to 95 years from the original copyright date by granting automatic 67-year renewals to most of these works when their original 28-year term expires. The 1998 act did not restore copyright protection to works that had already fallen into the public domain.

The Congressional action to extend copyright terms once again in 1998 was surprisingly controversial. Although the extension brought U.S. law into line with that of many European countries, it was vigorously opposed by a coalition of law professors, librarians and others who felt it would unduly deny future generations of creative persons the right to adapt and expand upon established works by imposing an excessive delay before copyrighted works fall into the public domain. They questioned whether allowing a copyright to run for 70 years beyond the author's lifetime instead of 50 would really encourage authors to do more or better work. But on the other hand, they contended, the term extension had a serious downside, preventing others from doing derivative works for 20 more years. To buttress their argument, they pointed to the U.S. Constitution, which authorized Congress to establish copyright protection only for limited times. Is 120 years--or even 95 years--what the framers of the Constitution meant by limited times?

In response to these arguments, the recording industry and other copyright owners contended that creative works should not fall into the public domain while they are still popular. They pointed out that many songs had been falling into the public domain that were still widely performed. Foes of still longer copyright terms replied that even popular works *should* become everyone's property *someday*, and that the framers of the Constitution never intended for that someday to be 95 or 120 years later. In the end, Congress agreed with the industry's advocates, not those arguing against this new shrinkage of the public domain.

In 2002, the U.S. Supreme Court agreed to hear a case challenging the extension of copyright terms as unconstitutional. A decision is expected by mid-2003.

The Copyright Owner's Exclusive Rights

Once you have a copyright, you own a variety of property rights that are protected by federal law. First of all, the copyright owner has the exclusive right to reproduce the work and sell copies. In addition, the copyright owner may abridge, expand, revise or rearrange the copyrighted work. And the copyright owner has the right to perform or display the copyrighted work. The owner also has the exclusive right to create *derivative works*, which are works based on a previous copyrighted work (for instance, a novelization of a motion picture or a movie script based on a novel). The owner can sell (or give away) any or all of these rights.

A copyright owner may also make arrangements that amount to renting out the work by allowing someone else to use the work in return for the payment of *royalties*. Granting first North American serial rights to a magazine allows the author to earn royalties for an article's initial publication while retaining ownership of the copyright. That allows the author to use the work in a later anthology, for instance. As explained later in this chapter, the republication of printed works in electronic form (by posting them on the Internet or an information service such as Lexis-Nexis, for example) has created new copyright questions. Many publishers have routinely republished works in electronic form under contracts granting North American serial rights without paying authors any additional royalties. By 2000, court decisions had forced publishers to rewrite their contracts to cover the republication of works in electronic form.

In some of the performing arts areas, it is also commonplace to give others the right to arrange and perform a work in return for the payment of royalties. In fact, the law requires those who own the copyrights to musical works to grant anyone permission to make *sound recordings* (i.e., CDs and tapes) of their music once it has been publicly performed. This is called *compulsory licensing*. The recording artist merely pays the prescribed royalties for each copy of the recording that is sold; the copyright owner cannot allow one performer to record a song while denying that right to others. The amount of these royalties is specified in the Copyright Act, although copyright owners sometimes agree to accept lower royalties to encourage well-known artists to record their songs. Those who record copyrighted music under the compulsory licensing provision of the Copyright Act must perform it essentially as written; they cannot normally make major changes without the consent of the copyright owner.

There is no similar compulsory licensing system for most other kinds of copyrighted works, such as written materials, audiovisual works and works of art. Moreover, the compulsory license does not apply to *synchronization rights* (i.e., the process of combining music with the visual images in a movie or video). The producer must get specific permission to add music to a movie or video--if the copyright owner is willing to grant permission. However, the 1976 Copyright Act did establish a compulsory licensing system in one new area: cable television. The copyright problems of both music and cable television will be discussed more fully later in this chapter.

In the motion picture, television and music industries, incredibly complex business arrangements have been developed to compensate the owners of the many copyrights that go into modern productions. Often there are separate arrangements with the authors of an underlying short story or novel, screenwriters who adapt the work, those who write, arrange and perform the music and lyrics, choreographers and many others. And these arrangements cover a variety of different rights. For example, the producer of a television show obtains (and pays for) the synchronization rights to include music in the show. However, the *performance rights* for the same music are another matter: ordinarily each television station must pay for the performance rights, because the producer does not purchase these rights. Broadcasters would prefer to have *source licensing*--in which the producer of the program obtains the performance rights--but that is not the usual arrangement. Most broadcasters obtain *blanket licenses* from music licensing agencies for all of the copyrighted music they put on the air. All-news and talk radio stations often obtain *per-program licenses*, which are less expensive for stations that air little music.

The case of *Stewart v. Abend* (495 U.S. 207), a 1990 Supreme Court decision, illustrates the great complexity of the copyright arrangements in the entertainment industry. This case involved the right of a group headed by actor Jimmy Stewart to re-release an old movie, *Rear Window*. The problem was that Sheldon Abend had purchased the rights to the short story on which the movie was based from the heirs of the story's author after the author died. The original 28-year term had expired, and the heirs had renewed the copyright (as permitted under the 1909 copyright law, which was in effect when this movie was made). The high court supported Abend's contention that Stewart's group had to negotiate again for the rights to the original story after the copyright renewal. The original sale of the rights to the story was valid only during the first copyright term, the court held.

Lawyers for the major Hollywood studios strenuously objected to this ruling, arguing that it would make it prohibitively expensive to re-release many old movies--or to use old story lines or music in new movies. The Copyright Act now deals with this problem by providing a *derivative works exception*. Under this provision, the original author regains ownership of a copyright when it is renewed, but the owners of derivative works (such as a movie based on a copyrighted story) do not lose their rights when the copyright on the underlying work is renewed and reverts to the original author.

On the other hand, when a movie's copyright expires and it falls into the public domain, the underlying screenplay falls into the public domain as well, according to a federal appellate court decision (*Batjac Productions v. GoodTimes Home Video Corp.*, 160 F.3d 1223).

Although the Supreme Court's *Stewart* decision alarmed many Hollywood studio lawyers, another 1990 court decision concerning the contractual arrangements that govern copyright ownership in the motion picture industry troubled them even more. In *Buchwald v. Paramount Pictures Corp.*, a Los Angeles Superior Court judge overturned many of the financial provisions of standard studio contracts that govern compensation for writers and others whose creative work goes into motion pictures.

The case began when humorist Art Buchwald sued Paramount for taking his ideas and much of his script for *Coming to America*, a successful 1988 movie starring Eddie Murphy. Buchwald won his case, and he and a partner shared a $900,000 judgment. However, the most notable aspect of the decision was the fact that the judge heard evidence about standard studio contracts for several months, and then made a sweeping decision that the contracts themselves are so unfair as to be inherently invalid.

A similar controversy arose concerning another Paramount hit, *Forrest Gump*.

In 1995 *Forrest Gump* grossed an estimated $660 million worldwide, but Paramount was claiming that there were no net profits--by relying on contractual provisions and accounting methods similar to those assailed by the judge in the *Buchwald* case. Winston Groom, author of the underlying novel on which *Forrest Gump* was based, retained the attorney who represented Buchwald and asked for a share of the money generated by *Forrest Gump*, regardless of whether there were any "net profits" under the studio's accounting methods. His contract, like Buchwald's, gave him only a percentage of net profits, not a share of the gross receipts. Groom's dispute with Paramount made headlines not only because of the movie's huge success and alleged lack of net profits, but also because actor Tom Hanks and the producer each had earned an estimated $40 million from the film under contracts that gave them percentages of the gross.

Paramount quickly reached a settlement with Groom for an undisclosed sum of money--thus ending the potential for another embarrassing lawsuit like Buchwald's.

"Works Made for Hire"

Returning to the exclusive rights of copyright owners, there are many instances when those who create artistic and literary works sell some or all of their rights to others instead of retaining those rights themselves. Often the author or creator of a work cannot afford to publish it and promote it properly. Thus, he or she makes a deal with a publisher to get the work into print--and in return the publisher asks for an assignment of the copyright. That means the publisher and not the author then owns the copyright to the work.

That is a common arrangement. However, there are some potential hazards in copyright law that may trap unwary creators of copyrighted works. One is the Copyright Act's *works made for hire* provision. The law says that if a person creates a work within the scope of his or her employment, the copyright belongs to the employer, not to the creator of the work. For example, if you are a staff writer for a newspaper, the publisher owns the copyright on the stories you write on the job unless you can negotiate a contract that says otherwise. Any time you create something on the job, that principle applies.

Few people would question the fairness of that part of the "works made for hire" rule, but what about writers and others who do free-lance work? What about the composer who accepts a commission to write the score for a new musical production? The law says that such a person is presumed to be on his own and not creating a "work made for hire." However, there can be questions about whether a person is actually an employee or a free-lancer. Also, contracts offered by publishers and others who buy creative works are often written to offset this presumption. If your contract says you are doing a "work made for hire," someone else may end up owning all rights to your creative efforts rather than just the first reprint or performance rights you intended.

In 1989 the Supreme Court ruled on the "works made for hire" provision of the Copyright Act in the case of *Community for Creative Non-Violence v. Reid*, (490 U.S. 730). The court had to deal with a situation that is not uncommon among free-lancers, including writers, photographers, artists and composers. In many instances free-lancers agree to produce a work on assignment without having a clear arrangement for copyright ownership. Under the Copyright Act's "works made for hire" provision, such works are presumed to belong to the creator if he or she is truly *independent* but not if the person is more like an employee than an independent contractor.

The Supreme Court ruled that if the creator of a work is an independent contractor as that term is normally defined in other areas of law, he or she is entitled to the copyright--unless the creator and whoever commissioned the work have a contract that says otherwise.

Some copyright experts considered the Supreme Court's test for independent contractor status to be so liberal that many media corporations reassessed their policies on copyright ownership. The court seemingly tipped the scales in favor of those who create works in free-lance situations. Many free-lance works that corporations assumed they owned may now legally belong to the original creator instead.

The *Reid* case involved a dispute between James Earl Reid and Community for Creative Non-Violence (CCNV), an organization that commissioned Reid to do a sculpture for display at a Christmas pageant in Washington, D.C. His sculpture, entitled "Third World America," depicted a homeless family sleeping on a grate in a street. CCNV contended that because it contracted with Reid to do the sculpture, supervised his work, and then paid him, he was really an employee and therefore CCNV owned the copyright to the sculpture. Reid contended that he owned the copyright--and therefore had the right to profit from reproductions of the sculpture.

The court ruled that Reid retained the copyright. The court's language suggested that those who are not on an organization's regular payroll almost always retain the ownership of works they create unless there is a contract that spells out some other arrangement. The crucial factor in the entire "works made for hire" area of copyright law at this point appears to be the contract between the free-lance creator and the person who commissions the work and pays for it. If the contract clearly says who owns the copyright, that contract is enforceable. If, however, the contract is vague or silent about copyright ownership--or if there isn't any contract--the law will presume that the free-lance creator owns the copyright. This does not affect works created by employees rather than free-lancers: an employer still owns an employee's job-related creative endeavors unless there is a contract that gives copyright ownership to the employee.

In 2000, a widely publicized dispute between recording artists and record labels illustrated some of the pitfalls and complexities of the "works made for hire" provision of the Copyright Act.

A member of Congress who had many recording industry executives among his constituents quietly inserted a provision into an omnibus federal budget bill adding sound recordings to the list of works that could be works made for hire. When several well-known recording artists found about it, they cried foul. An obscure provision of the Copyright Act says an "author" who transfers ownership of a copyright to someone else has the right to cancel that transfer after 35 years, thus retrieving ownership of the copyright.

Because recording artists, like authors, routinely sign contracts that transfer the copyrights on their works to a publisher (or in this case, a record label), that provision gives them a chance to recover their copyrights much later in life, when they and their works may have become famous and their copyrights highly valuable assets. But the law says only the "author" of a work has the right to retrieve the copyright. And under the "works made for hire" provision of the Copyright Act, the copyright owner and not the creator of a work is the "author" of a work made for hire.

Congress responded to the ensuing public outcry by quickly acting to delete sound recordings from the list of works that can be works made for hire.

Federal Copyright Law Preemption

One of the most significant changes in copyright law that resulted from the passage of the 1976 Copyright Act is that now both published and unpublished works are protected under the federal system. Previously, the federal law protected only published works, leaving unpublished materials protected only by the varying state laws that developed from what was called *common law copyright*.

That meant there were different rules and sometimes two different copyright offices with which to deal because some states set up their own registration systems to protect the copyright on unpublished works.

That dual system of state and federal copyright protection also caused both state and federal courts to stretch their definitions of the word "published" to protect authors. If someone handed out 100 copies of a short story to friends or potential publishers, was it published? If the author remembered to put in the copyright notice, federal courts tended to rule that it was published so the federal copyright system could be used to protect the work from would-be infringers. But if, on the other hand, the author failed to insert the notice, the work would fall into the public domain if "published." Thus, state courts tended to bend the rules to find that such works were really unpublished so they could provide common law copyright protection to otherwise unprotected authors.

The 1976 law eliminated this sort of double standard. As soon as a work is *fixed in a tangible medium of expression*, it is protected by the federal law. This means that as soon as a work is written down on paper, saved on a computer disk, recorded on film or tape, or placed almost anywhere else outside the creator's mind, it can be copyrighted under the federal law. One need not wait until the work is published to secure protection--federal copyright protection is immediately available. To secure this protection, you merely include a copyright notice in the draft of the work--and you may register the unpublished work if you want the strongest possible protection. But even without the copyright notice, under 1988 amendments to the Copyright Act the author is protected from all but innocent infringers.

In short, the 1976 Copyright Act completely abolished the state common law copyright system for works published after January 1, 1978 (the effective date for the 1976 law). As of that date all state laws relating to copyrights were *preempted*. That is, all such laws were superseded by the federal law and ceased to be valid for new works. Congress always had the authority to abolish state common law copyright protection and assume complete jurisdiction in this field; in the 1976 Copyright Act Congress finally did so, thus greatly simplifying the American copyright system.

THE FAIR USE DOCTRINE

If there were no exceptions to the hard and fast rules of copyright law, no journalist, historian or teacher could do his or her job very well. No one could quote even one sentence from a copyrighted work for the purposes of teaching, scholarly criticism or even reporting the news. Because of these problems, the *Fair Use Doctrine* exists--and creates a major exception to the copyright rules.

Basically, the Fair Use Doctrine is a legal concept that was originally created by the courts to allow some copying of copyrighted works in spite of the seemingly absolute rules against it in the 1909 Copyright Act. The courts recognized that such things as quoting brief passages for scholarly criticism or satire were reasonable and did not interfere with the copyright owner's financial return.

The 1976 Copyright Act specifically recognized the Fair Use Doctrine and established guidelines for determining which uses of copyrighted works are fair ones. Congress even addressed the tough issue of photocopying and attempted to establish some basic rules in that area.

To decide if a given use of a copyrighted work is a fair use, the Copyright Act says these four factors must be considered:

1. The purpose and character of the use, including whether it is for profit or for a nonprofit educational purpose;
2. The nature of the copyrighted work;
3. The percentage of the total work that is used;
4. The effect the use will have on the value or profit-making potential of the original work.

This four-part test is vague and general; it often takes a court decision to determine whether a given use of copyrighted material is an illegal copyright infringement or a legal fair use. To clarify some of the resulting uncertainties, there have been several voluntary agreements between representatives of copyright owners and various other interests (such as education) on what constitutes a fair use.

For instance, as Congress was completing its revision of copyright law in 1976, representatives of educators, authors and publishers met to decide what would constitute a fair use of a copyrighted work in a classroom. Under their agreement, teachers are permitted to photocopy as much as a chapter of a book, an article from a newspaper or magazine, a short story, an essay or poem, and charts, graphs, drawings or similar materials--but only for their own use.

For classroom use, the agreement permits teachers to reproduce one copy per student provided the work copied is sufficiently brief (usually under 2,500 words for prose, 250 words for poetry) if the original copyright notice is retained and if the copying is a spontaneous one-time activity. The teacher is required to ask for permission (or buy copies of the copyrighted work) before using it a second time. There are also limits on how many times during a single semester a teacher may distribute classroom sets of copyrighted works, and such copying may not ever be a substitute for requiring the students to buy either an anthology or a "consumable" item (such as a workbook or a test).

This agreement does not carry the force of law; a court would be free to rule that more (or less) copying than this constitutes a fair use. These guidelines are mentioned in the legislative history of the 1976 Copyright Act, but not in the act itself. The act itself vaguely acknowledges that teachers have a right to make copies for their classes under the Fair Use Doctrine. However, another provision of the law exempts teachers from copyright liability when they perform or display copyrighted works as part of their teaching activities--unless the copy of the work they use or display was itself pirated (as it would be when a teacher shows an illegally copied motion picture or television program).

During the 1990s another issue involving classroom copying became controversial: the use of course packages in college classes. In 1991 a federal court ruled that Kinko's Graphics, a major producer of these course packets, had to pay royalties for virtually all of the copyrighted materials (such as magazine or journal articles and book chapters) included in these custom anthologies of previously published materials (*Basic Books v. Kinko's Graphics Corp.*, 758 F.Supp. 1522). The court held that such large-scale copying was *not* a fair use. The result is that companies like Kinko's--and college bookstores--now charge higher prices for course packets so royalties can be paid to each copyright owner.

In 1996, the advocates of free copying for classroom use thought they had won a great victory when the sixth circuit U.S. Court of Appeals refused to follow the *Kinko's* decision in *Princeton University Press v. Michigan Document Services* (see 74 F.3d 1528). In this case, the court's 2-1 majority seemingly gave teachers and copying services carte blanche to copy magazine and journal articles as well as large parts of books for inclusion in course packets by holding that such copying is a fair use, not a copyright infringement.

Armed with this decision, many copying services geared up for a bonanza of royalty-free copying. But then the celebration ended: the full panel of judges sitting on the sixth circuit voted to set aside the earlier ruling and rehear the case *en banc* (with all judges participating). The judges then voted 8-5 to overturn the earlier decision and ruled that large-scale copying for course packets is indeed an infringement, not a fair use (*Princeton University Press v. Michigan Document Services*, 99 F.3d 1381).

Another fair use question concerns photocopying by libraries. The Copyright Act is rather specific about this because an important court decision had allowed wholesale reproduction of copyrighted works by libraries--something Congress wished to curtail. That case (*Williams and Wilkins v. U.S.*, 487 F.2d 1345, 420 U.S. 376) was initiated by a publishing house whose medical journals were being photocopied on a massive scale by federally funded medical libraries so the libraries could avoid purchasing additional copies. The publishing house lost its case: in 1973 a federal court said the dissemination of medical knowledge was so important that this copying was a fair use. The case was appealed to the U.S. Supreme Court, but because the high court divided 4-4 (with one justice not participating), the judgment of the lower court stood.

Alarmed at the *Williams and Wilkins* case, publishers lobbied in Congress to win restrictions on library photocopying into the 1976 Copyright Act. The result was another compromise, with the rules for photocopying by libraries spelled out in considerable detail. Basically, the law now says it is a fair use for a librarian to make copies of damaged or deteriorating works that cannot be replaced at a reasonable cost, and to provide single copies to those who request them, provided the request is for only a small portion of a work. An entire work that cannot be purchased at a reasonable price may also be copied at a patron's request.

These rules contain a number of other qualifications and restrictions that will not be summarized here. Significantly, however, they apply only to copying done by library staff members, not copying by members of the public who use coin-operated machines. The Copyright Act exempts librarians from liability for copyright infringements by unsupervised library patrons, as long as a warning about infringements is posted near the self-service copy machine.

Obviously, the law on photocopying was written in this fashion in tacit recognition that there is simply no way to prevent private individuals from engaging in coin-operated infringements--just as there is no way to prevent private audio or video taping of copyrighted materials that are broadcast (a separate problem that is discussed later).

Fair Use and Historical Events

Many problems have arisen as courts tried to apply the Fair Use Doctrine. One of the most important involves the conflict between copyright law and the public's right to know. Several court decisions have addressed these questions.

One of the best-known tests of the Fair Use Doctrine came in a 1966 federal appellate court decision, *Rosemont Enterprises v. Random House* (366 F.2d 303). In that case, Rosemont (a company set up by billionaire industrialist Howard Hughes) was trying to prevent publication of a biography about Hughes, who intensely disliked publicity.

Rosemont learned that the biographer was relying heavily on information gleaned from several old *Look* magazine articles about Hughes. The company quickly bought the copyright on those articles and then sought an injunction to prevent publication of the new biography as an infringement of the copyrighted articles.

A trial court ruled in Rosemont's favor, but the federal appellate court reversed that decision, holding that a copyright owner has no right to, in effect, copyright history. The appellate court noted that the magazine articles were only a fraction of the length of the book and that there had been extensive independent research for the book. The court brushed aside the argument that the book, like the original copyrighted magazine articles, was aimed at a popular market and was not merely an instance of scholarly criticism (something that earlier court decisions had recognized as a fair use).

Ultimately, the court ruled that there is a legitimate public interest in the doings of the rich and powerful, and that this interest outweighs the copyright consideration in a case such as this one. Random House was allowed to publish its book about Howard Hughes without incurring liability for a copyright infringement.

Another fair use case involving an issue of even greater public interest arose a few years later, *Time Inc. v. Bernard Geis Associates* (293 F.Supp. 130, 1968). That case involved amateur photographer Abraham Zapruder's film of the assassination of President John F. Kennedy in 1963. The highly unusual and revealing film was purchased by Time Inc., and published in *Life* magazine. Of course, it was copyrighted.

Later, author Thomas Thompson was publishing a book advocating a new theory about the assassination, *Six Seconds in Dallas*. Bernard Geis, the book publisher, offered to pay *Life* a royalty equal to the entire net profits from the book in return for permission to use *Life*'s still photographs made from the copyrighted film, which was central to Thompson's theory. *Life* refused.

The book publisher then hired an artist to make charcoal sketches from the copyrighted photographs, and these appeared in the book. Time Inc., sued for copyright infringement. The federal court said the use of charcoal drawings instead of the photographs themselves did not eliminate the copyright infringement, but the court also pointed to the legitimate public interest in the assassination of a president and said this was a fair use of the copyrighted pictures. To rule otherwise would prevent a full public discussion of the controversial issues raised by President Kennedy's assassination.

More recently, the Assassination Records Review Board declared the Zapruder film to be U.S. government property and an arbitration panel ordered the government to pay Zapruder's heirs $16 million for the film. Critics assailed that sum as outrageous, especially since the government was buying only the physical film, not its copyright. The copyright eventually reverted to the Zapruder family, and the family has been criticized for charging those who need to use the images (documentary filmmakers, historians, journalists and others) high license fees.

A somewhat similar copyright dispute arose in the late 1990s, when the estate of Dr. Martin Luther King, Jr. sued CBS for using nine minutes of Dr. King's famous 16-minute-long "I Have a Dream" speech in a documentary history of the twentieth century. The estate contended that CBS was guilty of copyright infringement for including the segment. CBS responded by arguing that the speech, which was heard live by an enormous audience and has been quoted widely ever since it was delivered in 1963, is such an important public event that no one should be able to prevent others from using it for journalistic purposes. However, a federal appellate court overturned a judge's decision to dismiss the lawsuit and said the King estate could pursue its claim against the network (*Estate of Martin Luther King v. CBS*, 194 F.3d 1211).

Fair Use and Unpublished Works

If President Kennedy's assassination was such an important issue that republishing photographs of it was a fair use, the same cannot be said of publishing previously unpublished excerpts from President Ford's memoirs about his decision to pardon Richard Nixon of all Watergate offenses.

In a case that pitted journalists against authors and book publishers, the Supreme Court ruled in 1986 that *The Nation* magazine was guilty of copyright infringement for "scooping" *Time* magazine and a book publisher by publishing a preview article about former President Gerald Ford's memoirs.

In *Harper & Row Publishers v. The Nation Enterprises* (471 U.S. 539), the court said the unauthorized use of about 300 words of verbatim quotations from Ford's memoirs before they were published elsewhere constituted piracy, not a fair use.

Ford contracted with Harper & Row to publish his book, and *Time* magazine agreed to pay $25,000 for the right to publish excerpts in a magazine article. Shortly before the *Time* article was to appear, *The Nation* somehow obtained a copy of Ford's manuscript and published an article based on the memoirs. The article focused on Ford's explanation of his controversial decision to pardon former President Richard Nixon for his role in the Watergate scandal.

Time then refused to publish (or fully pay for) its article about Ford's memoirs, since *Time* had been "scooped" by another magazine. Harper & Row then sued *The Nation* for copyright infringement.

Reversing a lower court, the Supreme Court ruled that *The Nation*'s story went beyond news reporting and was not protected by the Fair Use Doctrine. The court emphasized that journalists are free to publish summaries of copyrighted manuscripts, since neither facts nor ideas can be copyrighted. But publishing 300 words of verbatim quotations before the authorized publisher could get the memoirs into print was not a fair use.

The court implied that a similar article--even one containing 300 words of direct quotations--would be a fair use rather than a copyright infringement once the author's original work was in print. However, by publishing the excerpts as news before the original work was published, *The Nation* excessively cut into the profit potential of the original work, the court held.

In ruling as it did, the high court had to strike a balance between the First Amendment right of the mass media to cover the news and the right of an author to profit from his copyrighted creative efforts. This conflict between freedom of expression and the right of an author to profit from his work has existed as long as there have been copyright laws. And this Supreme Court ruling will surely not settle the issue.

Writing for the court, Justice Sandra Day O'Connor said:

> The obvious benefit to author and public alike of assuring authors the leisure to develop their ideas free from fear of expropriation outweighs any short-term 'news value' to be gained from premature publication of the author's expression.

Journalists generally viewed the *Harper & Row* decision as a serious defeat for their interests because it limited their right to quote extensively from the unpublished writings even of a former president. Although it does not prevent them from quoting a public official's writings *after* publication--or perhaps paraphrasing a person's unpublished works--much newsworthy (and historically important) information about the famous is locked up in their unpublished writings.

Journalists, historians and others with an interest in the unpublished works of the famous became even more alarmed when federal appellate courts began expanding on the *Harper & Row* rule to limit the right to quote from the unpublished works of famous people. Perhaps the most controversial of these cases involved the works of the late L. Ron Hubbard, founder of the Church of Scientology. In that case, *New Era Publications v. Henry Holt & Co.* (873 F.2d 576, 1989), the court allowed a firm affiliated with Scientology to prevent the use of 41 unpublished writings of Hubbard in Russell Miller's biography, *Bare-Faced Messiah*. The biography offended Scientologists by portraying their founder as a bizarre and sometimes dishonest messianic figure--and quoted his own correspondence with government agencies to back up those charges.

By ruling that those quotations were not protected by the Fair Use Doctrine, the court in effect allowed Scientologists to censor an unflattering portrayal of Hubbard. While the court allowed the book itself to be published and allowed the use of a number of other quotations from Hubbard's writings, the passages that were ordered deleted were important to the author's thesis. And perhaps most troubling to journalists and historians, this allows those who control the unpublished works of celebrities to pick and choose--allowing authors of sympathetic biographies to quote from their works while denying the same privilege to those doing more objective biographies.

Organizations representing book publishers, historians and journalists began urging Congress to amend the Copyright Act to re-legalize the use of quotations from the unpublished works of important historical figures. After several years of discussion--and several more appellate court decisions--many journalists and scholars were even more uncertain of when they could and couldn't quote the unpublished writings of famous persons.

In 1992, Congress responded to this problem by adding this sentence to the Copyright Act: "The fact that a work is unpublished shall not itself bar a finding of fair use if such finding is made upon consideration of all the above factors" (i.e., the four-part test that is used to determine whether the Fair Use Doctrine applies in a given situation). Six U.S. Senators issued a joint statement intended to further clarify the law, reaffirming that the purpose of the new language was to overcome the uncertainty among journalists and scholars. They said that the Fair Use Doctrine does indeed apply to unpublished works when the four-part test is met.

See p 237

Given this message from Congress, the courts have generally been more sympathetic to the use of quotations from the unpublished works of the famous by journalists and scholars in recent years.

If quoting from an unpublished work may be a fair use, what about republishing a widely distributed work that the copyright owner later withdraws and wants to keep from being republished by others? That issue arose in a case involving *Mystery of the Ages*, a book by Herbert W. Armstrong, founder of the Worldwide Church of God.

After Armstrong's death in 1986, the church rejected some of his teachings as "racist" or in "ecclesiastical error." Armstrong left his entire estate, including the copyright to his book, to the church. Although at least nine million copies had been printed in book form or in a magazine serialization before Armstrong's death, church leaders tried to halt further publication of the book. A spinoff group that continued to follow the teachings of Armstrong, the Philadelphia Church of God, published a new edition of the book--and was sued by the Worldwide Church of God.

In *Worldwide Church of God v. Philadelphia Church of God* (227 F.3d 1110), a federal appellate court in 2000 upheld the Worldwide Church's copyright and rejected the Philadelphia Church's fair use claims even though the Philadelphia Church was giving copies away to promote the faith, not selling them. The Philadelphia Church was ordered to stop publishing the book, although copies are still available in some libraries and on at least two websites. The U.S. Supreme Court declined to consider an appeal of this decision.

The result: a religious group that owns the copyright to a religious work can use the law to prevent a rival religious group from publishing it, even if the first group has disavowed the work but the second group still considers it authoritative.

Fair Use, Television News and Video Clipping Services

Another controversial application of the Fair Use Doctrine has involved *video clipping services*--businesses that make video tapes of television news and public affairs programs for sale to individuals and organizations that are mentioned on television. The idea of a clipping service is nothing new: for years newspaper clipping services have monitored the print media for stories that mention their clients. Originally, these firms literally clipped stories from newspapers and sent them to public relations practitioners and others who needed to see what the media were saying about them or their clients. Modern clipping services often photocopy newspaper and magazine articles for their customers.

Video clipping firms do essentially the same thing for their customers--but with video tape. In addition to taping newscasts and providing copies to people and organizations that are mentioned on television, clipping services provide audio transcripts of television newscasts. Also, they prepare "photo boards"--still photographs taken from the video every few seconds, each with a transcript of the accompanying audio. During the 1980s, the video clipping business enjoyed enormous growth. Everyone from prominent politicians to the Library of Congress now uses video clipping services to keep track of television news coverage. As a result, several video clipping services that started out as small businesses in somebody's basement mushroomed into million-dollar operations.

The growth of the video clipping industry led to lawsuits by television stations that objected to someone else taping their material, repackaging it, and selling it for a profit. In the early 1990s, several federal courts ruled that video clipping services are not protected by the Fair Use Doctrine--they are guilty of copyright infringement. Perhaps most notable of these cases is *Georgia Television Company v. Television News Clips of Atlanta* (983 F.2d 238, 1993). In that case, the court rejected a clipping service's argument that it had a First Amendment right to provide video clippings even if the Fair Use Doctrine does not apply to video clippings. Instead, the court said video clipping services were violating the Copyright Act.

After several defeats in court, video clipping services sought legislation to exempt them from copyright liability. Although many members of Congress use video clipping services themselves and were sympathetic, key Congressional leaders did what they often do when someone asks Congress to intervene in a dispute between two industries: they urged broadcasters and video clipping services to try to resolve their differences privately.

The major networks eventually authorized the clipping services to use their newscasts in return for relatively modest license fees. Meanwhile, broadcasters and the clipping services became involved in lengthy negotiations in an attempt to develop an industry-wide agreement covering the use of local stations' newscasts by clipping services.

A related controversy has arisen from the wholesale use of video news footage by competing news organizations. Whenever one station or network comes up with a particularly powerful video segment, everyone else rushes to get it on the air--and worries about copyright permissions later. The celebrated amateur video of the Rodney King beating by Los Angeles police officers is a prime example. George Holliday, the man who made the video, granted one Los Angeles television station (KTLA) permission to use the video--under terms that were later hotly disputed--but the video quickly appeared on stations and networks around the world. As a result, Holliday filed a copyright infringement lawsuit.

A federal judge dismissed Holliday's lawsuit in 1993, citing four grounds for doing so: (1) there was evidence that Holliday gave KTLA permission to use the tape and release it to other media outlets; (2) Holliday's consent should preclude his later claims of copyright infringement; (3) the use of his tape fell within the Fair Use Doctrine; and (4) the First Amendment permits public airing of certain works "of great importance to democratic debate." In connection with the First Amendment and Fair Use arguments, the judge cited *Time Inc. v. Bernard Geis Associates*, the case mentioned earlier in which Time Inc. was not allowed to prevent the use of drawings based on an amateur photographer's movie in a book about President Kennedy's assassination.

However, a federal appellate court alarmed many broadcast journalists by ruling in 1997 that the Fair Use Doctrine may *not* necessarily cover the use of another highly newsworthy video that was taken from a helicopter during the riots that occurred in Los Angeles after the first trial and acquittal of the officers who beat King. In *Los Angeles News Service v. KCAL-TV Channel 9* (108 F.3d 1119), the appellate court overturned a trial court's dismissal of a lawsuit stemming from the unauthorized use of video of the beating of Reginald Denny, a Caucasian truck driver, by African-American youths at the beginning of the riots.

The video was taken by Los Angeles News Service (LANS) and provided to several stations, but LANS refused to authorize KCAL-TV to broadcast the tape. KCAL then obtained the tape from another station and aired it without LANS' consent. When LANS sued for copyright infringement, KCAL argued that the riots were so newsworthy that the Fair Use Doctrine would permit the use of the tape. However, the appellate court held that other Fair Use factors besides newsworthiness had to be considered, including the economic effect of KCAL's use of the tape. To weigh all of these factors, a full trial would be needed, the appellate court ruled.

Under the *KCAL* decision, broadcast journalists who use even highly newsworthy video footage on the air without first obtaining a copyright clearance may risk a lawsuit.

In a related decision a year later, the same federal appellate court held that LANS could recover damages stemming from overseas use of the Reginald Denny video because it was copied illegally in the United States (*Los Angeles News Service v. Reuters Television*, 149 F.3d 987).

Parodies and Fair Use

When composers Marvin Fisher and Jack Segal wrote the song, "When Sunny Gets Blue," it probably never occurred to them that someone might rewrite the lyrics as "When Sonny Sniffs Glue." But the song, a big hit for vocalist Johnny Mathis in the 1950s, was a hit again with those new lyrics in the 1980s.

Radio personality Rick Dees included a 30-second excerpt of the tune--with his own lyrics--in a 1984 comedy album. In part, the lyrics went this way: "When Sonny sniffs glue, her eyes get red and bulgy, then her hair begins to fall."

Fisher and Segal weren't amused, and the resulting lawsuit, *Fisher v. Dees* (794 F.2d 432) produced a 1986 ruling by the ninth circuit U.S. Court of Appeals that clarified the scope of the Fair Use Doctrine.

Affirming a trial judge's decision to dismiss the lawsuit without a trial, the appellate court said the unauthorized revision of the lyrics was unmistakably a parody. It was not intended to tap the same market as the original song about a woman's depression after a love affair turned sour, the court ruled.

The composers had conceded that a brief excerpt--perhaps a single bar--would have been a fair use, but they argued that using most of the tune was excessive and therefore a copyright infringement.

The court disagreed. Judge Joseph Sneed wrote, "Although we have no illusions of musical expertise, it was clear to us that Dees' version was intended to poke fun at the composers' song, and at Mr. Mathis' rather singular vocal range." The court reaffirmed the principle that someone may do a parody of a copyrighted work without infringing the copyright.

However, a number of other courts have disagreed with that conclusion, especially where the parody yields large profits--and a literal reading of the *Fisher v. Dees* case would deny the copyright owner any share of the profits.

In 1994 the Supreme Court finally addressed this question, ruling that even a highly profitable parody may still be a fair use rather than a copyright infringement. The high court so ruled in a case involving a parody of a Roy Orbison song from the 1960s, "Oh, Pretty Woman," by the rap group 2 Live Crew.

In *Campbell v. Acuff-Rose Music Co.* (510 U.S. 569), the Supreme Court held that 2 Live Crew's commercial purpose in recording a parody did not necessarily make the new song (called "Pretty Woman") a copyright infringement rather than a fair use of the material borrowed from Orbison's original hit. The new song took the opening bass notes and the first line of the lyrics before launching into new material.

Writing for a unanimous Supreme Court, Justice David Souter declared that the 2 Live Crew song had sufficient "transformative value" to permit a trial court to find that it was a fair use rather than an infringement despite its commercial intent. Souter emphasized that the other parts of the fair use test must still be applied: the fact that a work is a parody with "transformative value" does not automatically make it a fair use.

The case was sent back to a trial court to consider the various fair-use factors, including the percentage of the original taken and whether the new work would hurt sales of the original by tapping the same market. Justice Souter noted that 2 Live Crew had originally sought permission to adapt Orbison's song--and was turned down. He said this fact does not necessarily resolve the question of whether the new song is a fair use or an infringement.

In short, the Supreme Court said that even a commercially successful parody of a copyrighted song may be a fair use rather than a copyright infringement, depending on how the other fair use criteria are weighed. And the court held that, as always in copyright infringement lawsuits, fair use questions must be decided on a case-by-case basis.

Another point that should be noted about "Pretty Woman" is that the 2 Live Crew recording was treated by the Supreme Court as a parody as opposed to a satire. A parody (borrowing from a copyrighted work *to poke fun at that particular work*) is more likely to be a fair use than a satire (borrowing from a copyrighted work to lampoon someone or something else rather than the copyrighted work itself). This distinction was illustrated by a 1997 federal appellate court ruling against the publishers of a rhyming summary of the O.J. Simpson murder trial, using a style obviously borrowed from the classic "Dr. Seuss" book, *The Cat in the Hat*. The court halted distribution of the new work, called *The Cat NOT in the Hat, A Parody by Dr. Juice* (Dr. Seuss Enterprises v. Penguin Books, 109 F.3d 1394). The court held that "Dr. Juice" mimics but does not parody Dr. Seuss' style.

The *Campbell v. Acuff-Rose* case did not address another troubling question about fair use and music copyrights: the use of sampling. In this era of digital technology, it has become increasingly commonplace for recording artists to sample the work of others and include it in their new recordings. It may take still another Supreme Court decision to determine when sampling is a fair use and when it is a copyright infringement.

Why are parodies and sampling not permitted automatically under the compulsory licensing provision of the Copyright Act? That provision allows anyone who pays the prescribed royalties to record a copyrighted song; it does not permit major revisions and adaptations without the consent of the copyright owner.

Another widely publicized case involving a parody--this one of a famous novel and motion picture--arose in 2001. Author Alice Randall wrote a book for Houghton Mifflin that is an African-American retelling of *Gone With the Wind*. Entitled *The Wind Done Gone*, it includes characters who closely resemble those in the Civil War classic. But it also has new characters, including Scarlett O'Hara's half sister--the daughter of plantation owner Gerald O'Hara (simply called "Planter" in the new novel) and a slave, thus putting a new spin on the story of *Gone With the Wind*.

The estate of Margaret Mitchell, author of *Gone With the Wind*, sued to halt publication of the new work, contending that it is an unauthorized derivative work and therefore a copyright infringement. A federal judge issued an injunction to prevent the new work's publication, but the 11th circuit U.S. Court of Appeals issued an order to set aside the injunction, allowing the new work to be published. The appellate court said the injunction against publication was "an unlawful prior restraint in violation of the First Amendment." That left the Mitchell estate free to pursue its lawsuit for monetary damages. The dispute was settled in 2002 when the estate agreed to drop the lawsuit. In return, Randall's publisher agreed to make an unspecified donation to Morehouse College, a historically black men's college in Atlanta.

Fair Use and Advertising

May a company show a competitor's copyrighted material in order to do comparison advertising? Is that a fair use or a copyright infringement?

By 2000, two different federal appellate courts had addressed this issue, and both held that a competitor's material may indeed be used in comparison advertising. In *Sony Computer Entertainment v. Bleem* (214 F.3d 1022), the ninth circuit U.S. Court of Appeals held that Bleem, a video game software producer, could display frozen images from games played on the Sony PlayStation video console in an attempt to show that its software is superior to Sony's.

The fifth circuit U.S. Court of Appeals ruled similarly in *Triangle Publications v. Knight-Ridder Newspapers* (626 F.2d 1171, 1980). In that case, the court allowed a newspaper to display the cover of *TV Guide* to compare its own TV program magazine with the national publication.

In the *Sony* case, the court ruled that a competitor may use single-frame screen shots for comparative advertising. The court did not grant Bleem a free hand to use computer generated simulations of the TV screen; the holding was limited to actual single-frame photographs of Sony's games taken from a TV screen.

Bleem's goal in its comparison advertising was to show that its games, which are played on a computer with a high-resolution monitor, have higher quality video than Sony's games, which use an ordinary, low-resolution TV set as a video display.

"Although Bleem is most certainly copying Sony's copyrighted material for the commercial purposes of increasing its own sales, such comparative advertising redounds greatly to the purchasing public's benefit with very little corresponding loss to the integrity of Sony's copyrighted material," Judge Diarmuid O'Scannlain wrote for the court.

In weighing the four factors that determine whether a particular use of a copyrighted work is a fair use or an infringement, O'Scannlain concluded that all four factors favored Bleem's use of Sony's screen images.

COPYRIGHTS AND MUSIC LICENSING

Mass communicators are finding themselves increasingly involved in the copyright problems of the music industry, whether they want to be or not. As indicated earlier, there is *compulsory licensing* in the music field, which means anyone can record copyrighted music by merely paying a specified royalty for each CD or tape sold. Also, once a song is recorded, anyone can play the recording without paying the recording artist for *performance rights*: the Copyright Act does not give recording artists the right to collect royalties for "performances" that consist of merely playing their *sound recordings* (with one notable exception, explained later). However, the law does recognize performance rights in the underlying music and lyrics that are used in a sound recording. The result: broadcasters have to pay for the right to play copyrighted music on the air, but the money goes only to composers and music publishers, not to recording artists and record companies (unless they also happen to hold the copyrights to the underlying music and lyrics). Business establishments that play music often must pay copyright royalties to composers and music publishers but not to recording artists for the same reason.

How can a composer or music publisher ever keep track of all the different radio stations and night clubs, for instance, that are using his or her copyrighted material? Wouldn't it be impossible to monitor every single radio station, let alone visit every club?

To solve that sort of practical problem, several music licensing organizations have been established to represent the interests of composers, lyricists and music publishers. The most important ones in the United States are the American Society of Composers, Authors and Publishers (ASCAP) and Broadcast Music Inc. (BMI). Using sampling techniques, both organizations keep track of whose music is being played on the air--and collect money for the copyright owners that they represent. Both ASCAP and BMI sell most broadcasters (and other users of copyrighted music) *blanket licenses* that allow them to use all of the music whose copyright owners are represented by ASCAP or BMI. (As noted earlier, some stations find it less expensive to purchase *per-program licenses* instead). Altogether, ASCAP and BMI control the copyrights to some four million songs and collect more than $300 million a year from broadcasters for the right to *perform* these songs by playing them over the air. They collect millions more for non-broadcast uses of copyrighted music. While ASCAP and BMI dominate the music licensing business, a third licensing organization, the Society of European Stage Authors and Composers (SESAC), has been seeking to increase its small share of the business--and recently signed up several well-known copyright owners as clients.

Given the large amount of money involved, there are recurring disputes (and lawsuits) over the collection and distribution of royalties for copyrighted music. But in the end, most broadcasters have little choice but to pay up: music is essential to their programming, and ASCAP and BMI between them control the copyrights to the vast majority of the copyrighted music that broadcasters want to play on the air.

ASCAP and BMI also send representatives out to collect royalties from the owners of night clubs and other business establishments where copyrighted music is played or performed. ASCAP and BMI have formulas based on such things as the size of the establishment and its business volume to determine the amount that each business has to pay for its *blanket license*. Even non-profit organizations such as schools and churches are required to pay royalties for certain uses of copyrighted music, although some uses of music in classrooms and at "services at a place of worship" are exempt under Section 110 of the Copyright Act.

A blanket license to use copyrighted music from both ASCAP and BMI costs radio stations about three percent of their net revenues after deductions. Stations buying only per-program licenses pay a higher percentage, but based only on revenue earned during the hours when music is played.

A 100-seat bar with one big-screen television set is charged about $500 a year for a blanket license, while a 600-seat hall that charges admission and has live bands pays about $4,000.

Under some circumstances retail stores must pay royalties for the music that is heard in their establishments. In fact, one of the more controversial questions in copyright law is whether store owners should have to pay royalties for merely playing a radio in their establishments.

For many years, the legal rule was that all but the smallest stores had to pay royalties if a radio was turned on. The Supreme Court once ruled that very small stores that played a "homestyle" radio were exempt from royalties (that occurred in *Twentieth Century Music Corp. v. Aiken*, 422 U.S. 151, 1975, a case involving a fast-food chicken shop with 1,055 square feet of total floor space). But a federal appellate court later ruled that this exemption did not apply to a chain of large clothing stores that had radios hooked to commercial-quality sound systems (*Sailor Music v. The Gap Stores*, 668 F.2d 84, 1981). Based on that case, ASCAP and BMI demanded royalties from virtually all retail chains, as well as individual stores larger than 1,055 square feet of floor space.

In 1991, however, two federal appellate courts ruled that large chains of retail stores are exempt from paying royalties if each store has no more than one homestyle radio playing, with small home-type speakers placed nearby. One of the cases, *BMI v. Claire's Boutiques* (949 F.2d 1482), involved a chain of 749 stores, mostly smaller than 1,000 square feet. Each store had a small radio and two speakers that were purchased from the Radio Shack chain. BMI contended that all of the stores in the chain had to be counted together, and that Claire's was really playing 700 radios, not one radio as permitted by copyright law. The appellate court didn't buy that argument, and ruled that under existing law, each store should be counted separately. Even the larger stores in the Claire's Boutiques chain were ruled to be exempt from paying royalties as long as they had only one radio and two speakers, the court ruled.

Shortly later, another federal appellate court went even further. In *Edison Brothers Stores v. BMI* (954 F.2d 1419), the court ruled that the size of the store isn't a crucial factor. The court held that this major retail chain, whose stores average 2,000 square feet, is exempt from paying royalties as long as each store plays a homestyle radio with speakers in or near the radio (as opposed to a commercial sound system with many speakers in the ceiling).

Alarmed at the prospect of American retailers en masse turning off their commercial sound systems and buying radios for their stores at Radio Shack to get out of paying copyright royalties, BMI appealed both cases to the Supreme Court. But the high court declined to take up either case. The result: it was perfectly legal for a store owner to play a homestyle radio with a couple of speakers without paying royalties.

After years of debate about this issue, Congress passed the Fairness in Music Licensing Act in 1998. Expanding on the two *BMI* court decisions, this law exempted small retail establishments, restaurants and bars from paying royalties for playing copyrighted music on radio or television sets in their establishments. Under a compromise between the business community and copyright owners, retail businesses smaller than 2,000 square feet and restaurants and bars smaller than 3,750 square feet are now exempt from paying royalties if all they do is play homestyle radio or TV sets. Even larger businesses can qualify for the exemption if they have no more than four TV sets or six speakers. However, these rules apply only to the reception of *broadcast music*. Business owners are not exempt from paying copyright royalties for the use of recorded or live music.

Under the law, playing recorded or live music in a business constitutes a separate *performance* of the copyrighted music, and the copyright owners are entitled to royalties. To collect these royalties, ASCAP and BMI file numerous lawsuits against retail stores (and club owners) who are using copyrighted music but refuse to obtain licenses from ASCAP and BMI. Rather than pay royalties for the privilege of playing music on the radio, of course, many business establishments instead buy a canned music service, which provides background music on tape for a flat fee that includes the cost of royalty payments to ASCAP and/or BMI.

Merchants who reluctantly pay money to ASCAP and BMI are sometimes even more annoyed when they learn that the money collected by ASCAP and BMI goes only to those who own the copyrights for the music and lyrics--not to the recording artists who perform the songs. But again, that's the way it is. Congress has repeatedly turned down the recording industry's requests to give performers a share of the royalties for the playing of their recordings by broadcasters and businesses. Congress' rationale has been that the on-the-air exposure helps sell more CDs and tapes, thus benefiting the recording artists.

Once ASCAP, BMI and other licensing agencies have collected the royalties from broadcasters, owners of business establishments and others, the money is distributed to copyright owners on the basis of formulas that take into account the amount of air time each copyright owner's material has been receiving. It is assumed that each song's popularity in night clubs and other businesses including retail stores parallels the song's popularity on the nation's radio stations.

CABLE TELEVISION COPYRIGHT PROBLEMS

Another major feature of the 1976 Copyright Act is a section dealing with the special problems created by cable television systems. In fact, one of the major reasons Congress finally passed the 1976 Copyright Act after years of stalemated deliberations was a pair of U.S. Supreme Court decisions on cable television and copyright law.

In the 1968 case of *Fortnightly v. United Artists* (392 U.S. 390), the Supreme Court had ruled that a cable television system is really nothing more than a sophisticated receiving antenna. Thus, cable systems--or community antenna television (CATV) systems, as they were then called--were not "performing" the copyrighted programming they picked up off the air, amplified, and delivered to their subscribers' homes for a fee. In so ruling, the Supreme Court exempted CATV systems from any obligation to pay royalties.

Then in a 1974 decision, *Teleprompter v. CBS* (415 U.S. 394), the Supreme Court went even further. It held that CATV systems were still not performing the programming even if they retransmitted it over great distances via microwave relay. Only if they videotaped the material rather than delivering it "live" would they be liable to pay royalties to copyright owners, the court ruled.

Alarmed by these two Supreme Court decisions, motion picture and television producers, broadcasters and others with a stake in the protection of copyrighted works banded together and began lobbying Congress for legislation to establish copyright royalties for cable television systems. They prevailed, and the 1976 Copyright Act was written to require cable systems to pay royalties for all distant television stations they import. The 1976 law did not require cable systems to pay royalties for picking up local television and radio signals and delivering them to their subscribers' homes. However, as Chapter 11 explains, the 1992 Cable Television Consumer Protection and Competition Act does allow broadcasters to demand compensation from local cable operators for the use of their copyrighted programming.

For many years, the royalties that cable systems paid for distant stations were determined by the Copyright Royalty Tribunal (CRT), an independent body established by the 1976 Copyright Act. Broadcasters and program producers often contended that the royalties were too low--and they regularly sued the CRT seeking higher royalties for the broadcast programming that cable systems deliver to their customers. In addition, many copyright lawyers thought that the CRT itself was one of the least effective federal entities ever created. In the end, Congress agreed and passed legislation to abolish the CRT in 1993. As a result, royalty rates are now determined by binding arbitration, and there is one less federal agency.

The royalties are set by an entity within the U.S. Copyright Office, the Copyright Arbitration Royalty Panel.

Arbitration is also used in many cases to determine royalty payments for one of cable television's main competitors: the direct broadcast satellite (DBS) industry. For years copyright law permitted satellite television providers such as DirecTV to pick up television network programming and deliver it only to subscribers in "white areas"--areas where it is not possible to receive a local station that carries network programming. The royalties paid by the satellite television industry for network programming are determined by arbitration if the networks and other program producers cannot reach an agreement with the satellite companies on royalty rates.

The "white area" issue became highly controversial in the late 1990s. The major television networks and local stations filed copyright infringement lawsuits against the satellite providers for signing up customers for network programming in communities that were by no means "white areas" but rather places easily within range of local TV stations. Their objection: when someone gets network programming from a distant station, typically in New York or Los Angeles, that cuts into the potential audience for nearby stations. For a time, satellite subscribers had to go to their local stations seeking permission to receive network television via satellite--a request that was not often granted: most local stations didn't want to lose any more viewers.

Finally Congress intervened in this dispute in 1999, passing a new Satellite Television Home Viewers Act. This law authorized satellite television providers to deliver local television stations to subscribers in each station's service area.

The new law allowed satellite TV services to begin carrying the major network stations and PBS immediately, without carrying all other stations in each market they served. In 2002, satellite services were required to carry all local stations in each market where they carry any signals. This created a problem for satellite providers because satellite TV signals are viewed in much of the United States simultaneously, requiring satellite systems to carry hundreds of stations--with each accessible only to subscribers in the station's local area. At this writing satellite services were working to increase their channel capacity enough to permit this. At one point Echostar proposed to put some local stations on a second satellite, requiring consumers to put up two separate dish antennas to receive all of their local stations. Amid protests from broadcasters, the Federal Communications Commission acted to halt that plan.

The Satellite TV Home Viewers Act enabled satellite services to compete on an equal basis with cable for the first time. Their inability to carry local TV stations, which are a regular feature of cable TV, severely handicapped them in their competition with cable until this law was enacted.

RECORDING TECHNOLOGIES AND COPYRIGHT LAW

While cable and satellite interests, broadcasters and program producers were battling in Congress, another equally intense battle over copyright protection has been waged on Capitol Hill: the fight over copyrights and new technologies, such as home video and audio tape recording and, more recently, the exchange of copyrighted materials on the Internet. And like the cable copyright dilemma, some of these battles over copyright protection were triggered by a controversial Supreme Court decision.

When video cassette recorders (VCRs) began to gain popularity in the late 1970s, motion picture and television producers became alarmed by the ease with which the public could tape programs off the air for later viewing. The producers saw the sale of home video tapes as a lucrative new market, and they felt that market would be jeopardized if consumers could simply tape movies and TV shows off the air for free.

In a long-anticipated Supreme Court decision, the court ruled in 1984 that home video taping is *not* necessarily a copyright infringement. In *Sony Corp. of America v. Universal City Studios* (464 U.S. 417), the court split 5-4 in ruling in favor of the estimated 20 million Americans who had VCRs in their homes by then.

Writing for the Supreme Court's majority, Justice John Paul Stevens pointed out that nothing in the Copyright Act specifically prohibits consumers from taping TV shows for later viewing, a practice commonly called "time shifting." Instead, such noncommercial video taping is a fair use of copyrighted programming, Stevens wrote in his majority opinion. Stevens said:

> One may search the Copyright Act in vain for any sign that the elected representatives of millions of people who watch television every day have made it unlawful to copy a program for later viewing at home, or have enacted a flat prohibition against the sale of machines that make such copying possible.

Forecasting the legislative battle that he knew would follow the Supreme Court's decision, Stevens conceded that Congress could "take a fresh look at this new technology just as it so often has examined other innovations in the past. But it is not our job to apply laws that have not yet been written," he added.

In so ruling, the Supreme Court reversed a federal appellate court decision that held private at-home video taping to be a copyright infringement. The lower court suggested that a flat royalty fee could be added to the price of each blank tape and each video recorder to compensate the entertainment industry for the copying that consumers would do.

Critics of the lower court decision pointed out that not all VCRs and blank tapes are used to tape copyrighted TV shows. Thus, they said, a blanket royalty would force many VCR owners to pay for copyright infringements they do not commit. As a result, such a royalty should more accurately be called a "tax" to support the entertainment industry, not a royalty, some contended.

Program producers replied by pointing to the potential for the sale of video tapes that might not be realized if consumers could freely tape TV shows. The industry needs those revenues to produce new and better shows, they said.

The Supreme Court's majority was clearly influenced by the fact that some uses of VCRs are clearly *not* copyright infringements. In fact, Justice Stevens noted that the television production community itself was divided on home video taping:

children's television host Fred Rogers had made it clear that he wanted those who could not view Mr. Rogers' Neighborhood at its scheduled time to tape it for later viewing!

In the end, the Supreme Court passed the buck to Congress by ruling that at-home video taping was not a copyright infringement under existing law. Predictably, both sides launched major lobbying efforts in Congress after the Supreme Court's 1984 decision. But Congress was not anxious to get involved in this politically touchy dispute. Legislation was introduced to collect royalty fees on the sale of VCRs and blank tapes, but it was never approved by Congress. As a result, noncommercial use of VCRs for time shifting is still a legal fair use. However, this does not mean that copying rented movies and keeping them indefinitely is a fair use. Nor was any non-home use of off-air video tapes made a fair use by the *Sony* decision.

Meanwhile, other groups of copyright owners have also lobbied Congress, seeking to protect their economic interests. A group called "The Coalition to Save America's Music" at one time tried to get Congress to add royalties to the selling price of blank audio tapes and audio taping equipment--on the ground that consumers are taping copyrighted music from friends' records and tapes (and also taping it directly off the air) instead of buying their own recordings. To no one's surprise, consumer groups responded by pointing to the many other uses for audio recorders besides taping copyrighted music, and argued that flat royalties on audio tapes would be unfair to everyone who uses a tape recorder for other purposes.

Despite years of controversy, Congress never acted to set up a royalty system for *analog* home audio or video taping. However, as *digital* audio recording equipment became less expensive, Congress revisited this issue.

In 1992, Congress responded to demands from the recording industry for additional copyright protection in the digital era by enacting the Audio Home Recording Act, which added a royalty fee to the purchase price of digital audio recording equipment and blank digital audio tapes or disks for home use, with the money allocated to record companies, recording artists, songwriters and music publishers. In return, the 1992 law said consumers could make one copy of a digital audio recording for non-commercial use, but not a second copy: the law imposed severe restrictions on "serial copying" (making multiple copies of the same tape or CD). The recording industry argued that, with the advent of digital audio recording, consumers could make virtually flawless copies of CDs (and eventually of digital radio broadcasts). This, they said, justified a new law to protect record companies.

Of course, evolving technology quickly made the Audio Home Recording Act irrelevant to most consumers: the advent of inexpensive CD-R units enabled personal computer owners to make copies of audio CDs (and CD-ROM-based computer software), copyright laws notwithstanding. And the restrictions on digital audio recorders contained in the Audio Home Recording Act made those devices unattractive to consumers. Why buy an expensive gadget that doesn't allow free copying when an ordinary home computer can copy music without all those nasty government-backed restrictions? In 2002, Congress was considering the difficult problem created by the sharing of copyrighted music files on the Internet; that issue is discussed later.

The question of sharing copyrighted works has many other dimensions. Representatives of some book publishers have also lobbied Congress, seeking the right to charge extra fees when books are placed in libraries where many people can read them instead of buying their own personal copies. Like home audio and video taping, the use of libraries cuts into the profits that copyright owners would otherwise realize, they contended.

Librarians, of course, replied that their budgets are hopelessly strained already, and that such added royalties would be a burdensome new tax on knowledge. Libraries, they noted, are not exactly a new invention. The nation's founding fathers knew about libraries when they drafted the first American copyright law in 1790, and they could have set up a royalty system if they thought the fact that libraries let people read books without buying them was unfair to copyright owners.

As all of these issues were debated in the courts, in Congress, in college classrooms, and probably in thousands of other places, some critics of the moves by copyright owners to enhance their profits began wondering where it would all end. Since photocopying machines are also used to copy copyrighted materials, some suggested that it would be just as logical to impose a flat royalty on reams of blank paper as it is to place such a royalty on blank audio and video tapes.

In 2002, it was becoming clear that the issue of video taping television programming is *not* settled. A consensus is emerging among industry groups that the digital hardware will include provisions to prevent home video taping once the digital TV transition is complete. At the very least, software codes will be included to prevent serial copying. But will consumers give up their analog TVs and VCRs if they cannot freely copy TV shows on the new digital hardware?

COMPUTERS, THE INTERNET AND COPYRIGHT LAWS

The mushrooming growth of the personal computer business has created many copyright dilemmas in recent years--problems involving both computer software and the Internet. When Congress enacted the 1976 Copyright Act, personal computers were primitive gadgets being built by a handful of hobbyists. Only a few years later, millions of personal computers had been sold to the general public and copyrighted computer software was being traded openly at almost every high school in America. When the Internet became wildly popular during the 1990s, still more copyright questions emerged.

At least five different legal questions have become controversial: (1) the protection of computer software copyrights, (2) the basic problems of digital copying and copy-protection, (3) the question of sharing copyrighted files over the Internet (particularly music and movies), (4) the problems of Internet broadcasting, and (5) problems that arose when publishers began placing their printed materials online.

Copyright Law and Computer Software

Like movies and TV shows, computer software has been copied by consumers on an enormous scale, prompting copyright owners to look for new ways to control what they see as a flagrant copyright infringement by the public. Moreover, several leading computer hardware and software companies waged a long--and ultimately unsuccessful--legal battle to keep competitors from making products that had a "look and feel" similar to theirs.

At first, it was not clear that certain types of computer software could even be copyrighted. A computer's "operating system," for example, is a complex pattern of binary numbers (ones and zeros) stored inside an electronic component known as a "read-only memory" (ROM) chip. Because these operating instructions for computers are readable only by the machines themselves and not by humans, some copyright experts questioned whether they could even be covered by copyright law (as opposed to patent law, which is normally what protects the designs of electronic and mechanical devices from infringement).

However, securing a patent is a difficult and time-consuming process, while registering a copyright is easy, as indicated earlier in this chapter. Thus, many computer manufacturers wanted to copyright their computer operating instructions rather than waiting and hoping to secure a patent eventually.

What brought this esoteric legal dilemma into focus was the appearance of the Apple II computer, an early personal computer for which thousands of programs were written. Few people questioned the rightness of extending copyright protection to these "application programs," programs that made it possible to play video games, do word processing, or solve complex mathematical problems on a personal computer. However, the Franklin Computer Company began making "Apple-compatible" computers, computers that used a basic operating system so similar to the Apple II operating system that the Franklin Ace computers would run programs written for the Apple.

Meanwhile, a number of companies in the Far East also began making Apple-compatible computers, some of them blatant copies of the Apple II's styling and electronic circuitry. Since some of these competing computers were sold for less than half the price of an Apple computer, the Apple Corporation began an aggressive legal campaign to halt the sale of Apple-compatible computers.

The legal rationale for this campaign was that Apple's operating system was a legitimately copyrighted product that no one else could duplicate without permission. Franklin and others defended themselves by pointing out that copyright law had not previously covered "useful devices" like a ROM chip containing computer code. To apply the Copyright Act to such things would be about like letting General Motors copyright the designs of the parts in its cars so no one else could make tires or carburetors that would fit on GM cars. Such things should be patented if they are really novel inventions, but if they are not novel enough to be patented, competitors should be free to copy the designs without fear of a lawsuit, Franklin and other Apple-compatible computer makers argued.

The question of whether a computer's encoded "operating system" could be copyrighted was resolved in two federal appellate court decisions--both decisive victories for Apple. In *Apple Computer Inc. v. Franklin Computer Corp.* (714 F.2d. 1240), a 1983 ruling of the third circuit U.S. Court of Appeals, the validity of Apple's copyright on its computer operating instructions was upheld. Writing for the court, Judge Dolores Sloriter rejected the argument that a pattern of ones and zeros embedded in a computer chip was not copyrightable. She said copyright protection "is not confined to literature in the nature of Hemingway's *For Whom the Bell Tolls*."

The ninth circuit U.S. Court of Appeals ruled in much the same way in a 1984 case, *Apple Computer Inc. v. Formula International* (725 F.2d 521). In this case, Judge Warren J. Ferguson wrote:

> The Copyright Act extends protection to 'original works of authorship fixed in any tangible medium of expression....' The computer program when written embodies expression; never has the Copyright Act required that expression be communicated to a particular audience.

Later, Apple took aggressive steps to keep others from making software that looked and operated like the software used on the Macintosh line of personal computers. In 1988, Apple sued Microsoft Corp. and Hewlett-Packard Co.--two major producers of competing computer software--for producing software using pull-down menus, icons and a "mouse" as a pointing device, all key features of the Macintosh system. Apple contended that these features are too close to the "look and feel" of the Macintosh.

A previous U.S. District Court decision, *Broderbund v. Unison World* (648 F.Supp. 1127), had held that a new computer program with too much of the same "look and feel" as an existing one could be a copyright infringement. After that ruling, Lotus Development Corp., creator of the Lotus 1-2-3 spreadsheet program, sued the makers of two competing spreadsheet programs because their spreadsheets used many of the same commands and looked much the same on the screen as Lotus 1-2-3.

Lotus and Apple both drew immediate criticism from many attorneys and software writers for filing these lawsuits. In both cases, those suing did not originate the "look and feel" that they were trying to prevent others from using. Lotus 1-2-3 closely resembles VisiCalc, a spreadsheet program that was widely used on early Apple II computers. In fact, one of the people who developed VisiCalc later helped design Lotus 1-2-3. And Apple was not the first computer maker to use pull-down menus with a pointing device and icons: Xerox and others used these ideas first. Perhaps more important, many critics felt Apple's desire to keep the Macintosh "look and feel" unique was like General Motors saying that other brands of cars could not have steering wheels--or a brake pedal to the left of the accelerator. If users are to be able to freely move back and forth among different brands of computers, all should operate in essentially the same way just as cars do.

In 1992, a federal judge dismissed the bulk of Apple's copyright infringement lawsuit against Microsoft and Hewlett-Packard, largely rejecting the idea that the "look and feel" of a computer program is something that can be protected under copyright law. The rest of Apple's lawsuit was dismissed in 1993--and Apple's appeals were not successful (see *Apple Computer Inc. v. Microsoft Corp.*, 35 F.3d 1435). In 1995, the Supreme Court refused to review the lower court decisions against Apple; the company had almost nothing to show for the ten years and millions of dollars it spent trying to win a legal monopoly on the "look and feel" of the Macintosh. By then it was clear that Microsoft could continue to produce its popular Macintosh-like Windows software, with or without Apple's blessing--and the U.S. Justice Department was investigating Microsoft rather than Apple for engaging in allegedly monopolistic business practices in the computer industry--an investigation that led the Justice Department to file a series of widely publicized antitrust lawsuits against Microsoft (see Chapter 12).

Meanwhile, Lotus also failed in its attempt to keep competitors from making programs with command structures similar to the Lotus 1-2-3 command structure. In *Lotus Development Corp. v. Borland International* (49 F.3d 807, 1995), the first circuit U.S. Court of Appeals ruled that Lotus could not copyright its command structure. The court ruled that the words and commands used to operate a spreadsheet are an uncopyrightable "method of operation," not a copyrightable creative aspect of the program. Elaborating on the court's decision in a concurring opinion, Judge Michael Boudin likened the command structure to the standard QWERTY typewriter keyboard layout used by almost all typewriter makers or the control buttons on a VCR, similarly used by most manufacturers. He said:

> If a better spreadsheet comes along, it's hard to see why customers who have learned the Lotus menu and devised macros for it should remain captives of Lotus because of an investment in learning made by the user and not by Lotus.

In 1996, the U.S. Supreme Court took up the Lotus case, but the justices deadlocked 4-4 after hearing oral arguments. Justice John Paul Stevens disqualified himself from participating in the case. A tie vote affirms the lower court's decision but denies it the full precedent-setting power of a Supreme Court decision.

In general, the trend today appears to be for the courts to take a narrow view of computer copyrights, thus allowing new competitors to enter the field with products similar to or compatible with the industry leaders' products. This is true in the video game field as well as the application software market. In 1992, two major federal court decisions expanded the right of independent companies to make cartridges that run on another company's video games in spite of the game-maker's copyright claims. First, a federal appellate court held that Nintendo could not prevent Galoob Toys from making a video game cartridge called "Game Genie," which plugs into Nintendo units and allows players to change the speed, mobility or number of "lives" of a video game character. The Game Genie is a fair use rather than an unlawful derivative work under copyright law, the court held (*Galoob Toys v. Nintendo of America*, 964 F.2d 965). If the Game Genie had been declared to be a derivative work, then the copyright owner (in this case, Nintendo) would have the exclusive right to produce it. But this decision did not resolve all of the issues involving Nintendo. That company and several of its competitors have been locked in a number of other complex copyright and patent infringement lawsuits that could drag on for many more years.

Another 1992 federal appellate court decision involving rival video game manufacturers further limited the right of any software producer to use the Copyright Act to avoid competition. In the case of *Sega Enterprises v. Accolade Inc.* (977 F.2d 1510), the court held that computer software companies may disassemble a competitor's computer code so they can determine how to make compatible products. The *Sega* case, which is widely regarded as a landmark case in the software industry, extended the Fair Use Doctrine to cover this kind of "reverse engineering." If the court had ruled that it is a copyright infringement to dismantle a competitor's software and examine its inner workings in order to make a compatible product, competition in the software industry would have been severely curtailed. However, the *Sega* case, like the Nintendo case, was not completely resolved by one decision. The appellate court sent the case back to a trial court to rule on several complex questions of patent law inherent in Accolade's reverse engineering activities.

In 2000, a federal appellate court again held that reverse engineering is a fair use and not a copyright infringement, allowing a company whose software emulates the functions of Sony's PlayStation game machines to disassemble Sony's copyrighted software in order to determine how to make compatible products (*Sony Computer Entertainment v. Connectix Corp.*, 203 F.3d 596).

The court suggested that Sony could file for a patent and not a copyright to protect its PlayStation game machine--and Sony quickly did just that. However, the court also noted that it is more difficult to obtain a patent than a copyright, stating, "If Sony wishes to obtain a lawful monopoly on the functional concepts in its software, it must satisfy the more stringent standards of the patent laws."

Given the complexity of the copyright and patent issues involved in these cases--and the enormous amount of money at stake--it is certain that these computer legal battles will continue, with unpredictable results. What is clear at this point is that the courts are reluctant to allow any company to use the Copyright Act to keep competitors from making compatible products in the high-stakes computer industry.

Internet Problems: Basic Issues

Inevitably, questions of copyright ownership in cyberspace have become controversial as millions of people began accessing the Internet during the 1990s. The problems became even more complex and controversial in 1999 and 2000 when millions of people began exchanging not only words and images but also music and digital video via the Internet, to the utter horror of copyright owners. Although there is much uncertainty in this newly developing area of the law, a few principles are clear.

The most fundamental principle is that a copyright is still a copyright, regardless of the means by which a copyrighted work is published, performed or distributed (although those three legal terms are being redefined in the cyberspace age). Also, the fact that a document is posted online somewhere without a copyright notice does not prove that the document is in the public domain. Under current law, no recently created work falls into the public domain unless the creator or other copyright owner expressly places it in the public domain. If there is no declaration that a work is in the public domain, the copyright owner could claim copyright infringement if he/she disapproves of the way someone uses the work. However, once a work is in the public domain, it's there for all purposes. The statement that a work is in the public domain, but only for non-commercial purposes, is not valid. If a work is in the public domain, anyone can use it for any purpose. On the other hand, a copyright owner can certainly retain the copyright and merely grant others a *general license* to use the work for certain specified non-commercial purposes.

In 1995, a task force under the direction of Bruce Lehman, the U.S. commissioner of patents and trademarks, released a 249-page "white paper" discussing the copyright, trademark and patent implications of cyberspace. The paper proposed a number of changes in copyright law that would increase the protection for corporate copyright owners--at the expense of writers, artists, librarians, and the general Internet-surfing public. Among other things, the task force proposed:

*To eliminate the first sale doctrine, which allows the buyer of a copyrighted work to resell it or lend it to others without having to pay additional royalties (this could undercut the ability of libraries to buy one copy of a book or magazine and then lend it to patrons as well as clarifying the right of copyright owners to prevent legitimate purchasers of a work from distributing it in cyberspace);

*To clarify the principle that the digital transmission or storage of a work in a computer, even if only temporarily, is copying and/or distribution of the work;

*To outlaw devices designed to defeat anti-copying technologies; and

*To allow libraries to make only three copies of a digital work, with one available for public viewing in the library (but not for borrowing or copying) while the other two are kept in a closed archive.

In 1998, the Supreme Court sidestepped the task force's proposal to eliminate the first sale doctrine, not only upholding it but ruling that it allows a discounter to buy American-made products that are sold at lower prices overseas and bring them back into this country as "gray market" goods, undercutting list-price retailers here (*Quality King Distributors v. L'Anza Research International*, 523 U.S. 135).

The task force declined to address the controversial question of holding online services liable for what their subscribers do. However, Congress included provisions in the 1996 Telecommunications Act under which Internet service providers (ISPs) can escape liability for both libel and copyright infringements committed by their millions of customers if they act promptly to remove allegedly unlawful materials. In passing this law, Congress recognized that it is impossible for ISPs to monitor everything that every user does online.

In 1998, Congress passed the Digital Millennium Copyright Act, a far-reaching new law that expanded on the Telecommunications Act, giving both copyright owners and ISPs extensive legal protection--but at the expense of those who post and use material on the Internet, including librarians, educators, website owners, the Internet-surfing public and even broadcasters.

The Digital Millennium Copyright Act has many provisions. Among other things, it brought the United States into compliance with the provisions of two World Intellectual Property Organization (WIPO) treaties signed several years ago. Perhaps the most noteworthy of these provisions is a requirement that VCR manufacturers start adding circuitry that will make it impossible for consumers to copy rental videos and pay-per-view television programming. Another little-noticed provision gives copyright protection to "cookies," the small files that are quietly placed on computers when they are used to surf the Internet, enabling some Internet hosts to ascertain what sites a computer user has visited. Some attorneys said this provision makes it a copyright infringement for a computer user to delete these cookies from his or her own computer, even though they may have been placed there without the user's knowledge or consent.

The Digital Millennium Copyright Act also established new rules governing digital copyrights, giving additional copyright protection to digital renderings of motion pictures, videos, sound recordings, photography and graphics. The act also banned many technologies that could circumvent encryption and copy-prevention schemes.

One of the most controversial features of the Digital Millennium Copyright Act concerns the handling of alleged copyright infringements on the Internet. The law exempted Internet service providers from liability for what their subscribers may post on the net if they act quickly to shut down sites containing alleged infringements. A copyright owner merely notifies the ISP that material on a particular site is a copyright infringement, providing a statement that he/she has a "good faith belief" that the use of the disputed material is an infringement.

The Internet provider must then notify the website owner and promptly shut down the site. The website owner, in turn, can oppose the shutdown only by stating *under penalty of perjury* that the challenged material is being removed by mistake or was wrongly identified. In contrast, the copyright owner is *not* obligated to declare anything under penalty of perjury. Nor is the website owner allowed to make a fair use defense of the use of the disputed material.

In effect, this allows copyright owners to shut down websites without ever going to court to prove that an infringement has in fact occurred. Internet providers are exempt from copyright liability--if they act as copyright enforcers. If they fail to play that role, they can be held liable for any infringement that may occur.

Critics of these provisions of the Digital Millennium Copyright Act have pointed out that the act was the result of a compromise between copyright owners and Internet service providers. Website owners, educators, librarians and others who advocate a broad Fair Use Doctrine were not at the bargaining table when this law was negotiated.

Still more controversial questions about the Internet and copyright law arose in the early 2000s. Two Internet start-up companies particularly incurred the wrath of the recording industry: Napster, an Internet-based music trading service, and MP3.com, which might be likened to an Internet juke box. Napster enabled millions of users to share music files--most of them copyrighted. MP3 allowed users to play music online with its "instant listening service." The larger problem of file sharing--"piracy" according to copyright owners--produced numerous lawsuits, countersuits, proposals for legislation and technical "solutions" intended to make various kinds of copying more difficult.

Internet Problems: File Sharing

No Internet start-up company more quickly exploded on the scene and caused panic in an industry than Napster, which popularized music file-sharing on the Internet.

The Napster site became enormously popular in 2000--and the record industry launched an all-out effort to halt music sharing by Napster's estimated 50 million users. By mid-2002, Napster was in bankruptcy. How did this happen?

The recording industry's all-out legal attack on Napster began with a request for an injunction in federal court to halt the file sharing. U.S. District Court Judge Marilyn Hall Patel initially granted an injunction in 2000, but the ninth circuit U.S. Court of Appeals issued a stay, allowing Napster to continue for a few more months while an appeal was heard. In 2001, the appellate court upheld much of the recording industry's case, clearing the way for Patel to curtail music sharing on Napster. In *A&M Records et al. v. Napster* (239 F.3d 1004), the appellate court held that when computer music enthusiasts exchange digital music files via Napster, that is often a copyright infringement. The court rejected Napster's contention that music sharing should be a fair use, just as home video taping television programs for later viewing is a fair use.

With the appellate court's blessing, Judge Patel ordered Napster to halt the exchange of copyrighted songs whenever a copyright owner asked Napster to do so. This order placed the burden on record companies to identify copyrighted songs and notify Napster. Then Napster had to prevent its users from exchanging each song as it was identified. As Napster complied, its listing of songs available for exchange rapidly dwindled.

A complicating factor was that at one time about 10 percent of the music being exchanged via Napster either was not covered by a current copyright or was exchanged with the copyright owner's permission. Sharing of that music was not affected by the court order. In fact, a major reason the appellate court rejected Judge Patel's earlier order to shut Napster down altogether was because not all music sharing facilitated by Napster was a copyright infringement--some of it was perfectly legal. In ruling that the non-infringing uses of Napster precluded a judicial decree to shut it down altogether, the appellate court was echoing its own earlier ruling when the recording industry tried to ban the sale of the Diamond Rio portable MP3 player (*Recording Industry Association of America v. Diamond Multimedia Systems*, 180 F.3d 1072). In that 1999 decision, the appellate court said it was inappropriate to ban the sale of a product that has substantial non-infringing uses.

By mid-2001, however, Napster was in a downward spiral. An independent Internet research firm reported that the average Napster user had 1.5 song files available online, down from an average of 220 songs in February. Meanwhile, most Napster users were gone: in mid-2001 Napster had an average peak of 320,000 users logged onto the system, down from 1.57 million in February. Many of the others had turned to alternate music-sharing systems which have no central coordinating point or are based overseas. The industry began an aggressive legal campaign against those systems, too, but it was more difficult than going after one high-profile, U.S.-based system.

As Napster's business prospects turned ever dimmer in 2002, the company sought additional backing from Bertelsmann AG, the German music firm that initially hoped to take control of Napster and revive it as a for-pay music downloading site. That turned out to be futile when Napster went into bankruptcy.

Meanwhile, several record labels announced their own Internet music distribution systems, most of which charge subscribers a monthly fee for the privilege of downloading music, while including technology to prevent subscribers from copying the music files or placing them on a CD. These ventures generally failed to attract a large following.

While the record industry was battling Napster, it was also fighting legal battles against other Internet music providers. In one such lawsuit, a federal judge ordered MP3.com, another Internet music site, to pay an astonishing $25,000 per CD (a total of perhaps $250 million) in damages to Seagram's Universal Music Group for copyright infringement. Ruling in September, 2000, Judge Jed Rakoff said he wanted to send a message to the Internet community to deter copyright infringement. Lawyers for MP3.com said they would appeal, pointing out that such a high damage award would surely bankrupt the company, which has already paid $20 million apiece to four other large record companies to settle lawsuits. MP3.com eventually reached a settlement in which its total payout was about $170 million.

MP3.com's website is in some ways similar to Napster, although MP3 allowed users to place copyrighted CDs in a huge data base maintained by the company. Napster, on the other hand, provided only an index and a linking service, allowing computer users to share music files with each other.

The news media reported in 2001 that of the first $80 million the record labels collected from MP3.com, none had been passed along to recording artists. Industry sources said the labels were uncertain whether to treat the money as licensing revenue, of which artists get half, or royalties, of which artists get a far smaller share. So they just kept it all while they tried to decide how much to pass on to recording artists.

In mid-2001, MP3.com announced that it was being acquired by Vivendi Universal, which became one of the world's largest record companies through a series of earlier mergers and acquisitions.

In still another lawsuit triggered by an Internet copyright issue, a federal judge ordered the 2600 Enterprises website to delete links that would help web surfers locate overseas websites offering the so-called DeCSS software to facilitate copying of DVD movies. The DeCSS software was written primarily by a Norwegian youth so he could view DVD movies on a Linux-based computer (as opposed to one running the Windows operating system). DeCSS overrides the copy-prevention features of DVDs, allowing them to be viewed and copied on Linux computers. The federal judge ruled that even linking to sites having the copying software is a contributory copyright infringement in violation of the Digital Millennium Copyright Act (DMCA). The defendants raised First Amendment questions and appealed the ruling--with the support of civil liberties and Internet advocacy groups such as the Electronic Frontier Foundation.

Acting in late 2001, the second circuit U.S. Court of Appeals rejected the First

Amendment claims and upheld the bulk of the judge's order. Ruling in *Universal City Studios v. Corley* (273 F.3d 429), the court concluded that the DMCA does not violate the First Amendment by banning not only software that defeats copy-protection schemes but also information about such software. In essence, the appellate court said it is up to Congress to weigh the First Amendment against the claims of copyright owners.

A further complication in the DVD controversy is that because the copying software was written to run under the Linux open-source operating system, it was quickly championed by advocates of Linux, for whom the freedom to distribute computer code and discuss its finer points is almost a religion. The Electronic Frontier Foundation argued strongly (but unsuccessfully) that there is a fundamental First Amendment right to distribute open-source software in spite of the DMCA.

Because of this free-exchange tradition, many computer enthusiasts were horrified and outraged in 2001 when a group of researchers who devised a way to defeat music copy-protection technologies (something they were invited to do by the recording industry) got a stern letter from industry lawyers telling them to suppress their findings. The researchers (students and professors at Princeton and Rice Universities, among others) were on the verge of presenting a paper at a computer security conference when the industry threatened legal action unless they withdrew their presentation. The legal threat came from the Secure Digital Music Initiative (SDMI), a group formed by the world's biggest record labels to develop a way to distribute copy-protected digital music.

The researchers were led by Professor Edward Felten of Princeton, an expert on encryption. He withdrew from the conference and then filed his own lawsuit, seeking a judicial declaration that the Digital Millennium Copyright Act, on which the industry based its threat, violates the First Amendment by preventing scholarly discussion of encryption and decryption technologies. His lawsuit was dismissed by a federal judge who ruled that Felten's rights were not violated because he did eventually publish his scholarly paper. Felten and his backers then asked a federal appellate court to reinstate the lawsuit.

By mid-2002, copyright owners were working on a number of fronts to curb unauthorized copying and consumer advocates were counterattacking. Backed by Hollywood studios, the Broadcast Protection Discussion Group was developing ways to prevent free, over-the-air television programs from being copied and placed on the Internet when they are broadcast in digital rather than analog form. If successful, this initiative could end or sharply limit the ability of consumers to do home video recording.

Meanwhile, record companies began marketing CDs in a copy-protected format without labeling them. The new CDs generally will not play on computers. That led consumer advocates to sue the industry, seeking an order requiring that the new CDs at least be labeled and also seeking compensation to consumers for alleged damage to their equipment caused by the new CDs. And technology buffs in England reported that Sony's proprietary CD copy-protection system could be defeated by scribbling around the rim of the disk with a felt-tip marker! There was no indication that it would work on all copy-protected audio CDs.

As this was happening, the Electronic Frontier Foundation sued the major studios and TV networks in mid-2002 in an attempt to define consumers' TV-recording rights in the digital age. The online civil liberties group asked a federal judge to declare that consumers can use digital recorders to watch shows after they are broadcast, skip all commercials, transmit recordings to members of their households and send copies of free TV broadcasts to anyone on the Internet provided they receive no compensation. This is a countersuit filed in response to an industry lawsuit intended to halt the sale of digital video recorders made by Sonicblue and ReplayTV that allow commercial-skipping.

On another front, a congressman in 2002 introduced legislation to protect the right of consumers to make copies of digital files, such as songs on a CD. Although the legislation by Rep. Rick Boucher (D-Va.) was given little chance to pass, it underscored concerns about the initiatives to limit consumers' rights. Boucher pointed out that under the 1992 Audio Home Recording Act the industry is already receiving a few cents of the purchase price of each blank recordable CD as compensation for copying done by consumers. Boucher criticized the industry for taking these fees and then pushing initiatives to prevent CD copying.

Webcasting and Copyrights

With little controversy, Congress quietly passed the Digital Performance Right in Sound Recordings Act of 1995, a law that ultimately forced many broadcasters to think twice about streaming their regular programming over the Internet. For the first time, this law gave record companies the right to receive royalties when their recordings are played over the air--but only on digital audio broadcast services, not ordinary AM and FM radio stations. As noted earlier, free, over-the-air broadcasters pay performance royalties only to the owners of music copyrights (via licensing agencies such as ASCAP and BMI), not to record companies and recording artists.

At first most broadcasters weren't particularly alarmed by this law because it didn't seem to affect them, but it made life more difficult for one of their competitors: satellite-based for-pay digital audio broadcasters. However, the law quickly became a huge problem for them once they started doing webcasting, streaming their over-the-air programming on the Internet.

In December, 2000, the U.S. Copyright Office issued rules explaining how the 1998 Digital Millennium Copyright Act and the 1995 Digital Performance Right law would apply to broadcasters. The new rules decreed that broadcasters, like other digital programmers, would pay separate royalties for streaming music on their websites, and that for the first time they would pay royalties not only to music licensing agencies such as ASCAP and BMI but also to record companies for the use of sound recordings.

The Copyright Office also ruled that broadcasters who stream their regular programming over the Internet must follow a series of restrictions on digital broadcasts imposed by Congress in the 1995 law. That law forbids the streaming of more than three songs from one album or four songs by one artist in a three-hour period, and also forbids identifying a song before it is played. The result: many broadcasters cannot put their over-the-air programming on the Internet without breaking the law because they routinely identify songs or recording artists before a song is played, and they often exceed the limitation on songs from one album or by one artist. (As of 2002, broadcasters and the recording industry were negotiating for waivers of some of these rules.)

In 2002, matters only got worse for many webcasters. A Copyright Arbitration Royalty Panel that had been established to set royalty rates proposed rates so high that most webcasters said they could not afford to pay them: 70 cents *for each playing of each song* for every 1,000 listeners for radio stations that were streaming their over-the-air programming and twice that--$1.40 per song--for non-broadcast webcasters. Many webcasters protested that the rates exceeded their total income from all sources and asked to pay instead a percentage of their revenue--as they already do to ASCAP and BMI.

Amidst the resulting controversy, the U.S. Copyright Office rejected the proposed rates and instead established the *same rate* for both broadcast streaming and non-broadcast webcasting. But the rate chosen was still 70 cents per 1,000 listeners for each playing of a song--the rate originally proposed for broadcast streaming. Advocates of webcasting said even that rate was so prohibitive it would force most webcasters to discontinue playing music. A group of webcasters said they would pursue the only recourse left open: a challenge of the rate decision in the U.S. Court of Appeals.

Perhaps the most shocking aspect of this for some webcasters was that the rates were made *retroactive* to October, 1998. Some predicted that bankruptcy would be the only way out for many webcasters.

Webcasters also faced other performance rights problems in 2002. For example, actors' unions were demanding additional payment if over-the-air commercials were also carried on the Internet.

Freelancers and Electronic Publishing

Another controversial question created by the digital revolution has involved the right of newspapers and magazines to place their content in online editions and electronic data bases without specific permission of freelance authors.

Until about 1995, most major publishers did not include a provision in the contracts signed by freelancers to cover electronic rights. The National Writers Union, an organization that represents about 3,000 freelance writers, sued the New York Times Co., other major publishers and the Lexis-Nexis computer database for using the writers' work electronically without specific permission.

The publishers contended that these electronic data bases were merely reproductions of the printed versions--and no separate copyright permission was required.

In 2001, the U.S. Supreme Court sided with the writers in *New York Times Co. v. Tasini* (533 U.S. 483). In this case, the court ruled that Jonathan Tasini, former president of the National Writers Union, and other freelancers, own the electronic rights to their works unless they specifically assign those rights to a publisher.

The case involved only material produced by *freelancers* as opposed to staff writers. Under the "works made for hire" provision of the Copyright Act, employers automatically own the copyrights to works created by employees within the scope of their employment. It also does not involve most freelance works published since 1995, when the major publishers began including specific provisions to authorize electronic republication in their standard contracts.

Responding to the court's decision, representatives of the *New York Times* pointed out that between 1980 and 1995, the years covered by the *Tasini* decision, the *Times* had published about 115,000 articles written by 27,000 different freelancers. Because of the difficulty of tracking down all of these authors and securing permission, *Times* Publisher Arthur Sulzberger, Jr. said the *Times* "will now undertake the difficult and sad process of removing significant portions from its electronic historical archive." Some historians, including documentary filmmaker Ken Burns and historian Doris Kearns Goodwin, who filed a brief supporting the publishers, also lamented the gaps in the historical record that would result from the *Tasini* decision if publishers are forced to remove freelance work from their data bases.

Sulzberger said publishers would ask Congress to amend the Copyright Act to allow electronic data bases to include pre-1995 freelance articles as well as staff-written articles and more recent freeelance work.

On the other hand, Tasini said his union would be happy to work out a licensing system for freelancers similar to that used by ASCAP and BMI to compensate music copyright owners, with freelancers compensated each time someone accesses the electronic version of a story or other material that appeared in the major media.

By 2002, it was clear that the historians' worst fears were coming true. The *New York Times* removed more than 100,000 articles from its online archive and by mid-2002 had only restored about 15,000 of them after coming to terms with authors. Many of the other authors either could not be located or had not reached an agreement with the newspaper. And many other newspapers that were not as concerned about being a newspaper of record as the *Times* simply deleted all pre-1995 free-lance materials from their online archives and made no attempt to strike deals with free-lance authors.

In joining Justice John Paul Stevens' dissenting opinion in the *Tasini* case, Justice Stephen Breyer said, "We may wipe out much of the history of the 20th century."

The history isn't really gone. For those with the time and money to do research page by page, the full text of many newspapers remains intact on microfilm in libraries. But for those who need the speed and global reach of online research, Justice Breyer's concern seems well-founded.

Other Internet Copyright Issues

Still other copyright problems have been created by cyberspace. A number of individual bulletin board system (BBS) owners have faced lawsuits because copyrighted materials were posted on their systems and could be downloaded. Several of these cases involved copyrighted software or digitized images. In one case, a

BBS owner was sued successfully by Playboy Enterprises for having 170 copyrighted images from Playboy publications available online.

Playboy has also aggressively pursued the owners of Internet sites containing images owned by Playboy. In 1998, Playboy won the largest statutory damage award in the history of American copyright law, a $3.74 million judgment against the owner of a site that allegedly distributed 7,475 Playboy-owned photographs over the Internet (*Playboy Enterprises v. Sanfilippo*, 1998 U.S. Dist Lexis 4773). In the late 1990s Playboy also won six-figure and seven-figure statutory damage awards against several other website operators.

Playboy also sued Terri Welles, the 1981 *Playboy Magazine* Playmate of the Year, in an attempt to keep her from identifying herself by that title on her website. However, a federal judge refused to grant a preliminary injunction in that case, holding that Playboy was unlikely to prevail in court even though Playmate of the Year is a registered trademark of Playboy. The judge said that a title such as Playmate of the Year becomes a part of a person's identity, like being an Academy Award winner, a former Miss America or a Heisman Trophy winner. To indicate this status on a website is a fair use under trademark law. Playboy appealed and the ninth circuit U.S. Court of Appeals affirmed the judge's ruling. In a later decision, the appellate court also held that Welles could not only identify herself as Playmate of the Year but that she could use words such as "playboy" and "playmate" in metatags--hidden keywords used by search engines. The court concluded that there were no suitable alternate words she could use in her metatags (*Playboy Enterprises v. Welles*, 162 F.3d 1169, 1998; 279 F.3d 796, 2002).

Still more perplexing copyright dilemmas have arisen in cyberspace. One that may have no solution is "chain e-mail," the common practice of forwarding messages to large lists of friends, clients or customers. Someone will put a copyrighted work online, often dropping the original byline and the copyright notice. He or she sends it to a few dozen friends, who then send it to others. Before long, thousands or millions of people have received the message.

To cite one example, in 1998 someone turned a Dr. Seussian doggerel about the Clinton-Starr-Lewinsky controversy, "Starr I Are," into chain e-mail, deleting the original author's credit. It was apparently written by a syndicated columnist who was later accused of plagiarism by some of the 100-odd newspapers that had paid for his original version of the work and who thought *he* had stolen it.

How can any author protect his or her work from infringement by chain e-mail? This is only one of the dilemmas involving cyberspace that must be resolved--if it can be resolved.

INTERNATIONAL COPYRIGHTS

So far, this discussion has concerned *domestic* copyrights in the United States. But copyrights are becoming more and more an international matter. However, for more than 100 years the United States refused to become a participant in the *Berne Convention*--the world's primary international copyright agreement. When the Berne Convention for the Protection of Literary and Artistic Works was established in 1886, the U.S. was probably the world's leading copyright pirate. American publishers freely republished European books without paying any royalties to the copyright owners. While most European nations agreed on a system of international copyright control, the U.S. simply refused to sign up.

How, then, have American works gained international copyright protection over the years? The U.S. has participated in another international copyright agreement called the Universal Copyright Convention (UCC) and also entered into reciprocal copyright agreements with individual countries. But perhaps more important, major U.S. publishers often arranged for the simultaneous publication of major works in Berne Convention member countries such as Canada to obtain full international copyright protection.

During the twentieth century the U.S. ceased to be a major copyright pirate and has instead become the world's leading *victim* of international copyright infringement. The result: U.S. copyright owners, including not only authors and movie-makers but computer software creators, began pressing Congress to join the Berne Convention. After 102 years of U.S. non-participation in the Berne Convention, Congress finally acted to allow this country to join--by approving the Berne Convention Implementation Act of 1988. On March 1, 1989, the United States officially joined the Berne Convention, becoming the 79th nation to do so. That gave American copyright owners protection in 24 countries with which the United States had no other copyright arrangement.

The Berne Convention offers far more copyright protection than the Universal Copyright Convention, of which the United States has long been a member. In essence, the UCC merely says copyright owners in any member country have whatever rights local citizens have in other member countries. If a country has little copyright protection, foreigners as well as that country's own citizens have little protection from piracy there. The Berne Convention, on the other hand, sets *minimum standards* for copyright protection, requiring each member country to provide at least that much protection.

The 1988 legislation made a number of revisions in U.S. copyright law to bring it into compliance with the requirements of the Berne Convention. For example, international copyrights are now protected under U.S. law *without registration*. But works published in the United States still must be registered before the copyright owner can sue an infringer.

Foreign copyright owners may sue for *actual damages* and other remedies (as opposed to statutory damages) without ever registering, although actual damages are often nonexistent in copyright cases (because the infringer often makes no profit). Domestic copyright owners may also sue for actual damages even if the copyright is unregistered when the infringement occurs--but they must still register before filing an infringement lawsuit, as explained earlier. Foreigners don't have to do that.

The complete elimination of copyright notice requirements was also required by the Berne Convention. Berne member countries must provide copyright protection *without any formalities*.

American copyright owners stand to gain even more international protection under the intellectual property provisions of the General Agreement on Tariffs and

Trade (GATT), which was signed by 117 countries in 1994. GATT is a worldwide agreement covering many aspects of international business; its intellectual property provisions cover patents and trademarks as well as copyrights. In general, the GATT copyright provisions closely parallel the Berne Convention rules, setting minimum standards for international copyright protection. Perhaps the most important change is that the GATT provisions, once ratified by the signing countries, will apply in many countries that never joined the Berne Convention. The GATT provisions are administered by the World Trade Organization through the World Intellectual Property Organization (WIPO). Over time, GATT will have a major impact on U.S. copyrights, patents and trademarks. Perhaps GATT's major weakness is that, like many global agreements, it may be difficult to enforce in some signing countries.

Because the GATT agreement is so far-reaching, copyright lawyers spent years trying to sort out how it affects U.S. law. One of the first issues to arise was the question of *copyright restoration*. Under GATT, a large number of foreign works that had fallen into the public domain under U.S. law had their copyright protection restored. This is true because the copyrights of many pre-1978 works that had expired under U.S. law were restored under the longer copyright terms provided by other countries and recognized by the U.S. legislation to implement GATT. This particularly affects those who use footage from old movies that were once in the public domain but may now be protected by copyright law again. A major concern is so-called "orphan works:" works whose copyright owners have vanished. Under the new rules, some of these old, formerly public-domain works again have valid copyrights--but there is no one available to grant permission for anyone to use these works. Companies that provide stock movie footage have been concerned that if they continue to use these ex-public-domain works without obtaining copyright clearances, owners of some of the reinstated copyrights may suddenly appear out of the blue and sue for copyright infringement.

In late 1996 still more international copyright questions were addressed at a major conference of the World Intellectual Property Organization. With delegates from about 160 nations present in Geneva, Switzerland, many of the world's copyright experts and government copyright officials met for three weeks to discuss a wide variety of complex copyright questions, many of them concerning new computer and satellite communications technologies. The result of this conference was two new worldwide copyright treaties that may ultimately have a major effect on U.S. law and the law in many other countries. For the most part, American delegates succeeded in preventing the adoption of treaty provisions that would greatly expand copyright protections at the expense of freedom of expression. Another WIPO conference was scheduled later to discuss some of the issues not resolved at the 1996 conference.

Despite all of the international agreements, Congress still has not fully addressed one major difference between U.S. law and the seemingly mandatory requirements of international copyright law: the recognition of *moral rights*.

Moral Rights and Other Issues

The debate over moral rights became heated when Congress voted to change U.S. copyright law to make it compatible with the requirements of the Berne Convention--more or less. In essence, moral rights give the creator of a copyrighted work some say over what happens to it later, even if the copyright is sold to someone else (such as a publishing house or a motion picture distributor).

Under American law, the copyright owner (who is often not the creator of the work) has the absolute right to change a literary or artistic work without the consent of the original author or artist. But under Article 6 of the Berne Convention, each member country must recognize moral rights, thereby giving the original artist the right to prevent the work from being changed without his or her consent.

The moral rights question has always been a major obstacle to American participation in the Berne Convention: U.S. copyright owners strongly oppose any recognition of moral rights, while groups of authors and artists want such rights. The moral rights issue received considerable publicity in connection with the colorization of older black and white motion pictures. Many of the actors and directors who made these movies view colorization as a sacrilege--like mutilating a classic painting. But the copyright owners see colorization as a way to make the films more appealing to a new generation of movie viewers. Cable entrepreneur Ted Turner was at the center of this controversy because his company colorized almost the entire MGM library of classic films. He purchased the copyrights to these films in the mid-1980s and then had them colorized, something he had every right to do, despite the bitter objections of many actors and directors.

For the most part, Congress sided with Turner and other copyright owners, refusing to recognize moral rights. When Congress voted to have the United States join the Berne Convention--still without recognizing moral rights--that action stirred a controversy among copyright lawyers. Some contended that signing the Berne Convention automatically gave legal recognition to moral rights in the United States, despite Congress' efforts to sidestep the issue. Others pointed out that the 1988 law specifically said joining the Berne Convention did not change American law on this point. And there was also the question of how the United States could legally sign a treaty while steadfastly refusing to recognize one of its major provisions.

Some copyright owners argued that U.S. *trademark* laws now give adequate protection to moral rights, and that the U.S. could comply with the Berne Convention's moral rights provisions without changing American copyright law. To support that claim, they pointed to cases such as *Lamothe v. Atlantic Recording Corp.* (847 F.2d 1403), a 1988 decision of the U.S. Court of Appeals. That case held that two rock musicians could use the Lanham Act, the federal trademark law, to sue a third musician who falsely claimed that he was the sole author of songs that they co-authored. They claimed that the third musician, Robinson Crosby of Ratt, falsely claimed sole credit for two songs on the album "Out of the Cellar."

On the other hand, many in the creative community scoffed at the idea that U.S. trademark law provides adequate protection for moral rights. Trademark law only requires accurate labeling, not keeping the works true to the original artistic intent, they pointed out. For example, U.S. trademark law would allow a Picasso painting to be cut into pieces and sold as long as each piece is truthfully labeled as a Picasso. Under the *Lamothe* decision, the copyright owner is still free to change a creative work without the creator's permission--as long as authorship credit is given. To the creators of copyrighted works, changing their artistic intent and still leaving their names on the work may be even worse than changing the work and dropping their names.

Obviously, the moral rights question is likely to remain controversial for many years. It may take a series of court decisions to clarify the legal implications of the U.S. decision to join the Berne Convention without recognizing the moral rights of those who create copyrighted works but later sell them out of economic necessity.

As for the issue of movie colorization, in 1988 Congress enacted a compromise law that pleased almost no one: the National Film Preservation Act. It created a National Film Preservation Board with representatives from 13 industry groups, including both the creative community and copyright owners. The board is authorized to nominate up to 25 films per year for inclusion in a National Film Registry. Each nominated film must be at least 10 years old, and only films that were released in theaters are eligible. The Librarian of Congress then chooses some or all of the nominated films for inclusion in the registry. If a film is included, it can still be altered (or colorized) by the copyright owner, but there must be a conspicuous statement included in the altered version saying that the original film has been altered.

In 1990, Congress went a step further in protecting the rights of visual artists--but still stopped far short of giving full recognition to moral rights. The Visual Artists Rights Act of 1990 gives sculptors, painters and other visual artists the final say over whether their names are used on their works. Thus, artists can require that their names be kept on their works, and they can prevent their names from being used on works that have been altered without their permission. Also, the new law gives visual artists the right to sue those who mutilate or destroy their art works--even if they no longer own the copyright. However, it does not apply to many works created before this law went into effect. Nor does it apply to "works made for hire:" if the owner of a building commissions an artist to do a sculpture for the lobby, for example, a future owner of the building can ordinarily remove the sculpture without violating the law. A federal appellate court so ruled in a 1995 case, *Carter v. Helmsley-Spear Inc.* (71 F.3rd 77).

The Visual Artists Rights Act does not change the law concerning the colorization of motion pictures.

UNFAIR COMPETITION

Earlier in this chapter we pointed out that news, factual information and ideas cannot be copyrighted. However, there is another kind of law that may prevent one news medium from systematically pirating its news from another. That legal action is called *unfair competition* or *misappropriation,* and it has often been used as a supplement to copyright law. Unlike copyright, which is now exclusively governed by a federal statutory law, unfair competition is a tort action that has developed primarily through state court decisions. There is no federal unfair competition statute and few states have enacted statutory laws in this field even today.

Unfair competition was recognized as a separate legal action largely as a result of a 1918 U.S. Supreme Court decision that came to be regarded as a classic ruling: *International News Service v. Associated Press* (248 U.S. 215). The case arose because INS, owned by the Hearst newspaper chain, consistently appropriated AP stories (this was possible because some Hearst papers were also AP members) and distributed them to INS customers as if they were INS stories. The Supreme Court acknowledged that the news cannot be copyrighted, but it ruled that no business may purloin its basic commodity from a competitor, "reaping where it has not sown," to use the court's language, which was a paraphrase of a passage from the Bible.

Following this Supreme Court precedent, a number of other courts have ruled similarly in similar situations, creating a new common law legal action for misappropriation. For instance, in 1963 the Pennsylvania Supreme Court decided a very similar case in the same way. In that case (*Pottstown Daily News Publishing Company v. Pottstown Broadcasting*, 192 A.2d 657), the court found unfair competition where a radio station had been pirating its news from the local newspaper on an ongoing basis.

However, some doubts were raised about unfair competition as an alternative to copyright law by two 1964 U.S. Supreme Court decisions, *Sears Roebuck and Co. v. Stiffel* (376 U.S. 225) and *Compco v. Day-Brite Lighting* (376 U.S. 234). These were unfair competition cases involving mechanical designs that could not be patented rather than news that could not be copyrighted, but the court's language was alarmingly sweeping.

The Supreme Court said the states simply could not create alternative forms of protection to fill in the gaps left by copyright and patent law. "When an article is unprotected by a patent or a copyright, *state* law may not forbid others to copy that article," the Supreme Court said (emphasis added). The Supreme Court seemed to be saying the entire field of patent and copyright law is federally preempted, thus denying the states any role in this area. And as already noted, even if the federal government did not preempt copyright law then, the new Copyright Act makes it clear that Congress intended to preempt copyright law in 1976.

However, a 1973 U.S. Supreme Court decision resurrected unfair competition as a viable legal action--if it was ever eliminated. In *Goldstein v. California* (412 U.S. 546), the court upheld a California law against record piracy at a time when copyright law did not cover sound recordings, despite the defendant's contention that the federal government had preempted the field under the *Sears* and *Compco* decisions.

In recent years there have been numerous unfair competition lawsuits in various states--and the courts have held that unfair competition still exists as a valid basis for a lawsuit, although it only covers a few activities that fall very close to the news piracy that led to the original *INS v. AP* case.

A new controversy over the concept of unfair competition arose in the 1990s when various companies began providing sports scores and statistics *during actual sporting events*. For a fee, both computer users and pager owners can receive this information in real time. The National Basketball Association--backed by other sports leagues--eventually sued over this practice, alleging misappropriation under New York's unfair competition laws.

In *NBA v. Motorola* (105 F.3d 841), a 1997 decision, a federal appellate court held that providing sports information in this way is neither a copyright infringement nor unfair competition. The court noted that only the broadcast descriptions of the games (not the games themselves) can be copyrighted. And these services are not even copying the broadcast descriptions, the court held. Instead, they monitor the broadcasts and compile their own statistics--using factual information that is available to all. In essence, the court said this was different from systematically taking someone else's news stories, rewriting them, and then selling them via a competing wire service. Even if the NBA develops its own real-time sports information service, others may monitor broadcasts to provide competing services, the court said.

Nevertheless, journalists should not overlook the danger of lawsuits for unfair competition. Given a pattern of systematic news piracy, courts in many states would still rule against a company that is guilty of "reaping where it has not sown."

TRADEMARKS

Another area of intellectual property law that fills a gap in copyright protection is trademark, tradename and service mark law.

There is a federal trademark law, the Lanham Act (officially, the Trademark Act of 1946). But unlike the Copyright Act, it is nonexclusive. That is, it does not preempt state trademark laws. In fact, many states have their own trademark statutes, and all states recognize at least some kind of inherent right of a business to adopt a name and prevent imitators from using it under the common law. A person who infringes someone else's trademark may be sued in federal court, in state court, or both.

These laws govern the slogans or other short phrases, logos and designs, symbols and names under which businesses operate and market their products and services. An understanding of this area of law is especially important for a student planning a career in advertising or public relations.

The basic purpose of trademark laws is to prevent customer confusion. A new company that adopts a logo or name that looks like or sounds like a famous trademark for a similar product is likely to run afoul of the law, even if the logo or name is slightly different.

The Lanham Act established a nationwide registration system for trademarks and service marks, which are basically a subcategory of trademarks. When a business wants to adopt a trademark, the first step is to conduct a search to see if any competitor or potential competitor is using a similar name. Before seeking a federal trademark, most businesses (or their lawyers) pay a commercial research firm to find out whether their chosen name is available by searching the voluminous files of past trademark registrations (and other sources of information on trademark usage, including the Internet). If no one else has registered the name, the business follows a registration and filing procedure not unlike that set up by the Copyright Act. As part of the registration process, proposed trademarks are published and rival businesses may challenge the registration of a new trademark if they wish.

What sort of names may and may not be registered under the Lanham Act? Generally, any name, phrase or symbol that distinguishes a firm's goods or services may be registered, but there are some exceptions. Flags and symbols for cities, states and countries cannot be registered, for instance. Nor may the name, portrait or signature of a living person be registered--except under circumstances where the name or likeness has already become distinctively associated with a firm.

In addition, purely geographic names and descriptive terms (for instance "first rate," "high quality," "blue ribbon," and "A-1") are usually unregisterable. One reason for this rule is that most popular names, descriptive terms and geographic names are so widely used that no one may gain a monopoly on their use nationally in connection with trade. This is not to say you can't open a business and call it "A-1 Auto Repair" or "Blue Ribbon Trophy Company," but you'll have a tough time getting it registered nationally as your exclusive trademark.

Even if a name is so widely used that no one can register it as a national trademark, someone may gain the exclusive right to use it locally. For instance, if you start a business called "A-1 Auto Repair" when there is already a business in the area called "A-1 Car Repair Company," you may be sued in a state court.

Because there have been so many different businesses seeking distinctive trademarks for so many years, the surest way to get a new trademark registered nationally is to come up with a new coined word. Several firms have done that over the years: Exxon, Citgo and Kodak, for example.

Assuming a business gets its proposed trademark past the hurdles of registration, the firm may use the trademark in various ways. The name may appear on products, in advertising and on the corporate letterhead. The fact that the trademark is registered under the Lanham Act is indicated by the little "R" in a circle after the word or phrase. However, trademarks may also be indicated in other ways. For instance, when registration has not yet been secured, a firm may indicate that it claims a word or phrase as a trademark by placing "TM" after the name (or "SM" after the name for a service mark).

Once registered under the Lanham Act, a trademark is valid for 10 years but must be reaffirmed after the first five years. Thereafter, a renewal every 10 years is required. There is no limit to the number of times a trademark may be renewed, as long as the trademark owner can show that it is still being "used in commerce." Unlike a copyright, a trademark can be maintained as private property indefinitely.

However, a trademark may also be abandoned or lost. Under the Lanham Act, failure to use a trademark for two years creates a presumption that it has been abandoned. Acquiescence in allowing others to use your trademark in a generic way can also result in its loss, which explains why trademarks such as "Xerox" and "Coca-Cola" are so vigorously defended by their owners. Should those words be allowed to become generally descriptive of all photocopying or all cola-type beverages, the owners could lose their exclusive rights to these names, as did the owners of ex-trademarks such as "aspirin," "cellophane," "cornflakes," "yo-yo" and "linoleum."

Companies do various things to avoid losing their trademarks through widespread usage as generic words. For instance, some companies advertise in magazines read by journalists to admonish writers and editors about the correct usage of their trademarks. The Xerox Corporation, for example, reminds journalists to capitalize "Xerox," and to use it as an adjective referring to a Xerox-brand product. Never use the word as a verb, the company insists. The company is outraged by statements such as, "Go xerox this for me."

Ideally, trademark owners want the news media to use their names as adjectives followed by a generic name for the product, such as "Dolby noise reduction system" or "Plexiglas acrylic sheeting." The Dow Chemical Company has tried to prevent writers from using the term "Styrofoam cup" (Styrofoam is a trademark owned by Dow) because most Styrofoam brand plastic foam is used for other things, not for cups.

What happens to writers who misuse a trademark? Journalists who break the rules may receive pointed letters from a trademark owner's lawyers--all as part of the company's effort to demonstrate that it is not acquiescing to the generic use of its trademark. However, a company's lawyers can do little more than write angry letters when the news media use trademarks as if they were generic terms. In fact, courts sometimes regard the widespread generic use of a trademark in the news media as one form of proof that the word or phrase has lost its special meaning.

However, *non-journalistic* abuses of trademarks are another matter. News writers may get away with misusing trademarks, but when one company misuses another's trademark in its advertising or on a product, a lawsuit is likely to result. Even book authors must be careful to use trademarks correctly. It would be quite legal for someone not associated with Ford Motor Company to publish a book called, "How to Repair Fords," as long as it is made clear that Ford is a trademark, and that the author is not claiming it as his or her own trademark.

Although federal registration of a trademark is obviously desirable if it can be secured, a person or business that has used a name over a period of time acquires some special rights with or without federal registration. In fact, Lanham Act registration is unavailable to purely local businesses, although most states have their own registration systems under which local trademarks may be protected. State trademark protection varies widely. But whatever the specific rules are in a given state, the courts will step in to prevent a new business from creating public confusion by imitating the name or trademark of an old, established one.

Under the principles of common law and equity trademark protection (which protect trademarks regardless of whether they are registered at the state or federal level or unregistered), the key issue in a lawsuit is whether a word or phrase has acquired a *secondary meaning* in connection with a certain product or service. There is a secondary meaning if the words connote something more than their dictionary definition because of the commercial usage. For instance, the word "playboy" has one meaning in the dictionary, but when applied to a magazine, it has a special meaning beyond that.

If a word or phrase is found to have a secondary meaning to a substantial number of people, no one else may use the name for a similar kind of business in that locality without creating confusion and misleading the public. With or without a trademark registration under federal or state law, the mere use of a tradename over time gives the user certain ownership rights: no business is entitled to pass off its product or service as someone else's. Even if a newcomer registers the name as a trademark first, the original user of the name will often prevail in court. The goal is to prevent a newcomer from fraudulently trading on the goodwill of an established business. This is the overriding objective of the common law of trademarks, of state trademark laws and of the federal Lanham Act.

What sort of words can acquire a secondary meaning? A good illustration of how trademark law works was provided by two federal appellate court decisions that were handed down on the same day in 1993: *Pacific Telesis Group v. International Telesis Communications* (994 F.2d 1364) and *Fruit of the Loom v. Girouard* (994 F.2d 1359). Pacific Telesis, one of the large regional telephone companies that emerged from the breakup of the American Telephone and Telegraph Company, began using "Telesis" as part of its name in 1983. Two years later, a new firm adopted "International Telesis" as its name and entered the telecommunications consulting business. Pacific Telesis sued, and the ninth circuit U.S. Court of Appeals eventually ruled that "telesis" (a Greek word meaning "event" or "fulfillment") is such a unique word when applied to the telephone industry that no one else in that line of business may use it without Pacific Telesis' permission.

On the other hand, the same court refused to give Fruit of the Loom, a large clothing manufacturer, the exclusive right to use the word "fruit" in the apparel industry. The dispute arose when businessman Ken Girouard created a company called Two Left Feet and began making thongs called Fruit Flops and bustiers called Fruit Cups. The court agreed that the full name, "Fruit of the Loom," has a secondary meaning. It is, in fact, one of the oldest trademarks still in use: it was first registered in 1871! However, the court ruled that the use of the word "fruit" by itself is not enough to constitute a trademark infringement, even when used by another clothing manufacturer. The court said there was little likelihood that consumers would confuse the two names or the two product lines.

Under certain circumstances not only a name or symbol but also a *color* may be protected as a trademark, according to a 1995 U.S. Supreme Court decision, *Qualitex Co. v. Jacobson Products Inc.* (514 U.S. 159). In essence, the court said that if a company uses a distinctive color for its products for a long enough time, the color may become sufficiently associated with the product in consumers' minds that it has a secondary meaning.

Sometimes even a distinctive *sound* can qualify for trademark protection. A few sounds have gained trademark protection: for example, the roar of MGM's lion, the phrase "AT&T" spoken over a musical sound and NBC's three-note chime--famous since radio days. Harley-Davidson, the motorcycle manufacturer, stirred controversy in 1995 when it sought to register the sound of the V-twin engine on Harley bikes. Several other motorcycle manufacturers challenged that trademark application, arguing that their own V-twin engines made virtually the same sound. After running up legal bills for five years, Harley-Davidson dropped its attempt to obtain federal trademark protection for its engine sound in 2000.

278 Copyrights and Trademarks

Another aspect of trademark law has provoked enough controversy and uncertainty to produce two Supreme Court decisions: the question of whether a business can keep a competitor from imitating its *trade dress*. In *Two Pesos v. Taco Cabana* (505 U.S. 763, 1992), the high court upheld a federal court judgment in favor of Taco Cabana, a Mexican fast-food restaurant chain that claimed Two Pesos imitated the appearance and decor of its restaurants. The Supreme Court unanimously ruled that a store's trade dress can have "inherent distinctiveness," and if it does, that "look" can be protected under the Lanham Act. That may be true even if the trade dress has not acquired a *secondary meaning*, the court ruled. But the court didn't really define inherent distinctiveness, thus creating uncertainty about what is and is not protected as a part of a company's trade dress.

In 2000, the U.S. Supreme Court revisited the trade dress question, ruling unanimously that clothing designers may not ordinarily use federal trademark law to prevent others from making similar-looking apparel. Ruling in *Wal-Mart Stores v. Samara Brothers* (529 U.S. 205), the court held that designers may not gain trademark protection for their designs merely by claiming that the product is inherently distinctive. Instead, they must prove that the public so strongly associates the design with a designer that there is a secondary meaning. This is generally very difficult to prove. The court said a product has a secondary meaning only when, "in the minds of the public, the primary significance of a (trademark) is to identify the source of the product rather than the product itself."

This decision leaves discounters such as Wal-Mart free to sell merchandise similar to high-end brand-name products as long as there is no actual counterfeiting or other deceptive marketing. Only if the public is deceived into believing they are buying the brand-name item is there likely to be a trademark infringement, the court indicated. A product can resemble a brand-name item such as the seersucker children's clothing decorated with hearts and flowers that Samara designed and Wal-Mart's supplier imitated in this case.

The *Wal-Mart* case limits the impact of the high court's earlier *Two Pesos* case. In *Two Pesos*, the court *upheld* a restaurant chain's right to protect the *trade dress* of its restaurants from imitators *without* proving the existence of a secondary meaning. But now the court has refused to protect the trade dress of products unless there is a secondary meaning.

Changes in Trademark Law

The Lanham Act was extensively revised by Congress in the Trademark Law Revision Act of 1988. Although many of the changes are highly technical, several have had an important effect on mass communications--particularly advertising.

Under the 1988 law, trademark owners may sue competitors who falsely malign their products or services for *treble damages* (i.e., three times the actual damages). However, in an effort to avoid undue restrictions on First Amendment freedoms, Congress limited this right to comparative brand name advertising by businesses, and not to political advertising or editorial commentary.

Most states have long recognized a right to sue for "trade libel" or "product disparagement." This law adds a *federal* legal right with a treble damage provision, making it easier for companies to deter false comparative advertising by competitors. Significantly, Congress rejected a proposed amendment to the new law that would have allowed *consumers* to sue for false advertising under the same provision of the law. Most states already allow consumers to sue false advertisers.

The revised version of the Lanham Act also has a provision allowing businesses to apply for trademark protection as much as three years before they actually put a product or service on the market by filing an "intent-to-use" application. In effect, this allows a company to reserve a name before launching the product or service. Under the old law, a product had to be in the marketplace before the trademark application could be filed. This forced companies to make a token distribution of their new products and services in interstate commerce, but to do so quietly to avoid alerting potential competitors before the tradename or logo could be fully protected.

Eventually Congress passed the Federal Trademark Dilution Act of 1995, which made additional changes in the Lanham Act. Under this law, a trademark owner can sue an infringer for "lessening of the capacity of a famous mark to identify and distinguish goods or services, regardless of the presence or absence of competition between the parties or likelihood of confusion."

Many trademark lawyers saw this as a major expansion of trademark law, allowing more lawsuits for "blurring" or "tarnishing" a trademark by someone who is not a competitor of the trademark owner. Blurring might occur when someone makes an unrelated product and uses a famous name, as Toyota did when it launched the Lexus, a car with virtually the same name as the pre-existing Lexis-Nexis computer data service. Tarnishment involves the use of a word or phrase that creates a negative association with an established trademark. Under the tarnishment concept, courts have halted such practices as the sale of "Enjoy Cocaine" posters using typefaces and colors similar to those in Coca-Cola's posters.

A number of states already have anti-dilution laws; now there is also stronger *federal* protection from trademark dilution. And once again, critics of the continuing growth of trademark and copyright law saw this as an example of the shrinkage of the public domain. As intellectual property law grows, there are fewer and fewer words, phrases and creative materials left that the general public may use without risking a lawsuit. That is one of the major dilemmas in this area of law.

Trademarks and Internet Domain Names

With the surging growth of the Internet in the late 1990s, a difficult new legal dilemma arose for trademark owners and others who wanted to register *domain names*--the names used in website locators and e-mail addresses. To cite just a few examples, "Xerox.com" is Xerox Corporation's domain name, just as "Ford.com" is Ford Motor Company's domain name and "Harvard.edu" is Harvard University's. Likewise, "fcc.gov" is the Federal Communications Commission's domain name. Adding "www." to any of these (or many thousands of other domain names) will take you to the organization's home page on the World Wide Web. The "Ford" or "Harvard" or "FCC" is the specific entity's domain name; the ".com" or ".edu" or ".gov" is called a *generic top-level domain name* and is shared by many organizations. Other currently recognized top-level domain names include ".mil" for military organizations, ".org" for non-commercial organizations and ".net" for entities loosely defined as computer networks. Many nations also have top-level domain names, such as ".us" for the United States.

By 2000, almost every large government agency, educational institution and corporation had a website--and wanted it identified by the organization's popular name or trademark. Hundreds of lawsuits have been filed by trademark owners and others to contest the ownership of domain names.

For many years Network Solutions Inc. (NSI), a Virginia-based company, had a government-sanctioned monopoly on registering domain names. By 2001 NSI had registered about 15 million domain names; the company received an annual fee directly or indirectly from each name registrant for maintaining the domain name data base. NSI gained its unique status through a contract with the National Science Foundation--and quickly became embroiled in controversy over its domain name registration policies. NSI's contract expired in 1998. However, NSI won a two-year extension by promising to share its registration authority with other companies that would be selected by a nonprofit corporation.

The Internet Corp. for Assigned Names and Numbers (ICANN), was then established with the backing of the U.S. government and the World Intellectual Property Organization, among others. It was given the authority to designate new name registrars who would share that task with NSI. In 1999, ICANN began accrediting private companies to handle registrations for the .com, .org, and .net domains. As a result, NSI faced competition from other name registrars; its monopoly was over. In 2000 ICANN also approved seven new domain names to supplement .com, .org and .net. Private companies have created additional domain names and managed to get them recognized, at least informally by Internet service providers.

ICANN also set up a global arbitration system so that disputes over domain names could be resolved quickly and without lawsuits. By 2001, this system was being widely used as an alternative to taking these disputes to court.

As NSI demonstrated when it had a monopoly, registering Internet names can be a lucrative business, but it also invites lawsuits: the company has been sued hundreds of times in disputes over domain names, which it has generally issued on a first-come, first-served system.

In some cases, individuals have registered hundreds of names with hopes of selling the names to trademark owners at a large profit. These people have been called "cybersquatters" and accused of "domain name hijacking." Instead of paying, several companies have sued--and usually prevailed based on proof that they hold a valid trademark in the name.

In one notable early case of alleged cybersquatting, Panavision International discovered that "Panavision" and "Panaflex" (two of its trademarks) were registered to a man in Illinois who had registered at least 240 different domain names--and was demanding payments in return for turning over the names to trademark owners. Among others, he had registered the names Delta Airlines, Neiman Marcus, Lufthansa and Eddie Bauer. He demanded $13,000 from Panavision to relinquish its tradenames. Panavision sued and got a federal court to order the "cybersquatter" to hand over the names "Panavision" and "Panaflex." The court concluded that he was guilty of various legal wrongs in registering others' trademarks, including violation of the Federal Trademark Dilution Act. In 1998, a federal appeals court agreed and upheld Panavision against the cybersquatter's claims (*Panavision International v. Toeppen*, 141 F.3d 1316).

When a domain name owner cannot be dismissed as a "cybersquatter," the legal problems become much more complex. For example, suppose two companies use the same trade name--but for different products. Who gets to be "Dove.com?" The makers of Dove soap or Dove candy bars? What about two companies that use the same name as a trademark for similar products, but in different geographic areas? Each one may have a valid regional trademark, but the Internet crosses all regional boundaries.

A federal appellate court had to deal with that kind of issue in a 1999 case, *Brookfield Communications v. West Coast Entertainment* (174 F.3d 1036). The case involved a dispute between two companies that had both used variations of the term, "movie buff," in their trademarks. Both wanted the domain name, "moviebuff.com". The court did a traditional trademark analysis and awarded the name to Brookfield because that company had used the name earlier. The court concluded that trademarks take priority over domain name registrations. Significantly, the court also held that Brookfield should have the exclusive right to use the "movie buff" name in *metatags* hidden in its web pages. The court held that it is a trademark infringement for a company to embed a competitor's trademark in metatags on its website so that search engines would lead net surfers to its site when they do a search keyed to the competitor's trademark. However, as noted earlier, another federal appellate court later upheld the right of former Playmate of the Year Terri Welles to use words such as "playboy" in the metatags on her personal website (*Playboy Enterprises v. Welles*).

Still another problem with domain names arises when an individual or a small company registers a legitimate family name or business name, only to learn later that a large corporation claims that name as a trademark, perhaps for an unrelated product. Large companies have been accused of "reverse domain name hijacking" when they use their power and wealth to intimidate a small company into giving up a name it may have used in business for years by threatening a costly lawsuit, even though there may be no trademark infringement.

Some companies have used the Federal Trademark Dilution Act to sue those who have registered a similar but not identical domain name--even when there is little chance of consumer confusion. For example, the Toys R Us company successfully sued an adult entertainment supplier whose domain name was "AdultsRus.Com." The court ordered Adults R Us not only to stop using the name but also to eliminate everyone else's electronic links to the name--a virtual impossibility in cyberspace (*Toys R Us v. Akkaoui*, 1996 U.S. Dist. Lexis 17090). Toys R Us argued, and the court agreed, that the use of Adults R Us would tarnish or dilute its trademark even though consumer confusion between the two businesses and their product lines was unlikely.

In 1999 Congress stepped into the ongoing disputes over domain names by enacting the *Anticybersquatting Consumer Protection Act*, a new law intended to ban (and criminalize) the practice of "cybersquatting"--registering someone else's trademark or a famous person's name as an Internet domain name in bad faith, hoping to make a profit by selling the name to its rightful owner.

This federal law allows fines of up to $100,000 for cybersquatting. The law also authorizes courts to order the cancellation of Internet names that were registered in bad faith, and it applies to names that have already been registered as well as new registrations. In short, the law establishes civil and criminal remedies for cybersquatting, allowing those who choose to go to court with domain name disputes (as opposed to using ICANN's arbitration procedure) to do so under ground rules favoring trademark owners.

The anticybersquatting law reduces the impact of a federal appellate court decision in 1999 which held that only owners of the most famous trademarks could prevent others from registering their names and using them as domain names.

In *Avery Dennison Corp. v. Sumpton* (189 F.3d 868), the court rejected an attempt by Avery Dennison, a maker of office labels and industrial fasteners, to stop Canadian businessman Jerry Sumpton from using the names "avery.net" and "dennison.net" as domain names. Sumpton registered some 12,000 common surnames as domain names, hoping to provide Internet users with e-mail addresses including their own names for relatively modest fees.

Avery Dennison sued, claiming that Sumpton was a cybersquatter who had improperly registered the company's trademark. The appellate court unanimously rejected that contention, holding that Sumpton's use of various surnames in no way infringed upon Avery Dennison's trademark. Avery Dennison claimed that Sumpton's use of its tradename amounted to trademark dilution in violation of the federal Trademark Dilution Act and parallel state laws. But the court held that only companies whose trademarks are truly "distinctive and famous" can prevent others from making noncompeting uses of their names as domain names. Sumpton is in the Internet service business, not the label-making business, the court noted.

"If dilution protection were accorded to trademarks based only on a showing of inherent or acquired distinctiveness, we would upset the balance in favor of over-protecting trademarks, at the expense of potential noninfringing uses," Judge Stephen Trott wrote for the court.

The *Avery Dennison* decision reversed the trend for courts to side with trademark owners at the expense of others who might have a legitimate reason for registering a domain name that also happens to be someone's trademark. In so doing, the court took a narrower view of who is a cybersquatter than had some earlier courts that considered this question. This decision made it harder for a company to prove that someone who has registered its tradename did so to profit from the trademark's value.

However, soon after this court decision gave purported cybersquatters an edge over trademark owners, Congress intervened with the anticybersquatting law.

While the battles over domain names continued, a separate trademark controversy arose over electronic *links*, which allow net surfers to click on a highlighted word or phrase and move quickly to an entirely different site. Several companies objected to the use of their trademarks by others in links--and filed lawsuits. In the most famous of these cases, Ticketmaster, the electronic ticketing agency, sued none other than Microsoft Corporation in 1997 for its inclusion of links to Ticketmaster in its web pages. Ticketmaster's main objection seemed to be that Microsoft routed surfers to Ticketmaster by way of other Microsoft-controlled sites that carried advertising (for Microsoft's profit, not Ticketmaster's). The case was settled in 1999 when Microsoft agreed not to link its Sidewalk city guides to pages within Ticketmaster's site.

In several other cases, web businesses have objected when someone else links to a page deep inside their sites ("deep linking") instead of to the opening page. That, of course, prevents customers from seeing their advertising messages. This issue is far from resolved, although there is a general consensus that linking in and of itself is perfectly legal.

Although normally legal, linking can also create copyright problems. In *Kelly v. Arriba Soft Corp.* (280 F.3d 934), a federal appellate court ruled in 2002 that the Fair Use Doctrine permits a search engine to reproduce small "thumbnail" copies of images from a website, but not the full-size images. Nor may a search engine link directly to the full-size images by *deep linking* in such a way that the full-size images appear to be part of a website other the one where they are posted.

Still other domain name and trademark disputes have arisen--and ended up in the courts. One is the use of a company's trademark on a website designed to *criticize* the company. Disenchanted former customers and former employees often set up websites to express their displeasure with companies. In one case, a website critical of the Bally Total Fitness Holdings Corp. was set up under the title, "Bally Sucks". It displayed Bally's logo with the word "sucks" printed across it. When Bally sued for trademark infringement and dilution, a federal court held that sites such as this one are protected by the First Amendment. The court rejected Bally's attempt to use trademark law to shut down the site (*Bally Total Fitness v. Faber*, 29 F.Supp.2d 1161, 1998).

These controversies and lawsuits over the Internet and trademarks may take many more years to resolve, as the law tries once again to catch up with a rapidly growing new technology.

ONGOING ISSUES

Copyrights and related areas of intellectual property law are full of unresolved questions. Several recent copyright law revisions were supposed to settle some of these questions, but today there are more unresolved issues than ever. Many of them stem from the globalization of mass communications and commerce, the dramatic growth of the Internet and other technical advances in recent years.

The explosion of the World Wide Web during the late 1990s created enormous copyright dilemmas. Some wonder whether *any* copyright can ever again be protected, given the ease with which millions of net surfers exchange files containing words, digital images, music and movies. How can the recording industry deal with the proliferation of ways to exchange copyrighted music on the Internet? Are the industry's anti-copying tactics, which some advocates of free expression on the Internet regard as draconian, appropriate? When CD burners became commonplace, did that mark the end of traditional copyright compliance?

Copyright owners have resorted to increasingly aggressive tactics to protect their copyrights in the digital age. Is that right? Is it wise to criminalize the noncommercial downloading of copyrighted materials? What about trying to prevent people from making back-up copies for personal use? Recently passed laws could make criminals of millions of people who think the copying they do is perfectly reasonable. What about copyright owners' attempts to suppress software that overrides copy-protection algorithms? Do scholars who break copy-protection codes have a First Amendment right to share their discoveries and discuss them at conferences?

What about webcasting? If the U.S. Copyright Office's rules on the webcasting of music are sustained in court, it will be impossible for some broadcasters to stream their over-the-air programming, and even harder for non-broadcast webcasters to survive. Is it right to ban routine broadcast practices such as identifying a song before it is played on the Internet to prevent copyright infringements by listeners? And should broadcasters even be required to pay separate copyright royalties to *record companies* (not just to the composers of the underlying music) when their broadcasts are digital? They never have for analog broadcasts.

These and many other copyright and trademark questions are being debated today. The Internet has given us an entirely different kind of world where the old definitions of publishing, distribution and performance do not fit the new realities very well.

Even before the Internet became so dominant, the dramatic growth of the personal computer industry itself created new copyright problems. Computer software companies have been concerned about the wholesale copying of their programs by consumers, just as motion picture producers are disturbed about the copying of DVDs. And software companies, like movie producers, realize they may not be able to stop these wholesale copyright infringements by millions of consumers. Almost as soon as a new copy-prevention scheme is devised, someone finds a way to crack it. And computer users have been annoyed at attempts by software companies to lock up basic command structures, not to mention operating systems, under copyright law. At least the battle over command structures has ended. Many computer users were delighted when the concept of copyright protection for the "look and feel" of a computer program was rejected by the courts.

Other new technologies have also created new copyright problems. Copyright owners complained for years that cable systems were not paying their fair share for the broadcast signals they intercept and sell to their subscribers. Under the 1992 Cable Television Consumer Protection and Competition Act, broadcasters were given the right to insist that cable systems pay for their use of local television signals, with cable systems, in turn, free to drop local stations that demand payment instead of paying them. (As Chapter 11 explains, stations may also choose to require local cable systems to carry their signals, but without payment.) Where that will lead--and whether the compulsory license for cable systems makes any sense now--is a question that Congress will surely have to address again. Another dilemma concerns satellite television systems. They now have the right to deliver local television stations into their own markets, for a fee. Should satellite providers be charged *the same fees* as cable systems for local signal carriage?

Still other complex problems involve international copyrights. The United States finally joined the Berne Convention after staying out of this important international copyright system for 100 years. But the United States still does not fully recognize the principle of moral rights as required of Berne member countries. Does this mean the United States will continue to inadequately address the moral rights issue? Creative artists often feel compelled to sell their copyrights. Once they do that, they usually have little recourse if their works are altered without their permission. Actors and directors were irate about the colorization of classic black and white movies, for example, but there was nothing they could do to stop it. Congress acted in 1990 to give some moral rights protection to visual artists--but pointedly declined to provide any relief to others whose creative works are altered without their consent.

More recently, the United States also signed the General Agreement on Tariffs and Trade (GATT) and is now a major participant in the World Trade Organization and the World Intellectual Property Organization (WIPO). That, too, is causing major changes in American copyright law. The legislation that was enacted to implement GATT immediately stirred controversy by restoring copyrights on many foreign works that were already in the public domain in the United States--works that were once available to all to use or adapt freely.

When Congress, acting at the behest of the music industry and other copyright owners, then proposed to bring American copyright law into line with the law in Europe by adding still another 20 years to the copyright term, there was widespread alarm among copyright scholars. These scholars said the copyright term was already longer than it needs to be to "promote the progress of science and the useful arts," to quote the Constitution's rationale for having copyright laws. Many wondered whether this wasn't still another case of copyright owners, who are often not the creators of copyrighted works, trying to milk every last possible penny of royalty money out of their investments--at the expense of the public interest. When George Washington signed the first U.S. Copyright Act into law in 1790, the copyright term was 14 years, renewable only for 14 more years. Even today, the term for a patent on an invention is only 20 years--not 75 years, much less 95 years.

Isn't there some point at which creative works--let's take music and movies as an example--become part of the culture that should belong to all Americans and not just the private property of investors who bought the copyrights years ago? Doesn't everyone feel a sense of personal attachment to certain songs and certain movies? Shouldn't all works be in the public domain at some point--perhaps sooner rather than later?

Copyright law raises still other issues. For example, what about the Fair Use Doctrine? The *Sony v. Universal Studios* Supreme Court decision held that the Copyright Act permits consumers to engage in "time shifting" by video taping television shows for later viewing. Such home taping is a fair use rather than an infringement, the court said. But what if the taping is done with a *digital* recorder? Under recent industry proposals, the right to copy free, over-the-air TV shows may be severely curtailed when the broadcasts are digital.

There are other questions about the Fair Use Doctrine. How much of a work may the news media quote? The Supreme Court held that quoting 300 words of a president's memoirs prior to their publication in book form was not a fair use. The *Harper and Row v. The Nation Enterprises* case raises troubling questions about the right of journalists to cover clearly newsworthy stories when crucial information is unpublished. Congress eventually amended the Copyright Act to make it clear that unpublished works may still be covered by the Fair Use Doctrine. However, there is still a possibility that a celebrity's supporters can use the Copyright Act to lock up history, preventing outside biographers from quoting relevant portions of the person's written works in any objective analysis of his/her life. No one may copyright factual information, but history is more than facts: much of it is embodied in the actual words of the person. When does the Fair Use Doctrine begin to protect history?

What about sampling by musicians? How much of a copyrighted song should someone be able to include in his or her new recordings? When does a parody become mere commercial exploitation? The Supreme Court has ruled, in the *Campbell v. Acuff-Rose* case, that a parody *may be* a fair use even if it is done for commercial gain. But *how much* of a song may a parodist use without infringing the copyright?

Trademark law also raises a number of questions. As more trademarks are established and registered, there will be fewer words and phrases left in the public domain, and the 1995 Trademark Dilution Act can only accelerate this privatization of words and phrases. If the owners of famous trademarks begin suing everyone who uses a similar word for a dissimilar product, will there be any words other than newly coined ones left to identify new products and services?

What about registering a *sound* or a *color* as a trademark? Should a motorcycle maker be able to register an engine sound as a trademark? If so, where does that leave competitors whose engines make a similar sound? If companies can own colors, won't we run out of colors for product cartons someday?

What about trademarks on the Internet? Should a trademark owner always prevail over anyone else who might register a domain name? What about a small company that has used a name for years and registers it as a domain name, only to be challenged by a giant corporation that uses the name as a trademark--perhaps for an entirely different kind of product? Should websites that use a company's trademark to criticize the company be protected by the First Amendment?

Copyrights and trademarks are inherently limitations on freedom of expression. Congress, the courts and, ultimately, the public must decide where the line should be drawn between free expression rights and the property rights of those who own copyrights and trademarks.

A SUMMARY OF COPYRIGHT LAW

What May Be Copyrighted?
Many types of literary and artistic works may be copyrighted, including prose (fiction and non-fiction), poetry, scripts, musical scores and lyrics, photographs, motion pictures, videos, sound recordings, computer software, maps, paintings, sculptures and advertising layouts.

What May NOT Be Copyrighted?
Factual and historical information (including news) may not be copyrighted, although a *description* of a news event (or a news production) may be copyrighted. In addition, ideas, processes, inventions and trademarks may not be copyrighted (but note that inventions and processes may be patented and trademarks may be protected under state and federal trademark laws).

How Does One Secure a Copyright?
Copyright protection is now automatic under U.S. law and international treaties. However, it is advisable to include a *copyright notice* (e.g., "copyright 2002 by J.J. Author") in a prominent place in the work. Whether the work is published or unpublished, doing that notifies any would-be infringer of the copyright.

Is It Necessary to Register a Copyright?
No, your copyright is valid without registration. However, if you register before an infringement occurs, you have more legal rights against the infringer than you would otherwise, including the right to win statutory damages and your lawyer's fees should a lawsuit be necessary. And in any case, you must register before filing a lawsuit. To register a copyright, send the proper registration form, two copies and the filing fee to the U.S. Copyright Office, Washington, DC 20559.

What Does a Copyright Give You?
The copyright owner has the right to reproduce, perform, revise or display the work for the duration of the copyright, which normally runs for the author's life plus 70 years or 95 years for corporate works. The owner may sell any or all of these rights. Under certain conditions copyrighted music may be recorded by anyone who pays the prescribed royalties (this is called *compulsory licensing*).

What Is the Fair Use Doctrine?
The Fair Use Doctrine allows anyone to make limited use of copyrighted works (e.g., quoting or photocopying a small portion of a work). Whether a given use is a fair one is determined by weighing: whether the use is commercial or educational in character, the nature of the original work, the percentage of the original that is copied and the effect of the use on the owner's profits.

CHAPTER SEVEN

Fair Trial-Free Press Conflicts

One of the most troublesome conflicts inherent in the U.S. Constitution is a problem called *fair trial-free press*. The Sixth Amendment guarantees a person accused of a crime "the right to a speedy and public trial *before an impartial jury*." On the other hand, the First Amendment gives the mass media the right to report crime news, including information and visual images that may prejudice an entire community against someone who has not yet stood trial and is still presumed innocent by the law. Or, as illustrated by the celebrated O.J. Simpson murder trial in 1995, live television coverage of a trial may leave a large segment of the population convinced that the defendant is guilty after a jury rules otherwise.

In recent years there have been many confrontations between the nation's courts and the news media over this problem. In attempting to control prejudicial publicity and assure fair trials for defendants in sensational cases, the courts have taken a variety of steps to limit publicity and thereby protect the Sixth Amendment rights of defendants. However, some of these steps limit the media's First Amendment freedoms. There is no easy solution to this conflict between two constitutional rights: both freedom of the press and the right to trial before an impartial jury are central to the American ideal of a free society.

PREJUDICIAL PUBLICITY AND FAIR TRIALS

Many judges and attorneys contend there is an overabundance of crime news in the media. Many believe such news is so sensationalized that some celebrity defendants may be denied a fair trial by an impartial jury. Some also believe the media can make it impossible for the prosecution (*the people*, if you will) to get a fair trial. The jury is supposed to consider only the defendant's guilt or innocence in the specific case before the court, not whether he or she is of high moral character generally. Thus, a suspect's past record is not ordinarily considered relevant evidence. But sometimes the media report inflammatory information about a suspect's past, information that may not be admitted as evidence when the trial actually occurs. Moreover, the media may report unsubstantiated details of an arrest or unverified test results. Or they may reveal the existence of a "confession" that may not be admitted into evidence in court if it was given under duress. On the other hand, the media may also reveal details about the prosecution's case that the jury is not supposed to consider. As a result, it may be very difficult to find unprejudiced jurors. Lawyers and judges sometimes feel that drastic measures are necessary to control what they see as irresponsible journalism that interferes with criminal defendants' constitutional rights.

However, defenders of the press often cite the important role of the media in keeping the public informed about modern society--a society with a high crime rate. They point out that the press performs an important watchdog role in monitoring the administration of justice. Even most judges will concede that covering the criminal justice system is an important function of the mass media. And, of course, judges cannot ignore the fact that the media's right to cover the news is constitutionally protected.

The O.J. Simpson Case and its Consequences

Perhaps no courtroom drama in American history better illustrates the problems of fair trial-free press than the criminal and civil trials of O.J. Simpson, the football legend and media celebrity. A criminal jury acquitted Simpson of killing his ex-wife and her friend Ronald Goldman in a brutal knife attack, while a jury in a later civil trial found him to be liable for the two deaths. The civil jury verdict, including a large punitive damage award, was later upheld on appeal (*Rufo v. Simpson*, 86 C.A.4th 573, 2001)

From the moment Simpson failed to surrender to police under a pre-arranged plan and was declared a fugitive, there was a worldwide media bonanza. At least 95 million viewers in the United States alone watched the two-hour pursuit leading to Simpson's arrest on live television. Within a few days, hundreds if not thousands of journalists were covering the story, and numerous incriminating details of the case were widely publicized. Almost all major American media outlets carried the tape or transcript of a 911 emergency call that Nicole Brown, Simpson's ex-wife, made a few months before she was killed, in which she said Simpson had broken down her door. Long before the trial almost everyone also knew that Simpson had entered a no-contest plea to misdemeanor wife-beating charges in 1989, and that Nicole had repeatedly called the police about earlier incidents in which Simpson allegedly beat her. The world even learned that in 1985 Simpson allegedly broke the windshield of Nicole's car with a baseball bat.

The publicity frenzy became so intense that in mid-1994 a judge took the extraordinary step of disqualifying the Los Angeles County Grand Jury from its normal role of hearing evidence and deciding whether to issue an indictment--on the ground that the grand jurors might be prejudiced by media publicity. Instead, the case proceeded to a preliminary hearing (which would not have been needed if there had been a grand jury indictment), with the major television networks providing gavel-to-gavel live coverage of the courtroom proceedings. And in another Los Angeles County courthouse a few miles away, a judge took the unheard-of step of postponing an *unrelated* murder trial, ruling that the Simpson publicity made it impossible for this other defendant to get a fair trial because the two cases were similar (like the Simpson case, this case involved a middle-aged African-American man accused of killing his younger, Caucasian ex-wife in a brutal knife attack that followed earlier incidents of domestic violence).

Once the Simpson trial began in 1995, the live television coverage repeatedly forced Judge Lance Ito to alter normal courtroom procedures. Time and again, millions of viewers got to see courtroom scenes on television that the jurors were not permitted to observe. As the trial increasingly focused on issues of race, police detective Mark Fuhrman was accused of using America's most inflammatory racial epithet more than 40 times. The jurors were not allowed to hear testimony about most of those times; Judge Ito ruled that its prejudicial effect would greatly outweigh its probative value as evidence. But Fuhrman's choice of words was a major story in the media for weeks. The jurors were sequestered--confined in a hotel and supervised to insulate them from the pervasive media publicity. However, they were allowed to have private conjugal visits. Can we ever know for sure that no visitor ever told any of the jurors the details of the Fuhrman controversy or other sensational developments in the case that occurred outside their presence?

Despite Judge Ito's efforts to assure that an impartial jury was selected, the news media carried many stories suggesting that some of the jurors were not impartial. When the jury rendered its not-guilty verdict, the event was viewed by the largest television audience in American history. Then the real controversy began--in the media and around the world.

Perhaps the one thing about Simpson's criminal trial that everyone on all sides agreed upon was that the media scrutiny was so intense that the American justice system may never be the same. Many believed that Simpson's real trial was in the mass media, and that the fair-trial, free-press issue is a more serious problem now than it has ever been before.

One of the early responses to the sensational media coverage of the Simpson case was a new law enacted by the California Legislature barring crime witnesses from selling their stories to the media before trial. That law was a direct response to the large sums of money several potential witnesses in the Simpson case were offered to sell their stories to media organizations, and it created a new controversy. The California First Amendment Coalition quickly won a federal court ruling that the new law is unconstitutional (see Chapter Three). The case also prompted California to adopt new rules restricting what lawyers can say to the media before and during a trial. About 40 states now have such rules.

Another response to the O.J. Simpson trial was that judges from coast to coast had second thoughts about permitting television coverage of celebrated trials. Exercising powers that they have in almost every state that allows cameras, judges barred television coverage of sensational trials after the Simpson criminal trial gained national attention. For example, in South Carolina television cameras were barred from the trial of Susan Smith, the woman who eventually confessed to drowning her two sons in a lake after first saying they were abducted. In California, cameras were barred from the trial of Richard Allen Davis, who was convicted of abducting and murdering 12-year-old Polly Klaas, although the judge did allow the announcement of the verdict to be televised. Cameras were also excluded from the retrial of the Menendez brothers, who were convicted of the brutal shotgun murders of their parents in Beverly Hills. Several states also reconsidered their basic rules permitting cameras in their courtrooms, although the rules in most states were not altered substantially.

When the families of Ron Goldman and Nicole Brown Simpson sought monetary damages from O.J. Simpson in a civil lawsuit, cameras were barred from the trial. Of course, the civil trial was very different from the criminal trial for many reasons. In civil cases, courtroom procedures, the rules of evidence and the standard of proof are all different than in criminal cases. For instance, a civil jury may rule based on *the preponderance of the evidence* without being convinced *beyond a reasonable doubt* as is required for a conviction in a criminal case. And, of course, many trial lawyers saw the very different composition of the jury as a crucial difference between the criminal trial that led to Simpson's acquittal and the civil trial in which he was held liable for the two deaths. Nonetheless, many observers also saw the absence of cameras as a significant factor in the dramatic reversal in the outcome of the case.

Lessons from the Rodney King Case

As a media event, the Simpson case even eclipsed the Rodney King beating. And yet, the King case also generated massive worldwide publicity, raising very serious fair trial-free press questions. The video tape of King's beating by Los Angeles police--and the massive rioting that occurred in 1992 when four officers were acquitted of most charges against them--became huge media events. Virtually everyone in America saw the video tape, and more than 80 percent of all Americans thought the officers were guilty, according to opinion polls. Then-president George Bush said of the taped beating, "it made me sick."

The beating of King, an African-American, by Caucasian officers greatly inflamed racial tensions in Los Angeles (and many other cities, because of the power of television).

So how do we find an impartial jury in a case like that? The first King trial was moved out of Los Angeles to a predominantly Caucasian suburban town. The jury heard testimony from more than 50 witnesses concerning the events that led to the beating and the rules governing police conduct. And they watched the video tape repeatedly. They concluded (unanimously) that three of the four officers had not been proven guilty of any crime *beyond a reasonable doubt*. The jury deadlocked on one charge against the fourth officer. But the verdict led to immediate violence in the streets; almost everyone assumed that the jury had been biased (just as millions of people concluded when Simpson's criminal and civil trials yielded opposite results). The first King jury may not have been convinced of the officers' guilt beyond a reasonable doubt, but most of the public surely was. Had not the officers' real trial--like O.J. Simpson's--occurred on television day after day?

In the aftermath of the riots that followed the first King beating verdict, the entire problem was analyzed again and again--and the media received a large share of the blame for all that seemingly went wrong in these cases.

Media critic David Shaw also faulted the media for failing to explain the context of the King beating:

> It would be difficult to deny... that the media--virtually all the media--did make mistakes in covering the King story. Often, for example, the media

referred to King as simply a "black motorist" who was beaten by police, rather than as someone who led police on a high-speed chase, drove recklessly, was intoxicated and allegedly appeared high on drugs and resisted being handcuffed--factors that clearly influenced the jurors who rendered not guilty verdicts....

Many others questioned whether the American system of justice can work in this kind of media-intensive environment. Thomas Rosenstiel of the *Los Angeles Times* said this of the problem:

> The jury system was conceived so that citizens could act as surrogates for the public to sit in judgment of crime. But with cameras increasingly trained wherever news is expected--from police cars, by citizen photographers and by free-lance camera crews who prowl the streets looking for footage to sell to TV stations--in a growing number of cases the public is beginning to believe that it can see and judge the crime for itself. And in these cases... citizens may no longer be so willing to accept the verdicts of their juries or their courts.

Rosenstiel wrote these words after the Rodney King case but before the Simpson case unfolded on television. When the Simpson criminal verdict was in, it was obvious that Rosenstiel had predicted what would happen. Americans did have strong opinions about what they saw on television. Day after day, television viewers saw for themselves that there was a "mountain of evidence" against Simpson, as the prosecutors pointed out to the jury, and they drew their own conclusions, as Rosenstiel said they might in this kind of case. Post-verdict opinion polls showed how deeply divided Americans were: about three-fourths of white Americans (and majorities of all other groups except African Americans) were convinced he was guilty. Among African Americans, the majority view was that Simpson was innocent, a victim of racism in the Los Angeles Police Department and the justice system.

Almost every key player in the case (and several prominent authors who were not personally involved) wrote books about the Simpson trial. Several of these became best sellers, further swaying public opinion against Simpson, who found that he could no longer command top dollar as a television commentator or advertising spokesperson. Even Alan Dershowitz, a prominent law professor who was a member of Simpson's "dream team" of defense attorneys, defended the role of the "dream team" in his book (*Reasonable Doubts*) by saying:

> A criminal trial is anything but a pure search for truth. When defense attorneys represent guilty clients--as most do, most of the time--their responsibility is to try, by all fair and ethical means, to *prevent* the truth about their client's guilt from emerging. Failure to do so...is malpractice.

Long before the Rodney King and O.J. Simpson cases forced this problem into the limelight, the Supreme Court had already dealt with fair trial-free press issues, and ruled that all defendants must be assured of a fair trial, media publicity notwithstanding. Although events of recent years may have dramatized the fair trial-free press problem as never before, the issues here are by no means new ones.

Early Fair Trial-Free Press Cases

The Supreme Court has struggled with fair trial-free press questions for more than 50 years. The court first took the drastic step of reversing a state court's murder conviction on the grounds of prejudicial publicity in the 1961 case of *Irvin v. Dowd* (366 U.S. 717). Even before that, the Supreme Court had expressed concern about the effect of publicity on trials (in *Shepherd v. Florida*, 341 U.S. 50, and *Stroble v. California*, 343 U.S. 181) and it had reversed a federal conviction due to prejudicial publicity in the 1959 case of *Marshall v. U.S.* (360 U.S. 310), but *Irvin* is especially noteworthy because it was a murder case and because it was the first state conviction to be reversed mainly due to prejudicial publicity.

The case involved Leslie Irvin, who was convicted of murdering six people near Evansville, Ind. and in nearby Kentucky. Irvin had been arrested on suspicion of burglary and writing bad checks a month after the murders. However, the county prosecutor--under political pressure to come up with a suspect--issued press releases calling him a "mad dog" and saying he had confessed to the murders. Since the murders themselves had received extensive news media coverage, the "confession" (which Irvin denied) led to a barrage of publicity in which he was branded "the mad dog killer." Other stories focused on Irvin's criminal past, revealing much information that would never be admitted into evidence at his trial.

The defense was granted a *change of venue* (a change in the location of the trial), but only to a nearby county where there had also been extensive publicity about the crimes and "confession." A second request for a change of venue was denied because Indiana law allowed only one change of venue. Subsequently, of 430 prospective jurors examined by the prosecution and defense attorneys, 370 admitted they had formed some opinion about Irvin's guilt. And of the 12 jurors finally seated to hear the case, eight admitted they believed Irvin was guilty before hearing any evidence in court but said they could be impartial anyway. Because they claimed they would be impartial, the defense could not show cause to have them discharged as jurors, and Irvin's lawyer had long since used up all of his *peremptory challenges* (requests to discharge prospective jurors without having to prove they would not be impartial).

The U.S. Supreme Court reviewed the case more than five years after Irvin was originally convicted and sentenced to death. (In the meantime he had escaped from Indiana's death row and been recaptured in San Francisco). The court found that Irvin had not received a fair trial and set aside his conviction. In 1962 Irvin was retried, convicted of one murder, and sentenced to life in prison, where he died in 1983.

Pretrial publicity again resulted in the U.S. Supreme Court reversing a murder conviction in 1963. Wilbert Rideau was arrested and charged with robbing a bank and killing a bank employee in Louisiana. During jailhouse interrogation by the local sheriff, he confessed the crimes. The session was filmed and the film was shown on local television three times. The Supreme Court held that it was a denial of Rideau's right to a fair trial not to grant him a change of venue after the people "had been exposed repeatedly and in depth to the spectacle of Rideau personally confessing in detail to the crimes...." The court said his real trial occurred on television, not in the courtroom (*Rideau v. Louisiana*, 373 U.S. 723). Rideau was eventually retried, convicted and sentenced to life in prison; he later became one of America's best known incarcerated writers.

The Sheppard v. Maxwell Decision

In 1966 the U.S. Supreme Court handed down the ruling on prejudicial media publicity that has come to be regarded as the landmark decision in this area, *Sheppard v. Maxwell* (384 U.S. 333). Dr. Sam Sheppard, a socially prominent Cleveland, Ohio, osteopath, was involved in one of the most famous criminal trials of his generation, a case that was the subject of a television documentary, a long-running fictionalized television series and a motion picture ("The Fugitive"). At the time, many called it "the trial of the century."

Sheppard's pregnant wife, Marilyn Sheppard, was murdered at their home overlooking Lake Erie in 1954. "Dr. Sam" said he was asleep on a downstairs sofa when he was awakened by his wife screaming upstairs. On the way upstairs to investigate, he was accosted from behind by a "bushy-haired" intruder who knocked him unconscious and fled.

Within a few weeks, the local papers were editorially demanding Dr. Sam's trial and conviction. The media literally took over the courtroom during his trial, and at one point the jurors' home telephone numbers were published in a gesture certain to build pressure on them for a guilty verdict. The press reported all sorts of "evidence" that was not admitted at the trial.

Some of the evidence that came out didn't help Dr. Sam. Although he initially denied it, at least one woman said she had an extramarital affair with him. And his account of what happened on the night of Marilyn Sheppard's murder was vague and confusing.

Sheppard was convicted and his conviction was affirmed by the Ohio courts. The U.S. Supreme Court declined to review the case at that point. However, when the high court took a new interest in the free press-fair trial problem in the 1960s, Sheppard's lawyers again asked the Supreme Court to review the case. This time the court did so, and in 1966--12 years after his original trial--Dr. Sam had his conviction reversed and was granted a new trial at which he was acquitted. Ironically, Sheppard's defense attorney at the second trial was a young F. Lee Bailey. Almost 30 years later, Bailey was a member of the "dream team" of defense attorneys who helped get O.J. Simpson acquitted at the next "trial of the century." But the Sam Sheppard story does not have a happy ending: four years after his acquittal, he died at age 46, after spending more than 10 prime years of his short life in prison.

In the mid-1990s, Cuyahoga County, Ohio authorities reopened the case as new evidence emerged pointing to Richard Eberling, who said he had done handyman work at the Sheppard home just before the murder, as the real killer. Eberling, who was later convicted and sentenced to life in prison for the murder of another woman, publicly denied killing Marilyn Sheppard. When forced to submit new blood samples for comparison to blood stains found in the Sheppard home, Eberling volunteered that his blood might have been there because he suffered cuts while replacing a storm window at the home. Meanwhile, a supervisor at a home health care agency where Eberling once worked was widely quoted as saying Eberling told her in 1983 that he killed Marilyn Sheppard. She said she went to the police soon after Eberling confessed to her, but they showed no interest in reopening the case then.

After Eberling died in 1998, a fellow prison inmate gave a videotaped interview in which he said Eberling had told him he did kill Marilyn Sheppard--and did it because she cried for help and bit him while he was raping her. The same inmate also said Eberling had earlier told a different version of the story, claiming he was paid by Dr. Sam Sheppard to kill Marilyn Sheppard.

Later other evidence surfaced that might have helped to acquit Dr. Sam. Although the police knew there was evidence of a forced entry into the home, they did not reveal it at the time of the trial. Nor did they initially reveal that there was a trail of blood from the bedroom where Marilyn Sheppard died down to the cellar, and that two of her teeth were broken outward, suggesting that she bit her assailant and he left the blood trail while fleeing. (Dr. Sam had no cuts when police arrived to investigate the crime, but Eberling was later observed with a prominent scar on his left wrist). In 1959, Eberling was arrested for unrelated crimes and a ring belonging to Marilyn Sheppard was found in his home. In later years, Eberling dropped tantalizing hints while still denying that he murdered Marilyn Sheppard. In one letter, he wrote, "Sam, yes, I do know the entire story." Another time he wrote, "The Sheppard answer is in front of the entire world. Nobody bothered to look."

In 1997, modern DNA testing of 43-year-old blood samples from the Sheppard home and tissue samples from Dr. Sam's body provided still more evidence that Dr. Sam's account was accurate and Eberling was the real killer. The DNA tests indicated that blood stains found around the home, including a stain on a wardrobe door two feet from Marilyn Sheppard's body, did not match Dr. Sam's blood, but they did match Eberling's.

In December of 1998, the Ohio Supreme Court allowed Sam Reese Sheppard, the Sheppards' son who has worked for many years to clear his father's name, to go to trial with a lawsuit alleging that Dr. Sam was wrongfully convicted and imprisoned.

In 1954, the Cleveland media had been anything but sympathetic to Dr. Sam's cause. By 1999, however, the media were taking a very different view of Sam Reese Sheppard's cause. For example, Joe Dirck, a *Cleveland Plain Dealer* columnist, wrote these words about Sheppard's case and the fair trial-free press issue in May of 1999:

> When he (Sam Reese Sheppard) looks around today, he sees a 24-hour mass media infinitely more pervasive and intrusive than they were in 1954 and just as eager to milk every cent of profit from stories with an exploit-

able level of sex and/or violence.

He sees a legal system in which prosecutors still sometimes value winning over justice, such as in Illinois, where recently yet another condemned man, the 12th, was released from death row after his innocence was established through DNA testing. Most of all, he sees society trapped in a culture of violence, bemoaning it on the one hand while celebrating and profiting from it on the other.

All the factors that combined to unjustly send his father to prison for 10 years, he believes, exist today, even more so. Defendants still get railroaded, the media still pile on, and the innocent still suffer.

"The case" is the perfect textbook example of how such excesses can lead to a terrible miscarriage of justice. In that sense, it may be even more relevant today as a cautionary tale, the son believes.

Although the media may have sympathized with Sam Reese Sheppard, the same cannot be said of the jury that heard his civil lawsuit in early 2000. The jury rejected Sam Reese Sheppard's attempt to clear his father's name and win money damages for his alleged wrongful imprisonment.

The eight-person jury declined to rule that Sheppard had proven his father's innocence by the preponderance of the evidence, as required in a civil case.

During nearly three months of testimony, Sheppard's attorney attempted to show that the original investigation of the murder 46 years ago was sloppy and that more recently acquired evidence, including new DNA tests, pointed to Richard Eberling as the real murderer. Eberling's DNA samples matched those at the crime scene, but not so conclusively as to rule out all other possible suspects.

Defending their original investigation and decision to prosecute Dr. Sam, Cuyahoga County, Ohio officials during the new trial called Dr. Sam "the playboy of the western world," offering evidence that he had at least two extra-marital affairs--and that his wife Marilyn may have also had an affair before her murder.

In the end, the jury took only three hours to rule that Sheppard had not conclusively proven his father's innocence. But this verdict failed to end the controversy: the public debate about the original Sheppard trials continued.

Whatever the ultimate verdict of history may be about Dr. Sam Sheppard, his case prompted a landmark Supreme Court decision on fair trial-free press. In an 8-1 opinion written by Justice Tom Clark, the court ruled that "the state trial judge had not fulfilled his duty to protect Sheppard from the inherently prejudicial publicity which saturated the community." The Supreme Court went on to instruct trial judges as to what they must do to ensure a fair trial. The court warned that failure to follow these safeguards would result in more reversals of convictions.

The Supreme Court's *Sheppard* decision suggested a number of specific things the nation's trial judges could do to protect defendants from sensational media publicity. The court said judges should do some or all of the following things to control publicity and protect defendants' rights:

1. Adopt rules to curtail in-court misconduct by reporters;
2. Issue *protective orders* (sometimes called *gag orders*) to control out-of-

court statements by trial participants such as lawyers;
3. Grant a *continuance* to postpone the trial until community prejudice has had time to subside;
4. Grant a *change of venue* to a place where there has been less prejudicial publicity;
5. *Admonish the jury* to disregard the media publicity about the case; or
6. *Sequester the jury* (confine them in a place where they will not be able to read about the trial in newspapers or hear about it on radio or television).

Basically, Justice Clark was suggesting two different kinds of remedies: remedies that *compensate for* potentially prejudicial media publicity, and remedies intended to *eliminate* such publicity--but at the expense of First Amendment freedoms. In the years following *Sheppard*, judges tried all of these things to control publicity. Some also began to do things the Supreme Court didn't recommend in the *Sheppard* case, such as closing their courtrooms to the press and public and holding preliminary proceedings--or entire trials--in secret. These judicial actions raised new constitutional issues.

"Gag" Orders and the News Media

Of all these remedies for prejudicial publicity, the one that generated the most controversy involved the suppression of information about the trial. In the *Sheppard* decision Justice Clark wrote:

> Neither prosecutors, counsel for defense, the accused, witnesses, court staff nor enforcement officers coming under the jurisdiction of the court should be permitted to frustrate its function. Collaboration between counsel and the press as to information affecting the fairness of a criminal trial is not only subject to regulation, but is highly censurable and worthy of disciplinary measures.

Responding to this mandate, jurists all over the country began issuing orders that they call *protective orders* or *restrictive orders;* journalists tend to call them *gag orders*. Originally, these orders fell into two categories: those directed against only the participants in the trial, ordering them not to reveal prejudicial information to the media, and those directed against the media, ordering them not to publish prejudicial information even if they lawfully obtain it. The first category (orders intended to dry up the media's sources of prejudicial information) usually have been upheld when challenged on First Amendment grounds. But the second kind (those purporting to exercise prior restraint of the media) have not fared as well and are rarely issued today.

In fact, in a television interview nine years after the *Sheppard* decision, Justice Clark said he did not mean that the media should be prohibited by judges from publishing information in their possession. Instead, gag orders were to be imposed only on those who might give prejudicial information to the press. Yet many judges imposed protective orders directly on the press after the *Sheppard* decision, citing the mandate to protect the rights of defendants as justification for doing so. More will be said of these orders shortly.

Other Remedies

The protective or gag order is just one of the remedies for prejudicial publicity recommended in the *Sheppard* decision, but it has surely been the most viable and controversial one. All of the others--which are really intended to compensate for prejudicial publicity instead of eliminating it--have limitations that sometimes render them impractical.

For example, a change of venue is expensive: it means all parties to the case, including witnesses, must travel a long distance for the trial, and it abridges the defendant's right to be tried in the place where the crime was committed, another constitutional right. Moreover, with today's pervasive mass media, the new community may be just as aroused about the case as was the community where the trial was originally scheduled.

Ordering a postponement of the trial also has major disadvantages. For one thing, it denies defendants their constitutional right to a speedy trial. For another, witnesses tend to become unavailable after a period of time. And finally, there is no assurance that the prejudicial publicity will not resume as the date of the long-delayed trial finally approaches. The community may harbor prejudices against a suspect for many years, and if anything a long delay may leave many persons more convinced than ever of the suspect's guilt.

Likewise, sequestering the jury has its drawbacks, although some states do sequester juries routinely in cases where the death sentence may be imposed. Nevertheless, many prospective jurors are unwilling to serve in a case where they will be isolated from the modern world for weeks or months. Moreover, sequestering a jury is expensive--the jurors must be provided food, lodging and entertainment. And finally, it has become almost impossible to completely insulate jurors from the mass media. The celebrated trial of Charles Manson and his followers for the murder of actress Sharon Tate and her friends provides a good illustration of the problems involved with sequestration. In the Manson trial the jury was sequestered, but on various occasions newspapers containing prejudicial stories appeared in the courtroom, in the restrooms used by the jurors, and on newsracks the jurors saw during the bus ride from their hotel to the court.

At one point, Manson himself held up a newspaper in court so that the jurors could see the main headline, which proclaimed, "Manson Guilty, Nixon Says." The judge immediately stopped the proceedings and asked the jurors if seeing that headline would influence their verdict and they all said it would not, but no one will ever know for sure if that was true.

Among the other ways to protect the defendant from prejudicial publicity are closing the trial or pretrial proceedings and directly questioning the jurors about their potential prejudices. The problems of closing the trial or pretrial hearings will be treated later in this chapter.

The difficulties of questioning the jurors about their prejudices (a procedure called *voir dire*) were already cited in connection with the *Irvin* case. Jurors may say they can be impartial when in fact they harbor strong prejudices based on the media publicity. Each side in a criminal trial is allowed to dismiss only a few jurors on peremptory challenges (i.e., without having to prove they are prejudiced). As the *Irvin* case illustrated, in a sensational case the defense may use all of its peremptory challenges and still be stuck with jurors who cannot be shown to be prejudiced but who are *not* impartial.

Furthermore, admonitions to the jury to disregard publicity they may see or read--another of the means of protecting the defendant's rights suggested in *Sheppard*--can hardly be expected to ensure that the jurors will not base their "guilty" or "not guilty" verdict on what they learn from the media as well as what they hear in court. Jurors being human, they will usually consider everything they know about the case in reaching a verdict, regardless of the source of that information.

This brings us back to protective (or "gag") orders, the most controversial but perhaps also the most practical means of protecting defendants from prejudicial publicity--because these orders may actually eliminate the prejudicial publicity rather than merely compensating for it.

"Gag" Orders as Prior Restraints

Protective (or "gag") orders were in the center of a bitter debate between the media and the judiciary from the time of the *Sheppard* decision until the U.S. Supreme Court finally clarified the constitutional issues involved a decade later in a case called *Nebraska Press Assn. v. Stuart* (427 U.S. 53, 1976).

Gag orders were widely used all over the country in the early 1970s. A judge who believed an upcoming case might generate extensive publicity would almost routinely issue an order forbidding all parties in the case to make statements to the media. Such orders usually prohibited disclosing a defendant's prior criminal record, discussing the merits of the evidence in the case and revealing the presence or absence of any confession. In many instances, this kind of information would be excluded as evidence at the trial, which would do little good if the jurors already know about it from watching television or reading the newspapers. But some judges went beyond these restrictions and actually attempted to censor the media by ordering publishers and broadcasters not to disseminate information they already had.

The Reporters Committee for Freedom of the Press kept records on the issuance of protective orders in the 1967-75 period. That organization identified 174 instances in which such orders were issued, including 63 that prohibited statements by court participants, 61 closing court proceedings or records to the press and public, and 50 involving direct prior restraint of the media.

After a number of state and lower federal court decisions on the validity of gag orders, the U.S. Supreme Court finally ruled on the issue in the 1976 *Nebraska Press Association v. Stuart* decision. That ruling all but eliminated gag orders that directly restrained the press (as opposed to orders that merely prohibited trial participants from giving prejudicial information to reporters).

The case involved Erwin Charles Simants, an unemployed handyman with a purported IQ of 75. Simants borrowed his brother-in-law's rifle, walked to the house next door and murdered six members of the James Henry Kellie family. Simants turned himself in the day after the murders and confessed. However, there were serious legal questions about whether he had sufficient mental capacity to understand his rights; his confession was quickly challenged.

At the preliminary hearing, Lincoln County Judge Ronald Ruff ordered the media not to report any of the testimony. This gag order was appealed to District Court Judge Hugh Stuart by Nebraska news organizations. Stuart replaced Judge Ruff's order with his own.

Stuart's order prohibited the publication of certain kinds of prejudicial information. Later, the Nebraska Supreme Court modified the order to prohibit publishing only Simants' confession and any other facts "strongly implicative" of the suspect. The press was ordered not to even mention the existence of a confession.

The news organizations appealed the order to the U.S. Supreme Court. The high court ruled unanimously that this order was a violation of the First Amendment in that it imposed a prior restraint on publication. In striking down the order, Chief Justice Warren Burger, writing for the court, referred to previous prior restraint cases and wrote:

> A prior restraint, by contrast and by definition, has an immediate and irreversible sanction. If it can be said that a threat of criminal or civil sanctions after publication "chills" speech, prior restraint 'freezes' it at least for the time.

The chief justice continued, "The thread running through all these cases is that prior restraints on speech and publication are the most serious and the least tolerable infringements on First Amendment rights."

But the court did not totally rule out the possibility of protective orders being directed against the media in future cases. It said that in "extraordinary circumstances" such an order might be imposed. However, there must be sufficient evidence to reasonably conclude that:

1. There will be intense and pervasive publicity concerning the case;
2. No other alternative measure--such as a change of venue or continuance or extensive voir dire process--is likely to mitigate the effects of the pretrial publicity; and
3. The restrictive order will in fact effectively prevent prejudicial material from reaching potential jurors.

These guidelines from the *Nebraska* case were widely discussed again when a federal judge ordered Cable News Network not to broadcast tape recordings of conversations between former Panamanian dictator Manuel Noriega and his lawyers. Noriega was in jail awaiting trial on drug trafficking charges at the time. The judge's order, which amounted to a direct prior restraint, was quickly appealed by CNN, but the Supreme Court refused either to set aside the gag order or to take up the case at that point. The judge who had issued the order later reviewed the

controversial tapes and concluded that their broadcast would not interfere with Noriega's right to a fair trial, so he decided not to make the order permanent. However, in 1994 the U.S. Attorney's office in Miami filed criminal contempt of court charges against CNN for broadcasting excerpts from the tapes while the order was in effect, and a federal judge fined CNN for the broadcast (*U.S. v. Cable News Network*, 865 F.Supp. 1549).

The Noriega case was unusual: in most instances gag orders targeting the media are overturned on appeal. Within weeks of CNN's contempt of court conviction, three state appellate courts overruled gag orders targeting the news media (see *Ohio ex rel. New World Communications v. Character*, 23 Med.L.Rptr. 1479, *Jacksonville Television Inc. v. Florida Dept. of Health and Rehabilitative Services*, 23 Med.L.Rptr. 1254 and *Kansas v. Alston*, 887 P.2d 681).

Gagging Trial Lawyers

Although the *Nebraska Press Association* case limited the power of judges to restrain the press, it had little effect on their power to impose gag orders on trial participants. By the early 2000s, at least 40 states had rules regulating what lawyers may say publicly while they are handling a newsworthy case.

The American Bar Association has guidelines for professional conduct by lawyers. Among other things, these ABA "Model Rules" cover extrajudicial (out of court) statements. Although these rules are voluntary, many states' mandatory rules are based on them. The ABA rules were extensively revised in 1994.

Under ABA Model Rule 3.6, lawyers are forbidden to make out-of-court statements that the lawyer "knows or reasonably should know...will have a substantial likelihood of materially prejudicing an adjudicative proceeding in the matter." This rule applies only while a case is pending and only to lawyers specifically involved in the case; it does not apply to other lawyers or law professors who may comment on a case in the media. Nor does it apply to lawyers who write books (or comment in other ways) after a case is over.

There is a separate provision in ABA Model Rule 3.8 intended to prevent prosecutors from trying their cases in the media. Rule 3.8 directs prosecutors to "refrain from making extrajudicial comments that have substantial likelihood of heightening public condemnation of the accused."

Although these rules have been adopted by many states, enforcement is often lax. For example, prosecutors often make inflammatory (and newsworthy) comments about pending cases in spite of Rule 3.8. For that reason, many leading defense attorneys demanded a "right of reply." In its 1994 revision of these rules, the ABA House of Delegates voted to add language to Model Rule 3.6 creating a right of reply.

Rule 3.6 now allows lawyers to make "reasonable" statements to the extent necessary to mitigate "the substantial undue prejudicial effect of recent publicity not initiated by the lawyer or lawyer's client."

When this right of reply provision was adopted, Michael H. Dettmer, then president of the Michigan State Bar, predicted "a right of reply free-for-all, with press releases begetting press releases begetting press releases."

In some high profile cases, of course, that is precisely what has happened. Nevertheless, the ABA felt obliged to rewrite and in some ways liberalize its Model Rules because a Nevada state rule based on an earlier version of the ABA rules was declared unconstitutional in *Gentile v. State Bar of Nevada* (501 U.S. 1030, 1991). In that case, Nevada disciplined Dominic P. Gentile, a criminal defense lawyer, for making allegedly improper public comments after a client was indicted. Like the earlier ABA rule, the Nevada rule permitted attorneys to publicly describe the "general nature of the claim or defense," but only if it is done "without elaboration." Nevada Bar authorities punished Gentile for saying too much to the media. He appealed, and eventually the Supreme Court held that Nevada's rules were too vague and therefore violated Gentile's First Amendment rights.

The *Gentile* case triggered a divisive three-year controversy within the ABA. In the end, the ABA adopted new limits on what trial lawyers may say to the media about a pending case, but with the right-of-reply provision. After much debate, the ABA decided to retain a *substantial likelihood* test for public statements by lawyers: this forbids lawyers to say anything that would have a substantial likelihood of prejudicing a pending case. Some advocates of greater freedom for lawyers urged the ABA to adopt a *clear and present danger* test under which attorneys could only be punished if their out-of-court statements created a clear and present danger of prejudicing a pending case. Under that test, it would be much harder to prove that a lawyer's extrajudicial comments were improper--and lawyers would have greater freedom to make public statements about a pending case. However, those who favored tougher restrictions on lawyers' public statements prevailed.

Many of the same issues have been raised concerning ethical rules and state laws forbidding candidates in judicial elections to announce their views on political and legal issues issues that might come before them as judges. In *Republican Party of Minnesota v. White* (2002 U.S. Lexis 4883), the U.S. Supreme Court ruled in 2002 that Minnesota's restrictions on judicial candidates violated the First Amendment. The 5-4 majority rejected the argument that judges and prospective judges should always present the appearance of impartiality and instead ruled that judicial candidates, like other candidates for public office, have a right to speak about controversial issues, even if they might have to rule on some of those issues later. However, the high court did *not* decide whether judicial candidates have a right to pledge or promise that they will decide any particular case or issue a certain way. Many states have rules prohibiting such promises, and those rules are likely to be challenged on First Amendment grounds in future cases.

Voluntary Guidelines

During the 1960s and 1970s, the media and the judiciary engaged in a number of voluntary efforts to solve some of the fair trial-free press problems. In many states, bench-bar-media groups developed voluntary guidelines for media coverage of sensational criminal cases.

The American Bar Association created a committee under Massachusetts Supreme Court Justice Paul C. Reardon to recommend fair trial-free press guidelines. The Reardon Report--as it came to be known--was adopted by the ABA

House of Delegates in 1968. It urged that all parties to a criminal prosecution refrain from releasing prejudicial information to the press. Moreover, the report urged judges to use their contempt power against lawyers and others who release inflammatory statements to the media. The report also endorsed the idea of closed preliminary hearings when the information revealed at such hearings might interfere with a defendant's right to a fair trial. Finally, the Reardon Report urged local groups of lawyers, judges and journalists to develop voluntary guidelines for press coverage of criminal trials.

Although the Reardon proposals were widely opposed (and ignored) by reporters, they formed the basis for local guidelines in at least 23 states. However, the whole concept of voluntary bench-bar-press guidelines was thrown into controversy in 1981 when a judge in Washington state forced journalists to promise to obey the "voluntary" guidelines as a condition of being allowed to attend some courtroom proceedings. Any reporter who refused to make this pledge would not be admitted to the courtroom, the judge decreed. That meant reporters would be unable to report things they heard in an open courtroom--and it sounded very much like the kind of prior restraint the Supreme Court's *Nebraska Press Association* decision was intended to prevent. The result was outrage among journalists from coast to coast, and the order was appealed to the Washington Supreme Court. In *Federated Publications v. Swedberg* (633 P.2d 74, 1981), the state high court said the order was simply a reasonable means of avoiding a closed hearing while protecting the defendant's right to a fair trial. The court distinguished this case from the *Nebraska* case, ruling that no prior restraint was involved. Rather, the reporters' promise was merely a "moral one ...and not enforceable in a court of law."

That kind of judicial reasoning troubled a lot of journalists: any journalist who violated this "moral" obligation could be expelled from the courtroom, while more compliant journalists were allowed to remain.

A year later, another Washington Supreme Court decision eased the effect of the *Swedberg* case, holding that trial judges must weigh a number of factors before barring journalists from pretrial hearings or sealing the records of such hearings. For instance, judges must first consider alternative means of protecting the defendant's rights and also allow anyone present to object to the closure. Moreover, if the justification for the secrecy is anything other than a defendant's fair trial rights, there must be a much stronger justification for any secrecy (see *Seattle Times v. Ishikawa*, 640 P.2d 716, 1982). Nevertheless, few media groups were willing to agree to "voluntary" guidelines after this sequence of events.

CLOSED COURTROOMS

Soon after the Supreme Court's *Nebraska Press Association* decision, a new conflict between judges and journalists assumed crisis proportions. Judges began to bar the press and the public from preliminary hearings, hearings on motions to suppress evidence and sometimes even from trials.

Although it has been customary for courtrooms to be open to the public throughout American history, there are a number of circumstances that may lead to a courtroom closure. Courtroom closures to protect a defendant's right to a fair trial are the primary subject of this chapter. However, courtrooms are also closed at times to protect an individual's privacy, to assure the secrecy of information affecting national security, or to keep the details of a police investigation confidential--to cite just three examples.

In the late 1970s there were increasingly frequent instances of preliminary criminal proceedings--and even trials--being closed to the press and the public in an effort to curtail prejudicial publicity. Gag orders directed against trial participants do not always stop the flow of prejudicial information to the press, and the *Nebraska* case imposed limits on judges' power to gag the press directly. Therefore, judges increasingly saw closed pretrial hearings as the best way to limit prejudicial publicity in sensational cases.

In order to understand the judges' viewpoint, we should explain why pretrial hearings occur and what happens at these proceedings. A preliminary hearing is intended as a check on law enforcement officers and prosecutors. It is a hearing where the case against the accused is reviewed by a judge, not to determine guilt or innocence but merely to decide whether there is enough evidence to justify a full trial. This is supposed to be a shortcut out of the criminal justice system for defendants who should never have been charged with a crime in the first place. The purpose is *not* to decide if the accused is guilty beyond a reasonable doubt (the standard of proof required in a criminal trial) but instead to see if there is enough evidence to justify a trial.

As a result, only the prosecution presents evidence at most preliminary hearings. If there is enough evidence, a trial is scheduled, almost without regard to the strength of the defense's case. Thus, as a matter of strategy, the defense often waits until the full trial before presenting its side of the case. As a result, news coverage of a preliminary hearing is necessarily imbalanced in most instances since only one side has been heard. The defense does have the right to cross-examine prosecution witnesses, but even so, if the hearing is covered by the media, most of the news generated there is going to be unfavorable to the defendant, who may have to stand trial before jurors who read about the preliminary hearing in the papers.

Pretrial hearings on motions to suppress evidence are even more likely to produce prejudicial publicity. At these hearings, the defense asks a judge to throw out damaging evidence, often because it was obtained by an unlawful search or seizure. Or perhaps the challenged evidence is a confession that was secured through coercion. In any event, what good does it do to have the tainted evidence suppressed (i.e., ruled inadmissible at the trial) if prospective jurors learn about it on the evening news? For these reasons, many judges and lawyers feel strongly that hearings on motions to suppress evidence should be closed to the press and public.

In addition to preventing jury prejudice, closing preliminary court proceedings protects the reputations of defendants who have been charged with a crime but are not held for trial because the hearing reveals that the prosecutor has little evidence.

Few journalists would deny that there are powerful arguments for secrecy at the pretrial stage in criminal proceedings, except for one thing: more than 80 percent of all criminal prosecutions in America are resolved without the case ever reaching a full trial. Because the judge's ruling on a motion to suppress crucial evidence is the decisive step in many criminal cases, serious plea bargaining usually occurs after these pretrial proceedings. If key evidence is barred, the prosecutor may be inclined to accept a guilty plea to a lesser charge or even drop the charges. If the evidence is ruled admissible, on the other hand, the defendant may plead guilty as charged at this stage, perhaps in return for a promise of a light sentence. In the vast majority of criminal proceedings, the last chance the public will have to monitor the justice system is at the pretrial hearing stage.

As a trend toward closed pretrial hearings developed, a constitutional challenge to this practice reached the U.S. Supreme Court in the 1979 case of *Gannett v. DePasquale* (443 U.S. 368).

The Supreme Court upheld a judge's order barring a newspaper reporter from a pretrial evidentiary hearing in upstate New York. The case arose when two young men were charged with murdering a former New York policeman. They reportedly confessed the crime and were later indicted by a grand jury.

Because of the intense publicity surrounding the incident and the arrest, the defense and prosecution concurred in closing the pretrial hearing. When Judge Daniel DePasquale barred the press and public, the Gannett newspapers appealed the ruling. The state's highest court affirmed the order and Gannett asked the Supreme Court to hear the case.

In affirming the closure, Justice Potter Stewart, writing for a 5-4 Supreme Court majority, acknowledged that "there is a strong societal interest in public trials." His opinion also noted, "there is no question that the Sixth Amendment permits and even presumes open trials as a norm." However, Stewart continued, the Sixth Amendment right to a public trial belongs to the defendant and not the public, and it is a right the defendant may waive.

Justice Stewart agreed with the trial judge's decision that the press' right of access to this particular hearing "was outweighed by the defendant's right to a fair trial...because an open proceeding would pose a reasonable probability of prejudice to these defendants."

Justice Stewart's opinion was joined by Justices John Paul Stevens, Lewis Powell, William Rehnquist and Chief Justice Burger. The latter three also wrote separate concurring opinions. Justices Marshall, Brennan, Blackmun and White joined in a dissent which said, "Secret hearings ...are suspect by nature. Unlike any other provision of the Sixth Amendment, the public trial interest cannot adequately be protected by the prosecutor and judge in conjunction or connivance with the defendant."

Justice Powell's concurring opinion was noteworthy in that it said the press and public should have a right to challenge proposed courtroom closures. In the years since *Gannett*, many journalists have done precisely that, sometimes successfully. Many reporters who regularly cover the courts carry a card with them containing the correct legal phrasing of a motion to object to a courtroom closure.

Nevertheless, the *Gannett* decision stood as a precedent permitting judges to close at least pretrial hearings when they felt the danger of prejudicial publicity would outweigh the public's right to observe the proceedings.

As a result of this decision, there was an avalanche of closed hearings--and even trials--in 1979 and 1980. The Reporters Committee for Freedom of the Press counted 21 courtroom closures ordered or upheld on appeal in the first 30 days after the *Gannett* ruling was announced. Within the year, there were at least 100 more such courtroom closures around the nation.

Open Trials: Richmond Newspapers v. Virginia

Apparently alarmed at the reaction to *Gannett* by trial judges, several Supreme Court justices made public statements condemning the trend toward courtroom closures. And the high court quickly agreed to review another related case, this one involving a closure of a full trial in Virginia.

In this case (*Richmond Newspapers v. Virginia*, 448 U.S. 555, 1980), a county judge had cleared his courtroom of reporters and spectators before the fourth trial of a man who was charged with murdering a hotel manager. His first trial had been invalidated on a technicality, and the next two resulted in mistrials. Relying on a Virginia statute that allowed "the removal of any persons whose presence would impair the conduct of a fair trial," the judge simply closed the trial. The defendant was acquitted after a two-day closed trial because there were "too many holes" in the prosecution's case, the judge said.

Two jointly owned Richmond, Va., newspapers challenged the courtroom closure. Just a week after the *Gannett* ruling of the U.S. Supreme Court, the Virginia Supreme Court upheld the ruling closing this trial.

Ruling in 1980--a year to the day after its controversial *Gannett* decision--the U.S. Supreme Court voted 7-1 to overrule this trial closing, a decision that was widely seen as a major victory for the mass media. Not only did the high court invalidate the closing of this particular trial, but Chief Justice Burger's opinion for the court recognized for the first time that there is a constitutional right of access to information inherent in the free press guarantees of the First Amendment:

> We hold that the right to attend criminal trials is implicit in the guarantees of the First Amendment; without the freedom to attend such trials, which people have exercised for centuries, important aspects of freedom of speech and of the press could be eviscerated.

Moreover, Burger's opinion went to some trouble to make it clear that this public right to attend trials, although only an implied right and not one specifically stated in the Constitution, was nonetheless legitimate. Burger pointed to a variety of other constitutional rights the Supreme Court has recognized over the years, although those rights too were only implied in the Constitution. Burger noted that the rights of association and privacy, the right to travel, and the right to be judged by the "beyond-a-reasonable-doubt" standard of proof in criminal cases were only implied and not stated in the Constitution.

Although this opinion was joined by only two other justices, at least two additional justices recognized a right of the public to attend trials in a separate opinion in the *Richmond* case. However, Justice Rehnquist (the only dissenter) said the states should be free to set their own standards on the administration of justice and found no provision in the federal Constitution that prohibited the Virginia judge from doing what he did.

In overturning the closure of a trial in the *Richmond* decision, the Supreme Court avoided reversing its year-old *Gannett* ruling, leaving judges free to close pretrial hearings in some instances where a closed trial might not be permitted. In fact, on the same day the Supreme Court handed down its *Richmond* decision, the court declined to review a lower court decision authorizing another closed pretrial hearing in New York.

Moreover, the Supreme Court did not even flatly forbid closed trials in the *Richmond* case. Instead, the high court said trials could still be closed under certain extraordinary circumstances. "Absent an overriding interest (in closing the trial) articulated in the (judge's) findings, the trial of a criminal case must be open to the public," Burger's opinion held. The Supreme Court did not set forth any guidelines for determining when a trial should be closed, but the court did make it clear that a judge must pursue alternative means of ensuring the fairness of a trial before barring the press and public.

In short, the *Richmond* decision limits a judge's discretion in barring the press and public from a trial, while permitting trial closures in extreme circumstances if the judge can set forth valid reasons for his action. This decision may not have gone quite as far as many journalists hoped it would, but it nonetheless sharply curtailed the nationwide trend toward closed courtrooms that had developed in the year between the *Gannett* and *Richmond* decisions.

Open Courtroom Cases After Richmond

The *Richmond* decision was a vindication of the principle of open courtrooms in America. While there have been a number of controversial courtroom closures since that bellwether 1980 Supreme Court decision, the trend toward closed trials has been reversed. In fact, the Supreme Court has since handed down several more decisions overruling courtroom closures.

In 1982, the Supreme Court invalidated a Massachusetts law that automatically closed the courtroom whenever a juvenile victim of a sex crime was to testify. In *Globe Newspaper Company v. Superior Court* (457 U.S. 596), the court said judges must evaluate each trial closure on a case-by-case basis rather than automatically closing a trial whenever a young sex crime victim is testifying.

In a 6-3 decision, the high court found the Massachusetts law unconstitutional because it made the closure mandatory. The court took pains to point out that judges could exclude the press and public in individual cases where they found that a minor's well-being would be in jeopardy if the trial were open.

Writing for the majority, Justice William Brennan took note of the court's ruling in *Richmond Newspapers* that the public has a constitutional right of access to criminal trials. However, Brennan pointed out that this right is not absolute: a trial may be closed if a state can show two things: (1) a "compelling governmental interest" that requires the closure and (2) that the law requiring closure is "narrowly tailored to serve that interest."

Weighing the Massachusetts statute--as interpreted by that state's highest court--the Supreme Court concluded that it failed this two-part test because a case-by-case determination of whether a criminal trial should be closed would be sufficient to protect young victims. The mandatory closure provision was overbroad, the court held.

The case arose when a judge closed a rape trial in which the victims were three girls under age 18. The *Boston Globe* challenged the closure, and after several preliminary decisions the state Supreme Court upheld the mandatory closure provision of the Massachusetts law. The *Globe* appealed, setting up the U.S. Supreme Court's decision.

The gist of the *Globe Newspaper* decision is nicely summarized by one of the footnotes in the majority opinion:

> We emphasize that our holding is a narrow one: that a rule of mandatory closure respecting the testimony of minor sex victims is constitutionally infirm. In individual cases, and under appropriate circumstances, the First Amendment does not necessarily stand as a bar to the exclusion from the courtroom of the press and general public during the testimony of minor sex-offense victims. But a mandatory rule, requiring no particularized determinations in individual cases, is unconstitutional.

The ruling produced dissents from Chief Justice Warren Burger and Justice William Rehnquist, who felt the mandatory closure rule was not unconstitutional, and from Justice John Paul Stevens, who felt the case should not have been heard.

In 1984 the Supreme Court took another step to assure public access to the criminal justice system when it ruled that the jury selection process must also normally be open to the public. In the case of *Press-Enterprise Co. v. Superior Court* (464 U.S. 501), the court unanimously overturned a Riverside, Calif., judge's decision to close almost six weeks of jury selection procedures during a 1981 murder trial. The *Riverside* (Calif.) *Press-Enterprise* challenged the judge's actions.

The judge not only closed the jury selection process, but also refused to make a transcript of the proceeding public after the defendant was tried, convicted and sentenced to death for raping and killing a 13-year-old girl. The effect of the judge's decision was to ensure that the public would never know how the jury was selected for a trial that ended with a death sentence.

Writing for the Supreme Court, Chief Justice Warren Burger emphasized that the jury selection, like other aspects of criminal trials, has traditionally been open to the public--and should continue to be open in all but very unusual circumstances. He wrote:

> Proceedings held in secret would ...frustrate the broad public interest; by contrast public proceedings vindicate the concerns of the victims and the community in knowing that offenders are being brought to account for their criminal conduct by jurors fairly and openly selected.

However, Burger said there might be rare occasions when prospective jurors could be questioned in private in the judge's chambers to protect their privacy during discussions of "deeply personal matters." However, even then a transcript of the proceedings should be made available within a reasonable time unless that would further invade a juror's privacy. But to close the entire process for "an incredible six weeks" (as Burger put it) was going much too far.

Although the decision that the judge should not have closed the jury selection in this case was unanimous, three justices wrote separate opinions. Justice Thurgood Marshall said the jury selection and "all aspects of criminal trials" should be open, regardless of whether open jury selection procedures might embarrass a prospective juror. Justices Harry Blackmun and John Paul Stevens wrote a separate opinion emphasizing the importance of jurors' privacy rights.

A few months after the 1984 *Press-Enterprise* decision, the Supreme Court again reiterated that criminal proceedings other than the trial itself must normally be open. In *Waller v. Georgia* (467 U.S. 39, 1984), the high court overturned a judge's decision to close a lengthy pretrial evidence suppression hearing in a case where the police had searched numerous homes and conducted telephone wiretaps to gather evidence of gambling. The defendants argued that much of the evidence was unlawfully obtained, and they wanted it suppressed. Moreover, they demanded that the evidence suppression hearing be open to the public, but the judge refused to open the hearing. Then he admitted most of the evidence and convicted several defendants of various crimes.

The Supreme Court ruled that most if not all of this evidence suppression hearing, like the jury selection proceedings in the 1984 *Press-Enterprise* case, should have been open to the public. Only a little of the seven-day hearing involved material that might invade anyone's privacy, the court noted. In *Waller*, the court again emphasized the right of the public--as well as defendants--to have criminal trials and pretrial proceedings held in open court under most circumstances. The court reiterated its rule about judicial openness from the *Press-Enterprise* decision. The court said that when judges abridge the open-courtroom rights of the press, public and criminal defendants, they must have a compelling reason for doing so, they must explain that reason clearly, and they must close no more of the proceeding than is really necessary.

Two years after the original *Press-Enterprise v. Superior Court* decision, the Supreme Court handed down another important decision with exactly the same name--and on a closely related aspect of the open-courtroom issue. In this 1986 case, *Press-Enterprise Co. v. Superior Court (P-E II)* (478 U.S. 1), the Supreme Court ruled that preliminary hearings and similar pretrial proceedings must be open unless there is a *substantial probability* that an open hearing will prejudice the defendant's right to a fair trial.

The 1986 case, commonly identified as *Press-Enterprise II* to distinguish it from the 1984 case, involved exactly the same two parties: the *Riverside* (Calif.) *Press-Enterprise* and the Riverside County Superior Court. This time, the newspaper protested the closing of a 41-day preliminary hearing for a male nurse accused of killing a dozen hospital patients with massive drug overdoses.

In California and many other states, a preliminary hearing is held in most major criminal cases. As explained earlier, these hearings are conducted by a judge to determine if there is sufficient evidence to hold the defendant for a full trial. The preliminary hearing is the only significant court proceeding in the great majority of criminal cases: less then 20 percent of major criminal cases actually go to trial. Therefore, the preliminary hearing is often the only opportunity the public will ever have to learn of the evidence against the accused. California law permitted the closing of a preliminary hearing whenever there was a *reasonable likelihood* that prejudicial publicity would result from an open hearing.

Writing for a 7-2 majority, Chief Justice Warren Burger objected to the almost-routine closing of preliminary hearings in California. Noting that they are often lengthy proceedings, he said they should be open to the public unless "...there is a substantial probability that the defendant's right to a fair trial will be prejudiced by publicity that closure would prevent and ...(that) reasonable alternatives to closure cannot adequately protect the defendant's free trial rights."

Burger also declared that if the courtroom is closed during a preliminary hearing, it must be for as short a period of time as possible. He particularly cautioned against closing a lengthy preliminary hearing: "...Closure of an entire 41-day proceeding would rarely be warranted. The First Amendment right of access cannot be overcome by the conclusory assertion that publicity might deprive the defendant of (the right to a fair trial)."

In the aftermath of the Supreme Court's *Press-Enterprise II* decision, closed preliminary hearings have become rare--and judges are more reluctant to close other pretrial proceedings now. This ruling strengthens the growing body of constitutional law saying that the criminal justice system must be conducted openly, with the press and public invited to view the process.

In 1993, the Supreme Court reaffirmed the *Press-Enterprise II* decision, overturning a Puerto Rican law allowing closed preliminary hearings there. Puerto Rico, which has considerable local autonomy but is required to obey the U.S. Constitution, continued to hold closed preliminary hearings in felony cases whenever a defendant requested it, in spite of the *Press-Enterprise II* decision. Ultimately, a journalist asked to be allowed to attend a closed preliminary hearing and was turned down. He then challenged the constitutionality of the Puerto Rican court rules and prevailed when the U.S. Supreme Court held that Puerto Rico, too, must allow public access to these proceedings (*El Vocero de Puerto Rico v. Puerto Rico*, 508 U.S. 147).

All of the cases summarized up to now involved *criminal* court proceedings. In 1999, the California Supreme Court ruled in a widely noted case that *civil* courtrooms should usually be open to the public. In *NBC Subsidiary v. Superior Court* (20 C.4th 1178), the court overturned a number of restrictions that a judge had imposed on the press and public during a trial pitting actor Clint Eastwood against his former lover, actress Sondra Locke.

The California Supreme Court recognized a broad constitutional right of the press and public to attend civil court proceedings as well as criminal proceedings. In a sweeping decision, the state Supreme Court unanimously ruled that the First Amendment protects the right to attend civil trials.

Writing for the court, Chief Justice Ronald George traced the tradition of open courtrooms through history and relied heavily on the U.S. Supreme Court's landmark *Richmond Newspapers v. Virginia* decision in concluding that there is a constitutional right to attend civil court proceedings. Although *Richmond* specifically affirmed the public's right to attend only criminal trials, George noted that there are strong public policy reasons to recognize a similar right in civil cases. "(T)he public has an interest, in all civil cases, in observing and assessing the performance of its public judicial system, and that interest strongly supports a general right of access in ordinary civil cases," George wrote.

This marks the first time that any state's highest court has clearly recognized a constitutional right to attend civil court proceedings. It will surely have an impact in other states, making it more difficult for judges to justify closing civil court proceedings.

Access to Courtroom Documents

If the nation's courtrooms are supposed to be open to the public under most circumstances, what about public access to *court documents*?

In the aftermath of the Supreme Court's *Richmond* decision and the cases that followed it, a number of lower courts have ruled that the press and public have a right to see and copy court documents even in sensational cases. Actually, court documents have normally been open for public inspection ever since colonial times: both the common law and many state constitutions require that court records generally be open. Recent court decisions have reinforced that principle--and established that there is a *First Amendment* right of access to many court documents. No longer may a trial judge freely seal court records without even considering the public's right to know.

A good example of a court decision affirming the right of access to court documents as well as the right to attend courtroom proceedings is *Associated Press v. District Court* (705 F.2d 114, 1983), a decision of the ninth circuit U.S. Court of Appeals. This case arose when a federal judge closed some of the pretrial proceedings and also sealed many court documents in the celebrated federal drug case against automaker John DeLorean, who was accused of arranging a multimillion dollar cocaine deal to save his failing auto company.

The appellate court ruled that the judge's secrecy orders violated the public's First Amendment right of access to court documents and proceedings that have traditionally been open. The decision is especially noteworthy because of the court's specific recognition that the First Amendment includes a right of access to court documents. However, the court said this right must be balanced against other rights, notably the defendant's right to a fair trial. Reiterating earlier decisions, the court said a three-part test should be used in deciding whether pretrial secrecy is justified. Before sealing documents or barring the public from the courtroom, the judge must determine that:

1. Allowing public access would cause "a substantial probability that irreparable damage to (a defendant's) fair trial right will result;"
2. There are no alternative ways to protect the defendant's right to a fair trial; and

3. There is "a substantial probability" that the secrecy would actually prevent the defendant's rights from being violated.

In ordering the DeLorean records opened, the appellate court noted that there had been extensive publicity about the case in spite of the court records being sealed. The secrecy was not working and therefore could not be justified.

Also, in recent years the media have increasingly sought--and been granted--access to pretrial *discovery* materials and proceedings. As Chapter One explains, during the discovery process each side is permitted to obtain information from the other through a variety of techniques including depositions (in which witnesses answer questions under oath, with the responses recorded by a court reporter) and written statements of various types. Often these discovery materials are newsworthy--and crucial to the success or failure of a lawsuit. These materials frequently become a part of the public record, available for anyone to read or copy.

There has also been debate about the circumstances under which courts should allow broadcasters to copy and air audio and video tapes that are submitted as evidence. For example, in 1986 the ninth circuit U.S. Court of Appeals held that broadcasters have a limited right of access to taped evidence in the case of *Valley Broadcasting Co. v. U.S. District Court* (798 F.2d 1289). This case arose during the Las Vegas racketeering trial of reputed mafia kingpin Anthony "Tony the Ant" Spilotro, who was later murdered in a gangland-style execution in Chicago.

The trial judge refused to allow television station KVBC to copy taped evidence, but the appellate court ordered the judge to reconsider in light of KVBC's *common law* right of access to this material. (The court emphasized that Valley's reporters had no *constitutional* right to do anything more than attend the trial and copy a transcript of the evidence).

The appellate court said there is a "strong presumption" that broadcasters are entitled to copy taped evidence unless a judge has "articulated facts" to show that the copying would jeopardize a defendant's right to a fair trial. The court said there was no risk of the evidence being destroyed during the copying because the court's tapes were only copies of the FBI's masters. Also, the court saw no more risk of jurors being prejudiced by seeing the taped evidence on television than by watching the normal news coverage of the trial.

In the late 1990s there were several more appellate court rulings on the extent to which there is a right of public access to court records under common law principles.

In 1998, the ninth circuit U.S. Court of Appeals held that federal courts in the ninth circuit, including those in nine western states, must follow specific guidelines to determine when the press and public are entitled to see sealed transcripts of closed court hearings and similar court records.

In a case involving alleged criminal wrongdoing by former Arizona Governor Fife Symington, the court said judges must provide some safeguards before sealing records in newsworthy cases: "If a court contemplates sealing a document or transcript, it must provide sufficient notice to the public and press to afford them the opportunity to object or offer alternatives," Judge Sidney R. Thomas wrote for the court in *Phoenix Newspapers v. U.S. District Court* (156 F.3d 940). "If objections are made, a hearing on the objections must be held as soon as possible," he said.

The media objected to the sealing of transcripts of two hearings concerning alleged jury tampering during the ex-governor's trial. The appellate court held that there was no valid basis for the judge to keep these documents sealed even after the trial. In fact, the public had a right to know that two jurors had received threatening telephone calls, something that could have influenced their decision to convict the former governor, the court said. (In a separate decision, the court later overturned Symington's conviction because of problems in the handling of the jury at his trial.)

In another 1998 decision, the ninth circuit U.S. Court of Appeals held that the public also had a right to see the psychiatric evaluation of the notorious "unabomber," Theodore Kaczynski. In *U.S. v. Kaczynski* (154 F.3d 930), the appellate court held that the public's right to know outweighed Kaczynski's right of privacy. This decision was again based on common law principles, which require this balancing test to determine when court records should be open to the public. The court did not address another argument made by news organizations: that the press and public have a First Amendment right of access to documents as significant as Kaczynski's psychiatric evaluation. (Kaczynski eventually pleaded guilty to charges of making and mailing letter bombs that killed several people over a period of years.)

In short, the right of the press and the public to inspect court documents, obtain copies of videotaped evidence, and to attend courtroom proceedings has been often upheld since the Supreme Court put those rights in question with its *Gannett v. DePasquale* decision in 1979. Today a judge can deny public access to court documents and close courtroom proceedings only if it is clearly necessary to protect a defendant's right to a fair trial.

CAMERAS IN COURT

To the surprise of many Americans today, the kind of televised spectacle that unfolded in the O.J. Simpson trial could not have happened until recently: both television cameras and still photography were prohibited in almost all American courtrooms for many years, and those restrictions were not abolished until the 1980s.

Long before the Supreme Court addressed the fair trial-free press problem in the 1960s, there were recurring controversies about the effect the media had on the decorum of a courtroom. This debate centered on the presence of cameras and broadcast equipment in court. One of the early cases that dramatized the problem was the 1935 trial of Bruno Hauptmann, the alleged kidnapper and murderer of celebrated aviator Charles Lindbergh's young son. Although Hauptmann's trial did not take place until nearly two and one-half years after the kidnaping, the courtroom was so jammed with reporters and photographers that it was impossible to conduct orderly proceedings at times. There was a great deal of inflammatory publicity.

After Hauptmann was convicted and executed for the crime, a Special Committee on Cooperation between Press, Radio and Bar was established to recommend standards of publicity in judicial proceedings. In its final report, the committee said the Hauptmann trial was "the most spectacular and depressing example of improper publicity and professional misconduct ever presented to the people of the United States in a criminal trial."

At least partly in response to the Hauptmann trial, the American Bar Association in 1937 added Canon 35 to its recommended Canons of Judicial Ethics. That rule prohibited broadcasting and taking photographs in a courtroom:

> Proceedings in court should be conducted with fitting dignity and decorum. The taking of photographs in the courtroom, during sessions of the court or recesses between sessions, and the broadcasting of court proceedings are calculated to detract from the essential dignity of the proceedings, degrade the court and create misconceptions with respect thereto in the mind of the public and should not be permitted.

Canon 35 was later amended to prohibit television coverage specifically and also made applicable to hallways and other areas adjacent to courtrooms. In the early 1970s, it was revised again and incorporated into Rule 3A(7) of the ABA Code of Judicial Conduct, which replaced the old ABA Canons. At that point it permitted some television coverage of court proceedings, but only with the consent of all parties, and only then for use in educational institutions after all direct appeals were exhausted (which could be years later). Rule 3A(7) was eventually rewritten to allow much more extensive television coverage, but before that happened, journalists fought a long and frustrating battle for access to the nation's trial courtrooms.

These ABA rules, of course, were merely recommendations to the state and federal court systems; they were not mandatory. However, by the 1960s every state except Colorado and Texas had adopted rules forbidding most camera and broadcast coverage of court proceedings. And in 1946, radio broadcasts and photography were prohibited in federal courts by Rule 53 of the Federal Rules of Criminal Procedure. That rule was also later expanded to forbid television broadcasting and to prohibit photography or broadcasting in the "environs of the (federal) courtroom."

Stunned by these restrictions, broadcast journalists and photographers wondered why the First Amendment didn't protect their right to cover trials. The Supreme Court eventually ruled on these questions in a 1965 case, *Estes v. Texas* (381 U.S. 532). The case involved a Texas grain dealer with political connections, Billie Sol Estes. He was convicted of swindling a group of investors, but his conviction was reversed by the U.S. Supreme Court because two days of the preliminary hearing and part of the trial were televised under Texas' highly unusual court rules permitting it.

The television coverage of the pretrial hearing was obtrusive: there were bright lights, bulky cameras and cables trailing around the courtroom. Before the actual trial, the judge imposed some restrictions on the media, and the TV cameras were confined to a booth in the back of the room. However, it was still obvious to everyone in the courtroom that the cameras were there.

In reversing Estes' conviction, five Supreme Court justices said the television coverage had denied him a fair trial. Four justices agreed that the presence of television cameras inherently denied a defendant the right to a fair trial. The fifth member of the majority, Justice John Marshall Harlan, said it might be possible to televise ordinary trials--but not celebrated ones such as Estes'. However, the court also predicted that future technical advances might make television cameras unobtrusive enough for use in courtrooms.

Admitting Cameras: Chandler

By 1980, broadcast technology had indeed advanced. Thanks to solid-state electronics, cameras became much smaller and usable with far less lighting than was required in 1965. As a result, the rules began to change. A few more states began admitting still photographers and video crews into their courts. By 1980, about 10 states allowed broadcast coverage *even without the consent of the defendant*, something the *Estes* decision would not have permitted in major cases. Clearly, it was time for a new Supreme Court decision.

In 1981, the Supreme Court responded to the changing technology by changing the rules on courtroom television coverage. That happened in *Chandler v. Florida* (449 U.S. 560), a case in which two police officers were convicted of using their squad car and police radios in a burglary of a restaurant. At the time of their trial, Florida allowed television coverage of criminal trials on an experimental basis. Although the two officers objected, much of their trial was videotaped, and portions were shown on television. The two officers, Noel Chandler and Robert Granger, appealed their convictions, contending that the television coverage denied them a fair trial.

The Supreme Court ruled against Chandler and Granger. Voting 8-0, the justices held that the presence of television cameras does not inherently violate a defendant's constitutional right to a fair trial, although they left open the possibility that a defendant could show that his or her rights were violated in a specific case. Thus, the Supreme Court refused to overturn Florida's rules allowing television coverage of trials even without the defendant's consent. The court said that the states were free to adopt such rules if they wished.

Writing for the majority, Chief Justice Warren Burger said:

> An absolute constitutional ban on broadcast coverage of trials cannot be justified simply because there is a danger that, in some cases, prejudicial broadcast accounts of pretrial and trial events may impair the ability of jurors to decide the issue of guilt or innocence uninfluenced by extraneous matter.

However, the Burger opinion made it clear that criminal defendants are entitled to protest their convictions if they can show that media coverage actually prejudiced the jury:

(The) appropriate safeguard against such prejudice is the defendant's right to demonstrate that the media's coverage of the case, be it printed or broadcast, compromised the ability of the particular jury that heard the case to adjudicate it fairly.

Chief Justice Burger cited the dramatic changes in broadcast technology between the 1960s and the 1980s. Burger made it clear that *Estes* had not prohibited all experimentation with cameras in the courtroom. He noted that Chandler and Granger had not shown that their right to a fair trial was actually jeopardized by the broadcast coverage.

As a result of the *Chandler* decision, the states that already allowed television coverage or still photography in their courtrooms were free to continue doing so, and a number of additional states authorized electronic and photographic courtroom coverage after that. Some of the states that previously permitted cameras in their courtrooms only with the consent of defendants dropped that requirement after the *Chandler* ruling was announced.

Obviously, the *Chandler* decision was a victory for the media, but it is important to remember what it did and did not say. It simply said there is no constitutional prohibition on cameras in the courtroom. It did *not* say the broadcast media have any special right of access to the nation's courts. Rather, *Chandler* said that the states are free to allow cameras in court if they choose to do so. Even then, when a particular defendant can show that media coverage denied him a fair trial, he is entitled to a new trial.

The response to the *Chandler* decision came quickly. In 1982 the American Bar Association recognized the new trend and revised Rule 3A(7), which previously urged the states to impose severe restrictions on broadcast and photographic coverage of criminal trials. As rewritten, the rule says the states may allow judges to permit photographic coverage if certain safeguards are met. It specifies that the coverage must be "consistent with the right of the parties to a fair trial" and must be handled so that cameras "will be unobtrusive, will not distract trial participants, and will not otherwise interfere with the administration of justice." However, this rule is still voluntary and not all states adhere to it.

In 2001 all 50 states were allowing television or still photographic coverage of some court proceedings. South Dakota became the 50th state to admit cameras when the state Supreme Court announced in 2001 that it will allow video and audio coverage of oral arguments. However, only 40 states allow camera coverage of criminal trials as opposed to appellate court proceedings, and a few of those permit cameras *only with the consent of the defendant*, something that is rarely granted. On the other hand, at least 35 states allow trial judges to admit cameras to their courts even if a defendant objects.

Cameras in Federal Courts

The last major holdout in admitting cameras has been the federal court system. However, the federal courts have been under increasing pressure from members of Congress as well as media representatives to open their doors to the electronic media. In 1990 U.S. Chief Justice William Rehnquist went on the record as "by no means averse to the idea" of allowing cameras in federal courts. Writing a letter to a member of Congress who was concerned about this question, Rehnquist took a position opposite to that of former Chief Justice Warren Burger, who once said cameras would be allowed in federal courts "over my dead body."

Responding to these changes, the federal judiciary in 1991 began a three-year experiment allowing cameras in two U.S. (circuit) Courts of Appeals and six federal trial courts, but only during civil trials and appellate proceedings, not criminal trials. During the experiment, the media were required to use pooling arrangements: usually only one photographer or video crew was allowed in a courtroom. Also, the rules required photojournalists to wear "appropriate business attire" in court.

The federal experiment with cameras was extended through Dec. 31, 1994 by the U.S. Judicial Conference. However, the conference declined to extend the experiment beyond that date or to make it permanent. For a time, cameras were again barred from almost all federal court proceedings.

The Judicial Conference back-pedaled a little in 1996, adopting new rules under which each federal appellate court may decide for itself whether to admit cameras to *appellate proceedings*. The 1996 rules discourage federal *trial courts* from admitting cameras even during civil cases, but they do not flatly forbid cameras except during criminal cases. By 1999 federal appellate courts in the second circuit in New York and the ninth circuit on the west coast voted to admit cameras, while the other federal circuits declined to do so.

Advocates of cameras in federal courts were encouraged when Congress voted to have Timothy McVeigh's trial in the Oklahoma City federal building bombing case, which was held in Denver in 1997, shown to families of victims back in Oklahoma City by closed circuit television. Even though the video was not televised for the public to see, it was an instance of a video camera being allowed in a federal *criminal* trial, something that had been prohibited across the board. Some hoped it might lead to a relaxation of the ban on cameras at federal criminal trials.

On the other hand, opponents of cameras in the courts argued that the lack of television coverage was a major factor in the speed and efficiency of the trial, in which McVeigh was convicted and sentenced to die. Many contrasted the McVeigh trial with the months-long O.J. Simpson murder trial, in which almost everyone involved seemed to be playing to the cameras at times.

In recent years Congress has considered legislation to open federal trial courts to cameras several times. Some members of Congress were predicting that the legislation would pass in 2002. An earlier bill to allow cameras in federal courts gained powerful support when the American Bar Association endorsed the idea of having television cameras in courts to provide "gavel to gavel" coverage from the U.S. Supreme Court down to the local level. Advocates of greater electronic media access to federal courts were encouraged by the fact that the U.S. Supreme Court released audio tapes of oral arguments in *Bush v. Gore*--the case that ultimately determined the outcome of the 2000 presidential election. No one seriously suggested that the airing of those tapes caused any problem for the court. But it did allow millions of people to hear for themselves the arguments in this crucial

Supreme Court case.

While camera access to federal courts remains limited at this writing, photographers and the electronic media have won the right to take cameras and television equipment into state courtrooms from coast to coast. The media made considerable progress in this area during the 1980s and early 1990s.

Rethinking Courtroom Cameras

During the late 1990s many lawyers and judges had second thoughts about admitting cameras to trial courts; several states reconsidered their rules after the O.J. Simpson case. Fortunately for the media, the Simpson case did not lead to wholesale changes in the rules allowing cameras in most states. In fact, in both Virginia and Georgia, measures to ban cameras were defeated after the Simpson trial. But the Simpson case clearly stirred new concerns and rekindled old ones, especially in New York.

In New York, the Simpson case had a major impact. New York allowed cameras in its trial courts on an experimental basis starting in 1987, and the experiment was renewed several times. In 1995, the state legislature seemed ready to make the experiment permanent until the Simpson murder trial captured the nation's attention. Amidst that spectacle, the legislature balked--and almost barred cameras altogether. But on the day before the third extension of the camera experiment was to expire in 1995, the legislature relented and voted to extend the experiment once again.

In 1997, a panel appointed by New York Gov. George Pataki studied the issue extensively and recommended that cameras be allowed in the state's trial courts on a permanent basis. However, defense attorneys, victims' rights advocates and civil rights advocates formed the New York Fair Trial Coalition and began lobbying for a ban on courtroom cameras, calling the 10-year-long experiment "an abysmal failure." In mid-1997, the legislature allowed the experiment to end, thereby closing the state's trial courts to cameras.

In spite of the official ban on cameras in New York trial courtrooms, New York judges have sometimes allowed cameras during especially newsworthy cases, including the trial in 2000 of four policemen charged with killing Amidou Diallo, an unarmed West African immigrant. The judge in that case ruled that the ban on cameras was unconstitutional, a holding that set no legal precedent but was encouraging to the media nonetheless. Judge Joseph Teresi seemed concerned about the potential for misunderstanding of the Diallo trial, which was moved from the Bronx, where Diallo was killed in his apartment lobby, to Albany. Judge Teresi also surely knew that the prosecution would have a difficult time securing a guilty verdict under the legal ground rules. Central to his thinking in opening the court to cameras seemed to be the hope that the outcome would be better understood if the millions of New Yorkers who were troubled by this racially charged case could actually watch the trial on television.

If the televising of the Simpson murder trial had great impact in places like New York, it also had some impact in California itself, where the state Judicial Council set up a task force to reconsider the question of cameras in the courtroom.

The task force urged severe restrictions on cameras in California trial courts, including a ban on camera coverage of almost all pretrial proceedings. The Judicial Council rejected that proposal and retained a system in which it is up to the judge in each case to decide whether to admit cameras. However, judges were given strict new guidelines to follow in making this decision, and media lawyers predicted that the new guidelines would lead to cameras being barred more often. Among other things, the new rules forbid camera coverage of jury selection and proceedings that are closed to the public.

ONGOING ISSUES

After several decades of controversy, the fair trial-free press problem is still with us, despite several Supreme Court cases holding that the First Amendment rights of the press and public cannot be ignored in an attempt to protect a defendant's Sixth Amendment rights. If anything, the problem has become more serious recently, as the sensational coverage of the Rodney King and O.J. Simpson cases illustrates.

The disturbing trend toward closed courtrooms was slowed considerably by the Supreme Court's *Richmond Newspapers v. Virginia*, *Globe Newspaper v. Superior Court* and *Press Enterprise v. Superior Court* decisions. However, courtroom closures remain a problem in some states. Judges still cite the threat of prejudicial publicity to justify closing the doors often. Too often, some would say.

Journalists have been fighting another access problem in the nation's courtrooms. For years, cameras, tape recorders and particularly television equipment were unwelcome in most courts. However, that changed dramatically in recent years. All states now permit cameras and broadcast equipment in their courts under some circumstances, although not necessarily in trial courts. That trend was encouraged by the Supreme Court's *Chandler v. Florida* decision, which said broadcast coverage of court proceedings is not inherently prejudicial to defendants.

The *Chandler* case didn't give the media any special right to take their equipment into the nation's courtrooms, however. The Supreme Court left it up to the states to decide when (and if) cameras will be admitted to their courtrooms. Most states now permit television coverage and still photography in their courtrooms, at least under some circumstances. However, the federal courts are still largely closed to photographic and broadcast coverage. And in states where the rules do not ban cameras, many judges have been reluctant to authorize television coverage of sensational cases in the years since the O.J. Simpson murder trial.

Fortunately for the media, another major fair trial-free press problem of the late 1960s and early 1970s has largely disappeared. Thanks to the *Nebraska Press Assn. v. Stuart* Supreme Court decision, "gag" orders have been imposed on the media only rarely in recent years. News sources in many celebrated cases are still subjected to gag orders, but most trial judges now recognize that directly gagging the press is usually an unconstitutional prior restraint.

Nevertheless, conflicts between the rights of a free press and the rights of those accused of crimes will surely continue as long as both the First and Sixth Amendments remain in effect. This is not a legal problem that is likely to be resolved soon--if ever.

Moreover, the fair trial-free press controversy has generated several related legal problems, including the threat of contempt of court that arises when a judge demands--and a journalist declines to reveal--the source of information that was leaked to the press in violation of a gag order. The next chapter addresses these issues, detailing the growth of shield laws and the increasing use of contempt of court citations against reporters in the years since gag orders became popular.

A SUMMARY OF FAIR TRIAL-FREE PRESS

What Is the Problem?
The First Amendment guarantees freedom of the press--and that includes the right to cover crime news. However, a person charged with a crime has a Sixth Amendment right to a trial before an impartial jury--a jury made up of impartial persons who will base their decision solely on what they learn in court.

Why Shouldn't Jurors Learn About a Case in the Media?
Much of the information that may be published in the media will never be admitted into evidence in court and is not supposed to be considered by a jury.

Why Do the Courts Ignore Some of the Evidence?
A court may only hear evidence that was gathered by lawful means, not evidence secured in violation of the constitutional ban on illegal coerced confessions and illegal searches. In addition, a jury is only supposed to decide whether a defendant is guilty as charged--not whether he is a good person in general. Information about a person's past is often irrelevant (but newsworthy).

What Has Been Done About This Problem?
The Supreme Court has urged trial judges to take various steps to control inflammatory publicity, such as "gagging" participants in trials so they will not reveal prejudicial (and inadmissible) evidence to the media. However, the Supreme Court has also ruled that closing the courtroom is not usually the solution. The court has held that trials and pretrial proceedings should be open to the press and public unless the trial judge determines that a closed session is absolutely necessary to protect the defendant's rights.

How Do Most Journalists Feel About This?
Many journalists oppose the judiciary's attempts to control publicity; they believe that these efforts interfere with the public's right to know about the administration of justice. They warn of the dangers inherent in secret court proceedings.

Are Cameras and Video Equipment Allowed in Court?
Many lawyers and judges question the propriety of photographic and television coverage of the courts. They feel this may turn a dignified proceeding into a circus, with lawyers and witnesses performing for the cameras. However, the Supreme Court has ruled that the presence of cameras in court does not necessarily violate the defendant's right to a fair trial. Most states now allow cameras in their courtrooms under some circumstances, although cameras are not permitted in federal criminal courts.

CHAPTER EIGHT

Newsgatherer's Privilege

Sometimes journalists become participants instead of observers of the legal system. Journalists have been jailed and sued for refusing to identify confidential news sources--and they have also been sued for identifying confidential sources. Journalists have seen their newsrooms ransacked by law enforcement officials in search of evidence, and contempt of court--a legal threat that seemed to be disappearing at one time--has reappeared as a major problem for the news media.

For a time, journalists had relatively few brushes with the law over their newsgathering activities. But the turbulent 1960s changed that. Within the militant social movements of that era, some journalists were afforded special favors. Trusted journalists were given inside information that no law enforcement officer could hope to obtain. Reporters at times witnessed unlawful activities and then wrote about them. Long gone was the day when journalists just interviewed the police and thought they had adequately covered crime news. Reporters were covering both sides and increasingly questioning what they were told by law enforcement authorities or prosecuting attorneys. As a result, reporters not only had access to more information of interest to the authorities than ever before, but reporters came to be viewed less as allies than as adversaries.

The Watergate era in the early 1970s intensified those trends. Investigative journalists unearthed confidential information of great social and political importance, and often published it without revealing their sources. The Iran-Contra scandal of the 1980s, like Watergate, was uncovered by investigative journalists, again creating problems of source confidentiality. And in 1991 the entire nation watched in amazement as Law Professor Anita Hill told the Senate Judiciary Committee of alleged acts of sexual harassment by Supreme Court nominee Clarence Thomas. Without the work of journalists who relied on confidential sources (and risked jail sentences for refusing to name those sources), the public would never have known of Hill's allegations.

In many of these circumstances law enforcement officials, grand juries, the courts and even Congress began demanding information from journalists. This inevitably produced conflicts because most journalists believe they have an ethical duty not to identify their confidential news sources. Without confidential sources, journalists contend, many important news stories could never be reported. It is commonplace for "whistle-blowers" (people with inside information about wrongdoing in government or business) to come forward and talk to a reporter in secret, something they could not do without a pledge of confidentiality. If reporters had to reveal their sources, many people with important information would not talk to them out of fear of the recriminations that might result.

For this reason, journalists often find themselves ethically obligated to protect the confidentiality of news sources. On the other hand, judges want all relevant information to be made available in court, and they are increasingly using their contempt of court power to enforce orders requiring journalists to supply confidential information. Judges often feel that journalists are no different from other citizens and should comply with subpoenas. But many journalists feel their moral and ethical responsibilities in this area are so compelling that they would rather go to jail than break a promise of confidentiality.

In treating this difficult problem, this chapter discusses two separate but intertwined legal issues: contempt of court as a legal sanction and the *newsgatherer's privilege*--the right of reporters to keep their sources and unpublished materials confidential. The chapter also addresses several related issues, including state *shield laws* (laws that sometimes excuse journalists from disclosing confidential information).

CONTEMPT OF COURT

Contempt of court is a very old--and very new--legal problem for journalists. Basically, it originated with the idea that a judge should be able to control the decorum of the courtroom, and should have the authority to summarily punish those who violate that decorum. American judges have had contempt powers ever since the founding of the republic, and English and colonial judges exercised the power considerably before that.

There are several different kinds of contempt of court, and the distinctions among them are sometimes crucial in cases involving the media. First, there is *direct contempt*, which involves an act that violates the decorum of the court or shows disrespect for the legal process. A citation for direct contempt usually results from either misconduct in or near the courtroom or from the refusal to obey a judge's order. A photographer who surreptitiously takes a picture in a courtroom where cameras are not permitted risks a citation for direct contempt of court. Similarly, a reporter who refuses to reveal a source of information when ordered to do so by a judge may be cited for direct contempt.

In addition to direct contempt, there is *indirect contempt* (sometimes called *constructive contempt* or *contempt by publication*), which involves a disrespectful act remote from the courtroom. From the early 1800s until the 1940s, one of the major legal threats to journalists was indirect contempt. Journalists were frequently cited for contempt because of what they wrote about a judge or the justice system. Unlike other public officials, judges had the power to punish journalists--directly and immediately--for publishing things they did not like, and some judges used that power freely. Surprisingly, the First Amendment was not seen as a constraint upon judges' contempt powers until a 1941 Supreme Court decision, to be discussed shortly.

Still another distinction may be drawn between types of contempt of court: contempt may be either criminal or civil in nature. *Criminal contempt*, as the name suggests, is a punishment for an act of disrespect for a court. That disrespect might be in the form of a photographer taking unauthorized pictures in court or a lawyer violating court rules in his zeal to win his case. In either instance, the offense would be an example of direct contempt of court and would lead to a criminal sanction. The punishment might be a fine or a jail sentence, or both. Indirect contempt is also treated as a criminal matter at times, as it often was in the days when journalists were punished for writing stories that judges found offensive.

Civil contempt, on the other hand, is not a punishment at all, although it may lead to a stay in jail. Civil contempt is a form of coercion: a person who is disobeying a court order is locked up until he or she decides it would be better to obey the court order. Thus, it can result in an indefinite sentence. The contemnor (the person cited for contempt of court) is free to leave any time--if he or she obeys the court order. But if this person stands on principle and steadfastly refuses to obey the order, the jail term could theoretically last for a lifetime in some states. Reporters who refuse to reveal their sources are often cited for civil contempt, and thus run the risk of an extended stay in jail if no compromise can be reached.

One thing particularly troubles many journalists about contempt of court: often the judge unilaterally defines the offense, determines that there has been a violation, tries and convicts the guilty party, and sets the sentence--all within a few minutes. Contempt citations may be appealed, and many involving journalists are, but the fact remains that judges have enormous power in this area. Unfortunately, that power is sometimes abused.

Nevertheless, a judge's contempt power has limits other than the recourse to a higher court. For example, if a criminal contempt sentence exceeds six months, the judge is not permitted to decide the case unilaterally--without a jury. The U.S. Supreme Court has ruled that there is a constitutional right to a jury trial in cases of "serious" criminal contempt, but not in "petty" cases--which the court has defined as cases involving jail sentences of six months or less (see *Bloom v. Illinois*, 391 U.S. 194, 1968; *Baldwin v. New York*, 399 U.S. 66, 1970). This constitutional limit doesn't necessarily affect civil contempt, which has no fixed term in many instances.

By the early days of this century, contempt of court had become a major problem for journalists. Anyone who criticized a judge or gave unsolicited advice about the handling of a pending case risked a jail sentence, so the media were often reluctant to subject the judiciary to the same kind of criticism as other officials.

Curtailing Indirect Contempt

In 1941 the U.S. Supreme Court handed down a landmark decision on contempt of court, a decision that stripped judges of their vast power to use indirect contempt against the media. The case, *Bridges v. California* (314 U.S. 252), resulted from two unrelated contempt citations, one against Longshoremen's Union leader Harry Bridges and another against the *Los Angeles Times*. Bridges sent a telegram to the secretary of labor threatening to call a massive West Coast dock strike if a court ruling unfavorable to him was enforced. Meanwhile, the *Times* published several editorials that judges disliked, including one entitled "Probation for Gorillas?" that admonished a judge to impose tough sentences on a group of Teamsters Union organizers.

Both Bridges and the *Times* were cited for indirect contempt, or contempt by publication. Deciding the two cases together, the Supreme Court ruled that these contempt citations violated the First Amendment. The court prohibited contempt citations for public statements in the future, unless it could be shown that the publication created a *clear and present danger* to the administration of justice. The court rejected an older test under which any publication with an "inherent tendency" or "reasonable tendency" to interfere with the orderly administration of justice could be punished. As a result, it became much harder for a judge to justify citing a journalist for indirect contempt of court.

A few years later, the Supreme Court overturned two more indirect contempt citations against newspapers in *Pennekamp v. Florida* (328 U.S. 331, 1946) and *Craig v. Harney* (331 U.S. 367, 1947). In *Pennekamp*, the Florida Supreme Court had upheld a contempt citation against the *Miami Herald* for publishing editorials accusing local judges of being soft on criminals. The *Craig* case arose when a Corpus Christi, Texas, newspaper criticized a judge for his handling of a minor landlord-tenant dispute. In both cases, the U.S. Supreme Court reversed the contempt citations, reiterating that the clear and present danger test applies to indirect contempt citations. In neither case could the judge who issued the citation meet this test, the Supreme Court said.

In *Craig,* the court said the contempt power should not be used to punish newspapers for what they print "unless there is no doubt that the utterances in question are a serious and imminent threat to the administration of justice."

After those decisions, the use of indirect contempt against the media almost disappeared. For a time, about the only sort of contempt threat journalists faced was the kind that arises when a photographer is caught taking illicit courthouse pictures. To be cited for contempt, one almost had to advocate marching on the courthouse (see *Cox v. Louisiana*, 379 U.S. 559, 1965). In short, contempt of court citations stemming from what was published ceased to be a major legal problem for the media.

Direct Contempt and Journalists

Unfortunately for journalists, it wasn't long before a new contempt of court problem arose. After the *Sheppard v. Maxwell* decision in 1966 (see Chapter Seven), judges began to exercise more control over the conduct of the media in and around their courtrooms. Moreover, the *Sheppard* case encouraged judges to issue "protective orders" (or "gag" orders) directing trial participants not to reveal prejudicial information to the media. Naturally, when a reporter somehow obtains such information in spite of a gag order, the judge wants to know who violated the court order. More and more judges began asking journalists to identify their sources, citing them for direct contempt if they refused to answer such questions. The modern press-judiciary conflict over contempt and reporter's privilege had begun.

In the decade following *Sheppard*, hundreds of journalists were summoned before judges and questioned about their sources. In addition, grand juries as well as both prosecutors and defense attorneys began to view journalists as sources of useful information. During the discovery process in civil cases, journalists were called on to reveal their sources more and more often. In 1969 and 1970 alone, at least 166 subpoenas were issued seeking notes, tapes and film outtakes from the three national television networks. In the same two years, the *Chicago Daily News* and *Chicago Sun-Times* faced more than 30 subpoenas seeking information.

As time passed, this trend continued: in 1989 American news organizations received at least 4,400 subpoenas, according to a survey conducted by the Reporters Committee for Freedom of the Press. In 1993, the Reporters Committee concluded that the number had dropped slightly--to 3,500 subpoenas. More recent surveys showed an even greater decline in the number of subpoenas: 2,725 in 1997 and only about 1,300 in 1999. The Reporter's Committee said the declining number of subpoenas could indeed indicate that fewer subpoenas are being issued to the media--or merely that fewer news organizations are reporting the subpoenas received by their staff members.

Most of these subpoenas were for non-confidential information such as tapes of material that had been broadcast. However, several hundred subpoenas in each survey sought confidential information, forcing journalists to choose between violating their principles and risking judicial sanctions. In the early 2000s, journalists in some states were facing more threats of jail time for refusing to disclose confidential information than they had seen in many years. In 2001 and 2002, freelance writer Vanessa Leggett spent 168 days in jail--longer than any journalist in modern times--for refusing to divulge her confidential notes and tapes to a federal grand jury investigating a murder case.

What journalists have needed is a viable reporter's privilege, preferably at the federal level and in all states.

REPORTER'S PRIVILEGE

The term *privilege*, as used in this chapter, means an exemption from a citizen's normal duty to testify when ordered to do so in court or in another official information-gathering proceeding. In earlier chapters *privilege* was used in a different sense. In libel law, for example, privilege is a defense, a concept that allows public officials to make defamatory statements while performing their duties without fear of a lawsuit--and allows the media to accurately report those statements without the risk of a libel judgment.

In this chapter, however, privilege means an exemption from having to testify about confidential matters. The privilege concept is an old one that developed under the English common law. Several kinds of privilege were recognized under the common law, including the doctor-patient, lawyer-client and priest-penitent privileges. Each of these was established to protect a relationship that needed to be kept confidential for socially important reasons. These privileges have numerous exceptions, but all still remain viable today, at least under some circumstances. A doctor or lawyer, for instance, cannot be compelled to testify in court about many of the confidential things a patient or client may reveal. Likewise, in many instances a priest (or other member of the clergy) cannot be forced to testify about the things he/she learns from a parishioner during a confession or pastoral counseling.

While these privileges have been recognized for hundreds of years, the idea of a journalist's privilege developed mostly in the twentieth century. The common law traditionally did not recognize journalists as among the people who could invoke privilege. Maryland adopted a *shield law* (a statutory law shielding a reporter from the duty to reveal sources of information) in 1896, but it was some 30 years before the next such law was enacted anywhere in the United States. By 2000, shield laws had been enacted in at least 30 states, and these statutory laws are discussed later. However, some journalists began to argue that, even in the absence of a statutory shield law, the First Amendment protected their right to keep their sources confidential.

Is the First Amendment a Shield?

An appellate court first ruled on the argument that the First Amendment constitutes a shield law in a 1958 libel decision, *Garland v. Torre* (259 F.2d 545). Columnist Marie Torre made some unflattering statements about actress Judy Garland and attributed them to an unnamed CBS network executive. Garland sued for libel and demanded the identity of the source during the pretrial discovery process. Torre refused to name her source and a federal trial court cited her for contempt. She appealed, and the U.S. Court of Appeals upheld the citation; Torre was sentenced to 10 days in jail.

In an opinion by Potter Stewart (later a Supreme Court justice) the appellate court conceded that this case required a difficult balancing of two rights, but the information sought went to the heart of Garland's claim, Stewart said. Thus, the reporter's right to keep a source confidential had to give way to the right of a court to require the disclosure of relevant information.

After that decision, the idea of a constitutional privilege for journalists remained in limbo until the late 1960s. At that point the argument began to be seriously reconsidered in view of the flood of contempt citations of journalists. In 1970 and 1971, three court rulings on the issue were appealed to the Supreme Court. In one of these cases a court recognized a constitutional privilege, while in the other two the lower courts declined to do so. To resolve this conflict, the Supreme Court agreed to hear the three cases together.

The result was *Branzburg v. Hayes* (408 U.S. 665), an important 1972 decision that denied the existence of a journalist's constitutional privilege in cases such as the ones before the court. However, the ruling was confusing because the vote was 5-4, with only four justices rejecting a constitutional shield outright while another four (the dissenters) said there should be a qualified constitutional shield. The swing vote was provided by Justice Lewis Powell, who said the First Amendment should not excuse journalists from revealing their sources in these cases. However, Powell also suggested that the First Amendment might protect journalists' sources under some other circumstances.

The three cases that were consolidated in *Branzburg* involved widely varying circumstances, but all had one thing in common: reporters had refused to answer grand juries' questions about potential criminal activity they allegedly witnessed. The case where a court recognized a constitutional shield, *U.S. v. Caldwell*, involved Earl Caldwell, an African-American reporter for the *New York Times*. Caldwell had interviewed leaders of the militant Black Panther movement. In California, a federal grand jury investigating militant groups subpoenaed Caldwell to testify and to bring along his notes and tapes.

Caldwell refused even to appear. Not only would testifying breach his confidential relationships with his news sources, he said, but merely appearing would undermine that confidential relationship. Since federal grand jury proceedings are secret, the Panthers might never know for sure whether he kept his promises of confidentiality if he appeared.

Caldwell and the *Times* asked a federal district court to quash (set aside) the grand jury subpoena. The court granted the request only in part, and Caldwell appealed. The ninth circuit U.S. Court of Appeals ordered the subpoena quashed, ruling that Caldwell had a First Amendment right to keep his sources confidential. The U.S. government appealed to the Supreme Court.

In the second case of the *Branzburg* trilogy, *In re Pappas*, television journalist Paul Pappas was invited to a Black Panther headquarters in Massachusetts. He also promised not to disclose any information he was given in confidence. A county grand jury summoned him and asked what he had seen at Panther headquarters. He refused to answer many of the grand jury's questions, citing the First Amendment. The state Supreme Court rejected his argument and he appealed to the U.S. Supreme Court.

In the *Branzburg* case itself, *Louisville Courier-Journal* reporter Paul Branzburg observed two young men processing hashish and wrote a bylined story about it. The article included a tightly cropped photo of a pair of hands working with what the caption said was hashish. Later, Branzburg wrote an article about drug use in Frankfort, Kentucky. The article said he spent two weeks interviewing drug users. Branzburg was twice subpoenaed by grand juries, but he refused to testify, citing both a Kentucky shield law and the First Amendment. He challenged both subpoenas, but the Kentucky Court of Appeals ruled against him, declaring that neither the First Amendment nor the Kentucky shield law applied to his situation. The shield law, the court said, only applied to the identities of informants; it did not excuse a reporter from testifying about events he personally witnessed. Branzburg also appealed to the U.S. Supreme Court.

Consolidating the three cases, the Supreme Court said all three reporters had to comply with the grand jury subpoenas. Thus, the high court affirmed the lower court rulings in *Branzburg* and in *In re Pappas* while reversing the *Caldwell* decision. Four Supreme Court justices said flatly that a journalist has the same duty as any other citizen to testify when called upon to do so. However, Justice Powell, who provided the crucial fifth vote to reject a reporter's privilege in these cases, didn't go that far. He left open the possibility that the First Amendment might excuse a reporter from revealing confidential information under other circumstances. Powell said:

The asserted claim to privilege should be judged on its facts by striking of a proper balance between freedom of the press and the obligation of all citizens to give relevant testimony with respect to criminal conduct. The balance of these vital constitutional and societal interests on a case-by-case basis accords with the tried and traditional way of adjudicating such questions.

In short, the courts will be available to newsmen under circumstances where legitimate First Amendment interests require protection.

Thus, Powell felt a balancing process was necessary, with a constitutional shield for journalists available in some cases. One dissenter (Justice Douglas) took the absolute position that no restriction on freedom of the press was constitutional, not even the requirement that reporters testify in a court. The other three dissenting justices (Stewart, Brennan and Marshall) said they thought there should be a qualified journalist's privilege, based on the Constitution. These three justices said that, to justify requiring a journalist to reveal his sources, the government should have to show:

1. That there is probable cause to believe the journalist has clearly relevant information regarding a specific probable violation of law;
2. That the information cannot be obtained in some way that doesn't so heavily infringe on the First Amendment;
3. That there is a compelling and overriding interest in the information.

Even though these guidelines appeared in a dissenting opinion, they have been used by several lower federal and state courts in deciding journalist's privilege cases. The *Branzburg* decision, it turns out, was not quite the defeat for the media that it first appeared to be. The high court refused to create a constitutional shield law, but five of the nine justices (the four dissenters plus Powell) did say that the Constitution gives journalists at least a limited right to withhold confidential information. Since then, a number of lower courts have undertaken the balancing process suggested by Powell, often ruling that journalists' confidential information is privileged in situations different from the ones that led to the *Branzburg* ruling (grand jury investigations). In so ruling, courts have often looked to the guidelines in the *Branzburg* dissent.

Federal Rulings after Branzburg

Perhaps foreshadowing things to come, only a few months after *Branzburg* a federal appellate court looked to the dissenting and concurring opinions rather than the opinion of the court to find a precedent. Late in 1972, the second circuit U.S. Court of Appeals ruled that a case was sufficiently different from *Branzburg* to justify a different result. In *Baker v. F & F Investment* (470 F.2d 778), the court said a journalist has a constitutional right not to reveal his sources, at least under certain circumstances.

In *Baker*, the author of an article exposing the "blockbusting" practices of real estate agents (tactics calculated to panic white homeowners into selling out at low prices) was asked to reveal his source--but in a civil lawsuit between black home buyers and real estate firms. Since the source was in the real estate business, he could be subjected to harassment and economic harm if identified, the writer said. The appellate court allowed this writer to keep his source confidential, noting that unlike *Branzburg* (which involved grand jury investigations) this was a civil lawsuit to which the journalist was not a party. In this instance, the U.S. Court of Appeals said the First Amendment protected the author's right to keep his source confidential.

In the decades since *Branzburg* and *Baker*, courts have cited several rationales in addition to the constitutional argument for a reporter's privilege. Some federal courts have recognized a limited federal common law journalist's privilege within the Federal Rules of Criminal Procedure, the Federal Rules of Civil Procedure and the Federal Rules of Evidence. None of these rules actually mentions a reporter's privilege, but several federal courts have held that a qualified reporter's privilege is inherent in them. For instance, Rule 17(c) of the Federal Rules of Criminal Procedure authorizes courts to set aside subpoenas that are "unreasonable or oppressive." Rule 501 of the Federal Rules of Evidence recognizes the concept of evidentiary privileges. It doesn't specifically cite a reporter's privilege, but the Congressman most responsible for drafting Rule 501 said in Congress: "The language of Rule 501 permits the courts to develop a privilege for newspaper people on a case-by-case basis."

By the early 1980s federal courts from coast to coast had recognized a limited reporter's privilege on various grounds, including the First Amendment, the federal rules of procedure, federal common law or a combination of these. However, none of the federal courts recognized the sort of absolute privilege journalists wanted. Instead, the courts have weighed reporter's privilege claims against other considerations, often ruling that the privilege must give way--or at least that the media must let a judge examine the purportedly confidential information to determine whether it should be disclosed. In such cases, difficult confrontations between the press and the judiciary often result.

For example, in 1980 the third circuit U.S. Court of Appeals ruled against the producers of the CBS television program "60 Minutes" on a reporter's privilege issue. In *U.S. v. Cuthbertson* (630 F.2d 139, 1980), a federal judge in New Jersey ordered CBS to submit confidential materials to him for an in-chambers review. The judge hoped to determine whether the materials should be released to the defendants in a criminal case that stemmed from a "60 Minutes" story.

The *Cuthbertson* case resulted from a story entitled "From Burgers to Bankruptcy." It questioned the franchising practices of an East Coast fast-food chain, Wild Bill's Family Restaurants. A grand jury later indicted several Wild Bill's executives on various criminal charges. The executives subpoenaed CBS' outtakes and other unpublished information before their trial. The judge ordered CBS to provide much of the requested material for an in-chambers inspection. When CBS refused, the judge cited the network for contempt, and CBS appealed. The U.S. Court of Appeals affirmed the judge's order. The judge would have to see the materials in order to adequately weigh the defendants' need for them against the network's qualified privilege to keep them confidential, the appellate court ruled. Thus, the appellate court affirmed the contempt citation against CBS.

CBS asked the U.S. Supreme Court to review the lower courts' rulings, but the petition was denied. CBS reluctantly allowed the judge to review the requested materials.

Despite the *Cuthbertson* ruling, the federal third circuit has recognized a reporter's privilege in other circumstances. That circuit Court of Appeals has ruled that the privilege covers not only sources but also unpublished materials, and that it applies in both criminal and civil cases.

A year before *Cuthbertson,* the third circuit Court of Appeals affirmed a reporter's right to keep her sources confidential in a civil case, *Riley v. Chester* (612 F.2d 708, 1979). A police officer who was involved in a dispute with the local police chief made news by suing the chief. Then he subpoenaed a reporter to learn the source of a news story he considered unfavorable. However, the reporter, Geraldine Oliver of the *Delaware County (Pennsylvania) Daily Times*, refused to identify the source at a court hearing. Oliver was cited for contempt, but the appellate court overturned the citation because the identity of the source was not relevant enough to the case to override the qualified reporter's privilege. In so ruling, the court said that three requirements had to be met before a reporter should be required to disclose confidential information: (1) the information had been sought elsewhere; (2) the information could not be obtained from other sources; and (3) the information was clearly relevant to the case.

On the other hand, the third circuit refused to uphold the reporter's privilege in another 1980 decision, *U.S. v. Criden* (633 F.2d 346). In that case, Jan Schaffer, a Philadelphia *Inquirer* reporter, refused to testify about her conversations with a U.S. attorney during the "Abscam" case, in which many public officials were charged with bribery. The U.S. attorney admitted the conversations had occurred, and Schaffer was eventually cited for contempt. The third circuit Court of Appeals affirmed a contempt citation, noting that the issue here was not confidentiality (the source had already waived his right to confidentiality) but the conduct of the U.S. attorney in allegedly "leaking" word of the investigation to the press. In this criminal proceeding, the defendants were seeking a dismissal by alleging prosecutorial misconduct and sought Schaffer's testimony to show such misconduct. The appellate court ruled that the reporter's testimony was crucial to the case and thus affirmed the civil contempt citation. In so ruling, the court noted:

> When no countervailing constitutional concerns are at stake, it can be said that the privilege is absolute; when constitutional precepts collide, the absolute gives way to the qualified and a balancing process comes into play to determine its limits.

The third circuit then applied the three-part test it enunciated in *Riley* and found it satisfied. Thus, the court said the reporter's privilege had to yield to the defendants' Sixth Amendment right to a fair trial in this particular case.

In 1981 the U.S. Supreme Court refused to hear an appeal of the third circuit decision, in effect forcing Schaffer to choose between testifying and going to jail. However, all four of the Philadelphia "Abscam" defendants either were acquitted or had the charges against them dismissed. The contempt citation against Schaffer was dropped after she agreed to reveal whether she had in fact interviewed the U.S. attorney in the case, without revealing the content of the conversation. Nevertheless, the case was closed only because the defense attorneys said they no longer needed Schaffer's testimony--not because of any victory for the reporter's privilege.

Meanwhile, other federal appellate courts across America have also recognized a qualified reporter's privilege in the years since *Branzburg*. Like the *Criden* decision, these other decisions have emphasized the limited nature of the privilege, insisting that it must be balanced against other rights. For example, in *Silkwood v. Kerr-McGee* (563 F.2d 433, 1977), the tenth circuit Court of Appeals recognized the reporter's privilege and said it applied to a documentary filmmaker. The court overturned a trial judge's order requiring the filmmaker to reveal his confidential information because the party seeking it (the Kerr-McGee Corporation) had not diligently tried to secure it elsewhere first. In any future request for the filmmaker's (or any other journalist's) confidential information, the trial court was ordered to weigh: (1) the relevance and necessity of the information; (2) whether it went "to the heart of the matter;" (3) its possible availability elsewhere; and (4) the type of case involved. The *Silkwood* case attracted wide attention because Karen Silkwood was killed in an auto accident en route to testify to the Atomic Energy Commission about allegedly dangerous practices of her employer, the Kerr-McGee Corporation. In this civil lawsuit her heirs and others charged the company with violating her civil rights.

In a civil libel case, the first circuit U.S. Court of Appeals handed down yet another decision recognizing the existence of a journalist's privilege. In *Bruno & Stillman v. Globe Newspaper Co.* (633 F.2d 583, 1980), the court ruled on a dispute over pretrial discovery of a reporter's confidential sources by emphasizing the balancing of rights necessary in such cases. The court reaffirmed the existence of the privilege, but said the trial court had to balance the First Amendment interests involved against the plaintiff's need for the information. The case was remanded, with instructions for the trial judge to follow in deciding whether to order the newspaper involved (the *Boston Globe*) to disclose its sources for a series of stories criticizing the plaintiff's products (fishing boats).

The fifth circuit Court of Appeals also recognized the existence of a reporter's privilege in 1980, in *Miller v. Transamerican Press* (709 F.2d 524). But in that case, the Court of Appeals said the privilege had to give way to a libel plaintiff's need for confidential information without which he could not prove actual malice. Thus, that appellate court allowed the discovery of a magazine's confidential sources. The case resulted from an article in *Overdrive* magazine (a specialty magazine for truck drivers) alleging mishandling of the Teamsters Union's Central States Pension Fund. The appellate court upheld a lower court ruling that the identity of a source for the article "went to the heart of the matter" in the libel suit, since the plaintiff could probably not prove actual malice without checking on what the source told the article's author.

On the other hand, a federal district court in Washington, D.C., decided not to require a reporter to reveal his sources in a situation somewhat like the *Silkwood* case. In a 1979 decision, *U.S. v. Hubbard* (493 F.Supp. 202), the court recognized a *Washington Post* reporter's qualified privilege, and rejected the Church of Scientology's demand for the reporter's notes about an FBI investigation of the church. The court decided the privilege protected the reporter because the church could obtain the same information from FBI sources.

The U.S. Court of Appeals for Washington, D.C., followed up the *Hubbard* ruling with a 1981 decision that strongly endorsed the concept of a reporter's privilege, *Zerilli v. Smith* (656 F.2d 705). The case arose after U.S. Justice Department officials allegedly leaked wiretapped telephone conversations of Detroit underworld leaders to the *Detroit News*. Two reputed underworld figures sued the Justice Department and sought a court order requiring a reporter to reveal his sources.

The judge refused to issue such an order, and his decision was appealed. The appellate court affirmed the refusal, noting that the plaintiffs had not exhausted alternative means of securing the information. They had not queried Justice Department employees who had access to the tapes, for instance. In civil cases to which the reporter is not a party, a reporter is exempt from revealing his or her sources "in all but the most exceptional cases," the appellate court held.

The court said that to overcome the reporter's privilege, a civil litigant must show that: (1) the lawsuit is not frivolous; (2) the information sought is crucial to the case; and (3) all alternative sources for the information have been exhausted.

As more federal court decisions have helped to clarify the scope and limitations of the journalist's privilege, one other point has become increasingly clear: the privilege does *not* apply to a journalist's *eyewitness observations*. When a journalist happens to be an eyewitness to an event or activity that leads to a federal lawsuit, the courts have consistently declined to excuse the reporter from testifying about what he or she saw and heard. For example, in *Dillon v. City and County of San Francisco* (748 F.Supp. 722, 1990), a federal court reviewed the history of federal case law on reporter's privilege and concluded there was no legal basis for excusing a television cameraman from testifying about a confrontation that he witnessed between a citizen and police officers. The court pointed out that if the citizen were suing the police in a state court instead of a federal court, the California shield law would apply to the case, and it might excuse the photographer from testifying. However, state shield laws do not normally apply in federal cases.

In 1999, the second circuit Court of Appeals reaffirmed that reporter's privilege exists in the second circuit, which is important for journalists because that circuit includes New York, the home of many major print and broadcast news organizations. Ruling in *Gonzales v. NBC* (194 F.3d 29), the court upheld the privilege after initially denying its existence--but then held that NBC did not qualify for it in this instance. The case resulted from a 1997 NBC *Dateline* story about alleged police misconduct against minorities in Louisiana. The story led to a lawsuit against the police by a Hispanic couple, and they sought outtakes from NBC. The appellate court eventually ruled that the outtakes were relevant to a significant issue in the case and were unavailable elsewhere--and ordered NBC to comply with a subpoena for the outtakes.

The fourth circuit U.S. Court of Appeals also recently reaffirmed the existence of reporter's privilege (*Ashcraft v. Conoco Inc.*, 218 F.3d 282, 2000). The court said judges in the fourth circuit should determine whether the privilege applies by asking: 1) whether the information is relevant; 2) whether the information can be obtained by alternate means; and 3) whether the court has a compelling interest in the information.

Applying this test, the appellate court overruled a contempt citation that a judge had imposed on North Carolina newspaper reporter Cory Reiss for refusing to reveal who gave him sealed court documents. The appellate court ruled that the judge had not followed proper procedures in sealing the documents. Therefore, there was no compelling interest in determining who gave them to a reporter, the court held. The documents were clearly newsworthy: they revealed that Conoco had paid $36 million to settle a lawsuit alleging that it allowed gasoline to contaminate the drinking water used by 178 residents of a trailer park.

Upholding Reporter's Privilege: Shoen v. Shoen

Starting in 1993, a bitter family feud involving the founder of the U-Haul rental firm and two of his sons led to two landmark federal court decisions on reporter's privilege. When the second decision was announced in 1995, it was such a strong affirmation of journalists' rights that one communications lawyer was quoted in the press as saying, "it doesn't get any better than this."

The case began after author Ronald Watkins began doing research for *Birthright*, his book about the ugly battle between Leonard Shoen, the U-Haul founder, and his sons Mark and Edward. During the feud, Eva Berg Shoen, the wife of a third son, was brutally murdered at the family's vacation home in Colorado. Before Watkins interviewed him for the book, Leonard was widely quoted in the media as saying the two sons with whom he was feuding were responsible for Eva's death. They sued their father for libel and subpoenaed Watkins, demanding the notes and tapes from his interviews with their father.

Watkins appealed the subpoena, and the ninth circuit U.S. Court of Appeals ruled that an investigative *book author* such as Watkins could be protected by reporter's privilege. In *Shoen v. Shoen* (5 F.3d 1289, 1993), the court held that Watkins could not be forced to reveal his journalistic work product because the sons had not exhausted all other possible sources of the information they wanted. They had not even taken a deposition to obtain the information directly from their father before seeking it from Watkins. The appellate court said that a book author, like other newsgatherers, may invoke reporter's privilege under these circumstances. Like conventional news reporters, book authors have historically played an important role in bringing newsworthy events to light, the court noted.

The sons then obtained a court-ordered deposition from their father and went after Watkins' notes and tapes again. Watkins again refused to cooperate and was cited for contempt of court. Just before Watkins was to be jailed for contempt, the ninth circuit U.S. Court of Appeals intervened again. In *Shoen II* (*Shoen v. Shoen*, 48 F.3d 412, 1995), the court delivered another strong affirmation of the reporters' privilege concept. Here was a book author whose source was not confidential (everyone knew it was the elder Shoen). Nor did the source object to Watkins turning over his notes and tapes. Nonetheless, the court said a journalist could not be forced to turn over his research materials except as a last resort. The court adopted a new three-part test for cases such as this one (i.e., cases involving a reporter who is not a party to a civil lawsuit, who has no confidential sources, and whose sources do not object to the disclosure of the information sought). Reporters are often served with subpoenas under those circumstances.

Writing for the court, Judge Jerome Farris said that in this kind of case the party seeking to overcome the journalistic privilege must show that the information is "unavailable despite exhaustion of all reasonable alternative sources," is not cumulative (i.e., repetitive) and is "clearly relevant to an important issue in the case." The court said Watkins should not be compelled to turn over his notes and tapes because the information they contained was not clearly relevant to the sons' libel case and also because the notes and tapes were cumulative, duplicating information the sons had already obtained elsewhere.

Technically, the *Shoen* decisions are binding legal precedents only for federal courts in the states that make up the ninth circuit (seven western states plus Alaska and Hawaii). However, most federal appellate circuits have recognized a limited journalist's privilege. The consensus of the federal courts seems to be that journalists must sometimes reveal confidential information, but only if a party to a lawsuit clearly needs it and cannot obtain it anywhere else.

Because the journalist's privilege is limited, though, many news organizations are obliged to turn over such things as unpublished notes and video outtakes in response to subpoenas. The trend now is for attorneys representing news organizations to respond to subpoenas by attempting to negotiate a deal. Rather than fighting a legal battle over reporter's privilege that may or may not be winnable, attorneys often attempted to separate what is really crucial to journalists, such as protecting the identities of confidential sources, from what is often less crucial (e.g., protecting the remainder of a video segment that was aired in part). Often a deal is struck in which the news organization turns over some of the requested material in return for the right to keep sources confidential.

State Rulings on Privilege

In addition to the rulings by federal courts, a number of state supreme courts have recognized a journalist's privilege even in the absence of a statutory shield law. For instance, in 1977 the Iowa Supreme Court recognized a qualified First Amendment privilege for reporters. In a libel case, *Winegard v. Oxberger* (258 N.W.2d 847), the court roughly followed the three-part test in the *Branzburg* dissent, indicating that a reporter could refuse to reveal confidential information, at least in a civil proceeding, unless: (1) the information sought "goes to the heart of the matter" before the court; (2) other reasonable means of obtaining the information have been exhausted; and (3) the lawsuit in which the information is sought does not appear to be "patently frivolous." However, the Iowa Supreme Court weighed the case at hand and decided that three-part test was met, so the reporter was not excused from revealing her sources for several stories about a protracted divorce case that led to a libel suit.

A number of other state courts have also found a constitutional basis for a journalist's privilege, sometimes even in criminal proceedings when a defendant contended the information was needed for his or her defense. In so doing, some state courts have ruled that a qualified reporter's privilege is inherent in their own state constitutions as well as the federal Constitution. The Wisconsin Supreme Court so ruled in a murder case (*Zelenka v. Wisconsin*, 266 N.W.2d 279, 1978), although the court emphasized that the journalist's right to withhold confidential information had to be balanced against the defendant's need for the information. The case stemmed from a drug-related murder, and the defendant sought the identity of the source for an underground newspaper story that claimed the victim had been cooperating with narcotics officers. The state Supreme Court said the defendant had not shown that the privileged information would have helped him in his defense. Thus, the court upheld the reporter's right to keep a source confidential.

In 1982, the New Hampshire Supreme Court ruled in much the same way in another murder case: *New Hampshire v. Siel* (8 Med.L.Rptr. 1265). In that case two student journalists at the University of New Hampshire refused to release documents that would have revealed their sources for a story about the murder victim's alleged drug dealings. The state Supreme Court affirmed a judge's ruling that the materials sought from the student journalists would not have affected the outcome of the case.

Similarly, the supreme courts of Kansas, South Dakota, Vermont, Virginia and Washington have recognized at least a limited reporter's privilege in the absence of a state shield law (see *Kansas v. Sandstrom*, 581 P.2d 812, 1978; *Hopewell v. Midcontinent Broadcasting Corp.*, 538 N.W.2d 780, 1995; *Vermont v. St. Peter*, 315 A.2d 254, 1974; *Brown v. Virginia*, 204 S.E.2d 429, 1974; *Clampitt v. Thurston County*, 9 Med.L.Rptr. 1206, 1983; and *Senear v. Daily Journal-American*, 641 P.2d 1180, 1982).

Although California has a strong shield law in its state constitution, the California Supreme Court has also ruled that the concept of reporter's privilege sometimes protects journalists in situations not covered by the shield law. In a 1984 decision, *Mitchell v. Superior Court* (37 C.3d 268), the court ordered a trial judge to reconsider an order requiring a small newspaper to reveal its sources during a libel lawsuit. The case began after the *Point Reyes Light* published a series of articles critical of the Synanon Foundation, a purported drug rehabilitation program. The newspaper won a Pulitzer Prize for the stories, but Synanon sued for libel and then demanded names of the paper's sources during pretrial discovery.

The California Supreme Court conceded that the shield law did not protect journalists from having to reveal their sources when defending a libel case. But Synanon had a very weak libel case--and apparently was pursuing the lawsuit solely to learn the names of whistle-blowers within Synanon who had talked to reporters. The court said reporter's privilege should excuse journalists from revealing their sources when a libel case appears to be without merit or when the social importance of protecting the identities of sources outweighs a libel plaintiff's need for the information. This ruling was a major victory for journalists who believe they have an ethical duty to protect their news sources from reprisals.

On the other hand, some state supreme courts have flatly refused to recognize any journalist's privilege, even a qualified one. The Idaho Supreme Court, for instance, once refused to recognize any sort of First Amendment privilege for journalists, even in a civil libel suit (*Caldero v. Tribune Publishing*, 562 P.2d 791, 1977), although that court later moderated its stand on this issue. The *Caldero* case was particularly notable for the stridency of the court's language in condemning the concept of a reporter's privilege:

> In a society so organized as ours, the public must know the truth in order to make value judgments, not the least of which regard its government and officialdom. The only reliable source of that truth is a "press" ...which is free to publish that truth without government censorship. We cannot accept the premise that the public's right to know is somehow enhanced by prohibiting the disclosure of truth in the courts of the public.

Caldero was a libel case in which the plaintiff, a police officer, was criticized by a newspaper for shooting a suspect fleeing a minor crime. The officer, Michael Caldero, sought the identity of a source for the newspaper article during pretrial discovery, but the paper refused to reveal it. The Idaho Supreme Court affirmed a contempt citation against a reporter, flatly refusing to recognize any journalist's privilege.

However, three years after *Caldero*, the Idaho Supreme Court backpedaled on the privilege issue in *Sierra Life v. Magic Valley Newspapers* (6 Med.L.Rptr. 1769, 1980), another libel case in which the plaintiff demanded the identity of confidential sources during pretrial discovery proceedings. Here the *Twin Falls Times-News* published stories reporting on various legal actions taken against a life insurance company by other western states. The company never alleged that anything in the stories was false, but nonetheless a trial judge ordered the paper to name its sources during the pretrial discovery process. The paper refused, maintaining that the information was taken from public records and was accurate, and that sources within the company merely told reporters where to look to find these public records. When the paper refused to reveal the sources, the judge stripped the paper of all its normal libel defenses and entered judgment in the amount of $1.9 million for the plaintiff--still without any proof of the elements of libel (such as the negligent or malicious publication of a falsehood).

Faced with that situation, the Idaho Supreme Court felt compelled to retreat from its refusal to recognize a reporter's privilege, and it reversed the judge's action, reinstating the paper's defenses. The court acknowledged that a journalist's confidential information has to be shown to be *relevant* before it can be discovered. The court said the plaintiff had not shown that knowing the identity of the sources would help prove its libel case. This time, the Idaho Supreme Court was at least a little more sympathetic to the needs of the media:

> We recognize that the news media rely upon confidential sources in the preparation of many stories.... The ability to keep the identity of those

sources confidential is not infrequently a prerequisite to obtaining information. This interest, while legitimate, is not so paramount that legitimate discovery needs of a libel plaintiff must bow before it. But by the same token a trial court can be expected to exercise caution when it orders these sources be revealed. As the Supreme Court of the United States has suggested, the first question to be answered is whether the identity of the sources is relevant.

Thus, the Idaho Supreme Court afforded limited protection to journalists' sources in *Sierra Life*. Still, Idaho journalists enjoy far less protection from indiscriminate discovery or subpoenas than do journalists in many states. In states such as Idaho, journalists need a statutory shield law far more than they do in states where the courts have given them more constitutional protection.

STATUTORY SHIELD LAWS

Immediately after the *Branzburg* Supreme Court decision, a number of bills were introduced in Congress in an attempt to establish a federal statutory shield law. The plurality opinion in *Branzburg* emphasized that Congress would be free to enact a shield law even though the high court was declining to create one by judicial decree. However, Congress became hopelessly bogged down in the details of the proposed federal shield laws, and none was ever approved.

Two of the major problems that stymied Congress were the tough problem of deciding who should be covered and the "prescient witness" question. A prescient witness is someone who actually witnesses a crime, such as reporter Branzburg. There was a strong feeling in Congress that someone like Branzburg should have to testify about the unlawful activity he witnessed. But others in Congress felt such an exception would fatally weaken a shield law.

Moreover, Congress could never completely agree on the definition of a journalist. A shield law applicable only to mainstream journalists would have been politically acceptable, but it would have created serious new First Amendment problems. How could a federal law single out some journalists and give them a reporter's privilege without affording the same privilege to journalists working for less middle-of-the-road publications? On the other hand, many in Congress were simply unwilling to vote for any shield law that also protected "underground" journalists because such a law might help them develop even stronger ties to radical groups than they already had.

Also, Congress was unable to decide whether the federal shield law should be a strong one with few exceptions or a much weaker one with many exceptions. In addition, there was no consensus on the question of protecting reporters' notes and film outtakes as well as the identities of sources.

As a result of these unresolved issues, no federal shield law was enacted, leaving the question to the state legislatures and the courts to decide.

State Shield Laws

More than 30 states have enacted statutory shield laws, but these laws vary widely in philosophy and approach. Moreover, some state shield laws have been significantly altered by judicial interpretation. The highest court in one state (New Mexico) has gone so far as to overturn a statutory shield law as an unconstitutional encroachment on the information-seeking authority of the judiciary (see *Ammerman v. Hubbard Broadcasting*, 551 P.2d 1354, 1976). But another state (California) placed its shield law in the state constitution to make it safer from attacks on its constitutionality in the courts.

The following states adopted shield laws in the years shown here (listed in the order in which they adopted these laws): Maryland (1896), New Jersey (1933), Alabama (1935), California (1935), Arkansas (1936), Kentucky (1936), Arizona (1937), Pennsylvania (1937), Indiana (1941), Montana (1943), Michigan (1949), Ohio (1953), Louisiana (1964), Alaska (1967), New Mexico (1967), Nevada (1967), New York (1970), Illinois (1971), Rhode Island (1971), Delaware (1973), Nebraska (1973), North Dakota (1973), Minnesota (1973), Oregon (1973), Tennessee (1973), Oklahoma (1974), Colorado (1990), Georgia (1990), South Carolina (1993), Florida (1998) and North Carolina (1999). Many of these statutory laws have been extensively revised since their original enactment and, as just noted, many have been heavily modified by judicial interpretation.

In view of the widely varying judicial interpretations, it is difficult to generalize about state shield laws. Some appear to be very strong but have been fatally weakened by court decisions. Others have been upheld and even strengthened by court decisions. Generally, shield laws fall into three groups: (1) absolute privilege laws, which seemingly excuse a reporter from ever revealing a news source or other confidential information in a governmental inquiry; (2) laws that only apply the privilege if information derived from the source is actually published or broadcast; and (3) qualified or limited privilege laws, which may have one or many exceptions, often allowing the courts to disregard them under certain circumstances. Any list of which states' shield laws fall into each category could well be outdated before it is printed, in view of the frequent court decisions in this area.

Perhaps the best way to summarize state laws is to provide a checklist of things a good one should cover. You may wish to review your state's shield law (if any) and particularly the court decisions (listed after the law itself in your state's annotated statutes), using the research method described in Chapter One. In evaluating your state's statute and court decisions, determine if the law includes these provisions:

1. Coverage for all journalists, including newspaper, wire service, magazine, broadcast, free-lance and foreign reporters;
2. Coverage of all communications media, including newspapers, magazines, sporadically published newspapers and magazines (some "underground" publications are published only irregularly), wire services, broadcasters, book publishers, cable systems, online media, documentary film producers, etc.;

3. Applicability to all sources of information, regardless of whether the information is ultimately published or broadcast;

4. Applicability to journalists' "work product", i.e., notes, unpublished photographs and tapes, film outtakes, rough drafts, etc.;

5. Applicability to all official proceedings, including grand jury investigations, legislative and administrative proceedings, criminal and civil court proceedings (including the discovery process, even if the reporter is a litigant as in a libel suit);

6. Applicability even if the confidential source waives confidentiality by revealing his or her identity to a third party;

7. The absence of any exceptions that would create loopholes to exclude some reporters or some proceedings.

Obviously, few state laws include all of these provisions, but many journalists believe their needs would be best served by one that does. Still, state shield laws mean little until they are interpreted by the courts.

The Courts and Shield Laws

Sadly, the reality about shield laws is that many lawyers and judges don't like them. Judges sometimes find themselves dealing with reporters who possess important information--information that might well affect the outcome of a case--but who simply refuse to fulfill what judges see as a civic responsibility by disclosing it. Some judges wonder how a court can seek the truth under those circumstances, and they view shield laws as obstacles to justice, laws made by people who are, after all, politicians. Shield laws, they feel, strip the courts of some of their authority to do an important job. Many judges seem perfectly willing to weigh a journalist's privilege against other interests; some are willing to create such a privilege judicially in the absence of a statutory law, as already explained. However, when a legislature makes the decision for them--and makes the privilege absolute under all circumstances--judges tend to look for loopholes.

Perhaps the sentiment of the legal establishment was best summarized many years ago by John Wigmore, the preeminent scholar on the law of evidence. Speaking in 1923 about the nation's first shield law, enacted in Maryland in 1896, he said: "the (Maryland) enactment, as detestable in substance as it is in form, will probably remain unique."

Wigmore's prediction was wrong, of course, but the sentiment has been shared by generations of lawyers and judges. To them, a shield law--or any other law that exempts someone from testifying--may seem to be an obstacle to justice. For years judges have been whittling away at the older common law evidentiary privileges of doctors, lawyers and clergymen, and they have shown great ingenuity in interpreting the language of state shield laws to reduce their impact.

Probably the most notable example of a court decision overturning a shield law is *Ammerman v. Hubbard Broadcasting*, the New Mexico case cited earlier. In that decision the state supreme court said the legislature doesn't have the power, under the state constitution, to restrict a judge's authority in this way. Thus, the court simply invalidated the whole shield law by declaring it to be a *procedural* rule. The legislature has no authority to dictate procedural court rules to the judiciary, the court said.

However, amidst an outcry from journalists and their supporters, the New Mexico Supreme Court later added a provision to the state's Rules of Court to replace the invalidated shield law. The new court rule (Rule 11-514) is similar to many of the newer state shield laws in its scope. Basically, Rule 11-514 excuses journalists from disclosing their sources' names and other confidential information unless: (1) the information is "material and relevant" to a pending case, (2) the information is not available elsewhere, (3) the information is crucial to the party seeking its disclosure, and (4) the information is so important that the need for it outweighs the "public interest in protecting the news media's confidential information and sources."

No other state's highest court has gone quite as far as New Mexico's did in overturning a statutory shield law, but several other courts have handed down decisions narrowing the scope of state shield laws or broadening their exceptions. For instance, New York courts repeatedly carved out judicial exceptions to that state's shield law in the early years after its enactment in 1970. By 1973, the courts had created a prescient witness exception and ruled that the law didn't apply unless a reporter had promised confidentiality to a source. They also ruled that the law didn't apply if the information came to a reporter unsolicited (see *WBAI-FM v. Proskin*, 344 N.Y.S.2d 393, 1973). In New York, more than a dozen reported court decisions have gone against journalists who were seeking to keep sources or information confidential under the state's shield law.

Responding to that trend, in 1990 the New York Legislature effectively overruled many of these court decisions by strengthening the state shield law. As revised, the shield law protects not only the names of sources but also virtually all other unpublished information, including reporters' notes, film and video outtakes, and information that came to a reporter unsolicited. Such information need not be revealed by a journalist except if it is proven necessary in a criminal case and is unavailable elsewhere.

Across the continent in California, the pattern is much the same as in New York. State courts repeatedly narrowed the scope of a seemingly absolute shield law, even though the law itself was strengthened. First, an appellate court said the law simply didn't apply when a judge was trying to find out who violated a judicial "gag" order. The legislature doesn't have the authority to pass a law that makes it impossible for courts to investigate violations of their orders, the court held (*Farr v. Superior Court*, 22 C.A. 3d 60, 1971). Later, another California appellate court said the shield law didn't apply when the information might help exonerate someone charged with a crime, because the defendant's constitutional right to a fair trial was paramount. Thus, the reporter would be required to bring in the requested information for a judge's inspection in his chambers, with the judge entitled to release the information if he deemed it significant to the case (*CBS v. Superior Court*, 85 C.A.3d 241, 1978). In 1980 the people of California voted to place the shield law in the state Constitution, where it was somewhat safer from judicial modification.

However, judges continued to carve out exceptions to the California shield law, despite its constitutional status. For instance, in a 1982 case, *KSDO v. Superior Court* (136 C.A.3d 375), a California appellate court ruled that the shield law protects journalists only from contempt of court citations and not from other legal sanctions (such as the loss of otherwise valid defenses in libel cases). The problem of shield laws and libel cases is also discussed in Chapter Four.

In 1990, the California Supreme Court created another significant exception to that state's shield law, ruling that it does not necessarily cover reporters who have evidence that could help exonerate the accused. In *Delaney v. Superior Court* (50 C.3d 785), the court said the shield law ordinarily applies to eyewitness observations and other non-confidential information as well as confidential information in a journalist's possession. However, the court went on to say that the shield law does *not* apply when a judge determines that the information is crucial to the defendant in a criminal case: the defendant's fair-trial rights take priority and the journalist can be forced to testify--or jailed for contempt of court if he or she refuses.

On the other hand, the California Supreme Court later ruled that the *Delaney* principle does not apply to the prosecution. Prosecutors have no due-process right to circumvent the shield law and force journalists to testify or provide evidence in their possession (*Miller v. Superior Court*, 21 C.4th 883, 1999). As a result, the defense may be able to get around the shield law at times when prosecutors cannot, although at least one later case held that the prosecution must usually be afforded the right to cross-examine a journalist who testifies for the defense--or else the defense cannot use evidence obtained from the journalist.

The California Supreme Court has also ruled that in civil cases in which a journalist is not a party (i.e., the journalist is not suing anyone or being sued), the state shield law provides absolute protection from contempt of court citations (*New York Times Co. v. Superior Court*, 51 C.3d 453, 1990). In such civil cases, journalists are not legally required to reveal confidential information at all. However, if they do not, they may encounter certain legal problems, despite the existence of the shield law. For example, under California law a journalist may sometimes be sued for monetary damages by the losing party in a civil case if the journalist refuses to provide evidence that would help that party win the case.

In New Jersey, an equally large loophole was created in the state shield law by a state Supreme Court decision--but then the law was significantly strengthened. In the celebrated Myron Farber case (discussed later), the court said the shield law must give way when a criminal defendant seeks evidence held by a journalist. At the very least, the journalist must submit the material to a judge, who is to make an in-chambers evaluation and decide whether to release the information (*In re Farber*, 394 A.2d 330, 1978).

In the aftermath of the *Farber* decision, both the New Jersey Legislature and the state Supreme Court have acted to *strengthen* that state's shield law. In *Maressa v. New Jersey Monthly* (445 A.2d 376, 1982) and *Resorts International v. New Jersey Monthly* (445 A.2d 395, 1982), the state Supreme Court ruled that the shield law is virtually absolute in libel cases. In the *Maressa* ruling, the court said:

Twice in recent sessions, the legislature has made evident its intent to preserve a far-reaching privilege in this state. And twice in recent terms, this court has construed the shield law to protect confidential information to the extent allowed by the United States and New Jersey Constitutions. Absent any countervailing constitutional right, the newsperson's statutory privilege not to disclose confidential information is absolute.

Another state in which the courts have not only affirmed but strengthened a shield law is Pennsylvania, where the state Supreme Court significantly expanded the shield law's scope in *In re Taylor* (412 A.2d 32, 1963).

The Pennsylvania law specifically protected only "sources of information," but the court interpreted that language to include notes and other unpublished materials, even if they did not reveal the news source. Moreover, Pennsylvania state courts have liberally interpreted a phrase in the law that exempts reporters from revealing their sources "in any legal proceeding." "Any legal proceeding" really means what it says, the Pennsylvania courts have ruled.

Furthermore, a federal court deciding a case that arose in Pennsylvania chose to observe the state shield law in *Steaks Unlimited v. Deaner* (623 F.2d 264, 1980). That decision is not surprising, inasmuch as federal courts are supposed to apply most types of state law in "diversity of citizenship" cases (i.e., cases decided in federal rather than state courts only because they involve citizens of two different states). The Pennsylvania shield law did not apply in the federal case from Pennsylvania discussed earlier (*Riley v. Chester*) because it was not a diversity case. *Riley* was a federal civil rights case. The same was true in the *Dillon v. San Francisco* case, where a federal court declined to follow the California shield law.

In Minnesota, the state shield law was severely narrowed by a 1996 Minnesota Supreme Court decision, *State of Minnesota v. Turner* (550 N.W.2d 622). In that case, the court held that the shield law protected only the names of news sources and not other confidential information such as reporters' unpublished notes. In response, the Minnesota media launched a coordinated campaign to persuade the legislature to strengthen the shield law--and the legislature did so in 1998. The amended version of the Minnesota shield law specifically protects confidential information as well as the names of sources. Like many shield laws in effect today, the revised Minnesota shield law requires journalists to disclose otherwise-confidential information if it is clearly relevant to a court case, cannot be obtained elsewhere, and is so important that there is a compelling and overriding interest requiring disclosure.

In Florida, which never had a statutory shield law until 1998, the provisions of the new shield law are similar to those in the revised Minnesota law. In Florida, the shield law allows exceptions if the information sought is relevant, is unavailable elsewhere, and there is a compelling reason to force a reporter to testify.

In 2000, the Illinois Supreme Court held that the Illinois Reporter's Privilege Act, as the state's law is called, did not protect two reporters from revealing their news sources to a grand jury. The court held that the reporters' testimony was relevant and vital in a criminal investigation where the key issue was whether a city official had committed perjury by denying that he was one of their sources (*People v. Pawlaczyk*, 724 N.E.2d 901).

To summarize, journalist's privilege is in a state of change and uncertainty. Many states have shield laws, but even in these states reporters are often called upon to reveal their sources or other confidential information. On the other hand, in some states without shield laws the courts have judicially recognized a limited reporter's privilege, but the courts in other states have refused to take that step. On the federal level, a number of courts have recognized a qualified privilege as a matter of federal common law in the years since the Supreme Court's *Branzburg* decision.

JAILED JOURNALISTS: THREE NOTABLE CASES

Given the wide variety of laws and court decisions on shield laws, perhaps the best way to illustrate how this legal problem can affect a journalist is to describe the events that led to three of the best-known cases that have already been mentioned: the cases involving Bill Farr, a former *Los Angeles Herald Examiner* reporter (later with the *Los Angeles Times*), Myron Farber, a *New York Times* reporter, and Vanessa Leggett, a freelance book author whose 168 days in jail for refusing to reveal confidential information stands as a modern record.

The Bill Farr Case

In 1970 reporter Bill Farr was covering the trial of Charles Manson and his counterculture "family" for the sensational murders of actress Sharon Tate and a number of other persons. A protective ("gag") order was in effect, but two of the six attorneys in the case gave Farr a copy of a statement by a prospective prosecution witness who said Manson planned to torture and murder several more show business celebrities. Farr published the story and the trial judge, Charles Older, demanded to know who had violated the court order by giving Farr the information. Invoking the California shield law, Farr refused to name his sources. Judge Older accepted Farr's response at the time.

However, Farr later left the *Herald Examiner* and became a special investigator for the Los Angeles County District Attorney. Judge Older summoned Farr after the trial and again demanded the names of the sources, contending that the shield law applied only to currently employed reporters. Farr still refused to comply and was cited for contempt of court.

At this point a complex series of legal maneuvers began--and lasted for a decade. The Farr case eventually produced four appellate court decisions. In the first of the four (*Farr v. Superior Court*, cited earlier), a California appellate court in 1972 carved out a giant exception to the state shield law. The court said the legislature had no power to enact a law that would prevent a judge from finding out who had violated a court order. For the legislature to pass such a law is a violation of the autonomy of the judiciary as a separate and equal branch of government, the court ruled. Thus, the shield law was invalid in Farr's situation. The court sidestepped the question of whether the shield law should apply to former reporters, but the legislature quickly amended the law to close that possible loophole.

Still, the court had said the shield law didn't apply to Farr's situation. He had to reveal his sources or go to jail. He chose jail and began serving a potential life sentence for civil contempt after the California and U.S. Supreme Courts declined to review the first appellate ruling. However, after Farr had spent 46 days in jail, he was released by order of U.S. Supreme Court Justice William O. Douglas pending a second appeal.

After almost two more years of legal maneuvering, another California appellate court decision was handed down: *In re Farr* (36 C.A.3d 577, 1974). In that case, the court recognized the possibility that Farr might spend the rest of his life in jail rather than obey the court order by revealing his sources.

A procedure had to be created to allow the release of civil contempt prisoners whose violation of a court order was based on *a clearly articulated moral principle*. The appellate court said a hearing should be held to decide if: (1) Farr was refusing to obey the court order because of a moral principle; and (2) continued incarceration would not induce him to obey the court order. If Farr was obeying such a principle and was committed to stand firm regardless of the prospect of continued jailing, the trial court had to change the contempt citation from civil contempt (which has no time limit) to criminal contempt (with a maximum sentence of five days in this case).

At Farr's "moral principle" hearing, an array of media celebrities testified on Farr's behalf. A judge agreed that Farr was obeying such a moral principle and ended the civil contempt citation. The next day, however, Judge Older (the original judge who cited Farr for contempt) initiated a new criminal contempt proceeding and eventually sentenced Farr to five more days in jail and a $500 fine. That sentence was delayed while Farr again appealed. The U.S. Court of Appeals rejected Farr's challenge to the constitutionality of his contempt citation, deciding that the court's need to find out who violated the original court order outweighed Farr's journalistic privilege (*Farr v. Pitchess*, 522 F.2d 464, 1975). Ultimately, a California appellate court set aside the new contempt citation on the ground that it constituted a multiple prosecution for the same event (*In re Farr*, 64 C.A.3d 605, 1976).

At that point, Farr was free of the threat of additional jail time. However, even then his legal troubles were not over. Two of the six trial lawyers who had handled the Manson case filed a $24 million libel suit, contending that he had libeled them by saying two of the six lawyers had given him the information for the story that started the whole escapade. A trial judge dismissed that libel suit in 1979, but the two attorneys appealed the dismissal. In 1981--a decade after Farr's legal troubles began--an appellate court finally affirmed the dismissal of the libel suit.

In addition to enduring a decade of litigation, Farr was left with another problem: paying a huge bill for legal expenses. The *Los Angeles Times* covered Farr's legal fees after he became a *Times* employee, but not the legal expenses he incurred before that time.

The Myron Farber Case

Compared to Bill Farr's legal battle, Myron Farber's troubles were short-lived but nonetheless painful, both for Farber (who eventually spent 40 days in jail) and the *New York Times* (which was assessed $285,000 in fines). The case arose from stories Farber wrote for the *Times* in 1976, investigating a series of mysterious deaths at a New Jersey hospital some 10 years earlier. The stories were largely responsible for the indictment of Dr. Mario Jascalevich for murder.

About halfway through the doctor's six-month trial in 1978, his attorney got a subpoena ordering Farber and the *Times* to release information from interviews with witnesses at the trial. Farber and the *New York Times* refused and were cited for criminal and civil contempt of court. Farber was fined $1,000 and ordered jailed until he chose to provide the subpoenaed information. The *Times* was fined $100,000 plus $5,000 a day until the court order was obeyed.

Farber and the *Times* appealed the orders to the New Jersey Supreme Court, contending that both the First Amendment and the New Jersey shield law, a seemingly absolute one, protected them. The state Supreme Court denied their appeal, ruling that the shield law does not apply when a criminal defendant needs information from a journalist for his defense. The court ordered Farber and the *Times* to submit the requested material to the trial judge to examine in his chambers so the judge could decide whether the material was necessary to the defense or if it should be kept confidential.

Both Farber and the *Times* refused to comply. Farber went to jail and the *Times* continued paying $5,000 a day until the trial was concluded and the case was given to the jury, which eventually acquitted Dr. Jascalevich. After that, all of the other civil and criminal contempt citations were dropped. Eventually the governor of New Jersey pardoned both Farber and the *Times* and refunded the fines paid by the *Times*.

Some journalists were critical of Farber's and the *Times*' handling of this dispute, particularly because Farber struck up a lucrative book-publishing deal involving the Jascalevich case and because the whole confrontation might well have been avoided, given a little more diplomacy on all sides. Nevertheless, both Farber and the *Times* paid a high price for their principles, as did Bill Farr. Myron Farber's legal troubles didn't last nearly as long as Farr's, but he missed breaking Farr's record for jail time by only a few days.

Fortunately, few journalists have paid as high a price as Farr and Farber for protecting their sources. In fact, jail sentences for journalists are still unusual. But on the other hand, numerous journalists and news organizations lacking the resources available to the *Los Angeles Times* and *New York Times* have been forced to reveal confidential sources simply because the money to fight a costly legal battle was not available.

Moreover, after the *Farr* and *Farber* cases it became more commonplace for journalists to be forced to choose between revealing confidential information and going to jail. James C. Goodale, a New York lawyer who specializes in press law, reported a study of the problem at a Communications Law Symposium of the Practising Law Institute. He said he had identified 67 instances in which a reporter was ordered to reveal confidential information between September, 1982 and September, 1983. Although journalists eventually avoided revealing any confidential information or going to jail in 37 of the 67 cases, Goodale said the 67 cases represented about twice as many confrontations between reporters and the courts as occurred only a year earlier. He said more and more lawyers--both prosecutors and defense attorneys--were viewing journalists as fair game when subpoenas are being issued.

As noted earlier, thousands of subpoenas are issued to news organizations each year, and journalists comply with many of them. Most television stations routinely comply with subpoenas seeking tapes of material that has been aired, and an increasing number comply with subpoenas seeking tapes that were not aired to avoid fighting a difficult and expensive legal battle.

In addition, there have been enough instances of journalists being jailed for refusing to reveal their sources that most such incidents are not covered by the national news media as extensively as they once were. But the 1990 jailing of San Antonio, Texas, television journalist Brian Karem made national news because he faced a *six-month* sentence--a sentence the U.S. Supreme Court declined to set aside. However, Karem's jailing ended after only two weeks of his jail term. At that point he identified his news source (with her permission) and was freed.

In 1992, the issue was in the news again because two journalists risked a jail sentence for contempt of Congress by refusing to reveal their sources for Anita Hill's then-secret sexual harassment charges against Supreme Court nominee Clarence Thomas. A showdown was averted when key senators decided not to force the issue by issuing subpoenas to the reporters--subpoenas that would have resurrected a controversy that had already divided the nation. But the incident again illustrated the difficult problems journalists can face when they refuse to identify confidential sources.

The Vanessa Leggett Case

Perhaps no journalist who ever faced a subpoena for refusing to reveal confidential information started with less backing and ended up with more national recognition than Vanessa Leggett, who was jailed for 168 days in 2001 and 2002 for refusing to reveal her notes, tapes and confidential sources to a federal grand jury investigating a murder in Houston.

Leggett, who spent several years investigating the murder of Houston socialite Doris Angleton, was not initially recognized as a journalist by some. Although she was writing a book about the murder, she had not yet signed a contract when she was subpoenaed. Nor did she have many previous publication credits, although she had won a writing award for early work on her book and she taught a college writing class. But as her case unfolded, it became clear that she was indeed a journalist--a newsgatherer intending to communicate a newsworthy story to the public.

Leggett spent many hours interviewing Roger Angleton, who was accused of murdering Doris Angleton, the estranged wife of his wealthy brother, Robert Angleton. Roger apparently confessed during his interviews with Leggett--and then committed suicide shortly before his trial. Prosecutors brought charges against Robert for allegedly arranging the murder but he was acquitted in state court.

When a federal grand jury began investigating the case, Leggett was served with a subpoena. She refused to comply, citing her need for confidentiality as a journalist. She was cited for contempt and jailed in a federal detention center.

When it became clear that she was prepared to stay in jail indefinitely to protect her notes, tapes and confidential sources, the local and national media rallied to her cause.

A prominent Houston attorney for whom Leggett had worked as an investigator defended her, with support from attorneys representing news organizations, but both a federal judge and the fifth circuit U.S. Court of Appeals rejected Leggett's First Amendment claims. In an unpublished opinion that set no legal precedent, the fifth circuit refused to set aside her contempt citation, declaring that reporter's privilege does not apply to federal grand jury investigations--or even to criminal proceedings. The Supreme Court later declined to hear an appeal of this questionable decision; federal prosecutors argued that the case was moot because Leggett was out of jail by then.

Leggett was only released from jail because the grand jury adjourned in early 2002 without issuing any indictments. A second federal grand jury was convened later and did indict Robert Angleton, but without issuing a subpoena to Leggett.

By 2002, Leggett's own story of personal courage was making national news. Among other honors, she received the prestigious PEN First Amendment Award in New York and signed her long-sought book contract. Because of the length of time she was incarcerated for nothing more than protecting journalistic confidentiality, her case reopened the long-standing debate about the lack of a federal shield law--and about the weakness of reporter's privilege in the cases where a newsgatherer needs confidentiality the most.

LAWSUITS BY NEWS SOURCES

Ordinarily, when journalists promise confidentiality to a news source, they will go to great lengths to keep that promise. But on rare occasions a reporter--or perhaps an editor--will decide that a source's name is so important to a story that the name must be used, despite the fact that the source was promised anonymity.

Such a situation led to a landmark Supreme Court decision in the 1991 case of *Cohen v. Cowles Media Co.* (501 U.S. 663). By a 5-4 vote, the Supreme Court ruled that the First Amendment does *not* protect the media from being sued by a news source if a promise of confidentiality is broken, regardless of the newsworthiness and relevance of the name to an important story.

The case began in 1982 when Dan Cohen, a public relations aide to the Republican candidate for governor of Minnesota, gave several reporters documents that revealed petty misdeeds many years earlier by the Democratic candidate for lieutenant governor (an arrest at a protest rally during the 1960s and a $6 shoplifting conviction that was later set aside). Cohen leaked the information to the press just before the election.

Although the reporters promised not to identify Cohen, the editors of the Minneapolis *Star Tribune* and St. Paul *Pioneer Press* decided to use his name. If they were to run the story anonymously, they felt they would be dealing an unfair last-minute blow to the Democrats. If they did not publish the story, they could be accused of a cover-up to aid the Democrats. Thus, they felt the fairest way to handle the story was to run it and identify the source as a Republican activist.

When Cohen's name was used, he was immediately fired from his job. He sued for breach of contract, arguing that the promise of confidentiality was an enforceable contract under Minnesota law. A jury awarded him $200,000 in actual damages and $500,000 in punitive damages.

The two newspapers appealed, arguing that they should have a First Amendment right to publish truthful information about an event as newsworthy as an election--without risking a lawsuit afterward. The Minnesota Supreme Court agreed and overturned the entire jury verdict, ruling that the First Amendment indeed does protect the media from liability for publishing the name of the source for a clearly newsworthy story. The state court also ruled that Cohen could not sue for breach of contract under Minnesota law. However, the court said that a legal doctrine called *promissory estoppel* might allow Cohen to sue if the case were not barred by the First Amendment. In essence, promissory estoppel is a remedy for a person who does something in reliance on someone else's promise and is injured when that promise is broken, but who does not have a valid contract for some reason.

The U.S. Supreme Court overturned the Minnesota court's ruling. The high court said that promissory estoppel is a "generally applicable law" (i.e., a law that applies to everyone, not just the mass media). Generally applicable laws, the five-member majority said, apply to the media--despite the First Amendment. The First Amendment does protect the media's right to publish truthful information, but only if it is lawfully obtained. Writing for the majority, Justice Byron White said Cohen's information was not lawfully obtained because of the broken promise of confidentiality:

> ...(T)he truthful information sought to be published must have been lawfully acquired. The press may not with impunity break and enter an office or dwelling to gather news. Neither does the First Amendment relieve a newspaper reporter of the obligation shared by all citizens to respond to a grand jury subpoena and answer questions, even though the reporter might be required to reveal a confidential source.... The press ...may not publish copyrighted material without obeying the copyright laws.
>
> ...(T)he First Amendment does not confer on the press a constitutional right to disregard promises that could otherwise be enforced under state law....

The four dissenting justices disagreed with that line of reasoning, arguing that the story in question was so newsworthy that the use of Cohen's name was justified: voters had the right to know that the Republican gubernatorial candidate's public relations person was leaking stories to the press about a Democratic candidate. In his first major dissenting opinion as a Supreme Court justice, David Souter argued strongly for more First Amendment protection than the majority was affording to the mass media. Souter wrote:

> There can be no doubt that the fact of Cohen's identity expanded the

universe of information relevant to the choice faced by Minnesota voters ...(and) the publication ...was thus of the sort quintessentially subject to strict First Amendment protection. The propriety of his leak to respondents could be taken to reflect on his character, which in turn could be taken to reflect on the character of the candidate who had retained him as an adviser. An election could turn on just such a factor; if it should, I am ready to assume that it would be to the greater public good, at least over the long run.... Because I believe the State's interest in enforcing a newspaper's promise of confidentiality insufficient to outweigh the interest in unfettered publication of the information revealed in this case, I respectfully dissent.

Less than a year earlier, Justice Souter had replaced William Brennan, the author of *New York Times v. Sullivan* and many other key decisions upholding and expanding freedom of the press. While Souter may not have said all of the things Brennan might have said if he were still on the court, Souter's dissenting opinion surely was one with which Brennan would agree. In fact, in his early years on the Supreme Court, Souter joined in a number of decisions that belied his initial billing as a staunch conservative--including the court's decision to reaffirm the *Roe v. Wade* abortion decision in 1992. Perhaps this illustrates once again how dangerous it is to try to place Supreme Court justices in ideological categories--as both Republican and Democratic presidents have learned after making what they thought were safe (from their perspective) appointments to the high court.

The *Cohen* decision produced a variety of reactions among journalists. Many noted the irony of the press having to defend a lawsuit for *revealing* a source when reporters are much more likely to get into legal trouble for *not revealing* a source. And several media attorneys warned that the *Cohen* decision could encourage news sources who are unhappy with the way they appear in print or on television to sue the media, contending that they were promised confidentiality. Since most interviews between a reporter and a news source are private meetings between two people (with no witnesses available to corroborate either party's claims), such a lawsuit would end up being a credibility contest between the source and the journalist on the witness stand--with a jury acting as referees.

In the end, it will be up to each state to determine when news sources may sue the media for naming them. Some states may not allow such lawsuits except if there is a written contract promising confidentiality and it is breached (a remote possibility). Others, like Minnesota, may allow cases like this one to go to court on a promissory estoppel theory. The long-range implications of the *Cohen* case remain to be seen. What is clear now is that journalists have still another potential legal hazard to think about when they promise confidentiality to a news source.

For Cohen, the lawsuit finally ended in 1992--10 years after it began--when the Minnesota Supreme Court reconsidered the matter and held that he was entitled to collect the $200,000 in actual damages but no punitive damages. The state court said the promissory estoppel doctrine did apply in Cohen's situation.

NEWSROOM SEARCHES

For a time a related legal problem produced some alarm among journalists: law enforcement searches of print and broadcast newsrooms. In a disturbing 1978 decision, the U.S. Supreme Court ruled that the First Amendment does not create any privilege that would protect the media from newsroom searches even if no journalist is suspected of a crime (*Zurcher v. Stanford Daily*, 436 U.S. 547).

The case began in 1971 when a large group of demonstrators occupied the Stanford University Hospital and were forcibly ejected by Santa Clara County (California) sheriff's deputies and Palo Alto police. The *Stanford Daily*, the student newspaper at Stanford University, covered the incident, which was marked by considerable violence. A number of persons, including several law enforcement officers, were injured. Two days later, the *Daily* ran a special edition with a number of photographs of the disturbance.

The Santa Clara County district attorney's office got a search warrant and four police officers searched the *Daily's* office in the presence of several staff members. No member of the staff was suspected of any involvement in the violence, but the police searched the offices for additional photographs or relevant information. They found none.

The *Daily* staff sued the local officials in a federal civil action, alleging violations of the First, Fourth and Fourteenth Amendments. Both the federal district court and the ninth circuit Court of Appeals ruled in the student journalists' favor, but the Supreme Court reversed those rulings.

In a 5-3 decision, the Supreme Court said the Constitution does not prevent an unannounced search of a newspaper, even when no member of the staff is suspected of any crime. The court said that such a search is constitutional as long as the normal requirements of specificity and reasonableness are satisfied by the search warrant. Police would not be permitted to go rummaging through a newspaper's files indiscriminately, but if a warrant described specific evidence, the police could conduct a newsroom search in an attempt to obtain that evidence, the court ruled.

However, the Supreme Court made it clear that Congress or state legislatures could act to forbid newsroom searches; the high court merely said it wasn't going to forbid them judicially. Within days of the *Zurcher* decision, anti-newsroom search bills were introduced in a number of state legislatures and in Congress. Several states passed such laws within a few months, among them Illinois, California, Alaska, New Jersey and Virginia.

The Privacy Protection Act of 1980

Congress also passed a comprehensive federal law limiting newsroom searches, the Privacy Protection Act of 1980. This far-reaching federal law effectively overruled the *Zurcher* decision, outlawing most newsroom searches by federal, state and local law enforcement officials.

Under the Privacy Protection Act, law enforcement officials are prohibited from conducting searches and seizures involving "documentary materials" (photographs, tapes, films, etc.) held by newsgatherers except under very limited circumstances. The law allows such searches and seizures only when: (1) the person holding the information is suspected of a crime; (2) there is reason to believe the materials must be seized immediately to prevent someone's death or serious bodily injury; (3) there is reason to believe giving notice and seeking a subpoena would result in the materials being destroyed, changed or hidden; or (4) the materials were not produced as a result of a court order that has been affirmed on appeal.

The rules regarding a journalist's *work product* (e.g., notes and rough drafts) are even tougher. These materials cannot be seized except when the journalist is suspected of a crime or when necessary to prevent someone's death or bodily injury.

Anyone who is searched in violation of the Privacy Protection Act may sue the federal government and most state and local governments, but evidence secured in violation of the bill may nonetheless be used in court.

The law also directed the U.S. Justice Department to prepare guidelines for searches by federal officers involving evidence held by someone not suspected of a crime but also not working in a First Amendment-related area such as a newsroom.

Perhaps the major virtue of the Privacy Protection Act is that it usually requires law enforcement officials to get subpoenas instead of search warrants if they wish to obtain information from journalists.

Why is this distinction important? Search warrants are ordinarily authorized by judges unilaterally; the person who is the object of the search has no chance to argue against the issuance of the warrant. He or she first learns of the warrant's existence when law enforcement officers show up and enter the premises (by force, if necessary).

Subpoenas, on the other hand, are merely court orders directing someone to produce information. They can be challenged on legal grounds, and their issuance can be appealed. Granted, subpoenas are a major problem for journalists; some large newspapers and television stations have attorneys working nearly full time on the job of resisting subpoenas. Nevertheless, most journalists would much rather face a subpoena than have their offices raided by law enforcement officers armed with a search warrant.

At the very least, the Privacy Protection Act is an improvement over the situation in which journalists found themselves after the *Zurcher* decision. However, many journalists wish the law had been made even tougher: evidence secured during illegal newsroom searches should not be admissible in court, they contend. In the area of newsroom searches, as in the broader area of reporter's privilege, the major legal problems are not completely resolved.

ONGOING ISSUES

There is an inherent conflict between the need of journalists to protect their sources and other confidential information, on the one hand, and the need of the courts to obtain all relevant facts on the other. Judges believe they cannot mete out justice if they are denied access to crucial information. But journalists believe they must protect confidential information--for a number of socially important reasons.

At least two reporters have spent more than a month in jail to uphold their professional principles. And the jailing of journalists has become so commonplace that it is not always the headline news that it once was. It seems certain that new confrontations cases will continue to arise in many states.

Although more than 30 states have shield laws, the courts have repeatedly carved out judicial exceptions to these laws, requiring reporters to disclose confidential information despite the seeming applicability of a shield law. In a number of states, the appellate courts have significantly weakened state shield laws by judicial interpretation. In response to that trend, the voters in California, for example, placed their shield law in the state constitution. But almost as soon as that happened, the courts began whittling away at this new constitutional shield law just as if it were still merely an act of the state legislature.

However, there is a countervailing trend in the development of the reporter's privilege: a surprising number of both federal and state courts have recognized the privilege judicially, even in the absence of a statutory shield law. In no fewer than seven states lacking shield laws, the state's highest court has taken this step.

Moreover, federal courts in appellate circuits from coast to coast have recognized a reporter's privilege as a matter of federal common law if not constitutional law. This judicially created reporter's privilege is by no means absolute: the courts are reserving the right to weigh the privilege against other factors, such as the relevance of the requested information and the court's need for it.

Perhaps no case of a jailed journalist better illustrates the weakness of reporter's privilege than that of Vanessa Leggett, who spent 168 days in jail in 2001 and 2002, even though she was not accused of any crime. Her offense was asserting her need to protect her confidential notes, tapes and sources, and her case prompted a federal appellate court to flatly declare that reporter's privilege does not apply in federal grand jury investigations--or in criminal cases in general. Fortunately for other journalists, that legally questionable pronouncement came in an unpublished decision; it set no precedent.

Reporters and judges both feel there are important ethical principles at stake in this area. Like fair trial-free press, this issue represents an inherent conflict between two important rights, both of which must be respected in a democratic society. And like fair trial-free press, this dilemma is not likely to be resolved soon.

A SUMMARY OF NEWSGATHERER'S PRIVILEGE

What Is Contempt of Court?
Judges have the authority to punish persons who show disrespect for a court or disobey a court order by citing them for contempt. Criminal contempt is a punishment for a past misdeed; it results in a fine or jail sentence. Civil contempt is not a punishment but a form of coercion; persons cited for civil contempt may be jailed only until they obey a court order that they previously refused to obey.

Why Is Contempt a Problem for Journalists?
When a journalist promises to keep certain information (such as the identity of a news source) confidential, he/she has an ethical obligation to keep that promise, even if a court asks for the information. Thus, an ethical journalist may risk a contempt of court citation--and perhaps a jail sentence.

What Is Reporter's Privilege?
Because many important stories could not be researched without promising confidentiality to key news sources, journalists believe they should have a right to keep their film outtakes, unpublished notes and sources' names confidential. Reporter's privilege is the concept that a newsgatherer has at least a limited right to withhold this information, even when asked to reveal it by a judge.

What Is a Shield Law?
A *shield law* is a statutory law that excuses journalists from revealing confidential information when asked to do so in court. About 30 states have such laws, but some of them have so many exceptions that they provide a reporter little protection from a contempt of court citation. Also, courts have sometimes declined to accept shield laws, ruling that they improperly abridge the judiciary's authority.

Without a Shield Law, Does Reporter's Privilege Exist?
In *Branzburg v. Hayes*, a majority of the Supreme Court justices said a limited constitutional reporter's privilege exists under certain circumstances, but not under the circumstances that led to the *Branzburg* case (grand jury investigations where reporters allegedly knew of or witnessed unlawful activity). In the absence of an applicable shield law, a number of federal and state courts have recognized a qualified privilege for reporters to withhold confidential information. This privilege usually does not apply if the information is clearly relevant and necessary to the case and is unavailable from other sources.

Are Newsroom Searches Lawful?
Under the Privacy Protection Act of 1980, most newsroom searches by law enforcement agencies are unlawful. Newsroom searches are rare today.

CHAPTER NINE
Freedom of Information

Of the various legal battles modern journalists must fight, one of the most difficult and frustrating is the struggle for *freedom of information*. Without the freedom to gather the news, the freedom to publish is little more than a right to circulate undocumented opinions--a right to editorialize without any corresponding right to report the facts.

In recent years, the media have made significant gains in the battle for access to government meetings and records, but there have also been defeats. As governments have expanded in size, their sheer vastness has made it easy for them to conceal important information from public scrutiny. Moreover, the tendency of the federal government to keep secrets in the name of national security has grown drastically since World War II. Clinton administration officials estimated in 1995 that no fewer than 3.5 million documents a year were being declared secret for reasons of national security alone. Logically, the end of the Cold War and the overall easing of global tensions since 1989 should have reduced the need for government secrecy to protect national security. However, the threat of international terrorism inspired a new trend toward government secrecy in the era after Sept. 11, 2001.

Almost no one would argue that governments should release information that could assist potential terrorists, but if democracy itself is to work, the public still must be well informed about the activities and policies of government. How can the people intelligently compare the policies of rival candidates unless there is freedom of information? Without freedom of information, how can the people evaluate government policy toward countries such as Iran, Iraq and North Korea, cited by President George W. Bush as an "axis of evil" in a speech about the threat of terrorism after Sept. 11. Clearly, the need for national security must be balanced against the need for openness in government.

Moving closer to home, the same principle applies. Perhaps the threat of terrorism might justify secrecy about the inner workings of a nuclear power plant or a water treatment facility. But how can the voters know if the city budget is reasonable or the school board is following sound educational policies unless the public can know what those budgets and policies actually are and how they were determined?

Recognizing these needs, journalists and public interest groups have campaigned for openness in local, state and national government for years. That fight has produced dramatic improvements in public access to official records and proceedings. Today, all 50 states have laws requiring most agencies of state and local government to hold open meetings as well as laws guaranteeing public access to many government records. When World War II ended, only a few states had such laws.

On the federal level, millions of documents have been made public under the Freedom of Information (FoI) Act, a law that was not even enacted until 1966. In addition, many federal agencies that once treasured the privilege of holding private meetings to shape their policies are subject to the 1976 Government in the Sunshine Act. That law has many loopholes, but at least it has opened some formerly closed meeting room doors.

How significant are these laws? The number of requests for information under the federal FoI Act exceeds one million per year. Moreover, it would take a book as long as this one just to summarize all of the FoI Act lawsuits that occurred during the law's first 30 years of existence. But is the information that is ferreted out of once-locked government files under the FoI Act really important?

Using the FoI Act, researchers learned that the Central Intelligence Agency spied on Martin Luther King, Jr. and other pioneer civil rights leaders, and that longtime FBI Director J. Edgar Hoover used the FBI in efforts to discredit King. Other FoI Act inquiries revealed government experiments with mind-controlling drugs that killed at least two persons in the 1950s. Meanwhile, still other researchers using the FoI Act learned of the CIA's efforts to overthrow a government in Chile and to use journalists as foreign agents.

Journalists also used the FoI Act to expose the safety hazards posed by the Ford Pinto's gas tank, to help find out why the Hubble Space Telescope's mirror failed to work properly, and to alert citizens to the environmental hazards posed by the Department of Energy's nuclear weapons plants in several states.

The list of socially important government secrets uncovered because of the FoI Act is nearly endless. The FoI Act was used to discover long-concealed health hazards caused by radiation and the dangers of Agent Orange to Vietnam War veterans. It was also used to unearth important details of America's unsavory role in the Bay of Pigs invasion of Cuba and President Nixon's plans for military action in Cambodia.

Moreover, the federal FoI Act is just one law among many intended to open closed doors and unlock secret files, although it is a very important one. This chapter summarizes these freedom of information laws, and then surveys other problems journalists encounter in their quest for information.

THE FEDERAL FREEDOM OF INFORMATION ACT

When Congress enacted the federal FoI Act in 1966, its primary users were expected to be journalists. Certainly journalists who were alarmed at the growing trend toward government secrecy took the lead in lobbying for its passage. But ever since the FoI Act was approved, its main users have been corporations, academic researchers and private individuals with a special interest in a particular topic. Most of those actually filing formal requests for information are lawyers representing private clients, not journalists representing the public interest. In fact, historians and other academicians file far more requests under the FoI Act than journalists. FoI Act requests take time, and journalists tend to need information too quickly to wait for a formal request to be honored by a slow-moving bureaucracy. Perhaps the authors of the FoI Act were a little naive when they ordered government agencies to respond to FoI requests in 10 working days; critics have said that no government agency moves that quickly. Recognizing this fact, in 1996 Congress extended the time limit to 20 working days as part of a major FoI reform, which is discussed later.

What are the basic provisions of the FoI Act? It declares that a vast number of records kept by administrative agencies of the federal government shall be open for public inspection, and that copies are to be provided at a reasonable cost. Unless these "agency records," as they are called, fall within one or more of nine specific exemptions, they must be opened to the public on request.

To facilitate this process, a 1974 amendment to the FoI Act requires agencies to publish lists of their records and even their fee schedules for making copies in response to FoI requests. Fees may be waived or reduced when an agency feels that releasing a document would benefit the general public and not just one individual or company.

That provision has caused some controversy, since it allows agencies to charge one requester more than another for the same information. The FBI once charged the major wire services $9,000 for material that it provided free to one writer whose work was a public service (in the FBI's opinion).

A requester need not justify his FoI Act request, but those who can convince an agency that they are serving the public interest have a big advantage at the agency's cash register. In 1986 Congress amended the FoI Act to reduce the fees government agencies may charge news organizations and nonprofit educational or scientific institutions, while increasing the fees that commercial businesses must pay. Businesses must usually pay for the time government agencies spend searching for requested documents and reviewing them prior to their release. Journalists and nonprofit groups are usually excused from those charges altogether. Other non-commercial requesters may encounter different rules, depending on the agency they are dealing with. For some years the Federal Communications Commission, for example, did not charge non-commercial requesters for the first two hours of search and review time or for the first 100 pages released in response to a request. But after two hours and 100 pages, the meter started running.

Although federal agencies may give a price break to journalists and nonprofit groups, they are not supposed to consider the identity or purpose of a requester in deciding whether to release a particular document. The U.S. Supreme Court once said this: "Because Congress clearly intended the FOIA to give any member of the public as much right to disclosure as one with a special interest in a particular document ... the identity of the requesting party has no bearing on the merits of his or her FOIA request" (*Department of Defense v. Federal Labor Relations Authority*, 510 U.S. 487, 1994).

In an effort to avoid complying with the law, federal agencies have sometimes claimed that honoring a certain FoI Act request would be prohibitively expensive.

The courts have generally not heeded that argument, instead compelling agencies to comply despite the alleged cost. For instance, in a 1980 decision (*Long v. Internal Revenue Service*, 596 F.2d 362, cert. den. 446 U.S. 917), a federal appellate court held that the IRS had to supply requested information even if it would cost $160,000, as the IRS claimed.

For FoI purposes, the term "agency" is defined to include executive departments, military departments, government corporations, government controlled corporations, other executive agencies and independent regulatory agencies. In short, it covers just about the entire federal government except for Congress and the courts.

Once an agency receives a formal request for a particular record, it is supposed to respond by either providing the record or denying the request (and explaining why it did so) within 20 working days. However, the courts have repeatedly excused government agencies from this very short time limit, ruling that the deadline is "directory" rather than "mandatory." Thus, FoI Act requests may take a year or more, although a federal appellate court has ruled that an eight-year delay was too long (*Fiduccia v. Department of Justice*, 185 F.3d 1035).

If a request is denied, the requester has a right to appeal the denial, first through the agency's appeals procedures and then to the federal courts. Thousands of lawsuits have been filed in the federal courts under these provisions of the FoI Act. As a result of amendments to the FoI Act in 1974 and 1976, federal judges are empowered to review the requested documents in private in their chambers and then rule on the validity of an agency's decision to deny the request. The judge must decide if the documents properly fall within one of the nine exceptions, thus justifying government secrecy. Briefly, the nine exceptions are:

1. Documents that have been properly classified as confidential or secret in the interest of national security or U.S. foreign policy;
2. Documents relating to "internal personnel rules and practices" of federal agencies;
3. Matters that are specifically exempted from public disclosure by some other statutory law;
4. Trade secrets and certain other financial and commercial information gathered by government agencies;
5. Interagency and intraagency memoranda that involve the internal decision-making process (e.g., working papers and tentative drafts);
6. Personnel and medical files and similar documents that should be kept confidential to protect individual privacy;
7. Investigatory files compiled for law enforcement purposes, but only when the disclosure of such files would: (a) interfere with law enforcement; (b) deprive a person of a fair trial; (c) constitute an unwarranted invasion of personal privacy; (d) disclose a confidential source; (e) disclose investigative techniques and thereby permit someone to circumvent the law; or (f) endanger the life or safety of any individual;
8. Documents prepared by or used by agencies regulating banks and other financial institutions;

9. Oil and gas exploration data, including maps.

Obviously, many of these exceptions are so broad and all-encompassing that they can be used to justify massive government secrecy. In addition to the millions of government documents that are classified for national security reasons, millions more are confidential for other reasons. The exceptions for law enforcement files and internal memoranda, for example, have been widely used to withhold information from the public.

Using the FoI Act

Anyone seeking information under the FoI Act should make it clear in writing that he or she is making an FoI Act request, perhaps mentioning the act by its official citation: Title 5 of the United States Code, Section 552 (or simply 5 U.S.C. 552). The request should be as specific as possible, identifying the desired record exactly as the agency identifies it. Each agency publishes information about its record-keeping scheme in *The Federal Register,* available online and in many large libraries, to assist FoI Act users in properly identifying the records they seek.

An FoI request should first be directed to the official designated to handle FoI requests within a particular agency. If that fails, the request should next go to the agency head, unless the agency has specified a different appeals procedure.

If that too fails, the requester has little recourse except to go to court--or perhaps cultivate "sources" within the agency who may be willing to "leak" the material surreptitiously.

If a request for information under the FoI Act is denied, the person who made the request is supposed to receive a list of the documents being withheld with an explanation of the legal justification for withholding each document. This list is called a *Vaughn Index,* because a federal appellate court ruled that such an accounting is necessary in *Vaughn v. Rosen* (484 F.2d 820, 1973).

Under a policy adopted by the Bush administration after Sept. 11, federal agencies were directed to abandon a Clinton administration policy adopted in 1993 that required the release of information unless it is "reasonably foreseeable that disclosure would be harmful." Under the new policy, announced by Attorney General John Ashcroft on Oct. 12, 2001, government agencies are encouraged to keep information secret whenever there is a "sound legal basis" for doing so. This new directive cited the importance of "safeguarding national security, enhancing the effectiveness of law enforcement agencies, protecting sensitive business information and, not least, preserving personal privacy."

Ashcroft's new policy also said, "it is only through a well-informed citizenry that the leaders of our nation remain accountable to the governed and the American people can be assured that neither fraud nor government waste is concealed." But when requested information falls into a gray area where either openness or secrecy might be legally defensible, the new policy encouraged government officials to opt for secrecy by saying, "Any discretionary decision by your agency to disclose information protected under the FOIA should be made only after full and deliberate consideration of the institutional, commercial, and personal privacy interests that could be implicated by disclosure of the information."

It remains to be seen how this new policy will affect public access to government information. However, the new policy and the spirit of the times--with today's heightened concern for national security and personal privacy--seem likely to make life more difficult for journalists and others who need access to government information. Many journalists and civil libertarians were concerned about the trend toward government secrecy in the post-Sept. 11 era. For example, many were troubled by the secrecy that surrounded the detention of about 750 immigrants who were deemed security threats after Sept. 11, the secrecy of the military tribunals that were to be used to try some detainees, and the limited press access to the battlefields during the war in Afghanistan.

On the other hand, the Bush administration's new FoI Act directive did not rescind a second Clinton administration FoI policy, an executive order signed by President Clinton in 1995 that made major changes in the way federal agencies handle secret information. The executive order revised the rules under which agencies classify documents as secret for national security reasons. Among other things, the 1995 executive order requires agencies to declassify most documents after 25 years and make them available for public inspection. Agency heads such as the director of the CIA are permitted to make exceptions to the 25-year-disclosure rule, but only with the approval of a committee set up to review these exceptions. The 1995 rule exempts CIA documents that would reveal the names of its "intelligence sources" (i.e., spies) as well as Defense Department documents relating to such things as war plans. While FoI attorneys pointed out that the 1995 policy still gives agencies such as the CIA and Pentagon wide latitude to keep secrets, several were quoted as saying it was a distinct improvement over the old system--a change that will make millions of additional government documents accessible to the public under the FoI Act.

For anyone who plans to use the FoI Act, an extremely valuable booklet is available from the Reporters Committee for Freedom of the Press in Washington, D.C. Titled *How to Use the Federal FoI Act*, it includes government agency FoI directories and fee schedules, plus general instructions and samples of request letters, appeals letters, fee waiver requests and the legal documents needed to file a lawsuit.

FoI Lawsuits

If the time comes when an FoI Act lawsuit is necessary, the act includes a provision allowing a court to require the government to pay the requester's attorney's fees and court costs if the lawsuit is successful. And if the court finds that agency personnel acted capriciously in denying the original request, the Civil Service Commission is required to hold a proceeding to decide if the government employees who denied the request should be disciplined.

Of the numerous lawsuits filed under the FoI Act, a few should be summarized to illustrate the typical workings of the act and the role of the courts in interpreting it. The first exception (for national security) is a broad one that the courts have tended to uphold. In fact, judges have sometimes declined to even look at classified material in their chambers if an agency submits a convincing affidavit (a statement made under oath) to justify the need for keeping the document secret. In a 1977 ruling (*Bell v. U.S.*, 563 F.2d 484), a federal appellate court said such an affidavit should be given "substantial weight."

However, other courts have ruled that documents must have been properly classified for the national security exception to apply. In a 1974 case (*Schaffer v. Kissinger*, 505 F.2d 389), a federal appellate court held that Red Cross reports on South Vietnamese prison camps had not been classified under proper procedures and thus had to be released.

Nevertheless, the national security exception remains a gigantic and very troublesome loophole in the FoI Act. Numerous abuses of the national security classification system have been revealed over the years, among them instances where it was used to conceal corruption, government waste and bureaucratic bungling.

The Assassination Records Review Board, created by Congress in 1992 after years of protests about the federal government's insistence on keeping so many records about the assassination of John F. Kennedy secret, completed a lengthy review of classified records in 1998. The board concluded that the government had "needlessly and wastefully" withheld millions of records that did not need to be kept secret, and that this secrecy "led the American public to believe that the government had something to hide" about the Kennedy assassination.

The Pentagon's preoccupation with secrecy is at times even amusing. In his book, *Without Fear of Favor: The New York Times and Its Times*, Harrison Salisbury told a story about the Pentagon Papers case (discussed in Chapter Three). The government was trying to prove that publishing the Pentagon Papers would cause irreparable harm to national security, so an official communique from the National Security Agency's director was brought into a Washington courtroom in a double-locked briefcase. Inside the briefcase were three envelopes of diminishing size, each inside the next larger one. Inside it all was a very sensitive secret message. At the crucial moment of its unveiling, a *Washington Post* reporter pulled from his pocket a Congressional document that included the identical message, published long ago for all the world to read.

Another noteworthy illustration of the same point was the government's attempt to censor *The Progressive* magazine when it planned to publish an article on the hydrogen bomb, an article prepared from readily available public information. (That case is also discussed in Chapter Three). It has been suggested more than once that foreign spies in America should spend their time reading popular newspapers and magazines and browsing in public libraries rather than snooping around the Pentagon.

Nevertheless, the national security exception to the FoI Act must be taken seriously because it allows the government to withhold many important documents from public inspection, thus concealing not only legitimate military and diplomatic secrets but also much information that should be public in a democracy.

Among the other exceptions, several have stirred considerable controversy. The trade secrets and private business information exception, for instance, has prompted a number of double lawsuits with federal agencies caught in the middle. On one side, someone (often a competitor) is seeking information that may be covered by the trade secrets exception. On the other, the private company that originally submitted the information is suing to compel the government to keep the material confidential. The latter kind of lawsuit is called a "reverse FoI" suit.

Of more interest to journalists and scholars, however, have been the exceptions for law enforcement information, internal personnel rules and internal working documents. The federal courts have shied away from compelling law enforcement agencies to disclose information that they contend is essential to their investigatory functions. However, the courts have been somewhat less inclined to let federal agencies broadly interpret the exception for internal agency materials. On a number of occasions, agency efforts to maintain internal confidentiality have failed.

One notable case of this sort is a 1976 Supreme Court decision, *Department of the Air Force v. Rose* (425 U.S. 352). That case arose when legal researchers sought records of honors and ethics code violation hearings at the Air Force Academy, with the names of alleged violators deleted. The Supreme Court ruled that where there is a genuine and significant public interest in an agency's policies, those policies should be disclosed unless their revelation would jeopardize an investigation or prosecution. The court noted the clear Congressional intent that such information be made public as long as no individual's personal privacy rights are threatened.

Many other practical problems have become evident as federal agencies, information seekers and the courts have attempted to live under the FoI Act. One of the most important of these problems is the fact that agencies can escape the law by either destroying or concealing sensitive records, and public officials can sometimes circumvent it by simply taking their records home with them. There may be no way for anyone outside an agency to prove that a given document ever existed, if the agency steadfastly maintains that it didn't.

Moreover, in a 1980 decision (*Kissinger v. Reporters Committee for Freedom of the Press*, 445 U.S. 136), the Supreme Court ruled that former Secretary of State Henry Kissinger could keep his diary of official telephone calls secret because he took the diary home with him, unless the government itself should compel him to return it. In response to Justice William Rehnquist's majority opinion, the dissenting justices warned that this ruling would give major government officials freedom to completely escape the reach of the FoI Act by simply taking their important papers home.

In another major 1980 decision (*Forsham v. Harris*, 445 U.S. 169), the Supreme Court made it clear that private organizations doing research under government grants need not make their data public. The court ruled that such research data simply doesn't fall within the definition of "agency records" and is thus not covered by the FoI Act.

In 1982, the Supreme Court continued the trend toward a narrow interpretation of the FoI Act, handing down two more decisions that restricted public access to government information under the act: *FBI v. Abramson* (456 U.S. 615) and *U.S. Department of State v. Washington Post* (456 U.S. 595).

In *Abramson*, the high court ruled that some of the information compiled by the Nixon administration about its critics was exempt from disclosure under the FoI Act. The FBI had originally gathered the information for investigatory purposes, and the court said the information was covered by the law enforcement investigatory exception even though it was eventually recompiled and put to partisan political uses.

The *Abramson* decision produced dissents from four Supreme Court justices (Blackmun, Brennan, Marshall and O'Connor). In two separate opinions, they said the majority was in effect amending the FoI Act by its broad interpretation of the law enforcement investigatory exception. Justice O'Connor's opinion pointed out that the records in question were clearly not compiled in their present form for law enforcement purposes and therefore should not fall within the exception.

The *Washington Post* case expanded the scope of the exception for "personnel, medical and similar files." The court held that records indicating whether an individual holds a U.S. passport are a "similar file" that falls within the exception if the individual's interest in privacy outweighs the public interest in disclosure.

The case began when the *Post* sought to find out if two Iranian nationals living in Iran were also U.S. citizens with American passports. The State Department refused to provide that information, contending that to provide it would "cause a real threat of physical harm" to both men. The *Post* sued under the FoI Act. In deciding the case, a virtually unanimous court said:

> Although Exemption 6's language sheds little light on what Congress meant by "similar files," the legislative history indicates that Congress did not mean to limit Exemption 6 to a narrow class of files containing only a discrete kind of personal information, but that "similar files" was to have a broad rather than a narrow meaning.

Eight justices signed the majority opinion. Justice O'Connor concurred without joining in the court's opinion. The Supreme Court sent the case back to a lower federal court to determine if the privacy rights of the two Iranians outweighed the public interest in disclosure, thus justifying the government's nondisclosure of their citizenship status.

Again considering privacy issues, the Supreme Court ruled in 1997 that a government agency's mailing list should not be disclosed under the FoI Act (*Bibles v. Oregon Natural Desert Assn.*, 519 U.S. 355). The court balanced the public's right to know against the privacy rights of those on the list, and ruled that names on such a list should only be released when their disclosure would "shed light on an agency's performance of its statutory duties or otherwise let citizens know what their government is up to."

In 1985 the Supreme Court restricted the scope of the FoI Act in another way, this time by excluding many Central Intelligence Agency (CIA) records from disclosure under the FoI Act. In the case of *CIA v. Sims* (471 U.S. 159), the court ruled that the CIA may keep the identities of its sources of intelligence data secret even when national security is not involved.

The case arose when the Ralph Nader Public Citizen Health Research Group sought the names of researchers and institutions that participated in a CIA project involving mind-altering drugs during the 1950s. The project required researchers to administer drugs that are now illegal to unwitting subjects. Some of the researchers and institutions agreed to have their names released, but many others refused--and the CIA withheld their names. The Nader organization then sued to obtain the names.

The FoI Act has no specific exception to protect the identities of the CIA's sources. However, the blanket exception for information exempted from disclosure by another law (exception 3) has been used by the CIA to keep its sources secret. The law that established the CIA authorized the agency to keep its sources of information secret.

In ruling in favor of the CIA, the high court emphasized that intelligence work requires secrecy, and that the fear of being identified may lead intelligence sources to refuse to cooperate with the CIA. Thus, the court chose to liberally interpret the law allowing the CIA to keep its sources secret.

The Supreme Court drastically restricted public access to FBI records in a 1989 case, *U.S. Department of Justice v. Reporters Committee for Freedom of the Press* (489 U.S. 749). In one sweeping decision, the court ruled out public access under the FoI Act to the FBI's criminal histories on at least 24 million people. These criminal histories--often called "rap sheets"--are computerized compilations of personal information from various sources, including state and local law enforcement agencies.

The court's unanimous ruling creates a vast across-the-board exception to the FoI Act for records that might in any way affect personal privacy. Moreover, the court's language is so broad that it may apply to other government agencies and not just the FBI, severely limiting the FoI Act's applicability to records about individual people.

Explaining the court's decision, Justice John Paul Stevens wrote:

> (W)e hold as a categorical matter that a third party's request for law enforcement records or information about a private citizen can reasonably be expected to invade that citizen's privacy, and that when the request seeks no 'official information' about a government agency, but merely records that the government happens to be storing, the invasion of privacy is 'unwarranted.'

The Supreme Court said in this far-reaching decision that there is a difference between records concerning the activities of a federal agency itself and records maintained by the agency about individuals, with individual records broadly exempted from the FoI Act.

This ruling was widely assailed by journalists and others who pointed out that many of the most telling revelations about past government wrongdoing have come from records about individuals. The mere fact that the FBI is keeping records on some individuals not suspected of a crime may raise serious questions.

A few months later, the Supreme Court went still further, ruling that many documents obtained by the FBI from other government agencies are also exempt from disclosure. In a case called *John Doe Agency v. John Doe Corp.* (493 U.S. 146, 1989), the high court said the government could not be compelled to release certain documents concerning the Grumman Corp. because they were "compiled for law enforcement purposes." Grumman requested the documents from the Defense

Contract Auditing Agency during a federal grand jury investigation of aerospace industry accounting practices. The auditing agency responded by turning the documents over to the FBI, which then refused to release copies under the FoI Act exception for documents compiled for law enforcement purposes. The Supreme Court agreed that such documents should be exempt from disclosure.

Taken together, these 1989 rulings and several earlier Supreme Court decisions seem to be sending a message to the federal bureaucracy, and especially to the FBI: when in doubt, withhold information that is requested under the FoI Act. The court has repeatedly declared that the FoI exceptions "must be narrowly construed." The court even said that in the *John Doe Agency* case. But when faced with a specific request for government information, the court continues to rule that the exceptions allow broad government secrecy.

However, the Supreme Court backpedaled a little in a 1993 decision, *U.S. Department of Justice v. Landano* (508 U.S. 165). In that case, the court held that the exception for law enforcement records does not give the FBI an automatic right to refuse to release information that might identify a source. The court acknowledged that ordinarily FBI informants' names should be kept confidential, but the court said the FBI is not entitled to a legal presumption that this kind of information is *always* confidential. Instead, the FBI must consider such requests for information on a case-by-case basis.

Although many of the Supreme Court decisions interpreting the FoI Act have involved the national security and law enforcement exceptions, the high court has interpreted a number of other provisions of the law. In 2001, for example, the Supreme Court unanimously ruled that the Bureau of Indian Affairs cannot keep its correspondence with Indian tribes confidential under the FoI exception for "inter-agency and intra-agency memorandums or letters." In *Department of the Interior v. Klamath Water Users Protective Association* (532 U.S. 1) the court said communications between the BIA and Indian tribes are not comparable to communications between government agencies and their paid private consultants, which were previously ruled confidential under this FoI exception.

Other FoI Act Problems

Users of the FoI Act also encounter other practical problems with the act. One of them, as already noted, is the problem of delays in compliance. Many federal agencies have large backlogs of FoI requests, and the courts have not chosen to enforce the time limits contained in the act. This poses a particular problem for journalists as opposed to other users of the FoI Act. While a historian or a business enterprise may be prepared to wait a year or two for important information, that kind of a delay is often fatal for a journalist working on a timely news story.

Another problem with the FoI Act can be high court costs and attorney's fees. Those who sue the government for the release of documents and "substantially prevail" in court are entitled to have the government pay their costs and attorney's fees. However, if the lawsuit is not successful, the document requester is likely to have a large legal bill to pay.

366 Freedom of Information

The FoI Act doesn't say anything about those who seek documents having to pay the government's expenses if they lose. However, the general rules governing federal appellate court proceedings say that the winner is entitled to recover court costs (but not lawyers' fees) from the loser in any lawsuit that reaches a federal appellate court.

On the basis of these rules, the U.S. Justice Department sought--and eventually won--an order from a federal appellate court requiring singer Joan Baez to pay $365 of the government's court costs in an FoI Act appeal. Baez gained the release of about 1,500 pages of FBI records about her, but she sued to obtain additional files the government had kept secret. Although she lost, at first the appellate court refused to order her to pay the government's court costs. Then the court reconsidered and ruled that she had to pay (*Baez v. U.S. Justice Department*, 684 F.2d 999, 1982). This case was troubling to many civil libertarians, not because of the amount of money Baez was ordered to pay but because of the precedent it established.

Still another problem encountered by those who use the FoI Act is the legally sanctioned censoring of documents. The act permits agencies to delete portions of documents that fall within an exception while releasing the remainder of the document. The result is sometimes a document with page after page of blank space, interrupted only by conjunctions and prepositions.

Perhaps most serious of all, the federal bureaucracy has made a concerted effort to weaken the FoI Act in recent years. Both the FBI and the CIA have lobbied Congress for a blanket exception from the act, and efforts were under way to have Congress broaden the exceptions. Citing the cost of complying with FoI Act requests and alleged breaches of national security, some officials argued that public access rights should be sharply curtailed.

Congress never gave the FBI and CIA the blanket exception they wanted. However, in 1986 Congress did authorize the FBI and other federal law enforcement agencies to reject FoI Act information requests without confirming or denying the existence of the requested documents. Previously, the FBI often had to disclose the existence of a document in order to justify not releasing it. That, of course, gave useful information to people who wanted to know if they were the subject of FBI scrutiny.

In 1982 Congress restricted access to information involving the CIA by passing the Intelligence Identities Protection Act. That law made it a crime to engage in a "pattern of activities" with the "intent to identify and expose covert agents." While the law was apparently aimed at former CIA agents who reveal agency secrets--a troubling instance of prior censorship in and of itself--some journalists feared that the law was written so broadly that it could be used against the mass media as well.

Despite all of these difficulties, the FoI Act remains a valuable tool for information gathering. In its short history, this law has opened thousands of files to public scrutiny, files that otherwise would have remained locked indefinitely.

ELECTRONIC FREEDOM OF INFORMATION

The enormous growth of online communications and the Internet during the 1990s led to major changes in the way government agencies handle and disseminate information. And it led to radical changes in public perceptions about public records, creating new FoI problems.

On one hand, the Internet has made it much easier for governments to provide large amounts of information to the public. But on the other hand, it has led to unprecedented public demands for government secrecy: once a net surfer discovers a site that has personal information about individuals available online, thousands of others may learn about it in a few hours--and start demanding that the site be shut down. In many instances agencies have responded to these controversies by removing information from their online databases that was routinely available to the public in paper form for years. To the alarm of journalists, this has resulted in the loss of public access to newsworthy public information in many cases: the paper records may no longer exist, and the electronic version may be off limits to the public. And at the other extreme, many government agencies have put their public records out to bid, with the winning bidder given the right to computerize the records *and charge hefty fees for public access to once-free public records.* News organizations have fought battles from coast to coast over this shrinkage of public access to public records.

"Just as we move into a technological age in which public information can be distributed quickly and easily, we see privacy advocates pushing to keep much of that data secret and governments eager to sell off what's left to the highest bidder," said Kenneth A. Paulson, executive director of the First Amendment Center, during a panel discussion at a conference on computer-assisted reporting in 1997.

Electronic Freedom of Information Act Amendments

Responding to some of the new FoI problems and opportunities created by the Internet and the rapid growth of computer usage in and out of government, Congress extensively amended the FoI Act in 1996. By passing the Electronic Freedom of Information Act Amendments of 1996, Congress may have made the most important changes in the FoI Act since it was enacted 30 years earlier.

The Electronic FoI Act Amendments were widely reported in the media as merely requiring government agencies to make their records available in electronic form--on the Internet, on CD ROMs or in other ways. However, the 1996 law did much more than that.

The Electronic FoI Act changed the way federal agencies respond to FoI requests in three basic ways: (1) it requires agencies to make it easier for the public to identify and access government records, (2) it facilitates the computerization of the FoI compliance process, and (3) it completely reforms the timetable and procedures that agencies must follow in responding to FoI requests.

To assist the public in accessing federal records, the new law requires agencies to provide detailed indexes and guides to explain what records are available and where they may be found. Also, the new law divides government records that fall under the FoI Act into three categories: those that must be published, those that must be made available in agency reading rooms or placed online even if no one makes a request, and those that must be made available when there is a request.

To computerize the FoI compliance process, the 1996 law requires many agencies to set up "electronic reading rooms." Whereas those seeking government information previously had to go to an agency's headquarters in Washington and camp out in a "public reading room," in many instances the documents kept in those rooms are now online. As a result, anyone anywhere with a computer and Internet service can read the same documents at home. This one provision of the 1996 act alone vastly increased public access to federal records. In fact, it may have increased public access as much as the FoI Act itself did 30 years earlier.

The Electronic FoI Act Amendments also provide for other computer enhancements of the FoI process. In addition to flatly declaring that records kept in electronic form are fully covered by the FoI Act, the new law requires agencies to provide materials in a variety of computer formats.

The new act also addresses a longtime concern of users of the FoI Act: the tendency of government officials to black out huge portions of government records before releasing them. When electronic records are "redacted" (i.e., blacked out), it is often impossible even to tell that this has happened. Entire sections can be deleted--with no paper trail to show where the deletions occurred. The new law says that agencies must indicate where there have been redactions and how much was redacted where it is feasible to do so and where disclosing that information will not in itself reveal confidential information.

Finally, the 1996 act addresses the chronic problem of interminable delays in FoI responses. The new law gives agencies 20 working days instead of 10 to respond to FoI requests, but it also makes major changes in what agencies must do if they are going to miss this deadline. For one, journalists and a few others will be able to have their requests expedited in some instances. In addition, those whose requests are complex and may require considerable agency time will be given an opportunity to scale back or simplify their requests in return for faster processing. And requesters who face delays are supposed to be notified and given an estimated compliance time.

Aside from the specific details in the Electronic FoI Act Amendments, one of the most important innovations in the new law is the requirement that agencies identify the information that is repeatedly requested and avoid wasting time processing duplicative requests over and over again. The new law says that when an agency determines that particular information must be released under the FoI Act--and is likely to be requested again--the agency must put that information where the public can access it routinely (usually without even filing a formal FoI request).

FOI LIMITATIONS

Executive Privilege

Ever since the days of George Washington and Thomas Jefferson, American presidents and sometimes others in the executive branch have asserted a right to withhold information from Congress and the courts under a concept called *executive privilege*. The legal foundation for executive privilege is vague; chief executives won the right to keep many of their working papers confidential mostly because no one was really in a position to challenge that kind of secrecy.

Executive privilege has also been claimed by some executive officers of state and local governments. As it developed, the privilege generally covered not only military and diplomatic secrets but also many of the internal documents generated within the executive branch of government.

The executive orders issued by Presidents Harry Truman and Dwight D. Eisenhower in the 1950s to govern the rapidly growing national security classification system were justified largely by the concept of executive privilege. Those orders allowed military and diplomatic secrets to be classified on three levels: confidential, secret and top secret. Only persons who had been granted an appropriate security clearance were to be given access to this kind of information.

As the national security classification system grew, it became a complicated bureaucratic operation that annually locked up millions of documents, as mentioned earlier. The Pentagon Papers case (also discussed in Chapter Three) illustrates the problems in this area. The case arose when several newspapers obtained copies of a secret report about the Vietnam War. The newspapers' editors felt the public should know about the conclusions reached in the Pentagon Papers. They believed these papers were classified not so much to protect national security as to conceal the diplomatic errors of several presidents and their administrations.

In resolving the case, the Supreme Court allowed the papers to be published but did not generally rule on the concept of executive privilege itself. The FoI Act in effect recognized executive privilege by exempting from disclosure two kinds of information that executive privilege had covered: matters affecting national security and the internal working documents of federal agencies.

However, executive privilege was carried a step too far by the Nixon administration during the Watergate scandal, and the result was a U.S. Supreme Court decision that severely restricted its scope. As the scandal drifted nearer to the president himself, Nixon sought to invoke executive privilege to avoid releasing some very incriminating tape recordings to a court. The tapes included a number of conversations between Nixon and his aides, and Nixon realized how damaging some of them would be if made public. The Watergate special prosecutor contended that the tapes were needed in the prosecution of several Nixon aides.

Nixon's refusal to release the tapes, which he justified by citing executive privilege, was challenged by the special prosecutor, and the case reached the Supreme Court. In the resulting 1974 decision (*U.S. v. Nixon*, 418 U.S. 683), the scope of executive privilege was drastically curtailed.

In a unanimous decision, the Supreme Court ruled that executive privilege is absolute only in connection with military and diplomatic information that must be kept secret to protect national security. In other areas, the high court said, the privilege has to be balanced against other interests, such as the obligation of every citizen (including the president) to step forward with evidence of a crime that may be in his possession. Like the reporter's privilege, executive privilege has its limits.

The Supreme Court ordered the president to release the Watergate tapes. That, of course, accelerated the amazing chain of events that led to Nixon's resignation from the presidency later in 1974. As they were released, the tapes revealed ever more incriminating evidence that Nixon and his top aides had conspired to cover up crimes that were planned in the White House.

Thus, executive privilege is a less formidable justification for government secrecy today than it once was. However, these new limitations on executive privilege are of little help to the press and public, since the FoI Act still exempts so much of the information that was once kept secret under the justification of executive privilege.

Nevertheless, some of the internal government information that was once hidden by executive privilege is now available at least to the courts. And when such information is presented as evidence in court, it may become a part of the public record. The problem of public access to court records is discussed later in this chapter; Chapter Seven discusses courtroom closures to protect confidentiality.

The 1974 Privacy Act

Journalists and civil libertarians--normally allies on First Amendment issues--are often on opposite sides of one of the most troubling problems in the freedom of information area. When the public's right to know and the individual's right to personal privacy conflict, the two groups often sharply disagree. Organizations such as the American Civil Liberties Union (ACLU) argue strongly for laws assuring the secrecy of personal information collected by government agencies, even at the expense of journalists' access to information.

Congress attempted to deal with this problem by enacting the 1974 Privacy Act, the first comprehensive federal law intended to protect individuals from improper disclosure of personal information by government agencies. The Privacy Act was a response to the growing public alarm over the massive amount of personal information government agencies were placing in computerized data banks. Groups such as the ACLU argued that these data banks constituted a major threat to individual freedom. If the private information kept in these data banks were to fall into the wrong hands, flagrant abuses could occur, they pointed out. Journalists, on the other hand, feared that a strong privacy protection law would be misused by government officials as an excuse for needless secrecy. Bureaucrats could avoid public scrutiny of their own deeds (and misdeeds) in the name of protecting individual privacy.

As it was finally enacted, the 1974 Privacy Act (5 U.S.C. 552a) represents something of a compromise on this issue. The act applies to all information contained in hundreds of government record-keeping systems, placing strict limits on the manner in which the records are used. The act forbids federal agencies to release personal data from these record-keeping systems, or even transfer it to another federal agency without the permission of the person the information concerns.

The Privacy Act grants private individuals certain rights to inspect their own records in government data banks, with provisions allowing them to correct errors they discover. In addition, federal officials who improperly release personal records may be sued for damages, attorney's fees and court costs.

The Privacy Act includes a number of exceptions, allowing government agencies to release personal information without the affected person's permission for law enforcement purposes, for use by the census bureau and Congress itself, and for similar purposes. Significantly, the Privacy Act also allows the release of personal data that is defined as public information under the FoI Act. The Privacy Act was written this way to minimize its effect on the FoI Act.

As it turned out, the Privacy Act generally created only minor problems for most journalists, but problems nonetheless. One of the exceptions to the FoI Act excludes "personnel and medical files and similar files the disclosure of which would constitute a clearly unwarranted invasion of personal privacy."

That language is broad enough to give federal officials considerable leeway in deciding what personal information they must release under the FoI Act, and what they may withhold. Furthermore, the Privacy Act tends to discourage officials from releasing information in borderline cases because of the disparity between the consequences of violating the two laws.

The FoI Act allows those seeking information to sue officials who balk at releasing information, but only for attorney's fees and court costs. The Privacy Act, on the other hand, provides penalties for violations as well.

Thus, although the Privacy Act was written in such a way as to minimize restrictions on the release of information that would otherwise be accessible under the FoI Act, it does discourage openness in some cases. An official who errs in the direction of disclosing too little information faces no monetary penalty and only a vague threat of disciplinary action under the FoI Act; the official who errs in the direction of disclosing too much information faces monetary penalties under the Privacy Act.

Perhaps the most controversial data bank to which the Privacy Act provided personal access is the one maintained by the Federal Bureau of Investigation. One problem is that the FBI is often slow in releasing individual files, and when files are finally released they are often censored. (File censoring is permitted by the Privacy Act because these are, after all, law enforcement investigatory files). Moreover, there are several exceptions that sometimes permit the FBI to refuse to disclose even the existence of personal records. But nonetheless, the act gives private persons their first opportunity to learn something about the records the FBI may be keeping on them.

(Note that the Privacy Act gives individuals a limited right to inspect *their own files*. The Supreme Court's 1989 decision in the *Department of Justice* case held that the FBI has an across-the-board right to refuse to release files about individuals to *other persons*. That decision does not affect the right of an individual to seek access to his or her own file.)

The FBI's handling of personal information under the Privacy Act has stirred criticism from both civil libertarians and journalists. On at least one occasion, the FBI piously refused to release to journalists any background information on a well-known murder suspect. However, the FBI did issue 15,000 "wanted" posters to post offices, and these posters contained much of the information journalists were seeking.

In 1988, Congress strengthened the Privacy Act by passing the Computer Matching and Privacy Protection Act. This law governs the transfer of information between government agencies' computer data bases. A great deal of this information is transferred from one agency to another to cross-check whether individuals are entitled to government assistance they may be receiving. This law added a verification requirement to prevent individuals from losing their benefits through misidentification and other data-handling errors. It also established Data Integrity Boards in many federal agencies to oversee the use of computerized data-matching programs.

In 2001, new federal rules governing the privacy of medical records went into effect. The new rules, created under the Clinton administration and approved by Congress, were opposed by health industry groups such as insurers and hospitals, contending that they were too restrictive and costly to implement. After hearing arguments from the industry and privacy advocates, the Bush administration put the new rules into effect.

The new regulations require that doctors and other health-care providers obtain written consent from patients before sharing their health records even for routine purposes such as verifying bills to insurance companies. The rules also allow patients to see their own files and request corrections of errors. Patients must also be told how their health information will be used when possible.

A number of states already had medical privacy laws that included many of these provisions, but these rules established *nationwide* standards for medical record privacy.

The "Buckley Amendment"

At about the same time as the enactment of the 1974 Privacy Act and the 1974 amendments to the FoI Act, Congress also approved the "Buckley Amendment," more formally known as the Family Education Rights and Privacy Act (20 U.S.C. 1232g). That federal law, which is sometimes identified by its initials (FERPA), is often confused with the more general 1974 Privacy Act, and in fact the two have similar provisions. The Buckley Amendment was so designated because Senator James Buckley of New York led the effort to add it to the 1974 Elementary and Secondary Education Act amendments, a major federal-aid-to-education bill.

The Buckley Amendment gives parents the right to see their children's school records and forbids the release of these school records to outside parties without the parents' consent. Similarly, it allows students over age 18 to see their own school records, and requires their consent before these records may be released to outside parties. School systems that fail to obey the Buckley Amendment may be denied federal funds. In 2002 the U.S. Supreme Court made it clear that the denial of federal funds is usually the sole remedy for non-compliance: students cannot use the Buckley Amendment to sue schools that divulge their personal information (*Gonzaga University v. Doe*, 2002 U.S. Lexis 4649). The Supreme Court also clarified another aspect of the Buckley Amendment in 2002, ruling that it does not preclude such everyday classroom practices as having students grade each others' quizzes (*Owasso Independent School District v. Falvo*, 534 U.S. 426). The court said the law was intended by Congress only to cover permanent records maintained by teachers and other school employees.

The Buckley Amendment has had some impact on the newsgathering activities of the media, at times in absurd ways. Overzealous school officials have sometimes used it as an excuse to withhold newsworthy and non-sensitive information about students involved in athletics or other newsworthy extracurricular activities. But perhaps the Buckley Amendment's most serious effect on newsgathering has been to increase the secrecy of school disciplinary records. That has sometimes made it difficult to report on newsworthy disciplinary actions, such as those involving student athletes or political activists. Fearful of losing federal money, some school officials have tended to avoid risking any appearance of non-compliance with the Buckley Amendment.

Campus newspapers are sometimes accused of violating the Buckley Amendment by reporting on the academic eligibility of student athletes and student government officers, who are usually required to maintain a certain grade average to be eligible for their positions. The college administrators responsible for making sure that student officers and athletes are eligible are not always diligent in checking grade records. As a result, investigative journalists sometimes learn that a particular student leader is academically ineligible--and publish that newsworthy fact. That inevitably brings charges that the campus newspaper has violated the Buckley Amendment by revealing student grades, which are supposed to be confidential.

Controversies of this type have occurred at numerous colleges--almost invariably because college officials do not understand what the Buckley Amendment really does and doesn't say. The Buckley Amendment says schools that have *ongoing policies* of not keeping grades confidential *are ineligible for federal funds*. It does not forbid student newspapers to publish student leaders' grades to prove that they are academically ineligible. Nor does it say that a college could lose its federal funds just because the campus newspaper reveals a few student leaders' grades in a clearly newsworthy story about their fitness to serve.

Campus officials often cite the Buckley Amendment as a basis for keeping reports of campus crimes secret. However, there has been a national movement in recent years to force officials to reveal campus crime rates and in some cases information about specific crimes.

In 1990 Congress enacted the Crime Awareness and Campus Security Act, requiring all colleges and universities receiving federal funds to issue annual reports of crime statistics as well as descriptions of security arrangements. The law requires the use of uniform crime reporting procedures so that students and their families can compare the crime rates at different institutions as a factor in choosing a college. It does not require campuses to open their police records to the press, however.

Congress also revised the Buckley Amendment to declare that "law enforcement unit" records on college campuses are not "educational records" that must be kept confidential. However, this revision of the Buckley Amendment stopped short of requiring campus officials to make information about specific crimes public. It merely declared that the Buckley Amendment does not require such information to be kept secret.

The 1990 Congressional action did not settle the matter, however. On many campuses, administrators continued to cite the Buckley Amendment as a basis for keeping campus records concerning specific crimes and court proceedings confidential.

Initially, several courts responded by ruling that the Buckley Amendment cannot be used to justify keeping campus crime records secret if they are supposed to be open under state law. For example, a federal judge so ruled in a pioneering lawsuit filed by Traci Bauer, editor of the Southwest Missouri University *Standard*, to compel the administration to open these records (*Bauer v. Kincaid*, 759 F. Supp. 575, 1991).

Soon other student editors filed similar lawsuits to force administrators to disclose campus crime or court information under state freedom of information laws. By 1997, both the Ohio Supreme Court and the Georgia Supreme Court had ruled that campus officials had to release information about campus crimes or court proceedings in spite of the Buckley Amendment (see *The Miami Student v. Miami University*, 680 N.E.2d 956, 1997; and *Red & Black Publishing Co. v. Board of Regents of the University of Georgia*, 427 S.E.2d 257, 1993). Both courts concluded that the Buckley Amendment does not apply to campus crime and court records. Note that these cases did not create any new legal right of access to university crime and court records; that is governed by state FoI laws. But if such records would otherwise be public under the applicable state law, these courts held that the Buckley Amendment does not override state laws and transform crime records into "educational records."

Congress entered this controversy by adding language to the 1998 reauthorization of the Higher Education Act declaring more emphatically that the Buckley Amendment cannot be used to justify secrecy about violent crimes and certain other crimes committed on campus. If this information would otherwise be made public (under a state open record law, for example), Congress declared that the Buckley Amendment does not change that.

Perhaps even more important, the 1998 version of the Higher Education Act also included language requiring all colleges and universities receiving federal funds (including private schools with federally insured student loans) to create and maintain a log of criminal incidents reported to their campus police or security department--and make this log public. This log must include the nature, date, time, general location and disposition of each complaint. The log must be made public within two business days, and new information that is later discovered about an incident must be added to the log and made public within two business days. There is an exception for certain information that would identify a victim or jeopardize an ongoing investigation. The 1998 law also strengthened the requirements in the

1990 legislation that colleges and universities must publish an annual report of campus crime statistics.

The 1998 legislation is officially known as the Jeanne Clery Disclosure of Campus Security Policy and Campus Crime Statistics Act. It is named in memory of a Lehigh University student who was unaware of recent crimes on her campus and who left her security door propped open, enabling an intruder to enter her room and murder her. Reports of campus crime that are filed as required by this law are sometimes called Clery Act reports.

Unfortunately for the student press, that is not the end of the story. In 1998 the U.S. Department of Education filed its own lawsuit in federal court to override the Ohio Supreme Court decision and force university officials in Ohio to keep campus crime information secret when an offense is handed through campus disciplinary proceedings. The Department of Education pointed out that the Ohio Public Records Act exempts from disclosure any record that state or federal law requires to be kept secret. Contending that the Buckley Amendment *does* cover campus disciplinary proceedings, federal officials obtained an injunction ordering university administrators not to release records pertaining to these proceedings. In 2002, the sixth circuit U.S. Court of Appeals upheld that injunction, ruling that the Buckley Amendment does in fact require campus disciplinary records and proceedings to be confidential (*U.S. v. Miami University* (2002 U.S. App. Lexis 12830).

The *Miami* decision did not affect the requirement that all colleges and universities disclose general information about campus crimes as well as the police log, but it did uphold the rule that campus disciplinary proceedings are confidential under the Buckley Amendment. Inasmuch as they are confidential under the Buckley Amendment, that also makes them confidential under the Ohio Public Records Act because that law exempts from disclosure anything that is secret under another state or federal law, the court concluded.

The Student Press Law Center has a detailed report for journalists about covering campus crime available on its website (www.splc.org).

The Federal Advisory Committee Act

Congress enacted the Federal Advisory Committee Act (FACA) in 1972 in an attempt to control the growing use of secret advisory committees by the executive branch of government. It requires various non-government organizations that give advice to the government to hold open meetings and maintain public records. It covers a variety of advisory bodies--entities that include one or more persons who are *not* federal "officers" or "employees" and that give advice to the president or an agency in the executive branch of the federal government.

However, its usefulness was limited by a 1989 Supreme Court decision, *Public Citizen v. Department of Justice* (491 U.S. 440). The court ruled that Congress did not intend for the act to cover privately funded bodies such as the American Bar Association committee that reviews the qualifications of prospective federal judges. Thus, the ABA panel can continue to meet in secret and maintain secret records when it evaluates potential judges (including possible Supreme Court justices). The decision also means that many other private groups may meet secretly and make recommendations to government officials. The court did not overturn the Advisory Committee Act itself, but by ruling that the act does not apply to the ABA panel it may open the way for other groups to claim that they are exempt from the act's open-meeting and open-record provisions. This could curtail the public's right to know about many advisory group recommendations that shape federal government policy.

A highly publicized FACA case arose in 1993, when President Clinton established a President's Task Force on National Health Care Reform and named his wife, Hillary Rodham Clinton, to head it. The Task Force, which almost always met in secret, consisted entirely of senior government officials--except for the First Lady, who held no official government position (nor could she under the Anti-Nepotism Act, the law forbidding federal officials to appoint close relatives to government positions). In *Association of American Physicians and Surgeons v. Hillary Rodham Clinton* (997 F.2d 898), a federal appellate court had to decide whether the task force was subject to FACA--and thus required to hold open meetings.

The key issue was Hillary Rodham Clinton's status. If she did not qualify as a full-time federal "officer" or "employee", then FACA would apply to the task force (because one of its members would have been a private citizen, not a government official). But the court traced the history and status of "first ladies" and concluded that the first lady was the equivalent of a federal "officer" or "employee" even though she could not be paid or hold any official position while married to the president. As a result, her task force was not a private advisory body subject to FACA but instead an internal body within the Clinton administration, the court held. Therefore, it could meet in secret.

The decision prompted a lengthy concurring opinion by Judge James Buckley, who argued that Hillary Rodham Clinton could not be classified as a government official, but that FACA should not apply because this law unconstitutionally violates the president's right to obtain private advice about policy matters.

Criminal History Information

For many working journalists, another serious obstacle in gathering information has been the effect of state and federal privacy laws on access to information about persons accused of crimes. In 1976, the federal Law Enforcement Assistance Administration (LEAA) issued a controversial set of guidelines intended to restrict the release of personal information by law enforcement agencies. The guidelines required state and local police agencies receiving federal aid to develop policies governing the release of information about persons arrested or charged with crimes. The guidelines were prompted at least in part by the LEAA's efforts to establish a new nationwide computerized law enforcement information network. LEAA officials feared that the vast amount of personal information available through this new system would lead to abuses such as the indiscriminate release of individual criminal history information (records of past arrests and convictions).

Originally, the LEAA guidelines were intended to seal all criminal history records in the interest of individual privacy. But those rules produced strenuous objections by journalists. In their final form, the guidelines did not specifically tell local police agencies what their information policies had to be, but they did require these agencies to develop consistent policies.

As a result of the LEAA recommendations, some law enforcement agencies stopped releasing criminal history information to the press. Even current police blotter information that had traditionally been available was sometimes denied to the press. In many states, all records of arrests that do not lead to convictions--and even some records of arrests that do lead to convictions--are now sealed or simply destroyed. At least 47 states restrict access to criminal history "rap sheets" under some circumstances.

This is the area in which the disagreement between information-seeking journalists and privacy-oriented civil liberties groups tends to be the most clear-cut. ACLU leaders and other civil libertarians argue vehemently that a person should not be permanently stigmatized by public access to his or her police arrest record, particularly if the arrest does not lead to a conviction. When a record of an arrest has been legally expunged (erased), ACLU leaders are particularly emphatic in their contention that making information about it public is an injustice.

Many journalists, on the other hand, feel that while closing these records does protect individual privacy, it also allows wholesale abuses by law enforcement agencies. To support that assertion, they cite the dangers to civil liberties inherent in secret arrests and secret police activities. Also, they argue that society needs protection from persons with criminal records. They cite instances when privacy laws prevented employers from discovering their employees' criminal records, with the result that ex-convicts were placed in positions where they could commit similar crimes again. For instance, they point to a 1980 case in Texas where an employee of a mental institution raped a patient, and officials had been denied access to his criminal record (including a previous rape conviction) when they hired him.

This ongoing conflict will not soon be resolved. As Chapter Seven points out, there has been a long-term trend away from easy access to information about criminal suspects' past deeds, a trend prompted by the fair trial-free press dilemma at least as much as by the concern for personal privacy.

Federal Driver's Privacy Protection Act

With little public debate or even publicity in the news media, Congress passed a law in 1994 that significantly curtailed access to motor vehicle registration records and driving records. The federal Driver's Privacy Protection Act (DPPA), sponsored by Sen. Barbara Boxer, D-Calif., and Rep. Jim Moran, D-Va., was enacted as a part of the omnibus 1994 anti-crime bill.

This law requires every state to close its motor vehicle registration and driving records to the press and public, although there is an exception allowing insurance companies and private investigators, among others, to retain access to these records. Any state may pass legislation to opt out of the across-the-board federal secrecy requirements as long as individuals may arrange to have their own records kept confidential.

The DPPA was enacted as a public safety measure. To justify the bill, Boxer

378 Freedom of Information

cited the 1989 murder of actress Rebecca Shaeffer by a fan. The fan obtained her address from a private investigator who had access to California Dept. of Motor Vehicles records. However, journalists who opposed the bill pointed out that this rationale makes no sense: private investigators are exempt from the new secrecy requirements.

To journalists, the DPPA represents the loss of a powerful investigative tool. Columnist Dan Lynch of the *Albany Times Union* pointed to numerous important stories developed by reporters using motor vehicle and driving records. For example, the media have checked driving records to learn that some airline pilots and the captain of the Exxon Valdez (the tanker that ran aground, causing a disastrous Alaskan oil spill), among others, had drunk driving convictions and should not have been placed in jobs where they could endanger public safety. Lynch also pointed out that in New York City the media began checking the driving records of people involved in fatal accidents--and reported that many of them had dozens of suspensions or revocations, but were still driving.

As word of this law spread, leaders of several media organizations, including the Society of Professional Journalists, expressed concern that this law and others like it would severely erode the hard-won victories of the 1960s, 1970s and 1980s in the campaign for public access to government records.

Several states challenged Congress' authority to tell them how to handle driving records, but in 2000 the U.S. Supreme Court upheld this controversial law. Ruling in *Reno v. Condon* (528 U.S. 141), the court upheld the right of Congress to use the commerce clause of the U.S. Constitution as a basis for requiring the states to keep these records secret.

In a unanimous ruling, the court deviated from a recent pattern of overturning federal laws regulating conduct by the states. This time, the court held that the principles of federalism were not violated by an act of Congress for several reasons. The court concluded that selling driver's license information to advertisers and insurers, which a number of states were doing, amounted to commercial activity by the states that could be regulated under the Constitution's commerce clause.

By ruling as it did, the court reversed a decision by the fourth circuit U.S. Court of Appeals, which had upheld a challenge to the Driver's Privacy Protection Act by the state of South Carolina.

FEDERAL OPEN MEETING LEGISLATION

Another aspect of the struggle for freedom of information involves access to the meetings of government agencies. This is one of the oldest and most difficult information-gathering problems encountered by journalists. In theory, all public agencies should conduct the public's business openly, with citizens invited to listen in. But in practice many public officials find it tempting to make their decisions behind closed doors, announcing them in carefully worded press releases afterward. Obviously, if the press is to serve as a watchdog on behalf of the public, reporters must have a right to attend the meetings where public officials make their important decisions. To ensure this right, journalists have campaigned for open-meeting laws for many years--with some success.

In fact, at least 46 states already had open-meeting laws before Congress finally enacted such a law in 1976. That 1976 federal law, the Government in the Sunshine Act (5 U.S.C. 552b), requires about 50 administrative agencies to conduct some of their meetings in public.

The policy-making boards and commissions of these agencies must meet at announced times and places, with the public generally invited to attend. However, closed sessions are still permitted for 10 different reasons; the legal officer of the agency must specify the basis for each closed meeting.

The first nine grounds for secret meetings closely parallel the nine FoI Act exceptions, listed earlier in this chapter. They include such things as matters affecting national security, personnel matters, law enforcement investigations, discussions of trade secrets and the like. The tenth subject that may be discussed in a closed meeting is pending litigation and similar adjudicatory matters.

Whatever the reason for a closed meeting, the board or commission must vote to close a meeting before the public may be excluded, and the vote must be recorded. The agency must then keep accurate and complete records of what goes on during the closed meeting. In most instances, that record must be either a verbatim transcript or a tape recording of all proceedings. In some instances, however, detailed minutes are permitted instead.

When an agency holds a closed meeting, it must quickly publish the results of any votes, including a record of how each commissioner or board member voted.

Any person may initiate a lawsuit against an agency that appears to be violating the Government in the Sunshine Act, and federal district courts are authorized to issue injunctions ordering federal agencies to comply with the law. When a complaining party wins such a lawsuit, the federal court is authorized to require the federal government to pay his or her attorney's fees and court costs. However, the act contains no civil or criminal penalties for government officials who violate its provisions. In addition, the law specifically orders federal courts not to invalidate actions taken by agencies during illegal secret meetings. Thus, the federal open meeting law has virtually no "teeth" in it. As we shall see shortly, it is much weaker than many state open meeting laws in this respect.

Another major loophole in the Government in the Sunshine Act is that it does not prohibit government agencies from making their major decisions by circulating private policy memoranda among their commissioners. Some federal agencies decide many important matters by circulating memos and then merely announce their decisions at open meetings, which may occur only once a month or, in some instances, even less frequently than that. The Nuclear Regulatory Commission (NRC) and the Equal Employment Opportunity Commission (EEOC) have both been accused of using such tactics to evade the spirit of the Sunshine Act.

The Sunshine Act covers a number of well-known agencies in addition to the NRC and EEOC, including the Federal Communications Commission, Federal Trade Commission, Interstate Commerce Commission, Consumer Product Safety Commission, National Transportation Safety Board, Civil Service Commission, Securities and Exchange Commission, U.S. Postal Service board of governors and Federal Reserve Board. The act applies to the central policy-making board of each of these agencies but not to local or national staff meetings, even if those meetings involve important policy matters. Nor does it apply to cabinet-level departments or to some of the advisory bodies closest to the presidency, such as the National Security Council.

The Government in the Sunshine Act excludes most informal gatherings and unofficial meetings held by members of federal boards and commissions. In a 1984 decision, the U.S. Supreme Court ruled that it was proper for a majority of the members of the Federal Communications Commission to meet in private with communications leaders from other countries at an international conference. The court said the gathering in question was not a "meeting" and the international body itself was not an "agency" within the meaning of the law (*FCC v. ITT World Communications*, 466 U.S. 463).

In short, the federal open meeting law leaves much to be desired. It allows closed meetings for a wide variety of dubious reasons. Moreover, its enforcement provisions are notably weak, and it fails to cover many of the federal bodies that make the most important decisions. Nevertheless, it is a first step toward openness in the gigantic federal bureaucracy, a bureaucracy that once felt it had an absolute right to do the public's business in private without interference from meddlesome reporters or private citizens.

STATE OPEN MEETING AND RECORD LAWS

Although the federal FoI Act and Government in the Sunshine Act are important, most journalists find their own state FoI laws even more relevant than the federal laws. On a daily basis, thousands of journalists rely on state open meeting and public record laws to provide access to many of their most important news sources.

But while state public record and open meeting laws are of paramount importance to so many journalists, they are difficult to summarize in any detail in a national media law textbook. Not only do these laws vary considerably from state to state, but they are so often amended that no survey text can long remain accurate for all states.

If you are preparing for a career as a general assignment reporter, you will need to become familiar with the open meeting and public record laws of your state. You can locate these laws through an online search or by checking the index in your state's statutes or codes, which you will find in some public libraries and any law library. Look under such headings as "records and recording," "public records," "open records," "access to records," "meetings," "open meetings" or perhaps "freedom of information."

Most state open meeting and public record laws resemble the federal laws in many respects. In fact, many of the state open meeting laws were either adopted or extensively revised at about the time the federal laws were enacted. The mid-1970s saw a dramatic growth of such laws all over the United States.

State open meeting laws typically apply to the agencies of both state and local government. They usually require state boards and commissions, city councils, school boards and county governing boards to hold open meetings at regularly announced times and places. Any person is permitted to attend most of these open meetings, although some state laws have provisions authorizing public officials to remove anyone who creates a disturbance.

Virtually all state open meeting laws provide for closed or "executive" sessions. Most state laws spell out the circumstances under which these closed sessions are permitted, authorizing private meetings for matters affecting national security, personnel matters, discussions of pending lawsuits and usually various other subjects. Some states allow closed meetings for only a few reasons, while others allow them for many more.

An increasing number of state open meeting laws provide specific legal remedies for violations, allowing any citizen to sue the offending government body for an injunction to halt further illegal secret meetings. In addition, a number of state open meeting laws authorize the courts to invalidate actions taken at unlawful closed meetings, a provision the federal Government in the Sunshine Act lacks. Such provisions are important, because the possibility of having a major action overturned in court is a strong deterrent to holding secret meetings.

Another provision missing in the federal law--but present in many state open meeting laws--is criminal sanctions for knowing violations. In many states it is a misdemeanor for government officials to participate in a closed meeting if they know the subject at hand should be discussed only during an open meeting. However, criminal prosecutions remain rare because it is difficult to prove that a government body actually discussed an illegal subject behind closed doors and that the officials involved knew they were violating the law.

In some states, there is a state-level freedom of information commission that serves as a watchdog agency, enforcing the open meeting and public record laws. Other states have similar commissions, but without enforcement powers. And in others, enforcement is in the hands of the attorney general or local prosecuting attorneys. In some states--Ohio, for example--the courts have the power to remove officials from office for violating the open meeting laws.

State Public Record Laws

Likewise, the provisions of public record laws vary widely around the country. All 50 states have laws in this area. Most state public records laws define the term "public records" broadly enough to encompass a wide variety of documents maintained by agencies of state and local government. And most such laws allow general public access to these records without requiring that the person inquiring demonstrate any special interest or "need to know."

State public record laws consistently exempt certain kinds of records from public disclosure, most often personnel records, law enforcement investigatory records and records of juvenile courts, adoptions, parole matters, etc.

Most state public record laws specifically provide for judicial review in instances where public access is denied, and about two-thirds of the states provide criminal sanctions for officials who improperly deny public access. About one-third of the states require government agencies to pay the attorneys' fees of those who successfully sue for access to public records.

In all 50 states the comprehensive public record laws supplement other provisions for public access to government records. Long before it was fashionable to enact comprehensive open records legislation, various records were open to the public under the common law, and many of these miscellaneous common law provisions for public access have also been codified. Records that were traditionally open under the common law include records of the ownership of private land, birth, marriage and death records, and various court records.

In some instances, lawmaking in this area has occurred by vote of the people. For example, the people of Washington state enacted a public record law by popular vote in 1972. Meanwhile, California voters approved a constitutional amendment adding an "inalienable" right of privacy to Article I, Section 1 of the state constitution in 1974. In 1992, Florida voters approved a constitutional amendment creating a constitutional right of access to public records and meetings in Article I, Section 24 of the Florida Constitution.

As on the federal level, state public record laws have had to be reconciled with privacy laws. Most states have privacy statutes that limit public access to personal information in state data bases. These laws, sometimes given euphemistic titles such as "Information Practices Act," usually forbid state officials to release personal information without the individual's permission. Some of them go much further than the federal Privacy Act in sealing records that would otherwise be open under public records laws. California, for instance, enacted a voluminous Information Practices Act in 1977, and it prohibited the release of "disparaging" information about any individual. The result was a massive freeze-up of public information, and the problem was only partially solved when the media succeeded in getting the reference to "disparaging" information deleted two years later. Such laws have become a major obstacle for journalists, limiting disclosure of everything from hospital patients' records to errant motorists' driving records.

In 1999 the U.S. Supreme Court ruled on a case concerning access to public records under state law. In *Los Angeles Police Department v. United Reporting Publishing Co.* (528 U.S. 32), the court upheld a provision of the California Public Records Act forbidding the release of addresses of crime victims and persons arrested for a crime for commercial use.

The high court upheld California's right to release these addresses to non-commercial users while denying them to lawyers, insurance companies, drug counselors, driving schools and others who might use the information commercially. A provision of the California law requires law enforcement agencies to release such information to journalists, scholars and politicians, among others, while denying it to commercial users. The court pointed out that a state is under no obligation to release such information to *anyone*, much less to *everyone*.

The high court seemed deeply divided over the rationale for this decision, although the 7-2 majority said the state law was not invalid on its face. However, the court seemed to be inviting a future legal challenge based on the argument that the law is invalid as applied to companies such as United Reporting by denying them equal protection of the law.

As in the area of open meeting laws, it is impossible to describe all of the state record laws in detail. If you will need access to public records as a journalist--or if you will be responsible for controlling the release of personal information (as a hospital public relations officer, for instance)--there is no substitute for researching your own state's public records and privacy statutes.

ACCESS TO OTHER PLACES AND PROCEEDINGS

Having a strong public records or open meeting statute solves some of a journalist's information-gathering problems, but in a number of circumstances these laws are of little help. For instance, public records laws rarely govern the release of court records, and open meeting laws do not guarantee access to either the courts or the scene of a news event. These laws are of little value when a journalist needs to cross police lines to reach the scene of a disaster. Nor are they of any assistance when a journalist wishes to cover a controversial criminal trial or visit a prison where inmates are allegedly mistreated.

In the absence of a statutory law assuring journalists access to these places and proceedings, is there any constitutional right of access to the news? In several cases involving access to prisons, the U.S. Supreme Court has said there is no such right.

The high court decided two such cases, *Saxbe v. Washington Post* (417 U.S. 843) and *Pell v. Procunier* (417 U.S. 817), the same day in 1974. The court said prison rules against interviewing individual prison inmates were not a violation of the First Amendment. The *Pell* case arose in California when a policy that gave journalists freedom to interview specific prisoners was eliminated. That happened after an escape attempt in which several persons were killed. Thereafter, the media were only allowed to interview inmates selected more or less at random, not the inmates they wished to interview. Prison officials contended that media interviews had made celebrities of certain prisoners and helped provoke the escape attempt. The *Saxbe* case was a challenge to federal rules that similarly prohibited media interviews with inmates.

The Supreme Court said these anti-interview rules do not violate the constitutional rights of journalists since journalists have no special right of access to prisons. The court said neither journalists nor ordinary citizens have a right to freely visit prisons and interview inmates.

However, lower federal courts in California tried to avoid following this precedent, and the result was another Supreme Court ruling on prison access in 1978, *Houchins v. KQED* (438 U.S. 1). In that case, television journalists wanted to visit a portion of a jail where an inmate had committed suicide, a place where a psychiatrist said conditions were so bad that inmates could suffer psychological damage. Jail authorities denied access to the reporters and they sued, contending that prison conditions were a matter of legitimate public concern. A federal district court agreed, ordering authorities to let journalists see and photograph the controversial area of the jail. In the meantime, public tours of the jail had been initiated, but they did not include that area. The ninth circuit U.S. Court of Appeals affirmed the decision, but the Supreme Court reversed.

Writing for the majority, Chief Justice Warren Burger reiterated the Supreme Court's view that journalists have no constitutional right of access to prisons. He acknowledged that prison conditions are a matter of public concern, but he said, in effect, that the subject is none of the media's business:

> The media are not a substitute for or an adjunct of government, and like the courts, they are ill-equipped to deal with the problems of prison administration.

Burger said that if journalists wanted to find out about prison conditions, they should interview former inmates, prisoners' lawyers, prison visitors and public officials. In short, he said, the press has no constitutional right of access to places not accessible to the general public.

The *Houchins* decision was alarming enough, but a year later the court handed down its *Gannett v. DePasquale* ruling (discussed in Chapter Seven), allowing even pretrial courtroom proceedings to be closed to the press and public. However, during the 1980s the Supreme Court backed away from these denials of First Amendment protection for newsgathering activities. As noted in Chapter Seven, in *Richmond Newspapers v. Virginia* (the landmark 1980 decision holding that closed trials are not ordinarily permitted by the Constitution), the majority opinion included language suggesting that the court recognized a First Amendment right to gather news. "Without some protection for seeking out the news, freedom of the press could be eviscerated," the court said, quoting its 1972 *Branzburg v. Hayes* decision (see Chapter Eight).

In a concurring opinion in the *Richmond* case, Justice John Paul Stevens put it even more strongly:

> This is a watershed case. Until today the court has accorded virtually absolute protection to the dissemination of ideas, but never before has it squarely held that the acquisition of newsworthy matter is entitled to any constitutional protection whatsoever.

Many journalists saw *Richmond Newspapers v. Virginia* as a great victory for the right to gather the news. However, the majority opinion was somewhat less enthusiastic on this point than Justice Stevens' concurring opinion, and subsequent court decisions have not extended the concept very far beyond its original application (access to courtrooms).

In the early 2000s, many of these issues were debated again in connection with attempts by journalists to cover executions, including preliminary steps such as preparing an inmate for a lethal injection. As more and more states resumed capital punishment, this controversy grew--and ended up in court. In 1998, a federal appellate court upheld a prison warden's restrictions on the viewing of executions in California. Under these restrictions, journalists did not get to see anything more than the inmate on a gurney, already sedated and perhaps unconscious, in the final moments before the official pronouncement of death. The court ruled that journalists have no special right to view an execution, and that these restrictions were reasonable. The appellate court did suggest that there may be a First Amendment right, although a "severely limited" one, to witness capital punishment and ordered a lower court to reconsider whether the authorities' security concerns justify excluding the media (*California First Amendment Coalition v. Calderon*, 138 F.3d 1298).

As the controversy over media access to executions continued, a federal judge ruled in 2001 that California prison authorities had not justified their refusal to allow the media to view the entire process. The state again appealed.

Whatever the constitutional status of the right to gather the news, in or out of the prison system, Congress, state legislatures and local governments have often acted to grant journalists access to many sources of information. In fact, journalists have been granted access to prisons in most states; the Supreme Court was simply saying in *Houchins* that there is no *constitutional right* of access to prisons when the authorities decide to deny access. If state or local authorities choose to let journalists in, that's fine.

Another related access problem involves journalists' rights to cross police and fire lines to reach the scene of an accident or natural disaster. In virtually all states, journalists are afforded at least some special privileges of this kind, but they are usually treated as privileges, not rights. They can be denied by authorities.

However, when law enforcement authorities grant access to some favored journalists while denying it to others, another problem arises. May authorities play favorites among journalists without violating the First Amendment?

In a case involving access to police press passes, the California Supreme Court once allowed such favoritism. The *Los Angeles Free Press*, an "underground" newspaper with a paid circulation of nearly 100,000 at the time, sought the same press pass privileges as were routinely granted to other newspapers. The *Free Press* was turned down by local police, and that denial was upheld by the state Supreme Court in a 1970 decision, *Los Angeles Free Press v. City of Los Angeles* (9 C.3d 448). In so ruling, the court accepted the police contention that the *Free Press* didn't regularly cover police beat news except when it involved social issues. Thus, the police were able to convince the court that the *Free Press* didn't have the same need or justification for press credentials as more conventional kinds of newspapers. The court refused to recognize that the *Free Press* had any First Amendment right to hold police press credentials, even if they were routinely given to papers of which the police approved.

However, a federal district court in Iowa reached the opposite conclusion in a 1971 case, *Quad-City Community News Service v. Jebens* (334 F.Supp. 8). Local police there denied an "underground" paper access to police blotter information that was routinely available to other newspapers, but the court overruled the practice. The court pointed out that there were no written guidelines for determining who should be given access to police records and who should not. The police standards were too vague to be valid, the court said.

A few years later, a federal appellate court ruled on a similar question involving the granting of White House press credentials. In that case (*Sherrill v. Knight*, 569 F.2d 124), the Secret Service had denied press credentials to two "underground" newspaper reporters on the grounds that they had been convicted of crimes. Ruling in 1978, the appellate court refused to accept the Secret Service's argument that it had complete discretion in granting or denying White House press credentials. The court said the agency had to establish procedures for granting press passes. Reporters were to be told the reason for any denial and given an opportunity to reply.

Thus, these cases suggest that the police may grant information-gathering privileges to some journalists and not to others, but only if there are defensible guidelines to govern the awarding of these privileges. The decision cannot be arbitrary.

Access to Judicial Proceedings

Another difficult problem of access to information in recent years has involved the nation's judiciary. As Chapter Seven indicates, there was a nationwide trend toward closed preliminary courtroom proceedings immediately after the Supreme Court's *Gannett v. DePasquale* decision.

For a time, preliminary hearings were routinely closed in many states when a judge felt that prejudicial publicity would result if the hearing was open. Similarly, pretrial hearings on motions to suppress evidence were often closed, again to prevent publicity about evidence that may never be presented to a jury. However, since the Supreme Court's decision in the *Richmond Newspapers v. Virginia* case and several others that followed it, courtroom closures have become much less common--and less of a problem for journalists. The problem of closed courtrooms is discussed in Chapter Seven.

Another related problem for journalists is access to grand jury proceedings. Grand juries are bodies that hear evidence and decide whether to charge persons with a crime. All major federal criminal prosecutions begin with a grand jury indictment, and many of the most politically sensitive--and newsworthy--state cases are initiated in that fashion. (The Fifth Amendment to the U.S. Constitution requires grand jury indictments in major federal cases but not in state cases.)

Grand jury proceedings are almost always closed, in part to keep suspects from learning what is happening and fleeing before they can be charged and arrested. Grand jury transcripts (i.e., the official record of the grand jury proceeding) are also closed in most states, although some states make transcripts public after all of those charged with crimes are actually arrested. If no one is charged with a crime, the grand jury transcript remains sealed in most cases. And even in states that normally allow public access to the transcripts after all of those charged are arrested, courts may order the transcript sealed in newsworthy cases, such as those involving wrongdoing by public officials.

If a grand jury transcript is sealed, there is little a journalist can do to learn its contents, aside from engaging in such investigative reporting techniques as inquiring of persons who were present at the closed proceedings. Judges sometimes object to that kind of newsgathering, but what grand juries do is often newsworthy.

Other records kept by the judiciary are usually open under an old common law tradition, but there are important exceptions. Much news can be gleaned from the filings that occur in both civil and criminal lawsuits. The complaints and responses filed by those involved in lawsuits are usually public, and they may reveal newsworthy details about individuals' and businesses' plans, finances and past deeds (or misdeeds). One thing to remember about these documents is that they may not be protected by the qualified privilege libel defense until they are acted upon by a judge; reporters must be especially careful about reporting potentially libelous information contained in newly filed court records.

Some court records that involve personal matters are sealed in many states. For instance, probation department reports that recommend either jail terms or probation for persons convicted of crimes may be kept secret because they contain very personal information.

In addition, certain entire categories of court information may be off limits to reporters. For example, juvenile court proceedings are almost always closed, and the records that result are usually confidential. And some states have laws requiring the confidentiality of proceedings and records involving rape victims. As Chapter Three explains, some states have laws that forbid the media to publish the names of rape victims and juvenile suspects, although those laws are sometimes challenged on First Amendment grounds. The Supreme Court has said repeatedly that the states may keep such records confidential, but the media may not be prevented from publishing the information once it becomes public.

Access to Private Organizations

Everything we have discussed so far in this chapter involves access to *government* information. However, many newsworthy things happen in private business enterprises. For instance, when a corporation decides to open or close a plant, the economy of an entire city can be drastically altered. What right of access, if any, does a reporter have to investigate this kind of news?

Unfortunately, the answer is often "none." Private businesses need not admit reporters to their policy-making board meetings, and private business records are rarely open for public inspection. However, there are ways private corporate information can be researched.

Perhaps most important, almost all corporations whose stock is publicly traded are subject to very specific disclosure requirements under federal securities laws. The federal Securities and Exchange Commission is responsible for enforcing two important depression-era laws that require honesty and openness in the release of corporate information. These laws, the Securities Act of 1933 and the Securities Exchange Act of 1934, were passed to correct some of the abuses that led to the stock market collapse in 1929. The corporate takeover battles of the 1980s led to demands that these laws be made even stronger.

The Securities Act requires most corporations to file detailed reports on their management and business prospects with the SEC before they may offer their stock for public sale. The Securities Exchange Act requires publicly traded corporations to continue providing current information on their business and financial conditions even when they are not issuing new stock. A publicly held company cannot conceal either good news or bad news to defraud the investing public. Nor may a corporation's officers use what the securities laws call "insider information" to profit at the expense of unwary investors. For instance, when an oil company discovers a promising new field, its executives cannot quietly buy up a lot of stock at low prices before they publicly announce the discovery. And when a company is the target of a takeover bid (which often causes the value of its stock to increase), that fact must be disclosed in a timely manner.

As a result of these laws and the SEC's traditionally vigorous enforcement, major corporations must disclose a great deal of corporate information to the public. The 1934 Securities Exchange Act is no freedom of information law, but at least it does provide the press and public with far more information about corporate doings than might otherwise be available. In compliance with these laws, major corporations provide a steady stream of news releases that are supposed to be frank and forthright in describing the company's business prospects.

When it comes to businesses that are operated as purely private entities (such as sole proprietorships, partnerships and non-publicly traded corporations), there are few legal requirements for the public release of information. Such companies may adhere to an enlightened information policy on a voluntary basis, or they may not.

However, even the smallest and most secrecy-prone private firm has to deal with federal, state and local governments, and often its government filings can provide valuable information. The federal FoI Act and virtually all state public records laws exempt trade secrets and proprietary information from disclosure, but private businesses must file a variety of other documents that an inquiring reporter may be able to see and copy. For instance, often a private land developer will file detailed reports and plans in an effort to win local approval for a new construction project, generating public records that an alert reporter can use to learn many details about what would otherwise be a hush-hush deal. In addition, when a private company is involved in litigation, it must often disclose information in court records that it would never otherwise release. Such information also provides many an insightful story about a private business enterprise.

Access to Private Property

Another problem for journalists is the need to go onto private property to cover the news. When a disaster occurs on private property, for instance, journalists routinely go to the scene of the event along with law enforcement, fire and other emergency personnel. However, journalists have to be aware that they may be sued for trespassing or invasion of privacy for doing so. When there is no event as clearly newsworthy as a major disaster, the potential liability of reporters who trespass to get a story may be even greater. The growth of "tabloid television" greatly aggravated these legal problems, which are discussed in Chapter Five.

PRACTICAL SUGGESTIONS FOR JOURNALISTS

The procedures for using the federal FoI Act were discussed earlier, and the procedures under state public records laws are generally similar, but how does one gain access to a government meeting that is closed when it shouldn't be? In fact, how do you know for sure what is really happening behind closed doors?

The first step is to be absolutely sure what your rights are under the applicable open meeting law. Many journalists carry a copy of their state's open meeting and public records laws with them whenever they are on an assignment. When an agency you are covering goes into a closed session, insist on learning the specific legal basis for the closure. Make it clear that you understand the open meeting law too--and are prepared to assert your rights.

If a public agency still insists on going into a closed session when you doubt its legality, you have a dilemma. You should make it known that your employer is prepared to challenge any unlawful closed meeting in court, if in fact your employer will back you. If not, you have to decide if you are prepared to go it alone. Many state laws (and the federal Government in the Sunshine Act) provide for the government to pay your attorney's fees if you win, but if you lose, you may be out a lot of money. Moreover, you will probably have to spend a lot of money long before a court will award you any reimbursement of your attorney's fees.

There is, of course, a second problem: reporting what happens in a closed meeting. In many states and under the federal law, government bodies are required to keep either detailed minutes or a transcript of closed proceedings. Find out what the requirements are in your state, and make it clear you want to see the transcript or minutes at the earliest possible time. Failing that, many journalists simply wait out the closed meeting and then interview some of the participants, perhaps double-checking by separately interviewing others who attended the meeting.

For many readers of this text, the problem may be just the opposite of the one facing the reporter. You may be a public relations representative of the agency that is holding a closed meeting. Your responsibility as a professional is twofold: (1) you must make sure the officials of your agency are aware of their obligations under the applicable open meeting (and public records) laws; and (2) you must take steps to be sure that reporters have access to you and others in your agency so they can be accurately informed about what occurred during the closed meeting.

When there is secrecy, the information-gathering process places special demands on both the journalist and the public relations representative. Fortunately, in recent years more and more states have enacted strong open meeting and public records laws--laws that call for openness in government and seek to curtail the government secrecy that creates these problems.

ONGOING ISSUES

Secrecy is an inherent part of the management style of so many government officials that no experienced journalist really expects the battle for freedom of information to end--ever. Although America has had numerous FoI laws in effect for several decades, governments show no great enthusiasm for open meetings and records. At the federal level, there is a strong Freedom of Information Act and a Sunshine Act, but the Supreme Court has created substantial loopholes, allowing the federal bureaucracy to keep many documents secret.

On the state level, the freedom of information picture seems a little brighter.

All states have laws governing both open meetings and public records. However, it takes constant vigilance to force public officials to obey these laws. Given the slightest excuse, many government agencies will close their files and lock their meeting-room doors. In the coming years, a major goal in the FoI field will be to reduce the number of exceptions these laws recognize--and to add effective legal remedies for unlawful government secrecy--while warding off bureaucrats' attempts to rid themselves of the onerous task of doing the public's business in public.

On the other hand, journalists are sometimes caught up in the legal and ethical problems raised by the release of information that could hurt someone--information that may well be available under FoI laws. In 1989 a young actress was murdered near her home in Los Angeles by someone who obtained her home address from a detective agency with access to driver's license records. As a result, access to those records was restricted. The news media bore no responsibility for that tragedy. In fact, the news media usually do not reveal the home addresses (or even the names) of crime victims when the information would jeopardize the person's safety. But what about the case, discussed in Chapter Five, in which the *Los Angeles Times* reported the name of a woman whose roommate was murdered, and who saw the murderer escaping? The name was in a public record, readily available to anyone and everyone. But few murderers spend their time searching public records at the courthouse while they are hiding from the authorities. Should the name of an eyewitness to a murder be *published in a newspaper* while the suspect is still at large?

Like so many other issues that are both legal and ethical, freedom of information is not a simple issue. In a democracy, the public has a right to know what government officials are doing and how they are spending the taxpayers' money. The public watchdog function is one of the most important roles of the press. All too often government misconduct is hidden in the guise of protecting national security or individual privacy--or any of a dozen other high-sounding excuses for secrecy. Nevertheless, there are times when public access to information creates troubling ethical questions. Perhaps the media can best safeguard the public's right to know by aggressively fighting government secrecy, while at the same time exercising restraint in publishing information when the potential for private harm outweighs the potential for public good.

A SUMMARY OF FOI LAWS

What Are Freedom of Information (FoI) Laws?

Taken as a group, FoI laws are state and federal statutory laws that permit public access to the documents generated by government agencies and to the meetings of government bodies. While granting general public access, virtually all such laws also contain numerous exceptions, limiting public access to meetings and records that deal with certain subjects.

What Is the Federal FoI Act?

The federal FoI Act is an act of Congress requiring many federal agencies to open their records for public inspection and copying. Government agencies must publish lists of their records to assist FoI Act users in identifying the records they wish to see. Agencies now have 20 working days to respond to most FoI requests, but that deadline is often ignored. Information falling into any of nine specified categories is exempt from public disclosure.

How Does the Privacy Act Affect the FoI Act?

Theoretically, the 1974 federal Privacy Act does not limit public access to government records. Instead, it allows an individual to inspect many of his/her own records in government data banks, and it protects personal records from misuse. However, its practical effect is to restrict access to much information about individuals that might otherwise be accessible to journalists.

What Is the Government in the Sunshine Act?

The Sunshine Act is a law requiring the governing boards of about 50 federal agencies to hold open meetings. These boards must announce their meetings in advance and must allow the public to attend unless certain confidential subject matter is being discussed.

Do the States Have FoI Laws?

All 50 states have laws requiring government agencies to hold open meetings and permitting some public access to government records. These laws generally apply to both state and local government agencies, but they usually limit or deny public access to meetings and records dealing with certain subjects, most commonly personnel matters (the hiring and firing of employees).

What Can a Citizen Do If an FoI Law Is Violated?

The federal FoI Act and Sunshine Act both authorize private citizens to sue offending government agencies, with the agency required to pay a citizen's attorney fees and court costs if he/she wins the lawsuit. Many state laws have similar provisions.

CHAPTER 10

Obscenity and the Law

There is no more controversial problem in First Amendment law than the conflict between free expression and the right of the majority to set standards of sexual morality for everyone. The Supreme Court has made it clear that *legally obscene materials* are not protected by the First Amendment and may be suppressed by local, state or federal authorities. But if, on the other hand, a work is not obscene, it is constitutionally protected. Thus, it is essential to define obscenity--and yet that task has stymied the courts for many years.

The nation's highest court has had to intervene in this field repeatedly, sometimes reviewing specific works to decide if they are obscene on a case-by-case basis. It's an onerous and thankless task for a court whose other responsibilities are so lofty. In a moment of utter frustration, former Supreme Court Justice Potter Stewart once admitted he couldn't define obscenity, but added: "I know it when I see it."

Even if the Supreme Court has had trouble defining it, many people besides judges and professional pornographers need to know what is and isn't legally obscene. Print and broadcast journalists, cinematographers, photographers and advertising people, for instance, need to know the ground rules. Journalists are often accused of publishing something obscene when, in fact, the material in question falls nowhere near the legal definition of obscenity. There is a major debate underway concerning the presence of non-obscene but *indecent* material on radio and television and on the Internet.

The Supreme Court has held that governments may not ban non-obscene material from the print media or cable television even if it is "indecent" and offensive to many people. But as Chapter 11 explains, the Federal Communications Commission, acting under Congressional pressure, has restricted the broadcast of indecent material that would be perfectly legal in other mass media. In 1996, Congress passed the Communications Decency Act as a part of the broader Telecommunications Act, banning not only obscenity but also indecent material on any part of the Internet accessible to minors. This led many Internet users to protest the whole idea of government censorship of cyberspace. As explained later, the U.S. Supreme Court overturned the main provisions of this law in an important 1997 decision, *Reno v. ACLU* (521 U.S. 844). The court held that the Internet is entitled to the same broad First Amendment protection as the print media. But the Supreme Court later suggested that some regulation of the Internet to protect minors might be permissible (*Ashcroft v. ACLU*, 122 S.Ct. 1700).

The controversy about alleged indecency in cyberspace is only one part of a larger national debate that has developed recently over morality and alleged censorship in the arts. After artists whose works were offensive to many, including an artist who depicted a crucifix immersed in urine, won federal grants, Congress imposed restrictions on the content of works that are financially supported by the National Endowment for the Arts (NEA). Those who select grant recipients were directed to "take into consideration general standards of decency and respect for the diverse beliefs and values of the American people." Also, NEA grant recipients were required to sign anti-obscenity pledges under this controversial 1990 legislation.

At about the same time, the director of a major art gallery, the Contemporary Arts Center in Cincinnati, Ohio, was criminally prosecuted for exhibiting the work of photographer Robert Mapplethorpe, including some explicit homoerotic pictures. And in Florida, a federal judge declared "As Nasty as They Wanna Be," an album by the rap group 2 Live Crew, to be obscene, thus allowing it to be banned. To some Americans, these separate actions represented important steps toward eliminating something that they see as a blight: pornography. But to others, these were heavy-handed government attempts to censor, attempts by some people to dictate what others may create, view or listen to.

Like many earlier controversies about obscenity in America, these three have been resolved in the courts. A federal appellate court overturned the Florida judge's ruling that the 2 Live Crew album is obscene (*Luke Records v. Navarro*, 960 F.2d 134, 1992). In the Cincinnati case, the art gallery director was acquitted by a jury. Inasmuch as not-guilty verdicts cannot be appealed, that ended the litigation, but not the public debate concerning where art ends and obscenity begins.

The controversy over the NEA's decency standards led to a landmark U.S. Supreme Court decision in 1998: *National Endowment for the Arts v. Finley* (524 U.S. 569). By an 8-1 majority, the court held that the NEA rules are not an unconstitutional form of viewpoint discrimination by the government. This case is discussed later in this chapter.

All 50 states have laws to control obscenity, and federal law prohibits both the importation and mailing of obscene works. In addition, federal law bans the use of minors--or adults appearing to be minors--in sexually explicit films, videos, photographs and computer-generated images. The ban on adults who appear to be minors has generated a heated controversy--and more lawsuits, as explained later. Federal law allows heavy fines and lengthy prison terms for violators of these laws. Also, the federal Racketeer Influenced and Corrupt Organizations Act (RICO) allows the seizure of the assets of businesses that deal in obscenity. Separate laws allow customs agents, among other federal officials, to seize and destroy obscene materials.

Many state laws make producing, performing or selling obscene works a crime and also allow their seizure. But when these state and federal laws are enforced, the result is often a conflict between individual liberty and society's purported right to dictate moral standards for everyone.

As the ultimate interpreter of the meaning of the First Amendment, the U.S. Supreme Court often must resolve these controversies over obscenity. But in the years since the Supreme Court first tried to define obscenity in 1957, its attempts to define what is--and isn't--legally obscene have sometimes caused more confusion than enlightenment.

Given the difficulty of coming up with a legally sound definition of obscenity, many states and cities have looked for alternate ways to control the sale or exhibition of sexually oriented books, magazines and films. For example, many cities have attempted to zone adult businesses out of residential neighborhoods. And some communities have used nuisance laws against these businesses--with varying degrees of success.

This chapter traces the development of American obscenity law from its English and colonial roots to its current uncertain status.

EARLY PORNOGRAPHY BATTLES

In colonial America and Victorian England there were fervent but inconsistent efforts to eradicate literature that those in power considered obscene. As early as 1712, the Massachusetts colonial legislature passed a law that made it a crime to publish "any filthy, obscene, or profane song, pamphlet, libel or mock sermon."

Meanwhile, the English common law on obscenity was evolving through court decisions, and colonial courts and legislatures looked to the common law for guidance. The common law foreshadowed things to come in this field by failing to define obscenity and instead focusing on the alleged corruption of youth and threats to order.

By the mid-1800s, however, England and America were moving toward specific statutory laws aimed at obscene works. The Tariff Act of 1842 was the first federal law in America designed to restrict the flow of obscenity. It prohibited the "importation of all indecent and obscene prints, paintings, lithographs, engravings and transparencies." In 1857, it was expanded to include printed matter as well. The U.S. Post Office entered the field in 1865, when Congress enacted a law that made mailing obscene materials a crime.

Meanwhile, what was happening in England continued to shape American law. Lord Campbell's Act of 1857 and the first case tried under it produced a standard for obscenity that was followed in America as well as England for many years. Adopted as the Victorian period was beginning, the act prohibited obscene books and prints. It was tested in 1868 when a judge seized copies of an anti-Catholic pamphlet by a man named Henry Scott. Scott appealed to Benjamin Hicklin, recorder of London, and Hicklin ruled in Scott's favor. However, Britain's chief justice, Alexander Cockburn, reversed Hicklin's decision and ruled thus:

> The test of obscenity is whether the tendency of the matter charged as obscenity is to deprave and corrupt those whose minds are open to such immoral influences and into whose hands a publication of this sort may fall.

In short, Scott's work was held obscene because of how certain passages in the work might affect the most susceptible readers. And that concept came to be known as the "Hicklin" rule because the case was named *Regina v. Hicklin* (L.R. 3 Q.B. 360, 1868).

The Hicklin test was enthusiastically adopted by American courts in the late 1800s and early 1900s. The Hicklin test allowed a work to be ruled obscene based on isolated passages taken out of context, and it defined obscenity in terms of its effect on the *most susceptible* members of society. As a result, all sorts of once-respected classical literature became suspect. The country was in the mood for a moral crusade.

It wasn't long until a crusader came along to meet the need. His name was Anthony Comstock, and he developed a following as he campaigned for morality. He and his supporters spent four months in 1873 lobbying Congress; the result was what came to be known as the Comstock Law, or more officially the federal Anti-Obscenity Act of 1873. This act went far beyond the 1865 law, giving the U.S. Post Office the power to banish from the mails any "obscene, lewd, lascivious, or filthy book, pamphlet, picture, paper, letter, writing, print, or other publication of an indecent character."

Conspicuously absent was any definition of obscenity; that would be left up to the people at the post office who would enforce the law. And who would that be?

None other than Anthony Comstock became the post office's special agent to ferret out obscenity and banish it from the mails. He pursued his new duties with a passion, and once boasted that he had "destroyed 160 tons of obscene literature."

Not content to bar dirty books from the mails, Comstock organized citizens groups to suppress "immoral" books even if they weren't mailed anywhere. Two of the most famous of these groups were the New York Society for the Suppression of Vice and the New England Watch and Ward Society.

These organizations cared little about the distinctions between great literature and pure pornography; anything "immoral" was fair game. Anthony Comstock and his followers made the word "Victorian" mean prudish. For 70 years, almost any sort of material depicting or referring to any kind of sex was likely to be censored.

What about the First Amendment? Apparently it never even occurred to the Victorians that freedom of the press included any protection at all for erotic expression. But somehow, both literature and human life survived--and the Hicklin rule drifted out of style in the twentieth century.

CHANGING STANDARDS AFTER 1900

By 1920 times were changing, and so was the law. In that year a New York appellate judge ruled that a book must be evaluated as a whole rather than being banished because of isolated passages. Further, the judge said the opinions of qualified critics should be considered before a book is ruled obscene. That happened in *Halsey v. New York Society for the Suppression of Vice* (180 N.Y.S. 836).

Finally, in 1933 federal Judge John Woolsey refused to follow the most basic part of the Hicklin Rule, the idea that a work was to be judged by its effect on the most susceptible members of society. In reviewing James Joyce's great work, *Ulysses*, he refused to follow the Hicklin Rule, under which he would have had to rule it obscene. He said a work must be judged by its effect "on a person with average sex instincts" rather than by its influence on the most corruptible members of society. Moreover, he said the work had to be judged as a whole, not by looking at isolated parts.

In 1934 the U.S. Court of Appeals upheld that decision (*One Book Entitled 'Ulysses' v. U.S.*, 72 F.2d 705). The appellate court--with Augustus and Learned Hand, two famous jurists who were cousins, in the majority--handed down a ruling that all but abolished the Hicklin test. The appellate court affirmed Judge Woolsey's view that the work should be judged as a whole and weighed by its effect on the average person.

The Landmark Roth Case

By the 1950s, many state and federal courts had abandoned the Hicklin Rule in favor of the more liberal one suggested in the *Ulysses* decision, but the U.S. Supreme Court had not attempted to write a definition of obscenity that would square with the First Amendment.

In 1957 the Supreme Court reviewed a series of obscenity prosecutions and finally dealt with this issue. In *Butler v. Michigan* (352 U.S. 380), the court overturned a Michigan law that prohibited the sale of any book that might incite minors to commit depraved acts or corrupt their morals. In so doing, the court said that states cannot quarantine "the general reading public against books not too rugged for grown men and women in order to shield juvenile innocence." If that were allowed, the court said, the result would be "to reduce the adult population of Michigan to reading what is only fit for children."

Thus, the Supreme Court had taken its first step toward the ultimate elimination of the Hicklin Rule: it had said material cannot be forbidden to adults just because it may be considered bad for children.

Four months later, the Supreme Court handed down another obscenity decision, and this one has been viewed as the court's landmark ruling in the field. The case was *Roth v. U.S.* (354 U.S. 476, 1957). The case arose when a man named Samuel Roth was convicted under federal law for mailing circulars, a book and advertising material that were considered obscene. It was decided together with another case, *Alberts v. California*, in which David Alberts had been convicted of violating a California law against possessing obscene materials for sale.

The Supreme Court upheld both convictions, deciding that the laws under which they were convicted did not violate the Constitution. The court specifically ruled that obscene materials are not protected by the First Amendment.

However, Justice William Brennan's majority opinion also adopted a definition of obscenity that some lower courts had been following in lieu of the Hicklin Rule. The court said that henceforth no state could ban sexually oriented materials as obscene unless they were legally obscene under this new definition. Using the new definition, a court determines whether a work is obscene by asking:

whether to the average person, applying contemporary community standards, the dominant theme of the material taken as a whole appeals to prurient interest.

Thus, the Supreme Court specifically disavowed the Hicklin test, partly because it permitted judging obscenity "by the effect of isolated passages upon the most susceptible persons." The Hicklin test violates the First Amendment, the court ruled. However, the courts that tried Roth and Alberts both used proper definitions of obscenity, so their convictions were affirmed. Still, *Roth* is a very important case because it officially adopted a new definition of obscenity and made it binding everywhere in America.

The *Roth* case produced the first of a series of dissenting opinions on obscenity law by Justices Hugo Black and William O. Douglas. These two jurists took an absolutist position about the First Amendment. They said the First Amendment protects even obscenity. Thus, they argued that criminal prosecutions based on the content of the materials--or the bad thoughts they allegedly inspire--should be unconstitutional.

For years these two justices consistently maintained that obscenity laws are unconstitutional, a position free expression advocates heartily endorsed. However, on several crucial occasions their absolutist stance created problems: it enabled the high court to reverse obscenity convictions, but made it impossible for a majority of the court to agree on the reason for the reversal. The result was a series of plurality decisions that left the nation unsure what the law really was.

Shortly after the *Roth* decision, the Supreme Court was called on to review a number of other cases involving sexually explicit material. Soon a trend began: the Supreme Court repeatedly overturned lower courts' determinations that various works were obscene. In 1958 and 1959 alone, the high court reversed obscenity rulings involving a collection of nudist and art student publications, a magazine for homosexuals and another magazine that included nudity. The court also overturned a state statute prohibiting movies depicting adultery and reversed a ruling that held bookstore owners responsible for the content of all the books they offered for sale.

Obviously, these decisions represented a trend toward liberalism on obscenity. The Supreme Court continued to consider obscenity beyond the protection of the First Amendment, but fewer works were being adjudged obscene while more and more works were being given First Amendment protection.

Expanding the Roth Test

The *Roth* case was a landmark decision, and like many landmark decisions it left some questions unanswered. For instance, what is the definition of a community for "community standards"? Does it encompass a local area, or is it something larger than that? And what does it take to violate those community standards?

The Supreme Court addressed the latter issue in a 1962 decision, *Manual Enterprises v. Day* (370 U.S. 478). The case involved the Post Office's attempts to ban from the mail several magazines intended mainly for homosexuals. Although the majority opinion branded the magazines "dismally unpleasant, uncouth and tawdry," the court said they were not obscene and thus upheld their right to use the U.S. mail.

Under the federal obscenity law in force at the time, a work had to appeal to "prurient interest" and be "patently offensive" before it could be banned. The court said these publications were not patently offensive. The court also affirmed a position it had previously taken that mere nudity is not obscene.

That case left "community standards" undefined, but a 1964 Supreme Court decision, *Jacobellis v. Ohio* (378 U.S. 184), addressed that problem. Nico Jacobellis, a theater manager, was convicted of violating an Ohio law by showing an allegedly obscene French film, *Les Amants*. The court reversed Jacobellis' conviction, ruling the film non-obscene. It had been shown in about 100 cities, including at least two others in Ohio.

Justice Brennan, writing for the court's plurality, said the Constitution requires *national* standards on obscenity. "The federal Constitution would not permit the concept of obscenity to have a varying meaning from county to county or town to town," he said.

However, Brennan's reference to national standards attracted a strenuous protest from Chief Justice Earl Warren, who argued that local standards are precisely what was intended in *Roth*. "...(C)ommunities throughout the nation are in fact diverse, and it must be remembered that, in cases such as this one, the court is confronted with the task of reconciling conflicting rights of the diverse communities within our society and of individuals," Warren wrote.

As we shall see, Warren's view rather than Brennan's eventually prevailed, but for nearly a decade most judges assumed there should be national standards of obscenity, with local juries obliged to follow them no matter how much those standards differed from prevailing local sentiment.

"Fanny Hill" and "Social Value"

The constitutional law of obscenity was further expanded in 1966, when the Supreme Court ruled that a classic erotic work, *Memoirs of a Woman of Pleasure* (often called "Fanny Hill"), was not obscene. In *Memoirs v. Massachusetts* (383 U.S. 413), the Supreme Court was again unable to reach enough of a consensus for a majority opinion, but the plurality opinion authored by Justice Brennan suggested a three-part test for obscenity: the original Roth test, plus "patent offensiveness," and a requirement that the work be "utterly without redeeming social value."

In *Roth*, Brennan had said works that are obscene lack any "redeeming social importance," but the *Roth* decision did not specifically make the absence of "social importance" a part of the test for obscenity. However, lower courts began to consider that factor, and Brennan referred to it again in *Jacobellis*. Finally, in *Memoirs* Brennan said a liberalized version of the "redeeming social importance" concept was a constitutionally required part of the test for obscenity. He said a work could not be considered obscene if it had "social value." However, Brennan's opinion in *Memoirs* was still only a plurality opinion. Justices Black and Douglas continued to vote to overturn obscenity convictions--but on the rationale that the First Amendment protects even obscene materials.

But despite its lack of majority support on the Supreme Court, the "social value" test was very widely accepted after 1966. Like Brennan's concept of national standards, the "social value" test would eventually be abandoned by the Supreme Court, but for a time it made obscenity prosecutions extremely difficult. Proving that a work is "utterly without redeeming social value" is by no means easy. Almost any obscenity defendant could find an expert witness somewhere who would testify that the work in question has some sort of social value.

The *Memoirs* case involved what some might consider a classic bit of erotica. Written about 1749 by an Englishman named John Cleland (1709-1789), it is a first-person account of the activities of a high-class prostitute in London. The book attracted the censors of Massachusetts as early as 1821. By the 1960s, "Fanny Hill" had been translated into braille, placed in the Library of Congress, and purchased by hundreds of other libraries. And yet, the Massachusetts attorney general tried to have it "banned in Boston" again, nearly 150 years after the first such effort. This final attempt to ban "Fanny Hill" in Boston failed, of course, when the nation's highest court ruled that the book was not legally obscene.

Alternatives to Proving Obscenity

After the *Memoirs* decision, the Supreme Court moved away from attempting to define obscenity and looked to other factors in deciding three important obscenity cases.

In *Ginzburg v. U.S.* (383 U.S. 463), the court upheld the federal obscenity conviction of a well-known pornographer, Ralph Ginzburg. In so ruling, the court avoided dealing with the question of whether the publications he was convicted of marketing were inherently obscene and instead took note of the way he promoted his works. The court said there was abundant evidence of pandering, "the business of purveying textual or graphic matter openly advertised to appeal to the erotic interest of their customers."

Ginzburg originally tried to mail his publications from Intercourse and Blue Ball, Pennsylvania, but the post offices in those small towns couldn't handle the volume, so he settled for Middlesex, New Jersey. The court concluded that those mailing points were selected only for the effect their names would have on his sales.

Thus, the court affirmed an obscenity conviction based on the conduct of the seller rather than the content of the works.

The next year in *Redrup v. New York* (386 U.S. 767, 1967), the Supreme Court reversed three state obscenity convictions. In all three cases, a state court had assumed the material was "obscene in the constitutional sense," but the Supreme Court said those decisions were wrong. However, the justices could not agree on any one standard by which to judge obscenity.

As a result, the court backed away from defining obscenity and simply listed three categories of marketing that might justify state prosecutions without any finding that the works themselves are obscene. The three were: (1) the sale of sexually titillating material to juveniles; (2) the distribution of such materials in a manner that is an assault on individual privacy because it is impossible for unwilling persons to avoid exposure to it; and (3) sales made in a "pandering" fashion.

The result of *Redrup*, apparently, was that only hard-core pornography could be banned. The court seemed to be extending constitutional protection to materials that, though possibly obscene, were neither pandered nor forced upon unwilling recipients. The impact of the *Redrup* decision is shown by the fact that it was cited as a basis for the reversal of 35 reported obscenity convictions in the next year and a half. Some of these reversals came in additional Supreme Court rulings that were decided without formal opinions, with others in decisions of lower state and federal courts.

The Supreme Court affirmed its suggestion in *Redrup* about obscenity and juveniles a year later in *Ginsberg v. New York* (390 U.S. 629, 1968). There, the court upheld the conviction of Sam Ginsberg (not to be confused with Ralph Ginzburg) for violating a state law against selling to minors material defined to be obscene on the basis of its supposed effect on them. In affirming Ginsberg's conviction, the court accepted the concept of "variable obscenity"--that is, the concept that a state could punish someone for selling a work to juveniles that might not be obscene to adults.

Thus, the sum effect of these three decisions is to allow obscenity prosecutions under special circumstances, even though it had become almost impossible to prove a work was legally obscene to adults.

The Warren Court's Finale

In 1969 the Supreme Court handed down the last major obscenity decision of the liberal Warren era (Chief Justice Warren retired later that year). But that last decision went a long way toward protecting the private possession of obscene matter from government scrutiny.

In *Stanley v. Georgia* (394 U.S. 557), the court overturned an obscenity conviction that resulted from an amazing law enforcement "fishing expedition." Police searched Robert Eli Stanley's home in quest of bookmaking materials, but instead they found some possibly interesting films in a dresser drawer in his bedroom. They set up his projector, watched the films, and then arrested him for possessing obscene matter in violation of a Georgia law.

In the court's majority opinion, Justice Thurgood Marshall said this:

> Whatever may be the justification for other statutes regulating obscenity, we do not think they reach into the privacy of one's home. If the First Amendment means anything, it means that a state has no business telling a man, sitting alone in his own house, what books he may read or what films he may watch.

Marshall said, in effect, that there is a constitutional right to possess and use even obscene materials in the privacy of one's home. Also, Marshall wrote, the First Amendment protects the "right to receive information and ideas, regardless of their social worth."

However, the court warned that this ruling was not intended to abolish "*Roth* and the cases following that decision." This was a unique set of facts, and two years later the Supreme Court refused to extend *Stanley* to other situations. In the meantime, of course, Chief Justice Earl Warren had retired and the makeup of the court was shifting.

In two cases decided the same day in 1971, *U.S. v. Reidel* (402 U.S. 351) and *U.S. v. Thirty-Seven Photographs* (402 U.S. 363), the court backed away from the *Stanley* principle. In *Reidel*, the court upheld the constitutionality of the federal obscenity law's ban on mailing obscene matter even to consenting adults. Thus, the court avoided following the "right to receive" concept from *Stanley*. In *Thirty-Seven Photographs*, the court said customs officials could still seize obscene materials from a returning traveler's luggage, even if they were intended for private use.

Two years later, in *U.S. v. Twelve 200-foot Reels of Super 8mm Film* (413 U.S. 123, 1973), the Supreme Court was even more emphatic in saying the First Amendment does not give a private individual any right to bring allegedly obscene materials back from abroad. Once a person makes it home with his obscene materials he is safe, but if officials catch him en route, it is a different matter.

These decisions were widely criticized as inconsistent with the language of *Stanley*. The *Stanley* decision was only *distinguished* and not reversed, but it was obvious by 1973 that the Supreme Court's view of obscenity was changing. Richard Nixon had by then appointed four new justices to the Supreme Court, and he made it clear that one of the things he was looking for was justices who would crack down on pornography. A new and more conservative majority on obscenity matters was coalescing.

SETTING A NEW STANDARD

The new Supreme Court majority had an opportunity to make its own statement on obscenity law in 1973, and the result was a new landmark decision that revised much of what the Warren court had done, *Miller v. California* (413 U.S. 15). The four Nixon appointees and Justice Byron White made up a five-justice majority in this case, and Justice Brennan, long the author of important majority and plurality opinions on obscenity, began writing dissents.

In *Miller* and four other cases decided at the same time, the court revised the *Roth-Memoirs* test, abandoning the "redeeming social value" concept. The new majority also disavowed the idea of requiring nationally uniform "community standards," thereby freeing each state to adopt standards that might differ from those in other states--or even from one community to the next within a state.

The *Miller* case arose when Marvin Miller conducted a mass mail campaign to sell "adult" material. Five of his brochures were sent to a Newport Beach, Calif., restaurant, and the recipients complained to police. Miller was convicted of violating California obscenity law and appealed to the U.S. Supreme Court.

The high court took the occasion to write a specific new test for obscenity. The new test said a work is obscene if:

1. An average person, applying contemporary community standards,

would find that the work, taken as a whole, appeals to the prurient interest;

2. The work depicts or describes, in a patently offensive way, sexual conduct, and the applicable state law specifically defines what depictions or descriptions are prohibited; and

3. The work, taken as a whole, lacks serious literary, artistic, political or scientific value.

Thus, the court reaffirmed the first two parts of the test set forth in *Memoirs,* although the community standards could now be local. Also, the term "patently offensive" would have to be defined in statutory law. However, the third part of the *Memoirs* test, the "redeeming social value" concept, was abandoned in favor of "serious literary, artistic, political or scientific value," something slightly easier to prove in a criminal proceeding.

It was still only a 5-4 decision, but the *Miller* decision marked the first time since 1957 that a majority of the Supreme Court had been able to agree on "concrete guidelines to isolate 'hard core' pornography from expression protected by the First Amendment."

In abandoning national standards, Chief Justice Warren Burger emphasized the diversity of the communities of America. "It is neither realistic nor constitutionally necessary to read the First Amendment as requiring that the people of Maine or Mississippi accept public depiction of conduct found tolerable in Las Vegas, or New York City," Burger said.

One of the court's goals in allowing the states to adopt local standards, certainly, was to reduce the workload of the federal courts. The Supreme Court had been asked to review hundreds of obscenity cases, and the justices felt obliged to accept far more of these cases than they would have preferred. But if the court was seeking to get out of the obscenity business, it failed. In the years after *Miller,* the high court had to accept a number of additional obscenity cases.

In one of them, *Pinkus v. U.S.* (436 U.S. 493, 1978), the Supreme Court said that children should not be a part of the "community" when jurors determine "community standards," if the work was intended for adults. However, the court said adults with varying degrees of susceptibility to obscene materials should be considered in the determination.

The Supreme Court answered another important question about the *Miller* decision some years later in *Pope v. Illinois* (481 U.S. 497, 1987). In this case the high court clarified the way the three-part Miller test must be applied in state obscenity prosecutions.

The *Pope* case involved a challenge to the validity of an Illinois obscenity conviction in which all three parts of the Miller test were measured against prevailing community standards. Although *Miller* had said either statewide or local community standards could be used to determine whether a given work was obscene, that was only one part of the test. An Illinois court used subjective community standards to determine all three parts, including the question of whether the work had serious value.

The Supreme Court held that the measurement of "serious ...value" was to be based on *objective* standards. The court said a "reasonable man" test should be used to determine whether a literary work has serious value. Expert witnesses could be summoned to testify as to the serious literary, artistic, political or scientific value, if any, of a work. Writing for the court, Justice Byron White said:

> The proper inquiry is not whether an ordinary member of any given community would find literary, artistic, political, or scientific value in allegedly obscene material, but whether a reasonable person would find such value in the material taken as a whole.

This hardly represented a major change in obscenity law: an objective standard is usually employed to determine whether questionable works have serious value. However, in this case the court made it clear that the use of such a standard is required by the First Amendment. Without it, local communities could declare important literary works to be obscene by citing their own standards for seriousness. The result could be acts of censorship that would abridge First Amendment freedoms.

In so ruling, the Supreme Court was responding to its own experience with situations in which local juries did apply parochial standards in obscenity cases and rule a serious literary work to be obscene, forcing the appellate courts to intervene.

That is precisely what happened in *Jenkins v. Georgia* (418 U.S. 153, 1974). A jury convicted Billy Jenkins, a theater manager, of violating the Georgia obscenity statute by showing an Academy Award-nominated R-rated film, *Carnal Knowledge*. The film had occasional scenes of nudity and non-explicit scenes suggesting that sexual intercourse occurred.

The case reached the Supreme Court, which said the film did not depict sex in a patently offensive way and was thus not outside the protection of the First Amendment. Local juries must consider all parts of the Miller test, including the "patent offensiveness" factor, in determining obscenity, the court said.

But more to the point, perhaps, was the fact that this case forced the court to hedge on its commitment to local standards. If a jury in an isolated community somewhere decides a work that is considered a serious one everywhere else violates the local standards there, isn't that exactly what the court invited in *Miller*?

In the 1974 case of *Hamling v. U.S.* (418 U.S. 87), Justice Brennan dissented when the court affirmed a federal obscenity conviction, warning:

> National distributors choosing to send their products in interstate travels will be forced to cope with the community standards of every hamlet into which their goods may wander.

This threat is far from an academic one. In a 1978 case, an Oregon distributor of sexually explicit materials was forced to defend a federal obscenity prosecution in Wyoming because postal authorities thought the conservative community standards there would make a conviction easier to secure. At the request of an Oregon postmaster, a Wyoming postmaster solicited materials from the distributor, using a false name and address. Other than mailing the materials, the Oregon man had no contact with Wyoming, and he mailed materials to no one else in the state. But he was charged with violating the federal obscenity law in Wyoming and was forced to defend himself there. He eventually pleaded guilty to one count, and a federal appellate court felt it had no choice but to uphold the judgment, although the justices vigorously protested this "venue shopping" by federal officials.

The appellate court said, "...publishers and distributors everywhere who are willing to fill subscriptions nationwide are subject to the creative zeal of federal enforcement officers...." (*U.S. v. Blucher*, 581 F.2d 244, 1978). The decision was eventually set aside by the Supreme Court, but the fact that Blucher was prosecuted at all raises serious questions about the community standards issue.

For those who produced or appeared in nationally distributed books or films, this problem became a very serious one. For example, Harry Reems, male star of the widely known explicit movie, *Deep Throat*, was prosecuted for violating federal obscenity laws in Memphis, Tenn. The movie was not made there, and it was apparently shown there only twice (before the theater was raided by police). But Reems was caught traveling through town and criminally prosecuted--although his movie had been shown legally in hundreds of cities by then.

Aside from the problem of varying "community standards," doesn't this sort of thing also raise issues of fundamental fairness? Is a publisher or actor afforded "due process of law" when forced to defend himself hundreds or thousands of miles from where he lives and works, just because a copy of his allegedly obscene material made its way there?

These questions were being asked again much more recently, as the U.S. Justice Department launched criminal actions against a number of Los Angeles-based adult video producers by obtaining grand jury indictments against them in Tulsa and Dallas, not in Los Angeles.

In 1993 officials at the U.S. Justice Department said they were reconsidering the policy of indicting alleged pornographers in places far from where they live and work. However, a year later the Justice Department filed criminal charges in Memphis against a couple who lived near San Francisco because they maintained pornographic computer images on a private bulletin board system at their home in California. An undercover federal agent in Tennessee signed up for access and paid a fee to obtain a password--and then downloaded enough images to persuade a jury in Memphis to convict them on federal obscenity charges. Their convictions were upheld on appeal in *U.S. v. Thomas* (74 F.3d 701, 1996).

The court affirmed the principle that federal obscenity laws apply to digitized computer files and also ruled that the couple could be convicted under the community standards in Memphis rather than San Francisco. Although this case involved a bulletin board system and not a site on the Internet, it raised questions about liability for pornographic materials that are posted on the Internet and downloaded by someone far away, in a place with different local community standards.

Although federal prosecutors still engage in forum shopping at times, the lower courts everywhere must follow the Supreme Court's instructions in *Pope v. Illinois*: they must decide the "serious... value" part of the *Miller* test on the basis of an *objective* analysis of what is and isn't serious value. That cannot be determined by local community standards alone. This is why the U.S. Court of Appeals overturned a federal judge's determination that 2 Live Crew's album, "As Nasty as They Wanna Be," was obscene. In *Luke Records v. Navarro*, cited earlier in this chapter, the appellate court noted that the judge based his determination of community standards in South Florida on his own experience in the community. And the sheriff who was seeking to have the album declared obscene offered no expert testimony that it lacked serious literary, artistic, political or scientific value. But the defense produced several experts on music, literature and African-American culture who testified that the album did indeed have serious value. In view of that, the appellate court ruled that the sheriff had failed to prove that the 2 Live Crew album was legally obscene.

Pornography and Minors

While the courts were wrestling with the problems of community standards, another trend has been developing in obscenity law: a nationwide crackdown on the production and distribution of films and other works depicting minors in sexually explicit roles. By the early 1980s the federal government and at least 20 states had passed laws to ban the use of minors in such roles even if the work was not legally obscene.

In 1982, the Supreme Court ruled on the constitutionality of these laws in *New York v. Ferber* (458 U.S. 747). The high court carved out an exception to the normal rules on obscenity, upholding a New York law that permitted criminal prosecutions for those who produce or sell printed matter or movies in which minors perform sex acts, without any proof of obscenity.

The court ruled that the states have the right to prohibit children from appearing in sexually explicit scenes regardless of the literary merit or non-obscene nature of the work. Where such a scene is needed for literary or artistic reasons, the court said "a person over the statutory age who looked younger could be utilized."

In urging the high court to find the New York law unconstitutional, civil libertarians and the book publishing industry warned that such laws could be used to prosecute those who produce many socially important works, including motion pictures such as *Taxi Driver*. The Supreme Court did not heed their arguments, choosing instead to give the states a relatively free hand to regulate the use of minors in sexually explicit roles.

In 1990, the Supreme Court again allowed the states to adopt more restrictive rules for minors than for adults. In *Osborne v. Ohio* (495 U.S. 103), the court carved out an exception to the *Stanley v. Georgia* ruling (discussed earlier). *Stanley* had created a right to possess even obscene books or movies in the privacy of one's own home without government interference. In *Osborne*, the court said Ohio could prosecute a person for the mere private possession of sexually oriented materials in his own home *if the materials involved children*.

In a controversial 6-3 ruling, the court rejected arguments that upholding the Ohio law could open the way for laws to punish parents who possessed nude photographs of their own children. The majority held that the Ohio law was not unconstitutionally broad or vague. (The Ohio law contained an exemption allowing parents to possess photographs of their own children).

Writing for the court, Justice Byron White said the need to control child pornography was so "compelling" that the states were free to enact laws that might be unconstitutional under other circumstances.

What about sexually explicit videos starring an actor or actress who claimed to be an adult at the time the videos were made, but who turns out to have been under age? There have been several legal battles over that issue involving actress Traci Lords, who made a number of adult videos before she was 18, using false documents to misrepresent her age. The 1977 Protection of Children Against Sexual Exploitation Act seemingly made it a federal crime to produce or distribute sexually explicit materials involving minors, regardless of whether the producer or distributor knows that a performer is under 18. However, a federal appellate court ruled in 1988 that producers of videos could present evidence that they were deceived about a performer's age in their defense (*U.S. v. U.S. District Court*, 858 F.2d 534). And in 1994, the Supreme Court reinterpreted the 1977 law and ruled that it does not permit the criminal prosecution of anyone who does not know that a person appearing in an adult video is under age (*U.S. v. X-Citement Video Inc.*, 513 U.S. 64).

Congress offered prosecutors a way around the safeguards for film and video producers in the *X-Citement Video* decision by passing the Child Pornography Prevention Act of 1996. In sweeping terms, this law banned not only the use of minors in sexually explicit roles (even non-obscene ones) but also images that "*appear to depict* a minor engaged in sexually explicit conduct." The law established stiff fines and prison sentences not only for the producers of films, videos, photographs or computer-generated images that appear to depict a minor engaged in sexual activity but also for persons who merely possess such a film, video or image.

The Child Pornography Prevention Act was immediately challenged in court by civil libertarians, booksellers, photographers, adult film producers and others who said it could be used to prosecute anyone who possessed a copy of many mainstream movies, including not only *Taxi Driver* but also *The Exorcist, Dirty Dancing, Animal House* or *The Last Picture Show*, among many others. There were media reports that a filmmaker doing a remake of *Lolita* in 1998 had a prominent First Amendment lawyer present for six weeks of production and editing in an attempt to avoid running afoul of this law. Several nude scenes featuring an over-18 "body-double" for the 15-year-old lead actress were cut at the lawyer's insistence. He reportedly feared that even using an adult double would create the appearance of a minor involved in a sex scene, thereby violating the law.

Explaining the intent of the 1996 law, Senator Orrin Hatch, R-Utah, its primary sponsor, said that computer-generated images are virtually impossible to distinguish from photographs, often making it difficult for law enforcement authorities to act against child pornography because no minor's face is identifiable. However, he said, computer images pose the same dangers as unretouched photographs of child pornography: they can be used to seduce children into sexual activity and to encourage pedophiles to prey on children.

In 2002 the U.S. Supreme Court overturned the provision of the Child Pornography Prevention Act that banned computer-generated images and other images that only "appear to" depict a minor engaged in a sex act. Ruling in *Ashcroft v. Free*

Speech Coalition (122 S.Ct. 1389), the court voted 6-3 to overturn that part of the law.

Writing for the majority, Justice Anthony M. Kennedy agreed that the Child Pornography Prevention Act is overly broad and vague. Congress had tried to justify the ban on computer simulations on the ground that while no actual children are exploited in the creation of such images, real children could be harmed because the images could feed the prurient appetites of pedophiles. But Kennedy's majority opinion upheld a lower court's conclusion that the government had failed to show a link between computer-generated images and the exploitation of actual children.

This decision does not affect provisions of the Child Pornography Prevention Act and parallel state laws banning the creation, sale or mere possession of images of real children engaging in sex acts--those laws remain intact. It doesn't even affect provisions of the federal law that ban the use of computer morphing techniques to alter images of real children to make it appear that they are engaged in sex acts. Nor does the decision limit the power of the authorities to prosecute those who produce, sell or possess computer-generated or other images that are legally obscene. The issue here was prosecutions based on images that are not legally obscene and do not involve the use of real children as models.

Soon after the Supreme Court's *Ashcroft v. Free Speech Coalition* decision, a bipartisan group of lawmakers joined Attorney General John Ashcroft in proposing a new federal law that might circumvent the Supreme Court's decision. For Ashcroft, this issue has become something of a personal cause: he was a strong supporter of the Child Pornography Prevention Act as a U.S. Senator in 1996. As attorney general, he oversaw the federal government's effort to defend the law in the Supreme Court. And he quickly emerged as a leader of the movement to enact a new law.

The Senate and House considered two approaches. In the Senate, the focus was on banning computer-generated as well as real images of *pre-pubescent children* engaged in simulated or real sex acts. By concentrating only on younger children, Ashcroft and his allies hoped to pass a law that would survive a court challenge. The legislation as of mid-2002 would criminalize the possession of "a visual depiction that is, or is virtually indistinguishable from, that of a pre-pubescent child engaging in sexually explicit conduct." A pre-pubescent child is defined as one who "does not exhibit significant pubescent physical or sexual maturation."

In the House, a bill was approved in mid-2002 that would place on the defendant the burden of proving that a real child had *not* been used to produce erotic images that appear to be of children. The Electronic Frontier Foundation and other Internet civil liberties groups questioned the constitutionality of this approach. They also wondered whether the bill would achieve its sponsors' goal of banning child pornography because it is relatively easy to produce erotic images of computer-generated children without using any real children--and then to circumvent a law like this one by documenting the computer-based production methods.

OTHER FORMS OF CENSORSHIP

Postal Censorship

From the Comstock era to the *Blucher* case, many federal efforts to suppress allegedly obscene materials have centered on the postal service. However, postal censorship has its limits.

A classic example is the time when the Post Office tried to censor *Esquire* magazine, which was more sexually oriented then than it is today--but hardly hardcore pornography. The case began in 1943 when the postmaster general refused the magazine second class mailing privileges.

A federal appellate court reversed that postal decision, and the Supreme Court agreed. Justice William O. Douglas, writing for the court, said, "Congress has left the postmaster general with no power to prescribe standards for the literature or the art which a mailable periodical disseminates" (*Hannegan v. Esquire*, 327 U.S. 146, 1946).

After that adverse ruling, the postal service backed away from most efforts to censor popular publications, but it was given a new role in obscenity law enforcement in 1968. At that point Congress passed the Pandering Advertisement Act (39 U.S.C. 3008), a law allowing postal patrons to demand that their names be removed from objectionable mailing lists after they receive material they consider sexually offensive. The Post Office is required to force mailers to remove names from their lists in compliance with these requests.

The Supreme Court upheld that law in 1970, in *Rowan v. Post Office* (397 U.S. 728). Congress strengthened the law in 1971, allowing postal customers to have their names removed from offensive mailing lists even before the first sexually objectionable item arrives in the mail.

The U.S. Post Office has also engaged in various other forms of censorship. For example, for many years it was unlawful to mail unsolicited advertisements for contraceptive devices. However, *Bolger v. Young Drug Products Corp.*, a 1983 Supreme Court decision that is discussed in Chapter 13, overturned those regulations on First Amendment grounds.

Censorship on Military Bases

Issues of freedom and control have long been controversial in the armed forces. Much has been said and written over the years about the freedom (or lack thereof) of those serving in the U.S. Army, Navy, Air Force, Marines or even the Coast Guard. In the late 1990s, a controversy arose over the military's rules against fraternization and adultery--rules that were sometimes used to discipline, discharge or even imprison armed forces personnel for private, off-duty consensual sexual conduct that would be considered of no concern to most civilian employers. Amidst this controversy, Congress passed new legislation in 1996 to ban the sale or rental of non-obscene but sexually oriented videos, films and even magazines such as Penthouse and Playboy at PXs (stores) on military bases.

Under this legislation, called the Military Honor and Decency Act of 1996, a censorship board was set up by the Department of Defense to determine which movies and magazines should be banned. During the controversy that resulted from all of this, magazine publishers, civil libertarians and others challenged the 1996 law. In 1997, a federal judge ruled the law unconstitutional and barred its implementation. Then a federal appellate court voted 2-1 to overrule that decision and uphold the law, declaring that military stores "are nonpublic forums in which the government may restrict the content of speech, so long as the restriction is reasonable and it does not discriminate among particular viewpoints" (*General Media Communications v. Cohen*, 131 F.3d 273, 1997). In 1998, the U.S. Supreme Court declined to review the appellate court decision, leaving the law intact--and the military free to ban the sale or rental of sexually oriented videos and publications in their stores.

Films, Obscenity and Censorship

Motion pictures have created special censorship problems ever since the cinema emerged as a form of entertainment and art. From the early days of magic lantern shows to the modern era of adult films, irate citizens have demanded censorship to protect public morals.

The movies have been criticized for irrelevant escapism--and for being too relevant. From the 1920s until the 1960s, it was commonplace for cities and states to operate film censorship boards that blatantly engaged in prior restraint of motion pictures, something that would have been unconstitutional if applied to almost any other communications medium. That practice ended gradually, as the Supreme Court extended more and more First Amendment protection to motion pictures. More recently, some newspapers have refused to carry ads for movies of which they disapproved, and cities have tried to zone offensive theaters out of town.

Meanwhile, of course, films of all kinds have appealed to the millions, often while bureaucrats were trying to shut them down. At one point in the 1970s, more than half a million Californians had paid to see the controversial adult film, *Deep Throat*, in Los Angeles County, while local authorities were censoring it in neighboring Orange County.

But censorship crusades by no means began when the modern motion picture rating system was introduced and films were first given adults-only ratings in the 1960s. Amidst a furor, Ohio authorities censored a film and then won the Supreme Court's blessing in 1915. In fact, that case (*Mutual Film Corp. v. Industrial Commission of Ohio*, 236 U.S. 230) set a precedent that stood up for 37 years: movies were not protected by the First Amendment, the court said.

Justice Joseph McKenna, writing for a unanimous Supreme Court, said, "The exhibition of motion pictures is a business pure and simple." Thus, movies should not be regarded as part of the press. Instead, they were mere entertainment and did not purvey ideas or public opinion. Moreover, movies had a special capacity for evil, the court said.

The *Mutual Film* decision was both a cause and the result of mediocrity in the film industry. Because early films were unsophisticated and often lacking in artistic quality, the Supreme Court had no problem dismissing them as frivolous entertainment and not a vehicle for significant ideas. But at least in part because of the Supreme Court's ruling, American films remained a frivolous form of entertainment for many years.

It was not until 1952 that the Supreme Court finally said films were a vehicle for important ideas, and it took an Italian film to make the high court change its mind. New York authorities banned a Roberto Rossellini film called *The Miracle*, in which a peasant girl encounters a stranger she believes to be the Biblical Joseph and gives birth to a child she imagines to be the Christ child.

The film was initially licensed for showing in New York, but religious leaders led by Cardinal Francis Spellman launched a major protest. In the face of this pressure, the film board reversed itself and prohibited further showings, declaring the film to be "sacrilegious." That decision was appealed, and in *Burstyn v. Wilson* (343 U.S. 495), the Supreme Court said for the first time that films are "a significant medium for the communication of ideas," and afforded them First Amendment protection.

The court said *The Miracle* could not be banned, but the ruling did not preclude the later censorship of other films. Unfortunately, no specific guidelines for review boards were provided, and the licensing of films continued for another two decades in many states and cities.

Thus, several more film censorship cases followed. In *Times Film Corp. v. Chicago* (365 U.S. 43, 1961) the Supreme Court upheld the constitutionality of a film precensorship system, but in 1965 in *Freedman v. Maryland* (380 U.S. 51) the court demanded procedural safeguards of film censors. In the meantime, however, both the Supreme Court and lower courts reviewed a number of other film censorship cases, often overruling specific instances of prior restraint.

Times Film involved a challenge to Chicago's licensing system by the producer of a movie that obviously would have been granted a license: a movie version of a Mozart opera. But Times Film refused to submit the film to the licensing board and instead challenged the system. The Supreme Court upheld the city's power to license films, finding films beyond the scope of the *Near v. Minnesota* ruling on prior censorship (see Chapter Three).

However, four years later in *Freedman v. Maryland* the Supreme Court backed away from giving carte blanche to film censors. The case arose from a challenge to Baltimore's censorship system, which was much like Chicago's. As in the Chicago case, the film in question (*Revenge at Daybreak*) was not sexually explicit, but it still had to be licensed.

However, this time a movie exhibitor made a more convincing case: he argued that the procedures were unfair and slow. In fact, it could take so long to get a license, he argued, that everyone who wanted to see the film would have gone somewhere else to see it before it was legal to show it in Baltimore.

The Supreme Court agreed and overturned the Maryland system because it lacked adequate procedural safeguards for movie exhibitors. The court said any licensing system would be required to: (1) operate very quickly; (2) assure prompt judicial review, with any final censorship order made only by the court; and (3) place the burden of proof on the censor rather than the film exhibitor.

Maryland rewrote its licensing procedures in an effort to comply with the

Freedman decision, and in 1974 the Supreme Court affirmed a federal court ruling upholding the new procedures (*Star v. Preller*, 419 U.S. 956). The new procedures gave the censorship board five days to grant or deny a license. Denials had to be submitted to a court for review in three days, and an appeal of a court decision allowing censorship was given top priority on the appellate calendar. Also, the licensing board had the burden of proof to show that the film was obscene.

Thus, Maryland was able to retain its movie licensing system. However, the Maryland system was later abandoned, as were most others around the country. Few cities and states were willing and able to operate movie censorship systems that complied with the stringent requirements of the *Freedman* decision. Several more licensing systems were overruled by lower courts after *Freedman*.

From a filmmaker's point of view, it was a good riddance. Local censorship boards were notorious for banning films that were by no means obscene but that simply offended the moral, religious or racial sentiments of the censors.

However, film censorship is still constitutionally permissible if adequate procedural safeguards are provided. And that, of itself, alarms many who believe movies should have the same First Amendment protection afforded to other mass media. Of all of the major mass media, only motion pictures may be routinely subjected to government *prior restraint* based on their content. Granted, the broadcast industry faces other forms of government control that are intended to prevent the airing of sexually explicit material and offensive language. In fact, broadcasters are forbidden to carry much material that is perfectly legal in the nation's motion picture theaters (this problem is discussed in Chapter 11). However, even broadcasters do not face prior restraints: government censors could not lawfully preview the programs for decency before they are aired. Only motion picture exhibitors have had to deal with the problem of direct prior censorship by the government.

Meanwhile, the motion picture industry has attempted to ward off even more heavy-handed government control with a vigorous policy of self-regulation. Beginning in the 1920s, the Motion Picture Association of America maintained a tough code governing movie content, and a code committee exercised censorship powers over movies. Critics attributed the irrelevance and frivolity of early American movies more to the influence of this industry body than to direct government controls.

In 1968 the MPAA shifted to a more permissive approach. Rather than attempting to censor movies, the MPAA introduced a rating system that would simply advise theatergoers about the content of each movie in advance. The rating system, with its ubiquitous G, PG, PG-13, R and NC-17 ratings, has largely accomplished its objective of protecting unwilling persons from offensive material while allowing others to see more explicit movies.

This rating system, however, has raised new questions. For example, participation in the rating system is voluntary, but the ratings are sometimes used as the basis for laws regulating the video business. Some states have considered laws that would forbid renting R or NC-17 rated videos to minors, and Utah banned the showing of such movies on cable television. As Chapter 11 explains, the Utah law was eventually overturned by the Supreme Court. If laws are to be enacted that base censorship decisions on these ratings, that means the MPAA--a private entity dominated by a few large film companies--will be engaging in prior restraint without any constitutional safeguards for movie producers and exhibitors, much less for the general public.

This is particularly true because an unfavorable rating (or having to release a film with no rating at all) can be a financial disaster for a movie distributor. In fact, the rating system itself was revised in 1990 to eliminate the old X rating after several high-budget movies received the X rating. In the minds of many theatergoers, an X rating meant that the film was basically an adult film with hard-core pornographic scenes. Few newspapers would even accept advertising for X-rated films.

The MPAA revised the system after such movies as *Wild Orchid* and *Henry and June* were given X ratings. The association simply eliminated the X rating altogether and replaced it with NC-17 (no children under 17 admitted). Although critics of the movie industry contended that this was nothing more than a cosmetic change, the NC-17 designation lacked the stigma of the old X rating--and most newspapers began accepting ads for some NC-17 movies. Ironically, *Wild Orchid* and several other movies of that period that had initially been given X ratings were edited to qualify for R ratings before their release in mainstream theaters. (*Henry and June* was released with an NC-17 rating and was shown in many theaters that did not normally carry X-rated fare).

Censorship of the Internet

In the late 1990s and early in the new century, a new issue concerning censorship and pornography gained worldwide attention: the question of censoring pornographic or "indecent" messages and discussions on the Internet. As noted earlier, Title V of the Telecommunications Act of 1996 (known as the Communications Decency Act of 1996) prohibited not only obscenity but also "indecent" or "patently offensive" material on any part of the Internet that is accessible to minors. Transmitting such material to a site on the Internet accessible to minors was declared to be a crime punishable by a $250,000 fine and two years in prison.

Amidst a worldwide online protest of government censorship of the Internet, several lawsuits were quickly filed to challenge this law, and two federal courts barred its enforcement in mid-1996. The Supreme Court heard an immediate appeal, and in 1997 the high court ruled that the key provisions of the Communications Decency Act are unconstitutional (*Reno v. ACLU*, 521 U.S. 844).

In a decision that was unanimous in most respects, the high court declared for the first time that the Internet is entitled to the highest level of First Amendment protection, like newspapers and books. The extension of full First Amendment protection to the Internet--in contrast to the limited First Amendment protection available to most of the electronic media--is perhaps the greatest victory the Supreme Court has given to free expression advocates in many years.

Those who challenged the Communications Decency Act included a diverse list of organizations: the American Library Association, the American Civil Liberties Union, the Electronic Frontier Foundation, newspaper publishers, book publishers, writers' groups and large corporations such as Apple Computer and Microsoft.

Many of their spokespersons were jubilant about the sweeping nature of the Supreme Court's decision. They had expressed concern that the law was so broad and vague that it could be used to criminalize many Internet sites and prevent the discussion of topics such as abortion, breast cancer and AIDS prevention.

The Supreme Court agreed. All nine justices voted to overturn the act's provision banning the display of patently offensive material at any site where minors could see it. Seven of the nine also voted to overturn a section prohibiting the transmission of indecent material if minors could receive it.

Writing for the majority, Justice John Paul Stevens said, "The interest in encouraging freedom of expression in a democratic society outweighs any theoretical but unproven benefit of censorship."

Stevens also noted that on the Internet "any person with a phone line can become a town crier with a voice that resonates farther than it could from any soapbox" and that "the same individual can become a pamphleteer." Therefore, he said, there is "no basis for qualifying the level of First Amendment scrutiny that should be applied to this medium."

Concurring in part and dissenting in part, Justice Sandra Day O'Connor, joined by Chief Justice William Rehnquist, said she too found much of the law to be unconstitutionally broad and vague. But she said she would uphold the part of the law that forbids the deliberate transmission of indecent material from an adult to minors--provided all of the recipients are minors. She likened the Communications Decency Act to a law requiring a bookstore owner to stop selling sexually oriented magazines to adults if a minor should walk into the store.

The court did not comment on the provisions of the Communications Decency Act banning obscene materials. In fact, those provisions were not even challenged in the *Reno v. ACLU* case. As explained earlier, if something is legally obscene, it is not protected by the First Amendment and may be barred from all media including books, magazines and newspapers. But many words and images that are offensive to many people are not obscene in a legal sense.

What is historic about this case is that it rejected the federal government's attempt to ban *non-obscene material* from the Internet if it is indecent or patently offensive and thereby make the Internet legally equivalent to the broadcast media, not the print media.

In 1999, the Supreme Court upheld a section of the Communications Decency Act banning obscene e-mail (*ApolloMedia Corp. v. Reno*, 526 U.S. 1061). In a one-sentence order, the Supreme Court affirmed a lower court ruling that interpreted the e-mail ban to apply *only* to obscenity and not to indecency.

In the *Reno v. ACLU* case the court also noted that there are other less intrusive means of protecting children from adult material on the Internet, including filtering software that can be installed on a home computer by parents to keep their children from accessing adult sites.

Internet filtering software became the focus of a new round of lawsuits and eventually a new federal law. Some libraries and schools started installing filtering software on their computers in 1998 and 1999. Civil liberties groups sued several libraries for installing such software, arguing that it violates the First Amendment rights of library patrons, and several courts ordered libraries to abandon filtering software (for example, see *Mainstream Loudoun v. Board of Trustees*, 24 F.Supp.2d 552). On the other hand, several lawsuits were filed by parents demanding that libraries use filtering software; these lawsuits have usually been unsuccessful. In the absence of filtering software, some libraries began requiring all children who access the Internet on a library terminal to have parental consent, with parents signing an acknowledgement that their children may be able to access adult sites.

In 2001, Congress approved a new law called the Children's Internet Protection Act. It directed the Federal Communications Commission to adopt new rules under which libraries and schools must install Internet filtering software to be eligible for federal aid for web access.

After the FCC complied with Congress' mandate, the American Library Association and civil liberties groups joined in a lawsuit challenging this new law. They contended that it violates the First Amendment by denying students and library patrons access to many non-obscene websites, including some that aren't even adult-oriented in their content.

A specially convened three-judge federal court in Philadelphia agreed, declaring the Child Internet Protection Act unconstitutional in 2002. Ruling in *American Library Association v. U.S.* (2002 U.S. Dist. Lexis 9537), the court held that the law is overly broad because it can block access to many Internet sites that contain protected speech.

The court explained, "Any public library that adheres to CIPA's conditions will necessarily restrict patrons' access to a substantial amount of protected speech in violation of the First Amendment."

An appeal of the decision of this special federal panel would go directly to the U.S. Supreme Court. The decision applies only to public libraries, leaving school libraries still subject to the Internet filtering requirement as a condition of federal funding.

Even before the Children's Internet Protection Act was passed in an attempt to mandate library filtering, Congress attempted to get around the *Reno v. ACLU* Supreme Court decision. In 1998, Congress again tried to ban sexually explicit materials at Internet sites accessible to minors by passing the Child Online Protection Act. This time, Congress avoided the indecency concept and banned material "harmful to minors"--and only from commercial websites that are accessible to minors.

This law was immediately challenged by the same coalition of civil libertarians and others who challenged the Communications Decency Act, and they made essentially the same argument again: that because it is so difficult to keep minors away from any Internet site, this would force many sites to engage in self-censorship. A federal judge issued an injunction to prevent the new law from going into effect until a trial could be held on the constitutional arguments raised by those challenging the law.

In 2001, a federal appellate court upheld the injunction, declaring that with today's technology there may be no constitutional way to deny minors access to objectionable websites. The appellate court focused on the global nature of the Internet in upholding the injunction against the Child Online Protection Act, concluding, "the standard by which (the act) gauges whether material is harmful to minors is based on identifying contemporary community standards (which) essentially requires that every web publisher subject to the statute abide by the most restrictive and conservative state's community standards in order to avoid criminal liability."

The U.S. Supreme Court reversed the appellate court in 2002 and suggested that the use of community standards on the Internet does *not* violate the First Amendment. However, the high court did not uphold the law itself. Instead, the court left the injunction against enforcing the law intact until a lower court can consider several First Amendment questions raised by those challenging the law.

Ruling in the case of *Ashcroft v. ACLU* (122 S.Ct. 1700), a deeply divided court agreed to send the case back to a lower court for reconsideration but agreed about little else. Although the court voted 8-1 to allow community standards to be used to judge websites, several justices in the majority issued separate opinions expressing concern about the potential for conservative communities to censor what Internet surfers may view elsewhere.

While the controversy over Internet content and the Communications Decency Act focused worldwide attention on the United States, a complicating factor is that because communication via the Internet is instantaneous and worldwide, other countries can pass laws to censor it, too. Already, online services have been forced to limit their content to accommodate restrictions imposed by the governments of other countries. In one widely publicized incident, CompuServe was forced to deny its American subscribers access to about 30 sexually oriented sites on the Internet to avoid violating German laws. While such restrictions are often temporary and do not affect most private two-way communications between individuals in the United States, they do affect the content of user groups and chat rooms. Also, according to media reports some countries have government agents monitoring Internet communications into and out of the country so that the originators or recipients of messages considered subversive can be caught and punished. With the growing popularity of Internet cafes in many parts of the world, that would seem to be a daunting task.

Censorship by Government Grant?

As noted earlier, in 1998 the U.S. Supreme Court ruled in *NEA v. Finley* that it does not violate the First Amendment for those who award government grants for the arts to consider "general standards of decency and respect for the diverse beliefs and values of the American people."

The court was ruling on a challenge to standards Congress directed the National Endowment for the Arts (NEA) to adopt in 1990. The new rules were a reaction to a public outcry over the funding of several controversial artists by the NEA. Four performance artists who were initially denied federal grants under the new standards, including New York performance artist Karen Finley, challenged the rules.

In upholding the grant criteria, the Supreme Court overturned decisions by two lower federal courts that had held the rules to be an unconstitutional form of viewpoint discrimination. Writing for the Supreme Court, Justice Sandra Day O'Connor said, "Congress has wide latitude to set spending priorities." She noted that libraries routinely choose to spend tax dollars to buy certain books while rejecting others, including those considered indecent or unsuitable for children.

Justice O'Connor ruled that the grant system is not unconstitutional on its face. She also emphasized, though, that the system *could be* implemented in a way that would involve unconstitutional viewpoint discrimination, but there was no evidence of that before the court.

During oral arguments in the case, Justice John Paul Stevens noted that the government funds campaigns to promote the message, "Just Say No to Drugs" through billboards and other media. "They are financed only to say 'No to drugs,' not 'Yes to drugs,'" Stevens said.

Justice Antonin Scalia wrote a concurring opinion in which he said, "*Avant-garde artistes* such as respondents remain entirely free to *pater les bourgeois*; they are merely deprived of the additional satisfaction of having the bourgeoisie taxed to pay for it." In essence, Scalia's opinion said, of course deciding who gets government arts grants involves viewpoint discrimination. But in this context that does not violate the First Amendment.

The lone dissenter, Justice David H. Souter, argued that the NEA criteria inevitably involve viewpoint discrimination that does violate the First Amendment because the federal government has not justified it.

As a practical matter, the *NEA* Supreme Court decision may have little effect on the arts: the four artists who challenged the rules received their grants early in the litigation, and the NEA no longer gives much of its money to individual artists. Instead, arts-oriented groups and organizations receive most of the grant money, and they are screened by panels of experts and community representatives. An art gallery or an orchestra is more likely to win a federal grant than an individual performance artist like Karen Finley. But the case raises many questions about the proper role of government funding of the arts, and about whether any grant selection process really is--or could be--free of viewpoint discrimination.

MUNICIPAL PORNOGRAPHY REGULATION

Given the difficulty of defining obscenity and winning criminal convictions under state and federal laws, many local governments have attempted to control bookstores and theaters they consider offensive in other ways.

Nuisance Laws

One method used by local governments is to ask a court to declare an adult-oriented business a *public nuisance*. In such a civil action, a city may be able to win a court-ordered closure by meeting a lower standard of proof than is required in criminal cases.

However, the U.S. Supreme Court placed constitutional limits on this approach in a 1980 decision, *Vance v. Universal Amusement* (445 U.S. 308). The case involved a Texas nuisance law that was construed to authorize closing down adult movie theaters merely because they had shown obscene films in the past. It was not necessary to prove that any film currently showing was obscene. The court said the Texas law lacked adequate procedural safeguards to protect the movie exhibitor's rights and that it posed an unconstitutional prior restraint.

On the other hand, the U.S. Supreme Court ruled in 1993 that federal officials have the legal authority to shut down a chain of adult businesses and seize its assets after a few items are ruled legally obscene. The court's 5-4 majority held that this is a *subsequent punishment* for the crime of selling obscene matter, not an unlawful *prior restraint* in violation of the First Amendment (*Alexander v. U.S.*, 509 U.S. 544). In this case, the Supreme Court majority upheld the right of federal agents to use the Racketeer Influenced and Corrupt Organizations (RICO) Act to seize the assets of adult book and video stores once some of the materials are ruled legally obscene. However, in a companion case decided the same day, the Supreme Court ruled that such a forfeiture of assets could be so excessive as to violate the Eighth Amendment, which forbids cruel and unusual punishments and "excessive fines" (*Austin v. U.S.*, 509 U.S. 602). Based on that ruling, the high court sent the *Alexander* case back to a lower court to decide whether seizing 100,000 books and videos after only seven items were ruled obscene might constitute an excessive fine.

Women's Rights and Pornography

In the 1980s several cities considered laws that would control pornography in another way--by declaring that its existence violates the civil rights of women. Such a law was actually adopted in Indianapolis. In effect, this law gave women the right to complain of civil rights violations when material that they found offensive was offered for sale at local stores or shown in local theaters.

However, the American Civil Liberties Union, among other groups, protested that these laws flagrantly violated the First Amendment. If material that is not legally obscene under the Miller test is censored as a result of civil rights complaints, the result would be an unconstitutional denial of freedom of expression, they contended.

In 1986, the Indianapolis law was ruled unconstitutional by the U.S. Supreme Court. In *Hudnut v. American Booksellers* (475 U.S. 1001, affirming 771 F.2d 323) the high court summarily affirmed a U.S. Court of Appeals decision to that effect without giving the case a formal hearing.

In overturning the law on First Amendment grounds, the lower court pointed out that the law could be used to outlaw classic literary works such as Homer's *Iliad* because they depict women as "submissive objects for conquest and domination." Such works could be banned under the law regardless of their literary, artistic or political value. "The state may not ordain preferred viewpoints in this way," the Court of Appeals concluded.

Zoning, Decency Laws and Adult Businesses

Various communities have also attempted to control adult-oriented businesses through their zoning powers and public decency laws, and they have enjoyed some success. The use of zoning to control such businesses has been encouraged by several Supreme Court decisions, starting with a 1976 case, *Young v. American Mini-Theatres* (427 U.S. 50). That case arose in Detroit, where city officials attempted to limit the number of adult-oriented businesses that could exist in a given neighborhood. The Supreme Court said this was constitutionally permissible, even if the city didn't define obscenity with great precision, since the city wasn't forbidding adult materials altogether but simply controlling the time, place and manner of their distribution.

Encouraged by that ruling, hundreds of other American cities adopted zoning restrictions on adult businesses, sometimes zoning them out of town altogether. However, in 1981 the Supreme Court made it clear that communities could not use zoning to banish adult entertainment entirely without violating the First Amendment. That ruling came in the case of *Schad v. Mt. Ephraim* (452 U.S. 61).

In that case, the Supreme Court overturned a New Jersey community's ban on live entertainment as a violation of the First Amendment. Under its zoning powers, the city attempted to outlaw nude dancing and other forms of live entertainment. Overruling the local ordinance, the court said that mere nudity does not make entertainment obscene. The majority said the city could ban all forms of entertainment (including motion picture theaters), but that local officials could not use their zoning powers to forbid nude dancing while allowing other forms of entertainment. The court pointed out that this case was different from the Detroit case, in which adult-oriented businesses were merely dispersed around town and not banned altogether.

While the *Schad* decision held that nude dancing is not necessarily obscene, and therefore does have some First Amendment protection, a decade later the Supreme Court hedged a little in another case involving nude dancing, *Barnes v. Glen Theatre* (501 U.S. 560, 1991). The *Barnes* case was a challenge to Indiana's public decency law which, like similar laws in many cities and states, prohibits nudity in public places, including private business establishments such as bars. Based on *Schad* and other court decisions, authorities in most states assumed that these laws against public nudity did not apply to performances onstage or other activities in the performing arts. However, in *Barnes*, a deeply divided Supreme Court upheld the application of a public decency law to nude dancing in a bar, although only three justices could agree on a legal rationale for doing so.

In essence, the three justices who joined in the court's main opinion in the *Barnes* case said that nude dancing, while marginally an expressive activity protected by the First Amendment, could be banned in a bar or other private establishment because the limitation on expressive activity was "incidental" to the state's larger goal of banning public nudity to prevent crime, protect public morals and the like. They seemed to feel that First Amendment freedoms were not seriously impaired here because all an erotic dancer had to do to avoid violating the law was to wear "pasties" and a "G-string," as Chief Justice William Rehnquist put it. Rehnquist, whose opinion was also signed by Justices Sandra Day O'Connor and Anthony M. Kennedy, said that it was a small limitation on free expression rights to require dancers to wear *some* clothing, and that there was a very important government purpose for such public decency laws.

Justice Antonin Scalia concurred, but said he thought nude dancing should be completely beyond the protection of the First Amendment. Justice David Souter, on the other hand, also concurred in the court's decision to uphold the Indiana law, but on narrower legal grounds. Unlike the other four justices who voted to uphold the anti-nudity law, Souter seemed to be drawing a line and saying he would not support a broader ban on nudity in the visual or performing arts. And the four dissenting justices (Byron White, Thurgood Marshall, Harry Blackmun and John Paul Stevens) would have overturned Indiana's public decency law as a violation of the First Amendment.

The *Barnes* ruling was widely assailed by advocates of full First Amendment protection for the performing arts, but praised by groups that favor restrictions on what they view as obscenity or indecency in the arts. However, the case did not signal any immediate change in broader applications of obscenity law to the performing arts because five justices (Souter plus the four dissenters) appeared unwilling to support an across-the-board ban on nudity in the arts. Also, the *Barnes* decision has no direct effect on the court's earlier pronouncements about the use of zoning ordinances to control the location of adult businesses. In the *Schad* case 10 years earlier, the court had overturned an across-the-board ban on nude dancing and other forms of live entertainment under zoning laws. And that ruling has not been overruled.

Nor was *Barnes* the Supreme Court's final ruling on nude dancing in private clubs: in 2000 the court addressed the issue again--and again upheld a government's right to ban nude dancing in private clubs. In *City of Erie v. Pap's A.M.* (529 U.S. 277), the court overturned a Pennsylvania Supreme Court decision that an Erie, Pa. ordinance violated the First Amendment. In a 6-3 decision, the high court said that Erie did *not* violate the First Amendment when it banned nude dancing at a club called "Kandyland" and required erotic performers to wear at least "pasties" and a "g-string."

Of the six justices in the majority, four said nude dancing is expressive activity that is entitled to some First Amendment protection. However, they concluded that "secondary effects"--neighborhood problems associated with nude dancing establishments such as crime and illegal drug use--justified the city's requirement that performers wear minimal clothing. As in the *Barnes* decision, the plurality stopped short of ruling that all nudity in the performing arts could be banned. Instead, they said only that Erie officials had adequately justified their ban on nude dancing in private clubs by showing its ill effects on the community. Justices Antonin Scalia and Clarence Thomas concurred in the decision but said they would not extend any First Amendment protection to nude dancing.

Writing for the plurality and quoting portions of an earlier Supreme Court decision, Justice Sandra Day O'Connor said that although "society's interest in protecting this type of expression is of a wholly different, and lesser, magnitude than the interest in untrammeled political debate, and few of us would march our sons or daughters off to war to preserve the citizens' right to see specific anatomical areas exhibited at establishments like Kandyland," nude dancing is nonetheless entitled to some First Amendment protection.

In short, it is constitutionally permissible for a city to ban nude dancing in private clubs based on a "secondary effects" rationale, and to ban all adult businesses in residential areas or near churches and schools. However, many courts have now ruled that a city cannot use its zoning powers to force all adult-oriented businesses to get out of town. To completely banish adult businesses, local officials would have to prove that each one is engaged in producing, exhibiting or selling legally obscene works. In some states, even that isn't enough: the most local authorities can do is to have each legally obscene work banned on a case-by-case basis--a very costly and cumbersome process.

Nevertheless, in 1986 the Supreme Court reaffirmed the right of local governments to use zoning ordinances to exclude adult theaters in all but remote areas, even if the practical result is to make it impossible for any adult business to make a profit.

In *Renton v. Playtime Theatres* (475 U.S. 41), the court ruled 7-2 that the city of Renton, Wash., could prohibit adult businesses within 1,000 feet of any park, school, church or private residence. This meant that adult businesses could only operate in one isolated and largely vacant area of the city.

The court rejected arguments by adult business owners that this zoning policy would force them to locate only in an unprofitable "industrial wasteland." The court said that as long as some sites are available for adult businesses, cities may prevent them from locating in most neighborhoods.

Writing for the court, Justice William Rehnquist said that sexually explicit speech does not deserve as much constitutional protection as political speech. Therefore, stringent time, place and manner restrictions on adult businesses are constitutional even when similar restrictions on other kinds of speech might be unconstitutional. In essence, the court was recognizing a "hierarchy-of-speech" theory in which sexually explicit communications are near the bottom of the list.

The court also accepted Renton officials' argument that their zoning policy was needed to prevent urban decay, despite the fact that the fear of blight was based on the experiences of other cities and not on local experience. A lower court had overturned the Renton ordinance partly because the prediction of urban decay near adult businesses was not based on local experience.

In 1990, the Supreme Court decided a trio of cases on local regulation of adult businesses, declaring that cities must provide a variety of procedural safeguards for adult businesses that they seek to regulate or ban (*FW/PBS Inc. v. City of Dallas*, 493 U.S. 215). Relying heavily on the 1965 film censorship case, *Freedman v. Maryland*, the court overturned a Dallas, Texas, ordinance because it did not strictly limit the city's censorship powers and provide for a prompt judicial review of city restrictions on adult businesses. But the court reaffirmed the basic principle that local governments may regulate these businesses. Local officials have the right to use their zoning laws to isolate adult businesses in out-of-the-way places. However, if adult theaters and bookstores are to be banned altogether, the materials they sell or show must be ruled legally obscene. That requires persuading a jury that each book, magazine or movie is obscene in a legal sense and not merely pornographic or indecent.

In 2002, the U.S. Supreme Court once again addressed the use of zoning to curb adult businesses without proving that the materials they offer are obscene.

Ruling in *City of Los Angeles v. Alameda Books* (122 S.Ct. 1728), the court upheld key portions of a Los Angeles ordinance that prohibits adult stores from providing video viewing booths as well as selling books and videotapes if the combined business causes more problems for the neighborhood than a video store or video viewing parlor would by itself. The court rejected the argument that such an ordinance violates the First Amendment.

The court voted 5-4 to allow cities to ban the combination of the two types of business at a single location, responding to the city's argument that a concentration of adult businesses in one place can cause more crime and urban blight than a single business would, and that the sale of videotapes and providing a place for customers to view the tapes are really two different businesses. However, the case was only a limited victory for L.A. officials: the Supreme Court ordered the case back to a lower court for a trial where city officials will still have to prove their claims about the crime and blight this "adult superstore" would allegedly cause.

ONGOING ISSUES

In this new millennium, the overriding issue about obscenity and the First Amendment is really a very old one: who should have the right to decide what is obscene in a diverse, democratic society? Like much of communications law, the rules governing allegedly obscene matter have undergone rapid change in the last few decades. But the underlying issue in this area remains unchanged. We have seen the spectacle of book-burnings throughout American history, and they are continuing. We have even seen *the same book* banned in three centuries.

Today, there is a movement away from the tolerance for erotic expression that marked the recent past. Criminal prosecution again awaits some of those who produce, sell or display sexually oriented books, movies, music and visual images, materials that some see as art and others regard as filth. In trying to strike a balance between First Amendment freedoms and moral standards, aren't we debating the same issues today that have been debated ever since the first erotic drawings appeared on the walls of caves? Perhaps our answers today are different from those of earlier times. Or are they? Has anything really changed since prehistoric times, except perhaps the technology we use for the explicit depiction of sex?

Speaking of technology, what about the implications of cyberspace? At a time when a graphic image or a text file can be sent to thousands or millions of computers in 50 countries in an instant, whose rules should govern the content? Should the content of the Internet be limited to words and images that will offend no one anywhere in the world who owns a computer and a modem? Do such words and images exist? Should the laws of one country limit what Internet users in other countries can read? Should adults be limited to such words, subject matter and images as may be suitable for the children who will inevitably surf the net? And how should federal obscenity laws be applied to cyberspace? Should a computer server owner in San Francisco, for example, be criminally prosecuted in Memphis because an undercover federal agent sitting at a computer in Memphis can access the system in San Francisco, apply for a password, log on, and download materials that might violate the community standards in Memphis?

On the other hand, did Congress overstep the bounds in passing the Communications Decency Act? Was the Supreme Court right to rule it unconstitutional, extending full First Amendment protection to the Internet--and thereby allowing the Internet's free-wheeling worldwide discussion groups to continue uncensored? Is it appropriate for the Internet to have the same broad First Amendment freedom as the print media? If so, what about legislation to ban virtual child pornography such as the Child Pornography Prevent Act, which was recently rejected by the Supreme Court.

What about government grants for the arts? Is it right for the government to set standards that include a "respect for the diverse beliefs and values of the American people?" Doesn't that inevitably constitute viewpoint discrimination? Is viewpoint discrimination wrong in this context? Should the government force the people to pay for art through their tax dollars, even if many people disapprove of the art? If the government is going to give grants to support the arts, can the winners be selected in a way that does not run afoul of First Amendment freedoms?

Although the issues of censorship and freedom are not new, the explosion of digital communications technology has given them a new currency. Will we ever reach a consensus about the appropriate limits of erotic expression, if in fact there should be limits?

A SUMMARY OF OBSCENITY AND THE LAW

Does the First Amendment Protect Obscenity?
The Supreme Court has consistently held that the First Amendment *does not* protect materials that are legally obscene, but it does protect materials that may be indecent or offensive but not legally obscene. Thus, the crucial issue is defining obscenity. If a work is legally obscene, it may be censored and its producer may be punished. If not, it is protected by the First Amendment and cannot be censored.

What Was the Hicklin Rule?
For many years, obscenity in both England and the United States was defined by the Hicklin Rule, which looked to a work's effect on the *most susceptible* members of society to determine if it was obscene. Also, the Hicklin Rule classified a work as obscene even if only isolated passages were obscene, regardless of the literary merit of the work as a whole. This rule was abandoned after the *Ulysses* decision, in which a federal court refused to follow it and instead ruled that James Joyce's classic work, taken as a whole, was not obscene to average persons.

What Was the Roth Test?
Handed down by the Supreme Court in 1957, the Roth test defined obscenity by asking, "whether to the average person, applying contemporary community standards, the dominant theme of the material taken as a whole appeals to prurient interest." The result was that First Amendment protection was extended to many works that might have been classified as obscene in an earlier era. And during the 1960s, the Supreme Court expanded on its Roth decision. For a time, it appeared that "community standards" were national standards, and that a work could not be censored unless it was "patently offensive" and "utterly without redeeming social value."

What Was the Miller v. California Decision?
In 1973, a new conservative majority on the Supreme Court redefined obscenity, abandoning both the idea of national standards and the "social value" test. In its place, the Supreme Court said a work is legally obscene if: (1) it meets the original Roth test; (2) it describes sexual conduct in a "patently offensive" way; and (3) the work, taken as a whole, lacks serious literary, artistic, political or scientific value. The court made it clear that local community standards could vary from place to place, although works that have serious value as determined by objective standards cannot be censored anywhere.

May the Distribution of Non-Obscene Erotic Works Be Restricted?
Cities may use zoning laws to restrict adult businesses to certain areas. Also, minors may be forbidden to appear in or purchase non-obscene erotic works.

CHAPTER 11
Regulation of Electronic Media

The legal status of the electronic media is unique. While broadcasters, cable systems and satellite television providers share almost all of the legal problems of the print media, they must also deal with a federal agency whose specific task is to supervise and regulate them.

Like publishers, broadcasters may be sued for libel, invasion of privacy, or copyright infringement. Likewise, they share with other media the problems of advertising regulation, antitrust law and restrictions on their access to information. However, the electronic media must also contend with direct government regulation by the Federal Communications Commission. A broadcaster must get a license from the FCC before going on the air and must renew it periodically. Cable systems are not formally licensed by the FCC, but they are subject to various federal laws, FCC regulations and rules imposed by the local governments that grant their franchises. In between license or franchise renewals, broadcasters and cable system operators must comply with hundreds of government regulations covering everything from the content of their programming to the technical quality of their signals. The print media face no similar rules.

Furthermore, as some broadcasters and cable operators have learned, a license or franchise renewal is by no means automatic. RKO General fought a 20-year legal battle against government sanctions that nearly forced the company to forfeit 13 radio and television licenses worth perhaps a billion dollars on the open market. In the end, RKO lost its license to operate a television station in Boston--a license worth at least $150 million--and was forced to sell a number of other stations at bargain basement prices.

RKO General was accused of serious wrongdoing: the government's actions against RKO General were not exactly unprovoked. But can you imagine the government ordering the *Boston Globe*, *New York Times* or *Los Angeles Times* to stop publishing forever? Although that kind of thing happens to newspapers in some countries, it would be unthinkable in America. And yet, that can happen to broadcasters here, as the RKO General case shows.

How did the federal government acquire such life-and-death power over the broadcast industry? The answer lies in the nature of the *radio spectrum*. Only a limited number of frequencies are available, and the number of stations that may transmit at one time without causing interference is also limited. The idea that this justifies government regulation of broadcasting is called the *scarcity rationale*. Early in the twentieth century Congress relied on this rationale when it decreed that the entire radio spectrum would be used to serve *the public interest, convenience and necessity*. Congress was saying that those who were chosen to use the limited space available in the radio spectrum had a special obligation to the public.

As a result, the Federal Communications Commission was established to regulate broadcasting and other non-governmental uses of the radio spectrum. Over the years, the FCC assumed broad authority over the electronic mass media under the scarcity rationale. However, today there are many new technologies of mass communication, and the entire philosophy of broadcast regulation--including the scarcity rationale itself--has been re-examined by the FCC, Congress and the courts. Some have even proposed that the FCC itself be abolished, with the federal government phasing out almost all of its regulation of the electronic media.

As things stand now, the FCC has two primary functions: authorizing various individuals and organizations to transmit in the radio spectrum (the licensing function) and regulating those licensees (a supervisory function). Although cable television systems use wires rather than the airwaves to deliver programming to their subscribers, the FCC has broad jurisdiction over cable systems too. How the FCC acquired its regulatory powers and how it exercises those powers are the major topics of this chapter.

For many years, the FCC tended to believe it was fulfilling its mandate if it issued licenses and wrote ever-more-complex rules to regulate the conduct of licensees. That all changed in the 1980s, as the FCC took a series of controversial steps to deregulate the broadcast and cable industries. Instead of trying to ensure public service through government regulation, the commission began looking to marketplace forces to achieve that goal. The FCC adopted the philosophy that competition is healthy, and that more competition equals better public service. To foster competition, it juggled its frequency allocations to make room for more broadcasters. The FCC also authorized a variety of new broadcast-like services that it hopes will offer the public new alternatives in programming. During the 1990s, on the other hand, the FCC adopted a much tougher regulatory stance, abandoning some of the deregulatory moves of the 1980s and imposing a variety of new content controls on broadcasters--raising new questions about the First Amendment rights of the broadcast media.

In 1996, Congress approved the long-awaited Telecommunications Act, the most comprehensive piece of communications legislation enacted since 1934. In the 1996 law, Congress took major steps to foster new competition among broadcasters, cable systems, telephone companies and others who offer communications services. Many provisions of this law free the communications industries from long-standing government rules and regulations. But Congress also endorsed new government controls on broadcast content, including the widely debated V-chip system to allow viewers to exclude sexually oriented or violent programming.

All of these new developments have created new problems, not only in the United States but also in other countries as the communications business has become an increasingly global enterprise. For that reason, the international regulation of mass communications has become increasingly important in recent years.

BROADCAST REGULATION: A GLOBAL VIEW

Although this fact is sometimes overlooked, some of the most basic decisions concerning broadcasting are made at the international level and not by the FCC. Radio and television signals freely cross international boundaries, and broadcasters cannot operate with blatant disregard for the interference they might cause in other countries.

For this reason, many basic issues in telecommunications policy are decided on a worldwide basis. By treaty, the International Telecommunications Union (ITU), headquartered in Geneva, Switzerland, has overall responsibility for international administration of radio and television matters. Its approximately 150 member nations hold World Radio Conferences every few years to discuss major international issues. At such a conference in 1992, for example, the ITU's members made policy decisions significantly affecting telecommunications around the world: the conference decided on frequency assignments for a variety of satellite communications services and also selected frequencies for a new digital audio broadcasting service that will supplement and could replace some of today's AM and FM radio stations. Digital audio broadcasting is discussed later in this chapter.

Allocating frequencies is usually a primary function of these international conferences. No nation may simply place its radio and television stations on whatever frequencies it wishes; frequency assignment policies must be set on a global basis to avoid incompatible uses. Each country is free to decide which station transmits on a given channel in the AM, FM or television bands, for instance, but the decision about how much of the radio spectrum is set aside for broadcasting (as opposed to other uses) is made on an international basis.

In addition to worldwide telecommunications policy-making, there is regional coordination. For communications purposes, the world is divided into three regions. Region I encompasses Europe, Africa and the countries of the former Soviet Union. Region II includes North and South America, and Region III covers Asia and the Pacific (except for the former Soviet states). The United States regularly meets with its neighbors at Region II conferences to agree on radio and television frequencies in this hemisphere.

However, those meetings are not always amicable. In recent years the United States and its neighbors have experienced severe difficulties in coordinating broadcast channel assignments. For example, in the 1980s the Reagan administration announced intentions to create powerful radio and television stations named "Radio Marti," which would beam news to Cuba (or more correctly, the American version of the news). The stations were named after Jose Marti, a 19th-century Cuban freedom fighter.

Cuba regarded this as a blatant attempt to propagandize its people, so the Cuban delegation retaliated by walking out of an international conference on western hemisphere frequency coordination. Then Cuba turned on a number of powerful AM radio stations on frequencies used by American stations. The result was interference (some called it deliberate "jamming") to stations thousands of miles away from Cuba. For instance, one radio station in Des Moines, Iowa, saw its reliable nighttime range drop from a 700-mile radius to a mere 25 because a high-powered Cuban station began transmitting on the same frequency. Perhaps not coincidentally, that was the radio station where "Dutch" Reagan (as former President Ronald Reagan was once known) got his start as a sportscaster.

When that happened, American broadcasters began lobbying in Congress to stop the Radio Marti project. Congress finally passed a law requiring the Reagan administration to make Radio Marti a part of the Voice of America--with ground rules requiring that it provide objective news, not propaganda.

As the Radio Marti controversy illustrates, broadcasting has political and diplomatic ramifications that reach far beyond any country's borders. As a result, international cooperation is vital, particularly at a time when many nations are moving into new technologies such as broadcasting directly to home viewers from satellites. A single satellite positioned 22,000 miles above the equator can transmit a signal powerful enough to be received in an enormous area; a satellite transmitter may have a radio "footprint" that can cover half a continent, ignoring all boundary lines. Broadcasters and other users of the radio spectrum have always engaged in bloody battles for more turf, but today more than ever before those battles are becoming volatile international feuds.

THE RADIO SPECTRUM

Most of these electronic turf wars occur, of course, because of one simple fact about the radio spectrum: there are not enough channels to go around, either in the United States or abroad. Everyone is clamoring for more frequencies.

The Federal Communications Commission has recently launched a major effort to modernize its spectrum allocation policies--in the hope that room can be found for many new broadcasters and for more non-broadcast users of the radio spectrum. And Congress has passed legislation to release part of the radio spectrum that was once reserved for federal government use in an effort to make room for new communications technologies--and to bring in additional revenue through spectrum auctions.

When FCC policy makers discuss the radio spectrum, they use technical jargon. It is hard to avoid running into terms such as "Hertz," "megaHertz," "AM," "FM," "VHF," "UHF," "grade A contours," etc. Here is an explanation of these terms that may make the rest of this chapter more comprehensible.

AM means *amplitude modulation*; it was the original means by which sound was superimposed on a radio signal. *FM* means *frequency modulation*, a newer method of putting sound on a radio signal. Each method has advantages that will be noted later.

A *Hertz* (abbreviated Hz) is a unit of measurement, just as a foot, a mile or a pound is a unit of measurement. However, a Hertz is a measurement of frequency in the radio spectrum. Every station is assigned to transmit on a certain frequency or "channel." That frequency is measured in Hertz. One Hertz equals one electrical cycle per second. One *kiloHertz* (kHz) is 1,000 Hertz; one *megaHertz* (mHz) is 1,000 kiloHertz, or one million Hertz. The term Hertz, by the way, was chosen to honor Heinrich Hertz, a German scientist whose early research proved the existence of radio waves. Thus, the term Hertz is usually capitalized.

A station's frequency, expressed in kiloHertz or megaHertz, is its home address in the radio spectrum. For example, an AM radio station might operate on 1070 kHz (which is the same as 1.07 mHz). An FM station might operate on 94.7 mHz. Only one station can transmit on each frequency in a given geographic area; if two or more stations transmit on the same frequency, interference will result and neither station can be heard by many listeners. Therefore, each radio and television station has a unique frequency on which no one else may transmit in that station's service area.

A station's service area is determined by measuring or calculating the strength of its transmitted signal at various locations and then plotting the measurements on a map. For example, a TV station's *primary service area* is based on its *grade A contour*, which is nothing more than a circular plot showing where the station's signal drops below a given strength. The area inside that circle is where the station delivers a "city-grade signal." A station's *grade B contour* is a larger circle, encompassing an area where the signal is weaker but still viewable. The FCC has to assure that each station has an appropriate service area. Also, knowing the signal contours enables the FCC to determine where other stations that will operate on the same channel can be placed. If two *co-channel* stations (i.e., two stations sharing the same frequency) are placed too close together, harmful interference will result.

Different types of stations have different service areas. AM radio signals propagate (travel from the transmitting antenna to listeners' receivers) differently than FM radio or television signals. Similarly, VHF (very high frequency) television signals propagate differently than UHF (ultra high frequency) signals. Thus, VHF and UHF television stations may have different service areas even though their transmitters are located in the same place. As digital television broadcasting is phased in, all of these service area designations will change. Because the loss of even a small amount of its service area can cost a station thousands of viewers (and potentially millions of dollars in advertising revenue), the new digital service area designations were hotly contested during the late 1990s.

Further complicating matters for radio stations, an AM radio broadcaster's service area may be different at night than it is in the daytime. AM radio signals propagate mainly by *groundwave* during the day. That means signals literally travel along the surface of the earth. AM stations with high-power transmitters have a reliable groundwave range (called the *primary service area*) of roughly 100 miles, depending on the terrain.

At night, local groundwave propagation still occurs, but AM radio signals also travel by *skywave* propagation. That means some of the transmitted energy travels out toward space and is reflected back to distant points on the earth by the ionosphere (the Earth's upper atmosphere). AM radio signals also travel out toward space during the daytime, but the ionosphere absorbs most of the energy and very little is reflected back during daylight hours.

As a result of this skywave propagation, high-powered AM radio stations can sometimes be heard well at distances of 700 miles or more at night. In the early days of radio this was a tremendous advantage because it allowed persons far away from any station to hear some radio broadcasts. However, as the spectrum filled up it became a major problem; one powerful station can interfere with all others over an enormous area. The FCC had to require many radio stations either to reduce their power or go off the air altogether at night to prevent interference to distant stations. Today there are only a few dozen high-power *clear channel* stations on the AM dial, but those that remain are still authorized to serve a large geographic area (called the *secondary service area*) at night by skywave propagation. The skywave phenomenon also explains why a very powerful radio transmitter in Cuba can cause interference all over North America.

The radio spectrum also includes many other frequencies, each with their own unique characteristics. Above the AM radio frequencies, there is a region called the "shortwave" spectrum, which runs from about 2 to 30 megaHertz (mHz). Some shortwave frequencies are usable for worldwide skywave propagation even during the daytime. Beginning in the 1920s, they were used for international "shortwave broadcasting" as well as other commercial, government and military communications where long distances had to be spanned. Long-distance telephone services used shortwave radio in the days before microwave technology and communications satellites were developed.

Even today, more than a hundred nations do international shortwave broadcasting, although many shortwave broadcasters also stream their international programming over the Internet. On any given day or night, an American shortwave listener can hear such stations as Radio Moscow, Radio Australia, the British Broadcasting Corporation and our own Voice of America. Some, like the BBC and VOA, operate under government rules requiring that they practice objective journalism, but others do not. Almost all of these organizations broadcast in English (as well as many other languages), often on several different frequencies at once to cover different parts of the world.

Radio Moscow, traditionally one of the world's most extensive shortwave broadcasting operations, changed dramatically after the former Soviet Union itself was dissolved. Long known more for political propaganda than objective news, Radio Moscow began covering stories about the ills of the former Soviet Union--topics that were never even mentioned before--with astonishing bluntness.

However, relatively few people own shortwave receivers capable of tuning in these broadcasts. Had the Reagan administration's Radio Marti proposal merely involved shortwave broadcasting, the Cuban government probably would not have been so outraged by the idea. What was unique about Radio Marti was its placement right in the middle of the AM radio dial, where almost every Cuban could listen in. Florida and Cuba are so close together that it was not necessary to use the shortwave bands for Radio Marti: an AM station in the Florida keys can be heard in much of Cuba even during the daytime.

Above the shortwave spectrum is the VHF region, spanning 30 to 300 megaHertz. At these frequencies, there is little skywave propagation, so a broadcaster's service area extends only a little beyond the visual horizon. Stations with antennas on high towers, buildings or mountaintops achieve much better coverage than those with less favorable antenna sites. VHF television stations (channels 2-13) as well as FM radio stations use frequencies in this part of the spectrum.

The technology needed to use the VHF region, which is about 10 times as large as the AM and shortwave portions of the radio spectrum combined, became available prior to World War II. That was fortunate in view of the way demand for broadcast licenses escalated in those days. Also, it takes far more space to accommodate an FM radio station than an AM station. AM radio channels are 10 kHz wide; FM channels are 200 kHz wide. And television signals are true spectrum gluttons: a single channel is 6,000 kHz (or 6 mHz) wide--600 times the size of an AM radio channel. But that enormous channel width has been required to transmit high quality color video signals as well as audio.

If AM radio stations use so much less space than FM stations, why did the FCC allow FM to develop instead of creating a new and bigger AM broadcast band? FM has some important advantages, such as greater immunity to noise and the potential for higher sound quality. Perhaps if the decision were made today, the FM channels would be made narrower than they are, because good high fidelity FM sound is technically feasible with about one-fourth the bandwidth of the existing FM channels. But that decision was made many years ago when the demands for spectrum space were far fewer than they are today. To change it today would render obsolete millions of dollars worth of FM equipment.

Also, many FM broadcasters today are using the extra spectrum around their main broadcast signal for other purposes, such as private data transmission. Some stations make nearly as much money from these *subsidiary communications authorizations,* or SCAs, as the FCC calls them, as they do from broadcast advertising.

Likewise, by using new digital techniques it is possible to transmit a standard television picture in a channel much narrower than the standard 6 mHz--or to transmit a much higher quality television picture in a 6 mHz channel. Digital television stations can offer either high definition television (HDTV), which provides a dramatically better television picture than has been the standard for the last 50 years, or several channels of standard definition television on one 6 mHz channel.

Above the VHF portion of the radio spectrum, there is also a TV broadcasting allocation in the ultra high frequency (UHF) region, which runs from 300 to 3,000 mHz. But even in this vast amount of space, the demand for channels has exceeded the supply. For example, the frequencies from 470 to 890 megaHertz were originally set aside for UHF television channels 14 through 83. However, that tied up so much of the spectrum that other users (such as two-way police, fire and business communications) ran out of room. The FCC finally took back channels 70 through 83 and reallocated them for various two-way radio services and other uses. In some cities, the FCC also reassigned channels 14 through 20 for these other services.

Under the digital television channel plan adopted in 1997, the vast majority of the digital channels are in the UHF region, with most stations required to relinquish their old *analog* channels, many of which are in the VHF region, in 2006 or later. The analog channels are to be auctioned to the highest bidder.

As we continue to go up in frequency, there is a great deal of space still available in the microwave region (frequencies above 3,000 megaHertz), but the equipment cost goes up with the frequency while the communication range on the Earth's surface declines. However, these frequencies are ideal for satellite and space communications. Satellite television and computerized data communications take a huge amount of spectrum space, and it's just not available anywhere else. Direct broadcast satellites and "wireless cable" television systems both use this part of the spectrum.

When radio broadcasting was in its infancy, the major rationale for government regulation was that there just wasn't enough room for everyone. Even though we've learned how to use hundreds of times more spectrum space than we were using in the beginning, there still isn't enough room to accommodate everyone who would like to become an over-the-air broadcaster. And the demand for spectrum for non-broadcast services has become enormous. In recent years Congress has authorized the FCC to hold auctions to award licenses for many types of communications services. In 1995 and 1996 alone, various companies bid a total of about $20 billion for the right to use the spectrum for new personal communications services and other non-broadcast communications. The radio spectrum, like so many of our other natural resources, is limited--and the demand greatly exceeds the supply.

THE BIRTH OF BROADCASTING

When the pioneers of radio were conducting their experiments at the start of the twentieth century, they had no idea they were developing a new mass communication medium. Rather, they were looking for a way to send Morse code messages from one point to another without telegraph wires. In fact, for many years radio was called "wireless."

The first serious users for wireless radio communications were the world's navies and commercial shipping lines. By the early 1900s, Europe and North America were criss-crossed with telegraph wires, so the early inventors saw only one obvious need for wireless communication: at sea.

The first major legislation governing radio in the United States, the Radio Act of 1912, recognized this reality. It did not anticipate the development of commercial radio broadcasting, but it did provide for the licensing of shipboard and shore stations, among other things.

The 1912 act was prompted in part by the disastrous sinking of the luxury liner, the Titanic. The fact that the Titanic had a wireless station was credited with saving hundreds of lives, but many more might have been saved had the wireless stations of that era been better organized. There was a ship much closer to the Titanic than the one that came to its rescue, but that ship's wireless operator was off duty when the disaster struck, so no one aboard knew what was happening. Consequently, the 1912 Act required all large ships to be equipped with wireless and to have operators on duty full time. Also, the act established qualifications for wireless operators, set technical standards for wireless stations, and reserved certain wavelengths for government use and for distress signals.

After World War I, radio broadcasting developed almost overnight and almost by accident. Westinghouse and other equipment manufacturers supported stations such as Dr. Frank Conrad's widely noted Pittsburgh station, KDKA, mainly to promote the sale of more equipment, not to establish a new mass medium of communications.

However, in 1921 and 1922 radio broadcasting suddenly caught on much as the Internet caught on in the 1990s. Hundreds of stations rushed in to fill the available space in what is now the AM broadcast band. By the mid-1920s, there were so many stations that conditions were, at best, chaotic. Interference, not all of it accidental, reached intolerable levels.

Although the 1912 Radio Act had authorized the Department of Commerce to issue radio station and operator licenses, federal courts repeatedly ruled that Secretary of Commerce Herbert Hoover had no authority to stop issuing licenses when the entire AM radio band was occupied. Nor did Hoover have the authority to tell broadcasters which frequencies each could use. Some stations jumped from frequency to frequency in a frantic effort to avoid interference.

The AM broadcast band in 1926 or 1927 might be compared with the "Citizens Band" (CB radio) today in terms of interference. Like modern CB, the AM band then had layer upon layer of signals, with the louder ones covering up weaker ones and with signals suddenly disappearing and showing up elsewhere on the dial.

In a move that some in the industry have regretted ever since, the nation's broadcasters demanded government action to bring order out of that chaos. For five consecutive years in the 1920s, national radio conferences were held to make these demands. Most industries dread government regulation; here was an industry asking for government regulation.

Congress responded with the Radio Act of 1927, which set up a separate regulatory body for radio communications, the Federal Radio Commission. The FRC was composed of five commissioners, appointed by the president to serve as a policy-making board. Significantly, the FRC was given the authority to assign broadcasters to specific frequencies and to deny license applications when there was no room for additional stations. The FRC's staff was still housed within the Department of Commerce, but the commission nonetheless had wide authority.

The FRC quickly went to work creating order on the AM broadcast band. There were simply too many stations on the air, so the commission began gradually reducing the number. In deciding who should get a license, the FRC had several goals (listed in their order of priority):

1. To assure that everyone in America could receive at least one radio station;
2. To provide service to as many persons as possible from as many diversified sources as possible;
3. To provide outlets for local self-expression.

The FRC's authority was based on the Interstate Commerce Clause in the U.S. Constitution. For a time after the 1927 Radio Act was passed, some broadcasters contended that they were exempt from Federal Radio Commission regulation because their signals did not cross state lines. However, the FRC claimed jurisdiction over all broadcasters as *ancillary* to the regulation of interstate broadcasting: even purely local broadcasting could interfere with stations whose signals did cross state lines, the FRC said. The U.S. Supreme Court upheld the FRC on this point

(*U.S. v. Nelson Brothers.*, 289 U.S. 266, 1933).

Within a few years, the AM band was an orderly place, with each station assured an interference-free frequency, at least in its local area. The commission created several classes of stations to serve different purposes. First, certain powerful stations were designated as "clear channel" stations--stations that shared their frequencies with no one else anywhere in the country at night. These assignments went to stations that already had wide listening audiences and high-power transmitters. Their mission was to serve their metropolitan areas in the daytime and vast regions of the country at night.

Other stations were restricted to lower transmitter power and forced to share their frequencies with other broadcasters. At the bottom of the pecking order were daytime-only stations that had to leave the air at nightfall to make way for the clear channel giants.

Although the FRC was effective in achieving its major goals, it was replaced during President Franklin D. Roosevelt's "New Deal" administration. Roosevelt set out to systematically reorganize the federal government, and he felt the FRC should have both broader authority and a separate administrative staff.

To effect those changes, the Communications Act of 1934 was passed, establishing the basic regulatory structure that exists today. The FRC was replaced by the Federal Communications Commission. The FCC was given a separate staff, making it a fully independent regulatory agency. In addition to radio broadcasting, its jurisdiction was extended to include long-distance telephone service as well as virtually all non-governmental uses of the radio spectrum.

The FCC was specifically forbidden to "censor" broadcasting, but it was given extensive authority to regulate broadcasters in other ways. The most important power given the FCC, of course, was the power to grant or deny licenses. Broadcasters were required to renew their licenses periodically, an onerous burden they still must bear. The FCC was authorized to assure that broadcasters served "the public interest, convenience and necessity," a mandate the FCC used as a basis for imposing various programming requirements on broadcasters.

Within a few years, the Federal Communications Commission moved far beyond its original role as a traffic cop of the airwaves. The commission began not only saying who could use what frequency, but also issuing detailed rules to govern broadcasters' content and business practices. When the FCC adopted a package of "Chain Broadcast Regulations" (described in Chapter 12), the major networks said the FCC had gone beyond its authority. The networks went to court to test the commission's right to make such rules. In a landmark 1943 decision, the Supreme Court relied on the scarcity rationale to uphold the FCC's authority. The court said the agency was entitled to regulate broadcasting comprehensively, going far beyond its role as a traffic cop (*NBC v. U.S.*, 319 U.S. 190). That case (and other early court decisions) gave the FCC broad authority over all radio and television broadcasting as well as many other telecommunications services.

The FCC's authority is limited in certain respects. For example, the commission has little authority over government and military uses of the radio spectrum. A large part of the useful radio spectrum is reserved for federal government and military uses, including an enormous chunk of the VHF, UHF and microwave regions. Government uses of the spectrum are coordinated by the National Telecommunications and Information Administration. Earlier, the authority now exercised by the NTIA was exercised by various offices in the executive branch of government. Although the FCC consults with the NTIA on many spectrum use matters, the NTIA has the final say over most federal government telecommunications.

Some critics of this two-headed system think it is not the ideal way to serve the public interest. If federal government and military radio users were subject to FCC jurisdiction, the radio spectrum would surely be allocated differently than it is now. Commercial users of the spectrum chronically face severe frequency congestion. And they sometimes look longingly over the electronic fence, as it were, to the uncrowded green pastures of radio space where a few government users lazily graze. In fact, they sometimes do more than just look longingly over the electronic fence: Congress recently enacted legislation to reallocate a large segment of the government's radio spectrum (a total of 200 MHz) for various non-government uses. Much of this spectrum has been auctioned off to private companies for use in developing new communications technologies such as personal communications systems, which will offer local voice and data communications in competition with telephone companies and cellular providers. As noted earlier, these auctions are bringing in billions of dollars to the U.S. treasury: bidders are willing to pay high prices because so little spectrum is left to satisfy so many unmet needs. The best the FCC can hope to do is allocate scarce resources as fairly as possible, accommodating as many of the potential spectrum users as it can.

AN OVERVIEW OF THE FCC

The Federal Communications Commission's basic mandate has remained much the same ever since 1934, although the commission itself was reduced from seven members to five in 1982. The five commissioners serve as the agency's policy makers. They are appointed by the president, with the consent of the Senate, for five-year terms. Only three of the five members may come from one political party.

The commission has the power to adopt administrative regulations that have the force of law, so it is a lawmaking body. But it is a law enforcement and executive body as well. It makes judgmental decisions--often crucially important ones to broadcasters--in selecting among competing applicants for an available frequency. Moreover, it functions somewhat as a court would in weighing evidence in proceedings to penalize those who violate its rules. In short, the agency makes the rules, it enforces them, and it judges alleged violators.

However, the FCC's powers are limited. It must afford all parties who appear before it "due process of law" as required by the Fifth Amendment, and it must not violate the First Amendment--or any other part of the Constitution. Also, its jurisdiction is limited by the Communications Act of 1934, and its decisions may be appealed to the U.S. Courts of Appeals, and from there to the Supreme Court. On numerous occasions the federal courts have overturned decisions of the FCC.

When an FCC decision is appealed, the court must determine if the FCC exceeded its statutory authority or violated the Constitution, or if the agency "abused its discretion" by reaching a decision that was not justified by the facts.

FCC Procedures

As a rule making body, the FCC must follow specific procedures, as must other federal administrative agencies such as the Federal Trade Commission (see Chapter 13). When the commissioners need information on a particular subject, they may issue a *Notice of Inquiry*. Then they will await responses from interested parties. Or they may propose new regulations by issuing a *Notice of Proposed Rule Making*. These notices are published online on the FCC's website (located at "www.fcc.gov") and in the *Federal Register*, a daily publication of the federal government that announces actions by many federal agencies. After a rule making proposal is announced, interested parties are invited to respond with comments. Then anyone who wishes may react to the comments by submitting "reply comments."

After receiving written comments, the commissioners may also conduct a hearing at which oral arguments are presented. Finally, the commissioners vote on the proposed rule. If it is approved, the new rule becomes a part of the agency's official regulations, which appear in Title 47 of the *Code of Federal Regulations*.

If you have a special interest in any particular FCC rule, you can look up both the rule and the commission's detailed statement about the rule at the FCC's website or in the *Federal Register*, which you will find in any well-equipped law library and many large city libraries. The *Federal Register* is a huge publication, running to some 75,000 pages each year. However, FCC actions are indexed by subject and are thus easy to find. The FCC's website also includes this information--and much else that was never readily available before.

Although the major policy decisions are made by the five commissioners, the bulk of the FCC's work is carried out by the agency's administrative staff. The agency does most of its work through several "bureaus," each of which has a separate area of responsibility. The FCC's bureau structure was reorganized during 1993 and 1994 and again in 1999. Still another restructuring was completed in 2002.

The *Media Bureau* is of primary concern to broadcasters and cable systems. It is responsible for licensing and supervising radio and television stations and cable television systems. It also handles many post-licensing matters concerning direct broadcast satellite systems. The bureau handles the paperwork of licensing and other administrative matters, referring only the most controversial questions to the commission itself. However, the commissioners and ultimately the federal courts often review the bureau's decisions.

The *Wireline Competition Bureau* regulates landline telephone and other "common carrier" communications. A common carrier is a utility-like operation that must serve everyone who seeks service and is prepared to pay for it. The states regulate these services within their boundaries through their own public utilities commissions; the FCC regulates services and rates. Its stated goals include fostering competition and promoting fairness in these industries.

The *Wireless Telecommunications Bureau* handles most domestic wireless and two-way communications services, including cellular telephone and similar services, paging, public safety communications, and amateur radio. It licenses and regulates most kinds of private, non-broadcast radio operations.

The *International Bureau* licenses shortwave stations whose signals routinely cross international borders. In addition, it licenses satellite communications systems (which also transmit signals that often cross international boundaries), and handles much of the work required for U.S. participation in World Radio Conferences and other international activities.

The *Enforcement Bureau* enforces the FCC's regulations, supervising everything from broadcasters' compliance with technical standards to the enforcement of local telephone companies' compliance with regulations designed to foster competition.

The *Consumer & Governmental Affairs Bureau* handles all kinds of consumer-related matters, responding to inquiries from individual consumers as well as maintaining contacts with state and local governments and industry groups.

In addition to these specialized bureaus, the FCC has a central administrative staff, a science and technology office, a large legal staff and a plans and policies office, among other offices and divisions.

Obviously, the FCC has vast responsibilities beyond the regulation of radio and television broadcasting. Only a small part of the FCC's regulatory energy is directed toward such high-profile activities as regulating the nation's television and radio stations.

BROADCAST LICENSING

Certainly the FCC's most intimidating power is its licensing authority, and particularly its power to revoke or refuse to renew an existing license that could be worth a fortune on the open market.

In recent years no area of broadcast regulation has changed more radically than the licensing process. For most of the history of broadcasting, the FCC decided who would get a broadcast license through elaborate procedures that involved *comparative hearings*--a process that could drag on for years or, in some instances, decades. Now the FCC is awarding new licenses by auctioning them off to the highest bidder and the comparative hearing process appears to be no more than a part of broadcast history, albeit an important part.

Actually, the FCC has two different licensing procedures, one for new license applicants and another for renewals of existing licenses. For an applicant seeking a new license, the process is complex, costly and time consuming, starting with an elaborate procedure to determine if a frequency is available.

The FCC has a *table of allocations* that determines whether a frequency is available for a new station in a particular community. An applicant for a new license must either seek a channel that is already allocated to an area but is not in use or convince the FCC to make a new assignment. The FCC will not consider such a request unless it can be shown that the new station will not interfere with any existing station. Every station has a defined service area in which it is protected from interference.

Under these rules, there are almost no frequencies available for either radio or television stations in the major metropolitan areas. For most people who want to own a radio or television station in a large city, there is no choice but to buy one from the present licensee--at a high price. But if there should be an available frequency, the FCC now conducts an auction, with the license going to the winning bidder.

Until recently, though, very different procedures were followed, and they should be described to illustrate how significant the changes have been.

In the old system, the FCC would accept applications for an available frequency and then sort through the qualifications and promises of competing applicants, often holding a comparative hearing to decide who would get the license. The winner would then receive a construction permit and eventually a license.

All applicants had to show that they would serve the needs of their communities in many ways, and license applicants provided a considerable amount of background information to the FCC in their applications. They had to convince the FCC that they qualified for a license in terms of character, financial standing, technical capability, programming plans, non-discrimination in employment and non-ownership of conflicting media. Applicants had to be U.S. citizens. These basic qualifications have not been changed radically: to be allowed to participate in an auction applicants must also submit evidence of their basic qualifications.

Until recently, these applications were reviewed against a variety of criteria and preferences in an effort to determine which applicant was the most qualified. After years of filing paperwork with the FCC, applicants often faced a comparative hearing at which an FCC official would weigh the merits of competing applicants' claims. By then, each applicant would have spent a huge amount of money on lawyers' and engineers' fees, among other upfront expenses.

At these comparative hearings, FCC officials applied a complex set of rules for evaluating the competing applications. The commission considered a number of factors, including these: (1) the need for a first broadcast facility in communities that have none; (2) the need for competition in a community with only one broadcaster; and (3) the desirability of having every frequency efficiently used, which means the applicant offering to serve a larger area would probably have an advantage. There were also a variety of other *preferences*, including a preference for what the FCC called "the integration of ownership and management," which meant the FCC favored local ownership and resident management: an applicant who intended to run the station would be favored over an absentee owner. The FCC also favored applicants who didn't own other broadcast properties, thereby disfavoring the large corporations that own most radio and television stations today. And, as explained later, the FCC granted preferences to women and minorities until these preferences were overturned by federal court decisions.

Given the complexity of this process, the FCC took various steps to streamline it over the years. One problem was that competing applications were often filed by investors who had little intention of winning a license and operating a station. Instead, these persons often applied merely to force serious applicants to buy them out by paying large "settlements." In 1990, the FCC changed the rules to ban settlement payments that exceeded an applicant's "legitimate and prudent expenses" (which might include engineers' and attorneys' fees, for example). This was intended to take away the financial incentive for speculators to file frivolous applications, the FCC hoped.

The FCC's efforts to streamline the process were helpful, perhaps, but they were not enough: in 1993 an important federal appellate court decision overruled almost the entire comparative hearing process, including the commission's preferences for local ownership and in-resident management. The court said those were "peculiarly without foundation" (*Bechtel v. FCC*, 10 F.3d 875). After the *Bechtel* decision, the FCC placed all contested applications for new licenses on hold until the criteria for evaluating them and the procedures for granting licenses could be revised. By 1997, hundreds of radio and television license applications had been in limbo for several years, and Congress directed the FCC to conduct auctions when there was more than one applicant.

Some of the applicants complained bitterly about the auction plan because they had already spent enormous sums of money on engineering and lawyers' fees, among other things, to meet the old requirements for a license--only to have Congress, a court and the FCC change the rules on them. Congress then directed the FCC to limit bidding in these first auctions to the pre-existing applicants, and to waive the normal rules restricting settlements among competing applicants, giving rival applicants six months to reach agreements among themselves. The FCC also allowed uncontested applicants to sell their applications to others who would step in, obtain the license and build a station. In early 1998, the FCC awarded new licenses or construction permits for about 90 television stations and 600 radio stations through this process. Next, the FCC conducted auctions for 118 television and radio channels in late 1999, most of them FM radio channels in smaller markets.

Congress authorized the FCC to award all remaining non-digital licenses by auction. Digital television licenses are being awarded to existing television stations without auctions, although new digital licenses may be awarded later by auction to parties not holding television licenses in that market. As a means of awarding new broadcast licenses, comparative hearings are no longer part of the process. However, a federal court created a snag in the FCC's plan to auction more AM and FM radio channels in 2001: the court held that applicants for non-commercial licenses could not be forced to bid against commercial applicants. In *National Public Radio v. FCC* (254 F.3d 226), the court left the FCC in the position of having to exclude non-commercial applicants from upcoming auctions altogether or else create a public service "point" system, with points somehow equated to the dollars that might be bid by commercial applicants for the same channels. A small part of the FM band is reserved for non-commercial stations, but non-commercial applicants have been free to seek channels elsewhere on the FM dial if no non-commercial channel is available. The FCC had not resolved this problem by mid-2002.

The FCC also has a number of other ownership policies that were not affected by the *Bechtel* court decision. For example, the FCC will not ordinarily grant a radio or television license to the owner of a daily newspaper in the same market area, nor will the commission license someone who already holds the maximum number of radio or television stations allowed in a given community. These rules, too, may change soon: the FCC is reconsidering its newspaper-broadcast cross-ownership rule and certain other restrictions on broadcast ownership, with a decision expected in 2003 (see Chapter 12).

Court Decisions on Licensing Preferences

For many years the commission gave a preference to minority group members and women in evaluating license applications, a step designed to help correct the traditional underrepresentation of women and minorities in broadcast ownership. That led to situations in which a woman or minority applicant was given a license in preference to white male applicants who believed they were better qualified--and were prepared to go to court to prove it. The resulting legal challenges to the preference system produced several controversial court decisions.

In 1990, the Supreme Court reaffirmed the minority preference rules in the case of *Metro Broadcasting v. FCC* (497 U.S. 547). The *Metro Broadcasting* case became a major test of federal government affirmative action policies in general, and the court surprised many broadcasters by voting 5-4 to uphold these minority preferences. A year earlier, the Supreme Court had ruled that many affirmative action policies of state and local governments were unconstitutional in *Richmond v. J.A. Croson Co.* (488 U.S. 469). In the *Richmond* case, the court ruled that state and local affirmative action policies, when challenged in court, had to be justified under a *compelling governmental interest* test. That test made it difficult to defend programs that favor one party over another on the basis of race.

But in the *Metro Broadcasting* case, Justice Byron White switched sides and provided the fifth vote to uphold the FCC's affirmative action policy on the ground that it was mandated by Congress and should *not* be judged against the tough *compelling government interest* standard. White was often reluctant to overrule government policies endorsed by Congress. As a result, the FCC's policy favoring license applicants who are minorities was upheld--for the time being.

However, in 1995--only five years later--the Supreme Court took the unusual step of reversing the *Metro Broadcasting* decision, ruling that federal affirmative action programs must indeed be justified under the *compelling government interest* standard. The 1995 decision, *Adarand Constructors Inc. v. Pena* (515 U.S. 200), held that any federal program granting a preference to members of one race over another must be justified by proof that it is an appropriate remedy for a specific, provable instance of previous discrimination. And all race preference programs are subject to *strict judicial scrutiny*, the 5-4 majority in *Adarand* ruled.

Justice Sandra Day O'Connor, writing for the majority, quoted her own opinion in the *Croson* case, in which she said strict judicial scrutiny of racial preferences is needed "to smoke out illegitimate uses of race by assuring that the legislative body is pursuing a goal important enough to warrant use of a highly suspect tool."

O'Connor noted that the Supreme Court upheld the relocation and internment of Japanese Americans during World War II and said, "any retreat from the most searching judicial scrutiny can only increase the risk of another error occurring in the future."

O'Connor also said that the Fifth and Fourteenth Amendments guarantee equal protection of the law to *individuals*, not groups. Thus, any government policy that favors one person over others on the basis of race is suspect.

The *Adarand* decision produced strongly worded dissents from four justices, John Paul Stevens, David H. Souter, Ruth Bader Ginsburg and Stephen G. Breyer.

For broadcasters, this decision had far-reaching consequences: it called into question the FCC's entire system of race-based preferences. Reed Hundt, the FCC chairman at the time, responded to the *Adarand* decision by pledging to reexamine all of the FCC's minority preference programs to make sure they met the tough new constitutional requirements. Almost immediately, the FCC dropped its minority and women's preferences for an upcoming series of auctions to award personal communications service (PCS) licenses. In previous PCS auctions, women and minorities had been given credits of up to 40 percent in the bidding, so that a bid of $6 million by a woman or minority group member would win the license over a bid of up to $10 million by a white male, for example. That preference was controversial because the whole point of the spectrum auctions was to raise money to reduce the federal deficit. Under the rules announced in mid-1995 when the PCS auction preferences were dropped, the next round of auctions was open only to small businesses--but with the licenses going to the highest bidder, without regard to gender or ethnicity.

Meanwhile, another aspect of the FCC's racial preference program was abolished by Congress shortly before the Supreme Court reversed itself on federal affirmative action programs in 1995. For more than 15 years, the FCC had a *tax certificate* program under which those who sold broadcast stations or cable systems could avoid paying the capital gains taxes on the sale if they sold to a company controlled by women or minorities. The rationale for this policy, like the rationale for the licensing preference, was to encourage more minorities and women to become station and cable system owners.

When the Supreme Court upheld the minority preference in the *Metro Broadcasting* decision in 1990, the court also upheld the tax certificate program in a companion case, *Astroline Communications v. Shurberg Broadcasting* (497 U.S. 547).

In early 1995, however, there was widespread media publicity about several instances in which large, wealthy corporations had received (or were about to receive) multimillion dollar tax breaks under the tax certificate program. For example, Viacom, one of the nation's largest cable system owners, was about to receive a $600 million tax break under the tax certificate program. Viacom was planning to sell its cable systems for $2.3 billion to a partnership headed by an African-American lawyer who had helped to create the tax certificate program in 1978 when he was working at the White House Office of Telecommunications Policy. Although he headed the partnership, thereby making Viacom eligible for the huge tax break, it turned out that most of the money for the deal was coming from two large corporations that were not minority-owned, including Tele-Communications Inc. (TCI), the nation's largest owner of cable systems at the time.

Legislation to eliminate the entire tax certificate program was quickly passed by Congress and signed by President Clinton, cutting off Viacom's tax break. Leaders at the FCC and in Congress later considered but did not ultimately approve a new tax certificate program with strict rules to prevent abuses.

Even before the Supreme Court created doubts about the validity of the minority preferences, the women's preference in broadcast licensing had been overturned by the U.S. Court of Appeals in Washington, D.C. In an opinion by Judge Clarence Thomas, now a Supreme Court justice, the appellate court voted 2-1 to declare the women's preference unconstitutional. The court ruled that the FCC had failed to prove the preference would really foster diversity of opinion or programming on the airwaves (*Lamprecht v. FCC*, 958 F.2d 382, 1992).

Court Decisions on the EEO Rules

In addition to the court decisions overturning preferences in broadcast licensing, the U.S. Court of Appeals in Washington, D.C. has twice rejected the FCC's attempts to impose on broadcasters equal employment opportunity (EEO) requirements over and above those that apply to other businesses.

Under the FCC's original EEO rules, each licensee was required to seek out women and minorities for its work force. For many years, the FCC required broadcasters to achieve at least 50 percent of "parity." For example, if 20 percent of the population of a station's service area was African-American, at least 10 percent of the station's workforce had to be African-American for the station to be in compliance.

In 1998, the U.S. Court of Appeals in Washington, D.C., overturned the FCC's entire EEO program is *Lutheran Church-Missouri Synod v. FCC* (141 F.3d 344). The decision resulted from the FCC's attempt to penalize two Lutheran Church-owned radio stations near St. Louis, Mo. for EEO violations and other alleged infractions. The church went to court, arguing that an FCC requirement to hire outside the church for all but on-air employees violated the First Amendment guarantees of freedom of religion. (This was an important issue because the percentage of church members falling into some minority categories was much lower than the percentage in the larger community).

The FCC had long justified its EEO rules by arguing that even low-level employees such as secretaries, if drawn proportionately from all races and both genders, would influence a station's programming and make it better reflect the diversity of America. Under that rationale, the Lutherans argued, the government was in effect forcing religious stations to modify their message by hiring non-believers. A three-judge appellate panel agreed, overturning the EEO program as unconstitutional.

After this court decision it is still unlawful for a broadcaster to *discriminate against* women and minorities in hiring. But the FCC cannot legally penalize a broadcaster for failing to meet the numerical EEO requirements, which in effect had required broadcasters to hire a certain percentage of women and minorities even if better qualified white males applied. The FCC asked the appellate court to reconsider the case *en banc* (i.e., with all judges instead of a panel of three hearing the case), but the court declined to do so.

In late 1998 the FCC ended the case by renewing the licenses of the two Lutheran-owned radio stations.

A few weeks before the *Lutheran Church-Missouri Synod* court decision, FCC Chairman William Kennard gave a speech at a broadcasters' convention challenging industry leaders to come up with new proposals to promote diversity in the industry. When the *Lutheran Church* decision was announced, many broadcasters said they would continue to work to diversify their staffs even without formal EEO requirements. Broadcasters responded to Kennard's appeal by proposing new financial incentives for minority investment in broadcasting and new efforts to recruit and train minorities, among other suggestions.

In 2000, the FCC adopted new equal employment opportunity (EEO) rules to replace the rules that were declared unconstitutional in the *Lutheran Church* decision. The new EEO rules required broadcasters (and cable and other "multichannel video" companies as well) to do broad outreach in an effort to recruit a diverse workforce. However, unlike the EEO rules that were rejected by the court, the new rules included no quotas.

Instead of requiring broadcasters to hire on the basis of race to meet specific quotas, the new rules required broadcasters either to engage in a series of outreach efforts specified by the FCC or to devise their own methods and then document what they did, and to file regular employment reports with the FCC. Addressing another concern of the court in the *Lutheran Church* case, the new rules permitted religious broadcasters to hire believers for all positions, not just on-air positions.

Even though the new rules contained no hiring quotas, many broadcast attorneys were alarmed at the very complex outreach and reporting requirements. Many feared that broadcasters would have difficulty complying--and might never know if they are out of compliance until the FCC launched an enforcement action. Eventually the National Association of Broadcasters, joined by the state broadcasting associations in all 50 states, challenged the new EEO rules in a lawsuit in the federal appellate court in Washington, D.C.

In early 2001, the court overturned the FCC's new EEO rules. In setting aside the new rules, the court rejected the FCC's requirement that broadcasters must create minority outreach programs and report the results to the FCC. Although the new rules did not include the numerical quotas that the court found to be unconstitutional in the FCC's original EEO rules, the court said the new minority recruiting rules were also unconstitutional.

"The rule (the new recruiting requirement) does put official pressure upon broadcasters to recruit minority candidates, thus creating a race-based classification that is not narrowly tailored to support a compelling governmental interest and is therefore unconstitutional," the court held.

In the new case, *MD/DC/DE Broadcasters Association v. FCC* (236 F.3d 13), a three-judge panel of the appellate court in Washington unanimously agreed with the broadcasters' argument that the new rules still forced broadcasters to recruit based on race rather than merit and made it difficult for broadcasters to know when they were in compliance--a violation of the due process clause of the Fifth Amendment.

The case was seen as a stinging rebuke to outgoing FCC Chairman William

Kennard, who had worked hard to implement new EEO rules during his tenure. The decision was rendered three days before Kennard stepped down to make way for Michael Powell, the new chairman named by President George W. Bush shortly after his inauguration.

The language in the *MD/DC/DE Broadcasters* decision is so sweeping that it left many legal observers wondering if any set of rules that requires broadcasters to recruit on the basis of race would be constitutional. The FCC, acting under its new chairman, asked the court to reconsider and reinstate the rules; the court denied that request.

The FCC then proposed still another set of EEO rules in 2001. Those proposed rules would require fewer reports from television and radio stations and cable systems, with no requirement at all to collect race and ethnicity data on job applicants. As of mid-2002, the FCC was still conducting hearings on this proposal for a third set of EEO rules.

Broadcast industry leaders, while generally applauding the court decisions that overturned the two previous sets of EEO rules, said they are committed to seeking out more minorities and women for positions in the industry, with or without FCC rules requiring it. One prominent industry executive also noted that the year 2000 saw a slight increase in minority ownership of radio stations in spite of the enormous consolidation of radio station ownership since 1996. But he also noted that ownership statistics can be misleading, pointing out that several large minority-controlled media companies no longer qualify as minority owned because they have launched public sales of their corporate stock--and minorities no longer constitute a majority of their shareholders.

License Renewal Problems

Almost as soon as a station is licensed, it must begin preparing for the next crisis in the relationship between broadcaster and government: renewal time. At that point, the broadcaster is supposed to show good stewardship in the use of its assigned frequency.

For many years, most broadcasters assumed that once they had a license from the FCC, it was theirs indefinitely. A license to broadcast in a big city (without any station equipment or any of the other accouterments of a going business) came to be worth millions of dollars. This is true despite the fact that a broadcast license is theoretically nothing more than an authorization to use a frequency for the balance of the license term. The 1934 Communications Act says a license never becomes a vested right. In fact, broadcasters have to sign an agreement acknowledging that their frequencies will remain public property indefinitely.

However, in actual practice the FCC virtually rubber-stamped most renewals for many years. To lose a license, one had to commit a serious crime or try to deceive the FCC (by falsifying a license application, for example). However, that changed somewhat in the 1960s and 1970s. Both the FCC and the courts began taking a new look at the licensing process. And the process changed again when the 1996 Telecommunications Act mandated new procedures for license renewals.

A key turning point in the 1960s was a federal court ruling, *Office of Commu-*

nication of the United Church of Christ v. FCC (359 F.2d 994, 1966; 425 F.2d 543, 1969). In that case, a public interest group requested a hearing to protest the renewal of a Mississippi television station's license on the ground that its programming evidenced blatant racial prejudice. The FCC refused to grant the group any standing to challenge the license renewal, but a federal appellate court ordered the FCC to hold a new hearing and allow the group to appear. Next, the FCC held such a hearing but placed the burden of proof on the citizen group. The federal court overruled the FCC again, declaring that the burden of proof should have been on the broadcaster to justify his performance. Then the court set aside the license renewal, and the station eventually lost the license.

After that decision, citizens' groups demanded and won standing to oppose a number of other license renewals, and sometimes rival applicants demanded a comparative hearing so they could attempt to show that they could make better use of the frequency. This was a new element in the renewal process; no longer could a broadcaster merely fill out the forms and rest assured that renewal would be a routine matter. The risk that an opponent might file a *petition to deny* a license renewal came to be a fact of life for broadcasters.

Further breaking the rubber-stamp tradition, the FCC shocked the broadcast industry by denying renewal to an incumbent television licensee in Boston in 1969. A rival group challenged the renewal of WHDH, and the FCC eventually decided the challenger could do a better job than the incumbent.

The policy of holding a comparative hearing when a renewal is challenged was not new, but the rules had so favored the incumbent licensee that challengers had little chance to win. If the incumbent licensee had provided even average service, that record was supposed to be given preference over the mere promises of a challenger. But in this case, the FCC ignored the broadcaster's record of average service and granted the license to a challenger who promised better things. In so ruling, the FCC noted that the incumbent licensee, also the owner of the Boston *Herald-Traveler* newspaper, had shown little interest in the active management of the television station. Really, the station was little more than a source of revenue for the newspaper. A federal appellate court affirmed the FCC decision in 1970 (*Greater Boston Television Corp. v. FCC*, 444 F.2d 841).

The idea that an incumbent licensee could lose a license to a challenger at renewal time, thus forfeiting a property worth millions of dollars, frightened the broadcast industry. The industry quickly had legislation introduced in Congress to strip the FCC of authority to hold comparative hearings unless it first decided the incumbent broadcaster had done an unacceptable job. But before Congress could act, the FCC abandoned its policy of holding comparative hearings in most challenged license renewal cases.

However, a citizens' group took the FCC to court over that change in policy, and in 1971 a federal appellate court overruled the FCC, ordering the agency to hold comparative hearings in most instances when a renewal was challenged (*Citizens Communications Center v. FCC*, 447 F.2d 1201). The court said that only broadcasters with service records "far above average" should be exempted from comparative hearings if their license renewals were challenged. Thus, the FCC resumed its practice of holding comparative hearings when licensees faced renewal challenges, although perhaps the agency did so halfheartedly. It was not until 1996 that Congress again intervened and directed the FCC to eliminate comparative license renewal proceedings.

During the 1970s and early 1980s, the FCC gradually refined its comparative renewal policy. Eventually the commission reached the point of saying that a licensee who had a "substantial" record of service (as opposed to a "far above average" record) was entitled to a renewal almost regardless of what a challenger might promise. Although that change may have been an exercise in semantics more than anything else, it led to more lawsuits.

In 1982, the U.S. Court of Appeals in Washington, D.C., affirmed this policy on license renewals in *Central Florida Enterprises v. FCC* (683 F.2d 503). The court agreed that the FCC is entitled to give considerable weight to an incumbent licensee's *renewal expectancy* if the licensee has a "substantial" record of service. In essence, the FCC was saying this: the better the incumbent's record, the greater should be his or her renewal expectancy. A licensee with a record of minimal service would get no preference over a challenger in a comparative hearing, while someone with a superior record would get a very strong preference.

During the 1980s the FCC simplified the license renewal process in other respects. For example, the FCC eliminated much of the paperwork and red tape that once made a license renewal such a bureaucratic headache for broadcasters. The process was streamlined so much that most broadcasters could take advantage of what became known as *postcard renewal*. Instead of a detailed report, broadcasters had to fill out a renewal application that looked somewhat like a two-sided oversized postcard. However, postcard renewal was probably something of a misnomer, because broadcasters also had to fill out other forms at license renewal time, including forms to document their compliance with the equal employment opportunity rules. The FCC required about five percent of all broadcast licensees to go through an "audit" in which a longer renewal application form is required.

Thousands of pages of paperwork--forms that some critics of the process said the FCC staff didn't have time to read anyway--were eliminated as a result of postcard renewal. However, a coalition of minority groups went to court to challenge the FCC's authority to eliminate the more detailed application form. They said the shorter renewal form excused most broadcasters from having to show any record of public interest programming at all. But in a 1983 ruling, the U.S. Court of Appeals in Washington, D.C., upheld the postcard renewal process (*Black Citizens for a Fair Media v. FCC*, 719 F.2d 407). The court said occasional "audits" were sufficient to ensure that broadcasters would meet their obligations.

Congress and the FCC both acted to ease the license renewal burden for broadcasters several times in the 1980s and 1990s. In 1981, Congress lengthened license terms from three years to seven years for radio stations and from three years to five years for television stations. The 1996 Telecommunications Act took this a step further, directing the FCC to extend license terms to eight years for both radio and TV stations.

In 1989 the FCC took another step to limit the cost and uncertainty of license renewals. Recognizing that many challengers were filing a petition to deny a license renewal only in the hope of getting the licensee to pay a large settlement and not because of legitimate concerns about the station's performance, the FCC imposed strict limits on financial settlements of license renewal disputes. In the future, licensees would not be allowed to pay challengers more than their actual expenses as a settlement. (In 1990, the FCC adopted the same restriction on settlements among rival applicants for *new station licenses*, as explained earlier).

Finally, the license renewal process was greatly simplified by Congress in the Telecommunications Act of 1996. Probably the most important change was the elimination of the comparative license renewal process. Broadcast license renewals are now a two-step process in which the FCC first determines if the licensee is entitled to a renewal. Others may still oppose the license renewal, but the FCC considers only the renewal/nonrenewal question, not competing applications from others who might like to have the license. Only if the FCC should decide a licensee has committed such serious offenses as to be ineligible for a renewal does the second step occur. During that second step, the former licensee is denied a renewal, and other applications for the channel are accepted.

The 1996 Telecommunications Act also made other changes in the renewal process. Among other things, it required broadcasters to submit a summary of comments received from the public about violence in the station's programming. And it mandated a three-point evaluation of license renewals by the FCC. In reviewing each renewal application, the FCC was directed to make sure that the station: 1) has served the public interest, convenience and necessity; 2) has not committed any serious violation of the rules; and 3) has not committed a series of minor violations that constitute a "pattern of abuse."

There are several other ways in which broadcasters have been required to show compliance with the FCC's rules to earn a license renewal. Among the rule violations that led to the most renewal questions was the failure to properly document compliance with the FCC's equal employment opportunity (EEO) requirements (which are no longer in effect) and with the rules governing the safety of the station's tower installation. One of the major safety questions is compliance with the FCC's rules on electromagnetic radiation safety. Broadcasters have to prove that their towers do not produce hazardous electromagnetic fields in areas accessible to the public.

How does a station show that it complies with all of the old and new requirements to obtain a license renewal? It may take some years--and some court decisions--to establish how the post-1996 renewal process is supposed to work. What remains true is that broadcasters are still accountable for their conduct at license renewal time. The RKO case is perhaps the most notable license non-renewal case in the history of broadcasting. It illustrates both how the system works and how dysfunctional the process can be.

The RKO Case

One of the most lengthy license non-renewal cases in the FCC's history unfolded in the 1970s and 1980s, when the commission decided to strip **RKO General**, once one of the nation's largest broadcasting corporations, of all of its stations, including major-market television stations in New York, Boston and Los Angeles.

In 1980, the FCC acted to take away the three big-city licenses--and also made it clear that RKO's other radio and television licenses would be in jeopardy when they came up for renewal.

This case did *not* arise just because someone challenged RKO's right to a renewal and used a comparative hearing to promise better service. Rather, the FCC took the initiative to terminate RKO's licenses because RKO and its parent company, GenCorp. (formerly General Tire and Rubber), were allegedly guilty of various unlawful activities. Nevertheless, the RKO case is important because of its financial impact.

RKO claimed the three television licenses in question were worth at least $400 million and immediately appealed the FCC's decision. In 1981 the U.S. Court of Appeals affirmed the FCC's non-renewal of the Boston license (*RKO v. FCC*, 670 F.2d 215), and the Supreme Court declined to hear the case in April of 1982. Thus, RKO reluctantly went off the air in Boston and handed the channel over to a new licensee.

However, the Court of Appeals sent the actions to terminate the licenses in Los Angeles (KHJ-TV, now KCAL) and New York (WOR-TV, now WWOR) back to the FCC for further consideration because the commission had not yet provided a "principled explanation for RKO's disqualification" to operate those two stations. In upholding the FCC decision to take away the Boston license, the appellate court explained:

> The denial of a license renewal to a major licensee in a major market is of manifest moment and financial impact. The FCC's decision has not been reviewed callously, and we have tried not to lose sight of the difficult issues in this case by sweeping the reasoning of the Commission under a rug of agency expertise or administrative convenience. The record presented to this court shows irrefutably that the licensee was playing the dodger to serious charges involving it and its parent company.

Of all the evidence presented in the case, apparently the most persuasive to the court was the FCC's documentary proof that RKO provided information to the commission in the early stages of the proceeding that the company itself contradicted in later filings. The commission cited an "egregious lack of candor" on RKO's part.

After the *RKO v. FCC* court ruling, RKO managed to make a deal with Congress to rescue its New York license. Congress passed special legislation that overruled the FCC and renewed WOR-TV's license on condition that it move its studios from New York to New Jersey. Because of New Jersey's proximity to both New York and Philadelphia, the state had not had even one commercial VHF TV station within its borders. For years, New Jersey residents (and their legislators) had been demanding a VHF television station of their own. Congress decided to solve that problem--and let RKO partially off the hook at the same time--by trading a guaranteed renewal for a move across the Hudson River. But even after WOR's move to Secaucus, N.J., some New Jersey leaders were still unhappy about the VHF TV problem: WOR was allowed to keep its actual transmitter site in New

York (atop the World Trade Center), and the station continued to maintain an advertising office in New York. Many New Jersey residents felt that WOR was still primarily a New York station, though it had a New Jersey mailing address.

RKO then sold WOR to a group headed by MCA Inc. for $387 million. Since RKO was about to lose its New York license without any compensation, Congress had in effect given an enormous gift to RKO by overruling the FCC and allowing the company to renew the license in return for the move across the Hudson River.

Meanwhile, the FCC accepted some 160 competing applications for RKO's other 13 licenses and declared that the ultimate fate of those stations would depend on the outcome of the non-renewal proceeding involving KHJ-TV in Los Angeles. But as these complex proceedings dragged on through the 1980s, the FCC attempted to solve this long-standing licensing dispute. In 1987 an FCC administrative law judge ruled RKO unfit to hold any broadcast licenses, but a year later the FCC voted to let RKO sell its remaining stations (instead of losing them without compensation through license non-renewal).

As RKO sold its stations, the company also negotiated settlements with the many competing applicants for its licenses. In most instances, RKO received about two-thirds of the selling price, with the other third going to competing applicants.

When the FCC voted to close the books on the RKO case more than 20 years after it began, Commissioner Patricia Diaz Dennis dissented from the vote to let RKO sell out instead of forfeiting its licenses. She said it sent the wrong message to other broadcasters (that if a company can delay a license revocation long enough, it can negotiate its way out no matter how bad its record is).

Perhaps the RKO case also illustrates the major contradiction in broadcast regulation. In theory, every frequency belongs to the public: the broadcaster has nothing more than temporary authorization to use it, a permit that may be revoked at any time. But in practice, broadcast licenses are immensely valuable pieces of property, items that can be sold for huge sums of money. Thus, on those rare occasions when the FCC does what the Communications Act clearly authorizes it to do and decides the public interest would be better served by not renewing a license, the result is an economic catastrophe for someone--or many people, including innocent lenders and stockholders.

For this reason, the FCC has developed sanctions short of non-renewal to punish broadcasters for wrongdoing. Probably the most viable of these sanctions is a short-term renewal. The commission may renew a license for as little as one year. When that happens, a broadcaster knows he or she is on probation and had better make some changes quickly.

Despite all of these considerations, the FCC served notice in 1999 that license non-renewal is still a viable option. In the first such action in a decade, the FCC voted in mid-1999 to deny a license renewal to a Miami, Fla. television station: WHTF(TV), owned by the Trinity Broadcasting Network.

The commission's majority ruled that the religious network was unqualified for a renewal because it misled the commission in the 1980s to get around the FCC's ownership limits. An FCC administrative law judge concluded that Trinity created a minority-front company to take advantage of higher ownership limits then in effect for minority-owned companies, and that Trinity later misled the FCC about its ongoing control over the minority company.

The commission earlier had held up license renewals for Trinity's entire network of 12 full-power and 300 low-power television stations while this issue was being adjudicated. In the 1999 vote, however, the FCC agreed to disregard Trinity's alleged deception in determining the network's eligibility to renew its other licenses.

However, Trinity appealed the loss of the Miami license to a federal appellate court, and the court reversed the FCC's decision in 2000 (*Trinity Broadcasting of Florida v. FCC*, 211 F.3d 618). The court concluded that the minority ownership and control regulations that Trinity allegedly violated were too vague to be the basis for a license revocation. As a result, Trinity was allowed to keep its Miami license, but Trinity still had to pay about $31 million to settle license renewal challenges that had been filed against several of its stations by private entities.

BROADCAST CONTENT REGULATION

Aside from its frequency allocation and licensing functions, the FCC's main job is to supervise the ongoing operations of its licensees. While a certain amount of that supervision involves technical matters--frequency stability, modulation percentage, power level, and such--a far greater concern to the public (and to most broadcasters themselves) is the FCC's rules governing *content*.

Although Section 326 of the 1934 Communications Act specifically forbids the FCC to "censor" broadcasters, over the years the commission has adopted a number of rules to regulate broadcast content. Also, both the 1934 Communications Act and the 1996 Telecommunications Act, among other federal laws, have provisions governing broadcast content.

Ironically, one of the FCC's major goals during the 1980s was to disentangle itself from content regulation. No government agency has the authority to tell newspaper and magazine publishers to print a specific amount or kind of material, or to open their columns to those with whom they disagree. Why, the FCC asked, should broadcasters be second-class citizens when it comes to First Amendment freedoms? Some consumer groups responded to that question by arguing that broadcasters are given a government-sanctioned monopoly and should have to provide some mandatory public service in return. After all, the FCC does select just one broadcaster to operate on a given frequency in each community, denying that privilege to all others.

Whatever the pros and cons of deregulation, during the 1980s the FCC eliminated many of its rules governing broadcast content on the ground that they were inappropriate if not unconstitutional. In the 1990s, on the other hand, the FCC reversed its philosophy and created several new content controls.

Therefore, this section is about regulation and deregulation. A number of important restrictions on broadcast content are still in force or have recently been added--restrictions that do not apply to most other communications media. But other restrictions, including the Fairness Doctrine, which was perhaps the most controversial content regulation of all, have been abolished.

The Law of Political Broadcasting

Probably the most important aspects of broadcast content regulation are the laws and rules concerning political broadcasting. The key provision is Section 315 of the Communications Act, often called the *Equal Time Rule* or "equal opportunity provision." It has been a part of the Communications Act ever since it was enacted in 1934. In addition to Section 315--which is an act of Congress and cannot be unilaterally rewritten by the FCC--there are many FCC rules that spell out the details of broadcasters' obligations during election campaigns. The FCC adopted a major revision of these rules in 1991.

Section 315 requires broadcasters to provide equal access to the airwaves to all legally qualified candidates for a given public office during election campaigns. It reads in part:

> If any licensee shall permit any person who is a legally qualified candidate for any public office to use a broadcasting station, he shall afford equal opportunities to all other such candidates for that office in the use of such broadcasting station....

The Equal Time Rule has a number of provisions, some of them troublesome for broadcasters. Section 315 specifically exempts "bona fide" newscasts, news interviews, news documentaries and, significantly, coverage of news events such as political conventions and debates between candidates. That means a broadcaster can cover news stories involving one candidate without having to include all other candidates.

In 1984, the FCC extended the exemption for news and public affairs programs to many talk shows, thus allowing them to host political candidates during election campaigns without having to give equal time to all other candidates for the same office. In its 1991 rewrite of the rules, the FCC expanded this provision by saying that Section 315 really only applies to "uses" of a station that are controlled, approved or sponsored by a candidate, such as political advertising.

Section 315 doesn't require broadcasters to give politicians free time for campaign advertising. Rather, it merely requires that all candidates be treated equally. If one is sold airtime for a certain fee, the Equal Time Rule merely requires that others be allowed to purchase equal time in the same part of the broadcast day for the same price. If the other candidates can't afford to buy the airtime, the station has no obligation to give them free time. But if one candidate is given free airtime, all other candidates for the same office must also be given free airtime.

The lack of a requirement that broadcasters give candidates free airtime is something that the FCC and the Clinton administration were anxious to change in the late 1990s. President Clinton and both of the men he appointed to the FCC chairmanship (Reed Hundt and William Kennard) frequently called on broadcasters to give major party candidates free airtime during their campaigns. The television networks and other leaders of the industry responded by pointing to the large amount of broadcast news programming that is already devoted to political campaigns. But that airtime is *controlled by broadcast journalists*, not the candidates. What the Clinton administration and the FCC were seeking is airtime to use as they please--without journalists controlling the format and asking potentially embarrassing questions. In effect, they were asking for *free advertising time* for political candidates.

Clinton mentioned this issue in his 1998 State of the Union message. The next day, FCC Chairman Kennard said the FCC would propose rules concerning free airtime for political candidates. That produced a storm of criticism from Congressional Republicans. The FCC responded by issuing only a Notice of Inquiry to solicit public comments without actually proposing new rules that would require free airtime for politicians.

If Section 315 were the only applicable provision of the Communications Act, a station could comply with the Equal Time Rule by simply excluding all political advertising. That would, after all, be providing all candidates *equal* time--none. However, another provision of the Communications Act places an additional requirement on broadcasters. Section 312(a)(7) says broadcasters may have their licenses revoked if they fail to provide *reasonable access* to candidates *in federal elections*. ("Federal" means elections for the House and Senate as well as the presidency and vice presidency.) As a result, a broadcaster cannot avoid the Equal Time provision by simply turning away all federal candidates; they must be allowed to purchase some airtime for political advertising. But the 1991 revision of the rules makes it clear that broadcasters are not obligated to provide "reasonable access"--or any access at all--to candidates for state and local offices. Section 315 does require broadcasters to "afford reasonable opportunity for the discussion of conflicting views on issues of public importance," but the FCC has interpreted that to mean only that each station must cover the issues--not provide access to candidates for any particular non-federal office. However, if a station does sell airtime to a non-federal candidate, it must offer to sell equal time to other candidates for the same office.

During the 1980 presidential election campaign, the constitutionality of Section 312(a)(7) was tested in court. The Carter-Mondale presidential campaign asked to purchase 30 minutes of airtime on each network in late 1979, about a year before the election. All three networks refused to honor the request, despite the provisions of Section 312(a)(7). CBS offered only five minutes during prime time, while NBC and ABC flatly rejected the request. The FCC then ruled that the networks had failed to meet their obligation to provide federal candidates "reasonable access" under Section 312(a)(7).

The networks challenged the FCC's ruling in court, and that led to an important 1981 Supreme Court decision upholding the commission, *CBS v. FCC* (453 U.S. 367). Voting 6-3, the high court affirmed the commission's authority under Section 312(a)(7) to order broadcasters to air federal candidates' political statements. The court upheld the FCC's determination that the campaign had begun, even though the general election was nearly a year away at the time the issue arose. Of course, the 1981 Supreme Court decision came far too late to help the Carter-Mondale campaign, but it represented a major victory for future candidates and a defeat for broadcasters.

The Supreme Court majority ruled that the First Amendment rights of candidates and the public outweighed the First Amendment rights of broadcasters in this particular context. Writing for the court, Chief Justice Warren Burger pointed out that the FCC need not (and does not) honor all requests for air time by federal office seekers, but Burger said the FCC was well within its statutory authority in ordering the networks to air the Carter-Mondale campaign statements in late 1979. In fact, Burger noted that the FCC had set forth specific guidelines for broadcasters to follow in determining when candidates would have a right of access to the airwaves under Section 312(a)(7). In this case, the FCC was justified in concluding that the three major networks had violated those guidelines, Burger said.

Because the Equal Time Rule only requires equal treatment for candidates running *in the same election*, stations may sell advertising during a non-federal *primary election* only to those running for the Democratic and Republican nominations and not to those seeking minor party nominations. In the primary, the minor party candidates aren't actually running against the Democratic and Republican candidates. However, during the general election campaign all candidates for the same office must be allowed to buy comparable airtime at the same rates. A federal appellate court provided this interpretation of Section 315 in 1970 (*Kay v. FCC*, 443 F.2d 638). But remember that in federal elections, all candidates must be offered "reasonable access" to broadcast airtime if they can pay for it. And once a broadcaster sells (or gives) airtime to *any* candidate, federal, state or local, other candidates in the same election must be treated equally.

Under these rules, it has become commonplace for broadcasters to accept advertising from federal candidates and candidates for the most prominent state and local offices, while rejecting advertising from all candidates for less important state and local offices.

Politicians and Lowest Unit Charges

Still another aspect of the political broadcasting rules has become a bookkeeping nightmare for both broadcasters and candidates: the *lowest unit charge* provision in Section 315(b). This provision requires broadcasters to charge candidates the lowest rate that they charge their most favored commercial advertisers for advertising within the 45 days of a primary election and 60 days of a general election. Note that this provision applies to *all* candidates, not just federal candidates.

The lowest unit charge rule means the candidates get the rate charged the largest volume advertisers, even if that discounted rate isn't normally offered to one-time or short-term advertisers. Prior to the 45- and 60-day periods, candidates may be charged rates "comparable" to those charged other advertisers, which means that a candidate doesn't get the quantity discount then without buying enough advertising to qualify for it.

In its 1991 rewrite of the political broadcasting rules, the FCC went to great lengths to clarify the lowest unit charge rule. In recent years, the sale of broadcast advertising has become far more complex than it once was. As well as volume discounts, most stations offer lower rates for *preemptible* airtime (that is, an ad that can be dropped if someone else comes along later and offers to pay more for the same airtime). On the other hand, someone who purchases *non-preemptible fixed* airtime is guaranteed that the ad will air at a specific time--but that kind of advertising costs more. Many stations have found that they can maximize their advertising revenue by using this system.

The FCC conducted an audit of stations' political advertising sales practices in 1990, and learned that many politicians were actually paying more than commercial advertisers because they were compelled to buy non-preemptible fixed airtime instead of preemptible airtime. That was defeating the purpose of the lowest unit charge provision in Section 315(b). In fact, the FCC found that candidates often weren't even told that preemptible time was available at a lower cost.

To remedy these problems, the FCC's 1991 rewrite of the rules requires broadcasters to tell candidates about all of the rates and classes of airtime available, and to allow candidates to purchase the least expensive airtime offered to anyone. And if a candidate's ads are preempted (i.e., taken off the air to make time for an advertiser willing to pay a higher rate), the station must provide a "make good" (i.e., get the candidates' ads on the air at another time) before the election if it has provided "time-sensitive" make goods to any commercial advertiser in the previous year. Also, the FCC ordered broadcasters to apply the same rules to candidates as to their most favored commercial advertisers in establishing priorities for protection against preemption.

"Aside from all of those provisions, the lowest unit charge rule is pretty simple," one communications lawyer said during a seminar at a recent convention of the National Association of Broadcasters.

Given the complexity of the lowest unit charge rule, there have been numerous disputes--and lawsuits--between broadcasters and candidates over political advertising rates. A number of candidates have sued broadcasters in state courts, alleging that they were overcharged for advertising in violation of the lowest unit charge rule. Even these lawsuits turned out to be far more complex than anyone (even the lawyers) expected.

In response to the lawsuits alleging overcharges for political advertising, the FCC issued a declaration that the FCC itself has exclusive jurisdiction over lowest unit charge disputes. The courts do not have jurisdiction over this, the FCC declared. Then the 11th circuit U.S. Court of Appeals dismissed the FCC ruling as an "agency opinion" that does not prevent the courts from hearing lowest unit charge lawsuits (*Miller v. FCC*, 66 F.3d 1140, 1995). But a few months later the 9th circuit U.S. Court of Appeals said the 11th circuit was wrong: the FCC's declaration is valid and deprives the courts of jurisdiction over these cases (*Wilson v. A.H. Belo Corp.*, 87 F.3d 393). While the courts quarrel among themselves, political candidates who think they were overcharged can take their complaints to the FCC for certain, and maybe in some parts of the country the courts will hear their cases, too.

Because the lowest unit charge rule applies only to candidates and not *ballot propositions*, some broadcasters who reject advertising from all candidates for minor state and local offices are perfectly willing to accept advertising for state and local ballot propositions--but at higher ad rates than candidates pay.

In 2002, Congress passed the long-debated Bipartisan Campaign Reform Act intended to eliminate abuses of "soft money" (unlimited, unregulated contributions to political parties as opposed to specific candidates from wealthy individuals, corporations or unions). One of its provisions is a ban on the use of soft money to fund "issue advertising" that may be heavily partisan and aimed at specific candidates. The Federal Election Commission later adopted regulations that eased the campaign finance reform bill's restrictions on the use of soft money. It remains to be seen how this will affect political advertising on television and radio.

Political Debates and Other Problem Areas

Another messy problem area under the Equal Time Rule has been candidates' debates. For many years, the rule was interpreted to require broadcasters who aired debates between the major candidates to give equal time to all of the minor candidates as well. The major networks said they could never afford the airtime to do that. In 1960, when John Kennedy and Richard Nixon held the first nationally televised presidential debates, Congress passed a law temporarily setting aside Section 315 so equal time would not have to be given to minor candidates.

In several subsequent presidential elections, no nationally televised debates occurred because Congress chose not to set aside Section 315 again. In 1964, for instance, the polls indicated that Lyndon Johnson was far ahead of his Republican challenger, Barry Goldwater. Johnson's strategists felt he had nothing to gain and a lot to lose if he debated Goldwater, so the Democratic majority in Congress refused to set aside Section 315. For various reasons there were no nationally televised debates during the 1968 and 1972 campaigns, either.

However, in 1975, the FCC reinterpreted Section 315 to say that a debate sponsored by a non-broadcast organization would be considered a bona fide news event, and hence exempt from the requirements of Section 315 (see *In re Aspen Institute and CBS*, 55 F.C.C.2d 697). That new interpretation, which came to be known as the *Aspen Rule*, was quickly challenged by Shirley Chisholm, a minor candidate in the 1976 presidential election, but a federal appellate court upheld the rule (*Chisholm v. FCC*, 538 F.2d 349, 1976).

Thus, in both 1976 and 1980, presidential debates were sponsored by the League of Women Voters and dutifully covered as bona fide news events by the networks. Had the debates been staged by a broadcaster or network, it would have been necessary to include (or give equal time to) perhaps 30 lesser-known candidates for president.

The FCC ruled in 1983 that broadcasters could sponsor debates directly instead of having them sponsored by third parties such as the League of Women Voters. At the same time, the FCC dropped rules that had restricted the use of debates or segments of debates in news programs. The League of Women Voters challenged that reinterpretation of the rule on debates, but lost in the U.S. Court of Appeals (*League of Women Voters v. FCC*, 731 F.2d 995, 1984).

Nevertheless, whether candidates' debates are sponsored by broadcasters or outside organizations, ethical questions arise when only certain candidates are invited to take part. Because of television's great influence, some would argue that any debate that excludes some candidates for an office violates the spirit if not the letter of the Equal Time provision. A particularly strong argument for this position can be made in state and local elections, where there may be only three or four candidates running (as opposed to the 30 or so who usually become legally qualified candidates in a presidential election).

The Supreme Court ruled on this aspect of the Equal Time Rule in a 1998 decision: *Arkansas Educational Television Commission v. Forbes* (523 U.S. 666). At issue was whether public television stations *licensed to a government entity* such as a state have a First Amendment obligation to include all candidates in a political debate--even the ones who have no realistic chance of winning.

By a 6-3 vote, the Supreme Court ruled that even government-owned television stations have no obligation to include all candidates in a debate. The majority held that government-run stations, like private ones, have the right to make news judgments about which candidates are viable enough to be included in a debate sponsored by the station.

Justice Anthony M. Kennedy, writing for the court, said that forcing public broadcasters to include all candidates "would result in less speech, not more" because debates simply could not be held if 20 or 30 different candidates for president had to be included in each debate.

However, Kennedy added that government-controlled stations have a special obligation to be "viewpoint neutral" in their standards for deciding which candidates to include in a debate, never excluding a prominent candidate because he or she might oppose abortion or affirmative action, for example.

Justices John Paul Stevens, David H. Souter and Ruth Bader Ginsburg dissented, arguing that for a government entity to exclude some candidates from a debate while including others "implicates constitutional concerns of the highest order." The dissenters were particularly troubled because the five Arkansas state-owned stations involved in this case did not have clear, objective criteria to be used in determining which candidates are viable enough to be included in debates.

This case was seen as particularly important for public broadcasters because about two-thirds of the nation's 350 public television stations are licensed to a state.

There are still other ethical and legal problems in political broadcasting. For example, the fact that news events are excluded from the Equal Time Rule allows incumbents to get extensive media coverage without other candidates having any similar opportunity. When Senator Edward Kennedy was challenging Jimmy Carter for the 1980 Democratic presidential nomination, he asked the FCC to require the networks to give him equal time to reply to one of Carter's nationally televised news conferences. The FCC turned Kennedy down, and a federal appellate court upheld that decision (*Kennedy for President Committee v. FCC*, 636 F.2d 432, 1980).

For many years, showing the old movies of actors who became politicians (e.g., Ronald Reagan) posed a serious problem for broadcasters: the Equal Time Rule required stations that aired movies in which a candidate appeared (even in a non-political dramatic role) to give equal time to all other candidates for the same office. A federal appellate court once upheld this interpretation of the rules (*In re Paulsen v. FCC*, 491 F.2d 887, 1974). However, the FCC's 1991 rewrite of the rules appears to have taken broadcasters out of this dilemma. The new rules declare that Section 315 applies only to "uses" of a station that are controlled, approved or sponsored by a candidate. Stations are now free to show old movies featuring actors-turned-politicians without giving equal time to opposing candidates.

Section 315 does not allow broadcasters to "censor" a political broadcast. If a candidate libels someone on the air, there is nothing the broadcaster can do to stop it. However, the Supreme Court has exempted broadcasters from any liability for defamatory remarks on such occasions (see *Farmers Educational and Cooperative Union v. WDAY*, discussed in Chapter Four).

This ban on censorship of political broadcasts also poses other dilemmas for broadcasters. For example, what happens if a candidate chooses to include language the broadcaster considers distasteful? Occasionally a candidate insists on including vulgar or offensive language in a political statement--language that a broadcaster could not ordinarily air without incurring the wrath of the FCC. In 1984, the FCC issued a statement declaring that despite Section 315 broadcasters can prevent a candidate from using language that is not normally permitted on the airwaves.

However, broadcasters sometimes must allow candidates to include material that offends some (or many) viewers. For example, in recent years a number of candidates who opposed abortions have included photographs of aborted fetuses in their advertising. Acting on the advice of the FCC, a number of stations refused to air these ads in prime time--even if an opposing candidate had advertised in prime time. In 1996, a federal appellate court held that this "channeling" of anti-abortion campaign ads to times when the audience is small violates the Equal Time Rule. The court said that political candidates have a special right of access, even if their ads are offensive (*Becker v. FCC*, 95 F.3d 75).

A number of other problems have arisen as broadcasters tried to apply the Equal Time Rule. For example, what happens when on-air broadcast employees run for public office? Suppose a deejay with a four-hour show runs for the city council. If he or she doesn't take a leave of absence, must all other candidates be given similar deejay shows?

The FCC's traditional answer to that question has been yes: the station must either take the broadcaster-candidate off the air during the campaign period or give all other candidates equal time--for free. In *Branch v. FCC* (824 F.2d 37), the U.S. Court of Appeals in 1987 upheld the FCC's interpretation of the rules. In 1988, the Supreme Court refused to review that decision.

The case involved William Branch, a reporter for television station KOVR in Sacramento, Calif., who wanted to run for the city council in a small nearby town. He was told he would have to take an unpaid leave of absence if he ran for office. Branch appealed to the FCC and then to court, but to no avail. The Equal Time Rule means what it says, even if a candidate is also a broadcaster, the court held.

The Fairness Doctrine

Probably no rule that the FCC ever adopted has been as controversial as the Fairness Doctrine, established in 1949 and abolished in 1987.

The Fairness Doctrine required commercial broadcasters to keep their public affairs programming reasonably balanced: when they covered one side of a controversial issue, they had to balance that presentation by seeking out and airing opposing viewpoints--even if they had to give representatives of opposing views free airtime. Many members of Congress, some public interest groups, and many others still believe the Fairness Doctrine was a good thing--and hope to see it reinstated someday. On the other hand, most broadcasters (especially broadcast journalists) have vehemently opposed it as a violation of their First Amendment rights because it allowed government bureaucrats to second-guess their news judgments.

When the FCC abolished the Fairness Doctrine in 1987, that may have been the FCC's most controversial decision ever: the Democratic majority in Congress voted to overrule the FCC and put the Fairness Doctrine into statutory law, only to have President Reagan veto that legislation. In 1989, Congress again considered legislation to reinstate the Fairness Doctrine--and President Bush made it clear that he, too, would veto any such legislation. But when Bill Clinton's victory in the 1992 presidential election gave the Democrats control of the White House as well as both houses of Congress, legislation to reinstate the Fairness Doctrine was again introduced. For various reasons, Congress never passed Fairness Doctrine legislation during the 1992-94 period. When the Republicans gained control of both houses of Congress in 1994, there was little likelihood that the Fairness Doctrine would be reinstated by an act of Congress.

Why do Democrats tend to favor the Fairness Doctrine while Republicans tend to oppose it? Traditionally, Republicans and conservative causes have had more money to buy airtime than Democrats and liberal causes. Perhaps it is not too much of an oversimplification to say that Democrats support the Fairness Doctrine while Republicans oppose it because it required broadcasters to give *free* airtime to liberal causes more often than conservative ones (because backers of conservative causes were more likely to have the money to *buy* airtime).

The Fairness Doctrine was always a vague, general policy. It led to relatively few disciplinary actions against broadcasters and almost no license non-renewals. One notable exception to that generalization involved a conservative religious radio station. The owner promised fairness to all religious faiths when he sought FCC permission to purchase the station, but then he followed a policy of presenting only one viewpoint. The license was not renewed, a decision a federal court upheld (*Brandywine-Main Line Radio v. FCC*, 473 F.2d 16, 1972).

However, most complaints of Fairness Doctrine violations were not even passed along to broadcasters by the FCC. The FCC received thousands of Fairness Doctrine complaints each year, and only a few of them resulted in an FCC inquiry, let alone a formal action against the broadcaster.

Unlike the Equal Time Rule, which requires broadcasters to sell *equal* time to opposing candidates, the Fairness Doctrine never required minute-for-minute equality of access. Instead, it merely said broadcasters had to provide overall balance in their programming by presenting varied opinions on controversial issues sooner or later. A broadcaster could cover one side of an issue today and the other next week.

While the Fairness Doctrine was unpopular with broadcasters, many of whom felt it not only abridged their First Amendment rights but also stifled the coverage of controversial issues rather than fostering it, some consumer and media watchdog organizations saw it as the public's only hope of assuring that broadcasters would serve the public interest and not just their own private commercial interests.

Why, then, did the FCC abolish the Fairness Doctrine after 38 years?

In voting to abolish the Fairness Doctrine, each of the commissioners made speeches filled with rhetoric about freedom of the press. But their basic arguments for eliminating the Fairness Doctrine boiled down to these three:

First, the Fairness Doctrine gave government bureaucrats the right to second-guess the news judgments of broadcast journalists, opening the door for potentially dangerous violations of the First Amendment. No government agency has similar authority to supervise the editorial judgments of the print media.

Second, the Fairness Doctrine actually deterred instead of encouraging full news coverage: the fear of having to provide free airtime to a variety of dissenting groups led many broadcasters to avoid controversial stories, or at least to tone them down to avoid offending anyone. These tendencies were evidence of the "chilling effect" the Fairness Doctrine had on the First Amendment rights of broadcasters. (Under a corollary to the Fairness Doctrine called the *Cullman Rule*, broadcasters were required to give free airtime to opposing viewpoints if no one representing a particular viewpoint could afford to purchase airtime).

Finally, some people argued that the scarcity rationale, which was traditionally used to justify broadcast content regulation by the government, was no longer relevant because of the large number of new program sources available to the public, including cable and other newer technologies.

In explaining the commission's 1987 decision to drop the Fairness Doctrine, Dennis Patrick, the FCC chairman at the time, said:

> Our action today should be cause for celebration, because by it we introduce the First Amendment into the 20th century. Because we believe it will serve the public interest, we seek to extend to the electronic press the same First Amendment guarantees that the print media have enjoyed since our country's inception. ...(T)he First Amendment does not guarantee a fair press, only a free press. ...(T)he record in this proceeding leads one inescapably to conclude that the Fairness Doctrine chills free speech, is not narrowly tailored to achieve any substantial government interest, and therefore contravenes the First Amendment and the public interest.

The FCC's action in 1987 was almost anticlimactic: the commission had conducted a massive investigation of the Fairness Doctrine in 1984-85, an inquiry that produced documentation of numerous instances in which the Fairness Doctrine had a chilling effect on the free expression rights of broadcasters, stifling rather than encouraging the coverage of important issues. But the FCC believed then that it lacked the legal authority to eliminate the Fairness Doctrine. The FCC's lawyers believed, as did almost everyone else, that the Fairness Doctrine had been codified by an act of Congress in 1959.

However, a year later the U.S. Court of Appeals in Washington, D.C. shocked the communications law establishment with its ruling in *Telecommunications Research Action Center v. FCC* (801 F.2d 501). Writing for the court, Judge Robert H. Bork (who was later nominated for the Supreme Court) ruled that the Fairness Doctrine had never been anything more than an FCC regulation; it was never codified by Congress, he said. Thus, the FCC was free to repeal it.

After the Fairness Doctrine was repealed, several opposition groups decided to use a lawsuit that was already under way as a vehicle to challenge the FCC's right to abolish the doctrine. The case was *Syracuse Peace Council v. FCC* (867 F.2d 654), which began when WTVH-TV in Syracuse, N.Y. carried several commercials advocating the construction of a nuclear power plant. The FCC ruled that the broadcaster violated the Fairness Doctrine by refusing to provide airtime for the Peace Council to argue against the nuclear power plant.

The broadcaster appealed the FCC's ruling to federal court, and the court sent the case back to the FCC with specific instructions to consider its First Amendment implications. The FCC did--and abolished the Fairness Doctrine itself. Then the Syracuse Peace Council--backed by pro-Fairness Doctrine groups--went back to federal court, contending that the FCC had no right to abolish the Fairness Doctrine. A number of groups that backed the FCC's decision to repeal the Fairness Doctrine intervened in the case.

In 1989 the Court of Appeals ruled that the FCC had the authority to abolish the Fairness Doctrine. However, the appellate court avoided addressing the big issue: whether the Fairness Doctrine violated the First Amendment. In 1990, the Supreme Court declined to review the *Syracuse* case, thus ending the legal challenge to the FCC's decision to abolish the Fairness Doctrine--but leaving open the possibility that Congress might someday act to restore the controversial doctrine.

Another major federal court ruling on the Fairness Doctrine occurred in late 1993, in a case called *Arkansas AFL-CIO v. FCC* (11 F.3d 1430). In that case, the 8th circuit U.S. Court of Appeals issued an *en banc* ruling (a ruling by all judges serving on that court instead of the usual panel of three judges) that again reaffirmed the FCC's authority to abolish the Fairness Doctrine. This court reaffirmed the conclusion of other courts that the doctrine had not been codified by Congress. The case stemmed from a request by labor unions and others that the FCC declare KARK-TV in Little Rock, Ark. guilty of failing to cover all sides fairly in a 1990 ballot referendum. The FCC said the station had no obligation to cover all sides because the Fairness Doctrine had been repealed. The court upheld the FCC's decision, but again stopped short of ruling that the Fairness Doctrine, if reinstated, would violate the First Amendment.

If Congress were to pass Fairness Doctrine legislation, that would surely lead to a new court test of the doctrine's constitutionality--where the First Amendment implications would have to be squarely addressed. It remains to be seen whether the Fairness Doctrine will ever be reinstated, but the controversy surrounding it refuses to die. In 1996, still another challenge to the FCC's abandonment of the Fairness Doctrine was rejected by the 9th circuit U.S. Court of Appeals (*Coalition for a Healthy California v. FCC*, 87 F.3d 383).

Shortly after the FCC eliminated the Fairness Doctrine in 1987, a coalition of media organizations asked the commission to clarify whether some related rules had also been abolished. The commission eventually declared, to the surprise of many, that the *Personal Attack Rule* remained in force, requiring broadcasters to continue notifying the victims of personal attacks (and in some instances, to give these persons free airtime for a reply). The FCC also reaffirmed its *Political Editorializing Rule*, which required broadcasters who endorse candidates to offer opponents free time to reply on the air.

The Radio-Television News Director's Association (RTNDA) challenged the constitutionality of the Personal Attack and Political Editorializing Rules in a lawsuit that was not resolved until 2000--13 years after the Fairness Doctrine itself was abolished and 20 years after the RTNDA first challenged these rules in court. In 1998, the FCC deadlocked 2-2 on a vote to abolish these two rules, with Chairman William Kennard not voting because he worked on this issue as a lawyer for the National Association of Broadcasters in the early 1980s. Given the FCC's tie vote, a federal appellate court asked the two commissioners who voted against abolishing the rules to provide an explanation for their votes that the court could consider in ruling on the RTNDA's long-delayed legal challenge to the rules. More time passed, and the court eventually asked the FCC to eliminate the two rules or justify their continuing existence. Still another year passed with no formal response from the FCC, although the FCC did temporarily suspend the two rules for 60 days during the 2000 election.

The appellate court decided that wasn't enough. In late 2000 the court overturned the Personal Attack and Political Editorializing Rules. The court said that the two rules "interfere with the editorial judgment of professional journalists and entangle the government in day-to-day operations of the media." Ruling in the case of *Radio-Television News Director's Association v. FCC* (229 F.3d 269), the court issued a strongly worded opinion ordering the FCC to eliminate the rules permanently because it had failed to justify their continued existence.

Broadcast journalists praised the decision as a major victory for their First Amendment rights. They argued from the beginning that these rules forced them to avoid covering certain issues and therefore had a chilling effect on freedom of expression.

FCC Chairman William Kennard said he was "disappointed" with the court's decision and said the FCC would monitor broadcasters' handling of controversial issues while studying "how best to ensure that the public receives balanced coverage." Kennard said the FCC might launch a new proceeding to adopt similar rules, something that the court said the FCC could do if the rules could be justified.

In early 2001, however, Kennard resigned, as is customary when a new president is inaugurated. His replacement, Michael Powell, quickly made it clear that he thought these two rules--and many of the FCC's other broadcast content controls--were contrary to the First Amendment.

Of course, nothing in the decision to abolish the Fairness Doctrine or the related rules affects the Equal Time provisions of the Communications Act (Section 315). Section 315 still requires broadcasters to offer all candidates for a given office equal opportunities to purchase airtime, as it has ever since the Communications Act was enacted in 1934.

The Supreme Court and the Fairness Doctrine

In the debate over the constitutionality of the Fairness Doctrine, both sides carefully reviewed the Supreme Court's few previous decisions on its constitutionality. In 1969, the high court upheld the Fairness Doctrine in the case of *Red Lion Broadcasting v. FCC* (395 U.S. 367). That case arose at the end of the 1964 presidential election when a radio evangelist named Billy James Hargis attacked Fred Cook, the author of a book that criticized Republican candidate Barry Goldwater. The attack was aired over Red Lion's radio station in Pennsylvania, and Cook demanded reply time under the Personal Attack Rule.

Red Lion replied by telling Cook, in effect, to buy an advertisement. Instead, Cook complained to the FCC, which ordered the station to give Cook reply time. Red Lion appealed, charging that it violated a broadcaster's First Amendment rights to be forced to provide airtime to someone like Cook.

The Supreme Court agreed with Red Lion that the case involved a First Amendment issue. However, the court said the First Amendment rights of the general public took precedence over the rights of broadcasters. Red Lion was ordered to give Cook time to reply to the personal attack.

In contrast, a few years later the Supreme Court said that the print media have no obligation whatever to give space to those with whom they disagree. In the landmark case of *Miami Herald v. Tornillo* (418 U.S. 241, 1974), the Supreme Court overturned a Florida law requiring newspapers to publish replies from political candidates who are personally attacked in print. The court said the print media have a First Amendment right to publish only one side of controversial issues and to attack people without granting them space for a reply, if they so choose. Thus, there cannot be a Fairness Doctrine or a Personal Attack Rule for the print media under the First Amendment.

Many broadcasters felt this disparity in editorial freedom made them second-class citizens under the First Amendment. Those who felt that way were encouraged in 1984 when the Supreme Court suggested that it was having second thoughts about the policies announced in the *Red Lion* decision.

In 1984, the Supreme Court addressed the First Amendment rights of public noncommercial radio and television stations--and suggested that it might be time to reconsider the constitutionality of the Fairness Doctrine itself. That happened in the case of *FCC v. League of Women Voters of California* (468 U.S. 364).

This case was a challenge to a Congressional ban on editorializing by public broadcasters, and the court said it violated the First Amendment. It was the first time the high court had ever overturned a federal content restriction on broadcasters on First Amendment grounds. And the court seemed to invite a review of the validity of many other broadcast content restrictions, including the Fairness Doctrine.

The court rejected the arguments of those who felt public broadcasters should not carry editorials expressing their own views because they receive government funds. Congress had banned editorializing by stations receiving federal funds on the theory that if they editorialized these stations would feel obligated to support the government's policies. In effect, these stations could become propaganda organs for the government, Congress feared.

The court disagreed with that rationale and said there were many ways public broadcasters could be insulated from political pressures that might influence their editorial policies without simply forbidding them to speak out on the issues.

Although the Supreme Court's decision came on a narrow 5-4 vote, the majority opinion was so sweeping that it raised doubts about the continuing validity of the entire range of broadcast content controls. Writing for the majority, Justice William J. Brennan included a footnote that said the court might have been prepared to reexamine the scarcity rationale that has justified the restrictions on broadcast content. Brennan wrote:

> The prevailing rationale for broadcast regulation based on spectrum scarcity has come under increasing criticism in recent years. Critics, including the incumbent Chairman of the FCC, charge that with the advent of cable and satellite television technology, communities now have access to such a wide variety of stations that the scarcity doctrine is obsolete. We are not prepared, however, to reconsider our long-standing approach without some signal from Congress or the FCC that technological developments have advanced so far that revision of the system of broadcast regulation may be required.

That signal came within the next few years, of course, when the FCC abolished the Fairness Doctrine. Should Congress or the FCC reinstate the Fairness Doctrine, the Supreme Court would very likely have to revisit these questions.

The Fairness Doctrine and Advertising

One other aspect of the controversial history of the Fairness Doctrine merits some mention: the era when it applied to some commercial advertising messages. There was a time when those who disagreed with advertising had a limited right to go on the air and present counter advertising, sometimes at a broadcaster's expense.

In 1967, the FCC ordered broadcasters who carried cigarette advertising (which was legal then) to provide free reply time to anti-smoking groups under the Fairness Doctrine. In *Banzhaf v. FCC* (405 F.2d 1082, D.C. Cir. 1968), a federal appellate court upheld that ruling. Although the court said its ruling was specific to cigarette advertising and did not necessarily make the Fairness Doctrine applicable to other advertising, the result of *Banzhaf* was an avalanche of other demands for airtime to reply to controversial advertising.

Congress banned cigarette advertising by broadcasters as of Jan. 1, 1971, ending an era of colorful counter advertising from the American Cancer Society, American Lung Association and others urging people not to smoke. Under the *Banzhaf* ruling, broadcasters had been required to carry one minute of counter advertising for each three minutes of cigarette commercials. As a result, these organizations received millions of dollars worth of free airtime during this period.

Soon the same court that decided *Banzhaf* ruled that the Fairness Doctrine might apply to television ads for cars with large engines requiring high-octane gasoline. The FCC was ordered to determine whether environmentalists who opposed gas-guzzling cars were entitled to free airtime or whether other programming adequately rebutted the message conveyed in auto advertising (*Friends of the Earth v. FCC*, 449 F.2d 1164, D.C. Cir. 1971).

The FCC extricated itself from the counter advertising dilemma in 1974 by issuing new rules reinterpreting the Fairness Doctrine. The new rules said that henceforth the Fairness Doctrine would not apply to commercial advertising for products. A court upheld that reinterpretation in a 1975 decision, *Public Interest Research Group v. FCC*, (522 F.2d 1060). But before that happened, the Supreme Court had handed down another important decision in this area, ruling that the First Amendment does not create a right to advertise on controversial subjects. This 1973 decision, *CBS v. Democratic National Committee* (412 U.S. 94, 1973), resulted from an appeal by the Democratic National Committee for assurances that it could buy network airtime to solicit money and argue the Democratic viewpoint on controversial issues.

The Supreme Court, voting 7-2, said unequivocally that broadcasters may reject editorial advertising if they wish. Neither the First Amendment nor the Fairness Doctrine gave any specific individual or group a right of access to the broadcast media (except in response to personal attacks), the Supreme Court ruled. Under the Fairness Doctrine, a broadcaster might have to seek out *someone* to present a view contrary to that espoused by the station in an editorial, for example, but the station had the right to choose who it would be.

Today, of course, broadcasters have no obligation even to carry opposing viewpoints under most circumstances now that the Fairness Doctrine has been repealed. But the *CBS v. Democratic National Committee* decision was an important early step toward the modern view that broadcasters have nearly complete editorial discretion under the First Amendment.

In the absence of the Fairness Doctrine, broadcasters--like newspaper and magazine publishers--have the right to determine which viewpoints will and will not be carried under most circumstances. Nevertheless, the Equal Time Rule still limits broadcasters' First Amendment freedoms to some extent. It still forces broadcasters to sell airtime to political candidates with whom they may disagree when a newspaper or magazine publisher would have no such obligation under the Supreme Court's *Tornillo v. Miami Herald* decision.

Fairness Regulation after the Fairness Doctrine

Even in the absence of the Fairness Doctrine, broadcasters remain generally accountable to the government for the fairness of their news and public affairs programming. That point was powerfully driven home to the CBS network--and to the FCC--in a 1998 decision of the U.S. Court of Appeals in Washington, D.C.: *Serafyn v. FCC* (149 F.3d 1213).

Under Section 309 of the Communications Act, the FCC may only grant a broadcast license when it determines that would be in the "public interest, convenience, and necessity." That section also authorizes any person to file a petition to deny a license application by alleging that granting it would not be in the public interest. As noted earlier, petitioners have often alleged that a station's *content* was so bad that granting a license would not be in the public interest.

The *Serafyn* case illustrates that allegations of unfair content are still a valid basis for a license challenge even without the Fairness Doctrine.

This case resulted from a segment on 60 Minutes about the Ukraine, a country that was formerly part of the Soviet Union. In a segment entitled, "The Ugly Face of Freedom," the CBS newsmagazine alleged that most Ukrainians are "genetically anti-Semitic" and "uneducated peasants (who are) deeply superstitious." To make its point, CBS interviewed people who agreed with that viewpoint and declined to interview people who disagreed and who offered to be interviewed. CBS also quoted the chief rabbi of the Ukraine in a way that he said was out of context, and translated the Ukrainian word for "Jew" as "kike." The 60 Minutes segment also contained factual errors concerning Ukrainian history and showed Ukrainian Boy Scouts marching overlaid with recorded sounds of marching boots reminiscent of Nazi Germany.

The network and CBS stations were deluged with protests from Ukrainian-Americans. The network and CBS-owned stations did not respond to the protests and in at least one case didn't retain the protest letters in a CBS station's public file as required by FCC rules.

Alexander Serafyn and other Ukrainian-Americans filed a formal complaint with the FCC alleging news distortion by CBS and demanding that the FCC not approve CBS' purchase of a television station in Detroit, Mich. The commission dismissed the complaint without holding a hearing on its merits.

Serafyn then challenged the FCC in the federal appellate court. The court ruled that the FCC improperly dismissed the Ukrainian complaints and ordered the FCC to reconsider the matter. CBS intervened in the case and protested that a government review of the fairness of its news programming would violate the First Amendment, but the court ordered the FCC to reconsider the complaint nonetheless.

"The commission neither applied the correct standard nor provided a reasoned explanation in its decision," Judge Douglas Ginsburg wrote for the court. While this ruling did not require the FCC to do anything more than consider the matter further, it illustrates that broadcast news content is still subject to government supervision in the post-Fairness Doctrine era.

Banning Indecency on the Airwaves

Although the FCC moved to deregulate broadcasting in many ways during the 1980s and 1990s, the commission also took several major steps to add new content regulations and to enforce existing rules more aggressively. By 2000, the FCC had added so many new content controls that the era of deregulation was becoming a distant memory for many broadcasters.

The FCC's actions against broadcast indecency are one of the most controversial examples of this. Under federal law, broadcasters may not air material that is obscene, profane or *indecent*. The FCC has expanded on that law by banning indecent subject matter, words and visual images from the airwaves, even though the material in question may not be legally obscene and thus cannot be banned from other media (including cable television, which has different rules governing adult programming, discussed later).

Although the FCC's ban on indecency has been in effect for decades, it was rarely enforced for many years. But in 1987 the FCC launched a crackdown on indecent language and content, imposing stiff fines on violators. That crackdown led to a series of court decisions and a major controversy involving broadcasters, citizens' groups, Congress and the FCC.

Perhaps the most newsworthy part of the FCC's crackdown on alleged broadcast indecency involved Howard Stern's syndicated radio program. Stations that carried Stern's controversial show have been hit with fines of about $2 million. Stations owned by Infinity Broadcasting alone were fined $1.7 million for indecency violations on Stern's show.

Meanwhile, the U.S. Court of Appeals in Washington, D.C. handed down four separate decisions on the FCC's indecency rules. In the end, the court issued an *en banc* decision (a ruling by all judges on the court, not the usual panel of three judges) holding that the FCC, acting on orders from Congress, could ban indecency from the airwaves at all times except during a "safe harbor" period between 10 p.m. and 6 a.m.--hours when relatively few children are in the broadcast audience (*Action for Children's Television v. FCC*, 58 F.3d 654, 1995). The 7-4 majority held that there is a compelling government interest in protecting children from indecent material that justifies banning broadcast indecency during the daytime when many children are in the audience.

A few weeks later, the same court upheld the FCC's handling of the indecency fines, some of which took the FCC as long as seven years to process (*Action for Children's Television v. FCC*, 59 F.3d 1249).

Long before this controversy over broadcast indecency began, the U.S. Supreme Court declared that indecent but non-obscene material could be banned from the airwaves during the daytime hours, even if the same material was perfectly legal in other media. In a famous 1978 case, *FCC v. Pacifica Foundation* (438 U.S. 726), the Court voted 5-4 to uphold a mild FCC sanction against Pacifica, a foundation that operates several noncommercial radio stations, including WBAI in New York City. WBAI aired a program on contemporary attitudes toward language, and it included a 12-minute monologue by comedian George Carlin entitled "Filthy Words." In it, Carlin named "the original seven words" that "you couldn't say on the public ...airwaves" and ridiculed society's taboos about the words, "shit, piss, fuck, cunt, cocksucker, motherfucker and tits." The program was broadcast at 2 p.m., preceded by a warning that some of the content might be offensive to some persons.

A man who said he and his son inadvertently stumbled on the monologue while listening to their car radio complained to the FCC, and the FCC eventually placed a warning notice in the station's license renewal file. The FCC did not find the language obscene but did decide it was "patently offensive" and indecent--and therefore inappropriate for the airwaves. Further such incidents could lead to a license non-renewal, the FCC said.

Pacifica Foundation appealed to the courts. The Supreme Court ruled that the language, though not legally obscene, was inappropriate for broadcasting, at least during the daytime. The court said the words were indecent even if they might be constitutionally protected under other circumstances.

Explaining its decision, the court made an analogy to nuisance law and quoted an earlier decision defining a nuisance as "merely a right thing in the wrong place--like a pig in the parlor instead of the barnyard." Then the court concluded: "We simply hold that when the commission finds that a pig has entered the parlor, the exercise of its regulatory power does not depend on proof that the pig is obscene."

Although the FCC did not initially regard this Supreme Court decision as a mandate to enforce the rules against broadcast indecency aggressively, that changed in 1987. By then most broadcasters assumed they could take the *Pacifica* decision fairly literally, avoiding the "seven dirty words" in the George Carlin monologue and little else. The industry also assumed that there was a "safe harbor" for adult-oriented programming after 10 p.m. because few children would be in the audience then.

Almost without warning, though, the FCC suddenly changed its enforcement policies if not the rules themselves in 1987. The FCC acted against three stations for allegedly indecent broadcasts then--and imposed sanctions on many other stations in the ensuing years.

The FCC's actions in 1987 were controversial, but the debate became more intense when the FCC adopted a strict round-the-clock ban on indecency under orders from Congress. That ban was later overturned by the U.S. Court of Appeals, although a subsequent ban on indecent programming only during daytime hours was upheld, as noted earlier.

In announcing its 1987 crackdown on indecency, the commission said it would no longer limit its enforcement to cases where the "seven dirty words" were involved. Instead, the commission said it would look to a much more general (and in the view of many broadcasters, vague) standard in determining what is and isn't indecent programming.

In its widely publicized actions against Howard Stern, the FCC initially issued warnings to two stations that carried the show in 1987. When Stern not only continued his sometimes-risque on-air remarks but also added more stations to his lineup, the FCC began imposing large fines on stations that carried his program. In 1992, the FCC hit Infinity Broadcasting, the owner of stations in New York, Philadelphia and Washington, D.C., that aired his show, with the largest fine in broadcast history: $600,000. And the fines continued until stations that carried Stern's show had been fined about $2 million. Perhaps what made this so controversial was that while Stern's material is offensive to many people, he also had an enormous following. His show has often been the top-rated radio program in cities from coast to coast.

Although Stern may have more detractors than defenders in the industry, the FCC's action against stations carrying Stern's show (and a series of other FCC actions against allegedly indecent programming) troubled many broadcasters. Not only did this raise fundamental First Amendment issues, but it also left broadcasters unsure what the rules really were. For many years the commission used only the general definition of indecency that the Supreme Court had employed in the *Pacifica* case:

> (Indecency is) language or material that depicts or describes, in terms patently offensive as measured by contemporary community standards for the broadcast medium, sexual or excretory activities or organs.

After the FCC announced its new position on indecency, many station owners--fearing for their licenses--issued new directives to their staffs, launching a crackdown on broadcast content. The industry asked the FCC for a more specific definition of indecency with specific guidelines, and the FCC said in the early 1990s that it had such a document in the works, but for various reasons it was not released in that era. That left many broadcasters with fears that their employees might blunder into an expensive violation of the indecency rule--quite by accident.

Shortly after Michael Powell became FCC chairman in 2001, he pledged to act on many long-delayed FCC initiatives. By April, the FCC completed and released its long-awaited clarification of its Indecency Rule. In elaborate (and graphic) detail, the commission spelled out what kind of material is--and isn't--prohibited on the broadcast airwaves in this policy statement.

The FCC retained the basic rule it has followed for many years: that legally obscene material is always banned from the airwaves, while indecent material is prohibited during the daytime when large numbers of children are likely to be in the audience (6 a.m. until 10 p.m.). The FCC retained its overnight "safe harbor" policy which permits indecent but non-obscene matter between 10 p.m. and 6 a.m.

Responding to chronic complaints from broadcasters about the vagueness of the definition of indecency, the FCC included in its new policy statement the full transcription of numerous broadcasts that were ruled indecent as well as others that were ruled acceptable for broadcast. Ironically, this again underscores the unique status of over-the-air broadcasting under American law. The policy statement includes much language that is strictly forbidden during the daytime on radio and TV--but it can be downloaded from the FCC's website and read by anyone, anywhere, anytime on any computer that lacks content-filtering software. (See www.fcc.gov/eb/Orders/2001/fcc01090.html)

Although broadcasters were generally relieved to have the FCC's clarification, many said it still lacked sufficient specificity to guide them in making day-to-day decisions. And some broadcasters were horrified by what happened next. The FCC fined KKMG(FM), a Pueblo, Colo. station, $7,000 for an indecency violation in mid-2001. The offense was airing the sanitized, for-broadcast version of Eminem's "The Real Slim Shady." That number, the biggest hit on *The Marshall Mathers LP*, his grammy-winning album, had been aired by hundreds of other stations. If that shocked many broadcasters, the FCC's next move shocked them still more: a few months later the FCC rescinded the fine and dropped the case against KKMG(FM) altogether.

That action left broadcasters again wondering where they stood. Was the Colorado station fined merely because someone filed a formal complaint? Why did the FCC then back down--really? What would happen if complaints were filed against other stations?

In the end, broadcasters cannot ignore the hazards of airing programming that the FCC considers indecent. If an errant deejay (or even a caller on a talk show) should utter the wrong words--and if someone files a properly documented complaint with the FCC--the broadcaster is likely to face a fine. If violations continue, the broadcaster's license could be lifted.

Perhaps one reason indecency enforcement actions are rare is because the FCC requires good documentation. Those who file complaints usually need a tape of the offending words or images along with a written transcript and specific information about when the offense occurred. If on-air indecency is spontaneous, as it often seems to be, how can any citizen activist tape the offending words or images--except by having a tape recorder running all the time? However, in 2002 FCC officials conceded that they sometimes act on "sufficiently descriptive" complaints even without a tape and transcript.

If the FCC should decide to act on a complaint, the broadcaster faces a potentially long FCC review process. The FCC notifies a broadcaster of a fine for any major infraction by issuing a *notice of apparent liability*. This can happen as much as three years after the offending broadcast is aired. The broadcaster then has 30 days to respond. Next, the commission may either leave the fine unchanged, reduce it or eliminate it, depending on the broadcaster's explanation of the alleged offense. In some instances, the FCC has delayed that decision for several years.

If the fine is not eliminated, the broadcaster must either pay up or face a civil lawsuit by the U.S. Attorney General's office to collect the money. Only after such a lawsuit is filed (which can be five years after the offending broadcast was aired) does the broadcaster get a full hearing in court on the merits of the fine. In the meantime, the FCC continues to threaten the broadcaster with ever stiffer fines if it does not comply with the FCC's interpretation of the rules--even though that interpretation has not been reviewed for constitutionality by any court. Even worse, the FCC can put the broadcaster's licenses in jeopardy or refuse to allow the company to acquire more stations--all without giving the broadcaster any opportunity to challenge the constitutionality of the fine in any court. For most broadcasters, it is far cheaper and safer to pay the fine and engage in self-censorship than it is to go through all of this.

Regulating Children's Programming

In addition to its rules on political broadcasting and indecency, the FCC has at various times enforced a number of other broadcast content regulations.

Programming and advertising aimed at children have been a prime example. After a controversy over children's television programming that lasted for more than 20 years, in 1996 the FCC adopted rules requiring all commercial television stations to offer at least three hours a week of regularly scheduled programming to meet the *educational and informational* needs of children.

Under the 1996 rules, each station must provide this special programming in segments at least 30 minutes in length between the hours of 7 a.m. and 10 p.m.

The children's programming is not supposed to be preempted, even for news or sports events, more often than 10 percent of the time. This poses a problem for stations on the west coast, because major sports events in the east often begin before the traditional Saturday morning children's program block ends in the Pacific time zone.

The children's educational programming must be clearly identified as such on the air. Also, stations are required to notify program guides, indicating the appropriate age range for each program. In addition, each station must have a staff member who acts as a children's educational programming liaison, and each station must file quarterly reports with the FCC to explain how the children's programming requirements are being met.

The adoption of these rules followed an extended controversy in which advocacy groups argued that all television stations have a duty to provide educational programming for children. The networks and major station groups responded by pointing to the various programming and community services they were already providing that had educational value for children. And some pointed out that for all of its vaunted quality, the educational programming offered on PBS has very low audience ratings. It may be of higher quality, but given a choice, most viewers have voted with their remote control units for other kinds of programming. (By 1999, that argument was reinforced by the Nielsen ratings, which showed that the major over-the-air networks were attracting only a small share of children's viewership of programs for children, with about half of that small amount going to Fox.)

The trade press and other First Amendment advocates expressed concerns about the implications of the new mandatory children's programming requirements for other reasons. Here, they noted, is a government agency dictating program content, telling commercial broadcasters to provide the kind of children's programming that *the government thinks children should be watching*--and then to promote it to persuade viewers to watch what's good for them instead of the programming they might prefer to watch.

By 2002, the networks' concerns about mandatory children's programming were greater than ever. With several cable networks offering children's programming full time, the four major over-the-air networks saw the ratings for their children's programming drop even lower. Two networks, Fox and NBC, sold their Saturday morning airtime--the traditional home of children's programs--to outsiders. Fox struck a deal with 4Kids Entertainment, the toy-licensing company that made more than $100 million from Pokemon. Under the deal, 4Kids can use the Fox Saturday morning time to promote its new toys and games over the air. Fox agreed to find another way to do the FCC-required educational programming, requiring 4Kids to provide only 30 minutes of such programming during the four-hour Saturday morning block. The rest of the block was used for programs that are in reality toy commercials, critics charged. NBC handed its Saturday morning time over to the Discovery Network, a move that stirred far less criticism than the Fox-4Kids deal.

The 1996 rules were by no means the first FCC initiative in this area. In 1974, the FCC issued a policy statement calling on broadcasters to discontinue certain practices, such as allowing children's show hosts to advertise products. The commission also urged broadcasters to voluntarily upgrade their offerings for children. And the FCC considered imposing stricter children's programming requirements on broadcasters throughout the 1970s. However, in 1983 the FCC reversed itself, voting to discard the 1974 policy statement and to reject any formal children's television programming requirements. The 1983 policy said that broadcasters had to provide programs for children, but the commission declined to establish any specific requirements for the amount of such programming that had to be offered. Instead, broadcasters were given wide discretion to determine what kind of children's programs to offer.

By the late 1980s, however, children's television programming had many critics, some of them in Congress. To them, much of the programming for children seemed like little more than thinly disguised commercials for toys that were marketed in conjunction with the shows. In 1988 Congress passed legislation limiting the amount of advertising in shows for children and also requiring broadcasters to provide quality children's programming as a condition of license renewal. The bill was vetoed by former President Reagan, but it was passed again in 1990. President Bush allowed it to become law without his signature.

Under this law, called the Children's Television Act of 1990, advertising on children's shows is limited to 12 minutes per hour on weekdays and 10.5 minutes per hour on weekends. This provision applies only to shows intended for children age 12 and younger. These advertising limits have been enforced aggressively. The FCC has conducted a number of audits of station compliance, and stations carrying excessive advertising have often been fined. In one 1999 action, the FCC fined two jointly owned Illinois stations, WRSP-TV in Springfield and WCCU(TV) in Urbana, $110,000 for 304 violations of the limits between 1994 and 1996. Another station, WDBD(TV) in Jackson, Mississippi, was also fined $110,000 for 158 violations of the limits between 1993 and 1998.

The 1990 law also requires broadcasters to prove at license renewal time that they have met the "educational and informational needs" of children age 16 and younger by airing programs *specifically designed for that purpose*. The limits on commercials also apply to cable television, including both cable network shows and locally produced programming.

The Children's Television Act also established a National Endowment for Children's Television to support educational programs. In addition, Congress directed the FCC to address the problem of toy-based shows and determine if they were improper *program-length commercials* because they so clearly promoted toys based on the shows' characters--a concern that was being voiced again a decade later.

Acting in 1991, the FCC adopted new rules concerning toy-based shows in response to the Congressional mandate. The rules forbid commercials within a show (or within one minute on either side of the show) for toys based on characters in that show. And the rules forbid hosts of children's shows from doing commercials on the premise that young children cannot distinguish commercials from the non-commercial segments of the show. The commercials must be separated from non-commercial segments of children's shows. But the FCC declined to ban toy-based shows altogether, a decision that was widely criticized by groups advocating quality children's programming.

The FCC responded by issuing a new notice of proposed rulemaking concerning educational programming for children in 1995. That proposal led to the three-hour mandatory children's educational programming requirement the commission adopted a year later.

Regulating Violent Programming

During the 1990s another of the most heated controversies about government regulation of broadcast content involved television and children: the debate about the so-called *V-chip* and the new television content rating system that had to be developed to implement it.

The Telecommunications Act of 1996 required all television set manufacturers to include the V-chip in all but the smallest television sets. The act also required the industry to come up with a "voluntary" rating system so programs with ratings for excessive violence or sexual content can be blocked by parents. Programs not rated as suitable for children were to carry an encoded signal to prevent television sets with the V-chip from receiving them unless parents (or whoever controls the TV set) enters the correct code to receive these shows. In 1998, the FCC adopted rules requiring manufacturers to include the V-chip system in all new TV sets as of January, 2000, except for sets with screens smaller than 13 inches.

In mandating the V-chip system, Congress and the FCC were responding to a public outcry about the high rate of violent crime and pregnancy among teen-agers in America. Congress apparently accepted the argument of many parents and others that at least part of the blame lies with violent and sexually oriented programming on television. The 1996 law gave the industry one year to come up with a "voluntary" rating system--or else the FCC would convene an advisory committee to set up the ratings.

Soon after the Telecommunications Act became law, the industry set up its own task force to develop a rating system for television shows, drawing on the experience of the Motion Picture Association of America with its rating system for movies. Jack Valenti, longtime head of the MPAA and an expert on the movie rating system, played a key role in developing the TV ratings.

The system developed by the industry committee, announced in late 1996, borrowed heavily from the movie rating system. Six different ratings were established: TVY (programs for young children), TVY7 (programs for children over age seven), TVG (programs for all ages), TVPG (programs that some parents may find unsuitable for younger children), TV14 (programs with material that many parents would find unsuitable for children under 14) and TVMA (programs that may be unsuitable for children under 17).

To the consternation of many, the original TV rating system did not provide the one thing that many groups critical of television programming wanted the most: program ratings specifically indicating violent or sexually oriented content or offensive language with letter ratings.

Industry critics, backed by key members of Congress and the Clinton administration, demanded changes in the rating system. In mid-1997, the industry agreed to modify the system, adding the letters V for violence, S for sexual content, D for suggestive dialogue, L for offensive language and FV for fantasy violence. The rating is displayed in a corner of the screen at the beginning of each rated show.

While all of this was happening, the whole idea of the government forcing broadcasters to develop a rating system was widely criticized by advocates of full First Amendment rights for broadcasters. Their main objections to the rating system, as listed in *Broadcasting & Cable* magazine, were these:

>*It infringes on (broadcasters') First Amendment right to free speech.
>*It will be almost impossible to rate and code every hour of television programming.
>*Television shows that are tagged with violent or adult-themed ratings may scare away advertisers.
>*Implementation of the V-chip will force the networks to rely on sitcoms because adult-oriented dramatic fare will inevitably attract ratings for violent or sexual content.
>*No one has ever adequately defined what constitutes a harmful violent act in television programming.

Perhaps the most basic concern about the V-chip is whether it will really work. "Unless a new V-chip television is going to come equipped with a pair of handcuffs, it won't stop kids from finding ways to watch forbidden shows," one network executive told the trade press after the 1996 law was passed.

In fact, one thing that delayed progress in developing V-chip technology was the difficulty of designing a programming system too complex for adolescents to figure out, but simple enough for most adults. Leaders of the Consumer Electronics Manufacturers Association predicted that many children and especially teenagers would devise ways to get around the program blocking.

When V-chip-equipped TV sets began appearing in stores in early 2000, merchants generally reported widespread consumer indifference to the V-chip system. By 2002, many in and out of Congress were questioning whether the V-chip system was really being used by many parents to block objectionable programming.

Regulating Format Changes

The FCC also has become involved in content regulation on some occasions when a radio station proposed to change a unique programming format. During the 1970s, the only classical music stations in several cities tried to abandon that format, spurring protests by classical music lovers. The FCC originally refrained from getting involved in these controversies. However, the federal courts began ordering the FCC to review format changes when a station abandoned a unique format and the change produced widespread protests. For instance, that happened in Atlanta (*Citizens Committee to Preserve the Voice of the Arts in Atlanta v. FCC*, 436 F.2d 263, 1970).

Then in 1974 the federal appellate court that serves Washington, D.C.--the court that has heard so many FCC appeals over the years--decided *Citizens Committee to Save WEFM v. FCC* (506 F.2d 246). The court, ruling *en banc* (with all judges on the court participating instead of just a panel of three), ordered the FCC to hold a hearing whenever a unique format is being abandoned and a substantial number of persons object.

However, two years later, the FCC issued a policy statement calling for the court to reverse itself and let the commission stay out of such disputes. The FCC said, "...the public interest in diversity of entertainment formats is best served by unregulated competition among licensees."

But the federal appellate court in Washington refused to back down, and the result was a Supreme Court decision on the FCC's proper role in broadcast format changes. Ruling in 1981, the Supreme Court affirmed the FCC's right to stay out of broadcast format disputes in *FCC v. WNCN Listeners Guild*, (450 U.S. 582). The court said entertainment programming was within the broadcaster's discretion. The seven-justice majority wrote: "We decline to overturn the commission's policy statement, which prefers reliance on market forces to its own attempt to oversee format changes at the behest of disaffected listeners."

The Supreme Court decision was a major victory for the broadcast industry, which has strongly supported the FCC's moves to deregulate the field, but it was a defeat for classical music lovers and others who feared that minority tastes will not be served if all broadcasters are free to tailor their programming for the audiences that are most attractive to advertisers.

Other Content Regulations

For almost 25 years, broadcasters were subject to another content control that was always controversial and, some said, never successful: the Prime Time Access Rule. It was adopted by the FCC in 1971 and abolished in 1995. Under this rule, the ABC, NBC and CBS networks were generally limited to three hours of evening programming during the four-hour period from 7 to 11 p.m. Monday through Saturday (6 to 10 p.m. in the central and mountain time zones), with exceptions for news events and special occasions. The rule only applied in the 50 largest metropolitan areas.

The FCC's stated objective was to create new opportunities for local programming by limiting the portion of the evening hours the networks could lock up. But local network affiliates generally relied on syndicated programming such as "Wheel of Fortune" and "Jeopardy" to fill the non-network time instead of doing local public affairs programs. (A syndicated program is one produced independently and then sold directly to local stations rather than to a network.) In abolishing the rule, the FCC noted that ABC, NBC and CBS "no longer dominate the television marketplace." Eliminating the rule freed stations to choose whatever prime time programming they wished, including reruns of network shows that previously could be aired during the access period only by independent stations.

Among the other FCC regulations governing content are rules governing sponsorship identification. Broadcasters must identify the sponsors of ads and disclose the fact if someone has paid for the airing of non-advertising material.

In 1992, the FCC adopted another rule governing broadcast content: a restriction on over-the-air hoaxes. The rule was enacted in response to several widely publicized incidents in which radio stations reported fake events. For example, a Los Angeles station aired a phony murder confession, a station in St. Louis reported during the Persian Gulf war that the United States was under nuclear attack, and a Virginia station reported that a large waste dump was about to explode. The potential dump explosion created a panic reminiscent of the one caused by Orson Welles' classic "War of the Worlds" broadcast in 1938. (In a special Halloween broadcast on network radio, Orson Welles dramatized H.G. Wells' tale about an invasion of Earth by Martians. In Welles' program, music was interrupted by authentic-sounding news bulletins that terrified millions of people, especially near the Martians' purported landing site in New Jersey.)

The FCC responded to the recent hoaxes by banning broadcast fabrications about crimes and catastrophes that "divert substantial public safety resources" or "cause substantial harm to public health and welfare."

Hoaxes raise troubling ethical questions, of course, but the FCC's response to these hoaxes again illustrates the limited First Amendment rights of broadcasters. Does any government agency have the right to forbid tabloid newspapers from publishing pure fabrications as news? Should the government be allowed to ban what it considers to be false stories in newspapers, or just on radio and television? Should hoaxes be banned in all of the mass media? When does a broadcast dramatization--a fictitious work--become a hoax and therefore illegal on the air?

Another kind of content that has been restricted is advertising and other programming that promotes gambling. The advertising of gambling is restricted both by FCC regulations and by various state laws. However, government-run lotteries may advertise on local stations in their areas, and charitable lotteries are generally exempt from these restrictions, as are promotions and prize drawings by businesses other than casinos. Under the Charity Games Advertising Clarification Act of 1988, only casinos and others whose gambling is an end in itself are now forbidden to advertise *by federal law*. However, the 1988 act left the states free to restrict or ban lottery advertising even if the advertising would be legal under federal law.

What constitutes a lottery? A lottery exists any time the three *elements of a lottery* are present. They are: (1) a valuable prize; (2) determining the winner at least partly by chance; and (3) requiring participants to pay some "consideration" to enter the contest. To get around these rules, many businesses have set up drawings with the disclaimer, "no purchase necessary," to eliminate the consideration element and make their drawings legal to advertise. In many states, that is no longer necessary for businesses not primarily engaged in gambling.

What happens if one state has a state-run lottery, and broadcasters in an adjacent state wish to carry its advertising? The U.S. Supreme Court ruled on the question of out-of-state lottery advertising in 1993, and held that a broadcaster in a non-lottery state cannot carry ads for a nearby state's lottery if the state of licensing forbids lottery advertising, even if the station has a large audience in the state that has a lottery (*U.S. v. Edge Broadcasting*, 509 U.S. 418). The case involved WMYK-FM, a radio station licensed to a North Carolina town only three miles from the

Virginia border. North Carolina has no state lottery and forbids lottery advertising. However, more than 90 percent of WMYK's listeners are in Virginia, which does have a state-sponsored lottery. Nevertheless, the Supreme Court upheld the laws under which the station was barred from carrying ads for the Virginia lottery. The court upheld North Carolina's right to ban lottery advertising on stations licensed in that state, and ruled that the federal law granting states the right to ban lottery advertising does not violate the First Amendment.

However, after the *Edge Broadcasting* decision, several courts, including the U.S. Supreme Court, took a more permissive view of casino gambling ads, if not government-run lottery advertising.

In 1997, a federal appellate court held that the statutory laws and FCC regulations banning casino advertising violate the First Amendment rights of Nevada broadcasters. In *Valley Broadcasting v. U.S.* (107 F.3d 1328), the ninth circuit U.S. Court of Appeals held that the many loopholes and exceptions in the ban on lottery advertising undermine the government's stated rationale for this restriction on broadcasters' freedom of speech. A few months later, a federal district court in New Jersey ruled similarly, overturning the ban on advertising by Atlantic City casinos (*Player's International v. U.S.*, 988 F.Supp. 497).

The U.S. Supreme Court then weighed in with its decision in *Greater New Orleans Broadcasting Association v. U.S.* (527 U.S. 173, 1999). The high court unanimously ruled that the federal government may not ban broadcast advertising for private casino gambling. This cleared the way for New Orleans broadcasters, and broadcasters in many other states, to carry casino gambling ads. The rationale of the decision, which is discussed in Chapter 13, appears broad enough to allow stations in states that do not have casino gambling--but do not prohibit gambling advertising--to carry ads for casinos in other states.

After the Supreme Court's *Greater New Orleans* decision, the FCC issued a statement saying that broadcasters are indeed free to carry gambling ads anywhere that gambling is legal--but hedged about the rights of broadcasters in states that prohibit gambling. Nevertheless, the FCC stopped enforcing the lottery rule, leaving broadcasters free to carry advertising for out-of-state casinos if their state does not forbid gambing advertising. However, this does not supersede the *Edge Broadcasting* decision, which refused to legalize lottery advertising by broadcasters licensed to a state that has no state lottery and prohibits lottery advertising.

Broadcasters are subject to many other laws that govern advertising in general. For instance, the federal Truth-in-Lending Act requires the full disclosure of all credit terms if any of the terms of a loan are mentioned in an ad, as explained in Chapter 13. Almost no one would quarrel with the wisdom of having laws requiring credit advertising to be truthful and complete. However, the required disclosures are sometimes so detailed that they cannot all be squeezed into a short broadcast advertisement.

In the late 1990s several other new federal controls on broadcast content were considered at the FCC. In addition to the new children's educational program requirements and the V-chip rules, in 1997 the FCC's then-chairman, Reed Hundt, advocated the following: (1) a ban on hard liquor advertising on radio and television; (2) at least one minute of free public service announcements (PSAs) during prime time every night on each network; (3) free airtime for political candidates; (4) a new "family hour" from 8 to 9 p.m. each evening, with programming limited to material suitable for families with children; and (5) other public interest requirements that broadcasters would have to meet in return for their new digital licenses. Although Hundt's successor, William Kennard, did not pursue several of these initiatives with Hundt's fervor, Kennard did endorse the proposal for free airtime for political candidates, announcing in 1998 that the FCC would launch a new inquiry into this matter.

Meanwhile, a presidential Advisory Committee on Public Interest Obligations of Digital Television Broadcasters was created in 1997 to offer suggestions concerning Hundt's fifth proposal. This committee released 10 recommendations in 1998; most were quite general. One was that the FCC should adopt minimum public interest standards for digital broadcasters (without suggesting what they should be), while another was that the FCC should require broadcasters to report their public interest activities four times a year. The committee also said Congress should create a trust fund for public broadcasting and set aside a TV channel in each community for educational programming. And the commission urged the National Association of Broadcasters to adopt a new voluntary code of conduct to replace one that was eliminated to settle an antitrust lawsuit in the early 1980s.

In the late 1990s, there was a national debate concerning the meaning of the term, "public interest." At the FCC, in Congress, and in the media, questions such as these were being debated: is it in the public interest for the government to require broadcasters to provide free airtime to political candidates? If so, should only major-party candidates get free airtime? What other things must broadcasters do to serve the public interest in the digital age? And who decides what is in the public interest? Is it Congress? The FCC? Broadcasters themselves? Above all, if government makes these decisions and tells broadcasters what to put on the air, where does the First Amendment fit into the equation?

There have been colorful speeches about the definition of the public interest at industry gatherings, with Chairman Kennard arguing forcefully for specific public interest obligations being defined by the FCC, while Commissioner Michael Powell, who followed Kennard as FCC chairman in 2001, argued just as forcefully that the First Amendment requires the government to leave such decisions up to broadcasters themselves.

CABLE TELEVISION REGULATION

Just as radio was the growth medium in the 1920s and television boomed in the 1950s, cable and cable-like technologies were the mass communications growth leaders in the 1980s and 1990s. In 1980, about one-fourth of all American homes were served by cable television systems; by 2000, about three-fourths were served by either cable or satellite television.

Cable began in the 1950s as something called "community antenna television" or CATV. In its early days, it was literally what its name implied: an elaborate antenna system serving a whole community. Because it offered little more than improved television reception, CATV first developed in rural areas far from the nearest television transmitters. By pooling their resources, the people of a community could afford a large antenna system and signal boosters to receive the weak signals from distant television stations. Each home was connected to this central receiving system via coaxial cable, a special kind of wire that will efficiently carry television signals a considerable distance.

When cable television got its start in the countryside, it had little appeal in big cities where reception was good. However, in the 1960s that began to change because of two trends. First, a growing number of people were forbidden to put up TV antennas at condominiums, apartment complexes and even some tracts of single family homes. Instead, they were offered cable hookups for a fee. But even more important, cable systems began offering a lot more than clear television reception: they began providing many additional channels of programming, including out-of-town "superstations," original made-for-cable programming and such special attractions as music videos, recent movies and sports events.

The History of Cable Regulation

Because cable systems do not actually transmit an over-the-air signal, they are not treated as users of the radio spectrum, and they need no FCC license to operate (although cable systems do receive programming via satellites that use the airwaves). Cable also has other advantages. For instance, the number of channels that may be offered via cable is limited mainly by the number of channels a television receiver or cable converter can cover. A local cable system can put programming on every one of those channels without interfering with other cable systems or over-the-air broadcasters.

Because of these factors, cable television was able to develop without much federal regulation--at first. However, by the late 1960s, broadcasters became alarmed at the growth of cable television systems. So did the producers of television programming, which cable operators picked up off the air at no charge--and then delivered to their subscribers for a fee. Two U.S. Supreme Court decisions held that cable operators did not have to pay copyright royalties for the material carried over their systems, since the court viewed CATV as nothing more than an adjunct of the television receiving function (see Chapter Six). The owners of copyrighted programming felt they were being deprived of a fair profit by these Supreme Court decisions, and Congress enacted the 1976 Copyright Act in part to remedy this situation. Cable systems now pay royalties for the copyrighted programming on non-local stations that they carry. Also, under the Cable Television Consumer Protection and Competition Act of 1992, they must pay, or at least obtain broadcasters' consent, to carry some local stations but not others, for reasons that are explained later.

As cable systems expanded and began carrying distant signals, broadcasters became alarmed about this new medium. If a cable system imported distant signals, that could mean economic losses for local broadcasters. At least some of the cable subscribers would watch distant stations instead of local ones, especially if a cable system offered subscribers high-budget stations based in large cities along with nearby low-budget stations. Also, of course, the added non-broadcast programming represented new competition for broadcasters, siphoning off part of their audience.

Given the embryonic status of CATV in the 1950s, the FCC had refused to assume jurisdiction over cable because CATV didn't involve a use of the spectrum and the commission had no specific statutory authority to regulate it. But by 1966 the FCC had changed its mind. To protect broadcasters and program producers, the FCC then issued regulations for cable television systems. The new regulations had many very technical provisions, but one of the most important was a strict limit on distant signal importation. For instance, cable systems were required to carry the nearest station affiliated with each network rather than more distant ones. The rules also spelled out the relationship between cable systems and local governments, which had been granting franchises (in effect, government-sanctioned monopolies) to CATV operators.

The FCC claimed the authority to make these rules by arguing that cable affected on-the-air broadcasters, and that regulation was necessary to carry out the commission's regulatory responsibilities to broadcasters. Legally, this was called "ancillary jurisdiction."

The FCC's cable rules were quickly challenged in court, and in 1968, the Supreme Court affirmed the FCC's authority to regulate cable television in *U.S. v. Southwestern Cable Co.* (392 U.S. 157). The high court found authority for the FCC's regulation of cable not only in the concept of ancillary jurisdiction but also in a provision of the Communications Act that places wire and telecommunications in general under FCC control.

Regulation, Deregulation and Reregulation

Given the Supreme Court's blessing, the FCC repeatedly expanded its cable rules, placing more and more restrictions on cable systems. Many cable operators felt these rules were intended to protect the FCC's major clientele, the over-the-air broadcasters, not to promote the public interest. By the early 1970s, cable systems were required to do these things: (1) provide local public and government access channels if they had more than 3,500 subscribers; (2) originate a minimum amount of local programming, again if they had 3,500 subscribers; (3) refrain from importing distant signals or "leapfrogging" over the nearest network affiliate in providing each network's programming (these were called the "non-duplication" and "signal carriage" requirements); and (4) respect syndication agreements by not carrying a distant station's syndicated shows if a local station had exclusive rights to the show.

In addition, each system had to get sort of a de facto license called a "certificate of compliance" from the FCC before it could conclude its franchise agreement with local government officials, and cable systems had to comply with most of the other requirements imposed on broadcasters, such as the Equal Time Rule, the Fairness Doctrine and equal employment opportunity policies.

Faced with these comprehensive (and costly) federal regulations, a cable system again challenged the FCC's authority to issue such orders. But in 1972 the Supreme Court voted 5-4 to affirm the commission's program origination requirements (*U.S. v. Midwest Video Corp.*, 406 U.S. 649). Ironically, the FCC had dropped many of its access and programming requirements during this lawsuit and did not immediately reinstate them afterward, although cable systems were still required to provide equipment to those who wanted to do programming on such public access channels as remained available.

During most of the 1970s the FCC continued to regulate cable systems heavily in an effort to keep them from doing anything to upset the commission's policy of defining television service in terms of local markets. In 1976, the commission issued new rules on public access and also required cable systems with over 3,500 subscribers to eventually provide at least 20 channels.

However, Midwest Video, the company that lost the narrow 1972 Supreme Court decision, again challenged the commission's rulemaking authority.

This time, Midwest Video won. In 1979 the Supreme Court overturned the FCC's new public access and channel capacity requirements (*FCC v. Midwest Video*, 440 U.S. 689). The court said these rules, in effect, made common carriers of cable systems, placing them under obligations the Communications Act forbids the FCC to impose on broadcasters. Moreover, the court said the rules went far beyond what was reasonably ancillary to the FCC's lawful responsibilities in broadcast regulation. In effect, the Supreme Court told the FCC to go back to Congress and get the specific authority to do these things if they were really in the public interest:

> The Commission may not regulate cable systems as common carriers, just as it may not impose such obligations on television broadcasters. We think authority to compel cable operators to provide common carriage of public originated transmissions must come specifically from Congress.

While this Supreme Court decision overturned the FCC's nationwide rules requiring cable systems to provide public access, that did not mark the end of public access. First of all, some cable systems continued to provide public access channels on a voluntary basis. In addition, Congress passed legislation in 1984 that reinstated many public access requirements.

After its setback in the second *Midwest Video* decision, the FCC decided it was time to undertake a major deregulation of the cable industry. As noted earlier, cable operators had long argued that the FCC's rules were more intended to protect broadcasters by stunting the growth of cable than to serve the public interest.

The FCC heeded the cable systems' arguments and deregulated cable in 1980. In particular, the FCC abandoned the restrictions on distant signal importation. This allowed cable systems to offer their subscribers a much wider choice of programming--but at the expense of small-market television stations, some of whose viewers preferred to watch metropolitan stations via cable.

In 1980, the FCC also deleted the *Syndicated Exclusivity Rule* (or "Syndex"), but only temporarily. The Syndex rule required cable systems to black out syndicated programs shown by distant stations (including "superstations") when a local station had an exclusive agreement to show the program.

In deciding to drop the Syndex rule, the FCC noted that the syndication rules were intended to protect producers when they had no copyright protection from cable systems. With cable systems by then required to pay copyright royalties for distant signals, the FCC majority felt the rules were obsolete. Charles D. Ferris, the commission chairman at the time, said the FCC action "removed the regulatory debris of a previous decade."

Ironically, this "regulatory debris" made a comeback a few years later: the FCC voted to restore the Syndicated Exclusivity Rule in 1988. Eliminating Syndex was unpopular with many broadcasters and program producers in 1980; that decision was infamous to these groups by 1988. (Note that the Syndex rule is different from the "Fin-syn" rule--the Financial Interest and Syndication Rule. Until it was abolished, the latter curtailed network syndication rights and program production; it is discussed in Chapter 12.)

When it restored the Syndex rule, the FCC noted that much of the programming of superstations consisted of reruns of old network programs that were also carried on local stations. "Instead of a rule of reruns, which is what we have now, I think we can, through Syndex rules, better achieve program diversity that will appeal to differing viewer preferences," said FCC Chairman Dennis Patrick.

The new Syndex rule differs from the old one in several respects. For one thing, it permits superstations to negotiate exclusive national syndication rights contracts. Under such a contract, only the superstation could carry a certain show. No local station would then be able to obtain rights to that show. The new rule also exempts cable systems with fewer than 1,000 subscribers and cable systems that carry "distant" stations from nearby towns when viewers can pick up the signals off the air with a good antenna.

The new Syndex rule took effect in 1990. Several cable system owners and superstations challenged the new Syndex rule in court, but in *United Video v. FCC* (890 F.2d 1173), the U.S. Court of Appeals held that the FCC had the legal authority to reimpose this rule.

In 1984, the Supreme Court ruled on another of the FCC's cable regulations, sharply curtailing the power of local governments to regulate cable content when the local rules conflict with the FCC's rules. In *Capital Cities Cable Inc. v. Crisp* (467 U.S. 691), the court overturned an Oklahoma law that prohibited cable systems from carrying advertising for wine and hard liquor, even if the advertising in question was legal where it originated. (Although the Oklahoma law banned wine and hard liquor advertising on that state's television stations, stations in several nearby states were allowed to carry it).

The Oklahoma law directly conflicted with the federal must-carry rules then in effect, which required cable systems to carry nearby television stations without altering the content of their broadcasts. Several cable systems near other states' borders were required by FCC regulations to carry television signals from out of state, including their alcoholic beverage advertising.

As a result, Oklahoma cable operators were in a classic Catch-22 situation. If they obeyed the federal must carry rules and carried alcoholic beverage advertising, they faced prosecution under Oklahoma law. If they obeyed the state law and blacked out such ads, they risked punishment for violating federal regulations.

The high court resolved this conflict by ruling decisively in favor of the federal rules. The court said that the FCC, like Congress, clearly has the authority to preempt state and local laws that conflict with federal purposes. In essence, the court said cable content was a federal matter, not subject to local rules that conflict with federal policies.

However, the court did not rule that state laws forbidding liquor advertising are inherently in violation of the First Amendment, although both broadcasters and cable operators had urged the court to reach that conclusion. Rather, the high court based its decision to overturn the Oklahoma law solely on the concept of federal preemption, not the First Amendment. Thus, a state may still forbid alcoholic beverage advertising as long as the state law does not conflict with any federal law.

But the *Capital Cities* decision did make it clear that state and local governments may not impose rules on cable systems that conflict with federal rules.

In 1988, the Supreme Court ruled on another aspect of the right of the FCC--and local governments--to regulate cable television. The court held in *City of New York v. FCC* (486 U.S. 57) that local governments could not impose more strict technical requirements on cable systems than those established by the FCC. The FCC had adopted standards for such things as signal quality and had prohibited local governments from setting different standards. The idea was to allow the cable industry to operate under uniform national standards rather than standards that might vary from town to town.

New York argued that the FCC's standards were too low and that a city should be free to set higher standards than the FCC's. The Supreme Court ruled that the FCC had the right to set uniform national standards and to prevent any city from establishing different standards.

Cable Television Legislation

Even before the *Capital Cities* decision, local governments and cable operators were lobbying in Congress, seeking a clarification of the roles of federal, state and local governments in regulating cable.

As local governments saw their right to regulate cable being eroded by the Supreme Court and the FCC, their leaders decided they needed cable legislation from Congress--even if it wasn't exactly the kind of legislation they had originally hoped for. They worked out a compromise with the cable industry; the two rival groups jointly endorsed an amended version of a cable bill that had been bogged down in Congress for two years. Called the Cable Communications Policy Act of 1984, it was enacted late in that year.

In this legislation Congress further curtailed the right of local governments to regulate cable systems. The law deregulated many cable subscription fees after a two-year transition period wherever cable systems had "effective competition," which meant merely that there had to be three local television stations that viewers could watch without cable, if they had a good antenna. In addition, the 1984 law barred local governments from charging franchise fees in excess of five percent of a cable system's gross revenues. In return for this rate deregulation, the law authorized many local governments to require public access, government and educational channels--something the second *Midwest Video* Supreme Court decision had prohibited in the absence of an act of Congress.

The Cable Communications Policy Act affirmed the right of local governments to award franchises, but it also protected cable operators from arbitrary franchise nonrenewals. The law also excluded telephone companies from the cable business except in rural areas (a provision that was eventually overturned by the 1996 Telecommunications Act), and it prohibited TV stations from owning cable systems in their service areas (although the FCC can grant waivers of these restrictions). And the law required cable operators to wire their entire franchise service areas, not just the most affluent neighborhoods where the potential for profit might be greatest.

The 1984 act left the cable industry free to grow with minimal government regulation. However, the FCC, Congress and local governments began hearing many complaints about poor service and skyrocketing rates charged by cable systems under deregulation. Critics began calling cable an "unregulated monopoly," because in most areas there was only one cable system, leaving consumers with no real choice if they wanted any of the non-broadcast programming that became available. Without either competition or government regulation of their rates, many cable systems were free to do just about whatever they wanted, and consumers were the losers, critics charged.

In addition to rapidly rising subscription fees, another thing that concerned many consumers was the manner in which the fees were apportioned between the basic tier of cable service and premium tiers. In many places, the basic tier included little more than broadcast signals (which consumers with antennas could receive for free), but it carried a high monthly fee. On the other hand, the premium cable channels, which consumers generally could not get anywhere else, were offered for only a small additional charge. The fees were not proportional to the cost of the programming to cable systems, critics said.

By 1992, the complaints about cable's rates and service were so widespread that Congress reregulated the industry, enacting the Cable Television Consumer Protection and Competition Act of 1992. The bill was passed just before the 1992 election, and then-President George Bush vetoed it. Congress mustered a two-thirds majority to override the veto, something that had never before happened during his presidency. Perhaps that indicated the degree to which Congress was hearing from angry constituents about the cable industry's alleged misdeeds. In a single act of Congress, the entire regulatory structure of the cable industry was revised. The law made sweeping changes in cable regulation--and in the relationship between the broadcast and cable industries. The era of cable deregulation was over--for the moment, at least. These are some of the highlights of the 1992 Cable Act:

Rate regulation - Local governments were empowered to reregulate basic cable rates everywhere except where there is "effective competition," which was defined as 50 percent of the households in an area having a choice between two cable or cable-like services, with the smaller of the two having a 15 percent or higher market share.

Rate rollbacks - The FCC was directed to adopt rules to reduce cable rates substantially. In 1993, the FCC adopted rules intended to reduce most cable systems' rates by about 10 percent, but the rules were so complex and voluminous that virtually everyone was confused. The full text of the rate regulations exceeded 500 pages in length! The rate rollbacks were expected to save consumers about $1.5 billion per year, but in some communities rates actually went up, not down. In 1994, the FCC adopted extensive amendments to its rate rollback rules. The result was additional rate reductions that averaged about seven percent, although the actual reduction still varied widely from one community to the next. The FCC exempted very small cable systems from some of the rate regulations. Many of these rate regulations were repealed in early 1999 under provisions of the 1996 Telecommunications Act.

Proportional rates - Cable systems were directed to charge rates that were proportional to their costs for various kinds of programming, and to fairly apportion the cost of the system itself among the various basic and premium channels.

Service standards - The FCC was directed to establish minimum service standards. Cable systems were told to have someone on duty to answer the telephone and respond to customers' complaints about poor reception, for example.

Nondiscriminatory program access for cable's competitors - The FCC was directed to adopt rules under which wireless and other non-cable video delivery systems would have fair access to the popular cable networks at a reasonable price. Those rules were originally scheduled to expire in 2002, but the FCC extended them until 2007, noting that large cable system owners still control much of the programming that cable's competitors must purchase for their customers.

Must carry/retransmission consent - In perhaps the most important single aspect of the 1992 Act, each television station was given the right to choose either "must carry" or "retransmission consent." If a station selected "must carry," all cable systems in its service area were then required to carry that station (although no cable system was to be required to set aside more than one-third of its channel capacity for commercial television stations). However, the station would receive no payment for the mandatory carriage of its signal by cable systems. On the other hand, each station could also choose "retransmission consent." Then local cable systems were not allowed to carry that station's signal without obtaining permission and, presumably, some form of payment to the station. In 2001, the FCC declared that the must carry provision of this rule applies only to broadcasters' traditional analog signal, not the new digital signal. Because more than two-thirds of all Americans get their television via cable or satellite, this could undermine the long-promised transition to high quality digital television broadcasting.

All stations were required to notify their local cable systems of their choice by mid-1993, and most large stations opted for retransmission consent. Then the serious negotiations began, with both sides well aware that if a station and a local cable system could not agree on a price, the cable system would be free to drop the station. In the end, virtually all television stations agreed to accept some form of non-cash compensation for carriage of their signals by cable systems. For the most part, the cable industry simply refused to pay for broadcast signals, and broadcasters found that they lacked sufficient bargaining power to win major concessions from cable companies. What broadcasters got in lieu of cash payments from cable systems was a variety of other kinds of compensation for the right to retransmit broadcasters' signals. Several major networks and broadcast station groups gained new cable channels. ABC, NBC and Fox got cable channels in this way. Some stations and smaller groups got free advertising or promotional time on the cable. CBS held out for cash payments for retransmission consent--and got nothing in the 1993 negotiations, although it did in later rounds (retransmission consent agreements have to be renegotiated every few years).

Retransmission consent was prominent in the news in 2000 when Time Warner, America's second largest owner of cable systems, blacked out ABC network programming for 36 hours during the crucial May ratings sweeps period. Disney-owned ABC and Time Warner were deadlocked over the terms under which Time Warner would carry ABC-owned stations in several major markets. The blackout, which affected several million viewers, produced a public relations nightmare for Time Warner. The FCC declared that the blackout was illegal, cities demanded customer rebates under their franchise agreements, and Disney gleefully urged irate Time Warner cable customers to switch to satellite TV in full-page newspaper ads. Disney even offered viewers free satellite dishes if they would leave Time Warner cable for satellite TV. And millions of Americans who didn't lose their ABC TV service seemed to enjoy this shoot-out between two of the world's biggest media conglomerates. In the end, Time Warner agreed to many of Disney's demands and signed a retransmission consent agreement.

Channel repositioning - Cable systems were ordered not to reposition television stations that select the must-carry option to a different channel than their on-air channel without the station's consent. In addition to their on-air channel, stations were given the right to choose a channel they occupied on the cable system as of certain earlier dates. (One of broadcasters' major complaints had been that it was impossible to advertise their programming and urge viewers to watch "channel two," for instance, if their signal was moved to various other channels by cable systems in their service area).

In addition to these highlights, the 1992 act included a variety of other provisions. Altogether, the FCC was required to write regulations governing no fewer than 28 different provisions of the new law.

The new rules were so complex that both the cable industry and its critics predicted that it could take a decade to straighten out all of the details of the 1992 Cable Act.

Faced with the prospect of such a massive reregulation, the cable industry filed numerous different lawsuits in an attempt to keep the 1992 law from going into effect. However, most of these lawsuits were not successful. By far the most important court test of the 1992 Cable Act came in *Turner Broadcasting System v. FCC*, a case that produced two Supreme Court decisions, one in 1994 (512 U.S. 622) and another in 1997 (520 U.S. 180). In the 1994 ruling, the high court voted 5-4 to uphold the authority of Congress to authorize the FCC to impose must-carry requirements on cable systems. In so ruling, the court chose not to follow several earlier decisions of lower federal courts that had said previous must-carry rules violated the First Amendment rights of cable operators.

The Supreme Court noted that cable operators often have a monopoly of the primary television delivery system in a community. If a cable system with monopoly power should drop a television station, that could deny the station access to the majority of the viewers it is licensed by the FCC to serve. The high court said that the government's goal of fostering universal, over-the-air television service for the entire public was sufficiently important to justify requiring cable operators to carry local TV stations, even if it meant deleting other, made-for-cable programming.

In the 1994 decision, the Supreme Court sent the case back to a lower court to reconsider whether cable systems that drop local TV stations really do threaten their ability to serve the public.

The Supreme Court reconsidered the *Turner Broadcasting* case in 1997 and again voted 5-4 to uphold the must-carry rules. In the meantime a lower court had amassed considerable evidence that without must-carry, many local stations would indeed lose up to two-thirds of their potential audience. And some would probably go bankrupt as a result. On this basis, the high court's majority concluded that must-carry was necessary to fulfill the government's objectives of assuring the survival of free local broadcast television and fostering competition in the TV programming marketplace. On the other hand, the burden this imposed on most cable operators was found to be minimal. Thus, the must-carry requirement was not an undue restriction on cable operators' First Amendment freedoms, the court held in its 1997 ruling.

As a result of the *Turner Broadcasting* decision, the must-carry provision of the 1992 Cable Act remains in effect, requiring all but the smallest cable systems to carry local TV stations. Meanwhile, many other lawsuits challenging various other provisions of the 1992 Cable Act were combined, and in an important decision in 1995, the U.S. Court of Appeals in Washington, D.C. rejected most of the cable industry's claims. In *Time Warner Entertainment v. FCC* (56 F.3d 151) the court upheld the FCC's rate rollbacks, which averaged 17 percent over two years.

The appellate court also upheld the FCC's authority under the Cable Act to regulate rates in both the basic tier of service (which usually includes local TV stations) plus the "enhanced basic" tier (which often includes such channels as CNN, ESPN and MTV). The court said it was reasonable for the FCC to regulate both to prevent cable systems from moving popular programming from tier to tier to escape rate regulation. Perhaps most important, the appellate court rejected the cable industry's basic argument: that many of these rules violate cable operators' First Amendment rights.

Another controversial issue was largely resolved in 1993 when several leading cable program providers settled antitrust lawsuits by agreeing to sell their programming to non-cable video services such as direct broadcast satellite (DBS) systems.

The Telecommunications Act of 1996 again revised the laws governing cable television in several respects. Among other things, the 1996 law repealed most of the FCC's cable rate rollbacks in early 1999. This allowed cable systems to set their own rates for all but the basic tier, which includes over-the-air TV plus public and educational channels. The FCC's rate caps were repealed immediately for small cable systems (those with less than $25 million in annual revenue) and for systems that face "effective competition" from a another provider of comparable video services.

This new deregulation of cable rates was questioned by consumer groups because cable rates had been increasing significantly in spite of the FCC's rate rollback orders. The FCC's rules included exceptions allowing cable operators to raise their rates to recover various costs. One study showed that TCI, which had 13.7 million cable subscribers, raised rates an average of almost 14 percent in 1995-96. Consumer advocates were further angered when the FCC revised its rules in 1996 so that only franchising authorities and not individuals had the right to complain to the FCC about cable rates. Because local authorities often have no interest in pursuing this matter, many rate hikes go unchallenged.

Cable Franchises and the First Amendment

The cable franchising process, in which local governments authorize a cable system to wire a community, crossing public streets in the process, has been the subject of a number of legal battles that raised First Amendment issues.

In *City of Los Angeles v. Preferred Communications* (476 U.S. 488, 1986), the Supreme Court partially upheld a U.S. Court of Appeals ruling that the local government franchising process may violate the First Amendment rights of cable operators as "electronic publishers." In so ruling, the high court accepted an argument that cable operators had been making for years--that their First Amendment rights cannot be arbitrarily abridged by local governments.

Preferred Communications announced that it wanted to provide cable service in a portion of Los Angeles where another company already held an exclusive franchise from the city. Preferred challenged the city's right to grant one company the exclusive right to communicate by cable while denying that right to all others. Preferred contended that the utility poles could easily carry more than one company's cables.

Preferred Communications argued that because the utility poles could carry several sets of television cables, the grant of a cable monopoly was comparable to the city council choosing one newspaper to serve the city and then denying distribution rights to all other newspapers. In essence, Preferred Communications was arguing that utility poles, like city sidewalks, are a First Amendment forum where local authorities must permit rival communicators to deliver their messages.

That argument had been made before without much success, but this time an appellate court accepted it, ruling that cable systems are engaged in a form of communication that deserves essentially the same First Amendment protection as newspaper and magazine publishing.

In its 1986 decision, the Supreme Court refused to go as far as the Court of Appeals did. In an opinion by Justice William Rehnquist, the court agreed that cable systems "plainly implicate First Amendment interests." However, Rehnquist refused to equate cable's First Amendment rights with those of newspaper publishers. Instead, he said cable's rights had to be balanced against "competing social interests," perhaps including a city's desire to award exclusive franchises.

The Supreme Court sent the *Preferred* case back to a trial court to reconsider. In 1990, a federal judge in Los Angeles ruled that the utility poles in Los Angeles could indeed support more than one set of cables. Therefore, the Los Angeles policy of allowing only one cable system to operate in a particular area is a violation of the First Amendment, the court ruled. Also, the judge overturned Los Angeles' requirement that cable systems provide public access channels and meet minimum technical standards. Those rules, too, violate the First Amendment rights of cable operators, the court ruled. As a result of the *Preferred Communications* case, in many instances it is now possible for new systems to go into business in competition with existing cable operators, with or without the city's blessing. However, the cost of establishing a new system is so high that it has happened in only a few cities.

Banning Indecency on Cable

The cable industry has won several more First Amendment victories in lawsuits challenging government attempts to ban indecent but non-obscene adult programming on cable channels.

In 1987 the Supreme Court ruled that cable systems cannot be forbidden to carry indecent programming by state or local governments. In *Wilkinson v. Jones* (480 U.S. 926, affirming 800 F.2d 989), the Supreme Court upheld a lower court ruling that Utah's state Cable Decency Act is unconstitutional.

The high court did not issue its own opinion or even hold oral arguments on the case. Nevertheless, by affirming a lower appellate court's decision, the Supreme Court gave this case the weight of a Supreme Court decision.

The Utah law that was invalidated had forbidden nudity or sex acts on cable systems except between midnight and 7 a.m. In overturning the law, the Court of Appeals had said "The scope of the language (in the Utah law) is so uncertain as to chill legitimate expression in a way that the (Constitution's) overbreadth doctrine forbids."

In 1996, the Supreme Court again addressed the question of sexually oriented programming on cable in *Denver Area Educational Telecommunications Consortium v. FCC*, 518 U.S. 727). In this case, the high court ruled on the constitutionality of three provisions of the 1992 Cable Act concerning "patently offensive" sexually oriented programming on cable access channels.

The high court upheld Section 10(a) of the 1992 Act, which said cable operators may ban patently offensive material on commercial leased access channels if they choose to do so. The court said this provision does not violate the First Amendment; it leaves cable operators free to carry such programs or reject them, just as cable operators have a First Amendment right to carry or reject other cable programming.

However, the high court overturned Section 10(b) and Section 10(c) of the 1992 Cable Act, ruling that both violate the First Amendment. Section 10(b) required cable operators who choose to carry patently offensive material on a leased access channel to segregate it on a single channel and block that channel to everyone except subscribers who specifically ask to receive it 30 days in advance. The court said this was an excessive burden on First Amendment freedoms: it would not allow a viewer to decide spontaneously to watch a specific program; nor would it protect subscribers who feared having their names appear on a list of persons who had requested to receive a "sex channel."

The Supreme Court also ruled that cable operators cannot censor sexually oriented programming on public access, educational and government channels, as Section 10(c) of the 1992 law required. The court said these channels have traditionally been a public forum, not subject to censorship.

The Communications Decency Act, which is a section of the 1996 Telecommunications Act, went further in regulating adult programming on cable, requiring cable systems that carry sexually explicit adult channels either to scramble them completely or carry them only between 10 p.m. and 6 a.m.

Complete scrambling is not technically feasible for some older cable systems because of "signal bleed" (which allows some non-subscribers to see a fuzzy picture or hear muffled audio in spite of the scrambling). That meant adult channels could only broadcast during the late-night hours under this law. Playboy Entertainment sued, alleging a First Amendment violation. A three-judge federal court ruled that the scrambling requirement violates the First Amendment. The court concluded that providing an additional blocking device to any household that requests one (which is permitted under another provision of the Telecommunications Act) is a less restrictive alternative to the daytime blackout requirement as a way to deal with signal bleed.

The federal government appealed, leading to still another Supreme Court decision and another decisive First Amendment victory for cable in 2000: *U.S. v. Playboy Entertainment Group* (529 U.S. 803). In this case, the high court voted 5-4 to allow adult cable programming in the daytime even if a cable system cannot prevent all signal bleed. The court's 5-4 majority said the provision allowing any subscriber who wants it to request an additional blocking device is sufficient to enable parents to keep their children from watching adult programming on a fuzzy, partially scrambled screen. The court noted that fewer than one percent of cable subscribers had requested the additional blocking device, despite the widespread mailing of notices of its availability, indicating minimal parental concern about signal bleed.

The majority said it was a violation of the First Amendment for government to deny non-obscene adult programming to millions of daytime viewers who want it when the extra blocking device is a less-restrictive alternative to government censorship for those who do not want even a fuzzy, partially scrambled picture arriving in their homes.

Writing for the court, Justice Anthony M. Kennedy said, "This case involves speech alone; and even where speech is indecent and enters the home, the objective of shielding children does not suffice to support a blanket ban if the protection can be accomplished by a less restrictive alternative." Kennedy also said parents have reacted to this problem "with a collective yawn."

NEW ELECTRONIC MEDIA TECHNOLOGIES

A number of promising new electronic communications technologies have appeared in recent years. Some seemed destined to fundamentally alter the television viewing habits of Americans, but failed to deliver. Some actually lived up to their promise. Others have become costly boondoggles that produced nothing but billion-dollar losses for their promoters.

Cable, of course, is hardly a new technology. But its emergence as the fastest growing video delivery system of the 1980s contributed to the disappointing early failures of direct broadcast satellites (DBS), multichannel multipoint distribution systems (MMDS) and other once-promising new technologies. By the late 1990s, though, new cable-like DBS and MMDS ("wireless cable") systems were competing with cable and over-the-air broadcasters in a high-stakes battle for preeminence as the key television delivery system of the future--a future likely to be dominated by another new technology, digital television (DTV).

Digital and High-Definition Television

After years of research, planning and debate, in 1997 the FCC acted to authorize the transition to digital television in the United States.

Under the FCC's rules, each existing full-power television station was assigned a new channel for DTV. The FCC ordered network-owned and network-affiliated stations in the largest markets to begin digital broadcasting in 1999. For various reasons, not all stations were able to meet this deadline, although about 200 stations were broadcasting DTV (in addition to their normal analog broadcasts) by 2001. Stations in smaller markets were given until May of 2002 to make the transition to DTV, but about two thirds of the 1,300 U.S. full-power television stations missed the deadline. The FCC granted hundreds of six-month waivers--and said future waivers would be much harder to get. All stations are supposed to vacate their analog channels in 2006 so the old analog channels can be auctioned to the highest bidder.

By 2002, however, it was clear that this deadline could not be met. Broadcasters are not required to relinquish their analog TV channels until 85 percent of their viewers can receive digital TV signals. And by 2002, fewer than one percent of American households owned a digital TV set. Meanwhile, about 33 million new analog TV sets--the kind that are supposed to become obsolete in 2006--are being sold every year.

Many in the industry hoped that consumers would purchase or rent set-top adapters if they don't buy the new digital TV sets. However, that doesn't allow for the reception of true high-definition television (HDTV) service--which was originally considered to be the main selling point for digital TV. HDTV offers a vastly improved TV picture on a wide, theatre-style screen. Nor does a set-top box guarantee full compatibility. In mid-2002 it was still uncertain whether the same set-top converters would receive all cable and over-the-air digital TV signals. Nor is it likely that cable systems will carry broadcasters' digital signals as well as their analog signals. In 2001, the FCC declined to require cable systems to carry both, to the dismay of broadcasters.

Under the FCC's rules for digital TV, each station may broadcast the long-promised high-definition television (HDTV) on its digital channel or instead deliver four or five standard quality programs simultaneously on one digital channel.

Many broadcasters indicated that they would do this during most of the broadcast day, thus providing the public with more programming choices than ever before.

However, lengthy battles over technical standards for digital television delayed the transition to DTV for broadcasters, cable systems, equipment manufacturers and consumers. No one wanted to make a huge investment in hardware that might become obsolete in a matter of months or, at most, a few years. Still another debate arose: content producers, including the major Hollywood studios, demanded that the digital programming include a copy protection scheme to prevent consumers from copying TV shows on digital VCRs if a show is coded to prevent copying altogether--or to limit the number of times the material can be copied. Some manufacturers and consumer advocates wondered if consumers would toss out their analog TV sets and VCRs--which allow unlimited copying--for digital systems that do NOT allow copying and don't even offer the long-promised advantage of higher quality video.

At a convention for broadcasters in 1998, FCC Chairman William Kennard said, "No consumer wants to buy five set-top boxes, six remotes and a $6,000 television set that doesn't work with cable." Commissioner Susan Ness added, "Will the true high-definition set that (consumers) just bought display the true high-definition signal that the broadcaster has just transmitted if the set is hooked up to cable? The answer had better be yes."

And there were other problems with digital television. Although some major market stations began digital broadcasting on schedule, many other stations, especially in smaller markets, were still wondering how to cover the multimillion dollar cost of converting to digital broadcasting when the 2002 deadline passed. It requires new studio equipment, new transmitters, and often new towers. Industry executives have estimated that switching to digital will cost the average station $8 to $12 million, with an additional cost of about $100 million each for the major networks. Because cable and satellite systems also plan to offer digital TV, many broadcasters agree that they must make the switch to remain competitive. Nevertheless, the cost seems staggering to many station owners.

In a speech to broadcasters in 1996, Fox network founder Rupert Murdoch questioned where the money to switch to digital TV would come from. "No one that I know has a proven business plan that will generate one extra dime to help pay for all the expense. HDTV in particular is an inherently defensive strategy designed to help free broadcasting hold on to existing viewers and advertising revenues."

Another thorny issue has been spectrum auctions. Broadcasters contended that they could not afford to purchase their digital channels and still offer free television service, supported only by advertising revenue. To obtain their digital channels without an auction, broadcasters have repeatedly acquiesced to government demands for changes in programming that the FCC and the Clinton administration considered to be in the public interest. Many of the recently proposed content controls (discussed earlier in this chapter) were widely seen as a *quid pro quo* for digital channel allocations without an auction. But many in government felt it was imperative to auction off the broadcasters' old channels quickly to help reduce the federal budget deficit. What happens, then, if the transition to digital television takes far longer than expected? What if very few viewers have digital TV sets by 2006--and the rest are in no hurry to make the switch?

Broadcasters face still other obstacles in offering digital television. One of the most difficult is turning out to be winning approval from local governments for new towers or modifications to existing ones. Each station needs a new antenna for digital broadcasting, and the new antenna cannot necessarily be installed on the same tower as the station's present analog antenna. In many areas, local governments have flatly refused to authorize new towers--or even new antennas on existing towers. Even broadcasters who have not been denied the right to put up the antennas needed for digital television have often faced long delays in getting permits from local governments--making it impossible for many to meet the FCC's deadlines for launching digital broadcasting.

In 2001, communications attorney Richard E. Wiley, a former FCC chairman who headed the committee that developed technical standards for digital TV, was saying the only way to jump-start digital TV might be an act of Congress like the All-Channel Receiver Act of 1962, which required all new TV sets to cover the UHF channels as well as channels 2-13. Only after that law was passed did UHF broadcasting become viable for the first time. Manufacturers replied that if they had to include digital reception capability, even the smallest TV sets would cost hundreds or thousands of dollars more than they do now.

Despite all of the obstacles, everyone agrees that there will be digital television and that consumers will watch it--someday. One encouraging sign was a plan proposed in 2002 by FCC Chairman Michael to end the HDTV logjam. His plan called for the four largest TV networks plus HBO and Showtime to provide HDTV programming during half of the prime time period, starting in the 2002-2003 season. Also, he called for the major networks' affiliates to pass through the networks' digital signals by January, 2003, and for cable systems to carry up to five channels of digital programming during half of their prime time schedule by the same date. Finally, he called for TV manufacturers to equip half of their 36-inch and larger sets with DTV tuners by Jan. 1, 2004, with all sets 13 inches or larger to include digital tuners by Dec. 31, 2006.

Will Powell's plan come to pass? In mid-2002, program producers, TV networks, equipment manufacturers and consumer groups were still deadlocked over copy protection standards for digital TV. Hollywood interests were adamant that all digital programming, including free, over-the-air TV, must be copy-protected. Consumer groups were just as adamant that the right to tape TV shows, taken for granted now by millions of analog VCR owners, must not be abridged.

So will Powell's timetable be met???

Cable-Telephone-Internet Convergence

Perhaps no part of the Telecommunications Act of 1996 could have a greater long-range impact on the American way of life than the provisions designed to open all of the communications industries to new competition. In the most important of these initiatives, this law allows telephone companies ("telcos") and cable systems to enter each others' businesses and preempts (i.e., overrules) state and local law and regulations that stand in the way.

Even before the 1996 law was enacted, a number of states had taken steps toward allowing cable companies to offer telephone service, and vice versa. The FCC had also taken some preliminary steps in that direction, too. But now Congress has declared that wide-open competition is to be the norm. This means:

*Local phone companies are allowed to operate cable systems, even in their own telephone service areas.

*Local phone companies may offer Internet access.

*Local phone companies may offer long-distance telephone service.

*Cable systems may offer local telephone service and broadband (high-speed) Internet access.

*Long distance phone companies such as AT&T are free to offer local telephone service and Internet access.

*Local phone companies are free to manufacture telephone equipment, something they were largely prevented from doing under the court order that broke up the nationwide AT&T monopoly.

To facilitate all of these dramatic changes in the communications business, the 1996 act overruled a variety of federal, state and local regulations and industry practices that might stand in the way. In 2002 the U.S. Supreme Court upheld the rules giving cable systems access to utility poles at low cost, even if the cable system is using the poles to deliver high-speed Internet access instead of television (*National Cable & Telecommunications Association v. Gulf Power Co.*, 534 U.S. 327).

In addition to all of these provisions, the 1996 act included a vast array of provisions designed to foster competition and prevent anticompetitive business practices. For example, "navigation systems" such as cable set-top boxes must be made available for purchase apart from cable service, and they cannot be engineered to provide cable a built-in advantage over cable's competitors. Also, the various companies will not be allowed to "cross subsidize" their new businesses with revenue from their established businesses in which they enjoy a near monopoly. And technical standards must not be set up by entities such as the research arm of the local phone companies in a manner that gives the phone companies a competitive advantage.

How quickly all of this new competition will develop is uncertain. But the 1996 act directed the FCC and other regulators to adopt literally thousands of rules that will make all of this happen as soon as possible.

Even before the 1996 act was passed, the FCC had taken steps to open television and telephone services to new competition. In its so-called "video dialtone" proceeding in 1992, the FCC authorized telcos to begin installing fiber optic cables that are far superior to the coaxial cables traditionally used by cable television systems. Using fiber optics, telcos can offer an integrated package of one-way and two-way voice and video services, including HDTV cable television, fast Internet access and telephone service.

Several court decisions overturned provisions of the 1992 Cable Act that prohibited telcos from offering video services within their telephone service areas, ruling that these restrictions violate the First Amendment (see, for instance, *Chesapeake & Potomac Telephone Co. v. U.S.*, 42 F.3d 181, 1994--a case the U.S.

Supreme Court at first agreed to review and then dropped when it became clear that the 1996 Telecommunications Act would open the way for telcos to offer video services within their telephone service areas).

Direct Broadcast Satellites

The number-one high-tech disappointment of the 1980s was the *direct broadcast satellite* (DBS) business. A decade later, DBS had become a dramatic success story--boosted by government regulators as a needed source of competition for cable.

Billed in the early 1980s as the television technology of the future, DBS at first was a dismal failure. All of the original DBS companies bailed out, victims of technical, financial and marketing problems that began almost as soon as DBS was first proposed as a serious medium of mass communication. All of the firms that were originally awarded licenses for direct satellite broadcasting dropped their plans in the face of prohibitive costs and serious questions about the economic potential of the service. Several would-be satellite program providers were forced to absorb multimillion dollar losses in the process. It was not until much later that DBS became a viable medium.

The concept underlying DBS is fairly simple, although the technology to accomplish it is complex and expensive. A number of satellites are positioned above the equator at an altitude of 22,300 miles. At that altitude each satellite would orbit the earth at a speed that exactly matches the Earth's rotation speed. The result: each satellite appears to remain stationary over one point on the Earth's surface, not moving at all. Such a satellite is said to be *geosynchronous*. This allows receiving dish antennas to be locked in position, permanently pointed at a satellite. If communications satellites were not geosynchronous, very costly tracking hardware and software would have to be used to keep every dish antenna pointed at a satellite that appeared to be moving around the sky.

Once a geosynchronous satellite is in orbit, transmitting stations on the ground send up signals on an "uplink" frequency. The satellite receives these signals and retransmits them back to earth on a "downlink," which is usually a different frequency.

Geosynchronous communications satellites are not new. Virtually all major cable systems, broadcasters, wire services and newspapers have used these satellites for years to relay programming or information. However, the early communications satellites operated with such low transmitter power that a very sensitive (and therefore large) dish antenna was required to receive the signal. Perhaps one reason the DBS ventures of the early 1980s failed is because consumers had to have large dish antennas in their yards (or on their roofs) to receive the satellite signals. Early satellite dishes were typically about 10 feet in diameter (and ugly, in the opinion of many homeowners' associations, local governments and neighbors).

What is new about DBS today is that there is a new generation of satellites with more powerful transmitters operating on higher frequencies, allowing good reception with dish antennas only two or three feet in diameter--small enough to be mounted inconspicuously in a window, on a balcony or in an out-of-sight corner of the roof.

While the DBS ventures of the 1980s all failed, several major players in the communications business launched new DBS systems in the 1990s; the DBS industry had a combined total of about 20 million subscribers in 2002--enough to have a major impact on the fortunes of cable companies.

DirecTV and EchoStar, the leading DBS providers, gained many new subscribers in late 1999 and 2000 after Congress passed a new Satellite Television Home Viewers Act that allowed satellite systems to carry local television stations, including those offering network programming. Before then, DBS providers were barred from carrying the major broadcast networks except in "white areas" far enough from any city to be out of range of over-the-air TV stations. This new law amended the Copyright Act to allow this; it is discussed in Chapter Six.

Under the 1996 Telecommunications Act, the FCC took other steps to help DBS systems provide viable competition to cable. For instance, the FCC overruled local zoning and deed restrictions that prohibited the small dish antennas needed for DBS. The FCC adopted rules requiring local governments, homeowners' associations and landlords to allow not only dish antennas but also TV antennas. The FCC rule governing apartments allows tenants to put antennas on balconies and other private areas but not on roofs or outside walls.

In addition to the growing number of consumers who now have small DBS dish antennas, there are still about two million homes equipped with much larger dish antennas to receive television programs from satellites. But most of them are not receiving DBS programs as such. Instead, they are receiving satellite programming that is intended primarily for delivery to the public via cable systems, not for direct at-home reception by consumers. Congress acted several times in the 1980s to allow consumers to receive this programming--for a subscription fee. Most owners of these larger dish antennas are in rural areas not served by cable systems.

Other Technologies

Another once-promising new technology was the *multipoint distribution service* (MDS), sometimes called "wireless cable." MDS systems (or MMDS, *multichannel multipoint distribution systems*) use microwave frequencies to transmit television programs over the air to subscribers who pay a fee for the service. Each subscriber receives a special antenna and converter in order to receive MDS signals on an ordinary television set.

During the 1980s, MDS ventures were launched in many of the nation's major cities; by the 1990s many of the pioneers were gone. Many were unable to obtain satellite television programming at a reasonable price (many of the program providers with close ties to the cable industry were unwilling to sell their programming to another delivery system that competes with cable until they were required to do so by the 1992 Cable Act and other laws). In the final analysis, it appears that the growing market penetration and economic strength of the cable industry made it impossible for early MDS systems to compete.

However, by the early 2000s new multichannel MDS systems had gained some market share in competition with cable: MMDS systems had about two million subscribers nationwide. The 1996 Telecommunications Act required local authorities to allow small outdoor MMDS antennas, just as they must allow DBS dishes and TV antennas.

Another new technology that may gain some market share is the *local multipoint distribution service* (LMDS). LMDS systems are something of a combination of MMDS and cellular telephone technology. They deliver television programming from "cells" whose transmissions cover only a five- or six-mile radius. This allows LMDS systems to deliver programming custom tailored to local areas, with each "cell" having different programming than surrounding cells.

The FCC adopted rules for LMDS in 1997 and began auctioning spectrum for this new technology in 1998.

Perhaps the new video technology that has captured the public imagination more than any other is Internet-based television broadcasting using streaming technology. Many television broadcasters are moving aggressively to add streaming to their existing websites so they can do full-blown broadcasting on the Internet. They are well aware that other industries (including newspaper publishers, among others) are also moving rapidly toward video streaming on the Internet. Many foresee the day--perhaps only a couple of years in the future--when viewers can choose among a host of new sources of video programming via the Internet, including competing video-based local and national newscasts from newspapers and broadcasters. This kind of convergence may force policy-makers to rewrite all of their definitions of broadcasting--and publishing. Broadcasters and newspaper or magazine publishers may become direct competitors on the Internet, with both offering interactive (two-way) broadcasting.

However, webcasting has encountered its own obstacles. For one, there are copyright problems that stand in the way (see Chapter Six). Another problem is that Hollywood unions have demanded separate compensation if commercials that were intended for over-the-air broadcasts are also streamed on the Internet. This created a host of contractual and economic problems.

Meanwhile, the telephone and cable industries are rapidly merging (see Chapter 12) and announcing grandiose plans to spend billions to wire customers' homes with new fiber optic cables to facilitate all of this.

Still another video delivery system is called *satellite master antenna television* (SMATV). In reality, SMATV is little more than a privately owned cable system, but it has a separate legal status--and has enjoyed some financial success. SMATV systems operate in large apartment and condominium complexes all over the country, providing residents with a private cable-like service.

SMATV involves nothing more than a good antenna for over-the-air television reception, plus a dish antenna to pick up satellite-relayed premium cable services, such as movies, sports and news channels. The programming is then routed to individual residences by coaxial cable.

SMATV is not really a new technology, but it became much more popular after the FCC dropped all licensing requirements for receive-only dish antennas in 1979. Also, the cost of a satellite television receiving system declined sharply during the 1980s. This made it much easier for apartment complex owners to set up SMATV systems instead of providing access to a local cable system.

Several lawsuits also encouraged the growth of SMATV systems at the expense of community-wide cable systems. In 1982, the Supreme Court overturned a New York "cable access" law that forced landlords to permit cable installations in their apartment buildings for a $1 fee. In *Loretto v. Teleprompter Manhattan Cable Corp.* (458 U.S. 419), the court said this was a confiscation of private property without proper compensation. As a result, New York cable operators were required to negotiate with each landlord. And landlords were free to exclude cable from their buildings, offering their own private SMATV systems instead.

Thousands of SMATV systems are now in operation. Many are profitable, and their subscribers can tell little difference between SMATV and a conventional cable system. Both offer much of the same programming for about the same price.

A technology that is sometimes labeled as "new" is low-power television (LPTV). LPTV is really nothing more than a new kind of conventional television broadcasting that was introduced during the 1980s. The FCC acted in 1982 to allow "mini-stations" to serve small towns and localized areas in larger cities. The idea was that these stations would transmit with low power and would operate efficiently with low overhead and bring TV service to communities that had little or no local service. To help them do that, the FCC freed LPTV stations of many regulations that apply to full-power stations. LPTV stations are authorized to serve a radius of 10-15 miles from their transmitter sites. By the early 1990s, more than 2,200 LPTV stations were on the air or under construction.

However, by 2000 LPTV faced a threat from digital television: new interference from high power digital stations. In some communities LPTV stations were forced to change to less desirable channels, accept new interference, or even curtail their operations to avoid causing interference to new digital television stations, which have legal priority over LPTV stations. Eventually LPTV stations were given some protection from the new DTV stations, but only LPTV stations that were broadcasting at least 18 hours a day, with three hours of local programming, were given this protection. Only about 400 of the 2,200 LPTV stations meet these standards.

Another emerging communications technology is digital audio broadcasting, formally known as the Digital Audio Radio Service (DARS). DARS offers many channels of high-quality sound, delivered to consumers by satellites.

Four companies applied for digital audio broadcasting licenses. The FCC had set aside frequencies in the UHF spectrum for DARS and adopted rules for the new service. In 1997, DARS spectrum auctions were held. The two winning bidders offered a total of $173 million for their spectrum. The two companies, XM and Sirius, launched their services in 2001, charging subscribers about $10 a month for 50 to 100 channels of programming. Car radios capable of receiving it may eventually cost only about $100 more than ordinary car radios. This service is to provide nation-wide radio programming rather than local programming.

In 2000 the FCC created still another kind of broadcasting: low-power FM radio. Recognizing that most existing radio stations are owned by large corporations, the FCC is planning to license very low power stations to serve small communities or small areas within larger communities. This plan is discussed more fully in the section on broadcast ownership in Chapter 12.

Perhaps the oldest "new" technology of all is AM radio broadcasting. Long dismissed as an outdated technology that could not deliver good sound quality, AM radio may yet make a comeback, with the backing of the broadcast industry and the FCC. The FCC has allocated 10 new channels for AM radio just above 1600 kHz, where the AM band ended almost from the beginning of AM broadcasting. In addition, the commission set a higher standard for audio quality on the new channels, and set up a priority system for awarding frequencies to existing stations, with a preference for a few daytime-only stations in large cities lacking a full-time station and to stations having interference problems on their present channels.

ONGOING ISSUES

As the discussion of new technologies illustrates, the electronic media face enormous legal, economic and policy questions today. We may be in the midst of a communications revolution even more far-reaching than the one that brought us television 50 years ago. With cable or satellite TV and VCRs in at least three-fourths of all American homes, and with digital television, Internet-based television and digital audio broadcasting all here or coming soon, many of the old rules of broadcast law and economics are obsolete. The day when three major television networks could dominate home entertainment in America is past. In 1979, ABC, CBS and NBC commanded 91 percent of the prime time television audience. By 2002, the "big three" networks' share of the prime time audience was well below 50 percent and still declining.

Recognizing these trends, the Federal Communications Commission has tried several different approaches to broadcast regulation in recent years. Some would say the FCC has moved in fits and starts, taking a zig-zag route toward no discernable destination.

In the early years of television, the FCC attempted to promote the public interest by fine-tuning the Fairness Doctrine and other content controls. Then the FCC started calling the old rules "regulatory underbrush" and launched a broad deregulation of electronic communications. During the 1980s and early 1990s, the FCC looked mainly to the marketplace for answers, while attempting to provide a "level playing field" for broadcasters, cable and other audio and video delivery systems.

In 1961, then-FCC Chairman Newton Minow made his legendary and controversial "vast wasteland" speech to the nation's broadcasters. He lectured the broadcast industry for worrying too much about making money and not enough about serving the public. He said the FCC would be looking for better public service at license renewal time. But in the 1980s, a Reagan-era FCC chairman said television was merely "a toaster with pictures," and thus not in need of much federal regulation.

As a result, in the 1980s the FCC adopted policies reflecting the philosophy that marketplace forces would assure quality and diversity in programming--and thus better public service. The commission deregulated both the broadcasting and cable industries. Many of the rules and policies that were sacred cows for years were unceremoniously discarded, victims of a new philosophy.

In the mid-1990s, some critics of government regulation--including Newt Gingrich, then-speaker of the House of Representatives--were even talking about abolishing the FCC and eliminating almost all remaining federal regulation of the electronic media. But across the Capitol Mall at the White House and over at the FCC's headquarters, there was very different rhetoric: the talk was of adopting new rules to make sure broadcasters serve the public interest in a digital age.

Are the federal rules, new and old, really "regulatory debris?" Is deregulation a good idea? What about abolishing a rule like the Fairness Doctrine? Should broadcasters be as free as newspaper publishers are to cover the news as they see it? Or should the government decide how not only broadcasters but also other media cover the issues of the day? If broadcasters must serve the public interest, who decides what is in the public interest? The government? Broadcasters themselves?

Does the answer to these questions change for the new media owners who are now buying their spectrum at auctions? Is it logical to impose public interest obligations on digital audio radio service (DARS) providers when they have just paid upwards of $90 million each to purchase their channels? If the government can still regulate their content, exactly what did the digital audio systems buy with that money?

If the 1980s were an era of deregulation, things were very different in the 1990s, when Congress and the FCC implemented or proposed an unprecedented array of new content controls. The Telecommunications Act mandated the V-chip based on television shows' ratings. At about the same time, the FCC either implemented or proposed many new content controls: three hours a week of mandatory children's educational programming, free airtime for politicians, public service announcements in prime time on every network every night, a ban on hard liquor advertising and a new family hour.

Many of these are intended to make television "friendly to kids," as former FCC Chairman Reed Hundt once put it. But they raise anew all of the questions about government control of broadcast content. Does the federal government really know what is best for the nation's children--or adults, for that matter? Does that justify government control of broadcast content? If so, is it right for over-the-air broadcasting to be singled out for government controls that do not apply to other media? And above all, will it work? Can parents armed with a new TV set and a V-chip programming device really keep their kids from seeing the TV shows that their friends are watching? Will many even try? How long will it be before kids figure out how to program the V-chip themselves, or maybe find a home where the parents don't care or aren't around?

Cable has also seen regulation, deregulation, reregulation--and then more deregulation. In the 1990s Congress reregulated cable on a large scale--by enacting the 1992 Cable Television Consumer Protection and Competition Act. The act and the FCC regulations to implement it represented by far the most complex and burdensome regulatory scheme cable has ever faced in America. The question that remains, of course, is whether the public really won or lost under this regulatory regimen. The cable industry said that with the rate rollbacks, retransmission consent fees and other new costs, there would be little money left for new programming and technology. Broadcasters and some public interest groups, on the other hand, pointed to a litany of alleged abuses by cable systems during the cable industry's "unregulated monopoly" era. "They had it coming," some said of the tough rules cable faced under the 1992 act. But the battle is not over: the 1996 Telecommunications Act repealed some of the most onerous new regulatory burdens imposed on cable by the 1992 act. Cable was regulated before 1984, deregulated from 1984 to 1992, reregulated in 1992, and then deregulated to some extent in 1996. Will the pendulum continue to swing back and forth like that? Is on-again, off-again government regulation good public policy?

In the new millennium, it's sometimes a little difficult to tell whether we are in an era of deregulation or reregulation. On one hand, the 1996 Telecommunications Act was intended to foster competition so government regulation will be less needed. But those provisions required thousands of new rules and regulations to implement. Congress and the FCC both are saying that because competition is good, the media marketplace should be opened to new voices. But nobody has really answered the big question: will all of these new audio and video services really give us better programming or just a more vast "wasteland?"

What about the telephone companies? They say they can offer an unprecedented level of service with fiber optic cables, including high-speed Internet access. But is this competition really going to provide consumers better and less expensive service? What about letting local phone companies offer long-distance service while long-distance companies get into local phone service? Don't we risk replacing regulated monopolies with unregulated near-monopolies as the various communications companies merge? Perhaps the antitrust laws will prevent some of that (see Chapter 12).

As the Internet comes to dominate so many areas of communications, are we moving into still another new era without rules or road signs to tell us where we're really going? It may be that the one-way mass communications process we have known ever since the "penny press" era of the 1830s will largely disappear--rendered obsolete by two-way information systems that will come to dominate our lives and supplant one-way communications. Already, the Internet has had a measurable impact on television viewing in households that are online. Moreover, interactive television will soon arrive, and some of the world's largest computer and communications corporations are trying to capture this potentially enormous new market. But who should provide these new communications systems? The telcos? Cable systems? Computer software giants such as Microsoft? A combination of the three?

One thing does seem clear about the Internet: it will remain free of many government content controls that are routinely applied to broadcasting. Under the *Reno v. ACLU* Supreme Court decision (discussed in Chapter 10), the Internet enjoys the highest level of First Amendment protection--the same protection enjoyed by the print media.

However, the Internet's broad First Amendment protection may lead to new questions--and new absurdities. There is a growing convergence of the media. Does this mean it's okay to have a four-letter word on a video screen if it arrived via the Internet, but not okay if it arrived via over-the-air television at, say, 6 p.m.? Does that make any sense?

If the Internet is free of government content controls, shouldn't broadcasters also have full First Amendment freedoms? And what about cable? If the same four-letter word arrives via cable, maybe it's okay if the viewer has subscribed to an adult channel, but not otherwise. And what about renting movies on video? Are the four-letter words suddenly okay--even words that could get a broadcaster fined $1.7 million? Do the indecency restrictions really protect children from words that they don't ever hear at school (or on the way home)?

Is the traditional scarcity justification for broadcast regulation still valid in this multichannel world? The primary factor limiting the introduction of new video programming services today is the economic saturation of the marketplace, not the physical saturation of the radio spectrum. The fact that the FCC receives more applications for broadcast licenses than it can accommodate may not be the overriding consideration today, given the alternatives to traditional broadcasting that now exist. Over-the-air broadcasting is just one of many delivery systems available to those who wish to disseminate video programming to consumers.

At this point the same economic factors that serve to limit the number of newspapers also set the limits on television-like services. Either industry could add numerous additional outlets--if the marketplace would support them. True, a broadcaster must have a government license while a newspaper publisher does not, but that hardly seems to be the issue: new television-like services are appearing all over the landscape while major newspapers are failing--or moving into electronic publishing on the Internet.

With audio and video streaming on the Internet, *anyone* can be a "broadcaster" now--no government license is needed. But to those who say that fact eliminates the scarcity rationale once and for all, the defenders of government regulation, including some FCC commissioners, reply, "what about the *digital divide*?" They contend that as long as not everyone has Internet access, and those who do not are disproportionately members of minority groups, the government must continue to regulate broadcasting under the scarcity rationale. And more cynical observers might wonder, "how free can webcasting be when the copyright royalties are prohibitively expensive?"

Many of these questions should be answered as we move through the twenty-first century. In fact, many of them *will* be answered--by changing technologies and marketplace forces if not by government policy makers.

A SUMMARY OF ELECTRONIC MEDIA REGULATION

Why Do Broadcasters Have Special Laws to Follow?

Broadcasters do not own their frequencies. The radio spectrum is a valuable and limited resource; long ago Congress declared that those who are given the privilege of using it must serve *the public interest, convenience, and necessity*. Broadcasters must obtain licenses from the Federal Communications Commission, the agency charged with regulating the electronic media.

Are License Renewals Automatic?

No. However, if the broadcaster's service record is considered "substantial," a renewal is almost a certainty. License renewal challenges by citizens' groups and others have become more commonplace than they once were, but non-renewals are still rare. In several instances, broadcasters have lost licenses for violating FCC rules or criminal laws, but more often even those guilty of serious offenses have been permitted to sell, transferring their licenses to someone else, to avoid a license revocation.

What Are the Major Rules Governing Broadcast Content?

The *Fairness Doctrine* was a policy of the FCC that for nearly 40 years required broadcasters to provide overall balance in their programming. It was abolished in 1987, to the great consternation of Congress and some public interest groups but to the delight of broadcasters who objected to government officials second-guessing their news judgments. The Fairness Doctrine should not be confused with the *Equal Time Rule*, a provision of the Communications Act that requires broadcasters to sell comparable airtime to rival political candidates at comparable rates. The Equal Time Rule has *not* been abolished. Television stations are also required to carry three hours per week of children's educational programming, while many broadcast hoaxes are banned and broadcasters are required to serve the public interest, as that is defined by the FCC, in various other ways.

How Is Cable Television Regulated?

Cable television systems need no FCC license as such, since they do not broadcast over the air. However, cable systems are subject to many FCC rules because their operations affect on-the-air broadcasting. Cable was deregulated during the 1980s, but in 1992 Congress reregulated cable, imposing a number of new restrictions on cable systems. The 1992 law mandated subscription rate reductions and *must carry* or *retransmission consent* requirements to protect local television stations. Cable systems also must have *franchise agreements*, which give cities and counties some control over cable systems. The 1996 Telecommunications act has repealed some of the rate reductions and other rules established by the 1992 law.

CHAPTER 12

Media Ownership Issues

Who owns America's mass media? Is local ownership better than chain ownership? Does the public suffer when the same company owns many newspapers, magazines, Hollywood studios, Internet services, radio stations, television stations and cable systems--or a combination of these?

Ever since William Randolph Hearst and the Scripps family built the nation's first newspaper chains a century ago, these have been controversial questions. Media critics often regard the ongoing trend toward centralized ownership of the mass media as a threat to journalistic freedom--and the public interest. Regardless of how well intentioned the management of a large media conglomerate may be, central ownership deprives the media of the independence that is so vital in a democracy, critics say. Others, of course, have defended the growing chain ownership of the mass media, pointing to the efforts of many owners to provide good management and public service to each community they serve. Also, there are economies of scale: a large company can do many things more efficiently than a small one. For example, a company that owns eight radio stations in one city can sell advertising, do programming and handle station engineering with fewer employees (and lower costs) than eight individually owned stations would have.

However, even the defenders of multimedia ownership concede that abuses have occurred, and government agencies have sometimes acted to correct these abuses. The Antitrust Division of the U.S. Justice Department, for instance, has often acted against monopolistic business practices in the mass media. And at times the Federal Communications Commission has acted to limit both chain ownership in broadcasting and cross ownership of print and broadcast media. At other times, however, both the Justice Department and the FCC have acquiesced when huge multimedia conglomerates merged with other equally huge corporations. Sometimes the FCC has even set aside its own rules limiting cross-ownership to facilitate these mergers. And Congress relaxed many media ownership restrictions in the Telecommunications Act of 1996, adopting the philosophy that companies should be free to grow and compete with other growing companies, all of whom are free to enter each other's areas of business.

Never have questions of communications media ownership and business practices been more controversial than they are at the beginning of the twenty-first century: in the early 2000s there have been almost daily news accounts of megamergers of communications companies--and of the biggest antitrust lawsuit in years: the Microsoft case.

AN OVERVIEW OF ANTITRUST LAW

Serious government regulation of monopolistic business practices in America began with the Sherman Act, enacted in 1890 to combat the abuses that were rampant in the post-Civil War era of industrialization. The Sherman Act is the nation's pioneering antitrust law; it forbids a wide variety of "contracts, combinations ...or conspiracies in restraint of trade or commerce."

In 1914 the Clayton Act was adopted, forbidding certain other business practices and expanding the federal government's antitrust enforcement powers. This law was strengthened in 1950 by the addition of the Celler-Kefauver Act, which prohibits one company from buying out a competitor where the result is more monopoly and less competition. Thus, business ownership as well as business practices have come under federal regulation.

Of the many business practices banned by these antitrust laws, a few should be specifically noted. For instance, *price fixing* and *profit pooling* are prohibited. That means it is generally unlawful for competing companies to enter an agreement either to charge non-competitive prices or share profits. Rival companies are supposed to keep each others' prices low by competing. They're not supposed to conspire to avoid price competition.

In addition, many *mergers*, *tying arrangements* and *boycotts* are illegal. A merger is an arrangement in which two businesses combine. Mergers are illegal when they substantially reduce competition, to the detriment of consumers or other businesses. Before a merger of large companies can occur, federal officials must review and approve the transaction.

A tying arrangement involves forcing customers to buy something they may not want in order to get something they do want and cannot readily get elsewhere. Boycotts take many forms, but one common type is a refusal to do business with a person or a company as a means of coercing that person (or company) to do something he or she wouldn't otherwise be willing to do.

These various business practices may or may not violate the law, depending on the specific facts of a particular case. In some antitrust cases, the courts apply the *rule of reason*, weighing the specific facts to determine whether a violation has occurred. This may involve a very complex economic analysis, often involving close judgment calls. In other cases, the *per se rule* applies: some business practices are so egregiously unlawful as to be per se antitrust violations.

Federal antitrust laws establish three different kinds of legal actions to be used against businesses that engage in monopolistic practices: (1) criminal prosecutions by the U.S. government to punish wrongdoers; (2) civil actions by the U.S. government to halt monopolistic business practices; and (3) civil actions for *treble damages* by private individuals or other businesses that may have been injured by these practices. Treble damages means the victim of monopolistic business practices is entitled to recover three times his or her actual losses. This very strong remedy is intended to discourage violations of the antitrust laws.

All of these are provisions of *federal* antitrust laws. They apply to businesses engaged in interstate commerce and to local businesses whose activities in some way affect interstate commerce. The U.S. Justice Department's Antitrust Division is primarily responsible for enforcing these laws. However, where purely local businesses are involved, the jurisdiction over antitrust matters falls to the 50 states, all of which have at least some laws prohibiting monopolistic business practices within their borders. Also, state officials may sue to enforce the *federal* antitrust laws. For example, in 1990 the Supreme Court held that a state may sue to halt a merger between competing companies, even if the merger was already approved by the federal government (*California v. American Stores*, 495 U.S. 271).

In recent years, a number of American companies have also learned that antitrust enforcement isn't just a matter of satisfying federal and state regulators in the U.S. The European Union has a 20-member commission with the power to overrule mergers and acquisitions that will have an adverse effect on competition in Europe. More than one merger that won regulatory approval in the United States has been rejected by European authorities. With the globalization of world trade, no large American company can ignore European regulators and complete a merger or acquisition that has been disapproved in Europe.

The Microsoft Antitrust Case

Public attention was focused on antitrust law in the early 2000s more than at any time in recent history because of the *U.S. v. Microsoft Corp.* case. At the outset, the U.S. Justice Department and 20 states (later reduced to 18) jointly sued Microsoft, alleging a variety of unlawful business practices by the giant software company. Judge Thomas Penfield Jackson, who presided at the original trial, first determined that Microsoft in fact had a monopoly of personal computer operating systems with Windows. He then ruled that, as a matter of law, many of Microsoft's business practices were antitrust violations. For example, he ruled that Microsoft engaged in unlawful *tying arrangements*, improperly tying the Windows operating system with its Internet browser, Internet Explorer, to the detriment of Netscape, the competing browser. He also found that Microsoft charged computer makers more for Windows if they included competing application software than if they included only Microsoft products, and that Microsoft had its software engineers go to a lot of trouble to make Microsoft applications run better than competing applications under Windows--an effort to use the company's operating system monopoly to increase its market share in the applications business. He also ruled that several other Microsoft business practices were unlawful.

Having so ruled, Judge Jackson then issued orders to remedy these antitrust violations. Among other things, he ordered Microsoft broken up into two companies, one to develop and market the Windows operating system and another to do everything else Microsoft was doing. He also ordered Microsoft to sell the Windows operating system to all large computer makers for the same price, regardless of whether they included competing applications with their computers.

Judge Jackson then certified the case for a direct appeal to the U.S. Supreme Court on an expedited schedule. Microsoft opposed not only the judge's decision and his proposed remedies but also the direct appeal to the Supreme Court. The Supreme Court rejected the direct appeal, sending the case to the U.S. Court of Appeals in Washington, D.C.

In mid-2001, the appellate court unanimously overturned Jackson's proposed remedies, including the breakup of Microsoft. The court also disqualified Jackson from hearing the next round of proceedings in the case because he made inflammatory statements to the media several times. While the appellate court acknowledged that there was no evidence of "actual bias" by Jackson, the court said his comments would cause an "informed observer" to "question his impartiality."

However, the appellate court upheld Jackson's finding that "the company behaved anti-competitively... and that those actions contributed to the maintenance of its monopoly power" and also broke the law in other ways. So the case was sent back to the trial court to reconsider several issues, including appropriate remedies for Microsoft's antitrust violations, but with a different judge presiding (*U.S. v. Microsoft Corp.*, 253 F.3d 34).

The case was then assigned to Judge Colleen Kollar-Kotelly. Before she could hold new proceedings on the questions left unresolved after the appellate court decision, the U.S. Justice Department and nine states reached an agreement to settle the case. Judge Kollar-Kotelly ordered a 60-day public comment period during which supporters and foes of the settlement could comment on it. A federal law, the Tunney Act, requires such a public comment period when a antitrust lawsuit such as this one is settled. An unprecedented 30,000 written comments on the proposed settlement were filed with the court. They ranged from sophisticated legal arguments submitted by major law firms on behalf of corporate clients to short "I hate Microsoft" notes from individuals. At least two U.S. Senators, Orrin G. Hatch (R-Utah) and Patrick J. Leahy (D-Vt.) criticized the settlement, and the Senate Judiciary Committee held a hearing on it.

Meanwhile, nine other states that were parties to the antitrust lawsuit refused to go along with the settlement and sought tougher sanctions against Microsoft. Judge Kollar-Kotelly conducted a trial on their claims in the spring of 2002. A verdict was expected in mid-2002.

Meanwhile, Microsoft agreed to settle a group of private antitrust lawsuits by promising to give about $1 billion worth of software and refurbished hardware to schools in low-income areas, a proposal that drew wide criticism because the cost to Microsoft for making extra copies of its software would be next to nothing--and hardly an adequate sanction for Microsoft's monopolistic behavior toward its competitors. In early 2002, a federal judge rejected this settlement as inadequate, a move that forces Microsoft to renegotiate the deal or defend itself at a civil antitrust trial.

THE FIRST AMENDMENT AND ANTITRUST LAW

For about 150 years, Congress and the Department of Justice assumed that they had no right to regulate the business practices of the media because of the First Amendment, but that changed in the New Deal era. The economic depression of the 1930s, the formation of a labor union for journalists, and the Roosevelt administration's willingness to challenge business practices that earlier administrations ignored all contributed to new scrutiny of the media. By 1945, the U.S.

Supreme Court had twice ruled that the business practices of the mass media were very much within the government's purview. Both of these pioneering cases involved the Associated Press, the nation's largest news wire service.

The U.S. Supreme Court ruled that the First Amendment does not exempt the mass media from regulations that apply to other industries in a 1937 case involving labor laws, *AP v. National Labor Relations Board* (301 U.S. 130). The case arose when an Associated Press writer was fired for engaging in union organizing activities on behalf of the American Newspaper Guild. The guild complained to the NLRB, which found the AP guilty of an unfair labor practice. The wire service appealed the NLRB ruling, and the Supreme Court affirmed it, brushing aside the AP's argument that union activity was a threat to the agency's editorial freedom. The court said:

> The (National Labor Relations) act does not compel (AP) to employ any one; it does not require that (AP) retain in its employ an incompetent editor or one who fails to faithfully edit the news to reflect the facts without bias or prejudice. The act permits a discharge for any reason other than union activity or agitation for collective bargaining with employees.

Later in the opinion, the court added:

> The business of the Associated Press is not immune from regulation because it is an agency of the press. The publisher of a newspaper has no special immunity from the application of general laws. He has no special privilege to invade the rights and liberties of others.

A few years later, the Supreme Court again ruled against the AP's claims of a First Amendment exemption from government regulation in a landmark case involving antitrust law, *Associated Press v. U.S.* (326 U.S. 1, 1945).

This case arose when the *Chicago Sun's* application for AP membership was vetoed by its primary competitor, the *Chicago Tribune*. Under the AP's bylaws, each member was given what amounted to blackball privileges to prevent competitors from joining the wire service and gaining access to its worldwide news coverage. This policy had been in effect for nearly 100 years, but when it was used by such a prominent newspaper to blackball a well-known competitor, it invited government scrutiny.

The U.S. Justice Department challenged the exclusion of the *Chicago Sun* from AP membership as a violation of federal antitrust laws. The Justice Department pointed out that it was very easy for newspapers that did not directly compete with an AP member to join the organization. However, any potential competitor of an AP member was forced not only to get past the competitor's potential veto but also to pay a very large sum of money to join. Without joining the organization, a paper could not get AP news, since it was also against the bylaws to provide AP news to a non-member.

The case reached the Supreme Court, which ruled that these bylaw provisions indeed violated antitrust law. The high court emphasized that the First Amendment does not exempt the media from obeying laws regulating business practices:

> The fact that the publisher handles news while others (engaged in business) handle goods does not ...afford the publisher a peculiar constitutional sanctuary in which he can with impunity violate laws regarding his business practices.

Moreover, the court said, what the AP was doing amounted to a denial of the freedom to publish for many would-be members. Its bylaws, far from furthering the goal of freedom of the press, actually inhibited freedom of the press:

> Freedom to publish means freedom for all and not for some. Freedom to publish is guaranteed by the Constitution, but freedom to combine to keep others from publishing is not. Freedom of the press from governmental interference under the First Amendment does not sanction repression of that freedom by private interests.

After the Supreme Court had twice ruled against the Associated Press on questions involving the government's right to regulate its business practices, the Justice Department brought actions against a number of newspaper publishers who appeared to be violating federal antitrust laws.

NEWSPAPER ANTITRUST CASES

In the 1950s, two antitrust cases involving newspapers reached the U.S. Supreme Court, while several other important ones were decided by lower federal courts.

The first of these cases involved a newspaper accused of refusing to accept advertising from anyone who placed advertising with a local radio station. The case, *Lorain Journal Company v. U.S.* (342 U.S. 143, 1951), resulted in a unanimous Supreme Court ruling in favor of the government and against the publisher. Because the paper reached almost every home in its market area, its threat to refuse advertising from those who advertised on the radio station was a viable one: many merchants needed to advertise in the paper because there was no other way to reach a lot of their customers.

Defending its policies in court, the newspaper cited not only the First Amendment but also the well-recognized principle that a publisher has a right to refuse advertising. The Supreme Court dismissed these arguments, pointing out that antitrust law creates an exception to the publisher's right to refuse advertising. When the refusal to accept advertising is based on a desire to monopolize commerce, that right must give way to the right of other businesses to be free of monopolistic competition, the court said. A lower court injunction against the paper's business practices was affirmed, as was an unusual and slightly humiliating order that the newspaper publish a notice of the ruling every week for six months.

A decade later, the broadcaster that the *Lorain Journal* had tried to drive out of business won a treble damage civil suit under federal antitrust law (*Elyria Lorain Broadcasting v. Lorain Journal*, 298 F.2d 356, 6th cir. 1961), thus recovering three times its losses resulting from the paper's monopolistic practices.

However, a newspaper publisher fared better in another antitrust lawsuit that reached the Supreme Court in the 1950s, *Times-Picayune v. U.S.* (345 U.S. 594, 1953). In that case, the Justice Department challenged a tying arrangement in which an advertiser had to buy space in an evening paper, the *New Orleans States*, in order to get space in the same company's morning paper, the *New Orleans Times-Picayune*. A competing evening paper, the *New Orleans Item,* was the alleged victim in this tying arrangement.

When the case reached the Supreme Court, the justices voted 5-4 in the Times-Picayune Company's favor. The majority sympathized with the Justice Department's contention that this was a tying arrangement. However, the court said there was insufficient evidence of injury to the other paper to justify an antitrust action in this particular instance. This was true because the *Item* was profitable. In addition, the *Item* was gaining in ad revenue and actually carrying more advertising than its evening competitor, the Times-Picayune Company's *States*. The Supreme Court majority refused to view the *Times-Picayune* as a sufficiently "dominant" product for the tying arrangement to be unlawful. In short, the Justice Department failed to prove its case.

Was the Supreme Court right in this decision? Perhaps, but only a few years later the *Item* did fall upon hard times and was taken over by the Times-Picayune Company, forming the *New Orleans States-Item.*

Still another antitrust action against a newspaper arose in the 1950s, one that is remembered because it illustrates all three kinds of antitrust lawsuits permitted under federal law. The case, *Kansas City Star v. U.S.* (240 F.2d 643, 8th cir. 1957), resulted from a variety of questionable practices by the employee-owned Star Corporation, the publisher of Kansas City's only morning and evening daily newspapers and also owner of the leading network-affiliated radio and television stations in town. (A competing daily paper had gone bankrupt before these lawsuits were completed).

The company engaged in several monopolistic practices. For example, advertisers and subscribers had to buy a combination ad or subscription in both the morning *Times* and afternoon *Star* to get either one. You couldn't advertise in (or subscribe to) just one. In addition, some advertisers who also bought space in the competing paper before it failed were threatened with the cancellation of their ads in the Star-owned papers. Also, some advertisers were forced to buy ads in the *Times* and *Star* to get advertising on the company's radio and TV stations. In one case, a business partly owned by a major league baseball player was threatened with a blackout of news about the player on the sports pages if the business didn't discontinue its advertising in the competing paper.

Overall, it was a flagrant example of abuses by an ownership that wielded too much influence in one city. Critics of the situation suggested that being employee-owned doesn't necessarily make a newspaper more ethical than it might be if controlled by a huge out-of-town chain. Other observers saw irony in the fact that a newspaper founded by one of the most public-spirited publishers of the late

1800s--the great William Rockhill Nelson--would stoop to these depths. The *Star* gained its position of dominance because of Nelson's commitment to his community, only to abuse its power after the founder's death in 1915.

Whatever the *Kansas City Star's* distinguished past, the Justice Department took an unsentimental look at the present and filed both criminal and civil antitrust lawsuits. The Justice Department sought criminal sanctions against the corporation and some of its executives in addition to a civil order to halt the unlawful practices. A federal court of appeals affirmed criminal convictions of the corporation and the advertising manager in 1957. Shortly later, the company settled the civil suit by agreeing to sell off its radio and TV stations and to stop forcing advertisers to buy space in both papers to get space in either one.

Meanwhile, a variety of private treble damage civil suits were filed against the embattled company. The company eventually settled most of these lawsuits and returned to doing business more in the fashion founding publisher Nelson had in mind. An interesting footnote to this complex litigation is that, some two decades later, the employee owners sold the Star Corporation to Capital Cities Communications (a large media conglomerate) for $115 million, ending one of the last large-scale experiments with employee ownership in American journalism.

An antitrust lawsuit of another sort resulted in the mid-1960s when the Times-Mirror Corporation, publisher of the *Los Angeles Times,* purchased one of the last family-owned daily newspapers in Southern California, the *San Bernardino Sun-Telegram.* The Justice Department sued to force Times-Mirror to resell the *Sun* on the ground that its purchase by Times-Mirror substantially lessened competition in San Bernardino County. The city of San Bernardino is about 60 miles east of downtown Los Angeles and is the county seat of the largest county in America.

In a federal district court proceeding, the Justice Department showed that the only real competition the Sun Company had in much of that huge county came from the *Times.* Moreover, several other papers in the county either ceased daily publication or were sold to chains at about the same time. The court ruled that the *Sun*'s purchase violated federal antitrust law and ordered Times-Mirror to resell the paper. The judge's decision was affirmed without opinion by the U.S. Supreme Court in 1968 (*Times-Mirror v. U.S.*, 390 U.S. 712).

In compliance with this court decision, Times-Mirror sold the Sun Company to the Gannett Corporation, a large newspaper chain then headquartered in western New York. While Gannett owned far more newspapers than Times-Mirror, it had none in Southern California then. Therefore, this sale did not violate the law against acquisitions that tend to lessen competition.

This entire sequence of events disturbed observers of Southern California journalism for two reasons. First, in the name of preventing monopolies, the Justice Department forced an absentee owner 60 miles away to sell out to an absentee owner 2,500 miles away. Moreover, at that time Times-Mirror also owned the *Orange Coast Daily Pilot*, another suburban daily even closer to Los Angeles and even more directly in competition with the *Times* than the *San Bernardino Sun*. Certainly Times-Mirror's track record with the *Daily Pilot* had been a good one in terms of both community service and ethical business practices. Perhaps the Justice Department would have opposed Times-Mirror's acquisition of the *Daily Pilot* too, had it not happened before such acquisitions were given close government scrutiny.

Nevertheless, antitrust law is clear on this point: it's perfectly legal to buy newspapers in various markets all over America, but it isn't legal to buy nearby newspapers in overlapping markets. The fact that a management close to home may be better able to meet community needs than one thousands of miles away complicates the ethical issues here, but it doesn't change the law. On the other hand, the Justice Department has a lot of discretion in these matters. In recent years there have been other media takeovers, mergers and buyouts that would appear to be violations of antitrust law at least as flagrant as the *Los Angeles Times'* purchase of the *San Bernardino Sun*. The 1980s and 1990s were an era of deregulation and government acquiescence to mergers; deals that might not have been allowed by the country's antitrust guardians in the 1960s or 1970s were sometimes approved more recently. For example, the Justice Department made no attempt to intervene or even find other potential buyers in 1991 and 1992 when the *Arkansas Gazette* and *Dallas Times Herald* were both purchased and shut down by their crosstown competitors, the *Arkansas Democrat* and the *Dallas Morning News*, respectively.

However, during the Clinton era that approach to antitrust enforcement appeared to be changing. In 1995, the Justice Department went to court to halt the sale of the *Northwest Arkansas Times* in Fayetteville to a group with ownership ties to Donrey Media, the publisher of a competing paper in a nearby town, *The Morning News of Northwest Arkansas*. The Justice Department explained its action by issuing a news release that said, "Unless this transaction is blocked, the vigorous competition that has existed between these two newspapers for readers and advertisers will be substantially reduced or eliminated. That means the citizens of Fayetteville and Springdale will pay higher prices for their newspapers, and local businesses will pay higher advertising rates."

A federal judge agreed with the Justice Department's position and ordered the sale rescinded in mid-1995. A Justice Department spokeswoman said this marked the first time in 13 years that the agency had sued to halt a newspaper merger. The *Northwest Arkansas Times* was later sold to a company that did not own any nearby newspapers.

JOINT OPERATING AGREEMENTS

The late 1960s also produced another Supreme Court decision on antitrust law that disturbed many publishers. The case, *Citizen Publishing Co. v. U.S.* (394 U.S. 131, 1969), stemmed from a *joint operating agreement*, a kind of cooperative arrangement between once-competing newspapers that had become commonplace. Under a joint operating agreement, two newspaper publishers in the same town merge many of their business and printing operations but maintain separate editorial staffs so the two papers retain separate identities. The objective, of course, is to cut costs by only maintaining one expensive newspaper printing plant, for instance, instead of two. Obviously, it works best if one of the papers is a morning paper and the other an afternoon paper, so scheduling conflicts can be minimized. These arrangements often also include joint advertising sales, with advertisers offered a package deal and a discount if they place ads in both papers.

Such an agreement had existed between the *Tucson Daily Citizen* and the *Arizona Daily Star* since 1940. Not only did it involve a merger of production, advertising and circulation operations of the two papers, but it also involved profit pooling. In the mid-1960s, the *Star* appeared to be in financial difficulty, but a purchase offer from a large newspaper chain was rejected. Shortly later, the owners of the *Citizen* organized a new company and bought the *Star*. As a result of this series of events, the once-independent editorial staff of the *Star* found itself working for the owners of the *Citizen*.

The U.S. Justice Department challenged not only the change of ownership but the entire joint operating agreement as a violation of antitrust law. The case reached the U.S. Supreme Court in 1969, and the Supreme Court agreed that much of this cooperative arrangement was illegal. Justice William O. Douglas, writing for the court, said the only defense for acquisition of the *Star* by the *Citizen* was the "Failing Company Doctrine," which allows a company to buy out a competitor on the brink of bankruptcy. The rationale for this judicially created exception to antitrust law is that the rival company's failure would lessen competition anyway. However, Douglas said the Failing Company Doctrine didn't apply here because neither paper was failing at the time the joint operating agreement was initiated.

The decision was shocking to publishers all over America because joint operating agreements were then in effect in 22 cities, involving 44 daily newspapers. If this decision were left intact, many other joint operating agreements would also be illegal. Publishers said many of the participating newspapers would be forced to shut down because they could not afford to operate a complete business and printing facility on their own.

The American Newspaper Publishers Association, the major trade organization for the newspaper industry, went to work lobbying for a change in antitrust laws to legalize joint operating agreements. Congress obliged in 1970 with the *Newspaper Preservation Act*. Basically, this law legalized the 22 existing joint operating agreements, including the one in Tucson. In effect, Congress revised the law to overrule the Supreme Court's interpretation of it.

In addition to protecting the existing joint operating agreements, the Newspaper Preservation Act authorized the Justice Department to approve new agreements when it could be shown that at least one of the newspapers involved would fail without a joint operating agreement.

The Newspaper Preservation Act was bitterly opposed by the Justice Department, which contended it would allow publishers to enter anti-competitive arrangements even when they could survive on their own. Publishers of small newspapers also opposed it, fearing that the large papers in their area would offer joint advertising packages so attractive the smaller papers would be squeezed out of the marketplace. Also, labor unions in the newspaper field opposed the act because it authorized consolidations that would certainly eliminate jobs. Nevertheless, the act quickly moved through Congress and was signed by President Nixon.

Once enacted, the Newspaper Preservation Act was challenged on constitutional grounds by a small San Francisco newspaper, the *Bay Guardian*. This muckraking alternative paper contended that the joint operating agreement between the *San Francisco Chronicle* and *San Francisco Examiner* resulted in an unconstitutional infringement of its First Amendment rights by encouraging a monopoly that made it difficult for other papers to operate.

In a 1972 decision, a federal district judge rejected the *Guardian's* arguments, affirming the constitutionality of the Newspaper Preservation Act (*Bay Guardian Co. v. Chronicle Publishing Co.*, 344 F.Supp. 1155). However, the lawsuit against the San Francisco papers continued on other grounds and was eventually settled for an amount in excess of $1 million. Ironically, almost 30 years later Hearst sold the *Examiner* and purchased the rival *Chronicle*--and won an antitrust lawsuit challenging that transaction, which is discussed later.

New Joint Operating Agreements

In the years since its enactment, the Newspaper Preservation Act hasn't exactly produced an avalanche of applications for new joint operating agreements. In fact, the Justice Department approved only two such agreements during the 1970s, although a third pair of newspapers entered an agreement prior to receiving Justice Department approval. Two more involving major papers in large cities were approved during the 1980s, prompting court challenges in both instances.

The first application for a new joint operating agreement came in 1974, when the well-entrenched Anchorage (Alaska) *Times* and "failing" Anchorage *Daily News* asked permission to merge their non-editorial operations. The agreement was approved, but it did not help the *Daily News*: its circulation slipped to 12,000 (compared to 46,000 for the *Times*). Finally, the *Daily News* withdrew from the agreement, sued the *Times*, and sold a controlling interest to C. K. McClatchy, then the head of a strong newspaper chain in California. Taking over in early 1979, McClatchy poured money into the *Daily News,* modernizing and computerizing its operation. The editor, Katherine Fanning, who later became the first woman to be editor of a national newspaper (the *Christian Science Monitor*), upgraded the *Daily News* editorial product enough that it won a Pulitzer Prize. By 1980, its circulation was up to 30,000, while the *Times* had slipped to 44,000. And by 1990, the roles were completely reversed--it was the once-dominant *Times* that was a "failing newspaper." In an ironic turn of events, the *Times* ceased publication in 1992--after the *Daily News* agreed to carry some of the conservative columns and editorials from the *Times* in addition to its own for 10 years!

In 1979 the Justice Department approved another joint operating agreement, this one involving the "failing" *Cincinnati Post*, owned by the large Scripps-Howard chain, and the *Cincinnati Enquirer*, which was purchased during the approval process by the even bigger Gannett chain. Critics of the whole process wondered whether the *Post* was really failing or if perhaps two large chains simply saw a good way to cut their costs and enhance their long-term profit possibilities.

Meanwhile, a bizarre sequence of events unfolded in Chattanooga, Tenn., in 1980. The "failing" *Chattanooga Times* entered into a joint operating agreement with the *Chattanooga News-Free Press* without first securing the government's permission as required by the Newspaper Preservation Act. The two papers asked for Justice Department approval of their merger, but while the government was considering the issue, the *Times* abruptly fired 102 production employees, shut down its printing press, and in effect merged its printing operations with those of its crosstown competitor. After some embarrassing moments during which the Chattanooga publishers were chastised for their impatience, the Justice Department approved the Chattanooga joint operating agreement.

Seattle and Detroit Cases

One of the most bitter battles ever fought over a joint operating agreement unfolded in Seattle during the early 1980s. The financially troubled *Seattle Post-Intelligencer* and the *Seattle Times* sought government permission to merge their non-editorial operations in 1981. Under their proposed arrangement, the *Times* would publish weekday afternoons and Saturday mornings. The *Post-Intelligencer* would publish weekday mornings, while the two papers would produce a joint Sunday edition.

The proposal drew strenuous protests from a coalition of suburban newspaper publishers, major retail advertisers and employee groups, who contended the merger would result in price-fixing, excessively high ad rates, a decline in the quality of both papers and needless employee layoffs. Nevertheless, the plan was approved by Attorney General William French Smith in 1982. It was to go into effect shortly thereafter, but a federal judge granted a 60-day delay in the agreement's implementation so the opponents could challenge it in court.

In *Committee for an Independent P-I v. Hearst Corp.*, the foes of the merger won their case in federal district court, mainly because the Hearst Corporation, owner of the P-I, had not been willing to sell the paper to any of several qualified buyers who expressed an interest. Opponents of the plan contended that another owner could reorganize the paper and make it profitable as a fully separate newspaper.

However, in a 1983 decision, the ninth circuit U.S. Court of Appeals reversed the district court ruling, holding instead that it is not necessary to offer a failing newspaper for sale to justify a joint operating agreement. The ninth circuit said that Hearst had adequately shown that new management would not be successful in maintaining the paper as an independent entity. For that reason, the Justice Department's decision approving the merger was valid (*Committee for an Independent P-I v. Hearst Corp.*, 704 F.2d 467).

In its decision--a key ruling on the right of two newspapers to merge under the Newspaper Preservation Act--the court said that when there is sufficient evidence that a paper will probably fail under any ownership, the owner need not sell the paper to qualify for a joint operating agreement.

After the ninth circuit Court of Appeals ruled against them, opponents of the Seattle merger took their case to the Supreme Court, which refused to hear the case, thus ending the legal battle over the Seattle joint operating agreement.

Another legal battle over a joint operating agreement occurred in the late 1980s in Detroit, one of the few American cities that still had two truly competitive daily newspapers under independent ownership and control. In fact, it would have been hard to find another city with two competing papers as evenly matched in circulation and news coverage as the *Detroit News* and the *Detroit Free Press*.

The era of vigorous competition between the two--a Detroit tradition for a century--ended in a joint operating agreement in 1988. The *News*, which had just been purchased by Gannett, and the *Free Press*, owned by the Knight-Ridder chain, received the approval of Attorney General Edwin Meese to enter a joint operating agreement just before Meese left office. That cleared the way for the merger of all but the news departments of two of the largest and strongest newspapers ever to enter into such an agreement.

Just before the two papers were to be merged, a federal appellate court ordered the merger delayed pending an appeal of the legality of the joint operating agreement. A coalition opposing the merger, Michigan Citizens for an Independent Press, challenged the merger on the ground that neither paper was actually in danger of failing. The group contended that the two large newspaper chains had orchestrated a circulation war between the two papers that was certain to cause both to lose money--purely in an effort to justify a joint operating agreement.

Nevertheless, in *Michigan Citizens for an Independent Press v. Thornburgh* (868 F.2d 1285, affirmed 493 U.S. 38), the federal court ruled that the Justice Department had adequate legal grounds to approve the merger. The U.S. Supreme Court affirmed that ruling on a 4-4 vote with Justice Byron White not participating, thereby freeing the two Detroit newspapers to merge in 1989. (When the Supreme Court is equally divided, the lower court ruling in the case is automatically affirmed.)

In 1990, the Justice Department's Antitrust Division approved two more joint operating agreements, one involving the *Las Vegas Sun* and *Las Vegas Review Journal*, and another involving the *York (Pa.) Daily Record* and the *York Dispatch*.

Joint Operating Agreements and Newspaper Failures

By the early 2000s, the idea that joint operating agreements could save "failing" newspapers was widely questioned. While these agreements undoubtedly have saved some newspapers from oblivion (or at least postponed their demise), it was becoming clear that metropolitan daily newspapers (particularly afternoon dailies) are an endangered species--with or without joint operating agreements.

What happened in Anchorage (where a "failing" newspaper bailed out of a joint operating agreement and thrived while its non-"failing" competitor went broke) may have been unusual. However, joint operating agreements are not saving many failing newspapers. Of the original 22 joint operating agreements legalized by the Newspaper Preservation Act in 1970, only 12 remained in effect by 1995; the other 10 ended with the closing of one of the two jointly published newspapers.

In many other cities where there is a joint operating agreement, one of the two newspapers has only a tiny fraction of the circulation and revenue of the other. In San Francisco, for example, by the late 1990s the *Chronicle* had a circulation approaching 500,000, while the circulation of the *Examiner* was slipping downward toward 100,000. In 2000, the Hearst Corporation, owner of the *Examiner*, announced plans to purchase the *Chronicle* and shut down the *Examiner*--thereby ending the joint operating agreement and creating a newspaper monopoly in San Francisco. Facing an antitrust lawsuit, Hearst instead sold the *Examiner* to the publisher of a local alternative paper and an Asian weekly, under terms that led many observers to doubt that the *Examiner* could survive. Nonetheless, a federal judge eventually rejected a San Francisco politician's antitrust claims, upholding Hearst's sale of the *Examiner* and purchase of the *Chronicle* (*Reilly v. Hearst Corp.*, 107 F.Supp.2d 1192, 2000).

Even in Detroit, where the *News* was virtually even with the *Free Press* when their joint operating agreement was approved, the *News* has lost 40 percent of its circulation since that none-too-happy marriage.

Since the Newspaper Preservation Act was enacted in 1970, at least 162 daily newspapers in the United States have stopped publishing, leading some media critics to wonder, "did the Newspaper Preservation Act really preserve many newspapers?" Moreover, there are no more than 10 cities left in America with two or more independently published metropolitan daily newspapers, leading media economists to suggest that there can't be many new joint operating agreements.

One new joint operating agreement was announced in 2000 when the *Denver Post* and the *Rocky Mountain News*, rivals for more than 100 years, said they would merge all but their news departments under a new Denver Newspaper Agency.

Meanwhile, in many regions suburban dailies and especially weeklies are doing well while the nearby metropolitan daily or dailies are struggling. In fact, the leading newspaper antitrust question today may concern the tendency of the remaining metropolitan dailies to buy up all of the nearby weeklies or small dailies. Also, in some instances a newspaper chain has bought a number of adjacent suburban dailies in a metropolitan area in an apparent attempt to achieve efficiencies through joint advertising sales, production and even newsgathering. So far the Justice Department has not shown much interest in the antitrust implications of these trends.

BROADCAST MEDIA OWNERSHIP ISSUES

Few aspects of communications law have been as controversial and volatile in recent years as the questions of ownership and control of the electronic media. Congress, the FCC and the courts have all devoted endless hours to these issues. But then, that is not exactly a new phenomenon.

Just before the U.S. Justice Department challenged the Associated Press' exclusionary practices in the early 1940s, the Federal Communications Commission was taking a tough look at the way the networks (especially NBC) dominated radio broadcasting in America. Technically, the FCC has little authority over antitrust matters, but as part of its licensing process the commission is empowered to consider all factors that affect the "public interest, convenience and necessity." Thus, the FCC has the right to scrutinize the business practices and ownership patterns of broadcast licensees.

By the late 1930s, the FCC didn't like what it saw in radio broadcasting. Some

97 percent of all night-time transmitter wattage was controlled by three networks, with the vast majority of the most powerful stations affiliated with either the National Broadcasting Company or the Columbia Broadcasting System. In fact, NBC operated two different networks, both of which had affiliates in many major cities.

Even more disturbing, the networks imposed strict contractual controls on their affiliates. For instance, network affiliates were not permitted to carry any programming from another network. Moreover, affiliates were locked into five-year contracts with the networks--something the FCC found alarming in view of the fact that broadcasters were then issued licenses for only three years at a time. And the networks tied up virtually all of their affiliates' prime time programming. In addition, affiliates' rights to reject network programs were limited.

To end these abuses, the FCC issued a set of rules known as the "Chain Broadcasting Regulations" in 1941. These rules prohibited many of the questionable network practices. One provision was intended to force NBC to sell one of its two networks. NBC quickly took the FCC to court, charging that these new rules exceeded the FCC's authority and violated the First Amendment.

In *NBC v. U.S.* (319 U.S. 190), an important 1943 case that foreshadowed the *Associated Press v. U.S.* decision, the Supreme Court ruled against NBC on all grounds. The court said the First Amendment does not exempt broadcasters from government regulation of their business practices. Moreover, the court said, the FCC could properly issue rules to curb monopolistic network policies, despite the fact that enforcement of antitrust laws is beyond the commission's authority.

After this decision NBC had no choice but to sell one of its networks, so the "Blue" network--the one that NBC executives considered the weaker of the two--was sold later in 1943. That network became known as the American Broadcasting Company two years later, joining CBS and NBC to form the big three of broadcasting. The other radio network of the 1930s, the Mutual Broadcasting System, included a large number of affiliates, but most of them were in smaller markets. Mutual remained only a minor force in broadcasting.

Broadcast Ownership Restrictions

The FCC has adopted a variety of restrictions on broadcast ownership over the years to prevent monopoly control of the airwaves. However, the FCC's philosophy about this has varied greatly. The FCC first adopted tough restrictions on the number of stations one individual or company could own--and then abandoned many of those rules, little by little. The FCC has already liberalized several of its ownership rules, and more changes are likely in 2003.

The Telecommunications Act of 1996 directed the FCC to liberalize many of its remaining broadcast ownership rules. By 2002, the FCC was conducting a comprehensive review of its remaining ownership restrictions and seemed poised to eliminate many of them.

For many years no individual or company could own more than seven television stations, seven AM radio stations and seven FM radio stations nationwide. That rule was sometimes called the *Rule of Sevens*. In 1984, the FCC changed the number to 12 of each, thus creating the *Rule of Twelves*. The FCC liberalized the radio station ownership rules again in 1992, increasing the limit to 18 AM and 18 FM stations under one ownership. That limit was increased to 20 AM and 20 FM stations in 1994, with minority-controlled companies permitted to own up to 23 AM and 23 FM stations. The television station limit was left at 12 in 1992, although that limit was dropped a few years later.

Until recently, each liberalization of the ownership rules by the FCC elicited protests from Congress--and threats of legislation to reverse the FCC action. Then the roles were reversed. In the 1990s Congress directed the FCC to ease its ownership restrictions and it was the FCC that sometimes appeared reluctant to go along.

Under new rules established by the 1996 Telecommunications Act, there is no longer *any* limit on the number of radio or television stations one company may own nationwide. However, in the 1996 law Congress did retain a limit on the percent of the nation's television households one company's stations could reach, but that limit was also liberalized. Under the rules in effect between 1984 and 1996, one company could own stations that reached no more than 25 percent of the nation's television households. The limit was increased to 35 percent by the 1996 act. Note that this limit applies only to stations *owned* by a company; it does not apply to *affiliates*. Each of the major networks has affiliates that reach nearly all television households. Each network also has *network owned and operated stations*, most of them in the largest cities. The limit of 35 percent of the nation's TV households applies to these network-owned stations, and to stations owned by other broadcast groups.

The 35 percent limit has a "UHF discount" provision: only half of the households in a metropolitan area are counted toward the 35 percent cap if a company owns a UHF station rather than a VHF station there. (UHF is defined as channel 14 or higher.) Thus, one company could conceivably own stations that reach 70 percent of all television households if it owned only UHF stations. The rationale for this provision is that UHF stations draw smaller audiences. This is one of several FCC rules designed to encourage UHF station ownership.

The 35 percent limit came under attack by the major television networks in the early 2000s, and the FCC seemed ready to eliminate or further liberalize that and other ownership rules in the face of a series of adverse court decisions.

In early 2002 the U.S. Court of Appeals in Washington, D.C., ordered the FCC either to eliminate or re-justify the 35 percent cap. In *Fox Television Stations v. FCC* (280 F.3d. 1027) the court also overturned an FCC rule forbidding one company from owning both a TV station and a cable system in the same market.

The FCC also had another restriction on cable system ownership: a rule saying that no company could own cable systems serving more than 30 percent of all subscription TV households nationwide. In 2001, the U.S. Court of Appeals in Washington overturned that ownership restriction (*Time Warner Entertainment Co. v. FCC*, 240 F.3d 1126).

The same federal appellate court undermined still another aspect of the FCC's television ownership rules in a March, 2002 decision. Ruling in *Sinclair Broadcast Group v. FCC* (284 F.3d 148), the court rejected the FCC's justification for its television Duopoly Rule. The Duopoly Rule, rewritten in 1999, allows one company to own two television stations in the same market if there are eight competing "voices," which the FCC defines as television stations under eight different ownerships even after one company buys a second station. The court rejected this definition of "voices" as arbitrary and capricious because it ignores other media outlets such as newspapers, radio stations and cable television.

In mid-2002, FCC Chairman Michael Powell formed a series of committees to study the various ownership rules with the announced goal of either justifying or eliminating the remaining rules in 2003.

The 2002 review will also cover several other FCC rules, including a longtime ban on one company owning both radio and television stations in the same market. Although many longtime owners of both radio and television stations are exempt, this rule has been used to prevent some companies from acquiring both radio and television stations in the same market. The FCC has granted waivers of this rule from time to time, and the 1996 Telecommunications Act authorized the FCC to extend its existing waiver policy and grant waivers in the top 50 markets.

Although there is no longer any limit on the number of radio stations that one company may own nationwide, there are still local limits, although they too have been greatly liberalized. In metropolitan areas having 45 or more radio stations (counting both AM and FM stations), one company may own up to eight stations, although no more than five of them may be AM stations or FM stations. (This rule prevents any one company from owning eight FM stations or eight AM stations in one market). In markets having 30 to 44 stations, the limit is seven stations; no more than four of them may be either AM or FM. In markets with 15-29 stations, the limit is six stations, of which no more than four may be either AM or FM. In markets with fewer than 15 stations, one company may own no more than five stations or half of the total stations in the market, and no more than three may be either AM or FM. There is an exception for markets with three stations: one company may own two of them if the two are an AM-FM combination.

The liberalization of local radio ownership restrictions and the elimination of the nationwide radio ownership limits caused astonishing changes in radio broadcasting. Several large radio station groups quickly expanded, buying many more stations--and driving up the selling price of radio stations in the process. By 2002, Clear Channel Communications had grown from a small Texas company that owned a handful of radio stations to a giant national corporation that owned more than 1200 radio stations (about ten percent of all American radio stations).

Many new owners of station groups have combined various aspects of their stations' operations. For example, it is commonplace for station groups to program several stations jointly, manage them jointly, and sell advertising for them jointly. A company can now purchase several small stations surrounding a big city and do regional programming, including some simulcasting on the various stations. This allows a company to buy inexpensive small stations and compete with the giant metropolitan stations, encouraging listeners to tune in to whichever of the jointly programmed stations is loudest in their area. Critics say that something is lost in this equation, though: there is less local service to the small suburban towns that the individual stations once served exclusively.

The FCC's ownership rules also address another phenomenon in broadcasting: the use of time brokerage or *local marketing agreements* (LMAs) in which a station owner gives someone else the right to program the station. Like owning multiple stations in the same market, LMAs are attractive to station owners because of the cost savings possible if one station's staff can program and sell advertising for two or more stations. The ownership rules now say that a station operated under an LMA is treated as if the person or firm in control of the station actually owns it. Therefore, a company that programs stations under an LMA in a given city may not be allowed to own as many stations there.

Over the years the FCC also adopted a variety of rules restricting *cross-ownerships*. Cross-ownership is a situation in which one individual or company owns more than one kind of communications medium, usually in one market. The most notable of these rules is the newspaper-broadcast cross-ownership rule.

The FCC adopted the newspaper-broadcast cross-ownership rule in 1975. It banned new cross-ownerships between newspapers and television stations in the same market. The FCC allowed a number of companies that already owned both a newspaper and a television station in the same market to keep both.

From the beginning, this rule stirred criticism from all sides. Both broadcasters and newspaper publishers attacked the ban on new cross-media combinations. Consumer groups, meanwhile, attacked the FCC for not insisting on the breakup of more existing cross-ownerships. Lawsuits were filed by both those who felt the FCC had gone too far and those who felt the FCC hadn't gone far enough.

When the resulting case, *FCC v. National Citizens Committee for Broadcasting* (436 U.S. 775, 1978), reached the Supreme Court, the court unanimously affirmed the FCC's cross-ownership rule, thus satisfying neither group of critics. The court said the FCC had acted within its authority and had based its rule on appropriate grounds.

Since 1975, the FCC has granted only a few waivers to let multimedia owners get around the rule and acquire both a newspaper and a TV station in the same market. (The rule also banned radio-newspaper cross-ownerships, but waivers of that restriction became routine in the 1990s.) In 1998 the FCC reluctantly granted the Tribune Company a waiver to own a Miami, Fla. television and a newspaper in nearby Fort Lauderdale, and then said future waivers would be granted only rarely. However, the FCC backpedaled on this point after a biennial review of ownership rules in 2000, saying it would consider more waivers, especially in large markets with many media voices. Apparently the Tribune Company was counting on getting more waivers in 2000 when it took control of Times-Mirror Corp., publisher of both the *Los Angeles Times* and *Newsday* in New York. Tribune owns television stations in both cities.

In 2003, many of these broadcast ownership restrictions may be eliminated or revised substantially as a result of the FCC's comprehensive review of the rules.

Low-power Radio: an Alternative?

While large corporations were buying more and more stations, the FCC approved a plan to foster grassroots ownership of local radio stations. In 1998, FCC Chairman William Kennard called for a study of a proposal to allow *microradio* stations, which would be extremely low power locally owned stations that would serve a small community or a small area of a larger city. The proposal was seen as a response to the growing popularity of "pirate" radio stations that simply go on the air without a license.

At a time when some big companies own hundreds of radio stations, it has not been easy for an individual to obtain a radio license: the few new licenses that are available are being auctioned off at high prices, and existing stations also sell for enormous sums of money. In recent years, more and more people who feel they have something to say and nowhere to say it have built bootleg radio stations to broadcast a few hours a day--until being caught by the FCC. FCC officials said they shut down nearly 100 pirate radio stations during 1997 alone. To do that, the commission assigned a large part of its enforcement staff to shut down pirate radio stations.

A driving force behind the pirate radio movement was a station calling itself "Radio Free Berkeley" in California. When the FCC sought a court order to shut that station down, the station's lawyer argued that the lack of any provision for low-power radio broadcasting violated the First Amendment. A federal court at first refused to order Radio Free Berkeley off the air; it took the FCC two years to persuade the court to issue a permanent injunction against this pirate station. By the time the court finally ordered it off the air in mid-1998, Radio Free Berkeley was legendary on the Internet: imitators were springing up all over the country, with the help of free advice--and transmitter "kits"--from Radio Free Berkeley's founder.

Apparently believing that this indicated a need for low-power, minimally regulated radio stations to serve local areas, Kennard said the FCC would consider authorizing such stations. The whole idea was bitterly opposed by many licensed broadcasters concerned about interference problems from the new stations. Many broadcasters feared that, once authorized, low-power radio stations would be impossible for the FCC to control. Such stations would show up all over the radio dial on channels not authorized for them, broadcasters predicted.

Despite these concerns, in 2000 the FCC created the low-power FM radio service. In an effort to open up the airwaves to local community groups who are largely excluded from corporate-owned broadcasting, the FCC approved two classes of LPFM radio stations with maximum power levels of 10 watts and 100 watts. The new 10-watt and 100-watt stations will be heard well over a radius of 1-2 miles and 3.5 miles, respectively.

The new LPFM stations are to be noncommercial. Owners of existing radio and television stations, cable systems and newspapers are not eligible for these licenses. The licenses will be granted only to local entities at first, but non-local ownership will be allowed later. No entity will be allowed to own more than 10 LPFM stations nationwide.

To make room for LPFM stations, the FCC relaxed the mileage separation rules that protect broadcasters from interference that might be caused by nearby stations. However, Congress intervened, attaching a provision to a large federal spending bill that restricted the new low-power FM radio stations mainly to smaller markets where they can operate without violating the FCC's original mileage separation rules. Public radio stations and commercial broadcasters, fearing that the new LPFM stations would cost them listeners by causing new interference, banded together and lobbied Congress to restore the old interference standards. Congress complied, although the measure passed by Congress did allow the FCC to relax its interference standards on a trial basis in nine markets and license more LPFM stations in those places. But in most major markets, the old standards were reinstated, leaving almost no channels available for LPFM stations.

The Financial Interest and Syndication Rule

Another ownership restriction that has been eliminated is the long-controversial *Financial Interest and Syndication Rule* (often simply called the "Fin-Syn" rule). It was adopted in 1970 and was controversial from its inception until it was eliminated in several stages during the 1990s.

The Fin-Syn rule limited the right of the three then-dominant networks to produce and syndicate their own entertainment programming. Because the syndication rights to network television shows are worth billions of dollars, there has been an ongoing power struggle between the networks and Hollywood's program producers, and the Fin-Syn rule has seen almost as many revisions and court challenges as the Fairness Doctrine.

In essence, the original 1970 Fin-Syn rule curtailed the in-house production of entertainment programming by the major networks. And it prohibited the networks from acquiring a financial interest in the independently produced shows they aired. Also, the rule barred the networks from controlling and profiting from the syndication of "reruns" of network shows. The idea was to allow the independent program producers to keep the profits from off-network syndication. The FCC believed the networks had so much negotiating leverage that they would never allow independent producers to control the syndication rights without a federal rule requiring it.

The independent producers argued that they made little or no profit from the networks' initial use of their shows because the networks' payments barely covered production costs. The producers said they earned most of their profits by syndicating the shows to local stations for use as reruns. Thus, the producers said they needed the Financial Interest and Syndication Rule to keep the networks out of the syndication business.

Under this rule, many of Hollywood's independent producers prospered during the 1970s and 1980s. But by the 1990s, ABC, CBS and NBC were no longer dominant. Their share of the television audience had dropped from above 90 percent to something less than 50 percent. More and more viewers were watching made-for-cable programming, independent stations and new broadcast networks, especially Fox. It was clear that the three leading networks did not have the economic clout or the stranglehold on the viewing audience that they once had.

The FCC responded to the changing economic picture by eliminating the Fin-Syn rule in a series of steps taken between 1991 and 1995.

By 2000, the effect of abolishing the Fin-Syn rule had become clear: of 37 new series chosen for the fall, 2000 season by ABC, CBS and NBC, 24 were either owned or co-owned by the host network, according to reports in the trade press.

EARLY BROADCAST ANTITRUST CASES

Although the main efforts to regulate broadcast ownership and business practices have come from the FCC, the U.S. Justice Department has occasionally challenged broadcasters' business practices too. One notable early example was a case that reached the U.S. Supreme Court in 1959, *U.S. v. Radio Corporation of America* (358 U.S. 334). In that case, the Justice Department contended that RCA, parent company of NBC, had used NBC's clout as a network to force Westinghouse Broadcasting to trade its Philadelphia television station for NBC's less valuable station in Cleveland.

The case was an indirect result of the FCC's 1953 rules on multiple station ownership. When the FCC limited each owner (including the major networks) to five company-owned VHF television stations apiece, each major network wanted its five network-owned and operated stations to be in the largest possible market areas. At the time, Philadelphia was the nation's number four market; Cleveland was number 10.

The Justice Department claimed that NBC had threatened to lift the NBC affiliations from Westinghouse's Boston and Philadelphia stations unless Westinghouse agreed to the Cleveland-Philadelphia exchange. Also, the government said NBC had refused to grant Westinghouse an NBC affiliation for its Pittsburgh station until Westinghouse agreed to the unfavorable trade. In short, the Justice Department claimed NBC had exercised monopolistic power to coerce Westinghouse into making a bad deal, even though NBC had paid Westinghouse $3 million to make the trade more even. The two stations had identical frequency assignments: both operated on VHF channel three.

RCA responded by arguing that the FCC had approved the entire transaction, and that the FCC was fully aware of all of the facts when it did so. RCA contended that the Justice Department was barred from bringing the antitrust suit because the FCC had considered the antitrust questions before approving the deal in the first place. A federal court dismissed the suit, agreeing with RCA's contentions.

The Supreme Court reversed that dismissal. The high court pointed out that while the FCC is permitted to consider antitrust factors in approving or disapproving a change of ownership, it is not a law enforcement agency. The fact that the FCC approved the trade does not bar the Justice Department from later challenging it, the Supreme Court ruled.

The case was sent back to the federal district court for trial, but meanwhile the FCC took a new look at the situation and decided to use its licensing power to straighten things out. Acting in 1964 (eight years after the original station trade), the FCC refused to renew the license of the Philadelphia station unless NBC rescinded the trade with Westinghouse. NBC had attempted to extricate itself from the entire controversy by arranging another trade, this time offering the Philadelphia station to RKO General in return for RKO's Boston station. The FCC disapproved that trade, and instead ordered NBC to return the Philadelphia station to Westinghouse ownership, in turn accepting the Cleveland station back. This FCC-mandated second exchange occurred in 1965.

Although the *RCA* case reached the Supreme Court and created a nationwide controversy, there were relatively few Justice Department antitrust actions against the nation's broadcasters until recently. Fortunately or unfortunately, the Justice Department has often deferred to the FCC on matters of broadcast ownership, despite the FCC's lack of authority to enforce antitrust laws except indirectly through the licensing process.

There has also been one Supreme Court decision concerning cable television franchising and antitrust law. Ruling in the 1982 case of *Community Communications v. City of Boulder* (455 U.S. 40), the high court said cities are not exempt from antitrust lawsuits when they grant exclusive cable franchises. State governments have long been exempted from antitrust laws, but the court said that exemption does not automatically extend to local governments. However, it appears that the states remain free to grant antitrust immunity to local governments in spite of this decision.

The case involved a situation in which Boulder, Colo., authorized Community Communications to provide cable service in a small part of the city where TV signals were weak. About 13 years later, Community Communications sought permission to serve more of the city. The city passed an emergency ordinance forbidding the firm to expand and then drafted a cable ordinance under which other firms would be invited to apply for a city franchise.

Community sued, charging that this refusal to let it do business in much of the city--and the possibility that another company might be given a government-sanctioned monopoly--violated federal antitrust laws. The high court did not decide whether the city's action was actually illegal. Rather, it held that the city was not inherently exempt from such a lawsuit. The case was sent back to a lower court to reconsider the antitrust issues involved. As Chapter 11 notes, the Supreme Court has since ruled that exclusive cable franchises violate the First Amendment under some circumstances in *Preferred Communications v. City of Los Angeles*.

MASS MEDIA MERGERS AND ANTITRUST LAW

The last two decades have been times of unprecedented corporate mergers and acquisitions. With federal regulators clearly taking a relaxed attitude toward antitrust enforcement during much of this period, corporate America became engulfed in high-stakes consolidations. However, in certain cases the Justice Department has acted aggressively to control corporate mergers.

The mass media were deeply involved in this trend. There were numerous takeovers and buyouts of media corporations, often raising antitrust questions that would have led to enforcement actions by the federal government in an earlier time. During the mid-1990s, the three largest television networks were all purchased or merged. General Electric took control of NBC, Westinghouse purchased CBS and Walt Disney Co. purchased Capital Cities/ABC. Then in 1996 the Westinghouse-CBS combination merged with Infinity Broadcasting to create one of the nation's largest and most powerful radio groups (second in size only to the radio empire created by Clear Channel Communications).

In 1999 CBS announced still another megamerger: it joined up with Viacom in a merger under the Viacom name, bringing together CBS, Westinghouse, Infinity, Paramount Pictures, MTV, Nickelodeon, 35 television stations about 163 radio stations, Blockbuster, several major production companies, two broadcast networks (CBS and UPN) and several other cable networks--all under a single ownership. The FCC said in mid-2000 that it would modify its rules to allow the two networks to be operated jointly under common ownership. The FCC completed that action in 2001, allowing each of the largest networks to own a smaller network.

Meanwhile, Time Warner, itself a media conglomerate created by a previous high-stakes merger, took control of Turner Broadcast System, Ted Turner's media conglomerate. And in 2000 America Online, the leading Internet service provider and owner of Netscape after a previous merger, announced that it would take control of the entire Time Warner empire in a deal originally valued at an incredible $181 *billion*. By the time the merger was completed, its value was reduced to $99 billion due to the rapid decline in the value of technology stocks in late 2000. Even so, a merger of that magnitude triggered widespread concern within the federal government, among public interest groups and elsewhere, especially after Time Warner blacked out ABC programming for 36 hours during a compensation dispute with Disney in May, 2000 (see Chapter 11). The AOL-Time Warner merger won final government approval in early 2001, a year after the merger was announced. To win regulatory approval, AOL Time Warner had to make a number of concessions, including agreeing to open its broadband network to AOL's competitors.

While broadcasting companies were consolidating rapidly, so were other communications companies. In 1996 SBC Communications, the parent of Southwestern Bell, acquired Pacific Telesis, the parent of Pacific Bell, for about $17 billion, in the first-ever merger of two "Baby Bells," the regional telephone companies that were once part of AT&T. Three years later, SBC won regulatory approval to purchase still another "Baby Bell," Chicago-based Ameritech Corp. for $61 billion. This gave SBC access to a huge number of local telephone customers. Soon Bell Atlantic and Nynex, two more giant regional phone companies announced a merger.

Still another megamerger made headlines in 2000 because the U.S. Justice Department objected to it--and ultimately filed an antitrust lawsuit to prevent the merger from being completed. In this case, Worldcom, which had recently merged with MCI, a leading long-distance telephone service provider, announced plans to merge with Sprint, another large long-distance provider, in a deal valued at $129 billion.

While SBC and others were building telephone juggernauts, there were a host of mergers of cable multiple system owners (MSOs). And AT&T then became the nation's largest cable MSO by merging with what was then the nation's largest MSO, Tele-Communications, Inc., in a deal valued at $48 billion. Then in 1999 AT&T merged with MediaOne Group, another cable giant that was created by previous mergers, in a deal valued at $57.2 billion. The two AT&T mergers gave the giant telephone company cable access to 60 million American homes; AT&T

officials said they would market local phone service, Internet access and cable service to these households. Clearly, other giant communications conglomerates have the same kind of services in mind.

Some of these purchases and mergers alarmed many policy-makers not only because of their sheer size but also because of the prices being paid for cable systems. In some of these mergers cable systems were sold for up to $5,000 per household served. Even if a cable operator paid nothing for the programming it delivers to subscribers and had absolutely no other operating costs, it would take many years to collect enough subscriber fees at present-day rates just to pay off the $5,000 purchase price for each cable household. Clearly, these megacorporations were looking toward huge future profits from Internet ventures to recoup their investments.

By 2000, another issue had emerged. Local governments began using their authority to approve or disapprove transfers of franchises as a way to force open access to the high-speed Internet services offered by cable systems. Several cities, including Portland, Ore., refused to approve the transfer of local cable franchises to AT&T until AT&T agreed to allow open access. This directly challenged AT&T's business plan, which was to gain a large share of the Internet business with its broadband cable system. Eventually a federal appellate court ruled that Portland and other cities may *not* require cable companies to open their lines to competing Internet service providers (*AT&T v. City of Portland*, 216 F.3d 871). The court held that only the FCC has the authority to order cable companies to open their lines to competitors. In 2002, the FCC concluded a lengthy review of this question and declared that it would not force cable companies to open their lines to competitors in most instances. Also in 2002, cable operators won still another victory in the access battle when the U.S. Supreme Court ruled that cable systems are entitled to reduced-cost access to utility poles even if they intend to use the access to provide Internet service as well as television service (*National Cable & Telecommunications Association v. Gulf Power Co.*, 534 U.S. 327).

These mergers were just of a few of the largest of many media consolidations in recent years. In terms of both the billions of dollars involved and the number of media outlets affected, many of these mergers and purchases eclipsed the mergers of the 1980s--which at the time seemed breathtaking in their size and complexity.

In the earlier round of mergers, press baron Rupert Murdoch's News Corp. purchased most of the old Metromedia chain's broadcast properties and then bought the 20th Century Fox film studio. Murdoch then used the former Metromedia television stations as the springboard when he launched the Fox network and expanded his empire again and again with subsequent mergers.

In the early 1990s Rupert Murdoch continued his high-stakes media acquisitions, announcing a stunning deal with New World Communications in which a dozen television stations switched to Fox, abandoning affiliations with the big three networks. In some cases, that left ABC, NBC or CBS without a VHF affiliate in a major market. CBS was especially hard hit: it lost eight affiliates in the Murdoch-New World deal. That triggered a frenzy of network affiliation-switching deals around the country.

Murdoch's ongoing campaign to make Fox competitive with the other networks led to one of the most controversial ownership battles in broadcast history. NBC, apparently alarmed by another Murdoch deal that would have led to four NBC affiliates switching to Fox in 1995, filed a complaint with the FCC questioning Murdoch's compliance with the FCC's 25 percent limit on foreign ownership of U.S. radio and television stations. The issue had first been raised two years earlier by the National Association for the Advancement of Colored People when Fox tried to buy a Philadelphia television station--in a deal that fell through.

In response, the FCC Mass Media Bureau launched an investigation of News Corp., Murdoch's company, some 10 years after approving the purchase of the Metromedia stations (now the Fox Television Stations) by Murdoch and News Corp. (Murdoch, who was born in Australia, became a naturalized U.S. citizen just before he purchased the stations. News Corp., which put up most of the money to buy the Fox stations, is based in Australia but controlled by Murdoch--an American citizen.)

The investigation turned ugly; Murdoch and his defenders called it a "witch hunt" (a term Murdoch used publicly). The Mass Media Bureau proposed a restructuring of the ownership of the Fox stations that would have cost Murdoch about $500 million in taxes. However, at least three of the FCC's commissioners refused to go along with that proposal. In the end, the FCC found Murdoch's Fox Television Stations to be in violation of the 25 percent limit on foreign ownership, but the FCC also noted Murdoch's accomplishments in establishing a fourth network, something the FCC had advocated for years. The Commission invited Murdoch to seek a waiver of the foreign ownership limits based on his contributions to the public interest. This might have seemed like a minor problem for one of the world's most powerful media tycoons. However, the controversy delayed Murdoch's plans to purchase up to six more television stations, and at least one of the deals fell through. Meanwhile, the other networks were busy signing their affiliates to new 10-year contracts--before Murdoch could woo any more of them away. In the meantime, Murdoch announced another stunning deal that didn't need the FCC's pre-approval: a $2 billion partnership with MCI that would give MCI a 13.5 percent interest in News Corp.--and give Murdoch the capital for more bold acquisitions.

In mid-2001, Murdoch won regulatory approval of another broadcast merger: a plan to acquire 10 television stations owned by Chris-Craft Industries.

Meanwhile, there were big-ticket mergers in the advertising industry. For example, Benton & Bowles joined D'Arcy MacManus Masius Worldwide to become D'Arcy Masius Benton & Bowles. And foreign investment in the American entertainment industry became commonplace as two Japanese electronics giants took control of U.S. entertainment firms: Sony bought a controlling interest in Columbia Pictures and Matsushita became the corporate parent of MCA, Inc. At about the same time, a number of major newspapers were purchased by large media conglomerates, with the result that there were fewer and fewer independently owned newspapers left in the United States.

How did the antitrust laws and the FCC's cross-ownership rules affect all of these big-ticket mergers and buyouts? The Hart-Scott-Rodino Antitrust Improvements Act of 1976 requires prior government approval for all large corporate mergers and acquisitions. Both the Justice Department and the Federal Trade Commission must be notified before the merger can occur. And when a merger involves broadcast properties, FCC approval is required as well.

For the most part, these mergers drew few protests from the antitrust lawyers at the Justice Department, and the FCC routinely issued waivers of some cross-ownership rules, allowing these deals to go through. Eventually, though, many of the merged companies did have to sell some of their newly acquired properties to comply with the rules.

Moreover, in 1996 and 1997 the Justice Department carefully monitored the frenzy of radio and television buyouts, mergers and consolidations. On several occasions the Justice Department refused to approve mergers that fully complied with the FCC's rules and the Telecommunications Act. For example, in 1996 Justice refused to approve a merger that would have given one company (American Radio Systems Corp.) control of eight radio stations in Rochester, N.Y.--the maximum number permitted by the FCC's ownership rules. Justice Department officials pointed out that the company would control 64 percent of the radio advertising revenue in the Rochester market. Moreover, the company would have six of Rochester's eight most powerful radio signals. The Justice Department refused to approve the consolidation until the company sold three of its eight stations.

Much the same thing happened in the Cincinnati market, where a 1996 merger would have given Jacor Communications control of a 53% market share of radio advertising. Jacor had to sell a highly rated station to get the Justice Department's blessing for its merger.

In explaining these actions, Justice Department officials said they were looking at many factors to determine whether proposed mergers were "pro-competitive" or "anti-competitive." Factors that could make a merger "anti-competitive" might include an excessive radio advertising market share, dominance of a popular format (e.g., owning all of the album-oriented rock stations in a market), owning too many of the most powerful stations in a market, or even dominance in a certain age group that was highly desired by advertisers.

Perhaps the bottom line with all of these mergers and takeovers is that both the FCC and the Justice Department have broad discretion in deciding when to let two big companies join forces and when to play hardball with them.

ONGOING ISSUES

At a time when the nation's giant media corporations are maneuvering for bigger shares of the mass communications marketplace, there are major unresolved issues in media ownership and antitrust law.

The 1980s and 1990s saw massive media takeovers with little intervention by the Justice Department--which is supposed to act under the antitrust laws to prevent mergers and consolidations that lessen competition. At other times, relatively small mergers have received considerable scrutiny at the Justice Department.

Just what sort of merger is "anti-competitive" rather than "pro-competitive?" Does it really lessen competition when one company owns program production facilities, hundreds of broadcast stations, cable systems, television networks, national magazines and newspapers? What about foreign ownership of American communications companies? The FCC has rules limiting foreign ownership of broadcast stations, but not Hollywood production companies. Does foreign ownership in Hollywood have any implications for the public interest? Should the limits on foreign ownership of radio and television stations be liberalized?

Given the massiveness of the corporations that control so many of today's media, is there a place for something like *microradio*? Is the FCC's low-power FM radio plan a good way to democratize radio? Or will it lead to anarchy on the airwaves, as many broadcasters fear?

On the other hand, do the traditional ownership restrictions make sense in a marketplace that offers so many new choices in home entertainment programming? Should there be any cross-ownership rules today? Are these rules really in the public interest? It is not clear whether the recent actions to eliminate ownership restrictions in broadcasting will produce more or less public service in the long run. Critics contend that huge corporations such as Clear Channel Communications, which owns about 1,200 radio stations, stifle creativity in radio and dictate music playlists that do not take into account local preferences. Charges of radio payola and favoritism were being raised once again in the early 2000s. In 2002, Congress responded by considering legislation that would rein in big media companies and curb some of their alleged abuses. But these big companies are undisputably more efficient smaller ones. From the public's standpoint, is something important lost--or gained--when one company owns many radio or television stations?

What about open access to cable systems' broadband Internet services? Should corporate giants like AT&T, which is now not only the biggest long-distance telephone service provider but also the biggest cable system owner, have to open their networks to competing Internet providers? They paid top dollar for cable systems precisely to gain a monopoly on broadband access to America's homes and businesses. Should they be allowed to recoup this investment by profiting from their monopoly status? Or does the public interest require open access?

These are important questions--questions that will affect all of our lives. Fortunes may be made and lost, and the public interest may be served or disserved, as private industry and government regulators struggle with these questions.

A SUMMARY OF OWNERSHIP ISSUES

Do Antitrust Laws Apply to the Media?

For many years, publishers contended that the First Amendment exempted them from antitrust laws, but the Supreme Court ruled otherwise in 1945. Today, the mass media are subject to the same antitrust laws as other businesses.

What Business Practices Are Unlawful?

Antitrust laws forbid improper price fixing, profit pooling, tying arrangements, boycotts and certain other coercive business practices. Also, mergers that substantially reduce competition are unlawful.

What Is a Joint Operating Agreement?

Under a *joint operating agreement*, two competing newspapers merge their business, advertising and printing operations while maintaining separate editorial staffs. Some publishers say they could not stay in business without such arrangements. The Supreme Court once ruled that a joint operating agreement violated antitrust laws, but then Congress passed the Newspaper Preservation Act, legalizing existing agreements and setting up a procedure for the approval of new ones.

What Is Cross-Ownership?

Cross-ownership occurs when one party owns a combination of newspapers, broadcast properties and/or cable systems in the same metropolitan market area. Under FCC rules that have been upheld by the Supreme Court, new newspaper-broadcast cross-ownerships are forbidden, although waivers have been granted. Many other ownership combinations were also forbidden at one time. In recent years many of these restrictions have been eliminated.

What Are the Broadcast Ownership Restrictions?

Under the Telecommunications Act of 1996, there is no limit to the number of radio or television stations one company may own nationally. However, no company may own more than two television stations or eight radio stations in a large metropolitan area. In smaller markets the number of radio stations a company may own is correspondingly lower. No company may own television stations that reach more than 35 percent of the nation's television households. The FCC is currently reconsidering many of these rules.

How Will the New Technologies Affect Media Ownership?

As new technologies such as fiber optics, satellite communication, digital television and high-speed Internet access develop, the print and electronic media are converging, and the corporations behind these technologies are merging, with each seeking to offer as many communication services as possible.

CHAPTER 13

Advertising and the Law

Like broadcasting, the advertising industry has specialized legal problems not shared by other mass communications industries. In addition to all of the legal problems other communicators face, advertisers--like broadcasters--have a federal agency assigned to look after them: advertisers have to get along with the Federal Trade Commission. But to a growing extent advertisers must also deal with other federal agencies and state-level advertising regulators, sometimes including the chief law enforcement officers of many states working together.

In recent years the advertising industry has fought many battles with government regulators and even won a few. However, advertisers' victories in the regulatory arena seem minor compared to the dramatic triumphs they have achieved before the U.S. Supreme Court, which has completely rewritten the constitutional law of advertising and commercial speech since 1975.

THE FIRST AMENDMENT AND ADVERTISING

For many years, the prevailing rule was that advertising had no First Amendment protection. If a particular expression of fact or opinion could be dismissed as *commercial speech*, it could be arbitrarily suppressed by law. The *commercial speech doctrine*, as it came to be known, simply said advertisers were at the mercy of every arm of government, without the guarantees of freedom the Constitution afforded to most other kinds of speech and publishing.

That has all changed, starting in 1975. The U.S. Supreme Court handed down a series of decisions between 1975 and 1980 that established substantial First Amendment protection for commercial speech. During the 1980s, the Supreme Court wavered at times, sometimes upholding government restrictions on advertising in decisions that seemed inconsistent with the cases from the 1970s. But in the 1990s, the Supreme Court again strongly reaffirmed the First Amendment protection of commercial speech. In 1996, the high court handed down a decision on liquor price advertising that was so broad it appeared to give commercial speech *almost* the same First Amendment protection as noncommercial speech.

This line of cases is one of the best examples of American law growing through judicial precedent to be found anywhere in the mass communications field.

The starting point for this summary is a 1942 Supreme Court decision that denied First Amendment protection to commercial speech, a landmark ruling that stood for many years. That case is *Valentine v. Chrestensen* (316 U.S. 52). It stemmed from a bizarre situation. Just before World War II, a man named F.J. Chrestensen acquired a surplus U.S. Navy submarine and tried to dock it at a city-owned wharf in New York City. City authorities wouldn't let him, so he had to arrange for other dock facilities. Next, he started advertising guided tours of the submarine, but city officials wouldn't let him distribute his handbills on city streets because an anti-litter ordinance banned all but political leaflets. So he added a note criticizing city officials for refusing him dockage to the back of the handbill. Then he took the city to court for denying his right to distribute literature. The Supreme Court had just ruled in favor of that right in the first of the Jehovah's Witness cases (see Chapter Three).

When his case reached the Supreme Court, Chrestensen was in for a surprise. The high court said his back-of-the-handbill political statement was really a ruse to justify a purely commercial advertisement. And that was different from the Jehovah's Witness cases. Where purely commercial advertising is involved, the First Amendment does not apply, the court ruled.

For many years, *Valentine v. Chrestensen* was regarded as the prevailing judicial precedent on commercial speech. In fact, when the landmark *New York Times v. Sullivan* libel decision was announced in 1964, the court went to some trouble to explain why the *Valentine* rule didn't apply (the *Sullivan* libel suit was based on an advertisement). The court said the ad involved in the *Sullivan* case was an idea ad supporting the civil rights movement, not an ad for a purely commercial product or service as in *Valentine*. Thus, the *Valentine* rule still denied First Amendment protection to commercial advertising for another decade, despite *New York Times v. Sullivan*.

In 1973, the Supreme Court again denied First Amendment protection to commercial advertising, this time in a case involving the "help wanted" ads in a large newspaper. In *Pittsburgh Press v. Pittsburgh Commission on Human Relations* (413 U.S. 376), the Human Relations Commission ordered the newspaper to stop classifying its employment ads as "Jobs--Male Interest" and "Jobs--Female Interest." The newspaper contended that there were editorial judgments inherent in the decision to classify job openings that way, and that those judgments were protected by the First Amendment.

The Supreme Court disagreed, ruling that the classified ads are not only commercial speech but commercial speech promoting an illegal form of discrimination as well. The court had no difficulty in ruling that whatever First Amendment considerations might be involved were secondary to the city's right to outlaw advertising for an illegal commercial activity.

An interesting follow-up note to this case is that in 1979 the Pennsylvania Supreme Court ruled against the Human Relations Commission when it tried to stop the *Pittsburgh Press* from accepting "help wanted" ads from individuals who wished to indicate their age, sex, race or religion in the ad. The commission objected to such language as "salesman age 30," "born again Christian seeks work in Christian business," or "white woman seeks domestic work." The state high court said the job seeker had a First Amendment right to communicate such information as this, even though an employer isn't supposed to consider these factors. The U.S.

Supreme Court declined to review this second *Pittsburgh Press* decision.

Early Victories for Commercial Speech

Only two years after the original *Pittsburgh Press* decision, the Supreme Court handed down the first of its major decisions extending First Amendment protection to commercial speech (*Bigelow v. Virginia*, 421 U.S. 809, 1975). The case began in 1971 when Jeffrey Bigelow published an ad in *The Virginia Weekly* for an abortion service in New York, where abortions had just been legalized. The Supreme Court's *Roe v. Wade* decision, which held that abortions could not be banned in any state, did not occur until 1973. Both abortions and abortion advertising were illegal in Virginia in 1971.

Bigelow was prosecuted for violating the Virginia law. He appealed his conviction; the U.S. Supreme Court used his case to rewrite the Commercial Speech Doctrine. The high court emphasized that the service in question was not illegal where it was offered, and said the readers had a First Amendment right to receive this information. The court distinguished this case from *Pittsburgh Press* by pointing out that the commercial activity in question in the *Pittsburgh* case was illegal. But above all, the Supreme Court in *Bigelow* declared that this message did not lose the First Amendment protection it would otherwise enjoy merely because it appeared in the form of an advertisement. The high court said that in the future there would have to be a *compelling state interest* to justify laws prohibiting any form of commercial speech that has a legitimate purpose.

A year later the Supreme Court took another giant step toward protecting commercial speech under the First Amendment. In *Virginia State Board of Pharmacy v. Virginia Citizens Consumer Council* (425 U.S. 748, 1976), the Supreme Court overturned Virginia's state law against advertising the prices of drugs. Many other states had similar prohibitions on drug price advertising, but the Supreme Court again emphasized the First Amendment right of consumers to receive information as it overturned the state regulations.

Again, the court said the information in question was protected by the First Amendment despite its commercial nature. At that point, it seemed clear that the old *Valentine v. Chrestensen* doctrine was dead: commercial speech did have constitutional protection. However, while the court recognized the importance of price advertising to the free enterprise system, it also emphasized that this ruling in no way affected the right of governments to control false and misleading advertising.

In 1977, the Supreme Court handed down several more decisions strengthening the First Amendment protection of commercial speech. First, in *Linmark Associates v. Willingboro* (431 U.S. 85), the Supreme Court said homeowners have a First Amendment right to place "for sale" signs in front of their homes. The town of Willingboro, N.J. had outlawed "for sale" signs at a time when the area's racial composition was changing. There was considerable "white flight" and city officials wanted to discourage panic selling by white homeowners. One way to do this, the city felt, was to keep it from appearing that entire neighborhoods were for sale. A real estate firm challenged the constitutionality of the ordinance.

In defending the ordinance, city officials pointed to the social importance of racial integration and the evils of "white flight." Also, they said, homeowners who really need to sell their homes have other ways to advertise (by listing their homes with realtors or using newspaper classified ads, for instance). Nevertheless, the Supreme Court ruled against the city. In an opinion written by Justice Thurgood Marshall, the majority said the city could not constitutionally deprive its residents of the information that a for sale sign offers. "If the dissemination of this information can be restricted, then every locality in the country can suppress any facts that reflect poorly on the locality...," Marshall wrote.

Although the *Linmark* decision held that homeowners have a First Amendment right to put up "for sale" signs, many cities continued to restrict real estate signs in various ways to combat "white flight." For example, some towns allowed "for sale" signs but banned "sold" signs on the theory that the presence of a lot of "sold" signs would also send the message that many homeowners are leaving. In 2000, Philadelphia, Pa. real estate brokers abandoned a six-year effort to get that city to drop its ban on "sold" signs and filed a lawsuit that resurrects old questions about government suppression of real estate signs.

In addition to *Linmark*, in 1977 the Supreme Court handed down a commercial speech decision that was not at all surprising in view of its ruling in *Bigelow v. Virginia*. In *Carey v. Population Services International* (431 U.S. 678, 1977), the court overturned a variety of New York laws that restricted advertising of contraceptive devices. Even though these devices were legal in New York, state laws prohibited advertising, in-store displays and even sales of these products except by licensed pharmacists. Even pharmacists could not sell these devices to anyone younger than age 16. The Supreme Court found First Amendment violations in these laws and said there was no compelling state interest to justify them, as required in *Bigelow*.

In 1980, the Supreme Court established a new legal test that has been used ever since then to determine the validity of government restrictions on commercial speech. That happened in the case of *Central Hudson Gas and Electric v. Public Service Commission of New York* (447 U.S. 557).

The *Central Hudson* case challenged rules adopted by the New York Public Service Commission in 1977 in an effort to promote conservation and discourage energy use. Among other things, the commission prohibited advertising by utilities that might encourage consumption of utility services rather than conservation. The Central Hudson Gas and Electric Company challenged this wide-ranging regulation of its advertising. The company lost in the New York Court of Appeals, which ruled that the ban was justified because the need to conserve energy outweighed the slight free speech issue involved.

The U.S. Supreme Court reversed the New York court, holding that the ban on promotional advertising would have only a "highly speculative" effect on energy consumption or utility rates, and that a total ban on such advertising was going too far. If there was any doubt by this time, the court said commercial speech is constitutionally protected if it concerns "lawful activity" and is not misleading or fraudulent.

If commercial speech is constitutionally protected, how can the courts determine if a particular government restriction is proper under the First Amendment? In the *Central Hudson* case the Supreme Court said courts should evaluate government restrictions on advertising under these four criteria: (1) whether the expression is protected by the First Amendment (if it involves deception or unlawful activities, it is not protected by the First Amendment and may be banned without considering this test); (2) whether the claimed governmental interest that justifies the restrictions is substantial; (3) whether the regulation directly advances the governmental interest in question; and (4) whether the regulation is more broad than needed to fulfill the governmental interest.

This test has been cited in hundreds of cases since it was handed down in 1980 in the *Central Hudson* case, as both state and federal courts have had to rule on a variety of government restrictions on advertising.

At the same time as its *Central Hudson* decision, the high court ruled on a separate case involving *noncommercial corporate speech*, as opposed to commercial speech. The court established a different test for judging the constitutionality of government restrictions on that type of speech. This topic is discussed later in the chapter.

Lawyers' Advertising as Commercial Speech

The Supreme Court has repeatedly addressed the First Amendment rights of lawyers and other professionals who wish to advertise--and who are subject to special rules restricting their right to do so. The Supreme Court first dealt with lawyer advertising in 1977, handing down one of its most far-reaching commercial speech decisions: *Bates v. Arizona State Bar* (433 U.S. 350).

That case overturned Arizona's ban on advertising by lawyers, a rule similar to those found in nearly every other state. The case involved a legal clinic run by two young lawyers. The lawyers were disciplined by the State Bar for advertising the prices of routine legal services, prices that were far below the "going rate" charged by other lawyers.

In ruling against the state bar, the Supreme Court again emphasized the First Amendment right of consumers to receive commercial information. The court said advertising by lawyers (and presumably other professionals) could not be prohibited unless it was misleading or fraudulent. However, the court expressed reservations about ads that say something about the quality of the services offered ("we're the best lawyers in town"), because such ads could well be misleading.

That warning about misleading advertising by professionals foreshadowed two more Supreme Court rulings, *Ohralik v. Ohio State Bar Association* (436 U.S. 447, 1978) and *Friedman v. Rogers* (440 U.S. 1, 1979). In *Ohralik*, the Supreme Court affirmed sanctions against a lawyer for soliciting new clients in a manner that is sometimes called "ambulance chasing." The court said the First Amendment does not prevent a state bar association from adopting rules against that sort of conduct.

In *Friedman*, the court went a step further, upholding a Texas ban on the use of trade names by optometrists. The court said a trade name could be misleading and that it did not provide consumers important information--as did the commercial advertising in question in earlier cases. The court said a trade name could be misleading because there could be a change of optometrists (and thus a change in the quality of service offered) without the name changing. Therefore, a state is not violating the First Amendment when it requires an optometrist to practice under his own name rather than a trade name, the court ruled. This case was viewed as a slight retreat by some, and critics pointed out that it was customary and completely legal for law firms, for instance, to continue to use the names of the founding partners long after their deaths. Isn't such a name really a trade name at some point? Wouldn't that also be misleading? The court didn't address that issue.

More recently, the Supreme Court has decided a number of other commercial speech cases involving advertising or solicitations by attorneys: *In re R.M.J.* (455 U.S. 191, 1982), *Zauderer v. Office of Disciplinary Counsel* (471 U.S. 626, 1985), *Shapero v. Kentucky Bar Association* (486 U.S. 466, 1988), *Peel v. Attorney Registration and Disciplinary Commission* (496 U.S. 91, 1990), *Ibanez v. Florida Department of Professional and Business Regulation* (512 U.S. 136) and *Florida Bar v. Went for It Inc.* (515 U.S. 618). Perhaps the fact that the Supreme Court has handed down so many rulings on lawyer advertising not only illustrates how deeply divided the legal community is on this issue, but also that lawyers tend to file lawsuits when they don't like things as they are.

The case of *In re R.M.J.* involved regulations that severely restricted lawyers' advertising in Missouri. The rules allowed lawyers to use only certain words to describe the kinds of law that they practiced, and the approved words were in legalese, not layman's terms. A lawyer could not advertise that he or she handled personal injury or real estate cases, for instance. An unnamed lawyer violated these rules and was disciplined. The Supreme Court overturned the disciplinary action, holding that the attorney's advertising was protected by the First Amendment. However, the court again re-emphasized the point that only nondeceptive advertising--by lawyers or anybody else--is protected by the First Amendment.

The *Zauderer* case began when Philip Zauderer, a Columbus, Ohio, lawyer, was disciplined for publishing newspaper ads that contained a drawing of the Dalkon Shield contraceptive, which has been linked to miscarriages, injuries and possibly cancer. Zauderer's ads said that he was representing numerous women in lawsuits against the manufacturer of the Dalkon Shield and would be willing to take more cases involving the controversial device.

The Supreme Court voted 5-3 to strike down Ohio's ban on the use of illustrations in lawyers' advertising. The court said, in essence, that bar associations could require lawyers' ads to be truthful and little more.

As it had in earlier commercial speech cases, the court said in the *Zauderer* case that consumers had a right to receive the message that local authorities wanted to suppress, and that the advertiser had a right to communicate it.

The court did uphold Ohio's right to discipline Zauderer for certain aspects of his advertising, however. For example, his ads promised that women who filed Dalkon Shield lawsuits would not have to pay any lawyer's fees if they lost, since he was handling the cases on a contingent fee basis. However, women who lost their cases were still obligated to pay certain court costs, and the Ohio disciplinary committee penalized Zauderer for failing to explain that in his ads.

In 1988 the Supreme Court's *Shapero v. Kentucky Bar Association* decision overturned restrictions on targeted direct-mail solicitations by lawyers. Kentucky and about 20 other states barred lawyers from mailing solicitations to people who might have a specific need for a lawyer (in this case, people facing the loss of their homes through foreclosures).

The Supreme Court again ruled in favor of advertising by attorneys in a 1990 case, *Peel v. Attorney Registration and Disciplinary Commission*. In this case, the court said Illinois could not prevent lawyers from advertising the fact that they are certified specialists in a particular legal specialty. In a 5-4 decision, a deeply divided court held that such advertising could be false or misleading under some circumstances. However, a majority of the court also agreed that an across-the-board ban on all such advertising even when it is truthful went too far.

In 1994, the Supreme Court followed that decision by ruling that the Florida Board of Accountancy could not prevent accountants who are also lawyers from advertising that fact. In *Ibanez v. Florida Department of Professional and Business Regulation*, the court held that Silvia Ibanez, who was a certified financial planner as well as a lawyer and an accountant, could advertise these credentials on her business cards and in her yellow pages listing. To deny her that right would be an improper restriction on commercial speech, the court held.

On the other hand, a year later the Supreme Court upheld another Florida rule that prohibits lawyers from soliciting business with targeted mailings to accident or disaster victims within 30 days of the incident. In *Florida Bar v. Went For It Inc.*, the court said it was not a violation of the First Amendment for Florida to forbid such solicitations because the state has a substantial government interest in "protecting the privacy and tranquility of personal injury victims and their loved ones against intrusive, unsolicited contact by lawyers," Justice Sandra Day O'Connor said in the court's majority opinion.

The 1980s: Hedging on Commercial Speech

The Supreme Court has ruled on commercial speech rights in several other contexts, with mixed results.

In 1981 the Supreme Court ruled on the right of local governments to outlaw roadside billboards in *Metromedia v. San Diego* (453 U.S. 490). The court overturned a San Diego city ordinance banning both political and commercial billboard messages. However, the court was deeply divided in deciding the case, and Justice William Rehnquist called the decision a "virtual Tower of Babel from which no definitive principles can be drawn."

Nevertheless, a majority of the justices did agree that San Diego's billboard ban was too broad because it banned all billboards containing political messages as well as purely commercial ones. The court left open the possibility that a narrower ordinance forbidding only commercial but not political billboards would be constitutionally permissible. But beyond that, the court's five different opinions seemed to shed more confusion than light.

In 1984, the Supreme Court again addressed the constitutionality of a local ordinance restricting political signs, but this time the court decided that such an ordinance did not violate the First Amendment. In *Members of the Los Angeles City Council v. Taxpayers for Vincent* (466 U.S. 789), the court said the city of Los Angeles has the right to ban political posters on public property. The court ruled that forbidding posters on city-owned utility poles and buildings was not an excessive restriction on First Amendment freedoms. The court said this decision was not inconsistent with the *Metromedia v. San Diego* decision, in which a ban on all billboards (including those placed on private property with the owner's consent) was overturned as a First Amendment violation. In contrast, the Los Angeles ordinance only prohibited attaching posters to public property, not placing signs and billboards on private property.

In upholding the Los Angeles ordinance, the high court said a city has the right to prevent the "visual assault on the citizens ...presented by an accumulation of signs posted on public property."

What about political signs on private property rather than public property? As Chapter Three explains, the Supreme Court has ruled that a city may not ban all signs on private property conveying political messages (see *City of Ladue v. Gilleo*, 512 U.S. 43).

In view of the earlier commercial speech rulings, the Supreme Court surprised no one when it decided *Bolger v. Young Drug Products Corp.* (463 U.S. 60) in 1983. The court overturned the post office's ban on mailing unsolicited ads for contraceptive devices. The court said such a ban denies consumers access to important information that the public has a constitutional right to receive. In the majority opinion, Justice Thurgood Marshall emphasized the importance of family planning and the prevention of venereal disease as social issues, and said the post office had not adequately justified the ban on mailing this material.

Unfortunately, Supreme Court decisions are often not as consistent and predictable as the commercial speech cases of the late 1970s and early 1980s seemed to be. In 1986, there was a surprise awaiting those who thought they understood the Commercial Speech Doctrine. In *Posadas de Puerto Rico Associates v. Tourism Company of Puerto Rico* (478 U.S. 328, 1986), the court announced one of its most widely noted and controversial decisions on commercial speech. The court *upheld* Puerto Rico's Games of Chance Act of 1948, which legalized casino gambling on the island but barred casinos from advertising locally, while allowing casino advertising aimed at tourists. The law was challenged by Posadas, a Texas-based partnership that operated the Condado Holiday Inn Hotel and Sands Casino. The Tourism Company, a public corporation responsible for enforcing the island's gambling law, twice fined Posadas for advertising locally, and the casino operator eventually challenged the constitutionality of the Puerto Rican law. The local "advertising" included such things as matchbook covers and elevator signs that used the forbidden word, "casino."

The high court's majority opinion--written by Justice William Rehnquist--not only affirmed the Puerto Rican law but also mentioned alcoholic beverages and cigarettes as products whose advertising could be further restricted without violating the First Amendment. The court said, in essence, that advertising of anything "deemed harmful" enjoys less First Amendment protection than other advertising, even if the product itself is legal. Ironically, a decade later the Supreme Court would reconsider that idea and hand down a series of decisions *upholding* the First Amendment rights of alcohol, gambling and tobacco advertisers--again illustrating the uncertainties in this area of law.

In defending their law restricting gambling ads, Puerto Rican officials said the law was designed to attract tourist dollars while minimizing the harmful effects of gambling on the health, safety and welfare of Puerto Ricans. They cited "the disruption of moral and cultural patterns, the increase in local crime, the fostering of prostitution, the development of corruption and the infiltration of organized crime" as evils that the ban on local casino advertising was designed to minimize.

The Supreme Court's 5-4 majority agreed that these were substantial government purposes--substantial enough to justify restrictions on commercial speech.

The ruling attracted strenuous dissents from four justices, including William Brennan, who said the Puerto Rican law was intended to "suppress the dissemination of truthful information about entirely lawful activity merely to keep its residents ignorant." And Justice John Paul Stevens contended that the law violates the First Amendment by discriminating among the mass media. "I do not understand why (the court) is willing to uphold a Puerto Rico regulation that applies one standard to the *New York Times* and another to the *San Juan Star*."

The Supreme Court's *Posadas* ruling was clearly a setback for the advertising, broadcasting and newspaper publishing industries, all of whom filed briefs urging the court to overturn the Puerto Rican law.

The court followed up the *Posadas* decision with another ruling that upheld restrictions on commercial speech in 1989, *State University of New York v. Fox* (492 U.S. 469). In this case, the court upheld the SUNY system's rules restricting commercial activities on campus. The rules forbid using campus facilities for many types of selling; a cookware salesperson was arrested for refusing to leave a dormitory on the SUNY Cortland campus where she was conducting a "Tupperware party" in violation of the rules.

The court not only upheld the SUNY rules but also used the case to declare that governments need not use the "least restrictive means" to regulate commercial speech. If political speech is involved, the least restrictive means test still applies, but the court's 6-3 majority held that governments have more leeway in regulating commercial speech under the First Amendment. The majority said that the *Central Hudson* test (described earlier) is satisfied if there is a "reasonable fit" between a government's purpose and the restrictions on commercial speech that are adopted to help achieve that purpose.

Dissenting, Justice Harry Blackmun (joined by William J. Brennan and Thurgood Marshall) objected to this rewriting of the law by the court:

> The majority holds that 'least-restrictive means' analysis does not apply to commercial speech cases, a holding it is able to reach only by recasting a good bit of contrary language in our past cases.

The SUNY decision continued the Supreme Court's movement away from upholding commercial speech rights in close cases. For a time in the late 1980s, the court appeared to be retreating from the sweeping protection it extended to commercial speech in the 1970s. But a very different trend emerged in the 1990s.

The 1990s: Expanding Commercial Speech Rights

The Supreme Court has reaffirmed and expanded the constitutional protection of commercial speech during the 1990s, beginning with a 1993 case involving advertising circulars. By 1996, there could be no doubt that truthful commercial speech about lawful activities enjoys substantial protection from government censorship.

In the 1993 case, *Cincinnati v. Discovery Network* (507 U.S. 410), the court said the city of Cincinnati could not flatly ban newsracks for commercial literature while allowing newspaper vending machines. As explained in the section on newsrack ordinances in Chapter Three, city officials had ordered publishers of free magazines that were predominantly advertising to remove 62 newsracks from city property while allowing about 2,000 newspaper stands to remain in place.

In a 6-3 ruling, the court said the city had not provided a reasonable basis for this action. Citing the SUNY case, the court emphasized that, even though commercial speech does not enjoy the same level of protection as noncommercial speech, it cannot be arbitrarily banned. The court again said a government that bans commercial speech must show a "reasonable fit" between a legitimate government purpose (such as safety or aesthetics) and the action taken. The majority was clearly troubled when the city tried to defend its action by talking about visual blight and litter--at a time when it was acting against only the 62 newsracks for free magazines, not the 2,000 newspaper stands. The court said the city had seriously underestimated the value of commercial speech under the First Amendment.

Writing for the court, Justice John Paul Stevens wrote:

Cincinnati has enacted a sweeping ban that bars from its sidewalks a whole class of constitutionally protected speech.... We conclude that Cincinnati failed to justify that policy.

While the *Cincinnati* case was a strong affirmation of the First Amendment rights of commercial speech, the majority stopped short of giving it full First Amendment protection. The court reaffirmed that a government may restrict commercial speech when there is a "reasonable fit" between the restriction and the government's legitimate goals. This is a far lower standard than a government must meet to justify censoring noncommercial speech on the basis of its content. Moreover, shortly after handing down the *Cincinnati* decision, the Supreme Court announced a decision in which restrictions on commercial speech were upheld: *U.S. v. Edge Broadcasting* (509 U.S. 418). In this case, the court upheld laws that prohibited a North Carolina radio station from advertising Virginia's state-sponsored lottery, even though more than 90 percent of the station's listeners were in Virginia. The court said North Carolina had a legitimate governmental interest in discouraging its citizens from gambling and held that the state's ban on lottery advertising advanced that interest, even though it also prevented many listeners in Virginia from hearing ads for their own state's government-sponsored lottery.

However, in 1999 the Supreme Court ruled that the ban on broadcast advertising of gambling cannot be enforced against broadcasters in states where such gambling is legal. As noted in Chapter 11, the high court unanimously overturned the ban on First Amendment grounds in *Greater New Orleans Broadcasting Association v. U.S.* (527 U.S. 173). The court reversed a lower court decision that had upheld the ban against New Orleans broadcasters, who wanted to carry advertising for local casinos.

Writing for the court, Justice John Paul Stevens said the federal law in question fails to meet two parts of the commercial speech test set forth in the *Central Hudson* case. Noting that there are exceptions to the ban on gambling advertising for Indian-owned casinos and state-run lotteries, Stevens said the law has so many loopholes that it does not materially advance the government's claimed interest in reducing compulsive gambling.

"The operation of Section 1304 (the ban on casino advertising) and its attendant regulatory regime is so pierced by exemptions and inconsistencies that the government cannot hope to exonerate it," Stevens wrote. He said the government "cannot overcome the presumption that the speaker and the audience, not the government, should be left to assess the value of accurate and nonmisleading information about lawful conduct. Had the government adopted a more coherent policy, or accommodated the rights of speakers in states that have legalized the underlying conduct, this might be a different case," he concluded.

Two years earlier, the ninth circuit U.S. Court of Appeals ruled in a Nevada case that the ban on gambling advertising violates the First Amendment (*Valley Broadcasting v. U.S.*, 107 F.3d 1328). That decision left broadcasters free to carry gambling ads in the western states in the ninth circuit. Now broadcasters in other parts of the country are free to carry casino gambling ads. The language of the *Greater New Orleans* Supreme Court decision suggested that even broadcasters in non-gambling states are free to carry casino gambling ads as long as there is no state law that forbids gambling advertising. In fact, after this Supreme Court decision, the FCC stopped enforcing its restrictions on gambling except in the situation that led to the *Edge Broadcasting* decision: a radio or television station in a non-lottery state still cannot advertise another state's lottery in violation of the law in the state where it is licensed.

Cigarettes, Alcohol and the First Amendment

To the amazement of those who remember the Supreme Court's language in *Posadas de Puerto Rico* about the low status of advertising for products and services "deemed harmful," the court has decisively upheld not only gambling advertising but also tobacco and alcoholic beverage advertising in recent years.

In 1995, the Supreme Court overturned the beer labeling rules enforced by the Bureau of Alcohol, Tobacco and Firearms in the U.S. Treasury Department. In *Rubin v. Coors Brewing Co.* (514 U.S. 476), the high court unanimously ruled that there is a First Amendment right to disclose the alcohol content of beer on the label, something that federal law and ATF policies prohibited.

Writing for the court, Justice Clarence Thomas acknowledged that the government had a substantial interest in curbing beer "strength wars." However, he said the ban was overly broad because there are other ways the government could prevent brewers from promoting their products by emphasizing high alcohol strength. Explaining the court's decision, Thomas said, "Here (Coors) seeks to disclose only truthful, verifiable and nonmisleading factual information concerning alcohol content."

If the *Coors Brewing* case in 1995 was a victory for those who engage in commercial speech and a defeat for government regulators, the Supreme Court went even further in affirming the First Amendment protection of commercial speech in a 1996 ruling that also involved alcoholic beverages: *44 Liquormart v. Rhode Island* (517 U.S. 484).

In a case hailed by many in the advertising industry as a decisive victory, the court unanimously ruled that Rhode Island cannot ban liquor price advertising. All nine justices agreed that even the 21st Amendment, which repealed nationwide Prohibition but allowed individual states to ban alcoholic beverages, does not allow the states to legalize alcoholic beverages and then ban their advertising. The 21st Amendment, the court held, does not override the First Amendment.

Although all nine justices voted to overturn Rhode Island's ban on liquor price advertising, the justices were divided in their reasoning. There was no single majority opinion of the court. But the court's conclusion was clear enough.

At least seven of the nine justices either disavowed the *Posadas de Puerto Rico* decision or "distinguished" it (which means they said it does not apply to this situation while not voting to overturn it). Justice John Paul Stevens wrote the court's plurality opinion. When a government bans a type of advertising instead of just regulating it, he wrote, the court must exercise "special care" in applying the *Central Hudson* test. It was clear that Stevens and the three other justices who joined in all or part of his opinion wanted to extend broad First Amendment protection to commercial speech--perhaps protection as broad as that afforded to noncommercial speech.

Justice Clarence Thomas went even further: he said the *Central Hudson* criteria need not be considered because restrictions on commercial speech such as these are *per se* unconstitutional. Thomas added, "All attempts to dissuade legal choices by citizens by keeping them ignorant are impermissible."

That language is a powerful affirmation of what the advertising industry has been saying for years; one advertising industry lawyer boasted that he had those words engraved on a plaque for his office.

Justice Stevens' plurality opinion was only a little more restrained. It said:

The First Amendment directs us to be especially skeptical of regulations that seek to keep people in the dark for what the government perceives to be their own good.

Four justices joined in an opinion by Sandra Day O'Connor which agreed that the Rhode Island ban on liquor price advertising was unconstitutional, but only because the ban failed to satisfy the *Central Hudson* test. O'Connor said there was no "reasonable fit" between the ban and the state's stated goal: discouraging alcohol consumption by keeping liquor prices high. One thing that clearly troubled several justices was the across-the-board nature of the Rhode Island law: it left open no alternate channels of communication for businesses that want to advertise liquor prices.

Given the four different opinions, *44 Liquormart* was not as clear an affirmation of the First Amendment status of commercial speech as it might have been. Nonetheless, commercial speech has come a long way since 1942--when the Supreme Court said it had no First Amendment protection at all.

The *44 Liquormart* decision created doubts about the validity of many other laws restricting alcoholic beverage and cigarette advertising. For example, the city of Baltimore enacted ordinances banning almost all billboards for beer and cigarettes. A federal appellate court had rejected lawsuits challenging the Baltimore ordinances, but in 1996 the Supreme Court ordered the lower court to reconsider in light of the *44 Liquormart* decision. The appellate court did reconsider--and still upheld the Baltimore ordinances. The court said Baltimore had a right to ban billboards that would encourage minors to smoke and drink illegally, while leaving cigarette and beer advertisers with alternate means of getting their message out to adults. The billboard advertisers then appealed to the Supreme Court, but the high court declined to take up the issue at that point (see *Anheuser-Busch Inc. v. Schmoke* and *Penn Advertising v. Schmoke*, 101 F.3d 325, cert. den. 520 U.S. 1204). That inspired many other cities and states to follow Baltimore's lead and restrict cigarette and alcoholic beverage advertising, particularly billboards and point-of-sale advertising.

Then the Supreme Court intervened again. In 2001, the court ruled that the regulation of cigarette advertising is federally preempted under the Federal Cigarette Labeling and Advertising Act, thereby invalidating hundreds of state and local laws banning or restricting tobacco ads. In *Lorillard Tobacco Co. v. Reilly* (533 U.S. 525), a case challenging restrictions on tobacco advertising in Massachusetts, the court ruled by a 5-4 vote that many of the state's regulations violated the First Amendment as well as being federally preempted

Writing for the court, Justice Sandra Day O'Connor said the states may not single out cigarette advertising for special restrictions. She said the states may still use their zoning powers to regulate all advertising, but they cannot target cigarette advertising without intruding into a federally preempted area.

This case marked the second time in about a year that the Supreme Court overturned a government attempt to regulate cigarette advertising or marketing. In 2000, the court said the Food and Drug Administration lacked the authority to curb cigarette marketing by regulating tobacco as a drug (in *FDA v. Brown & Williamson Tobacco*, which is discussed later). Neither ruling involved the Federal Trade Commission's authority to regulate cigarette advertising.

The *Lorillard* case was a challenge to Massachusetts regulations forbidding tobacco ads within 1,000 feet of any school, park or public playground and requiring retailers to post point-of-sale advertising at least five feet off the floor, out of the immediate sight of young children. The court overturned those rules, and in the process swept away state and local restrictions on cigarette ads in many other states by holding that the regulation of cigarette advertising is federally preempted.

The court also ruled that Massachusetts' restrictions on outdoor and point-of-sale advertising for cigars and smokeless tobacco, which are *not* federally preempted, are invalid because they violate the First Amendment. As the court did in overturning Rhode Island's ban on alcoholic beverage price advertising in *44 Liquormart* and the federal ban on broadcast ads for casino gambling in *Greater New Orleans Broadcasting*, the court once again refused to allow a "vice exception" to the First Amendment--abandoning the rationale used to justify Puerto Rico's ban on local advertising by casinos in the *Posadas de Puerto Rico* case.

In a concurring opinion joined by Justices Antonin Scalia and Anthony M. Kennedy, Justice Clarence Thomas was again the court's most outspoken defender of "vice advertising." "Harmful products, (like) harmful ideas, are protected by the First Amendment," he wrote. He also objected to the court's "uncertain course" on commercial speech, with "much of the uncertainty being generated by the malleability of the four-part balancing test of *Central Hudson*," he noted.

Justice O'Connor's majority opinion was more reserved, but it also said Massachusetts was violating the First Amendment as well as the federal labeling law because the rules were overly broad: the 1,000-foot buffer zone meant tobacco ads were banned virtually everywhere in the major cities. She cited *Reno v. ACLU*, the case in which the court rejected a ban on indecency on the Internet because it denied adults their First Amendment rights in the name of protecting children (see Chapter 10), and said the same principle applies to tobacco advertising. "Protecting children from harmful materials... does not justify an unnecessarily broad suppression of speech addressed to adults," she wrote.

The result: unless anti-smoking groups can persuade Congress to end the federal preemption, tobacco advertising will be governed by federal law--and by the industry's 1998 settlement of a massive lawsuit by 46 states against the industry. In the $206 billion settlement, the industry voluntarily agreed to discontinue billboard advertising, stop using cartoon characters or otherwise targeting underage smokers and to bankroll an anti-smoking billboard campaign. That settlement was not affected by the *Lorillard Tobacco* decision.

The Federal Cigarette Labeling and Advertising Act forbids only broadcast advertising of cigarettes while requiring health warnings in ads and on cigarette packages. If the federal law or FTC regulations were to be expanded to further curtail tobacco advertising, that, too, could raise First Amendment issues, given the court's recent rulings on "vice" advertising. Taken together, the *Greater New Orleans* case on gambling, the *Coors* and *44 Liquormart* cases on alcoholic beverages and now the *Lorillard Tobacco* decision on cigarette advertising illustrate just how far the court has come since its *Posadas de Puerto Rico* decision in 1986.

Forced Advertising and the First Amendment

Still another advertising issue involving First Amendment rights was addressed in two U.S. Supreme Court decisions and several lower court cases in the late 1990s and the early 2000s: mandatory assessments imposed on growers to pay for generic advertising of farm products. Many growers object to state and federal programs that force them to pay for advertising campaigns with which they may disagree.

In 2001, the Supreme Court ruled that a forced advertising program violated the First Amendment. Ruling in *U.S. v. United Foods Inc.* (533 U.S. 405), the court overturned a federal program that required all mushroom growers to pay for generic advertising. United Foods, a Tennessee mushroom grower, objected, preferring to do its own advertising that emphasized the quality of its mushrooms as opposed to those grown elsewhere.

Writing for the court, Justice Anthony M. Kennedy said that the advertising assessments constituted "compelled speech." He traced the history of prior cases involving such issues as government agencies forcing all workers to pay union dues that are used for political purposes in concluding that coerced speech is just as unconstitutional as a government ban on speech.

The *United Foods* decision was surprising to many court-watchers because only four years earlier the Supreme Court had upheld a California state program that required all growers to pay for generic product advertising (*Glickman v. Wileman Brothers & Elliot Inc*, 521 U.S. 457). Justice Kennedy distinguished the new case from *Glickman* by pointing out that the growers in the earlier case were part of an association that had a regulatory marketing scheme. No such arrangement exists in the mushroom industry, he pointed out.

Another factor about *Glickman* is that it drew a lot of criticism from First Amendment scholars--and the California Supreme Court found a way to get around it. In a follow-up to *Glickman*, the California court ruled that there may be a right under the state constitution to opt out of certain forced advertising programs even when there isn't under the federal constitution (*Gerawan Farming v. Lyons*, 24 C.4th 468, 2000). The California court pointed out that the state constitution guarantees the right to "freely speak... *on all subjects*" and rejected the idea of reduced constitutional protection for commercial speech.

The U.S. Supreme Court didn't go that far in *United Foods*, but the court did overturn one form of government-mandated advertising assessment.

CORPORATE FREEDOM OF SPEECH

While the Supreme Court was extending some First Amendment protection to commercial speech, the court also began to protect another kind of speech: *noncommercial corporate speech*. The court took a major step in this direction in 1978, ruling that corporations also have First Amendment rights. In *First National Bank v. Bellotti* (435 U.S. 765), the court overturned a Massachusetts law that forbade corporate advertising for or against ballot measures except when such a measure might "materially affect" a company's business. In reaching this conclusion, the court emphasized the importance of a free flow of information, even when some of that information comes from corporations rather than individuals. The decision raised doubts about the constitutionality of limits on corporate political advertising in about 30 other states.

Massachusetts tried to defend its ban on corporate political advertising by arguing that corporations have so much money they could drown out other viewpoints if allowed to advertise. However, there was no evidence presented to prove that, and the court wasn't persuaded. Another problem with the Massachusetts law was that it allowed corporations engaged in mass communications (newspapers, television stations, etc.) to say anything they pleased on political issues, but that freedom was denied to other corporations. The Supreme Court said that, if anything, banks and other financial institutions might be better informed on economic issues than the mass media.

Thus, *First National Bank v. Bellotti* was a major victory for corporate advertising. It didn't guarantee corporations any special right of access when the media refuse to accept their issue-oriented advertising (a problem discussed later in this chapter), but it did say that, where the media are willing to accept advertising from corporations, a state cannot prohibit it just because it comes from a company instead of an individual or a campaign committee.

As explained earlier, when the Supreme Court decided the *Central Hudson* case in 1980 (affirming the right of utility companies to advertise for more business, even if the advertising might encourage energy use rather than conservation) the court also handed down an important decision on noncommercial corporate speech: *Consolidated Edison v. Public Service Commission of New York* (447 U.S. 530). In that case, the court said the New York Public Service Commission could not prevent utility companies from sending their customers inserts with their bills that discussed "political matters" or "controversial issues of public policy."

Like the *Central Hudson* case, *Consolidated Edison* challenged rules adopted by the New York Public Service Commission in 1977. In this case, New York's highest court had held that the ban on inserts with bills was a reasonable regulation of the time, place and manner of speech.

The U.S. Supreme Court reversed the New York court on that point, ruling that the ban on bill inserts was an excessive restriction of corporations' First Amendment rights.

This was a major victory for the First Amendment rights of corporations. Unlike the *First National Bank* decision, which came on a narrow 5-4 vote, this case was decided by a 7-2 majority--with seven justices voting to uphold the right of corporations to speak out on the issues of the day. In addition, the court set forth legal guidelines that can be used to determine whether future restrictions on corporate speech are valid.

The court noted the distinction between commercial advertising, in which a company seeks to promote sales of a product or service, and noncommercial corporate speech, in which a company expresses its views on controversial social or political issues. When a government attempts to restrict noncommercial corporate speech as opposed to commercial speech, the Supreme Court established a more stringent test than the one applied to the regulation of commercial speech in the *Central Hudson* case. When noncommercial corporate speech is involved, the Supreme Court said government restrictions are justified only if one of these three conditions is met: (1) the restriction in question is a "precisely drawn means of serving a compelling state interest;" (2) the restriction is required to fulfill a "significant government interest" and merely regulates time, place and manner, leaving open "ample alternate channels for communication;" or (3) there is a narrowly drawn restriction on speech under a few special circumstances where disruption of government activities must be avoided, such as at a military base.

In 1986, the Supreme Court again reaffirmed that corporations have First Amendment rights in *Pacific Gas & Electric Company v. Public Utilities Commis-

sion of California (475 U.S. 1). In this case, the Public Utilities Commission (PUC) had ordered PG&E, a large utility company, to insert a utility watchdog group's materials with consumers' utility bills in place of the company's own newsletter four times a year. The court held that the PUC order violated the First Amendment rights of the utility company. Four justices joined in a plurality opinion that said the company's newsletter "receives the full protection of the First Amendment." They said forcing the company to insert an outside group's material in place of its own is unconstitutional.

A fifth justice (Thurgood Marshall) agreed that the PUC could not force a utility company to insert notices from outside groups with utility bills, but he also said that corporate communications should not enjoy full First Amendment protection. And three other justices dissented, saying they would have allowed the PUC to require utility companies to insert a watchdog group's materials with utility bills.

This was, in short, a mixed victory for corporate First Amendment rights, delivered by a deeply divided Supreme Court. And corporate speech rights fared no better in a 1990 Supreme Court decision, *Austin v. Michigan State Chamber of Commerce* (494 U.S. 652). In this case, the court affirmed a Michigan law that prohibited contributions to political candidates from the general treasury of a company or private association, while allowing contributions from special-purpose funds. The majority declared that this type of restriction on corporate speech does not violate the First Amendment, at least in part because it does allow corporations to endorse or oppose candidates through separate funds or political action committees. The court did *not* reverse its earlier rulings on corporate freedom of speech in this case. This case does, nonetheless, represent a limitation on the First Amendment rights of corporations and private associations.

What does all of this mean? It means that there is still a hierarchy of First Amendment protection, depending on the nature and source of the message. Commercial advertising still enjoys less constitutional protection than idea-oriented or "editorial" advertising and similar forms of noncommercial corporate speech. But even noncommercial corporate speech enjoys something less than complete First Amendment protection.

ADVERTISING AND MEDIA ACCESS

Is there a constitutional right to place an ad in the media? Or may an advertiser buy space (or time, in the case of broadcasting) only if those who control the media are willing to accept the ad? To put it another way, is there any right of access to newspapers or radio and television stations?

The answer to these questions has traditionally been simple and straightforward: there is no right of access to the media for either editorial or advertising purposes. However, it took several important court decisions in the early 1970s to settle that question. Even so, under certain unusual circumstances, a right to advertise may exist--particularly if the rejected advertiser can show that the refusal to place his material fell within a pattern of unfair or monopolistic business practices. Also, under certain circumstances government-sponsored media cannot deny public access.

A good starting point in summarizing the principles of advertising and access is a 1933 Iowa Supreme Court decision. It's ancient history, but it was a pioneering court decision in favor of a newspaper's right to accept or reject advertising from whomever it pleases. The case, *Shuck v. Carroll Daily Herald* (247 N.W. 813), simply ruled that a newspaper is a private enterprise, and its management has no duty to be a common carrier that serves everyone who may come along.

In the decades since, courts have repeatedly ruled the same way when would-be advertisers demanded space in commercial newspapers. For instance, in 1970 a federal appellate court turned down a labor union's appeal for access to the advertising columns of the *Chicago Tribune*. In that case (*Chicago Joint Board - Amalgamated Clothing Workers of America v. Chicago Tribune*, 435 F.2d 470), the court rejected the union's claim that major newspapers should be public forums. The union wanted to run ads protesting a department store's sale of imported clothing, but no daily newspaper in Chicago would accept the ads. The union argued that there should be a First Amendment right of access under those circumstances. Nevertheless, the federal court affirmed the publisher's right to reject advertising even if it means one side of a controversial issue will not be heard. The U.S. Supreme Court declined to review the decision.

In 1971, another federal appellate court ruled against a movie producer who objected to censorship of his ads by the *Los Angeles Times*. In *Associates & Aldrich v. Times Mirror* (440 F.2d 133), the court declined to rule that the newspaper had any obligation to publish movie ads at all, much less any duty to publish them exactly as submitted.

These decisions were setbacks for advocates of public access to the press, but an even greater defeat came in 1974, when the U.S. Supreme Court handed down its landmark decision on access to the print media. The decision, *Miami Herald v. Tornillo* (418 U.S. 241), overturned a Florida state law creating a limited right of access.

The case arose when Pat Tornillo, a Miami teacher's union leader, ran for the state legislature. The *Miami Herald* twice editorially attacked Tornillo. Tornillo demanded space for a reply. The law seemed to be on his side when he made this demand: Florida had a right-of-reply law requiring newspapers to publish replies when they editorially attacked candidates for office. The *Herald* turned Tornillo down and he sued, invoking the Florida law. The state Supreme Court ruled in his favor, and the newspaper appealed to the U.S. Supreme Court. The Supreme Court unanimously reversed the Florida ruling, affirming the newspaper's First Amendment right to control its content without government interference. Thus, the court invalidated Florida's right-of-reply law.

Writing for the court, Chief Justice Warren Burger said, "a responsible press is an undoubtedly desirable goal, but press responsibility is not mandated by the Constitution and like many other virtues it cannot be legislated." The First Amendment simply does not permit a government to tell a newspaper publisher what to print and what not to print, he noted.

Of course, this case involved a state's attempt to dictate editorial content rather than advertising, but the decision affirmed the publisher's right to control the content of his entire publication; the ruling was not limited to the news side. In the years since *Tornillo*, courts have continued to reject any right of access to the editorial and advertising columns of newspapers and magazines except when there was evidence of unfair or monopolistic business practices. (Note that this case applies to the *print media*. As explained in Chapter 11, *broadcasters* are subject to some mandatory access rules that do not apply to the print media.)

What sort of monopolistic business practices would cause a court to force a newspaper to accept unwanted advertising? A good example is provided by a series of lawsuits challenging the classified advertising policies of the *Providence Journal* and *Providence Evening Bulletin*. These papers did not accept ads from rental referral services, a policy they defended as necessary to prevent fraud.

In a complex series of lawsuits, several rental referral services challenged this policy. They claimed it violated federal antitrust laws because the Providence papers enjoyed a virtual monopoly in their market and were, in fact, competitors of the rental services (both newspaper ads and rental referral services help people find housing).

At first the federal courts upheld the Providence papers' policies as reasonable anti-fraud measures: they said the referral service challenging the policies was guilty of deceptive practices. However, in 1983 a federal appellate court ruled that there was no evidence of fraud by another referral service. Thus, the court said the Providence papers were violating antitrust laws by denying advertising space to this would-be competitor. However, by then this referral service had gone out of business, and a federal judge awarded just $3 as token damages. (See *Home Placement Service v. Providence Journal*, 682 F.2d 274, 1982, and 9 Med.L.Rptr. 2518).

The point: a newspaper that enjoys a virtual monopoly in its service area (as many papers do) risks an antitrust lawsuit if it denies advertising space to someone whose business might be viewed as being in competition with the paper. However, aside from potential antitrust situations, both print and broadcast media are generally free to reject advertising if they wish. As Chapter 11 explains, there are a few circumstances when broadcasters must accept advertising that the print media are free to reject. The most important of these is political advertising in federal elections, which broadcasters must accept under Section 312(a)(7) to the Communications Act. Newspapers and magazines, on the other hand, may turn down all political ads or even accept ads for one candidate and not others. There is no Equal Time Rule for the print media.

Under some other circumstances, however, advertisers feel they have more access to print than to the broadcast media. Many broadcasters voluntarily exclude ads espousing controversial ideas. A number of major corporations have attempted to place issue-oriented ads on television, only to be rebuffed. Several of them, notably Mobil Oil and the Kaiser Corporation, have purchased newspaper and magazine ads to protest their denial of advertising space in the electronic media. For whatever practical reasons, the print media have been much more willing to carry idea ads than broadcasters, although neither medium is ordinarily under any legal obligation to do so.

The print media are also more receptive to some other kinds of ads. For example, many broadcasters voluntarily reject hard liquor ads, and federal law has prohibited broadcast advertising of cigarettes since 1971. The print media routinely carry ads for these products.

If neither the print nor the broadcast media must ordinarily carry ads to which the management objects, does that settle the matter of public access to all media?

Not necessarily. One communications medium that has provided considerable public access is cable television. In fact, for many years cable public access rights were mandated by FCC regulations. The Supreme Court's *FCC v. Midwest Video* decision eventually overturned those regulations, saying the FCC exceeded its authority by adopting what amounted to common carrier requirements for cable systems.

However, state and local governments that issue franchises to cable systems may negotiate public access requirements as part of the franchising process, and federal law requires cable systems to provide public, educational and government access channels under certain circumstances.

Access to Government-Sponsored Media

Another exception to the rule that there is no mandatory access to the media involves government-run communications media. Under some circumstances government-sponsored media have an obligation to be *viewpoint neutral*, and that may involve accepting advertising that the staff might prefer to reject.

Starting in the 1960s, several state and federal courts recognized a limited right to advertise on city buses. When state action is involved, as it is with these media, courts sometimes ruled that the authorities were constitutionally required to accept controversial advertising. For example, a federal court in New York and a state court in California both prohibited public transportation systems from flatly denying space to advertisers whose ideas they disliked. (See *Kissinger v. New York City Transit Authority*, 274 F.Supp. 438, and *Wirta v. Alameda-Contra Costa Transit District*, 68 C.2d 51).

However, the idea that there should be any general right of access to state-run media was dealt a severe blow by another U.S. Supreme Court ruling, *Lehman v. Shaker Heights* (418 U.S. 298). In that 1974 decision, handed down the same day as the *Tornillo* ruling, the Supreme Court denied a political candidate's appeal for access to the advertising space on a city-run bus line. The bus line's policy was to accept only commercial ads, not political ads, and the Supreme Court denied that the First Amendment creates any right to advertise even on government-run media such as this. Although the Supreme Court has repeatedly said city streets and parks, for instance, are "public forums" protected by the First Amendment, it refused to rule that ad space on city-run buses is automatically a public forum.

On the other hand, if a state-run communications medium rejects one candidate's ads while accepting others, the person whose ads are rejected may still have a case under the Fourteenth Amendment's "equal protection" clause, the court said. But in the *Lehman* case, all political ads were rejected; there was no discrimination, and the advertising acceptance policies were *viewpoint neutral*.

As a result of the *Lehman* decision, courts in recent years have usually refused to order access to ad space even in government-run media, as long as those in charge follow their advertising acceptance policies consistently.

However, the problem of public access to a state-run communications medium sometimes takes a different perspective when the management creates a public forum by accepting some political and social issue ads, while rejecting ads from those whose ideas it dislikes. A federal appellate court so ruled in a case involving the Washington, D.C. public transit system. In *Lebron v. Washington Metropolitan Area Transit Authority* (749 F.2d 893, 1984), the court held that transit officials could not reject a photo montage critical of the Reagan administration by artist Michael Lebron after accepting a variety of other political ads.

In 1998, a federal appellate court reached the same conclusion when a public transit system rejected anti-abortion ads after accepting other ads concerning sex and family planning. In *Christ's Bride Ministries v. Southeastern Pennsylvania Transportation Authority* (148 F.3d 242), the court held that the transit system had created a public forum by its ad acceptance policies. Therefore, the court ruled that the transit system violated the First Amendment by rejecting an ad in which an anti-abortion group wanted to say, "Women Who Choose Abortion Suffer More & Deadlier Breast Cancer."

On the other hand, if a government medium consistently accepts only commercial advertising and does not create a public forum for political and social issue ads, it can reject such ads. In *Children of the Rosary v. City of Phoenix* (154 F.3d 972), another 1998 decision, a federal appellate court upheld the right of a city-run bus system in Phoenix, Ariz. to reject anti-abortion advertising because the buses consistently carried only commercial advertising.

It is not easy to reconcile all of the varying court decisions involving the right to advertise in state-run media, but the prevailing rule since *Lehman* seems to be that there is no such right unless an agency of government accepts some ads of a certain type and then arbitrarily rejects other similar ads.

In 1995, the Supreme Court called new attention to this issue by ruling that Amtrak is a government agency for First Amendment purposes in *Lebron v. National Railroad Passenger Corp.* (513 U.S. 374)--another case involving artist Michael Lebron. Thus, when Amtrak rejected Lebron's proposal to purchase space for a political ad on "The Spectacular," a large billboard in New York City's Penn Station (controlled by Amtrak), that raised a First Amendment issue, the court held. The case was remanded to a lower court to conduct a First Amendment-based analysis and determine whether Amtrak as a government agency had any obligation to accept the billboard display. The proposed display combined a photo montage and text to attack the family that owns the Coors Brewing Co. for their support of conservative political causes.

A federal appellate court reconsidered the case and said Amtrak's status as a government agency didn't change anything. In a brief opinion, the court concluded that the First Amendment was not violated because Amtrak had never accepted any political advertising for The Spectacular--and had no obligation to do so in the future. Therefore, Amtrak had the right to reject Lebron's display (see *Lebron v. National Railroad Passenger Corp.*, 74 F.3d 371, 1995). As noted earlier, the Supreme Court ruled in *Lehman v. Shaker Heights* that even government-run media are entitled to reject political advertising as long as they do so consistently.

FEDERAL ADVERTISING REGULATION

Beyond the issues of advertising access and commercial speech, advertising law is a field dominated by the Federal Trade Commission and, to an increasing degree, other federal agencies as well as state and local regulatory agencies.

Unquestionably, the FTC is the most important single regulatory agency for advertisers. Created by the Federal Trade Commission Act in 1914, this independent federal agency is responsible for overseeing many kinds of business activities in America. The 1914 act said: "Unfair methods of competition in commerce are hereby declared unlawful; the Commission is hereby empowered and directed to prevent persons, partnerships, or corporations from using unfair methods of competition in commerce."

The FTC's initial mandate was to prevent unfair business practices--but only for the protection of other businesses. It was not at first given the job of protecting consumers from fraudulent business practices.

Perhaps this was because of a very old tradition in American advertising. The prevailing attitude was "caveat emptor" (roughly translated, "let the buyer beware"). For several centuries, that meant advertisers were free to flagrantly exaggerate the merits of their products. Newspapers in the 1800s were full of fraudulent advertising, most notably ads for patent medicines. These medicines were trumpeted as cures for everything from colds to cancer, although many of them had no medicinal value at all.

The consumer who was deceived by this false advertising had few legal remedies under the common law; the only remedies available involved complicated lawsuits that were difficult to win. Most victims of advertising fraud had no choice but to accept their losses and vow not to be fooled again.

However, the Federal Trade Commission quickly made false advertising one of its main concerns. By the 1920s, the majority of its enforcement actions involved advertising. The FTC contended that false advertising was unfair to other businesses. For instance, in a famous case that went all the way to the Supreme Court, the FTC challenged a company that advertised clothing as "natural wool" when it was really only 10 percent wool. In *FTC v. Winsted Hosiery Co.* (258 U.S. 483, 1922), the court agreed that false advertising is a form of unfair competition, since it diverts customers from honest merchants' products to those of dishonest competitors.

However, a few years later the Supreme Court curtailed the FTC's crusade against false advertising by ruling that the agency had no authority to act on behalf of consumers in the absence of evidence that the false advertising was unfair to a competing business. That happened in 1931, in *FTC v. Raladam* (283 U.S. 643).

As a result, the FTC's powers were sharply reduced, but only temporarily. In two other cases during the 1930s, the Supreme Court upheld FTC actions against deceptive selling tactics (see *FTC v. R.F. Keppel & Brother*, 291 U.S. 304, and *FTC v. Standard Education Society*, 302 U.S. 112). And in 1938, Congress enacted the

Wheeler-Lea Amendment, authorizing the FTC to act against "unfair or deceptive acts or practices" that might mislead the consumer. Wheeler-Lea also expanded the FTC's enforcement powers.

The FTC operated under this enabling legislation until 1975, when its powers were again expanded by the Magnuson-Moss Act. That law specifically empowered the commission to act against fraudulent practices all the way down to the local level. No longer would it be limited to practices involving interstate commerce as it had been; instead, the FTC could pursue businesses that merely "affected" interstate commerce. In addition, Magnuson-Moss authorized the FTC to issue "Trade Regulation Rules," orders carrying the force of law that govern business practices in entire industries.

Under these broad new powers, the commission entered an unprecedented period of activism in the late 1970s, but some of its actions so angered many business leaders that they prevailed upon Congress to hold up the FTC's budget until the agency changed its policies. As a result, in 1980 the agency briefly had to lock its doors and cease all operations. Finally, it was given an operating budget, but with severe restrictions on its authority, in the Federal Trade Commission Improvements Act of 1980. The 1980s saw a much tamer FTC in action, pursuing advertising fraud with far less enthusiasm than was true a decade earlier. By the 1990s, though, the FTC returned to a more aggressive posture in enforcing the advertising rules.

Before discussing those trends, we should describe the FTC's basic structure and enforcement powers, and explain what it did to abuse those powers--in the opinion of Congress.

FTC Enforcement Tools

The Federal Trade Commission, like the Federal Communications Commission, is an independent regulatory agency. It is governed by a five-member commission, with an administrative staff of more than 1,000 persons. The five commissioners are appointed by the president with Senate ratification.

How does the FTC go about the task of enforcing the rules against deceptive advertising? First, the FTC uses a three-part analysis to determine if a particular advertisement is deceptive: 1) Identify each affirmative claim or material omission and ask the advertiser to document what the ad says; 2) determine whether the claim could mislead a typical consumer acting reasonably; and 3) determine whether the claim is "material" (i.e., is it likely to affect purchasing decisions?). In deciding this, the FTC looks at the "net impression" created by an advertisement.

How does the FTC even locate advertising messages that may be deceptive? In addition to relying on complaints from consumers and competitors, the FTC does a lot of its own monitoring of the traditional media and, increasingly, the Internet. Once what appears to be a widespread problem is identified, the FTC may conduct a *sweep*: a simultaneous law enforcement action targeting numerous businesses of a certain kind in a particular region. Often the FTC staff works closely with a state's attorney general in these actions. Investigators may "test shop" many businesses--or systematically surf the Internet for a particular type of advertising that is under investigation. These sweeps often yield dramatic results--and send a message to others that the FTC is out there looking for false or misleading advertising.

Once the FTC decides an advertising message is unlawful and that formal action is warranted, the commission may use a variety of enforcement tools. Although most involve legal actions, the FTC's most effective means of controlling fraudulent advertising is often publicity. Since an advertiser's whole purpose is to persuade a segment of the public to buy or believe something, one of the worst things that can happen to an advertiser is to have the same media that carry the ads also publish news stories reporting that a government agency thinks the ads are false.

But beyond the clout of its press releases, the FTC has a variety of enforcement powers. The agency often acts on the basis of complaints from consumers or other businesses, but whatever the source of a complaint, the first step in an enforcement action is usually for the FTC to notify an advertiser that it considers his or her ads deceptive or misleading. The advertiser may be provided a copy of a proposed *cease and desist order*, along with supporting documents. Rather than face the lengthy and costly proceedings that lead to the issuance of such a decree, the advertiser may well choose to sign a *consent agreement*, agreeing to discontinue the challenged advertising without admitting any wrongdoing.

Even though this is a relatively informal way to settle an FTC complaint, the consent agreement is placed in the public record. There is usually a 60-day period for public comment on it, after which the FTC may issue a *consent order*, which carries the force of law.

In some cases, the FTC is willing to let an advertiser merely sign an affidavit called an *assurance of voluntary compliance*. But under either this procedure or the more official consent order, the FTC usually negotiates with the advertiser to reach a settlement. The agency prefers to avoid its more formal proceedings when possible, not only to save staff time but also to halt the misleading advertising quickly enough to protect the public. A typical advertising campaign runs for only a few months; the entire campaign may be over long before the FTC can complete its formal proceedings.

However, if the advertiser refuses to sign a consent order, the agency may initiate formal proceedings. Those proceedings involve bringing the advertiser before an administrative law judge, who will hear both the commission's and the advertiser's arguments and issue a ruling. The commission has the right to review the judge's decision, and may issue a formal cease and desist order, which the advertiser may then appeal to a federal appellate court. Because these are civil proceedings, the defending advertiser isn't afforded the full rights available in criminal trials. For instance, an administrative law judge may decide the FTC is wrong and the challenged ads are perfectly legal. In a criminal trial, that would be an acquittal and would end the proceeding. But here, the FTC can rule that the ads are illegal and issue a decree anyway, ignoring the judge's findings. The advertiser has no recourse then, except to appeal the FTC decision to a federal appellate court.

Once a consent order or cease and desist order is in effect, the advertiser faces large civil penalties--sometimes $10,000 a day or more--for violating its terms.

In addition to these enforcement tools, the FTC uses several other procedures. For example, the FTC can bring a legal action against an advertiser in a federal district court, avoiding the delays inherent in the handling of cease and desist orders.

Another option is for the FTC to publish purely advisory *Guides*. These pamphlets tell advertisers how the FTC interprets the law on a given point, such as the use of testimonials in advertising or product pricing. Violating a *Guide* is not a violation of law, but *Guides* are valuable to advertisers because they provide insight into the FTC's current thinking on various advertising practices. Another similar FTC action is to issue *Advisory Opinions*. Like *Guides*, they are voluntary, but they differ in that they are issued in response to inquiries from advertisers rather than on the commission's own initiative.

A similar policy guideline--but carrying the force of law--is called a Trade Regulation Rule, or "TRR." These rules generally apply to an entire industry, requiring certain specific advertising practices and forbidding others. The liberal use of TRRs was largely responsible for the Congressional action to limit the FTC's authority in 1980.

During the 1970s the FTC also launched another major effort to control advertising fraud, this one through an *Advertising Substantiation Program*. In this program, the FTC required certain industries to document all of the claims in their ads, something that produced voluminous and highly technical reports in some cases.

In 1984, the FTC--under the guidance of James C. Miller, a new chairman who disagreed with many of the agency's earlier regulatory efforts--revised its advertising substantiation policies. Instead of demanding that entire industries substantiate their ad claims, the new policy called for the FTC to demand substantiation mainly from individual companies.

Two more of the FTC's most controversial approaches to enforcement have been *Affirmative Disclosure Orders* and *corrective advertising*. Affirmative disclosure involves requiring the advertiser to reveal the negative as well as the positive aspects of a product. In a pioneering case of this sort, a federal appellate court upheld an FTC order aimed at the makers of Geritol. Geritol was advertised as a "tired blood" cure for the elderly, and the manufacturer was ordered to reveal that it did little to help people with certain kinds of anemia (*J.B. Williams Co. v. FTC*, 381 F.2d 884, 1967).

The FTC required hundreds of advertisers to reveal similarly negative facts about their products after this decision. Banks and savings institutions were obliged to advertise that there were "substantial interest penalties" for early withdrawal of money, and automakers who quoted mileage ratings from government tests had to tell customers, "your mileage may vary."

Many advertisers found these requirements onerous and embarrassing, but corrective advertising angered the business community even more. Probably the most famous FTC corrective advertising order was one aimed at Warner-Lambert Company, maker of Listerine mouthwash. For nearly a century, Listerine had been advertised as a cure for colds and sore throats, a claim that medical research did not support.

The FTC ordered Warner-Lambert not only to spend $10 million on advertisements admitting that Listerine would not cure sore throats, but also to preface the correction with the phrase, "Contrary to prior advertising." Warner-Lambert appealed the FTC ruling, but the federal appellate court affirmed the corrective order--although the court did agree that saying "contrary to prior advertising" was just too much penance. Warner-Lambert was allowed to run its corrective ads without that confession of past sins (*Warner-Lambert Co. v. FTC*, 562 F.2d 749, 1977). Warner-Lambert asked the Supreme Court to review this ruling, but the high court declined to do so.

The FTC issued a number of other corrective advertising orders in the 1970s, including one that required the makers of STP oil additive to publish ads telling the public its claims that STP would reduce auto oil consumption were based on unreliable road tests.

Two decades later, the FTC again required a petroleum company to do corrective advertising. In 1997, the Exxon Corporation settled an FTC complaint by agreeing to run television ads informing consumers that its most expensive premium grade of gasoline does not keep engines cleaner or reduce maintenance costs. Exxon previously aired ads claiming its Exxon 93 Supreme gasoline "has the power to drive down maintenance costs" and "keeps your engine cleaner." In fact, all grades of Exxon gasoline contained the same engine-cleaning additives, which are similar to those in many other brands of gasoline, the FTC noted. While agreeing to do corrective advertising in 18 major markets, Exxon did not admit any wrongdoing in connection with its previous advertising.

The FTC ordered corrective advertising in another field in 1999, directing the manufacturer of Doan's back-pain medicine to spend $8 million on ads including the words, "Although Doan's is an effective pain reliever, there is no evidence that Doan's is more effective than other pain relievers for back pain." The FTC took this action because Doan's manufacturer, Novartis, and its predecessor, Ciba-Geigy Corp., spent about $65 million over a 20-year period on advertising claiming that Doan's was better for back pain than other pain relievers, a claim that could not be substantiated.

In 2000, the Bayer Corporation agreed to spend $1 million on consumer education to settle FTC charges that it made unsubstantiated claims in its aspirin ads. Bayer ads said that aspirin will prevent heart attacks and strokes without explaining that some persons may not benefit or may actually be harmed by an aspirin regimen. Bayer agreed to give free brochures to consumers to correct its advertising, and to do print ads to tell consumers of the availability of these brochures.

Other Examples of Enforcement Actions

In addition to these cases involving various forms of penance by advertisers, the FTC has acted against thousands of other advertising campaigns that the agency considered to be false, misleading or deceptive. A few examples will illustrate the FTC's approach to advertising regulation.

Perhaps the best-known FTC case for many years, in part because it produced a U.S. Supreme Court decision, was the "sandpaper shave case," *FTC v. Colgate-Palmolive Co.* (380 U.S. 374, 1965).

In one of the most famous television ads of the era, Colgate-Palmolive Rapid Shave was shown shaving the sand off of sandpaper. The only problem was that what the viewer really saw was sand being scraped off a transparent plastic sheet. The FTC contended that this was deceptive and ordered the ads halted. Colgate-Palmolive chose to fight the order and set out to prove that the sand really could be shaved off a sheet of sandpaper. The company did it, but it took a little longer in real life than in the ads: about 90 minutes.

The Supreme Court eventually upheld the FTC's conclusion that the ad was deceptive. In so ruling, the Supreme Court did not say that all television mockups are deceptive. But, the court said, mockups that are central to the point of the ad or enhance the product are deceptive. A common industry practice was to use mashed potatoes in place of ice cream because of the heat generated by television lighting. The court used that mockup to explain its point. Perhaps showing actors eating ice cream that was really mashed potatoes would not be deceptive if the point of the ad was to promote something else, but it would be deceptive if the point was to sell the ice cream by showing its rich texture and full color, the court said.

In the years since the *Colgate-Palmolive* decision, the FTC has acted against a wide variety of advertising practices. The FTC has gone after advertisers who used a number of other mockups, mockups that hardly seem as flagrantly deceptive as the Rapid Shave commercial. In one Lever Brothers commercial for All detergent, an actor was shown standing in a huge washing machine with a stain on his shirt. The water rose to his neck and then receded--and the stain vanished. The FTC said it was deceptive, since the whole process couldn't really happen that fast.

On another occasion, the FTC went after the makers of Prestone Anti-Freeze for a commercial showing the "magnetic film" in Prestone protecting a strip of metal from acid. The FTC objected because the acid used in the demonstration was not the same kind encountered in auto radiators and because certain other test conditions didn't duplicate what really happens in a car.

Often the FTC has based its complaints on ads that were literally true but nonetheless deceiving. As early as 1950 the commission acted against a cigarette manufacturer for advertising that a study found its brand lower in tar and nicotine than others tested. That was true, but the study also concluded that all brands tested were dangerously high in tar and nicotine. The ads were literally true but still misleading, the FTC said.

The FTC has also challenged advertising claims that were controversial and dealt with issues on which there was scientific disagreement. In 1974, the commission filed a complaint and sought an injunction against the National Commission on Egg Nutrition for publishing ads that said, "there is no scientific evidence that eating eggs increases the risk of heart and circulatory disease." A federal appellate court upheld the FTC's action to halt this advertising claim, although the court overruled an FTC order requiring future egg ads to say the health issue was controversial and that experts differed.

The FTC has also expressed considerable interest in misleading testimonials.

The commission requires that celebrities who endorse products actually use them, and that "experts" who give endorsements must really be experts. Moreover, the claims users make in endorsements must in fact be verifiably true. A grass-roots or "plain folks" ad cannot have someone saying he gets 50 miles per gallon from his Guzzlemobile Diesel when tests indicate it won't deliver over 40. In fact, an ad in which "Mrs. Holly Hollingsworth" of "Guzzle Gulch, Nevada" endorses a product must actually show Mrs. Hollingsworth, not an actress portraying Mrs. Hollingsworth.

In 1978, the commission even acted against entertainer Pat Boone for what the FTC considered to be a misleading endorsement of a skin-care product. The FTC accused the manufacturer, the advertising agency and Boone of participating in false and misleading advertising. The FTC charged that the product would not cure acne as the ad implied it would. The commission sought a $5,000 penalty from Boone, and he signed a consent order agreeing to pay the $5,000 into a fund to compensate customers who were misled by the ad.

This action, the first to hold a celebrity accountable for a misleading endorsement, was a major shock to other celebrities who endorse products. After the Boone incident, virtually all celebrities demanded *indemnification clauses* in their endorsement contracts. (Indemnification means the advertiser has to pay any penalty the celebrity might incur because of the ad.)

Nevertheless, two other well-known celebrities, actors George Hamilton and Lloyd Bridges, were sued in the late 1980s for appearing in ads endorsing an investment plan that turned out to be fraudulent. After the plan's promoters went bankrupt and investors lost millions of dollars, both actors settled the lawsuits by paying undisclosed sums to those who lost money by investing in the plan.

Like testimonials, comparison advertising has attracted the FTC's attention, especially during the 1970s. Traditionally, advertisers have hesitated to criticize each other's products, partly out of fear of lawsuits and partly because industry self-regulation codes discouraged the practice. But in 1979, the FTC issued a policy statement demanding that the advertising industry and broadcasters drop their restrictions on comparative ads and calling on advertisers to compare their products "objectively" against competing brands by name.

If the 1970s saw the FTC push aggressively into new areas such as advertising substantiation, corrective advertising and comparative advertising, the 1980s were an era of retrenchment. In fact, in the mid-1980s there was growing uncertainty about the FTC's basic rules defining what constitutes deceptive advertising. In 1983, FTC Chairman Miller released an "enforcement policy statement" that said the commission would henceforth only regard advertising as deceptive if it harmed a hypothetical "reasonable consumer." However, it was not clear what legal weight this new statement would carry, and it was widely criticized in Congress as inadequate to protect the public from false and misleading advertising.

By the 1990s, the FTC was again aggressively pursuing advertisers who were allegedly guilty of misleading consumers. For example, in 1993 the commission launched a highly publicized effort to stop five of the nation's largest commercial diet programs from engaging in deceptive advertising. The FTC accused the five of making unsubstantiated weight-loss claims and disseminating consumer testimonials that did not represent the typical experiences of consumers who used these programs. The FTC said the weight-loss firms had to include in their advertising disclaimers such as: "For many dieters, weight loss is temporary," or "This result is not typical. You may be less successful."

Three of the five firms signed consent decrees agreeing to comply with the FTC's demands. The other two, Jenny Craig and Weight Watchers, engaged in protracted legal battles against the FTC. Weight Watchers won at least a minor victory against the FTC in 1994 when a federal appellate court ruled that the company had the right to sue the FTC to challenge the agency's enforcement policies for the weight-loss industry. Weight Watchers charged that the FTC was changing its rules governing weight-loss advertising on a case-by-case basis instead of conducting a formal rulemaking proceeding to change its rules (*Weight Watchers International v. FTC*, 47 F.3d 990).

The FTC also challenged the dietary claims made by the Eskimo Pie Corp. in its "Sugar Freedom" line of dessert products. The FTC charged that the company falsely advertised its products as low or significantly reduced in calories although some of them contained up to 16 grams of total fat, 10 grams of saturated fat and 260 calories per serving. The FTC said the failure to disclose the fat and calorie content was deceptive in light of the company's ads suggesting that the American Diabetic Association had endorsed the desserts. In 1995, the Eskimo Pie Corp. signed a consent decree in which it agreed to disclose the total fat content of any product marketed for diabetics, and to refrain from falsely claiming that any of its products have been endorsed by any organization. For its part, the Eskimo Pie Corp. denied trying to misrepresent its products, but said it settled the FTC lawsuit "to get this issue behind us." The company also dropped the "Sugar Freedom" name from its products.

At almost the same time as its actions against weight-loss programs and the Eskimo Pie Corp., the FTC sought a $2.4 million civil penalty, the largest up to that time for a violation of an advertising order, against General Nutrition Inc., the operator of about 1,500 GNC stores. GNC was accused of violating previous consent orders by making unsubstantiated claims about various health-oriented products. GNC eventually signed a consent decree in which it agreed to pay the $2.4 million penalty and stop making unsubstantiated health claims for its products.

In 1999, the Mazda Corporation agreed to pay $5.25 million in fines and civil penalties--the largest such payment ever--for alleged violations of an earlier FTC order requiring the car maker to disclose the terms of its car and truck leases in its print and television advertising. Among other things, the FTC concluded that the disclosures were in small and unreadable print, offset by distracting images and sounds, and on screen for too short a time.

FTC Actions Against "Unfair" Practices

The commission increasingly looked beyond advertising that was merely deceptive or misleading and began to act against ads it considered unfair even though they were truthful, starting in the 1970s. Critics came to call this policy the *Unfairness Doctrine*, an obvious reference to the Federal Communications Commission's Fairness Doctrine in broadcasting.

The FTC's definition of what it considers unfair advertising was summarized in a 1994 policy statement. An advertisement is unfair if it: (1) causes or is likely to cause substantial consumer injury; (2) which is not reasonably avoidable by consumers themselves; and (3) is not outweighed by countervailing benefits to consumers or competition.

The FTC's authority to act against ads that are merely "unfair" was affirmed by the U.S. Supreme Court in a 1972 decision, *FTC v. Sperry Hutchinson Co.* (405 U.S. 233). The court said the FTC has the power to act against "business practices which have an unfair impact on consumers, regardless of whether the practice is deceptive ...or anti-competitive in the traditional sense."

After that ruling, the FTC initiated a series of controversial actions against "unfair" advertising. In 1979, for instance, the commission responded to bicycle ads in which it felt unsafe riding habits were shown by ordering the advertiser to distribute public service ads on bicycle safety.

The FTC also used its authority during this era to issue Trade Regulation Rules to ban allegedly unfair practices in a variety of industries. These campaigns stirred bitter opposition among businesses and eventually in Congress.

For example, in 1978 the commission initiated a very controversial proposal to severely restrict television advertising aimed at children. The proposed restrictions would have completely banned advertising aimed at young children and prohibited ads for sugared food products targeted to older children. At one point before the commission voted on the matter, the FTC chairman at the time, Michael Pertschuk, made public statements on the issue that were so prejudicial that national organizations in advertising sought--and won--a court order prohibiting him from voting on the matter. The order was reversed by a federal appellate court, but industry leaders never trusted him again.

The FTC also proposed rules forcing funeral directors to list all their prices and service options, as well as rules requiring used car dealers to inspect the cars they sell and post a list of mechanical problems on each car. On other occasions, the commission acted to break up Sunkist Growers, an agricultural cooperative, and launched campaigns against various trademarks, seeking to take them from their owners and have them declared generic words. The FTC also issued rules requiring trade and vocational schools to provide a great deal of information to incoming students, and let them withdraw with a prorated tuition refund during their programs.

The FTC's policy on corrective advertising had angered the advertising profession. The extensive use of the Unfairness Doctrine against advertisers intensified that feeling, as did the move to ban children's television advertising. Chairman Pertschuk's public pronouncements further united the business community against the commission. Finally, the rules aimed at morticians, used car dealers, the Sunkist cooperative and trade schools were the FTC's undoing.

Responding to nationwide protests about the FTC's regulatory zeal, Congress refused to appropriate a budget for the agency in 1980 and then enacted the restrictive Federal Trade Commission Improvements Act. This law extended the FTC's funding for three more years, but at a high price. It temporarily prohibited the

FTC from acting against advertising that is only "unfair" but not deceptive or misleading. Responding in part to the industry's complaints and in part to the Supreme Court's rulings extending First Amendment protection to advertising, Congress declared that FTC actions should not be aimed at truthful advertising.

In addition, the 1980 act halted the FTC proceeding on children's television until the commission published a new specific proposal aimed only at "deceptive" advertising, and ordered the FTC to publish the text of every proposed new rule at the start of the rule making proceeding. The FTC eventually terminated its study of advertising aimed at children in 1981 without taking any action.

The 1980 act specifically set aside the FTC's actions involving morticians and agricultural cooperatives such as Sunkist Growers (although the FTC later adopted extensive regulations concerning advertising by morticians). Moreover, the commission was ordered to give Congress advance notice of new proposed rules. The 1980 law also declared that Congress would have the power to veto future FTC regulations. Finally, the FTC was ordered to reduce the paperwork burden it had imposed on businesses and to stop trying to invalidate businesses' trademarks.

Taken as a whole, these revisions constituted a substantial curtailment of the Federal Trade Commission's power. Business interests lobbied heavily in Congress to harness the FTC; their campaign happened to fit in with the mood of the times. Certainly popular distaste for government regulation was a factor in Ronald Reagan's decisive victory in the 1980 presidential election.

FTC Chairman James C. Miller, appointed soon after Reagan took office, pledged to reverse many of the commission's policies of the 1970s. For instance, Miller urged Congress to retain the 1980 FTC Improvement Act's ban on FTC actions against advertising that was merely "unfair" and not deceptive. In the years that followed, Congress repeatedly debated the merits of the Unfairness Doctrine--and eventually allowed the FTC to act against unfair advertising again.

Congress exercised its power to veto FTC regulations in 1982, overturning the FTC's long-awaited rules requiring auto dealers to disclose known defects in used cars. However, later that year a federal appellate court ruled that Congress did not have the right to give itself this veto power. In 1983, the Supreme Court agreed, ruling in an unrelated case: *Immigration and Naturalization Service v. Chadha* (462 U.S. 919). With that one ruling, the high court invalidated some 200 different laws that gave Congress the power to veto actions taken by agencies in the executive branch of the federal government.

The proper role of the Federal Trade Commission has been a subject of ongoing Congressional debate ever since. By the early 1990s the FTC had abandoned the non-regulatory posture it assumed during the 1980s, and Janet Steiger, the FTC chairwoman in the first Bush administration, declared that henceforth the FTC would take a more aggressive posture in enforcing the advertising laws. She said the FTC wanted to eliminate the public perception that the agency was no longer interested in fighting false and misleading advertising.

The FTC followed through on that pledge. By 2000, the FTC was nearly as agressive as it had been in the 1970s, launching hundreds of regulatory actions against advertisers every year. The agency was especially targeting weight-loss and nutrition advertising, advertisers who made questionable environmental claims and almost any kind of false, misleading or unfair advertising that might appear on the Internet.

The FTC released industry-wide regulations to prevent false or misleading "green" or environmental advertising claims in 1992. Among other things, the new rules require those who claim a product has "recycled content" to document the amount that really is made from recycled materials. The rules also prohibit the use of terms such as "ozone safe" or "ozone friendly" if the product contains any ozone-depleting chemical, and they ban the use of terms such as "biodegradable" to describe products that will not degrade quickly when buried in a landfill.

The FTC, "Joe Camel" and Cigarette Advertising

One of the most controversial advertising campaigns in American history involved "Joe Camel," R.J. Reynolds' cartoon character used to promote the Camel cigarette brand. "Old Joe," or "Smokin' Joe," as his fans sometimes called him, first appeared in European advertising for Camel cigarettes during the 1970s. A massive "Old Joe Camel" campaign was launched in the United States in 1988--and drew immediate fire from critics of the tobacco industry. Their main claim: "Old Joe" unfairly targeted under-age smokers.

Before the controversy ended, the entire tobacco industry was fighting new restrictions on cigarette advertising from coast to coast--restrictions that ultimately led to a Supreme Court decision overturning state and local laws regulating cigarette ads: *Lorillard Tobacco Co. v. Reilly* (discussed earlier).

During the mid-1990s, the Federal Trade Commission spent several years trying to decide how to deal with cigarette advertising, and particularly how to handle "Old Joe Camel." In 1994, the FTC voted 3-2 not to pursue an unfair advertising complaint against "Old Joe." But three years later, the FTC voted 3-2 to reverse itself and bring legal action to halt the "Old Joe" campaign.

This strange case began after the attorneys general of 27 states jointly asked the FTC to halt the ads, contending that the "Old Joe" campaign resulted in a huge increase in smoking among teen-agers. Joined by various public health and consumer groups, they cited large statistical increases in overall smoking rates among teen-agers, and pointed out that Camel's market share among under-age smokers increased enormously after the "Old Joe" campaign began. They argued that this cartoon camel--this "debonair dromedary"--was enormously appealing to teen-agers. In refusing to halt the "Old Joe" ad campaign in 1994, a deeply divided FTC decided that R.J. Reynolds was targeting young adults rather than teen-agers and that, in any case, the company had a First Amendment right to use this cartoon character. In reaching that conclusion, the FTC's 3-2 majority rejected the recommendation of its own staff, which contended that "Old Joe" did encourage underage smoking. For its part, R.J. Reynolds vehemently denied that the "Old Joe" campaign targeted teen-agers, despite its stunning success with that segment of the market.

Soon after the 1994 FTC vote, *Advertising Age*, a leading advertising industry trade publication, took the unusual step of urging R.J. Reynolds to discontinue the "Old Joe" campaign in spite of the company's victory at the FTC. The influential trade journal said this step would be wise because "Old Joe" provided an easy target for antismoking groups that want to ban all cigarette advertising. A week later, R.J. Reynolds' president replied in a letter to the editor, refusing to halt the campaign.

By 1997, however, the public mood had changed. Cigarette manufacturers were on the defensive everywhere. And there was far more evidence that cigarette makers had indeed set out to target teen-agers. The FTC then reconsidered the "Old Joe" issue and voted 3-2 (with two new commissioners in the majority) to launch a legal action designed to banish "Old Joe" as an unfair advertising image that improperly targeted under-age smokers. The FTC not only voted to ban "Old Joe" but to order R.J. Reynolds to run a corrective advertising campaign to combat under-age smoking.

Meanwhile, R.J. Reynolds faced many other legal problems stemming from the "Old Joe" campaign. For example, in 1994 the California Supreme Court ruled that individual citizens could sue R.J. Reynolds for targeting minors with the "Old Joe" campaign on the ground that it encouraged them to violate state laws against under-age smoking. In *Mangini v. R.J. Reynolds Tobacco Co.* (7 C.4th 1057), the state court said lawsuits based on cigarette advertising are not federally preempted under the Federal Cigarette Labeling and Advertising Act. The California court said that, while this federal law does preempt most state regulation of cigarette advertising, it does not prevent lawsuits against advertising that would encourage "illegal smoking by youths." Although the U.S. Supreme Court later ruled that regulating cigarette advertising *is* federally preempted, the high court declined to review the California court's ruling at that point, clearing the way for the *Mangini* case to go to trial. When that happened, R.J. Reynolds began negotiating with representatives of antismoking activist Janet Mangini, the lead plaintiff, and various government agencies that joined in the lawsuit.

In 1997, R.J. Reynolds settled the *Mangini* case, agreeing to halt the "Old Joe Camel" ad campaign permanently in the United States. Although Reynolds had announced the end of the "Old Joe" campaign earlier, its demise was made a part of this settlement, along with a large cash payment to fund anti-smoking advertising aimed at teen-agers.

The FTC ultimately dropped its civil lawsuit against R.J. Reynolds after the tobacco industry reached its landmark $206 billion settlement with 46 states. The industry agreed to end billboard advertising, to stop using cartoon characters and to refrain from targeting underage smokers. The industry also agreed to compensate the states for some of the health costs associated with cigarette smoking. (The other four states--Mississippi, Texas, Florida and Minnesota--reached a separate $40 billion settlement with the tobacco industry earlier.)

Despite the tobacco industry's promises, the Federal Trade Commission reported in 2001 that the industry had dramatically increased its overall spending for advertising and marketing after the settlement. At about the same time, five states jointly sued R.J. Reynolds for allegedly breaching the terms of the settlement, accusing Reynolds of being the worst offender in the industry in marketing to young people. (In 2000, Phillip Morris, America's largest cigarette maker, had pledged that it would voluntarily stop advertising in about 40 magazines heavily read by teen-agers, a step that Reynolds, among others, did not take.)

Other Federal Regulators

Although the Federal Trade Commission has the primary responsibility for regulating advertising on the federal level, a number of other federal agencies also have responsibilities in this general area.

Under the Food, Drug and Cosmetic Act of 1938, the Food and Drug Administration is responsible for assuring the purity and safety of foods, drugs and cosmetics. One of the FDA's major duties is to act against false and fraudulent packaging and labeling practices. In this respect, its duties overlap those of the FTC, which is empowered to act against false food, drug and cosmetic advertising. The two agencies generally cooperate in sharing their regulatory responsibilities, with the FTC mainly enforcing the rules on advertising while the FDA enforces the labeling requirements. Product labeling or advertising that raises environmental issues may also be regulated by the Environmental Protection Agency. In 1994, the FDA and FTC agreed to use the same definitions in evaluating claims made in food advertising.

The FDA was in the limelight during the late 1990s because of its efforts to regulate tobacco as a drug--and to severely restrict cigarette advertising. The FDA adopted rules, backed by the Clinton administration, to limit cigarette advertising on billboards and in most magazines to plain black type, without illustrations. The FDA also ordered tobacco companies to stop sponsoring sporting events and concerts in the name of their tobacco brands (although they could still sponsor events using their corporate names). In addition, the FDA acted to ban cigarette vending machines and to require the tobacco industry to fund a $150 million educational campaign to discourage teen-agers from smoking. The campaign was to include heavy use of television.

Most of the FDA's tobacco rules never went into effect: they were immediately challenged in federal court. In 2000, the U.S. Supreme Court ruled that the Food and Drug Administration lacked the statutory authority to regulate tobacco as a drug. In *FDA v. Brown & Williamson Tobacco* (529 U.S. 120), the court overturned a number of the FDA's restrictions on cigarette marketing.

The court did not rule out the possibility of future Congressional action to give the FDA the authority to regulate tobacco as a drug. Instead, the court merely said the FDA had no such authority under existing federal law. Unless Congress changes the law, the FDA cannot enforce its regulations that restrict minors' access to cigarettes, among other things.

To reach its conclusion, the court's 5-4 majority traced the legislative history of the acts of Congress governing the FDA and concluded that Congress never intended to authorize the FDA to regulate tobacco as a drug. In fact, the FDA itself denied that it had the authority to regulate tobacco for many years before it announced the new restrictions on tobacco marketing in 1996.

The new Supreme Court decision did not affect the voluntary agreement of the tobacco industry to curtail its advertising as part of its settlement of lawsuits filed by the states: that agreement still stands. Nor did this case affect the Federal

Trade Commission's authority to regulate cigarette advertising. In fact, this Supreme Court decision didn't even directly affect most of the FDA's restrictions on cigarette advertising, as opposed to other aspects of cigarette marketing. In a separate action, a federal court earlier overturned the advertising portions of the FDA's rules. In *Beahm v. Food and Drug Administration* (966 F.Supp. 1374), a judge ruled that those rules exceeded the FDA's statutory authority.

The legal battle over cigarette advertising has overshadowed other regulatory actions by the Food and Drug Administration--actions that may be on firmer legal footing. For years, the FDA has refused to let the makers of dietary supplements claim that their products will cure or even treat the symptoms of diseases. These products, used by millions of Americans and sold not only by health food stores but increasingly by grocery and drug stores, represent a $6 billion business. Medications designed to treat specific illnesses must undergo rigorous testing; these dietary supplements are usually sold without any government-supervised testing to prove their effectiveness. In 2000, the FDA loosened its restrictions on dietary supplements, announcing that they can claim to treat symptoms of "common conditions" that are considered "passages of life" such as morning sickness in pregnancy or memory loss. These products still cannot be advertised as treatments for specific diseases without full testing and documentation, the FDA said.

The FDA suffered another setback in 2002. The U.S. Supreme Court overturned a federal law prohibiting the advertising of compounded prescription drugs. Acting in the case of *Thompson v. Western States Medical Center* (122 S.Ct. 1497), the court voted 5-4 to invalidate a provision of the 1997 Food and Drug Administration Modernization Act that bans compounded drug advertising.

Compounded drugs are combinations of prescription drugs prepared by pharmacists to meet the special needs of patients at the request of doctors. Under federal law, drugs may be compounded without the normal testing that is required of new drugs as long as the compounded drug is not advertised.

Explaining the court's rejection of this law as unconstitutional, Justice Sandra Day O'Connor wrote, "If the First Amendment means anything, it means that regulating speech must be a last--not first--resort. Yet here it seems to have been the first strategy the government thought to try."

In making this observation, Justice O'Connor was evaluating the ban on compound drug advertising under the classic *Central Hudson* test of the validity of government restrictions on commercial speech. She pointed out that there are several ways the federal government could achieve its stated goal--to prevent the mass production and widespread sale of compounded drugs that have not undergone the normal testing required of new drugs--without banning advertising. Thus, she wrote, this ban on advertising fails to meet the final part of the *Central Hudson* test: the ban is more extensive than necessary to achieve the government's goal.

Other federal agencies have the authority to regulate various aspects of advertising. The Federal Communications Commission has some authority in the advertising area, although much of it is indirect, derived from the FCC's licensing powers. For many years the FCC had specific guidelines that limited the amount of advertising a broadcaster could carry without risking special scrutiny at license renewal time. Those guidelines were eventually deleted as part of a comprehensive deregulation package. The FCC still has the right to consider the quantity and quality of advertising when it renews broadcast licenses, but there are no longer any specific quotas for broadcasters to follow except in the case of advertising in children's programs, as explained in Chapter 11. In practice, most broadcasters carry less advertising than the old FCC guidelines permitted, anyway.

The FCC also has several other rules that affect broadcast advertising, perhaps the most notable being regulations requiring sponsorship identification.

Another federal agency with authority over some advertising is the Securities and Exchange Commission. The SEC is responsible for preventing the release of incomplete or fraudulent information about corporations whose stock is publicly traded. Thus, the SEC has responsibility for advertising regarding offerings of stock and certain other investment advertising. The agency exercises its authority by acting mainly against the corporation whose advertising is judged false, often by canceling stock offerings. It requires those who advertise stock offerings to make it clear that a media ad is neither an offer to sell nor a solicitation of an offer to buy, since media ads don't lend themselves to the highly detailed reporting of corporate information that is required. That information is provided in a prospectus.

The U.S. Postal Service also has the authority to oversee advertising, especially that of mail-order businesses. If the post office decides a particular advertisement is fraudulent, it has the power to halt all mail addressed to the advertiser, stamp it "fraudulent" and return it to the sender. The post office has an administrative procedure for determining whether a business is engaging in mail fraud; its decisions may be appealed to the federal courts.

Still another federal agency with authority over advertising is the Bureau of Alcohol, Tobacco and Firearms, which regulates alcoholic beverage labeling and advertising, among other things. The bureau has stirred controversy in recent years by sometimes refusing to allow winemakers to make health claims (even claims they could document) or to use reproductions of paintings by noted artists that included nudity in wine labels or advertising. Although the bureau has the authority to ban "obscene and indecent" wine ads, critics have accused its staff of acting arbitrarily in some of these situations.

Another restriction on advertising is included in the federal Truth-in-Lending Act. "Regulation Z," adopted by the Federal Reserve Board to implement this act, requires advertisers to disclose a number of details about credit arrangements if the terms are mentioned at all in an ad. For instance, any quotation of an interest rate must include a declaration of the "annual percentage rate" (APR). Similarly, an ad that quotes a down payment or monthly payment must also disclose additional details of the financing: you cannot merely say a particular car sells for "$500 down and $200 a month" without disclosing the other terms and the APR. Real estate and auto ads often fail to comply with Regulation Z, and the FTC occasionally launches well-publicized campaigns to force advertisers to obey the law.

Federal Lawsuits for Damages

Still another sanction for false advertising was created by Section 43(a) of the federal trademark law, the Lanham Act (discussed in Chapter Six). Under the

Lanham Act's advertising fraud provisions, companies may file civil lawsuits against competitors whose advertising is false and detrimental to their business. Significantly, the Lanham Act now permits courts to award *treble damages* (i.e., three times the actual monetary damages) in these private false-advertising lawsuits. And the victims of false advertising may also win injunctions--court orders to halt the advertising.

A number of courts have awarded damages in federal false advertising lawsuits under the Lanham Act. The biggest advertising fraud judgment ever--$40 million--was affirmed by the U.S. Court of Appeals in *U-Haul International v. Jartran* (793 F.2d 1034, 1986). In that case, Jartran entered the move-yourself market with an aggressive advertising campaign, and U-Haul (Jartran's main competitor) sued. The court held that some of Jartran's claims were false and detrimental to U-Haul's business. The huge damage award was based on a projection of U-Haul's lost profits ($20 million) plus the amount of money Jartran spent on false advertising (another $20 million)!

Another huge damage award for false advertising--more than $12 million--was won by Alpo Pet Foods Inc. in a 1991 U.S. District Court decision. Alpo claimed that Ralston Purina falsely advertised that its Puppy Chow could help prevent a canine hip disorder (*Alpo Pet Foods v. Ralston Purina*, 778 F.Supp. 555).

The Lanham Act allows substantial damage awards not only against advertisers but also against *advertising agencies*, according to a 1992 federal court decision. In *The Gillette Co. v. Wilkinson Sword Inc.*, an unpublished decision of a federal district court in New York, the Friedman Benjamin advertising agency was ordered to pay almost $1 million in damages to The Gillette Co. for preparing ads that falsely claimed Wilkinson's shaving system provided a shave six times smoother than Gillette's.

Perhaps no advertising fraud case ever filed under the Lanham Act drew more media attention than the "pizza wars" case, *Pizza Hut Inc. v. Papa John's International Inc.* (227 F.3d 489, 2000). Papa John's ran an advertising campaign with the theme, "Better Ingredients, Better Pizza" and with follow-up ads comparing specific ingredients in its pizza and competitors' pizza. Pizza Hut sued, alleging that Papa John's ads were deceptive and intended to mislead customers. After a trial jury ruled in Pizza Hut's favor, Papa John's appealed. A federal appellate court overturned the verdict, ruling that Pizza Hut failed to prove that consumers were actually deceived sufficiently that their purchasing decisions were affected by Papa John's advertising claims, which the court called "typical puffery." Proof not only that consumers were deceived, but also that the deception affected their purchasing decisions, is an element of a Lanham Act advertising fraud case. The U.S. Supreme Court declined to review this case in 2001.

STATE ADVERTISING REGULATION

Virtually all states also have laws empowering their officials to act against advertising fraud. At least 45 states have adopted various versions of what has been known as the "Printer's Ink Statute," an advertising fraud law first proposed in

Printer's Ink magazine in 1911.

The statute makes advertising fraud a crime, giving state and local prosecutors the responsibility for enforcement. Because it is a criminal law that must be enforced by officials who often feel they have more serious crimes to worry about, enforcement has traditionally been lax.

Recognizing the shortcomings of this law, most of the states have enacted other laws giving consumers and competitors civil remedies in instances of advertising fraud: victims of false advertising generally may sue for damages under state law as well as the federal Lanham Act. In addition, some states have given local and state prosecutors civil enforcement responsibilities much like those the FTC Act gave to the Federal Trade Commission. In a few other states, separate agencies have enforcement responsibilities.

Some of these state laws are strong and vigorously enforced. But in other places local advertising fraud is largely overlooked. The major problem with these state advertising laws has always been inconsistent enforcement.

Nevertheless, anyone who prepares, publishes or broadcasts advertisements should be familiar with the local laws on false or misleading advertising. If you plan an advertising career, you should investigate your state's laws on the subject. To check your state's annotated codes or statutes, you can look in the index volumes under "advertising" or "unfair trade practices."

Filling a Regulatory Vacuum

During the 1980s the Federal Trade Commission drastically scaled back its efforts to prevent false or misleading advertising. Hamstrung by crippling budget cuts and commissioners who wanted the agency to tread softly in its enforcement efforts for philosophical reasons, the FTC came to be viewed as a paper tiger by many advertisers.

However, the chief legal officers in the 50 states launched a coordinated effort to step into this regulatory vacuum. In most states, the attorney general is charged with enforcing state advertising fraud laws; the attorneys general found that by acting together they could wield just about as much clout as the Federal Trade Commission did in earlier times.

Acting jointly through the National Association of Attorneys General (NAAG), the attorneys general adopted national guidelines for airline advertising in 1988 in an attempt to eliminate questionable airline advertising practices. Then NAAG went after what its members viewed as deceptive advertising by auto rental agencies: in 1989 NAAG adopted guidelines for policing ads by auto rental agencies. The 50 states were, in effect, putting national advertisers on notice that there are still nationwide rules to prevent advertising fraud--even if the FTC is no longer willing or able to enforce its own rules vigorously in every instance.

This coordinated effort to set up national standards for advertising truthfulness in the absence of FTC action was led by the attorneys general of California, New York, Texas and several other large states. The national rules governing auto rental advertising were announced in Washington, D.C., by California Attorney General John Van de Kamp, who said the NAAG's airline advertising guidelines led to a dramatic decline in deceptive advertising in that industry. At the same time, New York Attorney General Robert Abrams said the uniform national rules would tell car rental agencies clearly what is acceptable and unacceptable in their advertising. Texas Attorney General Jim Mattox also played a major role in combating false and misleading advertising.

By 1990, NAAG members had launched several other crackdowns on allegedly deceptive advertising. For example, they challenged dessert-maker Sara Lee for marketing as "Lite Classics" food items with no reduction in calories. They went after the Kraft Co. for marketing "Cheez Whiz" as cheese when it included ingredients not found in cheese. (The company agreed to call the product a "cheese food".) And they forced the Mobil Chemical Co. to stop selling Hefty trash bags as biodegradable when they would not biodegrade for many, many years in a typical trash disposal site. They also acted against cereal makers Kellogg and General Mills for making allegedly false health claims.

However, the state attorneys suffered a major setback in 1992 when the U.S. Supreme Court ruled that under the Airline Deregulation Act of 1978 only the U.S. Department of Transportation may regulate airline advertising (*Morales v. TWA*, 504 U.S. 374). In effect, the court said that in the absence of federal regulation, the airlines are free to do as they please in their advertising.

Writing for a 5-3 majority, Justice Antonin Scalia pointed out that the deregulation act prohibited the states from enforcing any laws "relating to rates, routes or services" of the airlines. Scalia concluded that advertising is "related" to fares; therefore, he said, only the federal government may regulate airline advertising.

That is *not* true in most other industries, though. This ruling had no effect on the other coordinated attacks on deceptive advertising by state attorneys general. The new pressure from the states has surely caused some advertisers to long for the old days when they only had to worry about one federal agency. Now they could be forced to defend themselves against advertising fraud charges in up to 50 different state legal actions at one time. Most advertisers feel that they have no choice but to follow the guidelines adopted by the 50 attorneys general. Ironically, soon after NAAG got its advertising regulation system going, the FTC itself became more aggressive in regulating advertising. For advertisers, the result could be more regulation than ever, with both NAAG and a revitalized FTC acting against allegedly false, misleading and unfair advertising practices.

SELF-REGULATION

Another important influence on the content of advertising is self-regulation, the voluntary methods the advertising industry and the media have developed to prevent the release of false and distasteful advertising.

In 1971, four major advertising and business groups united to form an organization known as the National Advertising Review Council (NARC). The council is a cooperative venture of the American Association of Advertising Agencies, the American Advertising Federation, the Association of National Advertisers and the Council of Better Business Bureaus.

This review board includes representatives of national advertisers, advertising agency representatives and non-industry or public representatives. It accepts complaints about advertising and asks advertisers to substantiate their ad claims. The council asks advertisers to change their ads if they cannot be substantiated. If they refuse, the council is authorized to present its findings to a suitable government enforcement agency, but that is almost never necessary.

Although the NARC's main tools are persuasion and peer pressure, it has dealt with hundreds of questionable advertisements and represents an excellent example of an industry endeavoring to keep its own house in order without government involvement.

The NARC is housed at the Council of Better Business Bureaus, which has a staff-level National Advertising Division to do much of the administrative work of handling truth-in-advertising issues.

For many years, the National Association of Broadcasters maintained similar voluntary codes for radio and television advertising and programming practices. Broadcasters who subscribed to these codes were allowed to display a "seal of good practice." At one time about 4,500 television and radio broadcasters were code subscribers.

The NAB codes set limits on the number of commercials broadcasters were to carry, and also set standards for the content of both advertising and non-advertising materials. The NAB "Code Authority" and "Code Board" enforced these rules, although their only real enforcement power was the ability to prevent violators from using the "seal of good practice."

However, in 1979 the U.S. Justice Department filed an antitrust lawsuit against the NAB, charging that the codes constituted a restraint of trade. By placing limits on the number of commercials and the amount of commercial time that would be permitted, the NAB codes artificially forced up ad rates, the government contended.

After losing the case in federal district court, the NAB signed a consent decree in 1982, agreeing to drop many of the provisions of the television code. To avoid any further potential antitrust liability, the NAB then decided to eliminate its codes altogether and to disband the Code Authority and Code Board.

Thus, the broadcast industry's major attempt at self-regulation fell victim to a government antitrust lawsuit. As Chapter 12 explains, almost any time competitors get together and agree to do anything that might limit competition, they risk running afoul of the nation's antitrust laws--no matter how noble their intentions.

In the print media, there is no industry-wide code of advertising practices. Various organizations have adopted codes of ethics, but they generally deal with editorial matters, not advertising. However, many major newspapers have their own policies on advertising acceptability, and these policies are very influential. The *New York Times* not only has an advertising acceptability policy but also a Department of Advertising Acceptability that reviews ads prior to publication. That department independently checks advertising claims and bars future ads from those found to have violated the company's standards.

The *New York Times* prohibits ads considered in bad taste and attacks on individuals or competing products, among others.

Many newspapers prohibited advertising by theaters showing X-rated pictures, a policy that survived a number of court challenges. In fact, one of the main reasons the Motion Picture Association of America adopted the NC-17 rating for adults-only movies was to get around these restrictions on advertising. Many newspapers that refused to accept ads for movies with X ratings are willing to accept ads for moves rated NC-17.

Nonetheless, newspapers are legally entitled to reject ads for adult movies if they wish. The *Los Angeles Times* banned X-rated movie ads and successfully defended that policy in lawsuits by movie exhibitors who contended it violated everything from the First Amendment to antitrust laws. Even though theater owners were able to prove that a number of other Southern California newspapers banned X-rated movie ads as soon as the *Times* did it, they were never able to convince a court that this constituted any sort of conspiracy to violate antitrust laws (see *Adult Film Association v. Times Mirror*, 97 C.A.3d 77, 1979).

ADVERTISING ON THE INTERNET

The explosive growth of Internet advertising during the late 1990s led to a variety of government initiatives to regulate that advertising.

Major regulatory efforts began in one area in response to a public outcry: Congress and many state legislatures have considered the problem of "spam," or unsolicited advertising by bulk e-mail. The technology of e-mail makes it easy to build an enormous mailing list--and to send a deluge of messages to everyone on that list. An advertiser can send messages to thousands of e-mail addresses almost instantly and at virtually no cost. It was inevitable that such a powerful technology would be abused.

By 2002 at least 24 states had passed laws to curtail spam and Congress was considering federal anti-spam legislation. Typically, the state laws are designed to help consumers avoid being overwhelmed by unsolicited e-mail. The California law, for instance, says those who send unsolicited advertising via e-mail must include "ADV" at the beginning of the subject line and open the message with a statement that recipients may call a toll-free phone number or reply to an e-mail address to halt all further e-mail from that advertiser. E-mail advertisers who fail to comply may be criminally prosecuted. One problem, of course, is the difficulty of regulating a worldwide medium: how can a state control spam within its borders when the bulk e-mailer who is sending the spam is half a world away?

Another problem with states regulating spam is that it may raise federal preemption or First Amendment questions. In 2001 the Washington Supreme Court upheld that state's anti-spam law in a case where a bulk e-mailer had been sending up to one million pieces of unsolicited e-mail a week promoting a $40 package he called, "how to profit from the Internet." The court declared that the anti-spam law did not violate either the First Amendment or the interstate commerce clause of the U.S. Constitution (*State of Washington v. Heckel*, 24 P.3d 404). In 2002, an appellate court also upheld California's anti-spam law (*Ferguson v. Friendfinders*, 94 C.A.4th 1255).

Consumer advocates have also been concerned about outright fraud in advertising on websites. The Federal Trade Commission has launched a series of sweeps that targeted Internet advertising. One of the FTC's chief concerns was false, misleading or unfair health claims on the Internet: by 1999 the FTC had notified the owners of several hundred sites that their health claims could violate federal law. In a 1999 announcement, the FTC said about one fourth of the sites that received such notices over a two-year period removed the questionable claims or shut down their websites altogether without any further federal enforcement action. The FTC said it was considering various options to deal with the others, including legal actions to halt false or misleading advertising.

In 2001, the FTC responded to the events of Sept. 11 by going after websites that were exploiting the fear of terrorism by making false claims about cures for various diseases. The FTC warned operators of about 40 websites to remove claims that dietary supplements can cure anthrax or smallpox and also went after operators of websites claiming that products such as zinc mineral oil can cure anthrax. Sites offering gas masks, protective suits, mail sterilizers and products to detect the presence of anthrax also were warned to drop deceptive claims.

The Federal Trade Commission also took another step to combat false and misleading Internet advertising: the FTC added a section to its own website addressing the issue. The agency's news release announcing the availability of this report is located at *http://www.ftc.gov/opa/2000/05/dotcom.htm* and includes a link to the full report. The report has links to examples and mock ads that illustrate the FTC's suggestions for Internet advertising. While the information available on this site is only the FTC's opinion and is not legally binding, it is dangerous for any advertiser to ignore the FTC's published guidelines. In fact, the FTC's report, entitled "Dotcom Disclosures," also has links to many of the FTC's advisory *Guides* concerning advertising of various types of products and services, which should be of special interest to advertisers in the affected areas.

In essence, the FTC's position is that all of the consumer safeguards that apply in other kinds of advertising also apply online. That means all of the normal rules concerning deceptive and unfair practices must be observed by Internet advertisers. Internet advertisers must be prepared to substantiate their claims. And advertisers must make "clear and conspicuous" affirmative disclosures in many instances.

ONGOING ISSUES

As America undergoes a new revolution in communications technology, major questions about advertising and media economics must be answered. In view of the growing subscriber base of cable and satellite television, plus the declining market share of free, advertiser-supported broadcasting, it is not a certainty that advertising will remain the dominant source of revenue for the mass media. In fact, millions of people now devote a lot of their television-viewing time to advertising-free video programming such as movies on video tape. And VCRs enable consumers to "zap" commercials that cost advertisers millions of dollars to put on the air. These trends raise many policy questions for the advertising industry and its regulators.

Criticism of cigarette advertising has been intense in recent years. R.J. Reynolds dropped its successful but very controversial "Old Joe Camel" advertising campaign in 1977. By 2002, there had been many other government efforts to regulate or forbid cigarette advertising. Does this really violate the First Amendment rights of tobacco companies, as the Supreme Court said in its *Lorillard Tobacco* decision? Are restrictions or an outright ban on cigarette ads an appropriate response to the problem of teen-age smoking? If so, what about teen-age drinking? Is the ban on cigarette billboards, which was included in the tobacco industry's settlement with the states, a good solution?

What role should Congress and the courts play in advertising regulation? Will the courts continue the trend, begun in 1975, toward constitutional protection for commercial speech? Or will the courts again say a message is protected only if its creator is in the business of selling ideas as opposed to selling products and services? Do the Supreme Court's *44 Liquormart, Greater New Orleans* and *Lorillard Tobacco* decisions mark the beginning of a new era of First Amendment protection for commercial speech, even speech promoting a "vice?"

And if the FTC fails to aggressively enforce the rules forbidding false and misleading advertising, what about the role of other regulatory bodies? What of the National Association of Attorneys General? Should the 50 states' chief legal officers--acting in concert through their national organization--take on the task of setting national advertising standards? Will Congress step in and forbid advertising for some "harmful" products or services? Also, what role will self-regulation play in the future of advertising?

What of the trend toward enormous damage awards in false advertising lawsuits under the Lanham Act? Will the threat of *treble damages* for advertising fraud lead to changes in the way advertising claims are verified before a campaign begins? Do these awards constitute a threat to the freedom to engage in robust, aggressive advertising?

Like other American mass communications industries, advertising will be evolving in the twenty-first century. Whether this century will be a new time of heavy regulation of advertising or perhaps a new period of freedom from government control remains to be seen.

A SUMMARY OF ADVERTISING AND THE LAW

Is Advertising Protected by the First Amendment?

Until 1975 it would have been safe to say that *commercial speech* was not generally protected by the First Amendment. However, since then the Supreme Court has extended some constitutional protection to commercial speech and greater protection to noncommercial corporate speech.

Is Media Law Generally Applicable to Advertising?

While advertising has its own unique body of law, the general rules of media law also apply to advertising. An advertisement may lead to a lawsuit for libel, invasion of privacy, commercial misappropriation, copyright infringement or trademark infringement, for instance.

Do Advertisers Have a Right of Access to the Media?

Generally, there is no right of access to the media. A publisher or broadcaster may accept or reject advertising at will, unless the acceptances and rejections fall into a pattern of unfair or monopolistic business practices. However, broadcasters (but not other media) must sell advertising to federal election candidates, and sometimes state-owned media are required to grant advertising access.

Who Regulates Advertising Content and Why?

The primary federal agency that regulates advertising is the Federal Trade Commission. To protect the public from false and misleading advertising, the FTC has a Congressional mandate to monitor advertising and act against practices it considers improper. For some years the FTC was less aggressive in acting against questionable advertising practices than it had been earlier, but it appears to be stepping up its regulatory activities now.

How Does the FTC Enforce Its Regulations?

The FTC has a variety of enforcement tools, including informal letters of compliance, consent decrees and formal cease and desist orders. The FTC may require substantiation of an advertising claim, and it may order corrective advertising if an ad has been particularly false or misleading.

Does Anyone Else Regulate Advertising?

A number of other federal agencies have authority over certain kinds of advertising. Also, all 50 states have statutory laws prohibiting fraudulent business practices; some states vigorously enforce these laws against false advertisers, but some are less diligent. The advertising industry has an elaborate system of self-regulation as well. In recent years the National Association of Attorneys General has begun coordinated legal actions against allegedly fraudulent advertising.

CHAPTER 14

Freedom of the Student Press

Almost all student media--no matter how well edited or produced--eventually face the wrath of administrators who don't like something that appears in print, online or on the air. Official reactions vary from telephone calls or irate interoffice memos to outright censorship.

Although the student press has been censored for as long as there have been student newspapers, instances of censorship appear to rise and decline in cycles. Until the 1960s, administrative censorship seemed almost routine on many high school and college campuses. And when it happened, the staffs and their faculty advisers could do little or nothing about it. However, the era of student unrest in the late 1960s changed that. Students in that period were unwilling to limit their expression to editorials bemoaning the lack of school spirit or attacking the quality of cafeteria food. Instead, many high school and college newspapers focused on issues such as war and peace, civil rights and later drug use, sex counseling and other sensitive issues. Amazingly, many of them got away with it, creating a legacy of First Amendment protection for student journalists--at least at the college level.

But the trend was clearly away from campus press freedom by the 1980s and 1990s. Most student editors then were far less concerned about the great issues of the day than their predecessors had been. Perhaps the Supreme Court was responding to the mood of the times when it severely curtailed the freedom of high school journalists in 1988.

The story of campus freedom begins and ends at the U.S. Supreme Court. The court first extended First Amendment protection to students in 1969; at least 125 other court decisions followed that precedent, repeatedly overruling administrative censorship of student publications and other forms of campus expression.

In case after case in the Vietnam war era, the courts ruled that public school and college administrators could not arbitrarily censor student expression as they once did. Whenever an instance of censorship involved state action (i.e., an act by a government employee such as a public school principal), the courts held that the First Amendment and other constitutional safeguards applied. At private institutions, on the other hand, school officials are not government officials; the courts have rarely found state action in their conduct. That creates a different problem which we will discuss later.

In the 1980s, the law came full circle: lower courts began wavering in their support of campus freedom, and then the Supreme Court handed down its famous (some would say infamous) *Hazelwood School District v. Kuhlmeier* ruling (484 U.S.

260, 1988), which held that the official student newspapers at high schools are not ordinarily protected by the First Amendment. The court did not extend this ruling to college newspapers. Nor does it apply to *unofficial* publications even at the high school level. In fact, the court didn't even give administrators a free hand to censor official high school newspapers where there is a state law or local school policy forbidding administrative censorship. Nevertheless, the *Hazelwood* case signaled a clear reversal of the trend in court rulings on student press freedom. This case is discussed more fully later.

This chapter is about some of these landmark court decisions on student press freedom. It should be said at the beginning that there are dozens--and perhaps hundreds--of confrontations between administrators and student journalists every year. Although many of these incidents involve blatant prior restraint that may not be legal even today, these acts of censorship often go unchallenged because no one has the money, the inclination or the legal resources to haul school officials into court.

THE FIRST SUPREME COURT DECISION

In many areas of media law, the basic principles can be traced to a few landmark Supreme Court decisions, and student press freedom is one of those areas. In 1969, the Supreme Court ruled on the case of *Tinker v. Des Moines Independent Community School District* (393 U.S. 503), often called the "black armbands case." The case arose when John and Mary Beth Tinker, ages 15 and 13, and a 16-year-old friend were suspended for wearing black armbands at school as a symbolic protest of the Vietnam War. The Des Moines school principals had heard of the pending protest and hurriedly adopted a rule against wearing armbands on campus.

The suspension was challenged on First Amendment grounds. Two lower courts upheld the school officials' action, but the Supreme Court reversed, declaring that their act was symbolic speech, protected by the First Amendment. The court said:

> First Amendment rights, applied in the light of the special characteristics of the school environment, are available to teachers and students. It can hardly be argued that either students or teachers shed their constitutional rights to freedom of speech or expression at the schoolhouse gate.

The court noted that the three students did nothing to disrupt the educational process. The court said, "In our system, state-operated schools may not be enclaves of totalitarianism. School officials do not possess absolute authority over their students."

However, the court did make it clear that the rights of students were not "co-extensive" with the rights of adults off campus. The court said freedom could be suppressed when its exercise "would materially and substantially interfere with the requirements of appropriate discipline in the operation of the school."

Applying the Precedent from Tinker

After *Tinker*, many more cases arose as students asserted their newly won constitutional rights. Some of the earliest post-*Tinker* cases were only federal district court decisions and hence of limited value as precedents, but students were winning lawsuits against school officials.

In a 1970 case, *Antonelli v. Hammond* (308 F.Supp. 1329), a federal court in Massachusetts said a college president could not impose prior restraint on a campus newspaper without elaborate procedural safeguards. John Antonelli, a student newspaper editor at Fitchburg State College, resigned rather than submit an article by black activist Eldridge Cleaver to a campus review board. College President James Hammond set up the board to pre-censor the paper for obscenity and to assure "responsible freedom of press in the student newspaper."

Antonelli sued Hammond and won: the court said the campus paper was protected by the First Amendment, and that the review board was engaging in prior censorship without adequate safeguards. Moreover, the court condemned a threat by Hammond to withhold funding if the paper wasn't "responsible."

The next year, another federal district court overruled the suspension of a student editor because of a cartoon critical of the college president and an editorial criticizing a local judge, in *Trujillo v. Love* (322 F.Supp. 1266). Dorothy Trujillo was an editor of a "laboratory" newspaper produced by the Mass Communications Department at Southern Colorado State College. The faculty adviser and department chair said the editorial and cartoon didn't meet the Canons of Journalism and were potentially libelous.

Trujillo challenged her suspension in court and won, because the court felt the paper was still a student forum protected by the First Amendment, despite its in-house "lab" character. The court said that if its status as a teaching tool rather than a First Amendment forum had been clearly spelled out and put into effect, the censorship and suspension might have been constitutional. However, the lab status wasn't clearly defined, and the paper had become a forum for expression protected by the First Amendment. No one realized it in 1971, but that dilemma--whether a student newspaper is a teaching tool or a First Amendment forum--would be crucial in the Supreme Court's *Hazelwood* decision nearly 20 years later.

Two More Supreme Court Rulings

During the early 1970s, the U.S. Supreme Court addressed the First Amendment status of college students in two more cases; both expanded students' rights on campus.

In the first of these cases, a chapter of the Students for a Democratic Society, a national student organization known for its militancy, sought official recognition as a campus group at Central Connecticut State College, and was turned down because of SDS' national reputation for disruptive tactics. Without official status, the group could not use campus facilities for meetings and other functions. The group sued, and in *Healy v. James* (408 U.S. 169, 1972), the Supreme Court said the local group couldn't be denied campus privileges merely because of the national organization's reputation. Public colleges "are not enclaves immune from the sweep of the First Amendment," the court said, ruling that the college president's decision abridged the students' constitutional rights.

A year later the Supreme Court decided another college student rights case, this one involving disciplinary action against the editor of an "underground" or alternative campus newspaper. In *Papish v. University of Missouri Curators* (410 U.S. 670), the high court overruled the expulsion of Barbara Papish, a graduate student and editor of the *Free Press*.

Papish had previously angered university officials by distributing her paper when high school students and their parents were on campus, but when she published an issue they regarded as particularly indecent, they took action. The edition that led to the expulsion had a political cartoon depicting a policeman raping the Statue of Liberty and the Goddess of Justice, and a headline entitled, "Mother Fucker Acquitted."

The Supreme Court ruled that neither the cartoon nor the headline was obscene. Nor did Papish's activities "materially and substantially" interfere with campus order, the court said. The court ordered Papish reinstated unless her expulsion could be justified on academic grounds, citing the *Healy* decision: "We think *Healy* makes it clear that the dissemination of ideas--no matter how offensive to good taste--on a state university campus may not be shut off in the name alone of 'conventions of decency.'"

COLLEGE PRESS FREEDOM CASES

Within two years of the *Papish* decision, three noteworthy federal appellate court decisions on student press freedom were handed down, and each affirmed student rights.

In *Bazaar v. Fortune* (476 F.2d 570, 1973), the fifth circuit U.S. Court of Appeals overruled the prior censorship of a literary magazine at the University of Mississippi. The magazine, edited by Eugene Bazaar, carried two short stories with earthy language, both dealing with racial themes. The magazine was sponsored by the English Department and was to be printed on campus, but the print shop superintendent noticed some of the content and called the university chancellor, Porter Fortune, who ordered it censored.

When hauled into court, university officials acknowledged that the First Amendment protected the Ole Miss student newspaper but argued that this magazine was different because it was produced by a class. The appellate court disagreed and ordered the university to allow its publication, although the court did allow the university to put a disclaimer on the cover ("This is not an official publication...").

At almost the same time, another press freedom case with racial overtones was decided by the fourth circuit U.S. Court of Appeals, *Joyner v. Whiting* (477 F.2d 456, 1973). That case arose when Albert Whiting, president of North Carolina Central University, cut off funds for the *Campus Echo* because editor Johnnie Joyner editorially opposed integration of this formerly all-black school. At one point Joyner also said whites were unwelcome on the paper's staff, and that the paper would not accept ads from white-owned businesses. Whiting said he feared the paper's editorial position would cause the school to lose federal funds.

The court said Whiting's actions violated the First and Fourteenth Amendments. Even though Joyner was using his freedom of the press to speak out against another constitutionally protected principle, the court said the First Amendment still applied. The court noted that Joyner's editorial stance had not produced any disruption of the campus. A college administration doesn't have to create a student newspaper in the first place, but once a paper is established, it can't be shut down just because the administration doesn't like its content, the appellate court said.

Two years later, the same federal appellate court that decided *Bazaar* overruled the firing of three student editors by a college president in *Schiff v. Williams* (519 F.2d 257, 1975). Kenneth Williams, president of Florida Atlantic University, fired the three editors because "the level of editorial responsibility and competence has deteriorated to the extent that it reflects discredit and embarrassment upon the university." The paper engaged in vilification and rumor-mongering "instead of accurately reporting items likely to be of interest to the university community," the president said.

In overturning the firings, the federal appellate court said this was an unconstitutional attempt to impose administrative control on the newspaper. Citing *Tinker*, the court said such control could be justified only under special circumstances where disorder might otherwise result. Even if these editors produced a paper full of poor grammar, spelling errors and bad writing, as Williams claimed, that would not lead to a significant disruption on the campus, the court said. And without the threat of disruption, censorship of college publications is unconstitutional, the court concluded.

All of these cases were decided in the years immediately following the era of campus unrest in the late 1960s. In later years, few disputes involving freedom of the college press reached the nation's appellate courts. However, in 1983 the eighth circuit U.S. Court of Appeals handed down a ruling that was a major victory for campus press freedom: *Stanley v. Magrath* (719 F.2d 279).

This case arose after the *Minnesota Daily* at the University of Minnesota published a humor issue in 1979. One article purported to be an interview with Jesus Christ, and it described him as a Jewish "cult hero." The article angered many Minnesotans, including more than a few on the campus itself. The university responded by changing its rules to allow students to withhold from their fee payments the amount destined for the paper.

Although the policy change had little effect on its actual income, the *Minnesota Daily* challenged the legality of this action on First Amendment grounds. Reversing a trial judge's decision in favor of the university, the federal appellate court ruled that the change in funding was an attempt to control the paper's content in violation of the First Amendment.

In 1984 the university and the student paper reached a settlement in which the University Regents agreed to pay the paper's legal expenses (a total of $182,000) and restore its funding. The agreement also provided for the university and the paper to set up a $20,000 fund to sponsor seminars on press freedom and responsibility.

By the 1990s, the principle that public college and university newspapers are protected by the First Amendment seemed to be well settled. But does the First Amendment protect the right of an off-campus newspaper to be circulated to students? That issue was addressed in *Hays County Guardian v. Supple* (969 F.2d 111), a 1992 case. A federal appellate court held that administrators at Southwest Texas State University could not use a rule against commercial solicitation on campus to severely restrict the distribution of a free, advertiser-supported community newspaper. The court noted that campus officials allowed unfettered distribution of the official student newspaper (which contained advertising) as well as many kinds of literature that did not include advertising. The court noted that the presence of ads in a newspaper does not reduce its First Amendment protection. The court also ruled that the campus had the characteristics of a public forum--a place where the distribution of newspapers could not be arbitrarily restricted. The court said college officials could adopt reasonable time, place and manner regulations, but they could not enforce distribution rules so restrictive that they severely curtailed a community newspaper's ability to reach students.

Taken as a group, the cases summarized in this section say that college journalists enjoy substantial First Amendment protection. It may be that a campus publication could avoid becoming a First Amendment forum, as the court suggested in *Trujillo*, but that rarely occurs even if a student publication is produced in an instructional setting with university funding. It has been suggested more than once that college newspapers are a little like Dr. Frankenstein's monster: campus officials don't have to create one, but once they do, it's very hard to control. Also, the federal courts have consistently held that independent newspapers produced by college students enjoy broad First Amendment protection.

During the 1990s, a new problem plagued many college newspapers: large-scale newspaper thefts that in some cases were condoned if not encouraged by campus administrators. By 2002, there had been incidents on at least 200 campuses in which someone or some group systematically removed the entire press run of a newspaper from the newsracks. Sometimes the act was a protest against a specific story or the newspaper's editorial policies in general, but on other occasions there was no discernible reason for the theft. In some cases, campus police acted to halt newspaper thefts and to apprehend those who cleaned out the newsracks. But on other campuses administrators ordered the police *not* to act and openly sided with the newspaper thieves. Since most campus papers are free for the taking, some administrators refused to accept that taking the entire press run was even a wrongful act, despite the fact that the cost of printing replacement copies runs into hundreds or thousands of dollars.

The Student Press Law Center responded to this problem by suggesting that campus newspapers include a statement saying individual copies are free, but multiple copies carry a substantial charge. This at least makes it more clear that taking the entire press run is theft. However, even that has not worked on some campuses: some administrators have decreed that such a statement would constitute the imposition of an illegal new student fee.

On most college campuses, administrators are well aware that they cannot directly censor the student press without risking a lawsuit and a lot of bad publicity. But with a wink and a nod, they can certainly encourage someone else to do the dirty work for them by rounding up all the copies of an offending newspaper.

Campus Advertising and the First Amendment

Another troubling question on some campuses is whether the campus media have the right to accept controversial advertising: what happens if the administration orders a campus newspaper to reject alcoholic beverage advertising, for example? Alternately, what happens if the staff decides on its own not to accept a certain kind of advertising?

This question has been litigated for more than 30 years. In the 1960s federal courts in New York and Wisconsin overturned state-supported school and college administrators' efforts to keep student newspapers from accepting ads that espoused controversial ideas (see *Lee v. Board of Regents*, 441 F.2d 1257, and *Zucker v. Panitz*, 299 F.Supp. 102).

Some of the same issues were raised in the 1970s when a federal appellate court rejected an appeal for access to the ad columns of the Mississippi State University newspaper in *Mississippi Gay Alliance v. Goudelock* (536 F.2d 1073, 1976). The Gay Alliance wanted to place an announcement of its services and was turned down by the staff. The court said this case was different from previous public school advertising access cases because here the staff, as opposed to the administration, rejected the ad. Hence, the court said there was no state action in this decision to reject advertising from a gay organization. But in addition, the court said previous court decisions had given the editors final say over the content anyway.

In 1997, another federal appellate court upheld the right of student publications to reject advertising--this time at the *high school* level. In *Yeo v. Town of Lexington* (141 F.3d 241), the first circuit U.S. Court of Appeals ruled that student editors at Lexington High School in Lexington, Mass. were free to reject advocacy advertising, in this case an ad from a group advocating sexual abstinence. The court said there was a clear record that the students and not school officials were in complete control of the school newspaper and yearbook, and that they made the decision to reject the ad on their own. The court held that there was no state action involved here; therefore, there was no legal basis for a right of access to the student newspaper and yearbook.

At the university level, there was considerable controversy about a federal appellate court decision in 2000: *Pitt News v. Fisher* (215 F.3d 354). In this case, the student-run newspaper at the University of Pittsburgh challenged a Pennsylvania state law forbidding businesses such as bars and liquor stores to advertise alcoholic beverages in student media.

The *Pitt News*' lawsuit was tenuous because the law directly targeted advertisers, not the media. Under the commercial speech doctrine, a state may regulate advertising for a product such as alcoholic beverages as long as the regulations satisfy the *Central Hudson* test. But the *Pitt News* argued that by reducing its ad revenue, the ban forced the paper to reduce its size--and that, the paper argued, was a First Amendment violation.

The third circuit U.S. Court of Appeals rejected that argument, ruling that there is no First Amendment right for a student newspaper to have any particular amount of advertising that would enable it to publish any particular number of pages. (The *Pitt News* said it lost about $17,000 in advertising revenue in 1997-98 because the ban forced local businesses to withdraw alcoholic beverage advertising from the campus paper.) The court pointed out that the paper was free to publish a calendar of events that might list local bars and even note which ones offer bargains on alcoholic beverages, as long as businesses didn't pay for such listings. On the other hand, if a business *did* pay for such a listing, the business (but not the paper) could be prosecuted for violating the state law, the court noted.

The *Pitt News* case raises many legal and ethical questions. For example, would the outcome of the case have been different if the university administration had ordered the newspaper to reject alcoholic beverage ads, over the staff's objections? If that happened at the college level, it might raise serious First Amendment questions that were not raised by *Pitt News v. Fisher*.

Campus Fees and Student Freedom

In 1995, the U.S. Supreme Court ruled on another aspect of student press freedom: the right of a religious student group to receive university printing subsidies if other groups receive such subsidies. In *Rosenberger v. Rector and Visitors of the University of Virginia* (515 U.S. 819), the high court ruled that the University of Virginia had to pay for the printing of a Christian student newspaper from its Student Activities Fund if it paid for the printing of other student groups' newspapers. In so ruling, the 5-4 majority held that the First Amendment's *establishment clause* (which has been interpreted to forbid government sponsorship of religious activities such as prayers in public schools) does not require a public university to withhold support from a religious student newspaper when it supports other publications produced by student organizations.

Writing for the majority, Justice Anthony M. Kennedy said the university was engaged in *viewpoint discrimination* in violation of the free expression provisions of the First Amendment because it favored student newspapers expressing certain viewpoints over others. The viewpoint discrimination inherent in the university's action was "a denial of the right of free speech and would risk fostering a pervasive bias or hostility to religion, which could undermine the very neutrality (toward religion) the Establishment Clause requires," Kennedy wrote.

The U.S. Supreme Court ruled on a related case concerning student fees at universities in 2000. This time the court held that a public university may grant money derived from mandatory student fees to controversial organizations as long as the money is available to various groups on a *viewpoint-neutral* basis. Ruling in *Board of Regents v. Southworth* (529 U.S. 217), the court rejected a challenge by conservative students to the University of Wisconsin's practice of awarding student fee money to groups with which these students disagreed.

Writing for a unanimous court this time, Justice Kennedy said that it does not violate the First Amendment for student fee monies to be given to groups that espouse controversial viewpoints. Although this does force students to pay fees that go to groups with which they may disagree, Kennedy said this is not unconstitutional as long as the fee-granting process is open to a wide variety of organizations with divergent viewpoints. This is different from a situation where students (or government employees) might be forced to pay fees to support only one specific viewpoint, Kennedy said. The court has held that government workers may not be forced to pay dues that support a union's political activities, for instance. In contrast, here the mandatory student fee money was given to many different groups with varying viewpoints--not just to a group representing one viewpoint.

The Supreme Court ordered a lower court to make sure that the fee-granting system at Wisconsin really is viewpoint neutral before reaching a final decision on this case. This case differs from the *University of Virginia* case in that the student-fee-awarding policy there was *not* viewpoint neutral: student fee money was denied to campus publications produced by religious groups while being awarded to groups producing non-religious publications.

Other College First Amendment Questions

By the early 2000s, a number of courts had upheld the First Amendment rights of students and others on college campuses in several other contexts. For example, in 2001 the seventh circuit U.S. Court of Appeals upheld the right of students to present a controversial play at the Fort Wayne campus of Indiana University-Purdue University in *Linnemeir v. Board of Trustees of Purdue University* (260 F.3d 757). The play, *Corpus Christi*, depicts a Christ-like figure as a homosexual and has much language that is offensive to many Christians. A group of residents sued to halt the student performance, contending that by allowing a presentation of anti-Christian material, the university was violating the First Amendment's establishment of religion clause, which requires separation of church and state.

The appellate court rejected that argument and allowed the play to be presented, ruling that to stop the play would violate the students' First Amendment free-expression rights. Writing for the court, Judge Richard A. Posner said, "The contention that the First Amendment forbids a state university to provide a venue for the expression of views antagonistic to conventional Christian beliefs is absurd. It would imply that teachers in state universities could not teach important works by Voltaire, Hobbes, Hume, Darwin, Mill, Marx, Nietzsche, Freud, Yates... and countless other staples of Western culture."

On the other hand, the ninth circuit U.S. Court of Appeals ruled in 2001 that a college violated the First Amendment by prohibiting the expression of Christian beliefs on campus. In *Orin v. Barclay* (272 F.3d 1207), the court said Olympic Community College in Bremerton, Wash. violated the free speech rights and free exercise of religion rights of anti-abortion demonstrators by forbidding them to discuss the religious basis for their beliefs. College officials imposed several conditions on two anti-abortion protesters, including a ban on "religious worship or instruction."

Writing for the court, Judge Richard Tallman said, "having created a forum for the demonstrators' expression, (Dean of Students Richard) Barclay could not, consistent with the dictates of the First Amendment, limit their expression to secular content."

The same court that decided the *Orin* case also ruled in 2001 that a college faculty member had a First Amendment right to post a newsletter that harshly criticized college administrators, sometimes in strident language. In *Bauer v. Sampson* (261 F.3d 775), the court rejected the contention of administrators that Irvine Valley College (Calif.) professor Roy Bauer's newsletter had violent "overtones" sufficient to justify disciplinary actions against Bauer. The court held that Bauer's newsletter would lose its First Amendment protection only if it contained a true criminal threat, which the court said it did not.

HIGH SCHOOL CASES BEFORE HAZELWOOD

Except for *Tinker* itself, all of the cases discussed so far involved press freedom at colleges, not high schools. During the 1960s and early 1970s, it appeared that the same First Amendment principles applied in both high school and college press freedom cases. However, in the late 1970s some courts began to uphold administrative censorship in high school cases, something that did not happen in college cases--even in later years. And of course, in 1988 the *Hazelwood* Supreme Court decision held that the First Amendment does not protect official high school publications. In a footnote, the court said it was not deciding whether the *Hazelwood* principle would apply at the college level. The court didn't directly address the status of unofficial high school publications. However, less than a year after the *Hazelwood* decision a federal appellate court reaffirmed the First Amendment rights of an unofficial high school publication.

Before the *Hazelwood* case, there was a long tradition of court decisions upholding high school journalists' First Amendment rights, particularly in cases involving unofficial or "underground" newspapers. Those cases merit some review here.

Overall, far more high school than college free press cases have been litigated: no fewer than 13 federal appellate court decisions have overturned censorship or discipline of student journalists by high school administrators. In almost all of these cases, administrators attempted to engage in prior restraint, often pointing to profanity or language they considered obscene as their justification. But the courts have repeatedly told school officials that neither profanity nor four-letter words constitute obscenity, and that the prior censorship was unjustified. The courts have often ruled that independent or underground newspapers were First Amendment forums that administrators could NOT arbitrarily censor.

In deciding these cases, often the federal courts have focused on school procedures for reviewing student publications. The courts have generally held that prior restraint is permissible on a school campus when it wouldn't be in the community at large, but to justify censorship administrators must bear a heavy burden of proof and provide students with many procedural safeguards--things school officials failed to do in virtually all of the cases that have been litigated.

However, the leading precedent in one federal appellate circuit (the seventh circuit, covering Illinois, Wisconsin and Indiana) seemingly forbids prior restraint of unofficial student publications except when prior restraint of a commercial newspaper would also be constitutional (i.e., almost never). In *Fujishima v. Board of Education* (460 F.2d 1355, 1972), the federal court overruled the suspension of two students who distributed a paper called *The Cosmic Frog*. The court said *Tinker* did not permit school officials merely to predict that a disruption would occur and use that as an excuse to engage in censorship:

> *Tinker* in no way suggests that students may be required to announce their intentions of engaging in certain conduct beforehand so school authorities may decide whether to prohibit the conduct. Such a concept of prior restraint is even more offensive when applied to the long-protected area of publication.

In so ruling, the *Fujishima* decision took issue with *Eisner v. Stamford Board of Education* (440 F.2d 803, 1971), an earlier ruling of another federal appellate court that said prior restraint would be acceptable if certain procedural safeguards were provided:

> We believe that the court erred in *Eisner* in interpreting *Tinker* to allow prior restraint of publication--long a constitutionally prohibited power--as a tool of school officials in "forecasting" substantial disruption of school activities.

Nevertheless, most federal courts have taken the *Eisner* view rather than the *Fujishima* view, ruling that prior restraint is permissible if there are sufficient procedural safeguards. But the courts have almost never found the procedural safeguards to be adequate.

Even in the *Eisner* case, the court overturned a Connecticut school system's censorship procedures because they did not provide for a quick administrative review or specify to whom and how literature could be submitted for prior review. Still, under the *Eisner* precedent, decided by the second federal appellate circuit (which includes New York, Vermont and Connecticut), students have less freedom from prior censorship than they do in several other appellate circuits. Each federal appellate court sets precedents that are binding in its region but not elsewhere, although other courts often follow non-local precedents.

The second circuit Court of Appeals also upheld an administrative censorship action in a 1977 case, *Trachtman v. Anker* (563 F.2d 512). That case isn't a student press case strictly speaking: a group of students wanted to distribute a questionnaire on sexual attitudes at a New York high school, and the court allowed the administration to stop them. However, the court said literature distribution was not the issue here; expert witnesses had testified that responding to the questionnaire could cause psychological harm to some adolescent students. In fact, one of the two justices in the majority joined the dissenting third justice in emphasizing that this should not be viewed as an "unintended" precedent for any future abridgement of student freedom of expression.

Nevertheless, a federal district judge in New York cited the *Trachtman* decision when he upheld a high school principal's decision to censor a student newspaper in 1979. In *Frasca v. Andrews* (463 F.Supp. 1043), a judge said he didn't want to second-guess a principal who predicted that disruptions might result from two items in the paper: a heated exchange between members of the school lacrosse team and the editors, and an article accusing a student body officer of incompetence.

In *Frasca*, a federal judge allowed a school official to forecast a disruption as a justification for prior censorship, precisely what the court prohibited in *Fujishima*. However, *Fujishima* is a seventh circuit case, and *Frasca* was decided in the second federal appellate circuit.

However, even the second circuit later ruled in favor of student freedom in *Thomas v. Granville* (607 F.2d 1043, 1979). In that case, the court overturned a disciplinary action against students who distributed an underground paper near (but not on) school property. The paper offended school officials because it had articles on masturbation and prostitution. However, no disruption resulted and the court said the students' constitutional rights were violated by the disciplinary action.

Elsewhere around the country, other federal appellate courts have generally fallen somewhere between the stance of the second and seventh federal appellate circuits on issues of student freedom. Courts in the fourth and fifth circuits (covering the Southern states) have almost always reversed school officials' efforts to censor publications or discipline editors, while emphasizing that they were not flatly prohibiting prior censorship of school publications. Fourth and fifth circuit cases that so held include: *Nitzberg v. Parks* (525 F.2d 378, 1975), *Baughman v. Freienmuth* (478 F.2d 1345, 1973), *Quarterman v. Byrd* (453 F.2d 54, 1971), *Gambino v. Fairfax County School Board* (429 F.Supp. 731, aff'd 564 F.2d 157, 1977) and *Shanley v. Northeast Independent School District* (462 F.2d 960, 1972).

In a number of these cases, the courts said prior restraint would be constitutionally permissible under something like the procedural safeguards required for motion picture censorship in *Freedman v. Maryland* (see Chapter 10). Thus, the *Baughman* decision emphasized the need for prompt review of any decision to censor, with clearly drawn guidelines describing the kind of material that could be censored. In the *Baughman* case, the court overturned a school policy that allowed prior restraint when material was libelous or obscene. The court said these were terms of art and much too vague to be applied by students and principals in censorship cases. Furthermore, since *New York Times v. Sullivan* and *Gertz v. Welch* (see Chapter Four), much that is seemingly libelous is also privileged, the court pointed out.

The *Nitzberg* case echoed the ruling in *Baughman*, but also said that when school officials want to justify prior censorship by forecasting disruptions, they must have clearly drawn criteria that may be used in predicting that a publication would cause such a disruption.

The seventh federal appellate circuit, which decided the *Fujishima* case, has also ruled on two other student press freedom cases, *Scoville v. Board of Education* (425 F.2d 10, 1970) and *Jacobs v. Indianapolis Board of School Commissioners* (490 F.2d 601, 1973). The U.S. Supreme Court agreed to review *Jacobs* but then set it aside as moot (the students had all graduated). *Jacobs* was especially notable because the appellate court emphasized that the use of earthy language doesn't make a publication legally obscene. In so ruling, the court cited the Supreme Court's *Papish* holding that mere four-letter (or 12-letter) words do not constitute obscenity.

Another appellate decision worth special mention is *Gambino v. Fairfax* (cited earlier). That 1977 decision is notable because it arose from a situation that must be repeated hundreds of times every year somewhere in America: the editors of an official campus newspaper faced censorship because what they wrote was considered too sensitive and controversial for high school students. Gina Gambino and her staff wanted to publish an article on contraceptive methods in the student paper at a high school in Virginia. It was headlined, "Sexually Active Students Fail to Use Contraceptives." The principal reviewed and decided to censor certain parts of the article, contending that sex education instruction was prohibited at the school. Therefore, the student paper shouldn't do something the teachers were forbidden to do in class, the principal contended.

A federal district court overruled the school's censorship, brushing aside the argument that the public forum doctrine shouldn't apply because the paper was part of the school curriculum, produced by a class. Despite its status, the paper was still a public forum protected by the First Amendment, the judge ruled. The fourth circuit Court of Appeals affirmed that decision.

However, the same federal appellate court upheld an act of administrative censorship when illegal drug use rather than birth control was the issue. In a 1980 case, *Williams v. Spencer* (622 F.2d 1200), the court affirmed a decision by school officials to halt distribution of an underground newspaper called *Joint Effort* because the paper contained advertising from a "head shop" that officials felt would encourage drug use. Citing the language in *Tinker* that students' rights are not "necessarily co-extensive with those of adults," the court affirmed school regulations under which the publication was banned. The court said a rule against distributing information dangerous to the health and safety of students was not unconstitutionally overbroad even though it did not specify the kind of material that could be censored. The court seemingly gave school officials broad latitude to justify censorship by contending that a story or ad in a publication might encourage drug use or something else allegedly dangerous or unhealthy.

Where do all of these cases leave us? Until 1988, it was clear that school officials could not arbitrarily censor student publications (not even official, school-sponsored student newspapers) without risking a reversal in court. However, as the era of militant student protest faded into history it became clear that the schools and the courts were reflecting changing social conditions. The conditions were right for a new Supreme Court decision on student press freedom.

Meanwhile, California enacted a statutory law to spell out the extent to which public school students enjoy freedom of the press--the first such law in the nation. Acting in 1977, the California state legislature declared that both official and underground school publications are entitled to some freedom. While this law says that the principle of freedom of the press applies to school newspapers, the law also authorizes prior censorship for libel, obscenity and material likely to cause rule-breaking or campus disturbances. This law, found in California Education Code section 48907, not only requires censorship of material falling in these categories, but places the primary responsibility for this censorship on the faculty adviser. The authorization for prior censorship is so broad that the American Civil Liberties Union opposed the law in the state legislature.

The ACLU was particularly annoyed because section 48907 reimposed prior censorship of school newspapers in California only a year after the state's Supreme Court had ruled that prior restraint was not permitted under a previous law guaranteeing free expression for students. The old law afforded students broad free-expression rights but didn't mention official school newspapers. Interpreting that law, the California Supreme Court overruled the administrative censorship of an underground newspaper in 1976 (*Bright v. Los Angeles Unified School District*, 18 C.3d 450). The paper had been censored because an article accused a school principal of lying. The court said prior restraint might be possible in the school setting, but not under the law in force then. The legislature closed that loophole the next year by enacting section 48907, thereby authorizing limited prior restraint of high school but not college newspapers.

THE SUPREME COURT CHANGES THE RULES

By the late 1980s it was clear that the mood of the country had changed. The student protest era was over, and most school officials were determined to reassert their authority. The Supreme Court decided it was time to help the authorities do precisely that.

In its first rulings on the First Amendment rights of students since the heyday of the student protest movement during the 1960s, the Supreme Court has sharply curtailed students' constitutional rights. Even before the landmark *Hazelwood* decision, the court began chipping away at students' First Amendment rights.

Ruling in 1986 in the case of *Bethel School District v. Fraser* (478 U.S. 675), the court held that a Washington state high school student could be disciplined for delivering a speech containing sexual innuendoes, even though the speech contained no four-letter words and was clearly not obscene in a legal sense.

The *Fraser* case began in 1983 when Matthew Fraser gave a speech at a Bethel High School assembly to endorse a friend's candidacy for a student body office. A state champion public speaker, Fraser avoided obscenity in the nominating speech, but he thoroughly amused those students who understood his innuendoes. However, school administrators didn't think it was funny: they suspended Fraser for two days and removed his name from a list of candidates in a student election to select a graduation speaker. Fraser won the graduation speaker election on a write-in vote and school officials permitted him to speak at his graduation--but only after he filed the lawsuit that led to the Supreme Court decision.

The lower courts ruled that school officials had violated Fraser's First Amendment rights by suspending him, but the Supreme Court disagreed. Writing for a 7-2 majority, Chief Justice Warren Burger said:

The schools, as instruments of the state, may determine that the essential lessons of civil, mature conduct cannot be conveyed in a school that tolerates lewd, indecent, or offensive speech and conduct such as that indulged in by this confused boy.

Burger took pains to distinguish this case from the landmark *Tinker v. Community School District* decision, in which the Supreme Court had strongly affirmed the First Amendment rights of students nearly 20 years earlier. Burger said this case was different because "the penalties imposed in this case were unrelated to any political viewpoint." In *Tinker*, students were punished for wearing black armbands to protest the Vietnam war.

It does not follow, Burger added, "that simply because the use of an offensive form of expression may not be prohibited to adults making what the speaker considers a political point, that the same latitude must be permitted to children in a public school."

Having ruled against Matthew Fraser, the Supreme Court had little difficulty disposing of the *Hazelwood School District v. Kuhlmeier* case two years later. The Supreme Court ruled against the editors of *The Spectrum*, the student newspaper at Hazelwood East High School in Missouri. Their principal censored two articles they planned to publish: a story about teen-age pregnancy that quoted students who had become pregnant, and an article in which students explained how their parents' divorces had affected them. None of the students' real names were used in the stories.

The Supreme Court held in a 5-3 decision that the principal was entitled to censor the articles even though they neither violated the rights of other students nor threatened to cause a campus disruption (the landmark *Tinker* ruling had permitted campus censorship for only these two reasons). Writing for the court, Justice Byron White said:

> We hold that educators do not offend the First Amendment by exercising editorial control over the style and content of student speech in school-sponsored expressive activities so long as their actions are reasonably related to legitimate pedagogical concerns.

White said school officials never intended for this student newspaper to be an open forum for student opinion like the "underground" and off-campus newspapers involved in so many earlier court decisions that upheld students' rights. Instead, White concluded, school officials "reserved the forum (i.e., the school newspaper) for its intended purpose, as a supervised learning experience for journalism students. Accordingly, school officials were entitled to regulate the contents of (the) *Spectrum* in any reasonable manner." White's majority opinion added:

> A school need not tolerate student speech that is inconsistent with its basic educational mission, even though the government could not censor similar speech outside the school.... (Judicial action to protect students' rights is justified) only when the decision to censor a school-sponsored publication,

theatrical production or other vehicle of student expression has no valid educational purpose.

How can the *Hazelwood* ruling be reconciled with the court's strong affirmation of student rights in the original *Tinker* decision? Justice White explained why the court thought this case was different:

> The question whether the First Amendment requires a school to tolerate particular student speech--the question we addressed in *Tinker*--is different from the question whether the First Amendment requires a school affirmatively to promote particular student speech. The former question addresses educators' ability to silence a student's personal expression that happens to occur on the school premises. The latter question concerns educators' authority over school-sponsored publications, theatrical productions, and other expressive activities that students, parents, and members of the public might reasonably perceive to bear the imprimatur of the school.

Justice William Brennan wrote a dissenting opinion in which he and two other justices who often took liberal positions on First Amendment issues (Thurgood Marshall and Harry Blackmun) condemned the message the majority was sending to students:

> The young men and women of Hazelwood East expected a civics lesson, but not the one the court teaches them today.... Such unthinking contempt for individual rights is intolerable from any state official. It is particularly insidious from (a school principal) to whom the public entrusts the task of inculcating in its youth an appreciation for the cherished democratic liberties that our Constitution guarantees.

Nevertheless, the precedent from the *Hazelwood* case is clear: the First Amendment does not ordinarily protect official student newspapers (and other school-sponsored activities, such as drama productions) from administrative control. However, this does not necessarily mean that school newspapers have no protection at all from administrative censorship: the Supreme Court ruling did NOT invalidate state laws and local policies that protect the free-press rights of student journalists. All the Supreme Court really said was that, in the absence of any other rules barring administrative censorship, the First Amendment does not protect student newspapers from such censorship.

In California, the case had no effect on the validity of Education Code section 48907, which prohibits administrative censorship of school newspapers unless the content is obscene, libelous or likely to cause disruptive or unlawful acts. A California appellate court specifically ruled that section 48907 remains valid after the *Hazelwood* decision (see *Leeb v. DeLong*, 198 C.A.3d 47, 1988). Shortly after the *Hazelwood* ruling, five other states--Arkansas, Colorado, Iowa, Kansas and Massachusetts--passed laws much like the one in California to provide students with some freedom from administrative censorship. By 1996, similar laws had been considered but not yet approved by the legislatures in more than 20 other states.

There is, however, a psychological effect when the Supreme Court hands down a ruling on an issue such as this. The *Hazelwood* decision will surely encourage school principals to censor student newspapers, regardless of whether they are legally permitted to do so under the local rules.

As a result of the *Fraser* and *Hazelwood* decisions, many of the earlier cases on student press freedom have less significance today. While the *Hazelwood* decision applies only to official school-sponsored activities, students who express controversial views in unofficial newspapers may be punished in ways that do not involve direct prior restraint--as Matthew Fraser was, with the Supreme Court's blessing. Students who feel strongly enough about an issue to go to the trouble of publishing an unofficial newspaper or tract often end up including offensive language as well as political rhetoric. Under the *Fraser* precedent, school officials may justify punishing them on the basis of the language alone.

Under the *Tinker* rule, school officials were allowed to abridge students' First Amendment rights only when the exercise of those rights might disrupt the orderly educational process or violate the rights of others. Under the new rule, no threat of a disruption is needed to justify censorship. Instead, school officials will apparently be permitted to restrict students' rights whenever there is a violation of what school officials consider to be the proper standards of good taste and decency for students.

The Fallout from Hazelwood

The *Fraser* and *Hazelwood* cases have far-reaching implications for the legal rights of students, implications that could extend well beyond a student's right to publish news stories about divorce and pregnancy or to give a speech containing a few sexual innuendoes. And *Hazelwood*'s impact is being felt at the college level. While the court in *Hazelwood* declined to address the status of student publications at the college level, a U.S. Supreme Court decision such as this one inevitably has some impact on courts that rule on the scope of First Amendment freedoms on college campuses.

Although no appellate court has upheld administrative censorship of a college student newspaper in the years since *Hazelwood*, one federal appellate court did say that if student activities (including campus newspapers) are part of the curriculum, they may not enjoy full First Amendment protection (*Alabama Student Party v. Student Government Assn.*, 867 F.2d 1344, 1989). Of course, long before the *Hazelwood* decision a federal court said essentially the same thing in *Trujillo v. Love* (discussed earlier). And a leading scholarly publication for college and university administrators who supervise student activities said in a 1996 article that *Hazelwood* does apply at the college level (see "Hazelwood v. Kuhlmeier: Supreme Court Decision Does Affect College and University First Amendment Rights," in *NASPA Journal*, Vol. 33, No. 4, p. 307). This article led many college administrators to believe they have a right to control the campus media--at a time when journalism educators were adamantly rejecting that idea.

In 2001, a federal appellate court decisively supported the journalism educators' position in a long-awaited decision, *Kincaid v. Gibson* (236 F.3d 342).

The sixth circuit U.S. Court of Appeals, in an *en banc* decision (i.e., a decision by all judges serving on the sixth circuit instead of the usual panel of three judges), ruled in early 2001 that Kentucky State University officials violated the First Amendment by impounding all copies of the KSU yearbook in 1994.

Earlier, a three-judge panel of that court ruled that KSU administrators did not violate the First Amendment because the yearbook was not a public forum protected by the First Amendment. Campus officials objected to the yearbook for several reasons, including its color (purple), the lack of captions for many of the photographs, and the inclusion of considerable off-campus material.

In the new ruling, the judges held that the KSU *Thorobred* yearbook is a limited public forum and may not be arbitrarily censored by administrators. Significantly, the court ruled that the U.S. Supreme Court's *Hazelwood v. Kuhlmeier* decision does not apply to student publications at the college level, at least in this particular instance. The eight-judge majority even said campus media that are nonpublic forums cannot be censored if the censorship is not *viewpoint neutral*.

To reach its conclusion that the yearbook was a limited forum entitled to substantial First Amendment protection, the majority analyzed KSU's written policy governing the yearbook, the actual practice of the university in overseeing it, the nature of the yearbook as expressive activity and the campus context.

The decision was widely applauded by journalism educators and other advocates of campus press freedom. As a legal precedent, it is binding only in the four states in the sixth federal circuit: Michigan, Ohio, Kentucky and Tennessee. However, it is sure to carry considerable weight elsewhere.

After the *en banc* decision, KSU officials settled the case by agreeing to pay the two students who had brought the lawsuit $5,000 each plus $60,000 in attorney's fees. KSU also agreed to release the impounded yearbooks and attempt to distribute them to the students who were entitled to receive them seven years earlier.

This case may help resolve the question of whether the *Hazelwood* principle applies to student media at public colleges and universities--and resolve it in favor of freedom from administrative censorship.

At the high school level, *Hazelwood* clearly opened the door for widespread administrative censorship where no local law or policy forbids it. And in 1989, a federal appellate court held that administrators may also control the content of the *advertising* in high school newspapers, yearbooks and athletic event programs. In *Planned Parenthood v. Clark County School District* (887 F.2d 935), the court upheld a decision by school officials to forbid advertising by Planned Parenthood clinics in Las Vegas school publications. The court declared that under the *Hazelwood* precedent, school officials could ban advertising as well as editorial content concerning "potentially sensitive topics, such as those related to teen-age sexual activity."

However, if school officials choose not to control advertising in school publications but instead leave decisions about advertising entirely up to the student staff, then there is no state action involved in a school newspaper or yearbook's rejection of a controversial ad. The students are then free to accept or reject advertising, as a federal appellate court ruled in *Yeo v. Town of Lexington* (cited earlier).

An Exception to Hazelwood

Even the broad sweep of the *Hazelwood* decision has its limits: there are still some circumstances under which school officials may violate the First Amendment by censoring a student newspaper.

In 1994, the New Jersey Supreme Court overruled an act of administrative censorship of an official school newspaper at a *junior high school*--on First Amendment grounds. In *Desilets v. Clearview Regional Board of Education* (647 A.2d 150), the state Supreme Court held that the principal of Clearview Junior High School did not have sufficient grounds to censor two movie reviews that were written by Brien Desilets, then an eighth grader, for publication in the *Pioneer Press*, the school's official student newspaper. The reviews concerned "Mississippi Burning" and "Rain Man," both R-rated films. Although the principal later conceded that he had no objection to the content of either review, he said he removed them from the school paper because of the movies' R ratings. School officials did not want to encourage junior high students to see R-rated movies, he said.

In the lawsuit that followed, the Appellate Division of the Superior Court of New Jersey held that this act of administrative censorship violated the First Amendment *in spite of the Hazelwood precedent*, and the New Jersey Supreme Court ultimately agreed. The principal and superintendent attempted to justify the censorship under the school board's policy on school publications by arguing that reviews of R-rated movies fell within the category of "material which advocated the use or advertised the availability of any substance believed to constitute a danger to student health." But nothing in either review said anything about any "substance" that could affect "student health." Nor is either movie about such subjects. School officials even conceded that a Clearview teacher who discussed "Mississippi Burning" in class and encouraged students to see it had done nothing improper.

The court distinguished this case from *Hazelwood*, rejecting the idea that school officials had a legitimate pedagogical reason for discouraging students to see R-rated movies when the rating system itself leaves that decision up to parents and when R-rated movies had been discussed in at least one class at that school--with the apparent blessing of school officials.

The New Jersey Supreme Court emphasized that the school officials involved in this case had no adequate policy governing issues such as the content of the school newspaper. The court chastised the state commissioner of education for failing to assure that the schools had clear policies on such matters.

The court did not hold that there is a First Amendment right of student newspapers to publish reviews of R-rated movies. Nor did the court challenge the basic holding of *Hazelwood*--that school officials can control the content of official school publications when they have valid pedagogical reasons for doing so. What the New Jersey Supreme court did say was that, given the lack of a sound policy, school officials did not have a valid basis for censoring this particular newspaper.

Unofficial Newspapers: Still Free

Only 10 months after the *Hazelwood* ruling, a U.S. Court of Appeals reiterated the principle that school officials still may not arbitrarily censor *unofficial* student publications. In *Burch v. Barker* (861 F.2d 1149, 1988), the appellate court overturned a Renton, Wash., school district policy requiring prior administrative review of all student-produced publications.

A group of students produced an unofficial newspaper called "Bad Astra" and distributed about 350 copies at a senior class barbecue at Lindbergh High School. A parent placed copies in faculty mailboxes as well. While the newspaper was generally critical of school officials, it contained no material that could be considered profane, obscene, defamatory or commercial, the court concluded.

Although Brian Barker, the school principal, said he did not object to the content of the newspaper, he placed letters of reprimand in five students' files because they circulated the paper without seeking prior administrative approval. But the court ruled that the school policy requiring prior review of all student publications was overbroad and therefore violated the students' First Amendment rights. To require such across-the-board administrative approval amounts to an improper prior restraint, the court said.

In overruling the school district policy, the court declared that this situation was not comparable to the *Hazelwood* case because the policy here applied to all unofficial publications--not just official publications as in the *Hazelwood* case. School officials cannot engage in wholesale prior censorship of unofficial publications without violating the First Amendment, the court ruled.

While the *Burch* case reaffirmed the principle that non-school-sponsored publications cannot be censored arbitrarily, it would not preclude administrative sanctions if a particular publication contained offensive content. In fact, the *Burch* decision emphasized that while a sweeping policy of prior restraint is unconstitutional, school officials remain free to punish students afterward if they distribute offensive or disruptive materials. And as the Supreme Court's *Fraser* decision indicated, school officials now have wide latitude in deciding what is and is not acceptable on a high school campus.

Unofficial Websites: Not Really Free

With the growth of the Internet, a new student press freedom issue has arisen: the censorship of *off-campus* student websites, often accompanied by on-campus disciplinary action against the students. This raises serious First Amendment questions, although precedent-setting appellate court rulings on this issue were non-existent as of mid-2002.

In a case that may be typical of many others, several students at Carbon County (Pa.) Vo-Tech High School produced an irreverent website called *The Babbitt* (**thebabbitt.com**). After a local newspaper and a television station did a story about the website in early 2002, school officials blocked the site on a server that provides Internet access to most Carbon and Lehigh County Schools and also threatened two students with disciplinary action.

In Great Falls, Mont., a high school senior was expelled and transferred to another school by the local school board in 2002 for posting photos on his personal website under the heading, "10 Hottest Freshman Girls."

FREEDOM AT PRIVATE SCHOOLS

This entire chapter has been devoted to freedom of expression at public schools and colleges. What about private institutions?

At private schools, the general rule is that freedom only exists if school officials find it in their interest to grant it: in the absence of *state action*, the First Amendment does not apply. When a private university newspaper is censored or its editors are fired, normally the worst the administration need fear is bad public relations. The school may face condemnation by professional media and journalistic organizations, but there is usually little chance for the aggrieved students to win a lawsuit.

This problem was well illustrated by a 1980 incident at Baylor University, a Baptist church-related institution in Waco, Texas. *Playboy* magazine was doing a photo feature on "Girls of the Southwest Conference," and a *Playboy* photographer was coming to town. University President Abner McCall warned that any Baylor student who posed nude for *Playboy* would be punished (and presumably expelled). The Baylor newspaper, the *Lariat*, editorially said that Baylor students should be free to make up their own minds about whether to pose. Then McCall told the *Lariat* editors not to cover the growing *Playboy* controversy any more. The editors rejected that blatant censorship, and several were fired. Shortly, more staff members and two journalism professors resigned in protest. One faculty member who resigned was abruptly ordered to leave Baylor in mid-semester. Before it was over, the Baylor incident stirred a national controversy, but the *Lariat* staff had no legal recourse. They were out.

Although the issues that provoke censorship aren't often as spectacular as the one at Baylor, censorship incidents are not unusual at private universities.

During the era of student activism, many lawsuits were filed alleging constitutional violations by private institutions, but the courts consistently ruled in favor of school officials--except in a very few cases where state action could be shown.

To establish state action, it must be shown that a government is deeply involved not only in funding the institution but also in its management. In separate cases (neither involving student press freedom as such), state action has been shown at two major private universities in Pennsylvania: Pittsburgh and Temple. However, in both instances the Commonwealth of Pennsylvania had entered agreements with school officials in which the state provided major funding in return for substantial reductions in tuition for Pennsylvania residents. Moreover, the state was given the power to appoint one-third of each institution's governing board. (See *Isaacs v. Temple University*, 385 F.Supp. 473, 1974; and *Braden v. Pittsburgh University*, 552 F.2d 948, 1977.)

Aside from the two Pennsylvania cases, court decisions establishing state action at private schools and colleges are hard to find. Once a New York court issued a memorandum opinion in connection with a settlement of a student discipline lawsuit against Hofstra University. The opinion discussed the procedural rights of students, but didn't address the basic issue of whether state action was present (*Ryan v. Hofstra*, 324 N.Y.S.2d 964, 1971).

On the other hand, a number of court decisions have held that state action does not exist at various private universities. For instance, in *Furumoto v. Lyman* (362 F.Supp. 1267, 1973), a court failed to find any state action at Stanford University, despite massive federal grants and a state charter. The seventh circuit Court of Appeals reached the same decision in *Cohen v. Illinois Institute of Technology* (581 F.2d 661, 1978).

In a 1982 decision, the U.S. Supreme Court may have settled the question of state action at private educational institutions. In *Rendell-Baker v. Kohn* (457 U.S. 830), the court ruled that state action was not present at a private high school for students with special problems, even though the school received 90 percent of its revenue from government funds. In a 7-2 ruling, the court made it very unlikely that state action can now be shown at any purely private school or college.

Thus, the conclusion seems clear: in the absence of an arrangement like those at Temple and Pittsburgh, there's no state action, and private school administrators may therefore ignore the First Amendment.

There is, however, one other possible recourse. In a law review article entitled "Common Law Rights for Private University Students: Beyond the State Action Principle" (84 Yale Law Journal 120, 1974), Paul G. Abrams and Peter M. Hoffman urged that the common law principles of private association law be applied to student rights cases. It is well established that a private association must operate in accordance with its own bylaws. When it fails to do that, its members may turn to the courts for help, they pointed out. That principle has not often been used by students, but it could be, given a university policy that guarantees freedom of the press and a clear violation of that policy. Perhaps in an appropriate case a court would follow Abrams' and Hoffman's reasoning and recognize that private university students have some rights, at least when the institution has adopted a policy that says they do.

PRACTICAL CONSIDERATIONS

So far, we've talked about student press freedom mostly in terms of lawsuits and the First Amendment. Because this chapter will certainly be read for guidance by students facing threats of censorship, a few practical observations are in order.

First, it should be emphasized that constitutional rights are only available to those who are prepared to fight for them--in court, if necessary. School administrators often ignore the First Amendment until forced to recognize that it exists. Student newspapers are censored every year without anyone doing anything about it.

It is unfortunate but true that winning one's constitutional rights can be expensive and time-consuming. If you experience censorship, you may have some tough choices to make. Ask yourself some questions. Is the censorship really unlawful?

High school administrators now have wide latitude to control the content of official student newspapers (but not unofficial ones) unless there is a state law or local policy forbidding censorship. College administrators have less latitude in controlling the student press, although that could change as a result of recent court decisions.

Also, how important is the item you've been told you can't publish? How would a judge react to it? Justice Oliver Wendell Holmes' legal maxim, "...hard cases make bad law," certainly applies here. Don't pursue a case that invites a bad legal precedent, one that could be used to deny freedom to students elsewhere. A well-documented story about malfeasance by the college administration is one thing; a column that uses four-letter words gratuitously is another.

After weighing these questions, there are some specific steps to take if you feel you have a case worth pursuing. First, go through all available channels. Consult your faculty adviser if you have one. If there is a publications policy board, take the case there. Only if all internal remedies fail is it time to consider a lawsuit. But if you reach that point, weigh your options again. Is there a local attorney willing to represent you on a low-cost basis? The American Civil Liberties Union has represented students in numerous First Amendment cases. The Student Press Law Center in Washington may also be able to offer advice--or help you find an attorney. If legal help isn't available, compromise may again be in order. But if, on the other hand, you really have a good case and a good lawyer, perhaps your name will someday appear in law books like this one.

ONGOING ISSUES

The question of student press freedom is a miniature version of many other questions addressed in this book. In trying to answer these questions, the Supreme Court extended First Amendment rights to students at public high schools and colleges--and then began to curtail those rights. Under the most recent court decisions, college students still enjoy broad First Amendment rights; those rights are much more limited at the high school level.

Underlying these legal principles there are questions on which there is no consensus. To what extent should students be protected by the First Amendment? When are prior restraints justified at a public school or college? Should the rules differ at high schools and colleges? Why should the rules be different for private schools? Should underground newspapers be treated differently than official ones?

If the rationale for extending First Amendment rights to students is the concept of state action, doesn't that run afoul of the idea that *the taxpayers* should have the final say about what goes on at a public school? Doesn't the school board serve as the democratically elected representatives of the general public? And isn't the school principal the school board's surrogate, charged with doing the public's bidding? Isn't the principal really the publisher of a school newspaper? In effect, the Supreme Court has ruled that the principal does have the powers of a publisher.

In other areas of law, the courts have often ruled that the First Amendment sets strict limits on government actions that deprive individuals of their rights, public opinion notwithstanding. To some degree, at least, those limits apply to school officials. In the end, perhaps the most basic question in student press law is this: should the schools be a microcosm of society at large, or should they be insulated places with stricter rules and fewer constitutional safeguards?

A SUMMARY OF STUDENT PRESS LAW

Does the First Amendment Apply to Students?
In the landmark case of *Tinker v. Community School District*, the Supreme Court extended First Amendment protection to students attending public schools.

Are There Limitations on Students' Freedoms?
The Supreme Court said high school students' rights on campus are not as extensive as those normally available off campus. Students' freedom of expression may be limited when necessary to protect the rights of others and to maintain an orderly educational process. The courts have generally extended somewhat broader First Amendment rights to college students.

Are Student Publications Constitutionally Protected?
Federal courts have consistently held that *unofficial* or "underground" high school publications are protected by the First Amendment and may not be arbitrarily censored by school administrators. The courts have sometimes refused to allow censorship even when such a publication included earthy language or controversial subject matter. On several occasions federal courts have held that the First Amendment protects official as well as unofficial student media *at the college level*. A notable example is *Kincaid v. Gibson*, a 2001 decision.

Has This Trend Continued?
The Supreme Court handed down several decisions during the late 1980s that marked a turning point in students' rights. In *Bethel School District v. Fraser*, the court said the First Amendment does not prevent school administrators from disciplining a student for using non-obscene but offensive language in a speech at a school assembly. In *Hazelwood School District v. Kuhlmeier* the court said the First Amendment does not prevent administrators from censoring official high school newspapers. The court said there is a difference between the free speech activities that public school officials must *tolerate* (as in *Tinker*) and the kind of speech the First Amendment requires them to *sponsor* by permitting it in official publications or at school activities. These cases may not apply at the college level. Nor do they supersede state laws and local policies that forbid administrative censorship in some states.

Are Private Schools Treated Differently?
The legal rationale for extending First Amendment protection to students was that public school officials' acts constitute *state action*. The First Amendment prohibits the denial of free expression rights by governments, not by private entities. Unless a private school official's conduct constitutes state action (which it rarely does), the First Amendment is inapplicable to private schools and colleges.

INDEX

Access to court documents, 311-313
Actual damages (defined), 20
Adams, John, 42
Adams, John Quincy, 47
Administrative law, 16
Advertising -
    Access, 546-551
    Access to government media, 549-551
    Broadcast advertising, 452
    Central Hudson test, 533,538,540,541, 542,543,545,564,581
    Cigarette advertising, 543,561-653
    Commercial Speech Doctrine, 530-546
    Compounded drug advertising, 564
    Consolidated Edison test, 545
    Corporate speech, 544-547
    Damages for false advertising, 565
    Fair use of copyrighted materials, 247
    Federal Trade Commission, 551-563
    First Amendment rights, 530-547
    Generic ads for farm products, 543
    Lawyers' advertising, 534-536
    Regulation Z, 565
    Self-regulation, 568
    State regulation, 566
    Student press access, 581
    Unfairness Doctrine, 558
Affirmative Action programs, 439
Alien and Sedition Acts, 41
Annenberg Washington Program, 171
Annotated codes, 31
Annotated codes (defined), 15
Anti-abortion websites, liability for, 84
Anticybersquatting Consumer Protection Act, 281
Antitrust law -
    Broadcast cases, 522
    Broadcast ownership rules, 515-519
    First Amendment, 505
    Hart-Scott-Rodino Act, 526
    Joint operating agreements, 510-515
    Mergers, examples of, 523-527
    Microsoft case, 504
    Newspaper cases, 507-510
    Overview of antitrust laws, 503
Apple Computer Inc., 257
ASCAP, 248
Ashcroft, John, 359
Assassination Records Review Board, 361
AT&T, 524
Auctions (of radio spectrum), 431,434
Audio Home Recording Act, 254
Berne Convention, 268-271
Berzon, Marsha, 84
Black, Hugo, 57,65,397
Blackmun, Harry A., 8,65,99,141,178,538

BMI, 248
Booth Rule, 208
Boy Scouts of America, 91-92
Brandeis, Louis D., 51,53,174,175
Brennan, William J., 7,65,73,93,137,140,147, 201,307,350,396,398,401,403,462, 538,589
Breyer, Stephen G., 8,439
Brief, appellate (defined), 25
Broadcast ownership rules, 515-519
Broadcasting -
    Advertising rates, 452
    AM radio expansion, 497
    Auctions (of spectrum), 431,434
    Broadcast ownership restrictions, 516-519
    Children's programming, 468,471,472
    Children's Television Act, 470
    Communications Act, 433-434,448,449, 450,460,478,479
    Comparative hearings, 437
    Content regulation, 449-470
    Cross-ownership rules, 519
    Digital Audio Radio Service (DARS), 496
    Digital must-carry requirements, 490
    Digital television, 489-490
    Direct broadcast satellites (DBS), 493
    Equal employment opportunity (EEO) rules, 441-443
    Equal Time Rule, 450-456
    Fairness Doctrine, 456-464
    Federal Communications Commission, 433,436
    Federal Radio Commission, 432
    Financial Interest and Syndication Rule, 521
    Format changes, 472
    HDTV, 489-490
    History of, 431
    Hoaxes, 474
    Indecency rules, 464-468
    International broadcast regulation, 426
    Internet-based television, 495
    Licensing, 436-449
    Local multipoint distribution systems, 495
    Lotteries, 474
    Lowest unit charge, 452
    Low-power radio proposal, 519
    Low-power television, 496
    Multipoint distribution service (MDS), 494
    New communication technologies, 488-492
    Ownership rules, 515-519
    Personal Attack Rule, 460
    Pirate radio stations, 519
    Political broadcasting rules, 450-463
    Political debates, 454

Political Editorializing Rule, 460
"Postcard renewal," 445
Preferences in licensing, 437-439
Presidential debates, 454
Prime Time Access Rule, 473
Radio spectrum, 427
Satellite Television Home Viewers Act, 252, 494
Scarcity rationale, 424
Section 315, 450-456
Telecommunications Act of 1996, 494
V-chip legislation, 471-472
Violence in the media, 471
Buckley Amendment, 372
Buckley Amendment and campus crime, 374-375
Bureau of Alcohol, Tobacco and Firearms, 565
Burger, Warren E., 65, 147, 194, 300, 306, 308, 310, 315, 316, 384, 402, 452, 547, 587
Burr, Aaron, 47
Bush, George, 73
Bush, George W., 61, 355
Cable television -
    Adult cable scrambling, 488
    Cable Communications Policy Act of 1984, 481
    Cable Television Consumer Protection and Competition Act of 1992, 251, 477, 482
    Cross-ownership rules, 517
    First Amendment issues, 486-488
    Franchising, 486
    History of, 476-480
    Indecency, 487
    Internet provider access, 525
    Must carry rules, 484
    Satellite master antenna television (SMATV), 495
    Syndicated Exclusivity Rule, 479
Cameras in court, 313-318
Campaign finance reform, 453
Campus crime statistics, 373
Cellphone eavesdropping, 190-191
Central Hudson test, 533, 538, 540, 541, 542, 543, 545, 564, 581
Certiorari, writ of (defined), 7
Chafee, Zechariah, 44
Chain e-mail, 268
Change of venue, 298
Charity Games Advertising Clarification Act, 474
Child Online Protection Act, 414
Child Pornography Prevention Act, 406
Children's Internet Protection Act, 414
Children's Online Privacy Protection Act, 215
Children's Television Act of 1990, 470
CIA, 67, 364, 366
Cigarette advertising, 543, 561-563
Civil cases (defined), 18
Civil War, 47
Clark, Tom, 296, 297

Clear and Present Danger Test, 51
Clery (Jeanne) Act, 375
Clinton, Bill, 8, 360, 376, 456
Clinton, Hillary Rodham, 376
Closed courtrooms, 303-311
Colorization (motion picture), 271
Commercial Speech Doctrine, 530-546
Common law, 13
Communications Act, 433-434, 448, 449, 450, 460, 478, 479
Communications Decency Act, 393, 412-415
Complaint (defined), 21
Compounded drugs, advertising of, 564
Computer Matching and Privacy Protection Act of 1988, 372
Concurring opinion (defined), 25
Consolidated Edison test, 545
Constitution, U.S., 11
Contempt of court, 323-326
Cooper, Thomas, 42
Copperheads, 48
Copyright law -
    Audio Home Recording Act, 254
    Berne Convention, 268
    Cable television, 251
    Compulsory licensing, 232, 248
    Computer technologies, 255
    Digital Millennium Copyright Act, 260, 265
    Digital Performance Right in Sound Recordings Act, 265
    Direct broadcast satellite questions, 252
    Duration of, 231
    DVD copying software, 264
    Fair use and advertising, 247
    Fair use and historical events, 239
    Fair use and news, 241
    Fair use and parodies, 245
    Fair use and religious works, 243
    Fair Use Doctrine, 237-248
    Fairness in Music Licensing Act, 250
    Federal preemption, 236
    Freelancers and electronic publishing, 266
    General Agreement on Tariffs and Trade (GATT), 270
    International copyrights, 268
    Internet issues, 259-268
    Internet music sharing, 262
    Internet streaming of broadcasts, 265
    Moral rights, 271
    MP3.com, 261
    Music licensing, 248-251
    Napster, 261
    New technologies, 252
    Notice, 226
    Overview, 225
    Proving infringement, 229
    Registration, 226
    Remedies for infringement, 227
    ReplayTV, 265
    Sampling by recording artists, 246

Sonicblue, 265
Television news footage, 243
Unfair competition, 272
Universal Copyright Convention, 269
Unpublished works, 241-243
Video clipping services, 243
Video taping, 252
Works made for hire, 234
World Intellectual Property Organization, 270
Copyright Arbitration Royalty Panel, 251
Copyright Royalty Tribunal, 251
Courts, federal, 2-7
Courts, state, 8
Crime Awareness and Campus Security Act, 373
Criminal cases (defined), 18
Criminal history information, 376
Cromwell, Oliver, 36
Cross-ownership, 519
Croswell libel trial, 47
Cyberspace, definition of, 163
Damages in libel cases, 111
Damages, types of, 18
Demurrer (defined), 22
Denny, Reginald, 245
Digital Audio Radio Service (DARS), 496
Digital Millennium Copyright Act, 260, 265
Digital Performance Right in Sound Recordings Act, 265
Digital television, 489-490
Digitally altered photos as news, 208
Direct broadcast satellites (DBS), 252, 493
Discovery (defined), 23
Discovery (pretrial procedure), 107, 151
Dissenting opinion (defined), 25
Diversity of citizenship (defined), 10
Domain names, 279
Douglas, William O., 57, 59, 65, 176, 397, 511
Driver's Privacy Protection Act, 377
Eisenhower, Dwight D., 8
Electronic Freedom of Information Act Amendments, 367
Electronic Frontier Foundation, 264, 265
Elements of libel, 114-118
Eminem (Marshall Mathers), 467
Emotional distress cases, 160, 199
En banc (defined), 5
Encryption software censorship, 102-103
England, censorship in, 35
Environmental Protection Agency, 563
Equal Time Rule, 450-456
Equity (defined), 17
Espionage Act (1917), 49
Ethics in Government Act, 68
European Union, 504
European Union privacy standards, 216
Executive privilege, 369
Fair comment libel defense, 116
Fair use and historical events, 239
Fair Use Doctrine, 237

Fairness Doctrine, 456-464
Fairness in Music Licensing Act, 250
Fair trial-free press -
   Access to court documents, 311-313
   Cameras in court, 313-318
   Closed courtrooms, 303-311
   Gagging judges, 302
   Gagging trial Lawyers, 301-302
   O.J. Simpson case, 289-292
   Rodney King case, 291-292
Farber, Myron, 345
Farr, William, 344
Federal Advisory Committee Act, 375
Federal Communications Commission (structure), 433-436
Federal Radio Commission, 432
Federal Trade Commission, 551-563
Federal Trademark Dilution Act of 1995, 279
Felten, Edward, 264
Ferguson, Gordon, 157
Ferris, Charles D., 479
Fiction in libel cases, 165
Fighting Words Doctrine, 70
Film censorship, 98-99, 409
Financial Interest and Syndication Rule, 521-522
Financial newsletters, 97
First Amendment, drafting of, 41
Flag desecration, 73
Food and Drug Administration, 563-564
Freedom of Access to Clinic Entrances Act, 83
Freedom of Information Act, 356-370
General Agreement on Tariffs and Trade (GATT), 270
Ginsburg, Ruth Bader, 8, 439, 455
Government in the Sunshine Act, 378
Grand jury transcripts, access to, 386
Group libel, 117
Hamilton, Alexander, 47
Hamilton, Andrew, 39
Hand, Learned, 54
Harlan, John Marshall, 65, 72
Hart-Scott-Rodino Act, 526
Hatch Act amendments, 69
Hate speech, 70
Hidden cameras, 184-190
High-definition television (HDTV), 489-490
Hill, Anita, 347
Hoffman, Dustin, 208
Holmes, Oliver Wendell, Jr., 50, 58, 596
Hughes, Charles Evans, 59, 63
Hughes, Howard, 240
Hundt, Reed, 440, 450, 475
Internet -
   Advertising, 266, 570
   Anticybersquatting Consumer Protection Act, 281
   Censorship of, 103, 393, 412-415
   Chain e-mail, 268
   Copyright issues, 259-268
   Internet Corp. for Assigned Names and

Numbers (ICANN), 280
Domain names, 279
Electronic FoI Act, 367
E-mail privacy, 217
FoI - privacy controversy, 367
Indecency on, 412-415
Legal research on, 28, 30, 32
Liability for anti-abortion websites, 84
Libel on, 163-164
Links and trademarks, 282
Metatags, 268, 281
Misappropriation questions, 217
Music sharing, 262
Napster, 262-263
Obscenity on, 404
Open access to cable systems, 525
Privacy issues, 215
Spam, restrictions on, 570
Streaming of broadcasts, 265
Unsolicited e-mail, 570
Internet-based television, 495
Jefferson, Thomas, 40, 43
Jehovah's Witness cases, 76-77
Joint operating agreements, 510-515
Judicial proceedings, access to, 386
Jury trials, 23
Kennard, William, 442, 443, 450, 460, 475, 476, 490, 519
Kennedy, Anthony M., 7, 74, 89, 92, 148, 178, 455, 581
Kennedy, John F., assassination, 240
King, Martin Luther, 240
King, Rodney, 244, 291-292
Kozinski, Alex, 84, 206
Ku Klux Klan, 56, 71
Lanham Act, 274-278, 565
Legal encyclopedias, 30
Legal precedent (defined), 2
Legal research methods, 27
Leggett, Vanessa, 326, 347
Levy, Leonard, 43
Lexis-Nexis Academic Universe, 28
Liability for readers' or viewers' crimes, 104-105
Libel -
Actual malice, 122, 136-141
Broadcast defamation, 167
Criminal libel, 168
Damages, 111
Defenses, 124
Discovery, 151
Elements, 114-118
Emotional distress alternative, 160
Expressions of opinion, 132
Fair comment defense, 116, 130
Fiction, 165
Group libel, 117
Insurance coverage, 164
Internet, libel on, 163
Libel reform proposals, 171
Long-arm jurisdiction, 154

Negligence, 122, 141
Neutral reportage, 135
Pretrial discovery in, 150
Private matters and libel, 146
Privilege defense, 126
Product disparagement laws, 162
Proving damages, 123
Quotations, altered, 148
Refining actual malice, 145
Retraction laws, 152
SLAPP lawsuits, 157-159
Summary judgment, 155-157
Technicalities, 159
Tobacco lawsuits, 112
Truth defense, 125
Uniform Correction or Clarification of Defamation Act, 153
Who may sue, 116
Lincoln, Abraham, 48
Linux operating system, 264
Literature distribution, 75-90
Local multipoint distribution systems, 495
Locke, John, 37
Long, Huey, 94
Long-arm jurisdiction, 154
Lord Campbell's Act, 38
Lotteries, 474
Lotus Development Corp., 257
Lowest unit charge, 452
Low-power television, 496
Madison, James, 42
Majority opinion (defined), 25
Mapplethorpe, Robert, 393
Marketplace of ideas, 36
Marshall, John, 46
Marshall, Thurgood, 7, 65, 96, 101, 400, 532, 537
McVeigh, Timothy, 317
Medical information, confidentiality of, 372
Meiklejohn, Alexander, 44
Mergers of media companies, 523
Metatags, 268, 281
Microsoft Corp., 257, 504
Military bases, censorship on, 408
Military Honor and Decency Act, 408
Mill, John Stuart, 49
Miller, James C., 554, 560
Milton, John, 35
Minow, Newton, 497
Moral rights, 271
Multipoint distribution service (MDS), 494
Murdoch, Rupert, 525
Music licensing, 248
Napster, 262-263
National Association of Attorneys General, 567
National Endowment for the Arts, 393, 415
National Film Preservation Act, 272
Ness, Susan, 490
Network Solutions Inc. (NSI), 280
Neutral reportage, 135
New communication technologies, 488
New trial, motion for (defined), 24

News sources, lawsuits by, 348
Newsgathering torts, 184, 190-191
Newspaper Preservation Act, 511
Newsrack ordinances, 93
Newsroom searches, 351
Noriega, Manuel, 108, 300
Obscenity -
    Child Pornography Prevention Act, 406
    Film censorship, 409
    Hicklin Rule, 394
    History of, 394
    Internet censorship, 412
    Military bases and censorship, 408
    Miller Test, 401
    NEA grants, 415
    Nude dancing, 418
    Nuisance laws, 416
    Postal censorship, 408
    Roth test, 396
    Women's rights, 417
    Zoning and, 418
O'Connor, Sandra Day, 7, 83, 87, 88, 89, 95, 96, 103, 125, 178, 242, 413, 415, 419, 439, 541, 564
Open meeting laws, federal (see Sunshine Act)
Open meeting laws, state, 380
Opinion in libel cases, 132
Original jurisdiction, 7
Outrage (basis for legal action), 199
Paparazzi photographers, restrictions on, 191
Pataki, George, 318
Patrick, Dennis, 458, 480
Pentagon Papers case, 64
Pertschuk, Michael, 559
Pirate radio stations, 519
Posner, Richard A., 190, 582
Postal censorship, 408
Postal Service, U.S., 397, 408, 565
Powell, Lewis, 177, 305, 327
Powell, Michael, 443, 460, 467, 476, 491
Preemption, federal (defined), 10
Presumed damages (defined), 20
Pretrial discovery and prior restraint, 107
Pretrial discovery in libel cases, 150
Pretrial motions, 22
Princess Diana, death of, 173
Prior restraints -
    Abortion protests, 82-87
    Anonymous political leaflets, 90
    Computer encryption software, 102-103
    Discriminatory taxation, 94
    Fighting Words Doctrine, 70
    Film censorship, 98
    Financial newsletters, 97
    Flag desecration, 73-75
    Freedom of Access to Clinic Entrances Act, 83
    Government employees, 67-69
    Hate speech, 70
    Literature distribution, 75-90
    National security, 64-67
    Newsrack ordinances, 93
    Pretrial discovery information, 107
    Privately sponsored parades and fairs, 90
    Publishing crime victims' names, 105
    Restrictions on crime information, 105
    Restrictions on demonstrations, 82-87
    Rock concerts, 100
    "Son of Sam" laws, 103
Prisons, access to, 383
Privacy Act of 1974, 215, 370
Privacy Protection Act of 1980, 351
Private facts cases, 192, 200
Private organizations, access to, 387
Private property, access to, 388
Privilege, newsgatherer's, 326-338
Privacy -
    Abortion and contraception, 177
    Booth Rule, 208
    Cellphone eavesdropping, 190-191
    Crime victims' names, 194
    Defenses, 213
    Disclosure of private facts, 192, 200
    E-mail privacy, 217
    European Union privacy standards, 216
    False light cases, 200-202
    Hidden cameras, 184-190
    History of, 173
    Internet misappropriation, 217
    Internet privacy and children, 215
    Intrusion, 181-190
    Juveniles' names, 194
    Misappropriation and news, 207
    Newsgathering torts, 184, 190-191
    Rape victims' names, 193
    Ride-alongs (law enforcement), 184-185
    Right of publicity, 203-213
    Survival of privacy rights, 211
Product disparagement laws, 162
Propagation, radio, 428
Prosser, William L., 180
Protective ("gag") orders, 297, 299-302
Public figures in libel cases, 142
Public record laws, state, 381
Punitive damages (defined), 19
Racketeer Influenced and Corrupt Organizations (RICO) Act, 393, 417
Radio Act of 1927, 432
Radio Marti, 429
Radio Moscow, 429
Ratings (motion picture), 411
Reardon, Paul C., 302
Rehnquist, William H., 8, 61, 71, 80, 85, 95, 107, 131, 154, 161, 185, 316, 362, 413, 418, 420, 486, 537
Remand (defined), 26
ReplayTV, 265
Reporters Committee for Freedom of the Press, 299, 306, 326, 360
Retraction laws, 152
Right of publicity, 203-213
Rock concert censorship, 100

Tort: wrongful act, injury or damage for which civil action can be brought

Rutledge, Wiley, 58
Rymer, Pamela, 84
Sanford, Bruce, 60
Satellite master antenna television (SMATV), 495
Satellite Television Home Viewers Act, 252, 494
SBC Communications, 524
Scalia, Antonin, 70, 92, 96, 176, 179, 416, 419
Scarcity rationale, 424
Securities and Exchange Commission, 97, 565
Sedition Act (1918), 49
Sept. 11, 2001 (response to), 34, 60, 355, 360, 571
Sheppard, Sam Reese, 295
Shield laws, 338-344
Shopping malls and prior restraint, 78
Siebert, Fred, 37
Simpson, O.J., 3, 289-292
Sixth amendment, 288
Slander defined, 113
SLAPP lawsuits, 157-159
Smith Act, 54
Smith, William Kennedy, 107, 195
Soldier of Fortune (magazine), 105
Sonny Bono Copyright Term Extension Act, 231
Souter, David H., 7, 91, 178, 246, 349, 350, 416, 419, 439, 455
Sovereign immunity, 13
Special damages (defined), 19
Stamp Act of 1765, 39
Stare decisis, 14
Statutory law, 15
Stevens, John Paul, 74, 77, 86, 98, 99, 146, 147, 160, 253, 364, 384, 413, 415, 439, 455, 538, 540, 541
Stewart, Potter, 65, 305, 327, 392
Student Press Law Center, 375, 579, 596
Student press law -
    Advertising restrictions, 580
    At colleges, 576-580, 590
    At high schools, 575-583, 590-594
    Buckley Amendment and campus crime, 374-375
    Campus crime statistics, 374-375
    Hazelwood aftermath, 587-594
    Hazelwood's applicability at colleges, 590
    Newspaper theft, 579
    Website censorship, 593
Summary judgment, 155-157
Summary judgment (defined), 22
Sunshine Act, Government in the, 378
Supreme Court, U.S., 6
Sutherland, George, 94
Syndicated Exclusivity Rule, 479
Takeovers of media companies, 523
Tashima, Wallace, 157
Taxation as prior restraint, 94
Telcos, communication services by, 491
Telecommunications Act of 1996, 164, 260, 393, 412, 439, 443, 445, 471, 485, 488, 492, 493, 494, 516, 519
Thomas, Clarence, 8, 347, 441, 540, 541, 543
Torts (defined), 18
Trademarks, 274, 279
Trademarks -
    Abandonment, 275
    Colors as trademarks, 277
    Federal Trademark Dilution Act of 1995, 279
    In general, 274-279
    Internet domain names, 279
    Lanham Act, 274-279
    Registration, 274
    Secondary meaning, 276
    Trade dress, 278
    Trademark Law Revision Act of 1988, 278
Treble damage lawsuits, 503, 565
Trinity Broadcasting Network, 448
Turner, Ted, 271
Unfair competition, 272
Unfairness Doctrine, 558
Uniform Correction or Clarification of Defamation Act, 153
Universal Copyright Convention, 269
Video clipping services, 243
Vinson, Fred, 54
Visual Artists Rights Act, 272
Voice of America, 429
Voir dire (examining jurors), 298
Vortex public figures, 142
Warren, Earl, 8, 55, 58, 398, 400
White, Byron R., 8, 65, 93, 147, 177, 193, 349, 402, 406, 439, 588
Wiley, Richard E., 491
Williams, Roger, 36
Winfrey, Oprah, 163
World Intellectual Property Organization, 270
Zapruder, Abraham, 240
Zenger, John Peter, 39